Also in the Variorum Collected Studies Series:

PATRICIA CRONE
From Kavad to al-Ghazali
Religion, Law and Political Thought in the Near East, c.600–c.1100

MICHAEL LECKER
People, Tribes and Society in Arabia Around the Time of Muhammad

MOSHE GIL
Related Worlds - Studies in Jewish and Arab Ancient and Early Medieval History

MICHAEL COOK
Studies in the Origins of Early Islamic Culture and Tradition

RAMZI BAALBAKI
Grammarians and Grammatical Theory in the Medieval Arabic Tradition

FEDWA MALTI-DOUGLAS
Power, Marginality, and the Body in Medieval Islam

ANDREW RIPPIN
The Qur'an and its Interpretative Tradition

MICHAEL LECKER
Jews and Arabs in Pre- and Early Islamic Arabia

M.J. KISTER
Concepts and Ideas at the Dawn of Islam

SHAUL SHAKED
From Zoroastrian Iran to Islam
Studies in Religious History and Intercultural Contacts

DAVID AYALON
Islam and the Abode of War
Military Slaves and Islamic Adversaries

WAEL B. HALLAQ
Law and Legal Theory in Classical and Medieval Islam

R.B. SERJEANT
Customary and Shari'ah Law in Arabian Society

VARIORUM COLLECTED STUDIES SERIES

Interpretation and Jurisprudence in Medieval Islam

Norman Calder

Norman Calder

Interpretation and Jurisprudence in Medieval Islam

Edited by
Jawid Mojaddedi and Andrew Rippin

ASHGATE
VARIORUM

Published in the Variorum Collected Studies Series by

Ashgate Publishing Limited
Gower House, Croft Road,
Aldershot, Hampshire
GU11 3HR
Great Britain

Ashgate Publishing Company
Suite 420
101 Cherry Street
Burlington, VT 05401–4405
USA

Ashgate website: http://www.ashgate.com

ISBN–10: 0–7546–5903–8
ISBN–13: 978–0–7546–5903–7

British Library Cataloguing in Publication Data
Calder, Norman
Interpretation and jurisprudence in medieval Islam. –
(Variorum collected studies series ; 862)
1. Islamic law – History – To 1500
I. Title II. Mojaddedi, J. A. (Jawid Ahmad) III. Rippin, Andrew, 1950–
340.5'9'0902

Library of Congress Cataloging-in-Publication Data
Calder, Norman.
Interpretation and jurisprudence in medieval Islam / by Norman Calder ; edited by Jawid Mojaddedi and Andrew Rippin.
p. cm.
Includes bibliographical references.
ISBN–13: 978–0–7546–5903–7 (alk. paper)
ISBN–10: 0–7546–5903–8 (alk. paper)
1. Islam – History.
I. Mojaddedi, J. A. (Jawid Ahmad) II. Rippin, Andrew, 1950– . III. Title.
BP25.C35 2007
297.209'02–dc22

2006016386

The paper used in this publication meets the minimum requirements of the American National Standard for Information Sciences – Permanence of Paper for Printed Library Materials, ANSI Z39.48–1984. ∞ ™

Printed and bound in Great Britain by TJ International Ltd, Padstow, Cornwall

VARIORUM COLLECTED STUDIES SERIES CS862

CONTENTS

b) Imāmī Shīʿism

This volume contains xiv + 410 pages

PUBLISHER'S NOTE

The articles in this volume, as in all others in the Variorum Collected Studies Series, have not been given a new, continuous pagination. In order to avoid confusion, and to facilitate their use where these same studies have been referred to elsewhere, the original pagination has been maintained wherever possible.

Each article has been given a Roman number in order of appearance, as listed in the Contents. This number is repeated on each page and is quoted in the index entries.

INTRODUCTION

Norman Calder's life and accomplishments have been documented and celebrated in the introduction to a volume dedicated to him, *Studies in Islamic and Middle Eastern Texts and Traditions in Memory of Norman Calder* (Oxford, 2000). The occasion of reprinting Norman's major articles in this volume does not call for further comment along those lines. Here, we wish only to draw attention to some of the distinctive qualities of Norman's work which so clearly come through in his journal articles and book chapters.

The pleasure that Norman took in the use of language, both as reader and writer, is apparent in all his work. It is revealed not only in his scholarly writings but also in his personal correspondence, where his irresistible humour is most clearly evident. One could argue that an appreciation of Norman's wit and humour is essential for a full understanding of his scholarly writings, not least his reviews of books which he did not rate highly. In a personal letter in 1987, he wrote the following comments:

> [A] glance at the format of this letter will reveal the shameful truth about my response to the loss of [...] a sabbatical. ... Whether this is a wise investment or (more likely) a squandering of hard-won financial assets remains to be seen. For the moment I and my Amstrad [computer] glower at each other. Holding on to the fact that the phrase "to boot a computer" has a specific technical meaning is, I find, difficult; and the temptation to put on my hiking boots prior to a literal (*zahiri*) reading of the instructions, very great indeed. [Abdel Kader] Shareef, *au contraire*, delights in his PC (an altogether more aristocratic child than mine) and attempted the other day to demonstrate its merits. My suspicions about the whole species were however confirmed when his too – in spite of added size, price and colour – acted sulky and spoilt. Told firmly to do X and following all the linguistic guidelines of the manual my Amstrad generally resorts to the sniffy repetition of a computer-speak message which, interpreted, means "shan't". You then have to work out how to placate, cajole and persuade it to action; a process that usually ends in depriving it of electricity as the only way of stopping it from getting over-excited and quite mad. This Firm Disciplinary Training has so far had no discernible effect on the manners or general social decorum of my machine. My ancient Adler [typewriter], temporarily shifted to the top of the filing cabinet, smirks quietly in anticipation of a triumphant return.

Norman's writing style and delight in language developed from his enthusiasm for the most influential works of modern literature. In particular, he had a deep respect for the art of writing novels. He was in the habit of discussing the merits of the most celebrated novels with colleagues, friends and students alike, and would often find ingenious ways of relating them to the texts of medieval religious scholarship that he was teaching and writing about. To learn that Norman had set himself the task of reading Proust in French one summer would hardly have come as a surprise therefore to anyone who knew him. The influence of intellectuals from outside the field of Islamic studies, such as Paul Ricoeur and Frank Kermode, is also evident in much of his work, at least in shaping its conceptual framework. Perhaps the most significant influence came from Erich Auerbach's *Mimesis,* which he recommended in the initial reading list given to students beginning doctoral research under his supervision. The notion that Islamic texts, like their biblical counterparts, are "fraught with background" motivates Norman's work, and thus what Edward Said says of Auerbach applies equally to Norman Calder: "...far from seeming heavy-handed and pedantic, he exudes a sense of searching and discovery, the joys and uncertainties of which he shares unassumingly with his readers."[1] Furthermore, one could argue that the following description of Auerbach's work by Said might also apply to Norman's method of analysis.

> In all these works, Auerbach preserves the same essayistic style of criticism, beginning each chapter with a long quotation from a specific work cited in the original language, followed immediately by a serviceable translation ... out of which a detailed *explication de texte* ... unfolds at a leisurely and ruminative pace; this in turn develops into a set of memorable comments about the relationship between the rhetorical style of the passage and its socio-political context, a feat that Auerbach manages with a minimum of fuss and with virtually no learned references.[2]

Jacob Neusner's work on the Talmud might be identified as another major influence on Norman's methodological approach. Norman's stimulating interactions with his colleagues in Jewish studies at Manchester (along with John Wansbrough's own interest in Neusner's work) refined his vision of how the analysis of a text might proceed: with the text as the starting-point and focus of analysis, the unfolding of its structural layers serves to identify the functions of the work and the presuppositions of the compilers.

---

[1] Edward Said, *Humanism and Democratic Criticism* (New York: Columbia University Press, 2004), 100.

[2] Ibid., 87.

The essays in this volume witness the refinement in methodological approach and the broadening of research interests during Norman's unjustly truncated career. Starting with the articles on Shīʿī *fiqh* (Chapters XVII, XVIII), products of his dissertation research, the emergence of a distinctive writing style and methodology becomes increasingly apparent. Idiosyncratically, Norman often selected for analysis seemingly inconsequential passages, thus baffling or at least amusing readers by what they might anticipate to be a mountain made of a molehill – but those were precisely the passages required to fulfil the task of illustrating the ingenuity and individual creativity of the authors. The analytical methods employed in the articles about Friday prayer (Chapter XIII) and *ijtihād* (Chapter XXI) become increasingly refined in later contributions, such as those about Sarakhsī on *zakāt* (chapter XIV), Nawawī on *muftīs* (Chapter XV) and Ibn ʿĀbidīn also on *muftīs* (chapter XVI). His articles on fundamental juridical texts and concepts (chapters VIII, XI, XII) are grounded in attention to the precise form of juristic arguments, an approach that becomes the basis of all his later work. This is also reflected in four articles which remain unpublished, although it is hoped that they will, before too long, appear in book form; the titles of those articles reflect the on-going project of his *Studies in Early Muslim Jurisprudence* (Oxford 1993): "The Ḥanafī law on fornication"; "Nawawī and the typologies of *fiqh* writing"; "Scholars, *muftīs*, judges, and secular power: the need for distinctions"; and "The Social Function of *fatwās*." Although Norman focused increasingly on Sunnī Islam, as his research interests broadened, he also continued to develop his doctoral research in Shīʿism with influential contributions to this field, such as his articles on 17th-century juristic theory (chapter XX) and *ijtihād* (chapter XXI), as well as venturing into modern developments with reflections on the position of Khumaynī in the Shiʿi scholarly tradition (chapter XIX).

Many of Norman's later essays reflect an accomplishment that few of us can ever hope to achieve: truly reflective pieces of writing that summarize vast intellectual trends and centuries of learning, using original schemes that are stimulating and innovative. Inspired by the work of John Wansbrough, Norman found himself attracted not only to the question of Islamic origins, as seen in articles on *tafsīr* and *midrash* (chapter VII), lexicographical issues (chapters V, VI, VIII, IX) and identity formation (chapter X), but also more philosophical issues, as illustrated by his wide-sweeping contributions which attempt to summarize and appreciate the accomplishment of major Islamic intellectual traditions. The reflections on Wansbrough's *Sectarian Milieu* (chapter I), the essay simply entitled "Law" (from an encyclopaedia of philosophy) (chapter III) and the chapter on "orthodoxy" (chapter II) all illustrate the mature expression of Norman's vision. The latter article has drawn praise for the thought-provoking manner in which it tackles the question of the entire understanding of the nature of Sunnī Islam, rejecting the commonly-held notion that Islam is an "orthopraxy" and arguing instead that the needs and demands of the community led to the expression of an orthodoxy which served to define membership in that community.

The quality of Norman's scholarship has usually overcome any misgivings and prejudices others might have had concerning his new analytical approach, as can be witnessed by the recent publication in the Islamic Republic of Iran of a Persian translation of his article on "Law: legal thought and jurisprudence," which first appeared in the *Oxford Encyclopedia of the Modern Islamic World* (New York 1995). It was published in the December 2005 (Number 22) issue of the cultural periodical *Ḥāfiẓ*, which is available at most news-stands in Tehran. The editor prefaces the translation by informing the reader of its previous rejection by other periodicals for containing non-religious accounts of the history of early Muslim jurisprudence, but nonetheless argues that its unabridged translation is in line with the journal's principles of academic integrity. The faithful translator adds to the text only a parenthetical ("God save us!") after a brief reference to the ideas of John Wansbrough.

Norman's most influential article, as far as such matters can be judged, is perhaps "*Tafsīr* from Ṭabarī to Ibn Kathīr" (Chapter IV), a title frequently invoked and whose insights into the nature of *tafsīr* as a genre and as an intellectual activity have created a new way of talking about the material. His own conception of this article was that this was about "tafsir approaches to narrative: there are no approaches to narrative that distinguish that genre from anything else, but I tiptoe around this disturbing fact, while heaping immoderate praise on Qurtubi, moderate praise on Razi and ire and vituperation upon Ibn Kathir." This was an article to which Norman was embarking on writing a sequel at the time of his death. Tentatively entitled "Freedom and constraint in Quranic exegesis: the juristic mode," its plan was sketched out with the following points:

1. Meaning of title: *tafsīr* as a literary genre in juristic exegesis
2. Period to be covered: 3rd to 13th century
3. Characteristics of this period; the dominant type of religious discourse is juristic
4. Characteristic of juristic tradition: *madhhabs* – *ijtihād* – *taqlīd*; the structure of the law (whatever its origins) exists independent of the Qur'ān text. Therefore: a) the results of juristic exegesis can always be given in advance; b) the process of hermeneutical argument is unlimited – *irrespective* of the answer it brings; since an erroneous process illustrates the need to recognize correct procedures; c) the exploration of hermeneutical processes has just got to be the real purpose of *tafsīr*.

An examination of the exegesis of Q 24/3 through the explanations of al-Qurṭubī and Fakhr al-Dīn al-Rāzī is then to be presented with the following observations: 1) citation of authorities – tradition speaks through the scholar; 2) multiplicity of authorities – hermeneutical pluralism; 3) Rāzī and Qurṭubī both admit the appropriate meaning: it is Rāzī's first remark, his problematic; it is more deeply buried in Qurṭubī. The observations here suggest the following characteristics: 1) exploration of tradition: the community speaks in pluralism; 2) citation of heroes – the establishment of tradition – *isnād* and *matn*; 3) agreement in narratives – not part of a search for true history since that is not embedded in truth; 4) exploration of language and rhetoric.

A further note is to be given. Because the fundamental purpose of *tafsīr* is exploration of tradition, through authorities, nothing is lost. Even a rejected tradition is eternally there, for adducing if necessary. How, then, can development take place? There can be no new results – no change or real development of norms. There can be no elimination of material; the trace is permanent and even an erroneous argument may be recycled. But what we see is a refinement of expression and argument and some differences in preference. This theory would then be tested with a more complex case: Q. 4:15/4:16/24:2 where there is an apparent contradiction and a need for abrogation. This is the easier way to deal with texts of *tafsīr*, as the problem is also found in works of *fiqh* where the aim is getting to the point. Qurṭubī would then be examined, followed by Rāzī. In both instances, the scholars will be shown to follow a process of *naskh* for their exploration.

Another planned article was to look more directly at "Law and exegetical discourse in Islam," comparing *tafsīr* and *sharḥ al-ḥadīth*, and was to argue that the two genres were independent structures.

* * *

The editors of this volume wish to express their thanks to Anne Hall, the executor of Norman Calder's estate, for her permission to assemble the articles in this format and to the publishers and editors of the works in which the articles first appeared for their cooperation in allowing this volume to appear. We also thank Mona Sedky Goode of Victoria for her work on the Indexes to the volume.

JAWID MOJADDEDI AND ANDREW RIPPIN

New Brunswick, NJ/Victoria, BC
July 2006

ACKNOWLEDGEMENTS

Grateful acknowledgement is made to the following persons, journals, institutions and publishers for their permission to reproduce the articles included in this volume: E.J. Brill, Leiden (I, XV); The Institute of Ismaili Studies, London (II); Taylor & Francis, Oxford, http://www.tandf.co.uk (III, XIX); Oxford University Press, Oxford (V, IX); Cambridge University Press, Cambridge (VI, X, XIII, XVI, XVII, XVIII); Peeters Publishers and Booksellers, Leuven (VII); Walter de Gruyter GmbH, Berlin (VIII); *Studia Islamica*, Department of Near Eastern Studies, Princeton University (XI, XXI); Institut für Geschichte der Arabisch-Islamischen Wissenschaften, Frankfurt am Main (XII); Danish Academy of Science and Letters, Copenhagen and Jakob Skovgaard-Petersen (XIV); British Institute of Persian Studies, London (XX).

I

[47] History and Nostalgia: Reflections on John Wansbrough's *The Sectarian Milieu**

History may be servitude,
History may be freedom. See, now they vanish,
The faces and places, with the self which, as it could, loved them,
To become renewed, transfigured, in another pattern.

T.S. Eliot

[48] *1. Introduction*

In the final chapter of *The Sectarian Milieu* (1978), John Wansbrough allowed his analyses of literary types to become also a question about the response of a religious community, Islam, to God's self-revelation. He expressed the question in terms of a possible dichotomy between two approaches to history: history as process and history as event. In the former case, the patterns of (specifically) salvation history would be not only perpetually relevant, but also would offer a positive orientation to continuity and development. In the latter case, history becomes nostalgia: revelation is once for all time, over, an event nostalgically recalled – time past contained in time past. The question was intimately related to a typology through which Wansbrough aimed to characterize the varied epistemologies of Muslim religious literature. Hazardous, no doubt, it was to move from the functions of literary criticism to those of social description, but Wansbrough's studies had on numerous occasions discovered the permeability and the ambivalence of that boundary (1978: 132).[1] His last transition was less concerned with the social reality of religion, than with the theological.[2] If the question was not quite inevitable, it had

* For copyright reasons, this article has been reset. References to the pagination of the original are indicated in square brackets.

1 The problem was warily acknowledged throughout *The Sectarian Milieu* (1978: 54–55, 146), less warily in *Quranic Studies,* which offered some conclusions about "the emergence of an independent and self-conscious religious community" (1977: x).

2 "The fourth and final chapter contains a tentative and emphatically provisional reply to the *theological* question of history as event or of history as process." (1978: x, italics added)

at least that appearance, and, once articulated, had also the effect, retrospectively, of placing the whole of Wansbrough's scholarship, in *Quranic Studies* and *The Sectarian Milieu,* under a single heading: the history of revelation, in its largest sense, in Islam. *The Sectarian Milieu* is a sequel to *Quranic Studies.* God's revelation is not just a book, certainly not when it is viewed through the conceptual structures of modern theology and modern literary criticism. It is, perhaps, an offer: either the retrogressive stasis of nostalgia or the constitutive ground of choice, servitude or freedom.

Wansbrough effects a strong reading of Islamic theology, strong both for the reader (Wansbrough) and for the text. In the former sense it is Harold Bloom's strong reading that is at issue: Wansbrough has appropriated a tradition and made it his own, and offers it in an unexpected guise to his readers – a strong reading because a creative and a personal one (Bloom 1973). But, in a manner closer to the theories of Hans-Georg Gadamer (1975: 245–274), Islam too is given strength in this reading. By a constitutive act of prejudgement, Islam is assumed to be worthy of as much sustained effort of observation and analysis as can be managed within the structures of contemporary modes of discourse. That Wansbrough struggles to be of his time [49] and to see Islam with an access of understanding that is available only to his time may be obvious, but might not reconcile Muslims *qua* Muslims, or historians *qua* historians, to the merits of his approach.

For those who have been trained only in the best and highest tradition of pre-modern Muslim scholarship, it could not be true that Wansbrough's assessment of Muslim literature gives a suitable expression of Islam. Nor indeed could this be true for those who deny or are indifferent to the value of a complex intellectual assessment of faith. But for those who recognize or affirm that faith requires intellectual expression, then only the most complex and revealing idioms of contemporary discourse will serve the need to re-express a traditional faith. Islam (like Judaism and Christianity) has been here before. It may come, initially, as a shock (a scandal perhaps) to a traditional believing Muslim to hear, first that the Qur'ān is not words uttered by Muḥammad in Arabia in the seventh century C.E., but words that emerged in a cultic or paraenetic context in the Fertile Crescent, over centuries; and then, worse perhaps, that this is a strong expression of the theological truth-claims of Islam. But, for those who are aware of the possibilities grasped in the late twentieth century for the intellectual restatement of traditional faiths and values, this transfer of the document of revelation from "event" to "process" is potentially a strong and attractive reading of revelation in Islam: revelation not passively received (the Prophet as God's puppet) but forged in the experience of the community. It may well be found, this scandalous affirmation articulated, that a similar message is already present in the tradition, only differently expressed.

For scholars in religious studies, revelation can never be perceived directly as an act of God, or a fact of history. God's self-revelation to a given community can only be accessible to scholarship as a historical process, effectively a literary one, and one in which the community partakes creatively. Irrespective of the degree of metaphor discovered in the notion that God writes himself, it is the writings of God's mediators that are available for analysis. Not even of the Qur'ān is it claimed that God dictated, and merely dictated, it. (The most sophisticated Islamic theology had a very complex understanding of the relationship between God's eternal speech, and the individual words of the Qur'ān [see note 6].) God's self-revelation is not different from the effort of the community to express its understanding of God, and since that (in all its highest forms) is necessarily a literary achievement, it will be subject to the usual constraints of language and its effective manipulation, and the usual conventions of literary type and genre. To know God, it is reading skills that are required. But the act of reading is a creative one: the message depends on the reader's interaction with the text. God is what the reader makes of his (God's) texts. Wansbrough has engaged in a reading of the literature through which the Muslim community [50] gave expression to its perceptions of God's revelation. And he gives that literature, generally, a strong and attractive reading – in spite of occasional dicta which reveal an ungenerous impatience with this or that aspect of the tradition.

For historians, those who look on texts as a source of facts, Wansbrough's complexity of thought and language, can seem of little value. His polemical stance can be read as denying any value or merit to the historian's task; and he seems indifferent to the problems he leaves aside, the blank spaces in history that seemed to yawn in the first decade after *Quranic Studies.* (They have become less frightening in recent years: historians can live and work in a less crowded world). In fact, Wansbrough is himself a historian; he moves rapidly and frequently from the texts he studies to the nature and qualities of the community that produced them. Though he claims frequently to be studying literature, there are purer ideals of what it might mean to study literature than he admits. Mostly, he is a historian of thought, and specifically of theological thought; that is, of one discipline of rational thought characteristic of humans as intellectual beings. In this respect it is easy to see why his language is complex and tortuous, and the struggle with words transparent: this is an ambitious project of assimilation of diverse literary forms, and complex theological messages. It is not (merely) history.

The question which Wansbrough articulates throughout the fourth chapter of *The Sectarian Milieu* relates to Muslim concern for the functional continuity of revelation (1978: 141). In asking about that concern he is effectively expressing his own, and it is possible to ask of him too whether he approaches Islam with "a sense of history" or "nothing more than nostalgia". That dichotomy might be translated into another modernist question, namely whether he approaches Islam as something alien (the other) or something the same (the self), whether its experience is, for him, merely out there, or, with something like the force of kerygma, also ours. But the question, of him, is too starkly put – he does both. And it may be, in the end, that the question that he poses of Islam is also too stark. It is not a promising pre-judgement of one of the world's great religions that it should fall clearly and wholly into an either-or situation in respect of revelation as process and revelation as event. In Wansbrough's approach to Islam, the insistence that the Islamic kerygma is a continuation of the biblical one (of the Hebrew and the Christian Bible) brings it closer to Western observers and elevates its status. Islam is discovered to share, at a level that is not simply heresy, error, or misunderstanding, a structure of concepts, beliefs, and literary forms which are familiar and seductive; it is a restatement of something that is constitutive of ourselves. But precisely that discovery of sameness may also be a motive for re-asserting difference. Wansbrough's reading of Islam (mostly) gives that tradition an intellectual and imaginative force [51] which makes it also a challenge, especially for believers, or for those who, without belief, have inadvertently taken over the prejudices of the academic tools they use. Some of Wansbrough's pre-judgements are not quite so valuable as others. "As an object of nostalgia the monotheist theophany, *particularly in its Jewish and Muslim forms,* is not inappropriate" (1978: 142, my italics). But nostalgia, for Wansbrough, is a weakness and a function of self-deception[3] and this casual ranging of the Jewish and the Muslim faiths against (implicitly) the Christian faith may reflect in him nothing more than nostalgia. So also his judgement that the rabbinic concept of Torah may be characterized "not as historical but as nostalgic" (1978: 146). Since these are pre-judgements, it is possible that in his formulation of the question, deemed "crucial" (1978: 141), whether Islam fell on this side or that of the history-nostalgia divide, the cards were already stacked in favour of a negative answer.

2. The liturgical reading of scripture

Wansbrough's interest in the Qur'ān is predominantly historical; he is more interested in the question of how it achieved its present form than in the question of how it is (or might be) read, given the form it currently has. His interest in formulae, at least in *Quranic Studies,* is such that he sees in them confirmation of "a composition made up of originally unrelated pericopes." The word *qul* (say), for example, has a number of possible functions, none of them consistently carried out, some of them more and some less inviting the suspicion of interpolation (1977: 14–15). Its overall effect is, perhaps, to enhance "stylistic homogeneity" in a text "characterised by the absence of logical structure." But there is more to *qul*

3 "So regarded, every historiography must contain an element of imposture, and thus not so far distant from the self-deceptions of nostalgia, however unconscious these might be." (1978: 142)

than this. Taking the text as a whole, and remembering that God is the speaker, the effect is one of direct address, from God to the receiver/reader. Its tone depends on context. In the remarkable sequence of three final suras, each beginning with *qul*, there is not simply an indication of "liturgical instructions, frequently prayer", but a particular literary effect which depends on context. From Sura 80 to Sura 112, the word *qul* occurs only once, as the first word of Sura 109. Shortly afterwards, picking up the possibility of *qul* as introductive, comes that final sequence of three suras whose first word is *qul*. The mood of the preceding section is predominantly dark and angry, the imagery apocalyptic and mysterious. The suras are short, transitions abrupt. The verses too are short, [52] rhythms strong, rhymes sharp and rapidly recurring. The overall effect of galloping, breakneck, towards a conclusion is echoed in the apocalyptic imagery, in the quickening rhythms, and in the deictic knowledge that the reading is coming to a close. In this context, the threatening content and harsh plosives of Sura 111, *tabbat yadā abī lahab wa-tabba* (perish the hands of Abu Lahab, perish he), give way quite remarkably to the assonance and tranquillity of *qul huwa ʾllāhu aḥad*. The long sequence of "l" sounds echoes through the repeated name of God and continues into *lam yalid wa-lam yūlad wa-lam yakun la-hu* ... The phonetic patterning mimics the sense, with its initial stress on one-ness, and its contrasting pattern of affirmation and negation. This close-knit pattern of sound, rhythm, and meaning achieves a neat effect of closure and enclosure with the repetition of *aḥad* (one) as rhyme word in the first and in the last verse. "Say he is God, one. God the eternal. Neither gave he birth, nor was he born. He has no equal. One." (The alternative reading, "he has no equal, none", is present in the Arabic vocal pattern, and enhances the sense of semantic plenitude given by this sura.) *Qul* functions here, importantly, at a phonetic and rhythmic level; but its effect is also informative. God has been speaking in a predominantly harsh voice, distant and threatening. With the word *qul* he moves towards intimacy, suddenly offering a verbal image of one-ness and at-one-ness, a decisive change in mood and pace. This mood of offering is repeated in the last two suras, which, here, are not simply prayers or liturgical chants, but gifts offered directly from speaker to reader, in an intimacy of giving and receiving – which owes all of its intimacy to the word *qul* and much of its effect to its context, after apocalypse, as an act of closure and parting.

The origins of *qul huwa ʾllāh aḥad* may be polemical, but it is not polemical in its present context. The origins of *qul aʿūdhu bi-rabb al-falaq* (say: I seek refuge with the lord of the dawn) may be cultic or routine prayer (and parallels to this form of prayer may be found external to the document of revelation [Mālik ibn Anas 1984: 693]), but, again, in context, and largely by virtue of the introductory *qul*, these prayers are transformed and become an effective act of closure. Wansbrough's perceptions about the linguistic and literary nature of the Qurʾān are often pinned to the question of origins, but are easily translated to the question of effect. For him "variant traditions", like compositional formulae, point to questions of collection and incorporation in a canon (1977: 20–27), but in the text of the Qur'ān they function as themes that recur, patterns of meaning that echo in the mind and build towards a whole.

The search for wholeness and unity in the Qur'ān is a feature of contemporary scholarship which has frequently rested at the level of sura (e.g., Mir 1993; Johns 1993; Abdel Haleem 1993). A resolution of that problem, however, must depend on an answer to the question of unity in the document as a [53] whole. Wansbrough's studies, in a number of ways, suggest an approach to the larger question. His analysis of the contents of the Qur'ān in terms of imagery associated with retribution, sign, exile, and covenant (1977: 2–12) is a strong argument that the document exhibits unity of subject matter. (I think the analysis could be developed but it will stand for now.) The explicit corollary that this work should be read in the light of the biblical tradition, where these themes have an earlier airing, is well-taken, and an obvious way of achieving a richer understanding (just as *Joseph and his Brothers, Ulysses,* and *The Four Quartets* gain a richer meaning for those who are conscious also of Genesis, the *Odyssey,* and the *Divine Comedy).* From the mixed messages that the Qur'ān has "stylistic homogeneity" and "absence of logical structure" or that it is "a torso" something positive may be retrieved, for these remarks point to genuine qualities of style and subject matter. This book is easily experienced as a linguistic and rhetorical unity; it is not characterized by the kind of logic found in theology or philosophy; and it is essentially allusive in the sense of pointing insistently outwards, towards a body of knowledge external to itself. Most illuminating of all to my mind is the observation, essentially of *The Sectarian Milieu,* that Muslim scripture is liturgical. Wansbrough says that its origins were liturgical, and proceeds to ask questions about the emergence of the text and its symbolic function within the community. He demonstrates in fact that its form is liturgical. This observation depends not only on the specific patterns of refrain and structural formulae (pausal phrase, incipit formulae, stereotyped collocation, etc.) which he analyses in *The Sectarian Milieu* (1978: 59–69) but also on the general demand made by this text for acknowledgement of rhythm at all levels of reading. The cadences, rhymes, and formulaic patterns of juxtaposed verses create small rhythmic patterns; but larger looser rhythms are created by refrains within a sura, by verbal collocations that transcend suras, by compositional formulae (like *qul)* and even by variant traditions.

The rhythmic quality of the text, manifest at the levels of phrase, verse, and unit of meaning, has a different recurrence in the ordering of suras. The transition from longer suras to shorter ones is not mathematically consistent, but it is one of the marked rhythms of the book, and it is a formal element that points towards an end, the pattern of ever shorter suras and faster transitions creating the expectation of a final closure – though it arrives unexpectedly, not breathless, but in the form of a parting gift. The length of verses within suras varies roughly in the same direction, so enhancing the effect of movement towards an end. Thematic material is also treated rhythmically, not with the logic of philosophy but perhaps with that of music. Motifs of various kinds, of law or narrative, of theology or eschatology, in the form of prayer, adjuration, polemic, etc., are introduced, elaborated and then dropped, to be repeated later, expanded perhaps, explored, [54] or transformed: the literary effect is of richness deriving from anticipation and from memory. Meaning and message in this work are intimately related to repetition and recurrence. But the repetition is not unchanging: on balance larger structural blocs give way to shorter, looser, more fragmented material (like the long suras and the long verses giving way to shorter), and there is a gradual instantiation of a dominant apocalyptic mood. Contained between a prayer and a prayer, drawing together time past (narrative), time present (law), and time future (apocalypse), rhythmic in its themes and in its language, with patterns of recurrence and patterns of development, and an overall flow towards a pre-ordained end, the intimate giving of its closure and parting – few books are so obviously unified, so obviously demand to be experienced as a whole. In the light of these observations, any focus on the unity of the sura may be counterproductive: the meaning of a sura will always depend on its place within the whole, on its sustaining and developing the overall rhythm, whether of language or theme.[4]

Books that constitute a unity are not necessarily complete, and not necessarily the product of a single authorial mind. (Proust's *A la recherche* is a unified work of art, though it would certainly have been longer had Proust lived; the Hebrew and the Christian Bibles can each be read as a unity, though in relation to each other they are either expanded or deficient.) The Qurʾān is experienced by Muslims, and derivatively by the rest of us, as a single complete work, offering some kind of unified experience. The primary locus of experience for Muslims is of course liturgical, as when the Qurʾān is recited throughout the month of Ramaḍān, or on other occasions of heightened community feeling, at the celebration of a marriage or a death. It is experienced in a more fragmentary manner at daily prayer and in the mosque. But the fragments presumably come together on significant occasions, when the whole is recited (and indeed traditional patterns of Muslim education began and still begin with the memorization of this document, as a whole).

---

4 Abdel Haleem's study of Sūrat al-Raḥmān (1993) does take account of the way that the motifs of this sura echo motifs and elaborations found elsewhere in the Qurʾān. I think he over-stresses the idea that because a sura can be shown to have some kind of integrity and unity, its component parts cannot have a history, e.g., of the kind suggested by Wansbrough. The discovery that the text of the Qurʾān has a redaction history is one thing. The discovery that it can be read in its final form as a unified literary structure is another.

To read something liturgically is not quite the same as reading either a novel or a poem. The rhythmic patterns and linguistic redundancy that we expect to find in liturgies, together with the humdrum familiarity of words repeated, will tend to lull the reader into an inattentive rest, away from meaning; but will occasionally move the reader to the unexpected recapture of meaning. Gabriel Josipovici (1988) thought that liturgy functions in some re- [55] spects like Proust's *A la recherche:* it calls upon the possibilities of involuntary memory, which is quite unlike the willed memory of the historian (or adults who recount their childhood, "recount" as opposed to "re-experience"). Liturgy "makes accessible to our daily selves a memory which is alive, which is quite other than the historian's memory." (Josipovici 1988: 150)

Now, liturgy is clearly a function of community, and it has a curious and many-sided participation in our memories. What is learnt in childhood as a verbal pattern, in a context of community worship, remains the same in adulthood; but, with experience and knowledge, this same thing gains greater access of meaning. The meaning of course is the meaning of the past, and the future. (In the liturgical experience of Jews, Christians, and Muslims, there is a striking sameness of message, which depends on recurrence of theme, motif, character, and detail.) The pattern of our lives (from childhood, through experience of births, marriages, and deaths, to adulthood and age – for time and transition is where liturgy is evoked) is measured out in liturgy – in narratives allusively recalled, in prayers of thanks and supplication, in reflections on law and theology, in fear and in hope – and its elements recur and are transformed in all these. The life of the individual fuses with the life of the community, the childhood and the age of each are brought into a single pattern.

> The liturgy allows the participant to lead his life without falling into the temptation of either nostalgia for the irrecoverable past, or the apocalyptic desire for a sudden end. It has neither the atavistic quality of the return to a dream time, nor the purely intellectual quality of the study of the past. It allows the individual to age naturally by recognising that he is made up of the past and yet exists now, and is always moving into an open future ... Memory and repetition make the past live again. (Josipovici 1988: 150)

Make the past live again, and bring the future into our present; time past and time future contained in liturgy. Or, potentially so. For we cannot always be awake to all of the potential meanings of a liturgical text. It is by virtue of its humdrum effects, its permanent presence throughout the indifferent days and weeks and years, that it develops the power to catch us by surprise. Reading liturgy, we are surprised by a meaning that is both memory and repetition; celebrating a festival, a birth, or a death, we are caught by a phrase that evokes our past and our future, and our community's.

Josipovici's concern to achieve a set of words that will set the Jewish and Christian communities, in their liturgical approaches to the Bible, free from the charge of nostalgia is not just a lucky accident for a student who wants to write about Wansbrough. In the last decades of the twentieth century, for believers and non-believers, the problems of community identity and continuity, and indeed the fundamental question of value and legitimacy in the experience of community, have become pressing subjects of discourse. Nostalgia is [56] one of the key words through which this concern is expressed. Wansbrough's portrayal of Islam does much to free that community from the accusations of nostalgia which, usually unarticulated and mostly unperceived, colour a majority of Western depictions of Islam. It is too often for them a static religion, its meaning contained wholly in its foundation experience.[5] But Wansbrough, in the end, also decides that Islam was a religion of nostalgia — albeit only after considerable wrestle with words and meanings. The decision matters, but is less important than the struggle to articulate the question and to isolate some of the themes and motifs that promise an answer. In his Preface, Wansbrough describes his achievement as "a tentative and emphatically provisional reply" to the question he had formulated (1978: x).

I have already suggested my own view that a more generous pre-judgement might have produced a different formulation of the question: not *whether* the Muslim concept of revelation (in the larger sense) reflected a sense of "event", "nostalgia", "once and for all time", or "history", "process", and "continuity", but *how.* The answer to that would be much more varied than is permitted within the relatively narrow limits explored by Wansbrough. And there is need for an important caveat. It is always possible to give a nostalgic reading to an event, to a book, or to a tradition. The question ought really to be in what ways (and they are many) the Islamic experience of salvation history (a primarily literary experience) was open to non-nostalgic readings. History might be servitude, it might be freedom: the resolution lies perhaps with the reader. What Wansbrough did in the end was to offer a list of dogma that tended to work either in this direction or in that. Against the notions of closure and nostalgia were (in some respects) the concepts of *naskh* (abrogation), *ikhtilāf* (variant views), *fiṭra* (natural faith), *umma* (community), *ijmāʿ* (consensus), *fitna* (strife), and, perhaps, *tawātur* (authoritative

---

5 It is possible that this reflects the dominance of a Protestant sensibility allied to a nineteenth-century historiography. Historians who attempt a biography of Muḥammad are particularly tempted by an essentialist approach to religion, as are those who attempt any history of the early community. The tendency is peculiarly noticeable in the concluding pages of Michael Cook's *Muḥammad,* and especially in his last sentence: "The bleakness which we saw in [Islam's] conception of the relationship between God and man is the authentic, unadulterated bleakness of the universe itself." (1983: 89) That bleakness can only be product of a literary game of excavation, it has nothing to do with the richness and diversity of historical Islam, and in no way reflects the meaning that the events of the Prophet's life had for Muslims. The Muḥammad Cook describes is simply not the Muḥammad who lived in the imaginations of Muslims through the generations.

transmission). They seemed inadequate to the task, especially when credal beliefs in Muḥammad as seal of the Prophets, the Qurʾān as immutable word of God, law as prophetical precedent acted in the opposite direction (1978: 134–6, 139–40). It is all "much closer to the [57] Rabbinic concept of Torah". And that concept "may be characterised not as historical but as nostalgic" (1978: 146).

3. The exegetical reading of scripture

The Muslim notion of revelation as event was eventually encapsulated in acknowledgement of a book as the immanent word of God. Wansbrough showed how that book might be understood as the result of a historical process. With its canonization, the process was transformed, but not in the sense of cessation. The book had to be read. Like all books, it could be read nostalgically, but, experienced liturgically, it had a potentially transforming quality in spite of any credal beliefs that acted in the opposite direction.[6] Further, the Qurʾān was not read only liturgically, it was also read scholastically, that is, in and through the literary genre of *tafsīr* (exegesis). If a liturgical reading depended on humdrum familiarity and on linguistic redundancy to make it work, the scholastic type depended on opposite qualities. It was based on a meticulous denial of redundancy and an insistent realization that every word was a significant bearer of meanings. Liturgy enables the integration of the individual in the community through experience; it evokes its response precisely by virtue of persistent casual reading. *Tafsīr* is also an experience of integration and community, but its effects depend on attention [58] to detail, focused discrimination, and deliberate, systematic rediscovery of the text's allusions.

---

6 The credal belief that the Qurʾān was the *immutable* word of God (Wansbrough's preferred word) was not in fact explored directly in relation to that concept. That it was the word (speech) of God in any sense at all (for God does not speak in the sense of articulating sounds) was sufficiently problematic. That it was, in some sense, the eternal and uncreated word of God proved to be, for the mainstream of Sunni theologians, not simply an added complexity but a way to achieve an intellectual resolution of a profound theological problem. By a series of careful distinctions, they were able to affirm both that the familiar written text was, and that it was not, identical with the eternal word of God. It was in fact a physical manifestation of an inner speech *(kalām nafsī),* and it was the latter which was the eternal and unchanging speech of God. The eternal speech of God did not permit of division. For many thinkers of the Ashʿari and Māturīdī traditions, the relationship between the articulated words and the eternal speech could be expressed in terms of the relationship between the word "fire" and the real thing "fire". The sound and the concept "fire" are signifiers *(dalla ʿalā)* and not identical with the thing that heats and burns; in a parallel manner, the words of the Qur'an signify the eternal (immutable) speech of God. The formula that expressed the credal belief was insisted on: *al-Qurʾān kalām Allāh ghayr makhlūq,* the Qurʾān is the speech of God, an uncreated thing — not quite the same as the assertion that the Qurʾān is the uncreated speech of God. A fairly conventional account of these matters can be found in the commentary of Saʿd al-Dīn al-Taftazānī (d. ca. 791/1389) on *ʿAqāʾid al-Nasafī* of Abū Ḥafṣ ʿUmar al-Nasafī (d. 537/1143) (1326: 87, see also Elder 1950). See also the neat articulation of Muslim theory by Weiss (1992: 65–69).

In summarizing mood, in a passage that proleptically signalled his concern with the question of history as process and history as event, Wansbrough affirmed that "the primary concern of Islamic literature is with the past. Even the utterly timeless quality of scripture was neutralised by the several varieties of exegesis, each designed to provide a temporal and spatial context for revelation." (1978: 130) But *tafsīr*, as a genre, certainly embraced more that the provision of a temporal and spatial context for revelation. At its best, it transcends and negates any interest of this kind. In his study of *asbāb al-nuzūl* (occasions of revelation), Andrew Rippin (1981) showed again and again that the play of narrative in an exegetical context did not place the text in a (single) historical event. It offered an explanation of the text through story. The narrative form gave vitality to a number of different theological concerns (not unlike the narratives of *Sīra* for which Wansbrough has, I think incontrovertibly, demonstrated a theological message) (1978: 1–49).[7] Variant readings, polemical argument, removal of ambiguity, resolution of metaphor, and simply edifying entertainment were amongst the factors discovered by Rippin to be relevant to and explanatory of the way that *asbāb* were used. The reader-response that tries to make of the *sabab* a historical referent demonstrating that something stated in the Qurʾān "really happened" is systematically frustrated. As Rippin says, the desire to see in *asbāb* material the provision of a historical referent may be a "misunderstanding based on reading too many modern concerns into medieval literature" (1981: 439). Where *sababs* are introduced into *tafsīr*, they are frequently more than one. While they may act to limit the possible readings of a verse, the information they convey is "far too varied and flexible to allow decisions [about the context or the significance of a verse] to be based primarily on it" (1981: 441).

Sababs do not represent the totality of narrative material that emerges in *tafsīr*. In the course of a complete *tafsīr* it is necessary for the exegete to recall and re-express a body of narratives relating to all of the prophets mentioned in the Qurʾān, including the Prophet Muḥammad, either directly, in response to an explicit allusion in the text, or indirectly, because law, theology, polemic, prayer, or linguistics generated a possibility of narrative recollection which was in the event seized and acted on. The narratives available to the tradition were varied in their details. The reasons for their recall and repetition were also varied: to entertain, edify, provoke thought, elucidate [59] theology, justify polemic, or manifest the rhetorical and linguistic capacity of the Arabic language. Loyalty to the history of the genre, while it acted in some respects to limit the capacity of a verse to engender narrative expansion, also ensured the preservation even of eccentric

---

7 Rippin points to the similar functions of narrative in Sīra, as analyzed by Wansbrough, and in *sabab* material (1981: 439).

I

views, which might eventually be incorporated into major arguments. The effect of all this is to force a literary reading of the Qurʾān, and to pre-empt a historical one. Narratives do not just tell, they work; and, as presented in *tafsīr,* they do not, except for a careless and indifferent reader, conduce to a nostalgic reading of the Qurʾān, but rather to a dynamic one.

Narratives are only a small part of exegesis. If, by virtue of their form, they necessarily evoke a concern with the past, that concern is neutralized in part by their diversity, which prompts the realization that they are narrative play, and in part by the other large concerns of exegesis: law, theology, and language. All of these are timeless structures, intellectual abstractions, redeemed from time, but not arrested: they draw upon and mesh with the patterns of narrative to create interlocking structures of timeless relevance. In my own study of a handful of narrative motifs related to the story of Abraham (1993: 104–106), I found that the exegetes characteristically played across the substantive disciplines of Islam (prophetic history, theology, law, eschatology, even, marginally, Sufism) and the linguistic ones (orthography, lexis, syntax, rhetoric) to create highly complex and individual patterns, which demonstrated that normative structures (of law, theology, and language) interacted endlessly with narrative structures – an intersection of the timeless and the time-bound. Every *tafsīr* is a new world, but it is also the old-made-explicit, both of its time and containing the past.

In a characteristic re-articulation of the question that bothered him throughout *The Sectarian Milieu's* fourth chapter, Wansbrough asked whether concern with historical consistency, with the success of a community as it moved through time, was an issue of interest to Islam. If such a concern could be shown, would not this represent a shifting of "the burden of proof ... from the foundation event *(nomos)* to the subsequent understanding of that event"? (1978: 136–137) In the subsequent intricate arguments that searched for acknowledgement of "history as revelation", (1978: 137–138) Wansbrough came gradually and uncertainly to his pessimistic conclusion about Islam. But it is precisely, it seems to me, in certain formal features of *tafsīr* that we can find demonstration of what Wansbrough seems to require – a demonstration that the Muslim community was not concerned merely with the contemplation of a past event but with the meaning of that event as discovered in and through the experience of the community. For it is not characteristic of *tafsīr* that the exegete stands alone before the text and offers a personal account of its meaning or an aesthetic appreciation of its form. Both the subjectivity of the personal and the abstracted objectivity [60] of the aesthetic appreciation are denied in the process of *tafsīr.* The exegete cites authorities. The authorities include the Prophet himself and his companions and successors, but also succeeding generations of scholars up to each receding present. The meaning of the Qurʾān was not the meaning it had once, even as articulated by the Prophet himself, but the meanings that had been discovered in it, after and including the initial input of the Prophet, through the efforts of scholars, through centuries.

It was the interpretative experience of the historical community (represented by its scholars) that counted, not merely that of individuals. The formal articulation of this message lies in the way that exploration and articulation of meaning is achieved in *tafsīr* through the citation of authorities (Calder 1993: 102–103). Not only in the discipline of *tafsīr* but also in that of *sharḥ* (commentary on *ḥadīth*, like the *Fatḥ al-Bārī* of Ibn Ḥajar al-ʿAsqalānī) and in all the literature of the law, the same message is re-expressed – that it is through the historical experience of the community and the acknowledged achievement of earlier scholars, by building on the insights (narrative and analytical) that they produced, that progress took place. This apparently backward orientation was in fact an orientation towards the future, for it was a legitimate expectation (and one proved in the event) of each new generation of scholars, that the best of them would be constitutive of the past of the coming generations.

For Muslims who experience the Qurʾān as liturgy, this single text, learnt in childhood as a pattern of sounds, takes on new meanings with age, experience, and knowledge. For the community as a whole, the text that was received in the childhood of the community gained, in *tafsir,* new and richer meanings through and within the history of the community. And all of the meanings were perpetually present, for each succeeding generation assimilated the achievement of the past. Though the process was inevitably one of caducity (Wansbrough 1987: 24),[8] it also ineluctably created the challenge and the rewards of pluralism. Augustine, in the childhood of Christianity, reflected on the capacity of scripture to permit of several true interpretations. In the context of these reflections he was led to a number of similes which cast light on the peculiar nature of reading scripture (neither novel nor poem, nor, in the present context, merely liturgy). Scripture, for Augustine, was like a spring whose narrow compass contained great rivers. Its reader, in her/his immaturity, was like a child in the bosom of her/his mother, or an unfeathered bird finding comfort and security in a nest (in, as it were, a [61] humble reading). But later, the words of scripture were shady shrubberies *(opaca frutecta)* whose hidden fruits were searched out and plucked by mature birds/readers (1912: 12.27). Elsewhere, the dark secrets of scriptural writing *(tot paginarum opaca secreta)* were woods where deer/readers retired, and wandered, fed, rested, and chewed the cud (1912: 11.2). The sense of scripture as a space whose depths are not gauged by the experience of one reader, as a forest whose different paths are differently explored by different readers, is repeated in the formal characteristics of *tafsīr.* An exegete defines the space not by offering her/his own experience, which could

8 "Caducity" is a term used by Wansbrough (drawing on Jorge Louis Borges) to describe the processes of academic summary, textbook simplification, and detachable conclusion which transform lengthy academic argument into a chapter, a paragraph, or a footnote in the history of scholarship.

only be limited, but by offering the experience of others, thereby embracing a larger sense of space. The scriptural woods had no doubt snares and pitfalls as well as nourishing fruit and pasture. For St. Augustine, the church guarded against these. For Muslims, it was the consensual debate of generations that constituted authority and determined the limitations of permitted readings of the Qurʾān.

The upshot of these remarks is to suggest that there is an answer to the question Wansbrough raised in chapter four of *The Sectarian Milieu* which is quite different from the one he proposes. The translation of event into process, the assertion of a dynamic and continuing concept of revelation, was achieved for Muslims through reading — specifically through the act of reading the Qurʾān – for that was the pre-eminent articulation of God's self-revelation. This experience was available to all Muslims, liturgically and it was available scholastically to an elite. The relationship between the two types of reading was intimate. The capacity of lay people to sense in their experience of liturgy a sudden illumination was affected by their knowledge of the possibilities, or their experience of the possibilities, of a scholastic reading. That reading in all its pre-modem manifestations was a deliberate, systematic appropriation of the possibilities of the past – not the experience of one life only but of many generations. It involved not just a return to the meaning of the text, a restatement and renewal of what the text alluded to, but a return through the experience of the historical community towards a reticulation of meanings. Nor was this acknowledgement of history an assertion of evolution and transformation (a means of disowning the past), it was rather an assertion of timeless relevance. The fullness of reading available to a particular generation carried with it and derived from the readings of the past. The reading of scripture, like the use of memory, was for liberation — for the possibilities of the present were constituted by the experience of the past. Between servitude and chaos, the scholastic reading of scripture was, at least potentially, freedom.

[62] 4. *The legal "reading" of scripture*

Though the literary genre of *tafsīr* was formally the most obvious attempt of the Muslim community to give its scripture an intellectual and a dynamic reading, it was not in fact the genre with the highest prestige, nor the genre that offered the widest possibilities of intellectual self-expression in Islam. That status was reserved for *fiqh*, for exploration of the law. From the third Islamic century to the thirteenth (ninth to nineteenth C.E.), this discipline and its attendant genres moved gradually to an ever more dominant position as both the end and the means of education. It was through and in this discipline that the greatest intellectual and literary achievements of Muslim religious thought were achieved, and through this discipline that educated lay-people glimpsed and appropriated whatever notions they had of a lasting and dynamic significance for God's final and supreme act of self-revelation — that of the Qur'ān. For *fiqh*, like *tafsīr*, presented itself as a reading of scripture. This reading too had the peculiar characteristic that the reader was not the individual, but the community. The meaning of the law was always a function of what the community had so far experienced in its ongoing search for significance.

The literature of *fiqh* has not until recently been much appreciated by the West. This is partly because the Western concept of law is small and narrowly practical by contrast with the Muslim concept of *fiqh* which is large and orientated towards educational and literary ends, as well as encompassing the Western sense of things legal.[9] Muslim exploration of divine law and its translation into literary form cannot be understood simply in terms of the desire to influence practice (important though that is). It can be understood wholly as the effort to transform the event of revelation into a process of understanding which has perpetual relevance, including but not restricted to the sphere of the legal (in the Western sense). Writing-jurists who explored the tradition they inherited and gave it for their own time a new expression represented the highest grade of intellectual recognized by the Muslim tradition. Ideally, they kept themselves free from the mundane and potentially compromising tasks of both the *muftī* (legal consultant) and the *qāḍī* (judge) – each of these representing a step towards a narrower and more practical assessment of the law.[10]

[63] The question of how the discipline of *fiqh* could be understood as a reading of the Qur'ān depends on a theological myth which emerged in its final form only late in the tradition. Its essential components are familiar, though the subtleties and details depended on differential development of terminology and argument in different juristic schools and periods. The following account is based largely on the terminology and conceptions of the Shāfi'ī tradition as enunciated by Yaḥyā b. Sharaf Muḥyī al-Dīn al-Nawawī (d. 1277 C.E.).[11] The Qur'ān (though complete in itself and a miracle of eloquence, etc.) was, as a source of law, insufficient but contained within itself numerous pointers towards what completed it, namely the Sunna of the Prophet. Qur'ān and *ḥadīth* (the literary embodiment of Sunna) together constitute divine revelation *(waḥy)*. The definitive acts of translation of the structures of revelation into the structures of the law were taken in the course

9 It may be worth remarking that in certain periods of Western history, the study of the law has been almost as central to cultural expression as it was in Islam; and in few periods has it been quite so narrowly defined as in the second part of the twentieth century.

10 For a neat and suggestive assessment of the roles of the *muftī* and the *qāḍī*, see Reinhart (1993). I have insisted on the further distinction between the author-jurist and the *muftī* (Calder forthcoming).

11 Much of the following discussion is derived from my forthcoming paper mentioned in the previous note.

of the third and fourth centuries by the founding imams of the great schools of law – Abu Ḥanīfa, Mālik, Shāfiʿī, and Ibn Ḥanbal. By a willing act of affiliation *(intisāb)* and submission *(taqlīd)* (almost always dictated by family and geography) the vast majority of subsequent juristic thinkers accepted the basic structures of one of those independent readings of revelation and built on it. This was not an act of blind submission, for they were able to recreate the hermeneutical principles which had conditioned that initial act of independent *ijtihād* (a technical term which stresses the supreme effort that was required to get from the texts of revelation to the norms of the law). The structures of the law, in the form of topics, concepts, and rules, were set out in the genre of *furūʿ al-fiqh;* the justificatory rules and hermeneutical principles which explained the structures of each school *(madhhab)* were set out in the genre of *uṣūl al-fiqh* (the sources of jurisprudence). Both genres were renewed from generation to generation through the work of the author-jurists. Every subsequent generation of jurists discovered the meanings of the Qurʾān not through a direct and unmediated reading of revelation, but first through submission to that immense act of independent *ijtihād* which was attributed to the founding imam, and second, through acceptance of the further hermeneutical discoveries of scholars within a particular tradition. With a radical and incisive statement of what was historically the case, but scarcely articulated (at least by Shāfiʿīs) before him, the Shāfiʿī scholar Abū ʿAmr b. al-Ṣalāḥ (d. 1245 C.E.) made the necessary point: the texts of the *madhhab* of the imam are in relation to the *muftī* like the texts of the law-giver to the independent *mujtahid* (Calder forthcoming [64] cited from al-Nawawi [n.d.: 1.76]). Where the founding imam had "read" the texts of revelation, the later jurist read the texts of the juristic tradition and found his way through these back to the meanings of the Qurʾān which were in this context nothing other than the *madhhab* itself, both its rules and the personalities who gave it diachronic existence.

This situation was explicitly acknowledged in the forms of juristic works. The vast bulk of these belong to one or other of the four schools of law. They re-express and justify the structures of the founding imam. They present the law through citation of authorities. They develop a literature of hermeneutical engagement symbolized in the production of *matn* and *sharḥ, mukhtaṣar* and *mabsūṭ*. Each generation offers either a summary or an expansion of the achievements of the past *(mukhtaṣar* and *mabsūṭ)* and marks its commitment by making a past summary the basis for a contemporary expansion *(matn* and *sharḥ).* The facts are familiar. The assumption that these facts reflect decline, decay, and ankylosis is the product of a failure (or simply absence) of reading on the part of Western scholars. One of the last great exemplars of the tradition is the *Ḥāshiyat Radd al-Muḥtār* (1979) of Muḥammad Amīn b. ʿUmar, know as Ibn ʿĀbidīn (d. 1836 C.E.), a commentary on a commentary on an epitome *(mukhtaṣar),* and a work of extraordinary and sustained vitality.

Fiqh is (or, at its best, can be) precisely a dynamic reading of revelation which effects the transformation of event into process, giving it ongoing significance. If the smaller works of *furūʿ al-fiqh* simply present a structure of rules (the achieved translation of history into norm), the larger ones deliberately re-embed those rules in narrative (an interplay of the time-bound and the timeless). In the largest works, the whole of the tradition is brought into play, a medley of narrative origins and juristic opinions which constitute a theological message. A part of this message is the denial of significant evolution (the latter a means of denying the relevance of the past to the present), which is the same perhaps as an assertion of eternal relevance. But a denial of evolution is not a denial of time. The experience of understanding which was given to earlier generations by virtue of their participation in the system and in life remained relevant to, in fact constitutive of the experience and the possibilities of the present. In this respect it is possible to discover (paradoxically if not perversely) in the principle of *taqlīd* a central principle of vitality in the tradition of *fiqh*. For *taqlīd* (in so far as it designates submission to the authority of a founding imam and loyalty to a juristic school) is an assertion of hermeneutical continuity which need not be incompatible with change (understood perhaps as an assertion of the radical relevance and contemporaneity of a message that is timelessly valid). But *ijtihād*, at least as defined in the classical works, is a principle of static discovery of the law which (except in some of its twentieth-century manifesta- [65] tions) is probably incompatible with change.[12] The act of independent *ijtihād*, carried out by the founding imams, was authoritative and in some sense final (albeit perhaps marginally incomplete). Its meaning, however, changed from generation to generation and depended on the hermeneutical experience of the community – on reading the works of the imams, whose authority, in turn, depended on their reading of the texts of revelation.

The modern philosophical (and theological) understanding of the situation of Islam is eased slightly if we adopt and adapt some of the perceptions of Gadamer on the subject of hermeneutics. Gadamer would categorize the Western perceptions of the late nineteenth century which discovered in *taqlīd* a concept of "blind imitation" as a result of a post-Enlightenment sensibility, which stressed rationality and was incapable of a theoretical appreciation of hermeneutics. "Authority, ... properly understood, has nothing to do with blind obedience to a command. Indeed, authority has nothing to do with obedience, but rather with knowledge." (Gadamer 1975: 248) The expression is polemical, but the message is illuminating. For Gadamer, tradition and authority provided the indispensable grounds of self-knowledge, identity, and moral choice.

---

12 See the analysis of *Ijtihād* offered by Chaumont (forthcoming).

> The fact is that tradition is constantly an element of freedom and of history itself. Even the most genuine and solid tradition does not persist by nature, because of the inertia of what once existed. It needs to be affirmed, embraced, cultivated. It is, essentially, preservation, such as is active in all historical change. (Gadamer 1975: 250)

History is freedom, not servitude, when it is realized in and through a living tradition.

This kind of perception must transform our understanding of Islamic literature of the later period. All of its formal characteristics (citation of authority, polyvalency, summary, commentary, super-commentary) and many of its pertinent theoretical observations (like Ibn al-Ṣalāḥ on the significance of the *madhhab)* can be understood as an articulation of commitment to the diachronic community, and an acknowledgement that this is the necessary ground for continuing thought. "Our historical consciousness is always filled with a variety of views in which the echo of the past is heard. It is present only in the multifariousness of such voices: this constitutes the nature of the tradition in which we want to share and have a part." (Gadamer 1975: 252–253) Whether the multifarious voices were merely an addition – the trailing consequence of further days and hours – or a means to provide meaning in the present through the offer of relevant experience (not the experience of one life only but of many generations) might well be a nagging [66] question. But even the most insistently dynamic text can be read, perversely, as merely an object of nostalgia.

The multifarious voices which Gadamer presumed to be present in any genuine and solid tradition are present in the Muslim juristic tradition as *ikhtilāf* (variant views). Implicit or explicit in every work of, say, specifically Ḥanafī *fiqh*, and precisely because of its asserting its own self-identity as Ḥanafī, was an acknowledgement of the other traditions: the Mālikī, Shāfiʿī, and Ḥanbalī schools. The processes of mutual acknowledgement became easier and more comfortable with the passage of time (until the historical disjuncture of the nineteenth century), and were allied to the processes internal to each tradition whereby different views within the tradition had also to be acknowledged. At an intellectual and literary level, the broad structures of thought were both regional and local. Central Asia was Ḥanafī, North Africa Mālikī; but the Mālikīs of Spain showed a different pattern of preference from those of Qayrawān, and the Ḥanafīs of India did not just ape the great, revered tradition of Farghānah. The Shāfiʿīs of the Yemen prided themselves on a local scholarly tradition which vied with that of Cairo. At a practical level, local patterns of accommodation varied from place to place in accord with the different historical experience of different places. The literary phenomenon of *ikhtilāf* within a hermeneutical tradition was an intellectual reflection of the reality of diverse development within a single community. Wansbrough acknowledged *ikhtilāf* as a factor pointing away from nostalgia and towards a dynamic concept of revelation but he made remarkably little of it (1978: 134–135).

A final instance of the dynamic aspect of *fiqh* may be found in the way it articulated community responses to other tendencies that emerged in the history of Islam. I refer specifically to those movements termed *salafī* and to Islamic mysticism. The negative aspect of the hermeneutical tradition *(taqlīd)* was distance from revelation, and it inspired at various points in Islamic history a call for a return to the original texts and/or the early generations. In the introduction to Muzanī's *Mukhtaṣar,* a work that enacts the patterns of *taqlīd,* Shāfiʿī was portrayed as rejecting precisely *taqlīd* for himself and for his followers (Schacht 1950: 6). In the career and opinions of Dawūd al-Ẓāhirī, and in the whole of the Ẓāhirī school, the position was advanced of rejecting school affiliation in favour of a return to a plain reading of the original texts (Goldziher 1971). In all movements designated *salafī,* and especially in the works of Ibn Taymiyya and his followers, there was an attempt to reject tradition in favour of a return to the earliest generations. It is a significant pointer to the essential nature of the Islamic tradition as a whole that its great and successful movements are characteristically named after scholars (Ḥanafī, Mālikī, Shāfiʿī, Ḥanbalī), and its marginal and retrogressive movements are named after ideas: Literalism and Primitivism (*ẓāhirī* and *salafī*). [67] The enduring struggle of orthodoxy against primitivism can be exemplified in a number of historical episodes and movements. One such is that movement of Shāfiʿī scholarship which began with ʿAlī b. ʿAbd al-Kāfī al-Subkī Taqī al-Dīn (d. 1355 C.E.), continued through the life and works of his son, ʿAbd al-Wahhāb b. ʿAlī Tāj al-Dīn (d. 1369 C.E.) and culminated in the extraordinary life and achievement of ʿAbd al-Raḥmān b. Abī Bakr Jalāl al-Dīn al-Suyūṭī (d. 1505 C.E.). The stress here on a tradition and not on an individual is important. For the total vision of Islam, the body of materials which constituted its historical message, was such as could scarcely be controlled by a single writer. The elder Subkī's personal encounter with Ibn Taymiyya (which had unarticulated ramifications throughout his work [1952]) was transformed into the vast embrace of his son's *Ṭabaqāt al-Shāfiʿiyya al-Kubrā.* This book of "generations" (biographies) which articulated loyalty to a particular *madhhab* was precisely the demonstration of the relevance of the diachronic community in its traditional patterns of affiliation that was required to deny the claims of the *salafīs.* This movement of Shāfiʿī thought culminated in the combination of encyclopedic grasp and determined modernism which characterized the achievement of Suyūṭī. In a relatively homogeneous civilization, like that of Islam prior to the nineteenth century, the full message of the tradition is not articulated by one scholar, but by the joint efforts of many, through the generations and in a single generation, by continuously maintaining the traditional genres and re-expressing their message.

The debate between Salafism and orthodoxy had one of its most frequent realizations in relation to Sufism. For, at least in some views, the latter seemed to be a part of the experience of the community which was not fully grounded in revelation, and it included an epistemological principle that was not accounted for within the scholastic tradition. The expression of that principle varied. It can be found in a neat, early formulation in the *Kitāb al-Luma'* of Abu Naṣr al-Sarrāj (d. 988 C.E.), who stated: "There is nothing known and nothing understood except it be contained in the Book of God, or transmitted from the Prophet of God, or revealed in the hearts of the friends of God – *fī-ma futiḥa 'alā qulūb awliyā' Allāh.*" (1963: 1–2) It is symbolized, for a later period, in the title of the *Kitāb al-Futūḥāt al-Makkiyya* "The Book of Meccan Revealings" – of Muḥyī al-Dīn Ibn 'Arabī (d. 1240 C.E.). It was in relation to the practices of the Sufis that Ibn Taymiyya clashed with the elder Subkī. One of the features of the *Ṭabaqāt* of younger Subkī was his incorporation of Sufis into the Shāfi'ī tradition. And it was in extending the embrace of orthodoxy to include Sufi innovations that Suyūṭī had one of his great areas of achievement. It was in fact characteristic of the orthodox tradition and especially of the three major (and possibly also the fourth) schools of law that they found accommodation with the Sufi tradition and fought against the *salafī.* The point is confirmed by the varied patterns of [68] reference, often casual, but sometimes insistent, that recur in works of *fiqh.* In the *Ḥāshiya* of Ibn 'Ābidīn, he carefully incorporates within his brief biographical remembrance of Abu Ḥanīfa the information, well-established by his time, that amongst those who followed the great imam in his juristic methodology were many of "the noble friends of God", including Ibrāhīm b. Adham, Ma'rūf al-Karkhī, and Abū Yazīd al-Bisṭāmī (1979: 1.58–59). Later in the same work, Ibn 'Ābidīn is inclined to find, in the followers of [Ibn] 'Abd al-Wahhāb, the *salafīs* from Najd, a re-incarnation of the Khawārij (1979: 4.262). But, for the achievement of and the followers of Muhyī al-Dīn Ibn 'Arabī al-Shaykh al-Akbar he offers a more complex, more accommodating, assessment, which fully admits their place within the Sunni tradition (1979: 4.238–240).

5. *Islamic epistemology*

These reflections have taken me a long way from the work of Wansbrough. But they have a direct relevance to the argument of the last chapter of *The Sectarian Milieu.* In so far as the literary disciplines of *fiqh* and *tafsīr* represent the great intellectual traditions of Sunni Islam, they offer an authoritative and a dynamic reading of scripture which is precisely a means for the preservation of revelation as event and for its transformation into process – a literary transformation, whereby event was preserved but given a continuing relevance, a new voice constituted for the present out of the past.

Wansbrough began chapter four of *The Sectarian Milieu* with the suggestion that the concepts of legitimation and redemption necessary for the study of Islam might be reduced to three types: *nomos, numen,* and *ecclesia.* Under the rubric *numen,* he gathered all types of legitimation as the product of private vision, so defining this term that it embraced both the experience of the Sufis and that of the philosophers. But, for the history of Sunni orthodoxy, the category is insufficiently discriminated: for the experience of the mystic was incorporated into orthodoxy, and became a part of the reality of being a Muslim, whereas that of the philosophers was largely rejected, preserved by the tradition only as the marker of a boundary, not to be transgressed. The central concept of legitimation of the philosophers is intellect, that of the mystics is experience-and-illumination — the first implying a one-way movement towards God, the second an experience of two-way communion. Whatever the theoretical ramifications of the two movements, the difference was found to be radical in the experience and in the analyses of the Sunni orthodox tradition and deserves some reflection in contemporary academic schema. Under the rubric *nomos,* Wansbrough brings together the ideas of scripture (timeless, eternal and immutable) and legislation ("including neither the possibility of appeal nor the promise of change" [1978: 131]). But [69] again, distinction is required: the tradition itself distinguishes between the texts of revelation and the interpretation of those texts which is law. Legislation is precisely what God did not in the event provide; the structures of the law had to be drawn out of the texts of revelation by the immense creative act of *ijtihād* of the founding imams of the schools of law. They left their names upon those schools, as a sign of the human role in creating the law.

A modified version of the concepts of legitimation and redemption required for the study of Islam might then be the following (and I would restrict their relevance, at least provisionally, to the description of literary types — they are the concepts required for the categorization of Muslim religious literature):

1. revelation/text/primitivism
2. community/authority/continuity
3. mystic experience/illumination
4. intellect/philosophy

This is not so neat as Wansbrough's schema, but its significance will be evident in the light of the foregoing. Those texts (and arguments) which lay an overriding stress on the return to revelation, to the literal meaning of the documents of revelation, or to the meanings that were worked out in the primitive community — the movements known as Ẓāhirī, Salafī, and, possibly, amongst the Shīʿa, Akhbārī — all belong to the first category. To the second category belong all the major literary types of Sunni scholasticism: *fiqh, tafsīr, sharḥ,* and *ṭabaqāt.* To the third category belong works of the mystic tradition. To the fourth belong works of the Muʿtazilite as well as of the philosophical tradition - both of them movements perceived to over-stress the intellect as an independent source of religious knowledge. The historical experience of Sunni orthodoxy was worked out primarily in the second category and, by an act of appropriation, in category three. Categories one and four represent the boundaries of orthodoxy. Their messages were preserved by the main tradition as a means to establish boundaries, which, in the manner characteristic of a non-institutional and non-hierarchic community of intellectuals, were preserved ambivalently in the shifting patterns of discussion in search of consensus. (By contrast, the modern experience of Islam in one of its predominant aspects, that deriving from the thought and activities of Jamāl al-Dīn al-Afghānī and Muḥammad ʿAbduh, has reversed the pattern: the preponderance of categories two and three have given way to the preponderance of categories one and four.)

Wansbrough insisted at various points that his categories of legitimation were not intended to pre-empt the question of nostalgia versus history: "[B]oth *ecclesia* and *nomos* may generate a notion of history as revelation, [70] but neither need do so." (1978: 138) But it seems to me that both in his selection and in his definition of categories Wansbrough built into his assessment of the structures of Islam the answer that he eventually drew out. In the subsequent catalogue of items and arguments that made his case, careful and cautious though the expression never ceased to be, he made curious selections. This is nowhere more evident than in his selection of *tawātur* as a possible means for transforming event into process. This argument begins with a suggestion that the relation between law and history is "not so much antithetical as aetiological" (1978: 150). Neither of these seems to me a fruitful term to describe the flexible patterning of narratives, norms, and justificatory argument that in fact, in the literature of *fiqh,* characterized the interplay of history and law in Islam. Wansbrough stated here, however, more clearly than anywhere else, what was required: "the afterlife of an event perpetuated by constant interpretation". This precisely was the way that "event" might be reformulated as "process". And this precisely, in my view, is what was offered by the disciplines of *fiqh.* But Wansbrough looked in the wrong direction, to *tawātur,* to test his case. Unsurprisingly, the tradition failed the test, for *tawātur* is not a principle of constant interpretation. *Tawātur* is the epistemological category whereby the Muslim community guaranteed preservation of the event, not interpretation thereof. Though the insight remains paradoxical in the light of Western scholarship's insistently negative perceptions of *taqlīd,* it is that concept that carries the burden of integrating event and process in the history of Islamic law.

6. Conclusions

The writing persona of Borges' "Pierre Menard" (Borges, whose ironical glance illuminates and lacerates) noted a type of parasitic book – "which situates Christ on a boulevard, Hamlet on La Cannebière or Don Quixote on Wall Street" – as "fit only ... to produce the plebeian pleasure of anachronism or (what is worse) to enthral us with the elementary idea that all epochs are the same or are different." (1962: 39) Only marginally less elementary, I fear, is the recurrent idea of the foregoing, namely that all epochs are the same *and* different. To have found that this is the message of the literature of Muslim orthodoxy (with the intimation, too, that it is also the message of this epoch's glance at another) is, possibly, the eventual caducity of the present essay. In that respect at least, and in spite of the format of sustained *ikhtilāf*, it fathers itself – for I suspect that only Wansbrough's consciously literary embrace of the Islamic situation could have prepared for even this imperfect assertion that what we do in studying Islam is read literature, and what we find in what we study is the reading of literature. And [71] the reading of literature (like the use of memory, history, and the writing of *fiqh)* is possibly the best we can manage in achieving redemption from time — and I have finally assumed that that is what Wansbrough was searching for when he contrasted the nostalgic and the processual approaches to history and revelation. Both the smallness of the task was known to Borges ("It may be that universal history is the history of a handful of metaphors") and its infinite capacity for extension ("It may be that universal history is the history of the different intonations given a handful of metaphors"). (1962: 224–227) A very different intonation is found in T.S. Eliot's *The Four Quartets* which offer their own precise meditation on time, history, memory and community:

> We die with the dying:
> See, they depart, and we go with them.
> We are born with the dead:
> See, they return, and bring us with them. (Eliot 1943: 39)

In spite of the Christianity and the Englishness that offer him his symbols ("On a winter's afternoon, in a secluded chapel/History is now and England" [1943: 38]), Eliot's search for the meaning of history by an incorporation and a translation of the experience of the past into the present is not so very different from either a liturgical reading of the Qur᾿ān, *tafsīr*, or *fiqh*. This reduction merits again the ironic depreciation of Borges ("There is no exercise of the intellect which is not, in the final analysis, useless" [1962: 43]), but finds perhaps a more hopeful expression in Eliot's introduction to a valedictory sequence of metaphors:

> We shall not cease from exploration
> And the end of all our exploring
> Will be to arrive where we started
> And know the place for the first time ... (Eliot 1943: 39)

The intellectual experience offered to the pre-modern Muslim by the literary genres of the scholastic tradition began with the memorized words of the Qurʾān, and, after exploration, returned to the same words with an access of meaning which derived from the history of the community, discovered to be always the same and always different. The modern Muslim, like the modern student of Islam, like Wansbrough, begins elsewhere. The end is where we start from.

[72] References

Abdel Haleem, M. A. S. (1993). Context and internal relationship: Keys to quranic exegesis, a study of *Sūrat al-Raḥmān* (Qurʾān chapter 55). In G. R. Hawting and Abdul-Kader A. Shareef (eds.), *Approaches to the Qurʾān,* 71–98. London-New York: Routledge.

Augustine (1912). *St. Augustine's Confessions.* (W. Watts, trans.). The Loeb Classic Library. London: W. Heinemann.

Bloom, Harold (1973). *The Anxiety of Influence.* New York: Oxford University Press.

Borges, Jorge Luis (1962). *Labyrinths: Selected Stories & Other Writings.* New York: New Directions.

Calder, Norman (1993). *Tafsir* from Ṭabarī to Ibn Kathīr: Problems in the description of a genre illustrated with reference to the story of Abraham. In G. R. Hawting and Abdul-Kader A. Shareef (eds.), *Approaches to the Qurʾān,* 101–140. London-New York: Routledge.

– (forthcoming). Al-Nawawī's typology of muftis and its significance for a general theory of Islamic law. *Islamic Law and Society.*

Chaumont, Eric (forthcoming). L'Ijtihad et l'histoire. In R. Gleave and E. Kermeli (eds.), *Islamic Law: Theory and Practice.*

Cook, Michael (1983). *Muḥammad.* Oxford: Oxford University Press.

Elder, Earl E. (1950). *A Commentary on the Creed of Islam: Saʿd al-Dīn al- Taftazānī on the Creed of Najm al-Din al-Nasafī.* New York: Columbia University Press.

Eliot, T.S. (1943). Little Gidding. In *Four Quartets,* 31–39. New York: Harcourt, Brace and Company.

Gadamer, Hans-Georg (1975) [1965]. *Truth and Method.* Garrett Barden and John Cumming (trans. and eds.). London: Sheed and Ward.

Goldziher, Ignaz (1971) [1884]. *The Ẓāhirīs, Their Doctrine and Their History.* (Wolfgang H. Behn, trans.). Leiden: E.J. Brill.

Ibn ʿĀbidīn, Muḥammad Amīn b. ʿUmar (1979). *Ḥāshiyat radd al-muḥtār.* Beirut.

Johns, A. H. (1993). The quranic presentation of the Joseph story: Naturalistic or formulaic language? In G. R. Hawting and Abdul-Kader A. Shareef (eds.), *Approaches to the Qurʾān,* 37–70. London-New York: Routledge.

Josipovici, Gabriel (1988). *The Book of God: A Response to the Bible.* New Haven-London: Yale University Press.

Mālik ibn Anas (1984). *Al-Muwaṭṭa' (Kitāb al-jāmi', mā yu'mar bi-hi min al-kalām fī al-safar).* Aḥmad Rātib 'Armūsh (ed.). Beirut.

Mir, Mustansir (1993). The *sūra* as unity: A twentieth-century development in Qur'ān exegesis. In G. R. Hawting and Abdul-Kader A. Shareef (eds.), *Approaches to the Qur'ān*, 211–224. London-New York: Routledge.

Nawawī, Yaḥyā b. Sharaf Muḥyī al-Dīn al- (n.d.). *Al-Majmū' Sharḥ al-Muhadhdhab.* 18 vols. Cairo.

Reinhart, A Kevin (1993). Transcendence and social practice: *Muftīs* and *qādīs* as religious interpreters. *Annales islamologiques* 27: 5–28.

Rippin, Andrew (1981). The quranic *asbāb al-nuzūl* material: An analysis of its use and development in exegesis. [Unpublished Ph.D. dissertation, Institute of Islamic Studies, McGill University.]

[73] Sarrāj, Abū Naṣr al- (1963). *The Kitāb al-Luma' fī 'l-taṣawwuf of Abū Naṣr 'Abdallāh b. 'Alī al-Sarrāj al-Ṭūsī.* R. A. Nicholson (ed.). London.

Schacht, Joseph (1950). *The Origins of Muḥammadan Jurisprudence.* Oxford: Clarendon Press.

Subkī, 'Alī b. 'Abd al-Kāfī Taqī al-Dīn (1952). *Shifā' al-Siqām fī Ziyārat Khayr al-Anām.* Haydarabad.

Taftazānī, Sa'd al-Dīn al- (1326 AH.). *Kitāb al-'aqā'id al-Nasafiyya.* India.

Wansbrough, John (1977). *Quranic Studies: Sources and Methods of Scriptural Interpretation.* Oxford: Oxford University Press.

— (1978). *The Sectarian Milieu: Content and Composition of Islamic Salvation History.* Oxford: Oxford University Press.

— (1987). *Res Ipsa Loquitur: History and Mimesis.* Jerusalem: The Israel Academy of Sciences and Humanities.

Weiss, Bernard G. (1992). *The Search for God's Law: Islamic Jurisprudence in the Writings of Sayf al-Din al-Amidi.* Salt Lake City: University of Utah Press.

II

The Limits of Islamic Orthodoxy

I will begin by setting out what it is that I am not going to discuss in this essay. The word 'orthodoxy' means 'right teaching'; but observing Islam, I am not in a position to judge between Sunnism and Shi'ism, to say whether one of them is orthodox and the other the non-orthodox tradition. What I think will be the case is that within the Sunni tradition, or within the Shi'i tradition, there might be some sense in which that tradition defines for itself a set of right beliefs and does not go very far beyond them.[1] The question I want to ask here is: what are the outside limits of 'right belief' for the Sunnis?

F.M. Denny, in his *An Introduction to Islam* (New York, 1985), claims that 'orthodoxy' is not the best term to use when characterizing Islam; it is better to use the term 'orthopraxy' meaning right practice. I do not think that this is true. From the point of view of a sociologist, it may well be true that in a given Muslim society there are practices which are rejected by that society. But I do not think that the practices of any particular Muslim society will represent orthopraxy, the focus of what it is to be a Muslim. In fact, theologically, it is clear that the Sunni tradition does not allow practice, works, to be taken into consideration in the definition of a Muslim. In order to achieve salvation as a Muslim, one has to have right belief in some sense or another. If one has right belief, wrong actions are not a barrier to achieving salvation. One may go to Hell for a short time, but all times are short by contrast with eternity, and all Muslims, or all Sunni Muslims, who have faith – I am not quite sure where the limits lie here – are guaranteed eventual arrival in Paradise, perhaps after a period in Hell suffering the consequences of their bad deeds. But their bad actions do not stop them from being Muslims. The Muslim jurists are careful to distinguish between those who fail, let us say, to pray five times a day – they do not cease to be Muslim – and those who deny the incumbency to pray five times a day who might be apostates. So I do not think that Islam, either in its social practice, or in its theological and intellectual traditions, is a religion of orthopraxy; it is a religion of orthodoxy. There is a right teaching somewhere which we might find inside Sunni Islam defined in a particular way, and inside Shi'i Islam defined in a different way.

One of the places we might look to discover the right teaching of Islam is to those books which are called *'aqida* or *'aqa'id* in Arabic. The word means 'creed' and the books (often booklets or pamphlets or even sections within larger books of a different genre) set out the agenda of beliefs that represent being a Muslim. There is a genre of such works which have been produced by both the Sunni and the Shi'i tradition. To move away from Islam for a moment to the Roman Catholic tradition. The Roman Catholic Church has a creed, a set of beliefs, 'I believe in one God, the Father', and so on, which is recited every day at the Mass. It derives from a number of Councils which were held in the 4th and 5th centuries. In the first five centuries of Christianity, there was debate about what it was you had to believe to be a Christian, and finally at, say, the Council of Chalcedon, a form of the creed was agreed on, under the authority of that Council and the Pope who convened it. Since then it has stayed exactly the same. For the last 1500 years, the same creed has been recited in the Mass day after day, week after week, century after century. The Catholics achieved that kind of focus and continuity because they have a formal hierarchy consisting of the pope, cardinals, archbishops, bishops and priests, who can be summoned together in order to make final and binding decisions about the articles of faith and the mode of their expression.

Islam, by contrast, does not have such a system of authority. There has never been a council in Islam and there are no clearly articulated hierarchies. In fact, we cannot find a single Muslim (or Sunni) creed which is believed in by all Muslims. There are probably hundreds of Muslim creeds; certainly dozens can be found in, for example, the university library at Manchester. Each of these creeds is written by a particular jurist; so we can find the creed of al-Tahawi, the creed of Ibn Taymiyya, the creed of al-Ash'ari, and the creed of Abu Hanifa. We can look at them and ask: where is the right belief of Muslims? The answer, however, would seem to be that there is not one. There is al-Ash'ari's view about right belief, al-Tahawi's view, Ibn Taymiyya's view, and so on. Throughout Islamic history there are different creeds written out by different scholars. The significant creeds are those that emerge within a discursive tradition, through an informal, consensual acknowledgement of value that is quite different from the formal procedures of the Roman Catholic hierarchy.

The creeds that were thus produced in Islam had, of course, much in common, not least the components of the *shahada*, the belief that God is one and Muhammad is the messenger of God. But there were also more recondite beliefs – for the Sunnis, for example, that God has real attributes and the Qur'an is the uncreated word of God. These are central focuses of the creed; but how that creed is expressed varies from person to person. How high up on the agenda of faith a particular item is brought changes from time to time. Sometimes it may seem that an issue thought to be primary in one century is gradually displaced, moves towards the bottom of the list, and may fall off the list altogether. For example, the earliest Muslim creeds have a great deal to say about faith and works, whether works count towards faith. The issue was contentious, but in the end an established pattern of variation emerged. There seemed to be agreement that works count towards getting quickly to heaven (though God's mercy and the Prophet's intercession were also important), but they do not count decisively in the question of whether one can achieve salvation. For the Sunni tradition, faith alone guarantees salvation, and the limit of faith is *shirk* or polytheism. Those who avoid *shirk* will go to heaven eventually.

There remained significant and articulated differences about the definition of faith and its consequences, even within the Sunni tradition. The question, however, became unimportant and did not have to be expressed in every creed; it certainly was not expressed at all in some later creeds. But since the creeds form a tradition of literature, a continuous and authoritative tradition, the issue could always be revived, and be invested with a new significance. This is one of the patterns of flexibility that lies in the Muslim tradition; certain items on the agenda of faith move up and down the scale of importance, perhaps lose their significance, but may later recover and require re-expression, and must then be re-expressed in a manner that is not inconsistent with the decisive presence of a literary tradition.

Every Muslim agrees that God is one, but how does one express this? Ibn Sina or Avicenna, as he came to be known in medieval Europe, produced a philosophical definition of God as the necessary existent (*wajib al-wujud*), a phrase which did not immediately find acceptance in Sunni theological circles. However, through the influence of those scholars who admired the philosophers, and especially through the infiuence of Fakhr al-Din al-Razi (d. 1209) who was clearly fascinated by Avicenna's writing in spite of its dubious status as an articulation of right belief, the notion of God as the necessary existent became acceptable to Sunni Islam. In later creeds, even of the Sunni tradition, God is not only one but also the necessary existent.

Thus, there are patterns of development in the articulation of right belief, and there are acknowledged areas of dispute internal to the community. Both the agenda of relevant items and the way of expressing individual items may change with the passage of time. Where then precisely is orthodoxy? Does it lie in this or in that articulation of the creed, in this or in that century, in this or in that terminology?

Just to simplify things for the moment, let us say that it lies inside the discursive tradition of jurists who write creeds. As you see, I come back here to a set of ideas that I have already introduced in contrasting Islam with Roman Catholicism, that Muslims are caught up in a discursive process, an ongoing process of interpreting their own past. They seem not to – and this may be a great advantage – come down to established formulae that are going to last for 1500 years, but to provisional assessments. No matter how vehement, forceful, elegant or sophisticated the articulation of this or that scholar, no matter even how influential, it is not a final articulation. The scholars of the community, in consultation with one another and listening to one another, gradually develop, change and move – though, perhaps, not too far. There is always a core of belief which is there: the belief that God is one, Muhammad is the messenger of God, and that God, in some more or less mysterious sense, has attributes which can be named and numbered.

The question of what Muslims meant by God's attributes was always a difficult one, but it is not possible here to illustrate how the scholars expressed their understanding of this belief. Possibly even more difficult was the question of the Qur'an and its status as, in some sense, the uncreated word of God. There is some evidence that, since the late 19th century, the question of whether the Qur'an is the uncreated word of God has moved down the agenda, perhaps indeed dropped off it. Many Sunni Muslims today do not even know that this was an important item of their credal system. Indeed, some major writers have suggested that it is not only unimportant but quite unnecessary to claim, in any sense, that the Qur'an is the 'uncreated' word of God. And yet that was one of the most important and top-ranking elements of the creed at various times in the past.

We come back then to the general point that the creed is a set of beliefs, elaborated in a discursive tradition by scholars, who are committed to and engaged with the tradition as the core of orthodoxy. But what are the limits, the outside limits, of this orthodoxy? When does one drop off the edge, as it were, and stop being a Sunni Muslim? At this point, let me relinquish the question and try a different approach. For even if we concede that the literary tradition of creeds represents the core of orthodoxy, there is something unsatisfactory about the concession. Something seems to have been left out: I mean the law. Islam, it seems obvious, is a religion of which the central theological feature is the law, and yet the creeds scarcely mention the law. It is a striking fact that many law books (both *furu'* and *usul*) contain expressions of creed, but the creeds do not contain expressions of law. There is perhaps a significant symbolism in that fact, in the context of our question about the outer limits of orthodoxy. Books of law contain expressions of the creed, but not vice versa (unless of course some formulation of the injunction to obey God and his prophets be seen as just this).

If we are looking for a definition of orthodoxy, we ought to look for one which includes at least some reference to the law. So here I will draw a line under everything I have said so far, and start again from a different angle. From a purely abstract point of view, we might be able to categorize religious belief amongst all peoples at all times in terms of a limited number of typological headings. Let me make an effort in that direction. I shall even claim, for the limited purposes of this paper, that all possible forms of religious belief can be caught under the following five headings: scripture, community, gnosis, reason, charisma.

Some people claim that the way towards knowledge of God is through scripture, that God has revealed His own being through a set of written texts which we can call scripture or 'revelation'. Others claim that God's self-revelation to man is not through scripture, or not primarily through scripture, but through the community, that one particular community has been chosen by God and within that community correct belief will be articulated and preserved, because that community is guarded by God and preserved from error. A third group claim that the way towards knowledge of God is through 'gnosis' – I am using that word here to stand for mystic knowledge, as when a particular person, a holy man, claims that he can, through prayer, ascetic exercises or whatever, achieve direct communication with God. A fourth group claim that the way towards understanding God is by using reason, and that human reason is an adequate way to gain a complete knowledge of God. Perhaps the Islamic philosophers are an example of this point of view. Finally, there are communities which state that God has appointed, throughout the generations, one particular person to express and guard His message, claiming perhaps that this person has special charisma and knowledge of God, and that he is, in some sense, protected by God and given right belief.

Now, what I have done is set out five categories which, at least in theory, we can look upon as pure categories. Theoretically, there might be a religion which says that the only way God reveals himself to man is, let us say, through charisma, that is, through the choice of a particular man who is the leader of the community and who will tell the community about God and their duties towards Him. But in practice, most religions are mixtures of the five categories. Religions will both have a scripture which is God's revelation and, perhaps, a theory that inside the community there will always be right belief and, perhaps combined with that, a suggestion that there will be some people in the community with direct contact with God, mystically. All the great religious traditions of the world, like Hinduism, Islam and Christianity, in fact, have all five elements in various mixtures. And the same is likely to be true, within Islam, in relation to the two great orthodox traditions of Sunnism and Shi'ism. We can, further, usually pinpoint within a large religious tradition certain movements that correspond to particular items in that five-part epistemology that I have just presented. If we ask ourselves how we have knowledge of God, the question leads, I think, to this kind of epistemological typology, and I suspect that every religion could be analysed in terms of these five epistemological categories.

Within Islam, the Twelver Shi'a and the Ismaili Shi'a in their various forms are communities which lay stress on charisma as being, in various degrees, the highest and most important form of our achieving knowledge of God. Within Islam, there are two communities again, two sets of people, who lay great stress on reason as the means for our achieving knowledge of God. One is represented by the philosophers like al-Farabi and Avicenna. The other significant group is the Mu'tazila, a historical group who flourished in the 9th and 10th centuries, and for some centuries thereafter. They are rejected by the Sunnis because, in their view, the Mu'tazila overstress the role of reason. In an Islamic context, the term gnosis, refers, of course, mainly to the Sufis.

Where do the Sunnis lie in this epistemological spectrum? The reader will perhaps already sense the direction of my argument. I wish to claim that the Sunnis lie somewhere between scripture and community, or rather that they encompass both categories. By so doing, I go slightly against the way some Western scholars present Sunni Islam. In general, they seem to present Sunni Islam as a community which relies on scripture. But I think they have not taken enough note of what actually happens when Muslims are engaged in thinking about, expressing and developing their religion, and that we have here a religion whose major understanding of God is expressed through acknowledgement of what happens inside the community, the ongoing community. In fact, I wish to claim of Sunni Islam that it is more a religion of community than of scripture.

What are the major components of Sunni Islam? This religion states that at a certain point in history, God sent a prophet called Muhammad. He was not the first prophet, there were many prophets before him: Adam, Noah, Abraham, Moses, Jesus. In fact, there were many besides that familiar list, for it is said that there were 124,000 prophets altogether. Of these, some 300 (Ibn Qutayba says 315 in his *Kitab al-ma'arif*) brought a scripture of some kind. As a result of these prophets, and in particular the Prophet Muhammad, we have scripture or revelation. Divine intervention in history, manifested in God sending prophets to diverse human communities through the ages, culminated, and in some sense ceased, with the mission of the Prophet Muhammad. As a result of his mission, the whole of humanity – for his summoning the whole of humanity was one of the distinctive qualities of Muhammad's mission – was left with two bodies of texts, the Qur'an and the *hadith*. These are, for Sunni Muslims, the content, the manifestation, of revelation. These are the texts to which Muslims appeal when they are expressing and interpreting their faith.

These texts are the residue of salvation history. I use the term 'salvation history' here to indicate that part of history which is brought forward by a religious tradition as being somehow part of the definition of that religion. When young Muslims are brought up, they may be taught their local or national history at school, but as Muslims they are also taught about Adam, Noah, Abraham and all the prophets, as well as the life of Muhammad, at an appropriate level for youngsters. There are stories of the prophets for children and there are stories of the prophets for adults. These stories are the central components of salvation history for Muslims. As a result of salvation history (a history which has now come to an end because Muhammad was the last, the seal, of the prophets) we have revelation, scripture. The precise term is not important here. The reference is to a bundle of texts which constitute authority. Out of these, at least in theory, the Muslim community derives a theology and a system of law, both explained and justified by reference to the Qur'an and the *hadith*, through engagement in the exegetical process.

Some Muslims would say, with justification, that what they derive from scripture and revelation is, in fact, a way of life. And this is true in so far as the interpretation of scripture and revelation leads to the whole practical and historical experience of the Muslim community. But I want to focus here on the intellectual experience of the Muslim community and on that aspect of their faith which claims that out of revelation, that is, the Qur'an and the *hadith*, come the intellectual traditions of theology, law and exegesis. It is, in fact, possible to propose that the whole intellectual tradition of Sunni Islam can be encapsulated in a list of literary genres, these being the genres, the traditions of writing, through which the Sunni community has given expression to its understanding of its relationship to God and his Prophet. Rather schematically presented, the complete list (and I emphasize that I am referring here specifically to the Sunni community) is as follows: *qisas al-anbiya*; *sirat al-nabi*; Qur'an; *hadith*; *fiqh*; *kalam*; *tafsir* and *sharh al-hadith*

The *qisas al-anbiya* (literally, 'tales of the prophets') refers to a literary genre which offers a retelling of salvation history for Muslims. A continuation of this aim, but a different genre (different that is by the nomenclature of the literary tradition itself), is discovered in the *sirat al-nabi* literature. This offers a biography of the Prophet Muhammad. There are, of course, many different realizations of the tales of the prophets, as there are many realizations of the biography of Muhammad. Each generation rewrites these materials differently. Later generations draw upon and comment on the works of earlier generations. Each generation deals differently with the fact that some are intellectuals and some are five-year olds. For a five-year old, you tell the stories of the prophets and the biography of the Prophet Muhammad in a very different way from when you are dealing with people older, more educated or more intellectual.

The body of revelation in Islam is represented by the Qur'an and the *hadith*. Beyond these, and in some way exegetically linked to them, there are the great intellectual genres of *kalam* which is Islamic theology, *fiqh* which is Islamic law, *tafsir* which denotes commentaries on the Qur'an, and *sharh al-hadith* which denotes commentaries on *hadith* literature. The fact that the Muslim community produced commentaries not only on the Qur'an but also on the *hadith* is a reminder that both these sources have the status of revelation, both requiring to be interpreted in search of meaning and significance.

Now, if you go to any traditional Muslim library, and in particular to a Sunni Muslim library, I think you will find that a majority of the books in such a library, in so far as they relate directly to religion, can be accommodated under these broad generic headings. In order to make that claim absolutely certain, I would have to add a commentary on my own categories. For example, one of the problems facing the Muslim community was that of setting the limits on acceptable *hadith*. There are a great many collections of *hadith*, some of which are central and universally accepted, while others are recognized as of immense and undisputed importance, and there are still others which have a marginal status and are a focus of discussion. So, one feature of Muslim tradition is that it acknowledges an indeterminately large body of *hadith* literature. Associated with this body of literature is a method of critical assessment which, in turn, is embodied in literature. There is a range of books and types of book which offer views on how to pass judgements on *hadith*. The most important of these books are perhaps those known generically as books of *jarh wa ta'dil*, books that offer a methodology for categorizing the transmitters of *hadith*, and so permitting an assessment of the *hadiths* themselves. For the purposes of this paper, I want to bundle all the books of this type under the general heading of *sharh al-hadith*. Just as I want to classify here the many different types of book that deal with the Qur'an, including specialist studies of its vocabulary, literary style, the incidence in it of abrogation, or such large studies as al-Suyuti's overview of the Qur'anic sciences (*al-Itqan fi 'ulum al-Qur'an*), as all part of *tafsir*. This is not a resource of despair – for the genres of Islamic religious literature could be more discriminately analysed and categorized – but a matter of practical convenience.

My aim in delineating these genres and in proposing that they form the bulk of the contents of a traditional library, is to suggest that the limits of Islamic orthodoxy are expressed in this list. This is what Islam, or specifically Sunni Islam, in its broadest sense, is about. It is about everything contained in the *qisas al-anbiya, sirat al-nabi,* the Qur'an, *hadith, kalam, fiqh, tafsir* and *sharh.* Anything that is brought in under these headings and held inside the discursive tradition of Muslim literary experience belongs within the limits of Islamic orthodoxy. And these are discursive limits, for the question of what can be held inside these works is not fixed by reference to one work, or the works of one century, one school or one geographical region. The canon of literature which expresses the orthodox tradition of Sunni Islam is fairly clear in its central components – and even there such controversial and apparently irreconcilable figures as Ibn Taymiyya and Fakhr al-Din al-Razi must be held inside the tradition – but it offers almost limitless extension in the direction of minor and contested figures, who might always be drawn nearer or further from the centre as time and scholarship move.

In such a large tradition, where the centre is in debate and the boundaries are contested, is anything, one may wonder, excluded? Can this exploration of the limits of orthodoxy demonstrate that some particular belief or set of beliefs falls outside of those limits? Let us consider, for a while, *tafsir. Tafsir* is a term that designates, in one range of use, commentaries on the Qur'an. A work of *tafsir* will contain the whole text of the Qur'an, divided up into segments; the commentator will present a segment and then he will tell you what the segment means – except that he will not tell you what the segment means; he will tell you what the people before him said the segment meant. Works of *tafsir* characteristically consist of reports intimating that so and so said that this part of the Qur'an means such and such. One finds a very similar phenomenon, a similarly literary format, in works of *fiqh.* The single text is broken up by the operation on it of time and scholarship. The possibility of a single meaning is lost, the message is rendered into fragments, and all the fragments are brought into the present, because we find that a single verse of the Qur'an may have ten different scholars commenting on it with ten different views as to what it means. There will be limits, but there is a tendency, as time passes, for the meanings of the Qur'an to grow bigger. And there is also a tendency for Muslims not to comment directly. When a scholar writes a large *tafsir,* he explores the views of earlier authorities, including of course the views of the Prophet himself, the views of his Companions, the views of the next generations, until at the end, he might say 'And my view is ...' or 'My preferred view is ...', thus expressing preferences within the tradition rather than pinning down the meaning of the Qur'an. It almost never happens – in fact, I would go so far as to say that prior to the 19th century it does not happen – that a Muslim scholar sits down with the Qur'an and, using his own intellect, literary skills and imagination says 'I think it means X'. When such a thing did happen, the scholar in question usually became open to accusations of heresy.

One man who did this is, perhaps, the Bab, I mean Sayyid 'Ali Muhammad Shirazi (d. 1850), the founder of the Babi movement, and indirectly, of the Baha'i faith. The Bab wrote a *tafsir* of the *Surat Yusuf* (*Sura* 12) of the Qur'an. What he seems to have done is to express his opinion, at least in the end. There are, in his work, some vestiges of what might be called the orthodox technique, but in the end he simply used the Qur'an as a prompt to express his own religious experience. In the course of his lifetime, he was both perceived to be, and in the end claimed to be, the founder of a new religion. It was a deviation from orthodoxy, an abandonment of tradition, which is symbolized in his failure to acknowledge in his *tafsir* the experience of the community – I mean here the intellectual experience represented in generations of exegetical activity. It is perhaps odd, and it does not sound like the religion we so often hear about, and yet it is insistently the case: the intellectual tradition of Islam is one which makes it a requirement that each succeeding generation look at and take into consideration the work of the preceding generations. It is not a religion which, from generation to generation, goes back to the original words of scripture and revelation. When a scholar makes this attempt to go back to the original sources and to look at them with an unprejudiced eye (if there is such a thing), people are not sure about this and, as in the case of the Bab, he is liable to rejection.

Even when people are less radical than the Bab, they still get pushed aside. Consider the fate, for example, of those movements within Islam called the Zahiri and the Salafi. The terms can be translated, respectively, as Literalist (implying a return to the literal meanings of the revealed texts) and Primitivist (a return to the values of the early community). The terminology records the perception of the mainstream tradition in respect of these minor traditions. They were perceived to have a backward orientation, an orientation towards the verbatim words of scripture or the primitive community. The main tradition was represented by the great schools of law (Hanafi, Maliki, Shafi'i and Hanbali) and by the main theological traditions (Ash'ari and Maturidi). The Salafi thinker, Ibn Taymiyya, who lived in the 13th and 14th centuries, has had a tremendous influence on 20th-century Islam; but he had very little influence in the centuries after his death. In the 19th century his thinking was revived and discovered to be a good thing, although earlier he was not regarded as a good thing.

Let me return to my assessment of the contents of a traditional Muslim library. Those who are familiar with such a library may have noticed that there is one major literary genre, one that has a significant presence in a Muslim library, that is missing. It is the genre of *tabaqat* ('generations'), biographical works, and I missed it out deliberately because, in recalling it now, it helps to make my point. One of the most productive literary genres in Islam, the *tabaqat* literature, though it has many specialist divisions, conforms basically to a single format: it chronicles the transmission of knowledge through the generations. Whether dealing with jurists, exegetes, experts in *hadith* or with all types of scholar, such works offer a diachronic realization of Islam; an assertion that the essential message is preserved, not solely within the revealed texts, but in the teaching about these texts that is transmitted from generation to generation through the ages. The genre of *tabaqat* is an essential part of the religious self-expression of Muslims, and as such it tends to confirm what I have been suggesting, that Sunni Islam is a religion in which although everything in one sense is taken back to scripture, in another sense it is ongoing. It is a religion which seems to demand of its participants that appropriate acknowledgement be granted to the community as it develops through time (and as it is represented by scholars). Every later participation in the forms of literature – and it is through established literary forms and genres that thought takes place – every later statement of faith or assessment of meaning in the Qur'an, takes into account the earlier statements worked out by the community. The epistemological categories of scripture/revelation and community are always balanced inside Sunni Islam, and always balanced, I would say, in favour of community, not scripture.

This does not quite end the problem. I have not yet, as it were, reached the limits of orthodoxy. My first step is to suggest that the limits of orthodoxy are represented by what is, or what can be contained within, the broad literary tradition that I have identified in the preceding paragraphs. But this literary tradition contains references to other literary traditions. For example, it contains references to the writings of the Mu'tazila, to the philosophers, to the Sufis, and sometimes to the Twelver and Ismaili Shi'is. And it seems to me that we might attempt to define the limits of orthodoxy not only by saying that it is here, inside the literary tradition of the Sunni community, but also that it is there, in those aspects of the other traditions which seem to be necessary for the Sunnis to define their own position. There is a sense in which the preservation and recall of the Mu'tazili position on God's attributes constitutes the necessary ground of the Sunni position. Certainly, there are very few attempts to state the Sunni position on the divine attributes which do not explicitly recall the Mu'tazili position, making it the focus of fine distinctions which distinguish and clarify the Sunni position. The explicit acknowledgement of parallel and erroneous traditions is a part of the orthodox tradition. And the articulation of orthodoxy could not be achieved without a discursive exploration of the boundaries that separate the orthodox tradition from those traditions that are acknowledged to deviate from it.

What is at issue can be caught in the notion of 'intertextuality', a term that denotes the way that texts refer to other texts. The reference to other texts can be implicit – in the sense that a novel implies the existence of a whole genre of such things – or it can be explicit. The implicit references are more interesting but also difficult to assess. What is clear and immediately useful for our present investigation is the fact that inside this body of literature, that which constitutes Sunni orthodoxy, are numerous explicit references to that other body of literature, the works of the Mu'tazila, the philosophers, the Shi'is and the Sufis. In so far as such explicit references are helpful and accommodating, then these alternative traditions are being given a place in orthodox Islam, in this context Sunni Islam. In so far as they are explicitly rejected, we are approaching a definition of the boundaries of orthodox Islam.

Now, as far as I have ever been able to ascertain, in so far as the Sunni tradition mentions anything about the Ismailis, it is with clear and explicit rejection. One of the clearest boundaries of Sunni Islam is that which separates it from the Ismaili faith. It is just possible that, in the 11th century, when al-Ghazali attacked the Ta'limiyya, as he called the Ismailis of his day, he was moved by his sense of the strengths of their philosophy to build up parallel strengths in his depiction of Sunnism, but there has been very little subsequent acknowledgement of the Ismailis. Unlike, say, the philosophers, Ismaili writers do not become a significant part of the discursive move towards self-definition by later Sunni thinkers. It is also true that the Twelver Shi'is are not particularly referred to, and not particularly liked in general, within that body of literature. From a Sunni point of view, the basic Shi'i error, their refusal to acknowledge the historical succession to the Prophet Muhammad, is frequently acknowledged, and this is, of course, a fundamental part of the depiction of Sunni tradition. But the great tradition of Shi'i writers, whether on law, theology or philosophy, remains almost unacknowledged within the Sunni tradition. In fact, I would be tempted to say that the epistemological category of charisma, as I have defined it above, is very clearly outside the boundaries of Sunni Islam, except possibly at a popular level where it has tried to accommodate certain beliefs about the exceptional status of 'Ali b. Abi Talib, though these are in a Sunni context often assimilated to Sufism rather than Shi'ism.

The Sunni tradition of *kalam* refers to the Mu'tazila frequently and tries to derive a kind of shifting position in which certain of the views expressed by the Mu'tazila are more or less acceptable to Sunni Islam. Some scholars such as Ibn Taymiyya were extremely negative about the Mu'tazila; on the other hand, another Sunni theologian, Fakhr al-Din al-Razi, was much more accommodating. He found it necessary to cite, explain and clarify a great deal of the Mu'tazili tradition in order to assess its compatibility with the Sunni tradition. Unlike Ibn Taymiyya, he is not vehemently negative about this alternative tradition, but rather holds on to it, makes it a means whereby to discover and express the possibilities of Sunni Islam. In one other way the Mu'tazili tradition produced books that were accommodated inside Sunni Islam. A famous example is the Mu'tazili exegete, al-Zamakhshari (d. 1144). Although his *tafsir* contained Mu'tazili ideas, it contained also so much that was good, so much that was interesting to the Sunnis, that they began writing commentaries on al-Zamakhshari's work in which they took seriously what he had to say. Here then, at the boundary between Sunnism and the Mu'tazila, the line is not so clear. There is a sense in which the boundary is discursive, such that certain patterns of advance and retreat can be noted and mapped. The Mu'tazili tradition, in some way, is a part of the history of Sunnism and a permanent element in Sunni self-definition.

How about the philosophers? Al-Ghazali, famously, set out reasons why the philosophers were unacceptable to him, but in so doing established for them an important place on the defining fringes of orthodoxy. And not everyone agreed with all of al-Ghazali's strictures. Again, Fakhr al-Din al-Razi is an important figure here. Fascinated by the work and the arguments of Avicenna, he wrote a summary of the *Tanbihat wa'l-isharat*, Avicenna's last and possibly his most brilliant literary achievement. By that very fact of writing a summary, Fakhr al-Din indicated that he, a Sunni theologian, was taking on board at least some of what Avicenna had to say, and, indeed, many of the ideas and much of the terminology of Avicenna appear in Fakhr al-Din's *tafsir*. Thus, a great deal of philosophical terminology and thought crept into the Sunni tradition and became internal to that tradition. Of course, it was not absolutely internal, because other Sunni writers disliked the philosophers intensely, notably Ibn Taymiyya. So inside Sunnism we have a kind of 'yes' and 'no' with regard to both the philosophers and the Mu'tazila; and in that sense reason as an epistemological category has a significant place, albeit a highly qualified place, within Sunni Islam.

What about gnosis? Here, let me just say that, as far as I can see, from the 12th century onwards, slowly but insistently, there emerges an increasing quantity of favourable reference inside that body of Sunni literature to the literature representing Sufism. Again, it is Ibn Taymiyya who represents the opposition movement. He clearly felt strongly that the Sufis, in some respects, were a danger to Sunni Islam. But that negative evaluation was matched by more positive evaluations elsewhere, above all perhaps by a general tendency in the major juristic schools to acquiesce in the religious aspirations of the Sufi tradition. By the 19th century, there had emerged a long tradition of references and statements which indicate that Sunni Islam, as represented by that body of literature defined above, is at ease with gnostic literature, as represented by a long, continuous tradition of specialist works, beginning with figures like Abu 'Abd Allah al-Muhasibi, Abu Nu'aym al-Isfahani, Abu Talib al-Makki, al-Qushayri and others, and finally embracing Ibn al-'Arabi, who as *al-shaykh al-akbar*, 'the greatest shaikh', becomes a symbol of Sufi literature in its most sophisticated and, perhaps, its most dangerous form. In spite of this, he is, on the whole, approved of.

That last point may be illustrated very briefly by reference to a Hanafi juristic work of the 19th century: the *Hashiyat radd al-muhtar* of Ibn 'Abidin (d. 1842), which is a commentary on a commentary on an epitome of the law – the layered glosses of the work incidentally neatly illustrate the stress on continuity, on preserving the tradition, on acknowledging diachronic continuity, which I have already identified as an essential part of the Sunni religious experience. But here I want to note more specifically a couple of contexts in which Ibn 'Abidin makes explicit intertextual reference to works of the Sufi tradition. In a brief biographical reference to Abu Hanifa, founder of the Hanafi school of law, Ibn 'Abidin recalls the information, well-established by his time, that amongst those who followed the great imam in his juristic methodology were many of 'the noble friends of God,' including Ibrahim b. Adham, Ma'ruf al-Karkhi, Abu Yazid al-Bistami and other famous Sufis. In proceeding to make some remarks on these figures, Ibn 'Abidin mentions the works of Abu Nu'aym al-Isfahani and al-Qushayri. By citing these works, he establishes that they too belong to the constellation of authoritative sources that validly tell us about the experience of the (Sunni) Muslim community. He is telling his readers not only that some of the most important early mystics who were contemporary with Abu Hanifa learnt their law from him, but that the literature through which the Sufi tradition gives expression to its identity is acceptable to that tradition within and through which Ibn 'Abidin gives expression to his identity. Both the story (history) and the intertextual reference signal an alliance between the juristic school of Abu Hanifa and the mystic tradition as represented by even al-Bistami, who was often looked upon with suspicion because he held rather extreme mystic views. The story of Abu Hanifa's relationship with mystics was developed still further, with special reference to al-Shadhili, eponym of one of the most powerful mystic orders of the 19th century. And so we see that there developed a kind of narrative tradition, a set of stories, which signal the relationship between Sufism and Sunni Islam. In a different context, Ibn 'Abidin takes up the question of the acceptability of the teachings of Ibn al-'Arabi. It cannot be said that he offers an easy acquiescence in the problematic philosophy of the great mystic, but he does offer a kind of acquiescence, a modulated recognition that there is nothing essentially alien to Sunni Islam in the ideas of Ibn al-'Arabi, if correctly understood.

In conclusion, let me offer a final statement about the limits of orthodoxy in Sunni Islam. At an intellectual level, the limits of orthodoxy are represented by the contents of that set of books defined above as constitutive of a traditional Sunni library, together with such aspects of the alternative traditions (Shi'is, Mu'tazila, philosophers, Sufis, etc.) as are acknowledged in the primary set. My own, in this context necessarily broad, analysis of these books permits a kind of conclusion, namely that Sunni Islam is primarily a religion of community, scripture and gnosis, marginally of reason, and hardly at all of charisma. The primary elements are community and scripture (in that order I am sure), because they are the fundamental epistemological categories of Sunni literature. Gnosis has to be added and brought up to a primary position because, on balance, the body of Sunni literature acknowledges the religious validity of the Sufi experience, though its expression depends on a different set of literary texts. The totality of the experience available to a Sunni Muslim includes both the scholastic tradition or, if you like, the exegetical tradition represented in the former body of literature, and the mystic tradition represented in the tradition of Sufi literature.

In coming to these conclusions, I am conscious of a difficulty, namely that the situation I have described is not demonstrably true of the 20th century. As a university teacher, teaching 'religion' within a secular educational system, I am concerned not with the discovery or the evaluation of religious truth, but rather with the analysis of texts. In an academic context, it seems to me, I can say nothing about the existence or the nature of God, or the possibility of salvation. About the nature of texts and the arguments, about the beliefs and opinions that mould them, I can say at least a little. It is even possible, in this context, to formulate questions about religious experience which permit of answers that are within the sphere of academic analysis, answers that might be demonstrably true or false, or at least, more or less adequate to the situation analysed. In this context, students come from all over the world, including all parts of the Islamic world, to participate in this exercise of academic analysis. In proposing, year on year, to read with my students either this book or that, I can choose, without difficulty, texts which are a great pleasure for me to read and a great pleasure for them to read. They are the texts which constitute the intellectual heritage of Muslims throughout the world, and for non-Muslims too they are a part of the human heritage, a part which we too can share and enjoy, even if we do not have faith. Whether Muslim students come from Saudi Arabia, Malaysia or Africa, or even Iran with its predominantly Shiʿi tradition, they are happy to read any work, from any of the literary genres that constitute Sunni Islam. But should I propose to read Ibn al-ʿArabi, I would certainly meet with some resistance, with some intimation that this is not central to, or even perhaps is not, a part of the Islamic tradition. That is, there is a tendency for some contemporary Muslims to reject one major part of the historical experience of their community. This – and here I take off my academic hat and, with due apology, put on a judgemental one – seems to me on the whole not a very healthy tendency. I am inclined to think that if you have a rich, complex and varied tradition, the needs of the 20th century hardly indicate that it should be restricted, rather that it should be accepted in all its richness. Contemporary Muslims are, as it were, offered by their tradition a massive, complex, sophisticated heritage, a generous profusion of modes of religious fulfilment, and any step towards making that heritage smaller must be a bad thing.

If we ask why there is a tendency for at least some modern Muslims to make their heritage smaller, we will I think find that it goes back to a very great man and a very important thinker, Muhammad ʿAbduh (1849–1905). He wanted to reform Islam and make it relevant to the modern world, and the method he chose was a method of rejection. It had some very positive results, but one of the things he rejected was the whole mystic tradition. He claimed that much mystic lore was nonsense, *khurafat*; he called upon his followers not to listen to mystics and to get rid of them. One can perhaps understand what he meant in terms of what mystic traditions were like, or how they appeared, in the late 19th century, but nonetheless it is not a particularly good point of departure for Muslims today trying to find their way forward as Muslims. Muhammad 'Abduh also, in fact, initiated a novel stress in the area of scripture versus community. I am inclined to say that the reality of the Islamic (Sunni) tradition is that they combine the epistemological characteristics of scripture and community, while laying greater stress on community. Muhammad 'Abduh implied that Muslims, in order to accommodate themselves to the 19th and 20th centuries, should go back to the beginning. The products of the great intellectual tradition were not to his mind so very wonderful; for him, much of what these jurists and theologians had produced was of little value, they could be safely and wisely discarded. The community should go back and start all over again with the Qur'an. The relevant juristic hero for Muhammad 'Abduh was not Abu Hanifa, Malik, Shafi'i or even Ibn Hanbal, great figures though they all were; it was Ibn Taymiyya. And his usefulness was that he offered a scourge for the intellectual tradition and a banner for revivalism; he represented, *par excellence*, the Salafi (Primitivist) tendency in Islam.

Now, perhaps Muhammad 'Abduh was right; perhaps this was a necessary way forward, a retreat the better to advance. But on the whole, I would be inclined to say that, at that point of transition, Islam started to become a smaller tradition; and that, in some respects, sadly, Muhammad 'Abduh is the cause of a smaller, more limited Islam than that which was on offer before, and which remains on offer inside not simply the Sunni scholastic (exegetical) tradition, but also inside those other traditions which the Sunni tradition hauls in its wake – the precious baggage, the inescapable burden, of experience.

NOTE

1. Some of the ideas discussed in this paper have been more formally developed in my 'History and Nostalgia: Reflections on John Wansbrough's *The Sectarian Milieu*,' in *Method and Theory in the Study of Religion*, 9 (1997), pp. 47–73.

III

Law

Western scholarship (even when written by Muslims) has rarely presented Islamic law in such a way as to demonstrate its values rather than the values of the observer. It is legal practice in the Western sense (which admittedly corresponds to the special concerns of some Muslim jurists) that dominates the standard introductions to the subject: Schacht (1950), Linant de Bellefonds (1956) and Fyzee (1964). Certain features of Muslim juristic discourse, those perhaps which are most revealing of its nature and its intentions, are in such works disregarded in favour of a search for practical rules (certainly present, but strangely hard, sometimes, to find).

The problem may be exemplified by reference to two excellent works of scholarship which appeared in the late 1980s. Nabil Saleh, in his *Unlawful Gain and Legitimate Profit in Islamic Law*, pursues an aim which he shares with many modern Muslims, namely that of "reasserting *Sharī'ah* as a valid and sensible corpus of commercial and civil laws" (1986: 4). What he wants to achieve is "a financial system based on Islamic ethics", the subject matter of his final chapter. What stands in his way, and it does stand in his way, is the tradition of Muslim juristic writing. He goes through it honourably; but its variation, its complexity, its extravagant exploration of detail, its constant citation of different authorities, its apparent irrelevance, sometimes, to practice, its cunning and witty accommodation, sometimes, to practice: all these things make his task difficult, and will alert his readers to the fact that "a valid and sensible corpus of laws" is not quite what these jurists had in mind. Baber Johansen's book *The Islamic Law on Land Tax and Rent* (1988) centres on a set of legal concepts which were exploited by (amongst others) the Ottoman jurist Ibn Nujaym (970/1563), in Egypt, as an expression of his opposition to certain government tax-collecting initiatives. (These were justified in turn by a different manipulation of the same concepts.) Johansen's depiction of development, juristic manipulation and social consequence is revealing, but revealing of something that is particularly interesting to Western scholarship, namely the use of the law in a political situation.

Ibn Nujaym did indeed produce a treatise which had direct relevance to the politics of his day. But when he transferred the arguments of that treatise to his great compendium of the law, *Al-Baḥr al-rā'iq*, the nature of the arguments changed. First, they took their place as a tiny part of the whole that is the law (by no means an insignificant message), and, second, they ceased to have an immediate activist import. They became a part of the tradition. They were thus of course preserved and might be used again, but, in their new context, they had become an element in a pattern, a pattern constituted primarily by citations from earlier authorities. (What a Muslim law-book characteristically reveals is the tradition.) In cases of established dispute, Ibn Nujaym may have had preferences, but his literary procedure was such as to open up to his readers what the tradition had discovered, through a pattern of argument and counter-argument that represented centuries of juristic effort and juristic debate. The concepts of the law were explored through the tradition's provision of scholarly analysis.

The centripetal (if rather distant) focus of scholarly comment was revelation. That consideration suggests a preliminary definition of Islamic law: it is a hermeneutic discipline which explores and interprets revelation through tradition. The last two words of that definition are the most important. For the most obvious shaping factor, in any work of Islamic law, is its engagement with the past of a particular tradition, and its loyalty to it So much is this true that the tendency of the following pages will be to modify that definition, and suggest rather that Islamic law is a discipline that explores tradition, and uses tradition to discover (and limit) the meanings of revelation.

No one would deny that the explorations of the law were intended to influence, and might be used sometimes to control, practice; but the great exponents of the tradition would not, I think, admit that their work was valueless just because no one paid (practical) attention to it. The impulse to explore the law was (also) for its own sake, as an act of piety complete in itself, and so intrinsically a part of the religious perceptions of the Muslim community, that they hardly gave it (what the modern analyst has none the less to discover) explicit articulation.

The connotations of the phrase "Islamic law" are in part a product of Western perceptions and have been introduced now to Muslim societies through linguistic calques like Arabic *al-qānūn al-islāmī*. There is no corresponding phrase in pre-modern Muslim discourse. There, the two terms which expressed the commitment of the Muslim community to divine law were *fiqh* and *Sharī'ah*. The first of these is the easier to define.

It always refers to the human, and more or less academic, activity of exploration, interpretation, analysis and presentation of the law, whether this takes place in books, in schools, in the mind or in formal response to a specific question. It is possible to write *fiqh*, to teach and study it, to think (about) it and to manipulate and apply its concepts. *Sharī'ah*, on the other hand, is a word whose connotations are divine. It can be used very loosely and broadly to refer to the Muslim religion, because it is God's religion. It connotes God's law even when the details of the law are unknown or immaterial. It inspires loyalty and commitment in a way that the word *fiqh* does not. In a very narrow and specific sense it can refer to God's law as an ideal: that which is somehow contained within revelation, that which the *fuqahā'*, practitioners of *fiqh*, are trying to find through their explorations and analyses. And it is sometimes used to denote the same things as are denoted by the word *fiqh* (books of *fiqh*, books of *Sharī'ah*), but with that added sense of religious loyalty which comes from its association with God and truth. In modern academic analysis of Islamic law, the word *Sharī'ah* is of little use: what we can study and describe is always *fiqh*.

Fiqh is most obviously available to us as a tradition of literature, though, behind this, there is a tradition of thought and of education, and some kind of aspiration to social control. There are two major types of *fiqh* literature, that known as *furū' al-fiqh* (branches) and that known as *uṣūl al-fiqh* (roots). The former sets out, or appears to set out, concepts and rules that relate to conduct, and arguments about them. Its headings are purity, prayer, fasting, alms, pilgrimage (the essential acts of worship, *'ibādāt*, and invariably the first five books of a work of *furū'*) and then such topics as warfare, marriage, divorce, inheritance, penalties, buying and selling, judicial practice, etc., in variable order. The whole is a conceptual replica of social life, not necessarily aspiring to be either complete or practical, but balanced between revelation, tradition and reality, all three of which feed the discussion and exemplify the concepts. The literature of *uṣūl* identifies the divinely revealed sources of the law (Qur'ān and *Sunnah*), auxiliary sources (like consensus – *ijmā'*), and the hermeneutic disciplines which permit the complex intellectual cross-reference between revelation, tradition and reality which is exemplified in a work of *furū'*. The hermeneutic disciplines are historical and biographical (related to abrogation and to the reliability of those who transmit *Sunnah*), linguistic, rhetorical and logical. The linguistic and rhetorical sciences were in the developed tradition finely articulated, and presented usually under simple antithetical headings: command and prohibition, general and particular, absolute and qualified, metaphor and truth, etc. The application of logic to revelation usually meant analogy (*qiyās*) and was variously developed by different schools and individuals. The Shi'ite tradition was inclined to reject analogy as a systematic means to develop the law, but shows a corresponding complexity in the application of other types of rational argument. Books of *uṣūl* characteristically culminate in a discussion of *ijtihād*, a term implying the exercise of the utmost effort to discover a particular item of the law through application of the hermeneutic rules (Calder (1983 and 1989); Hallaq (1984 and 1986)). It is probably true that the literature of *furū'* is larger than the literature of *uṣūl*, and more characteristic. (In the present chapter, and for reasons of space alone, the last two sections will be devoted exclusively to *furū'*.)

There is a third type of literature which has a role in the public presentation of Divine Law. It is that known as *ṭabaqāt* or "generations". Biographical in form, diachronic in organization, such books demonstrate the continuity of the tradition and the moral and intellectual status of its participating scholars. Their message is theological, though about history; it is that the lives and works of individual scholars derive meaning and significance from their place within an ongoing tradition of juristic thought. This is in fact the ubiquitous message of Islamic juristic literature: individual jurists are not engaged in a private dialogue with revelation, they are the heirs to a tradition. The discovery of meaning in revelation depends on conformity to that tradition. The *ṭabaqāt* literature defends, and of course defines, the tradition.

The five major schools of Islamic jurisprudence, the four Sunni schools (Ḥanafī, Mālikī, Shāfi'ī and Ḥanbalī) and the Imāmī (Twelver) Shi'ites, have expressed themselves through the same three literary types. A broad formal description of the works produced within one school (or tradition) will suffice (to a degree) for all, in spite of the many points of detail that mark their differences. All traditions also produced some specialist treatises and monographs, which can usually be accommodated within the three broad literary types identified above.

The *ṭabaqāt* literature has another, perhaps more prosaic, function. Books of this type vary from the extremely schematic list of names, dates, formal virtues, teachers, students and books produced which is the minimal requirement, to great sequences of anecdotes which, collected and juxtaposed on artistic principles, are intended to educate. (The *Ṭabaqāt al-shāfi 'iyyat al-kubrā* of al-Subkī – a Shāfi'ī jurist, d. 771/1370 – is an example of the latter type.) The education, reflecting the artistic impulse which works through contrived juxtaposition and variation, is miscellaneous, but is mostly about the law. Truths about the law which find academic, formal, complex articulation in works of *furū'* or *uṣūl* are rendered here through anecdote, sometimes witty, through poetic citations, through the recognition of scholar-heroes, through wondrous resolutions of tricky problems and through a vocabulary of description which carries subtle (or not so subtle) messages about the aims of the tradition.

Abū Ḥanīfah (150/767) was in the mosque one day, surrounded by a group of students who were shouting and arguing. "What, can't you keep them quiet in the mosque?" muttered an irritable passer-by. "Leave them," said Abū Ḥanīfah, "for only thus will they learn *fiqh*." The historicity of the story is immaterial; its message is about the nature of the law – something to be argued about. The same Abū Ḥanīfah was holding a session one day in Mecca, when he was approached by a man from Khurasan. "I am owner of considerable wealth," said the man, "and I have a son. I am inclined to provide him with a wife and to set him up in comfort. But I fear he will divorce her and so squander my wealth. I could buy him a slave-girl and provide him thus with a household, but he might free her and so again squander my wealth. What shall I do?" "Take him to the slave-market," said Abū Ḥanīfah, "and when a particular girl catches his eye, buy her for yourself, and then marry her to him. If, then, he divorces her, she returns to your ownership; and if he frees her . . . well, he can't, for she is yours." The teller of this story was delighted not just by the reply but by the immediacy of Abū Ḥanīfah's response (Dhahabī: 21, 22).

No conclusions may be drawn from this about marriage practice and family problems in third/ninth-century Khurasan. The story is a show-case for the exploration of concepts. It is generated by the dual system of acquisition of rights to legitimate sexual intercourse in Islamic law: marriage and slavery. A master has rights to intercourse with a slave-girl, unless she is married to another; he may in appropriate circumstances transfer those rights to another; only the owner of a slave can set her free; etc. The story can be explained by listing the relevant rules of law. It was preserved and valued because the legal concepts here set to work are embedded in a narrative fragment which has an earthy humour, and because they are neatly manipulated as a display of skill.

In developed Islamic societies (say, from the fifth/eleventh century onwards, but also before this) the only formal, public system of education had as its major components the teaching of revelation and the teaching of the law, that is the schools of law. There were ancillary disciplines, and various means of secular and private education, but most educated members of Muslim society had as their primary currency of cultural exchange the concepts of the law. Through these they shared their leisure time, and created conversation, wit and public display; and through these they were able to analyse their society and their religion, to express their personal and their public piety and to devise various modes of social control. *Fiqh* was a multi-functional discipline. In the way that it possessed the lives of Muslims, it was challenged and in the end complemented only by the structures of Sufism. These two disciplines, at an intellectual and a practical level, were the primary modes of Muslim self-realization prior to the modern period. They could, without lack of piety, be experienced as humorous or serious.

There were of course differences of approach within schools and across schools. The Ḥanafī school in particular enjoyed the law, willingly explored its concepts through hypothetical cases and far-fetched problems and lent itself to cunning contrivances (*ḥīlah*) which exploited the letter of the law in order to uncover its tolerant spirit (or not, as the case may be). All the traditions did this to some degree, the Ḥanbalīs being perhaps the most conservative and piously serious; and all were aware of the dangers of these attractions. The Mālikīs polemically frowned on the Ḥanafī predilection for hypothetical cases, but acknowledged the temptations even as they preserved (created?) the following story. An Iraqi (i.e. Ḥanafī) asked Mālik (179/795) about a man who had sexual intercourse with a dead chicken, which then produced an egg, out of which came a chick; is it permitted for him to eat the flesh of the chick? Mālik's recorded reply is remarkably mild, all things considered (al-Qāḍī 'Iyāḍ (1967): 150–1).

Islamic law, in the thousand years or so of its cultural dominance, was the product of a highly sophisticated civilization. It was intimately related to an educational system which was more or less homogeneous throughout all pre-modern Muslim societies. Its long-term flourishing was due to the inherent flexibility of a conceptual structure which served to describe revelation, tradition and society. If the main aim of the structure was religious, indeed theological (an articulation of the hermeneutic relationship between the ongoing Muslim community and the ever more distant moment of God's direct intervention in human affairs), that does not exhaust the social functions it served. These might be explained in terms of the cultural needs of a sophisticated society, and probably cannot be explained in terms of the historical origins of Islamic law. None the less explanations in terms of origins have been characteristic both of the Muslim tradition and of the Western scholarly tradition.

The distant origins of Islamic law are strictly inaccessible, in the sense that they belong to a period for which we have no written records. The earliest surviving juristic texts are a number of works ascribed to named authorities of the late second/eighth and early third/ninth centuries. These works already show distinct school orientations, covering three major (and several minor) traditions, the Ḥanafī, the Mālikī and the Shāfi'ī. Literary evidence for the existence of a Ḥanbalī school of law is hardly available before the latter part of the third/ninth century, and for an Imāmī Shi'ite school, the early part of the fourth/tenth. If the Muslim tradition has a historical theory (and it might be more accurate to say that the Muslim tradition offers a schematic paradigm whose function is educative) it is as follows. The words and deeds of the Prophet (his *Sunnah*) were preserved, in the form of discrete anecdotes (*Ḥadīth*), which were transmitted orally through the generations. These were the source of juristic discussion which was eventually transformed, via the notably creative contributions of Abū Ḥanīfah, Mālik, Shāfi'ī, Ibn Ḥanbal and, for the Shi'ites, such figures as the Imām Ja'far al-Ṣādiq, into the legal schools we now know. Development within the schools is acknowledged, e.g. by generalized reference to early scholars and later ones (*al-mutaqaddimūn, al-muta'akhkhirūn*), but never explored. Each school is concerned to demonstrate that its tradition can be harmonized with revelation (which is not the same thing as asserting that *Ḥadīth* are in fact, historically, the source of tradition). Historical considerations are almost entirely irrelevant to the aims of Muslim juristic writing.

By contrast, Western scholarship has amongst its foremost achievements Joseph Schacht's *The Origins of Muhammadan Jurisprudence* (1950). (The epithet is justified perhaps by the Muhammadocentric nature of Muslim juristic discourse.) His key observation is simply that the earliest legal texts (especially those of the Ḥanafī tradition) are not notably interested in relating law to Prophetic *Ḥadīth*, whereas later texts (especially those attributed to Shāfi'ī – 204/820) argue systematically that Prophetic *Ḥadīth* are the only justification for juristic rules. Islamic law, he thought, emerged in local Muslim communities as a discursive presentation of local custom (which may well have been thought of as Prophetic), and was only later transformed into a hermeneutic discipline requiring constant cross-reference between rule and *Ḥadīth*, i.e. between law and revelation (for *Ḥadīth*, like Qur'ān, is part of the revelation and quantitatively by far the greater part). A corollary of Schacht's theory is that much, indeed the bulk, of *Ḥadīth* material will be found to be the result of a search for justification, either of the pre-existent schools of law or of those who opposed them. This is perhaps confirmed by the fact that the literary production of *Ḥadīth* collections is mostly posterior to the life of Shāfi'ī, the earliest collection of great authority being that of Bukhārī (256/870).

Historically this means that the Muslim community was, from the late second/eighth to the early fourth/tenth centuries, engaged in a process of self-definition which was intensely focused on the components of and the relations between revelation (Qur'ān and *Ḥadīth*) and the various legal traditions. The literary witness to this process, according to Western scholars, was a number of juristic texts ascribed to early masters, an indeterminately large body of Prophetic *Ḥadīth*, and – perhaps – the canonical text of the Qur'ān (Wansbrough 1977). The stress on community creativity required by this model of historical development has been found theologically repugnant by many Muslims. It is none the less likely to be (broadly) true, and might not be intransigent to some developments of traditional theology. When the situation stabilized, so did the existential task. The Muslim community was committed to a number of divergent juristic traditions which, through polemical debate, had acquired a common sense of methodological purpose. That was the foundation of

Islamic law: a set of legal traditions more or less mutually self-recognizing (the Imāmī Shi'ites never quite fully integrated) and committed to the task of justifying tradition (and developing it) by reference to revelation. The literary products of the formative, pre-Classical period, though held in great veneration, are not the greatest achievements of the traditions. In spite of an insistence (not just Western) on the terminology of decline, the great achievements of Islamic jurisprudence are probably spread fairly evenly from the mid fourth/tenth to the thirteenth/nineteenth centuries.

The literature of *furū'* may be analysed as displaying two major types: *mukhtaṣar* and *mabsūṭ*, the former term designating an epitome or digest of the law, the latter an expansum or broad exploration of the law's details. The terms are given by the tradition, where they figure frequently as the titles of specific books: the *Mukhtaṣar* of Marwazī (Ḥanafī, 334/946), *al-Mukhtaṣar al-nāfi'* by 'Allāmah al-Ḥillī (Shī'ī, 726/1325), the *Mabsūṭ* of Muḥammad ibn Ḥasan al-Ṭūsī (Shī'ī 460/1067) or of Sarakhsī (Ḥanafī, 483/1090). They are also used by Muslim writers as I use them here, to designate types of literature. Even when the terms are not used, the typology is explicitly recognized and its components successfully indicated. Of the Yemeni scholar Ibn al-Muqri' (838/1434) it is recorded that he produced a work known as the *Irshād*. "It is a precious book on Shāfi'ī *furū'*, elegant in expression and sweet in diction, extremely concise and dense with meaning. He himself wrote a commentary on it, in which he flew to the circumambient horizons" (Shawkānī (1929), i: 43). Shawkānī's contrast between the *Irshād* and its commentary indicates precisely what I have in mind by distinguishing *mukhtaṣar* and *mabsūṭ*.

The earliest *mukhtaṣar*s were produced in the fourth/tenth century. The four major Sunni schools all produced at least one significant *mukhtaṣar* in this period. They are generally useful works, not notably refined. Some of them (say, the Ḥanafī *mukhtaṣar*s of Ṭaḥāwī (321/933) and Marwazī (334/946)) have survived only because they were incorporated into later and more important commentaries (*mabsūṭ*). Some have a functional adequacy which has secured for them centuries of practical (educative) use, notably the *Risālah* of the Mālikī scholar Ibn Abī Zayd al-Qayrawānī (386/996). The Shi'ah produced no similar work earlier than the *Nihāyah* of Ṭūsī, whose late date reflects the relatively late emergence of the Imāmī Shi'ah both as a definitive sectarian group and as a group committed to the normative Muslim discipline of the law. These early *mukhtaṣar*s are significant in at least three different ways. Firstly, they are the product of authors who were consciously aiming at analytic control of their material, presentational elegance and some formal artistry. They were successful only to a degree but the sense of authorial personality and achieved personal control is of considerable importance. Secondly, and in some degree of contrast, these works are summaries of a school achievement and express a school loyalty. They rise above the polemical difficulties and the methodological complexities of third/ninth century debate to state the basic programme of concepts and rules which define their school, their tradition, their loyalty. Thirdly, they are functional: they serve the needs of a curriculum, being clearly intended as primers for students, and requiring elucidation and explication from teachers. These are the forerunners of a literary tradition, intimately associated with an educational programme and a social elite whose members, sharing their knowledge of the law, were enabled to analyse, enjoy and give formal religious dignity to the society they lived in.

The genre of *mukhtaṣar* was fundamentally educative. Such works explained the basic concepts and structures of the law, while giving only hints as to how these could be applied or explored. Initially, writers aimed only at a classical elegance of exposition. Their works are marked by restraint and by sufficiency. Their concerns were to choose and to exemplify the basic concepts in order to create a vehicle that would successfully convey its educative message. Meticulous organization and careful recourse to divisions and subdivisions were prerequisites for successful literary production within the genre. It was a limited genre. The concepts of the law did not change through the centuries (though their application might). The (theologically guarded) sanctity of tradition ensured that the production of a single masterpiece, in Classical format, would dominate subsequent efforts, sometimes for centuries. Within the Ḥanafī tradition, the neatly decisive work of Qudūrī (428/1037) lent in various degrees elements of form, order, structure and locution to the succeeding masterpieces of Mawṣilī (683/1284), Nasafī (710/1310, or 701) and Shurunbulālī (1069/1659). Those who were trained in the discipline, who already knew the law, would find pleasure in such works in recognizing the formal skills of the writer, attested through neat deployment, subtle shifts in order, conceptual density and uncluttered precision.

Qudūrī, in his *Mukhtaṣar*, began his section on alms (*zakāt*) thus:

> *Zakāt* is mandatory for the free man who is Muslim, mature and sane; if he owns a minimum quantity of goods, with exclusive ownership; and if he has had them for a year. Children, the insane, and slaves who are buying their own freedom are not subject to *zakāt*. One who is in debt for a sum that equals the value of his possessions is not subject to *zakāt*.

Shurunbulālī, in his *Nūr al-īḍāḥ* offers the following:

> *Zakāt* is the transfer of specified wealth to a specified person. It is incumbent on the free man who is Muslim, subject to divine

> command, and owner of a minimum quantity of goods, whether in the form of coinage, metal, ornaments or vessels; or in the form of trade goods whose value is equal to the minimum quantity; if he is free of debt and after provision of his basic needs; the minimum quantity being of goods which are productive, or potentially so.

Clause by clause the concept of *zakāt* attracts layers of qualification which become densely suggestive of the problems that attend on God's command. It is highly unlikely for most Muslims, most of the time, that their actual performance of this duty conformed to this type of approach. A practical casualness is not at all incompatible with the conceptual search for qualified meaning and precise significance that is articulated by these carefully juxtaposed clauses. The grammatical and terminological density of the originals is weakened in the translations, which involve about twice as many words as are used in the Arabic texts. A careful reading however should induce some consciousness of how the later text has grown out of, and in some degree, away from, the first. The reader should be aware of the increased specificity, the thorough concretenes of "coinage, metal, ornaments, vessels", etc., and the neat placing of "provision for his basic goods". It is entirely appropriate to feel dissatisfied with "trade goods whose value is equal to the minimum quantity" (should it not be "equal to or greater than"?), and then to consider that the missing words would really, perhaps, be superfluous – as nothing at all should be in this kind of work. Between the first text and the second the law has not changed. What has bothered and interested the jurists is their ability to catch the law in a network of words. The syntactic disjuncture that places the final clause in Shurunbulālī's text is conveyed in Arabic by a variation in adjectival agreement which compels admiration for its marriage of concision and complexity. It is precisely this that the jurists wanted to achieve.

Clearly the genre lent itself to mannerism. With the passage of time, it inspired numerous masterpieces of structural, conceptual and syntactic dexterity that dazzle the reader as they invite him or her to share and delight in the writer's virtuoso mastery of a discipline. The mannerist works, unlike the "Classical" ones, do not have the immediate aim of explaining and elucidating the law; they are quite as likely to hide it, in order to entice the reader into that recreative exercise that consists in unpacking the meanings that have been meticulously – but never with recourse to vagueness or generalization – embedded in the intricate texture of language. One of the most successful such works (not in fact unduly tortuous) is the *Mukhtaṣar* of the Mālikī scholar Khalīl ibn Isḥāq (776/1374). From the time of its production till the thirteenth/nineteenth century, it dominated the Mālikī schools of North Africa and was universally recognized as a jewel.

> *Zakāt* is mandatory / on the specified minimum / of flocks / subject to ownership / and the passing of a year / both complete / whether provided with fodder / or working / or product of breeding / but not of coupling with wild beasts; / increase is included / though before the year by only a day / but not on less [than the minimum] . . .

"Woven on a magician's loom" said Ibn Ḥajar al-'Asqalānī (852/1448), trying to convey this work's patterned complexity (1966, 2: 175). The style is (part of) the message, and it should not be disregarded in a search merely for the rules. (These can be learnt elsewhere, and cannot be easily learnt from Khalīl.) Such books say that the law is a delight and a pleasure, and that it is a tortuous and inextricable mystery; they create perplexity and the joy of achieved understanding; they lead the mind away from the messy and the mundane to at least a momentary vision of perfection; and they are witty. The last quality seems inherent in the distancing effect of any virtuoso performance, and owes much to the ironic gap that opens between life and its consciously contrived juristic image.

For centuries young Muslims, aspiring to be educated, had to learn such books off by heart. It might now be lamented that this was a sacrifice of young and enquiring minds. But this was also, potentially at least, an invaluable cultural provision, and, if the text remained in the mind as a recourse, it was a constantly available solace and pleasure.

The multi-volume *mabsūṭ*, by contrast with the slim *mukhtaṣar*, is easy to recognize: their authors, like Ibn al-Muqri', "fly to the circumambient horizons". They multiply the details of the law. They may even (though it is not the most characteristic feature of these books) find the opportunity to relate the concepts of the law to the particular circumstances of their time.

Marwazī, Ḥanafī author of an early *mukhtaṣar*, distinguished between legitimate governors and "outlaws" (*khawārij*). If the former collected *zakāt*, while providing the people with adequate military protection, the duty of the people to pay *zakāt* was thereby accomplished. If, however, the outlaws despoiled the people of their goods, while claiming it was *zakāt* (but in fact using the ill-gotten goods for ill-advised ends), the duty of the people *vis-à-vis* God was not accomplished, and they should repeat their distribution of *zakāt*. This was hardly a friendly rule for the people, who, in the last case, were first despoiled, then had to pay their religious duties! Marwazī however may not have had "real" consequences in mind (he derived his rules in any case from the books before him). Engaging the concept *zakāt* with the additional concepts of governors and outlaws was a heuristic device, permitting exploration of the significance of *zakāt*.

The later jurist Sarakhsī, in his *Mabsūṭ*, a commentary on Marwazī, managed to free the people from their double burden.

> As to the collections made by the sultans of our time, these tyrants . . . Marwazī did not deal with them. Many of the religious leaders of Balkh promulgate the ruling, with regard to these governors, that payment is required a second time, in order to fulfil the duty due to God, as in the case of land attacked and conquered by outlaws. This is because we know that they do not distribute the collected wealth as it should be distributed . . . The more valid view is that these illegitimate collections fulfil for the owners of wealth the duty of *zakāt* – as long as they formulate, at the moment of paying, the intention of giving alms to them [i.e. to the unjust sultans]. This is because the wealth that they possess is the property of the Muslims, and the debts they owe to Muslims are greater than their own wealth. If they returned to the Muslims what they owe them, they would possess nothing. Accordingly they have the status of the poor [and are therefore legitimate recipients of *zakāt*].
>
> (Sarakhsī (1986), 2: 180)

This is a *ḥīlah* (a juristic contrivance), and a joke. At least a quiet smile is appropriate on recognizing how Sarakhsī exploits the idea of debt to render the luxurious tyrants into the category of the poor, who are the rightful recipients of *zakāt*. Here he has clearly an eye on reality, and has arranged (and developed) his concepts for the achievement of particular ends. The development of the law by the discovery of new conceptual distinctions (tyrants, added to governors and outlaws) and by the acknowledgement of dispute (*ikhtilāf*) is characteristic of how the traditions, all of them, expanded.

Development in this sense, however, relating the concepts of the law to the particularities of the day, could be only a small part of any given book. In many works of *furū‘* it is impossible to detect any responses that are particular to a given time and place. Formally such works are timeless. They have two major structural components. The first is the set of concepts that constitute the law. These are explored through the contrasting effects of terminological density and casuistic extravagance. The implicatory richness of a highly technical vocabulary is unravelled by making it work through cases, which may be hypothetical or practical, highly imaginative or trivially stereotyped. The casuistry is heuristic, a device for exploration, and it would, accordingly, be quite wrong to read such works as if they had immediate practical ends (though they sometimes did, and always contained that potential). The time-bound origins of a particular ruling are cancelled. The multiplicity of rulings thrown up by the tradition, or devised by the individual jurist, become a means to discover the facets through which a legal concept is revealed. Where the tradition offers dispute (*ikhtilāf*), it too becomes a device to achieve a finer and more qualified perception of what a concept implies.

The second structural component of a *mabsūṭ* is revelation and justificatory argument. These are always integrated to some extent in a *mabsūṭ*, but it is a matter of tradition and individual taste how much they are expanded and developed. Both concepts and revelation are theoretically static (in spite of some real development, at least of the former). This literary tradition too, therefore, in time, developed characteristics which might be described as mannerist. To attempt here a history of so large and long a tradition would be vain. The major illustration offered here is taken from the *Muhadhdhab* of the Shāfiʿī jurist, Shīrāzī (476/1083), a work emphatically Classical.

In the following passage, Shīrāzī considers the question how the owner of "hidden" goods (differing from "manifest" goods, flocks or crops, in not being easily accessible to government inspection) should organize the distribution of his *zakāt*. Paragraph division and numbering are mine, but the neatness of the fit is Shīrāzī's. Note how every paragraph is constituted by a rule and the argument which justifies the rule; how the *ikhtilāf* of paragraphs 2.0–2.3 is unresolved.

> Chapter on the distribution of alms
>
> 1.1 It is permissible for the owner of wealth to distribute *zakāt* on hidden goods by himself. Hidden goods are gold, silver, trade goods and precious stones. This ruling is based on the *ḥadīth* from ʿUthmān, that he said in the month of Muḥarram, This is the month of your *zakāt*, so he who has a debt, let him pay his debt, then let him pay *zakāt* on the remainder of his wealth.
>
> 1.2 It is permissible for him to appoint an agent to distribute on his behalf. This is because *zakāt* is a claim on wealth, and it is permissible to appoint an agent to execute it, as with debts between men.
>
> 1.3 It is permissible that he pay his *zakāt* to the Imām. This is because the Imām is the representative of the poor. His status is like that of a guardian to an orphan.
>
> 2.0 On the question which is the best mode of conduct, there are three views.
>
> 2.1 The best mode of conduct is that the owner of wealth should distribute his *zakāt* by himself. This is the evident meaning of the text [i.e. the *ḥadīth* quoted at paragraph 1.1]. Further he is secure in respect of his own paying, but not secure in respect of anyone else paying.

> 2.2 The best mode of conduct is that he should pay the Imām, whether the Imām is just or unjust. This is because of what is related concerning Mughīrah ibn Sha'bah. He said to a client of his, who had the stewardship of his property in Ṭā'if, What do you do about alms on my property? The client replied, "Some of it I distribute directly as alms, and some of it I give to the authorities." Mughīrah asked what he knew about the latter portion. The client explained, "They buy land and marry women with it." Mughīrah said, "Pay it to them; for the Prophet of God commanded us to pay them." Another reason: the Imām is more knowledgeable about the poor and the extent of their need.
>
> 2.3 Amongst our companions there are some who say that if the Imām is just, payment to him is the best mode of conduct, but if he is unjust, then distribution by the owner of the wealth is best. This is because of the Prophet's words, He who asks for it as it should be, let him be given it; he who demands more than he should, let him not be given it. Further, the donor is secure in paying it to a just Imām, but is not secure in paying it to an unjust Imām, for the latter may spend it on his own desires.
>
> (Shīrāzī (1959), 1: 175)

In the *ikhtilāf* of 2.0–2.3 there are three foci of concern: *zakāt* as a personal duty to God, *zakāt* as a communal duty implemented by the Imām and *zakāt* as a functional provision for the poor. The three "best modes of conduct" can be analysed as resulting from the elevation, in sequence, of each of these considerations to a dominant position. Shīrāzī has effectively shown his readers how the Shāfi'ī tradition (his "companions") understood (in this context) the concept of *zakāt*, and how this understanding can be justified by arguments of revelation, of reason and of analogy. If the "best modes of conduct" emerged into the tradition because they were responses to particular situations (as is not unlikely), it is precisely that particularity that has been removed, so rendering the casuistry exploratory and not practical. In the distribution of *zakāt* it is necessary to consider the duty to God, the rights and duties of the governor and the legitimate expectations of the poor. The message is perhaps that no one of these considerations unequivocally overrides the others. This is an abstract analysis of concepts and should not be mistaken for a set of practical rules. If, anywhere in Shīrāzī's work, we could learn anything about, say, the actual practice of his governors (and I think we can't), it would be an accident, and would not represent a part of his purpose in producing this book.

In a *mabsūṭ* then, the concepts of the law are explored, often by varying one or several items in a "case" which, at a given point, reveals the significance of the concept. The result of course is that many different concepts are explored at once in a dense reticulation of argument. Here, in order to illuminate the concept of *zakāt*, Shīrāzī relates it to the concept of "agent" (*wakīl*) (1.2) and to the concept Imām (1.3), and that in turn to the concept of guardianship of orphans. Fully alert readers should begin to ask themselves about the significance of these judgments and might formulate further questions, or cases, which could illuminate the relationship between God, the individual (his or her agent, etc.), the Imām, the poor, etc. It is precisely this multifaceted and more or less hypothetical exploratory activity that constitutes the bulk of a work of *furūʿ*.

There is none the less a distinguishable third component which is also constitutive of the material contents of a *mabsūṭ*. It is the tradition itself. The exploration of concepts and the relating of concepts to revelation is achieved through tradition, In the passage from Shīrāzī above, we are not to imagine that he himself devised the three "best views"; they were given to him by the tradition, here the Shāfiʿī tradition. His role was to organize and present them in the neat schematic manner that permits the reader to perceive and register their implications. (That this role was creative is not denied.) Often the role of tradition is rendered explicit by reference to named authorities. In the early centuries of juristic writing, the named authorities are likely to be, almost exclusively, the founding fathers of the school tradition, Abū Ḥanīfah and his two pupils dominate the Ḥanafī tradition, Shāfiʿī, Mālik and Ibn Ḥanbal the other Sunni schools. For each of the last three it is commonplace to find that they had two or more opinions about legal problems, or that one of their pupils or colleagues had a well-defended alternative view, worth preserving. A multiple set of authorities and judgments was a prerequisite, for it permitted a concept to be viewed from a number of angles, so engendering complexity (a jurist's delight), and opening up different possibilities of development. The Shiʿite tradition too, when it began to produce juristic literature, called upon a constellation of authorities, as well as a large and diverse set of *ḥadīth* from the Imāms.

With the passage of centuries, the quantity of tradition, the juristic literature itself, became immensely greater than the quantity of revelation. The symbolic importance of the latter was not diminished, but its place in the literature of the law became, necessarily, (even) smaller. Within the school traditions this was not perceived as a problem, though it did prompt, on occasion, fundamentalist reactions, amongst those who felt that revelation rather than tradition should be the immediate source of rules. The prime example of fundamentalist reaction is Ibn Ḥazm, the Literalist (Goldziher 1971), but the tendency recurred from time to time, within various schools, its most notable later representative being the Ḥanbalī Ibn Taymiyyah. Generally, however, inside the schools, the meaning of revelation was discovered through tradition. There is no doubt about the priority of the latter: the first loyalty of a jurist was to his school which alone revealed (!) to him the meaning of revelation (!). The theological implications of that fact can hardly be overstated.

In literary terms, the theological argument was expressed through a number of devices. In addition to those mentioned above, the most obvious is, perhaps, the use of commentary, supercommentary and gloss. These layered texts (increasingly present as the tradition got older) are in part product of a teaching device, in part reflect a delight in the contrasting effects of epitome and expansion, but mostly are a theological affirmation of commitment to tradition. The content of some early *mukhtaṣar*, embedded within a contemporary *mabsūṭ*, are thereby asserted to be identical with the full complexity of the law as it was understood in the later period. Serving the same purpose was the device of jigsaw puzzle composition. Ibn Nujaym's *Al-Baḥr al-rā'iq* is an example. The text of this work is created out of larger or smaller fragments derived (and acknowledged) from the whole tradition of Ḥanafī juristic writing. Explicit authorial intervention is reduced to a minimum and always takes the form of commentary on a citation. What might interest a Western scholar, the chronological order of these things, is quite disregarded. Though there is no doubt that Ibn Nujaym's complex manipulation of the tradition created something new (if only, sometimes, in form, for that too is part of the message), his methodology was designed to affirm the timelessnes of his conceptual explorations. Cut into the tradition at any point and the whole complexity of the law is there.

The law is a timeless structure of concepts, justified by reference to revelation, and fully present, at least by implication, in any articulation within the tradition, whether in a *mukhtaṣar* or in a *mabsūṭ*. Understanding of the law is achieved through understanding of tradition, not through independent or personal assessment of the meaning of revelation. A deeper understanding of the law (always the same as a greater delight in the law) can be achieved through consideration of the implications of *ikhtilāf* and the possibilities of conceptual subdivision. Direct response to revelation or to reality, though always possible, and sometimes detectable, are not particularly characteristic of how the law as a whole develops. With regard to many aspects of social reality, the juristic traditions are marked not by their aspiration to control and understand reality but by abnegation and indifference to development. Jurists, for example, never considered it their business to analyse the real problems faced by real governments in the creation of administrative and financial systems that would work. The efforts made in that direction were few (e.g. by Māwardī *et al.*, see Lambton (1981)), the achievements limited and the results largely disregarded by the mainstream of all the juristic traditions (Calder 1986). In spite of some remarkable exceptions, the jurists on the whole preferred to analyse the concepts and problems they inherited, rather than to take on or create new ones (Imber 1982). And they continued to analyse inherited concepts and problems even when these had no bearing on the practical life of ordinary Muslims. No Muslim who studied *fiqh* would fail to learn the taxonomy of camels (in the archaic and frozen vocabulary of the tradition), and the arithmetic of how to distribute *zakāt* on camels, no matter how little the personal need to know this. Knowledge counted. Shawkānī tells us, with evident admiration, that Ibn al Muqri', on one occasion, considered the implications of the dispute within the Shāfi'ī tradition as to the use of sun-warmed water for ablutions: his heads of analysis reached thousands (Shawkānī (1979), 1.43). There may be exaggeration here, but the point is important: a jurist merits praise when he takes a single given problem or concept of the law and by minute analysis reveals its implications, its thousands (!) of facets. The diamond-cutting analogy is not inappropriate, for the effect of (good) juristic prose is one of crystalline clarity and of dazzling virtuosity.

I have said above that *fiqh* is a multi-functional discipline. It is not too difficult to concede that its primary function is theological, though it is not now easy to recover the theological message of these works. Modernist and fundamentalist Islam has lost the taste, and denies the priorities of traditional writing on the law. Sayyid Quṭb (executed 1966), informal spokesman for the Muslim Brothers in Egypt, and widely acknowledged for his Qur'ān commentary, on numerous occasions expressed what many Muslims now feel, namely that the tradition has somehow failed them. "The *Sharī'ah*," he says, "has been revealed in order to be implemented, not to be known, to be studied, and to be changed into culture in books and treatises" (Quṭb (1971), 1: 746). The observation is pertinent because it acknowledges (correctly) that this, or something like it, is what the tradition did. There, again and again, the stress falls on the need to explore the law in order to know it better, and on the need to create elegant and self-consciously artistic literary forms that will reflect the law's complexity. Whereas the pre-modern writers affirm that tradition controls understanding of revelation, modernist Islam tends to say the opposite, that revelation is a means to get rid of the (burdensome and irrelevant) complexities of a tradition which, perhaps, it is implied, has not served the community well. In the course of the thirteenth/nineteenth century, and largely as a result of Islam's confrontation with Western culture, the tradition had been interrupted, and its message lost. The tenuous continuation of the pre-modern juristic tradition was perhaps less tenuous amongst the Shī'ah, where it provided the concepts that inspired the jurists' intervention in the Iranian Revolution of 1978. Generally, however, the emergence of secular education systems and the divergence of the intellectual elite of Muslim societies to other (and frequently more pressing) matters has ensured that the law (or rather *fiqh*, for the inspirational power of *Sharīʿah*, a concept potentially devoid of detail or specificity, has increased) does not dominate society as it once did.

Quṭb's remark shows that he thinks the *Sharīʿah* (*sic*) exists to be implemented. That stress on loyalty and action, prior to (even independent of) exploratory thought, is part of an activist programme to which he was committed, but it has reverberations throughout modernist Muslim writing, and has affected the perceptions of Western scholars. F. M. Denny is not the only observer to imagine that Islam is better characterized as a religion of orthopraxy than as a religion of orthodoxy (Denny (1985): 98). This is not true, and was traditionally denied by Muslim jurists and theologians. For them, the definition of a Muslim, and the possibility of salvation, depended on faith, not works. For the whole of the Sunni tradition there was no dispute that faith (alone) guaranteed salvation. Works of course were important; Muslims might be punished, according to some temporarily, in Hell, for their failures to conform to God's law (though they might, even then, be saved through the intercession of their Prophet). In practical life, even the simplest, and absolutely undisputed, parts of the law (say, to pray five times a day) are today (and were undoubtedly in the past) often disregarded by some Muslims who, though acknowledging their error, are not (as far as the casual observer can tell) unduly disturbed by their sins, nor rendered doubtful in their conviction of salvation. A Muslim did not have to be a qualified jurist to perceive the law as an ideal.

These remarks, and the general tenor of this chapter, are not intended to deny that the law, and all writing on the law, was expected, in some degree, to influence practice. No jurist was ever oblivious to the fact that conceptual exploration of the law, or theological affirmations about the importance of tradition, had implications for daily life. And every jurist acknowledged his duty, as a member of the learned elite, to provide explicit and unqualified guidance in respect of particular problems that were brought to him by the populace at large. If the jurist Shīrāzī was approached by one who explained his financial circumstances, and enquired about payment of *zakāt*, Shīrāzī would not then sit back to consider the possibilities of the law; he would, as a *mujtahid*, recognize the need to provide an answer. The need to make the law work, to some degree, was universally recognized, and generated bodies of literature distinct from those described in this chapter. Juristic responses to particular questions generated the literature of *fatāwā* (responsa). That literature has its own complexity, which cannot be discussed here. Some parts of the law were more than others integrated into the administrative structures of Islamic society, notably the office of the *qāḍī* and all that appertained to it. Monographs were produced in such fields in which the stress was less on exploring the law, more on the provision of practical advice and rules of expedient conduct. There was even a small and marginal genre of monographs on the structures of government, little though these, on the whole, attracted the attention of the tradition. Many jurists however participated in government (while many others refused to do so) and tried to create some kind of link between the structures of the law and the structures of practical administration.

But practice, in whatever area or form, could never be more than a clumsy, partial and imperfect realization of the divine command. A fuller (if perhaps still inadequate) expression of that command could be achieved in literature. The literature of the law is an exploration of God's self-revelation to and within a particular human society. In all its forms, aspects and implications it is about a divinely sanctioned social order and the (consequent?) possibilities of human social integration. It is not a description of "real" society, nor the provision of a corpus of sensible, practical rules; it is at least the transformation of these things into a theological argument. As much for modern Muslims as for modern academics the task of mastering that literature and translating its implications into an idiom suited to (soon) the fifteenth/twenty-first century is one that has hardly begun. The cultural complement to juristic literature, with its stress on society, is, within Islam, Sufi literature, which provides a corresponding stress on the private devotional life of individuals. It is in the integration of these two structures that most Muslims – including the jurists, who were frequently also mystics – have, historically, found self-realization as Muslims.

BIBLIOGRAPHY

Al-'Asqalānī, Aḥmad ibn Ḥajar (852/1448) (1966) *Al-Durar al-kāminah*, 5 vols, ed. M. S. Jād al-Ḥaqq (Cairo).

Calder, Norman (1983) "*Ikhtilāf* and *ijmā'* in Shāfi'ī's *Risāla*", *Studia Islamica*, 58: 55–81.

—— (1986) "Friday Prayer and the Juristic Theory of Government: Sarakhsī, Shīrāzī, Māwardī", *Bulletin of the School of Oriental and African Studies*, 49(1): 35–47.

—— (1989) "Doubt and Prerogative: the Emergence of an Imāmī Shī'ī Theory of *ijtihād*", *Studia Islamica*, 70 (1989): 57–78.

Denny, F. M. (1985) *An Introduction to Islam* (London and New York).

Al-Dhahabī, Muḥammad ibn Aḥmad Abū 'Abd Allāh (748/1347) (1947) *Manāqib al-Imām Abī Ḥanīfah*, eds M. Z. al-Kawtharī and A.-W. al-Afghānī (Hyderabad and Cairo).

Fyzee, A. A. A. (1964) *Outlines of Muhammadan Law*, 3rd ed. (Calcutta).

Goldziher, Ignaz (1971) *The Ẓāhirīs: Their Doctrine and Their History*, trans. and ed. Wolfgang Behn (Leiden).

Hallaq, Wael B. (1984) "Was the Gate of *ijtihād* Closed?", *International Journal of Middle Eastern Studies*, 16: 3–41.

—— (1986) "On the Origins of the Controversy about the Existence of *mujtahids* and the Gate of *ijtihād*", *Studia Islamica*, 63: 129–41.

Imber, Colin (1982) "*Zina* in Ottoman Law", in *Contribution à l'histoire économique et sociale de l'Empire Ottoman*, Collection Turcica (Louvain), 3: 61–92.

'Iyāḍ, al-Qāḍī (1967) *Tartīb al-madārik wa taqrīb al-masālik li-ma'rifat a'lām madhhab Mālik*, 4 vols, ed. A. B. Mahmoud (Beirut and Tripoli).

Johansen, Baber (1988) *The Islamic Law on Land Tax and Rent* (Exeter Arabic and Islamic series) (London, New York and Sydney).

Khalīl ibn Isḥāq (776/1374) *Al-Mukhtaṣar*, in Muḥammad al-Khurashī, *Sharḥ mukhtaṣar al-khalīl*, 8 vols (Beirut, n.d.; reprint Cairo, 1900).

Lambton, A. K. S. (1981) *State and Government in Medieval Islam: an Introduction to the Study of Islamic Political Theory: the Jurists* (Oxford).

Linant de Bellefonds, Y. (1956) *Traité de droit musulman comparé*, 3 vols (Paris and The Hague).

Al-Qudūrī, Aḥmad ibn Muḥammad Abu'l-Ḥusayn (428/1037) (1957) *al-Mukhtaṣar* or *al-Matn*, 3rd ed. (Cairo).

Quṭb, Sayyid (1971) *Fī ẓilāl al-qur'ān*, 8 vols (Beirut).

Saleh, Nabil (1986) *Unlawful Gain and Legitimate Profit in Islamic Law* (Cambridge Studies in Islamic Civilisation) (Cambridge).

Sarakhsī, Muḥammad ibn Abī Sahl Abū Bakr (483/1090) (1986) *al-Mabsūṭ*, 30 vols (Cairo, 1906; reprinted Beirut, 1986).

Schacht, Joseph (1950) *The Origins of Muhammadan Jurisprudence* (Oxford).

—— (1964) *An Introduction to Islamic Law* (Oxford).

Al-Shawkānī, Muḥammad ibn 'Alī (1250/1834) (1929) *Al-Badr al-ṭāli' bi-maḥāsin man ba'd al-qarn al-sābi'*, 2 vols (Cairo).

Al-Shīrāzī, Ibrāhīm ibn 'Alī Abū Isḥāq (476/1083) (1959) *al-Muhadhdhab fī fiqh al-Imām al-Shāfi'ī*, 2 vols (Beirut).

Al-Shurunbulālī, Ḥasan ibn 'Ammār (1069/1659) (1900) *Nūr al-īdāḥ*, in Aḥmad ibn Muḥammad al-Ṭaḥāwī, *Ḥāshiyyah 'alā marāqī al-falāḥ sharḥ nūr al-īḍāḥ* (Bulaq).

Wansbrough, John (1977) *Quranic Studies: Sources and Methods of Scriptural Interpretation* (London Oriental Series, 31) (Oxford).

IV

Tafsīr from Ṭabarī to Ibn Kathīr

Problems in the description of a genre, illustrated with reference to the story of Abraham[1]

1

Tafsīr is a literary genre with definable formal characteristics. The most fundamental of these is the presence of the complete canonical text of the Qur'ān (or at least a significant chunk of it), segmented for purposes of comment, and dealt with in canonical order. In a work of *tafsīr*, passages of comment invariably follow canonical segments. Canon and segmentation, lemma and comment: where these are not systematically present, then a work is not an example of the central tradition of *tafsīr*, though it may belong to the margins of that tradition. This formal structure is so fundamental as to require no exemplification. In sections 2 and 3 of this paper two further structures are proposed as constituting, together with this one, a sufficient description of *tafsīr*. Description is of course a mode of interpretation. The interpretation then which I set out in this paper is intended to be general, at least for the period under consideration, namely from Ṭabarī to Ibn Kathīr. Exemplification is restricted to commentary on verses which relate to the story of Abraham. This does not impair the generality of the description, for, as will be evident, quranic narrative provoked more than merely narrative responses: in the hands of a skilled and sensitive exegete any quranic verse might be found to have implications ranging across the scholastic disciplines. In Sections 4 and 5 of this paper the distinctive achievements of Muḥammad b. Aḥmad al-Qurṭubī and Fakhr al-Dīn al-Rāzī are demonstrated in the light of the structural description proposed in sections 1–3. Sections 6 and 7 are concerned primarily with Ibn Kathīr whose *Tafsīr*, I maintain, must be recognized as a significant deviation from the norms of the genre; perhaps as a major turning-point in its development. The structures which I propose as constitutive of the genre, and the tensions revealed by the varied manipulation of these structures, were recognized at least to a degree by participants in the tradition. Demonstration of this in section 8 permits also of some concluding remarks about the dynamics of the genre and its limits.[2]

2

> When Abraham said to his father *āzar* do you take idols as gods... (Qur'ān 6.74)

Without further reference and unpunctuated that verse permits a number of possible readings, the most obvious of which will take the word *āzar* to be the name of Abraham's father. But it was known from other narratives (historians, story-tellers, the Bible) that Abraham's father was called Terah (so in the English Bible; the Arabic versions were Tārah or Tārakh) and this prompted some creative reflection. Abraham's father had perhaps two names, just as Jacob was also called Israel. Or, in familiar idiom, Āzar was a *laqab* (nickname), Terah, an *ism* (proper name). Or vice-versa. Or, indeed, Āzar was the only correct name, a view ascribed to Ḥasan [al-Baṣrī]. Sulaymān al-Taymī and others suggested that *āzar* was a word indicating abuse or insult, corresponding to Arabic *mu'wajj*: 'Fool, do you take idols...?' Ḍaḥḥāk suggested that *āzar* was Persian, meaning old man; Farrā' that it corresponded to Arabic *mukhṭī'*(one who errs, wrong-doer). Jawharī proposed that *āzar* was a foreign word (*a'jamī*) derived from the Arabic (!) *āzara* meaning to help, and referred to the fact that Terah/Āzar helped his people to worship idols. Alternatively, it was related to an Arabic word meaning power or force (*quwwa*) and so generated the reading, 'Is it through force that you take idols...?' For Mujāhid, it was not the name of Abraham's father, but the name of an idol, and should be read in the accusative, hence, 'Do you take *āzar* as idols for gods?' Qurṭubī, from whose *Tafsīr* all these readings are taken, adds a rare but helpful personal comment here, that in this case *āzar* is to be understood as a generic, *ism jins*. For Tha'labī, Abraham's father was called Terah by his father but was given the name Āzar when he became overseer to the temple treasury under Nimrod.

All of these readings permitted the extra subtlety that they could be read either in the vocative or in the genitive after *li*: either, 'Abraham said to his father, Fool, do you take idols...' or, 'Abraham said to his father, a fool, Do you take idols...' In the first case, the word must be read *āzaru*, in the second case, *āzara* (not *āzari* since it was either a foreign proper name or an adjective of the form *af'alu*, not permitting full declension). Ascribed to Ibn 'Abbās were two readings which propose a different word juncture without deviating from the consonantal outline of the quranic text: *a-izran tattakhidhu* or *a-azran tattakhidhu*, meaning, 'Do you take Izr/Azr as idols...?'

Commenting on this verse, Qurṭubī named a total of eighteen authorities, producing thereby a large variety of possible readings, while giving scarcely a hint as to his preferred reading amongst this amplitude. That amplitude was precisely the point might be inferred from his mode of approach. He began his commentary with a citation from Muḥammad b. Muḥammad al-Juwaynī who claimed that there was no dispute (*ikhtilāf*) on the name of Abraham's father, which was Terah. Juwaynī then gave two variants, both introduced by the anonymous *qīla*, namely, (i) that *āzar* corresponds to *ya mukhti*', O wrong-doer, and is *marfū*', in the nominative/vocative, and (ii) that it is the name of an idol and is in the accusative, with ellipsis of the verb. Qurṭubī responds to this, first, by denying the claim that there is no dispute on the name of Abraham's father and then by multiplying the variant readings in the manner demonstrated above and providing them with named authorities. In effect, he rejects the over-simplified presentation of Juwaynī and affirms the need for named authorities and multiple readings.

This citation of named authorities and the consequent polyvalent reading of the text is the second structural characteristic of *tafsīr* which I propose as constitutive of the genre.[3] There were of course factors which limited the exploitation of this feature. Two such, open to all exegetes, were, simply, the exercise of choice (hiding variety) or the expression of preference (admitting while controlling variety). Amongst factors likely to strengthen the reductive tendency were a highly specialized concern with a particular (theological) message and/or a narrow focus on some scholastic disciplines and a consequent lack of interest in others. Zamakhsharī, for example, notoriously, combines a meticulous concern for grammatical nicety with a defence of Mu'tazilī theology. These factors condition both his expressed preferences (admitting variety) and choices (implying eschewal of some possibilities). Polyvalent readings remain the norm, though named authorities are considerably reduced. Similar factors, if vastly different specific concerns, affect both Fakhr al-Dīn al-Rāzī (section 5, below) and Ibn Kathīr (sections 6 and 7) both of whom allow dogmatic considerations to restrict some readings, while admitting, variously, substantial polyvalent readings and sufficient named authorities to establish their participation within the genre – not just *tafsīr* but specifically Sunnī *tafsīr*.

The process of citing authorities and providing multiple readings is in part a declaration of loyalty: it defines the tradition within which one works. It is also a means to establish the individuality or the artistry of a given *mufassir*: the selection, presentation and organization of citations constitutes always a process that is unique to one writer. Finally, it is, of itself, one element in a theological message: the possibility of the community and the text to contain multiplicity while remaining one community and one text is thereby asserted.

Submission to polyvalent readings implied the danger of a tradition grown unmanageably large. Factors of choice, preference and scholarly or dogmatic exclusion worked continuously against centrifugal forces (temporal and spatial diffusion as well as scholarly imagination and development of sectarian and popular beliefs). If the main tradition embraced diversity and made it a means to various ends, the need for monovalent readings – perhaps for very specific purposes – was not thereby cancelled. The work of Dīnawarī (308/920) within our period and the famous *Tafsīr al-Jalālayn* of Suyūṭī and Maḥallī in the 9/15th century are firmly monovalent; as is one of the three *tafsīrs* by Wāḥidī (468/1076). Felicitously described by A. Rippin as 'Arabic translations' of the Qur'ān, these works probably reflect the needs of a curriculum (educational) and derive their larger meaning from the *tafsīr* tradition as a whole: in relation to this they are always either introduction or summary.[4]

3

For many contemporary scholars of philosophy and literary criticism, the concept of hermeneutics has become the focus for a highly generalized understanding of the relationship between the reader and the text/ the present and the past/ the individual and the world. For them the 'text' is either friend (to a degree, Gadamer) or enemy (Bloom) or just an indefinitely malleable system of signs without truth, without origins (Derrida); it is approached with prejudice (*Vorurteil*), or anxiety and misprision, or licence. Stimulating at certain levels of analysis, these ideas cannot be made to serve the immediate aim of assessing the forms or the content of *tafsīr*.[5] Refreshing, by contrast, is the assumption by G. Vermes that it is usually possible to distinguish between a problem that arises because of something in the text and a problem that emerges because something external to the text is imposed upon it: giving rise, respectively, in his terminology, to pure and applied exegesis.[6] This distinction has some value at a basic descriptive level but will hardly sustain the burden of precise systematic analysis. Does the exegetical problem related to *āzar* arise from a 'real' problem within the text or from an external idea or belief which is imposed upon the text? The question hardly seems appropriate. The problem arises because something within the text is recognized as being at odds with something outside the text.

This must always be true of exegetical problems. Texts in isolation are not only unproblematic, they are meaningless. The text of the Qur'ān takes on meaning only when it is systematically juxtaposed to certain structures which exist independently (more or less) of the Qur'ān itself; notably the grammatical and rhetorical structures of the Arabic language, but also the scholastic disciplines of law, theology and prophetic narrative. In the case of *āzar*, the narrative structure within the text is apparently at odds with a known narrative structure external to the text. Resolution is achieved through such processes as (i) harmonization through narrative – Abraham's father had two names or he acquired one name later in life; (ii) differentiation: e. g. grammatical/lexical – *āzar* does not belong to the narrative structure but to the grammatical, being not a proper name but an adjective; or narrative/grammatical – *āzar* is the name of an idol or class of idols and the sentence exhibits transposition or ellision of a verb; and (iii) exclusion – the quranic narrative excludes the others. And so on. The problem is invariably one of bringing the internal structures and the external ones into some kind of harmony. (This was a process of course which prejudiced the independence of the scholastic discipines, not least those of grammar and rhetoric. In practice, the independent analogical structures of grammar and syntax were, just, preserved;[7] and so, marginally, and in spite of Ibn Kathīr, was the independent discipline of prophetic narrative.)

John Wansbrough, reacting in part to the weaknesses of established scholarship, proposed a typological approach to the historical development (diachronic) of *tafsīr*. His types are haggadic, halakhic, masoretic, rhetorical and allegorical.[8] The terminology is sectarian, though probably intended to reflect the universality of hermeneutic approaches. For purposes of synchronic description, of *tafsīr* in the classical, post-development, period, the hint is invaluable. The scholastic disciplines against which the quranic text must be measured are broadly incorporated in that list. Clearly, there is room for subdivision: it is usually possible to distinguish lexical, orthographic and syntactic devices under the heading masoretic (grammatical). And there is a minor usefulness in acknowledging a distinction between linguistic (instrumental) and theological (ideological) structures. In sum, I would propose that *tafsīr*, in the period up to Ibn Kathīr, can be described as a measuring of the quranic text against the following:

1 Instrumental structures:
  orthography, lexis, syntax, rhetoric, symbol/allegory
2 Ideological structures:

prophetic history, theology, eschatology, law, *taṣawwuf*

This is the third and most complex structural organization which constitutes the literary genre of *tafsīr*. The term 'prophetic history' is intended to cover the disciplines of prophetic biography, both *qiṣaṣ al-anbiyā'* and *sīrat al-nabī*. 'Theology' covers the normal subject matter of *kalām*. Orthography, lexis and syntax are the normal subject matter of the grammatical disciplines; allegory and symbol are most commonly dealt with in the Islamic intellectual tradition as a part of the discipline of rhetoric.[9] The list permits no doubt of finer articulation but adequately defines the standard and the marginal concerns both of *tafsīr* and of the Islamic scholastic disciplines. All of these subjects were independently studied for their own sake and permitted of indefinite extension beyond the constraints of the quranic text; and all were systematically subject to the centripetal force of the quranic text. The interplay of discipline and text was neither random nor absolutely constrained: it was controlled by the knowledge, interests, skills, sensitivity, imagination, even humour, of individual exegetes, as well as by their literary and sectarian loyalties. A *tafsīr*, after all, is a work of art. Symbolic and allegorical readings frequently coincide with *taṣawwuf*, but played a marginal role even in *kalām*-type discussions. On balance, they have only a limited role to play in the period discussed here, though capable of considerable expansion to serve the needs of a particular theological message (Rāzī) and increasingly present in *tafsīr* works of the later period.

The claim advanced here is then that the three broad structures presented in the first three sections of this paper constitute the fundamental rules-of-the-game for *mufassirs*. The qualities which distinguish one *mufassir* from another lie less in their conclusions as to what the quranic text means than in their development and display of techniques which mark their participation in and mastery of a literary discipline. Just as the skill of, say, a football player can be recognized only in relation to a complex body of rules (variously constitued by such things as white lines on grass or a complex and developing off-side rule) so too the literary skills of a *mufassir* must be assessed not in terms of the end product (the Qur'ān explained) but in terms of their skilful participation in a rule-governed activity. In the next section the individual skills of Ṭabarī and Qurṭubī are assessed in the light of these observations.

4

By God, I shall deal with your idols, as soon as you turn your backs. / He rendered them to pieces, except for a big one.... / They said, Did you do this to our gods, O Abraham? / He said, This big one did it; so ask them, if indeed they speak.

(Qur'ān 21.57–8 and 62–3)

Here, on a simple reading of the text, Abraham lies. Indeed it was not the only occasion. At Qur'ān 37.88ff., where the same episode is described, Abraham, having looked at the stars, said, 'I am sick'. And so they turned their backs on him – and he was able to carry out his intention. Characteristically elliptic, this narrative need not be interpreted as implying that Abraham lied: he claimed to be sick because he was sick. But the structure of narrative external to the quranic text – the tales of the prophets, *qiṣaṣ al-anbiyā'* – provided the missing details, broadly confirming that this was a deliberate misrepresentation intended to deceive. Independent also of the canon was a complex structure of theological dogma which equally demanded to be compared with quranic narrative; and one item within that structure stated that Prophets were free from sin (*ma'ṣūm*). How then might Abraham lie?[10]

The problem was not simply one of scripture versus dogma, for the tales of the prophets had a significantly larger content than the liturgical reflex of those tales contained in the Qur'ān. It was, granted the wide circulation of these stories, a matter of public knowledge that Abraham had lied at least three times. This inconcinnity between narrative and dogma gave rise to a prophetic *ḥadīth*, recorded in Ṭabarī, and eventually incorporated in the classical collections. The Prophet of God said, 'Abraham did not lie, save three lies, two with respect to God (*fī dhāt Allāh*), namely his saying, "I am sick" and "This big one did it"; and one with respect to Sarah, namely his saying, "She is my sister".'[11]

At Qur'ān 37.88–9, Ṭabarī explains the phrase, 'I am sick' (*innī saqīm)*, by stating that Abraham claimed to have the plague, this being a disease from which the people of Abraham fled. His aim in making this claim was to be left alone in the temple of the gods where he could destroy them. Ṭabarī supports this explanation with six reports, from five different authorities, which confirm and elaborate his view. Marginally present in Ṭabarī's reports is the motif of a festival (*'īd*): Abraham's people had a festival which required them to leave the town for celebrations; claiming to be sick, Abraham was left behind. This double motivation for the abandonment of Abraham in the town was variously harmonized by later authorities. In either case, Abraham had lied. This was proved for Ṭabarī by reference to the prophetic *ḥadīth* mentioned above, which, after all, explicitly states that Abraham lied three times. Ṭabarī acknowledges an opposing group who claimed that these words of Abraham were, not quite a lie, but a *mi'rāḍ* – an expression which, though misleading, is really true. In this case, it is envisaged that all men, being subject to death, are sick, though they suffer from no particular disease. Granted this, Abraham is saved from the accusation of lying. Ṭabarī, characteristically as we shall see,[12] prefers narrative to theology and considers this theological subtlety overruled by the plain meaning of the prophetic *ḥadīth*: *wa-qawl rasūl Allāh huwa al-ḥaqq dūna ghayrihi* – a statement not without a vicious irony when adduced to prove that Abraham lied!

Ṭabarī, comparing the quranic text against the structures of narrative and theology, simply prefers narrative. More discriminatingly expressed, there are four structures here juxtaposed: popular narrative, quranic narrative, theological dogma and prophetic *ḥadīth*. For Ṭabarī synchronic structures, they had in fact emerged historically in that order: the stories before the liturgy, the dogma before the *ḥadīth*.[13]

When Qurṭubī came to assess Abraham's statement, 'This big one did it' – *bal fa'alahu kabīruhum hādha*, he transposed the next two phrases and read, not, 'Ask them, if indeed they speak', but, 'This big one did it, if they speak; so ask them'.[14] Abraham, he explains, linked the alleged action of 'this big one' to the ability of the idols to speak: he – the big one – did it, if indeed these idols speak. This is an example of the rhetorical device *taqdīm wa-ta'khīr* (transposition), which, correctly understood, removes Abraham's remark from the category of lies and renders it a polemical argument designed to demonstrate the error of the beliefs of the idolaters. Abraham did not lie: it was a *ta'rīḍ* (= *mi'rāḍ*). This event, so understood, permits also a juristic deduction, namely that it is permissible to concede an untrue premise in the course of a debate with the intention of leading an opponent to admit the falsity of the premise. These remarkable discoveries of rhetorical virtuosity and debating technique do not exhaust Qurṭubī's analysis of this problem. There are also variant readings. From Ibn Sumayqa': read *bal fa'allahu*, 'perhaps he did it' (!). From al-Kisā'ī: pause after *bal fa'alahu* and then begin a new sentence; hence, 'He did it [who did it]; their leader is this one'. And anonymously (*qīla*): it is a rhetorical question and debating device, meaning, 'Why should they deny that this big one did it since they believe it is worthy of worship?'

Comparing Qurṭubī to Ṭabarī (and he has the advantage of some 350 years) it is evident that he displays a remarkably increased versatility in exploring what was originally a narrative/theological problem, a versatility marked by his playing across the disciplines. Ṭabarī seems stolid when compared with the richness of Qurṭubī's responses. It remains true that none of these grammatical, rhetorical and juristic niceties would have been discovered without the original inconcinnity between the 'plain' meaning of the text and established theological dogma. Sensibly relishing the possibilities offered by a denial that Abraham lied, Qurṭubī had however a problem: how to explain the prophetic *ḥadīth*, which, from his vantage point, is seen to have restricted Ṭabarī's reading. A lie, according to Qurṭubī, is the provision of information which is opposed to the facts. Here and in all the other alleged instances of Abraham's lying, it can be shown that his statements, when fully understood, are not opposed to the facts: they are instances of *mi'rāḍ*, not lies. However these practical deceptions have their influence on the status of the Prophet, sensibly diminishing his honour – *khafaḍat 'an maḥmad al-manzila*. Abraham's consciousness of this and his consequent sense of shame are reflected in a prophetic *ḥadīth* which describes Abraham's sorrow on the day of resurrection. Invited to exercise his prerogative of intercession (*shafā'a*), he pleads first for himself on account of his three lies. For, according to Qurṭubī, because of their extreme veneration for God, prophets feel sorrow for deeds that others would not repent of. It would have been more fitting to his status as prophet and friend of God, *khalīl Allāh*, that he should have clung to the truth and expressed things as they were, but, since a dispensation was granted to him, he accepted. The result of this train of thought is that, while Abraham did not sin, he certainly compromised himself and betrayed to a degree his high status. From this Qurṭubī infers that the status of *khalīl* was not achieved in its perfect form by any prophet prior to the prophet Muḥammad. The many-sided sensitivity of Qurṭubī's analysis is remarkable: drawing upon all the available *ḥadīth*, admitting the high rank, moral sensitivity and sinlessness of prophets, he weaves an exposition that finds richness in the quranic text and finally promotes the unique status of the Muslim Prophet. It is an outstanding exposition and might serve to illustrate why, within the tradition of scholastic exegesis, Qurṭubī's *tafsīr* has some claim to being the most complete fulfilment of its possibilities.

These possibilities are fully implied by the three structures described above. It is obviously true that the exploration of the text in relation to the disciplines (structure 3) is achieved to a considerable degree through the citation of authorities (structure 2). The personal input of an individual exegete is measured both by his selection and manipulation of past authorities and by his additions to these. In Qurṭubī, the additions, when detectable, are fully within the constraints of the formal devices implied by these structures. His genius lies in his presentation of past authorities, his embracing of polyvalent readings, his playing across the disciplines (solving narrative and theological problems by the discovery of grammatical and rhetorical devices etc.) and his even-handed sensitivity to all the scholastic disciplines (except *taṣawwuf*, which, though arguably scholastic in certain literary forms, is only marginally present throughout the *tafsīr* tradition until a very late date). In all formal respects, Qurṭubī belongs firmly within the tradition initiated and defined by Ṭabarī; his artistry, however, is measurably greater. Less measurable is the sense of playfulness, or irony, which can be detected in his work and is perhaps product of the security that comes from working in an established discipline, fully mastered.[15] It is in these senses that one might claim for his *tafsīr* that it is the most complete fulfilment of the possibilities of the tradition. Hardly surprising then that within a century these possibilities were significantly transformed by Ibn Kathīr. Prior to demonstrating the contribution to the tradition of the latter, it will be useful to consider the distinctive genius of Fakhr al-Dīn al-Rāzī whose *Mafātīḥ al-Ghayb*, though in all respects of the scholastic tradition, reveals just how that might be transcended in the interests of a distinctive theological message.

5

> Likewise we show Abraham the power of the heavens and the earth; and that he might be one of those who are certain.
>
> (Qur'ān 6.85)

Kadhālika (likewise), understood to imply a comparison – like this – demands an object of comparison: like what? For both Ṭabarī and Zamakhsharī, just as God had given Abraham insight into the truth of religion, or the truth about his father's idols, so, likewise – *kadhālika*, he gave him insight into or knowledge of the power of the heavens and earth. Ṭabarī: *kamā araynāhu al-baṣīra fī dīnihin... urīhi*.... Zamakhsharī: *mithlu dhālika 'l-ta'rīf wa 'l-tabṣīr nu'arrifu Ibrāhīm wa-nubaṣṣiruhu*.... But this meaning really requires a past tense, whereas the quranic text offers a present, *nurīhi*, a problem overlooked by Ṭabarī, and resolved by Zamakhsharī, who finds here a kind of historical present: *nurī ḥikāyatu ḥālin māḍiyyatin*. These were minor grammatical problems and inspired no great virtuosity in the tradition at large – except indeed in Fakhr al-Dīn al-Rāzī.

Initially interpreting *kadhālika* in the tradition of Ṭabarī and Zamakhsharī (*mithlu-mā araynāhu qubḥa 'ibādat al-aṣnām*...), Rāzī goes on to find in this phrase a complex intellectual nuance, *daqīqa 'aqliyya*. For, the light of God's glory shines eternally and without interruption in such a manner that the human soul (*al-arwāḥ al-bashariyya*) cannot be cut off from that light except there be a veil (*ḥijāb*) between them. This veil is constituted by preoccupation with anything other than God. By whatever degree that veil is diminished, by that degree is God's self-revelation (*tajallā*) made accessible to man. In discovering that the worship of idols was a preoccupation with something other than God, Abraham was diminishing the veil and so inevitably (*lā jarama*) he received a manifestation (*tajallā*) of the power of the heavens. What Rāzī wants to stress here, and what he claims is implied by the word *kadhālika*, is the very close connection between the turning away from idols and the realisation of God's glory. It is as it were through the one (*kadhālika* = in this manner, by these means) that the other is achieved. The word *kadhālika* is a pointer towards this spiritual and noble meaning, *wa-kāna qawluhu kadhālika mansha' li-hādhihi 'l-fā'ida al-sharīfa al-rūḥāniyya*.[16]

Concerning the apparently incongruous present tense for *nurīhi*, Rāzī knew and offered Zamakhsharī's explanation: it was by way of narrative about the past, *'alā sabīl al-ḥikāya 'an al-māḍī*. But he perceived a second explanation which was, he claimed, greater and more noble. This present tense shows us that God did not simply enable Abraham to see, by a single act of enabling. Rather, he engaged Abraham in a process whereby he approached (not reached) knowledge of God's glory and power (*ma'rifat jalāl Allāh wa-qudsihi*, etc.). Created things, though finite in their essences and attributes, are infinite in their signification (*jihāt dalālātihā*). As the Imām al-Ḥaramayn had pointed out, not only are the objects of divine knowledge infinite, but of each single known thing, God's knowledge is infinite. If this is true, Rāzī continues, of every single indivisible atom, then what can be said about the entirety of God's power (*kull malakūt Allāh*)? The significations of this power as to the qualities of his glory and majesty are infinite. Now, the instantiation of infinite knowledge in the human mind, all at once, is impossible. This knowledge is to be acquired in degrees, progressively, infinitely, without end. And this is why God said, not, 'We showed him the power of the heavens and the earth', but, 'We show him', meaning to indicate an eternal process. And this is what is meant by the words of the wise: 'The journey to God is finite, the journey in God infinite'.[17]

Like Qurṭubī, Rāzī has a fine sense of how textual problems can be solved by playing across the disciplines. Here, two problems which began at a grammatical level – and, for most exegetes, ended there – achieved resolution through a highly idiosyncratic theological reading. Unlike Qurṭubī, Rāzī is not even-handed in his sensitivity to the scholastic disciplines: he is competent in all, but he has a particular theological message which is insistently imposed, sometimes barely convincing (as with *kadhālika*?), sometimes brilliantly achieved (as with *nurīhi*?).

That mixture of scholastic competence and idiosyncratic message marks the peculiar nature of Rāzī's contribution to *tafsīr*: without the former, his work would hardly have achieved the (frequently grudged) influence that it did. Because the scholastic value of his *tafsīr* was indisputably remarkable, his ability to add to the tradition was secured.

God's showing the power of the heavens to Abraham was traditionally associated with a story, frequently told on the authority of Ibn 'Abbās (and recognizably a remote descendant of the Judaeo-Christian *Apocalypse of Abraham)*.[18] Rāzī's presentation of this story was controlled by the question whether it was to be interpreted as a physical revelation (as implied by the story-tradition) or an intellectual. Marking his conformity to the norms of the genre, he refers to past authorities (albeit with the casual and laconic *qālū*), cites Ibn 'Abbās by name, adequately summarizes the narrative and indicates objections to it by citing, specifically, the Qāḍī 'Abd al-Jabbār. That this revelation by God was an intellectual rather than a physical one is certainly implied, if only by the space given to this argument, but Rāzī is hardly dogmatic; the possibilities of the tradition are indicated, polyvalent readings are possible. But the intrusive and personal message will not be denied. Of the eight arguments which he adduces as characteristic of those who would read this verse as referring to an intellectual revelation, only the last really counts; and it is his and his alone. It is that all created things are originated and contingent (*muḥdatha wa-mumkina*); and that which is originated and contingent is in need (*muḥtāj*) of a creator (*ṣāni'*). If man but understood this, it would be enough as a deduction of the creator's existence. What God showed Abraham then was an intellectual understanding of things whereby he acquired an intellectual conviction of God's existence. 'It is as if... he (Abraham) scanned the *malakūt* with the eye of the intellect and heard with the ear of his intellect its witness as to its essential being-in-need (*iḥtiyāj* / *iftiqār*).'[19]

An intense intellectual conviction as to the world's contingency and a consequent realization of its need for and dependence on a non-contingent being is the spiritual source of Rāzī's mystical theology. It derives, of course, from Avicenna, and it implies an understanding of God as *wājib al-wujūd*, the non-contingent existent. Still following Avicenna, the relationship between God and man is presented through the imagery of light: God is an eternal light to which man's soul has potential access, along the lines described above, at *nurīhi*. Rāzī finds these things implied throughout the quranic text. The phrase, 'And that he might be one of those who are certain' *wa-li-yakūn min al-mūqinīn,* presented, for example, a grammatical problem: what was the function of the *wa*? Not markedly interested, Rāzī records the possiblities: the *wa* is superfluous or it initiates a new sentence exhibiting considerable ellision or it serves to distinguish the possibility that he might have become a *jāhil*, a non-believer, through the same perception. The first of these was Ṭabarī's, the second Zamakhsharī's solution; the origin of the third is unknown and Rāzī identifies no authority for it (or the others). It is the semantic implications of the word *yaqīn* that inspire him. *Yaqīn*, he affirms, is a word signifying knowledge, *'ilm*, achieved through contemplation and after the removal of doubt. Knowledge in fact is an intellectual process. Man's understanding of God and God's relationship to the world is achieved through a succession and accumulation of evidences gradually instantiating a dominance of certainty (*yaqīn*). The heart (*qalb*, but seat of ratiocination not love!) begins in darkness, but as faith is achieved through evidence (*dalīl/dalāla*), there is a gradual admixture of light in the darkness, an achievement of radiance and splendour (*ishrāq wa-lama'ān*). Just as the morning-light grows with the approach of the sun to its zenith, so a servant of God, in proportion to his contemplation of the degrees of God's creation, enjoys an ever brighter light of *ma'rifa* and *tawḥīd*. And whereas the sun of this world has a limit to its upward movement, such is not true of the sun of *ma'rifa*, *'aql* and *tawḥīd*. 'That he might be one of those who are certain': these words are an indication of the degrees of the light of divine revelation and the rising of the sun of knowledge and divine unity, *ishāratun ilā darajāt anwār al-tajallā wa-shurūq shams al-ma'rifa wa'l-tawḥīd*.[20] All of this is a variation on the processual achievement of revelation described under the phrase *nurīhi*. The context is scholastic but the presentation of the intellectual vision is marked by an intensity of language and a variety of images which, though always subject to precise intellectual control, reveal commitment.

The argument about the originatedness and contingency of observable creation, the consequent realization of need and dependency, and the understanding of God's existence (and nature) is likewise frequently repeated and referred to. Play on the key terminology of *iḥdāth*, *imkān*, *iḥtiyāj* and *iftiqār* constitute the whole of Rāzī's complex understanding of why Abraham's pointing to the setting of the stars constituted a valid intellectual argument against the worship of idols. Only one aspect of this argument need be noted here: it is Rāzī's explicit recognition that it is only the basic principles which are mentioned in the Qur'ān; the ramifications and subtleties are appropriate only to the discipline of discursive theology (*ammā al-tafrī' wa'l-tafṣīl fa-dhālika innamā yalīqu bi 'ilm al-jadal*). The principles mentioned in the Qur'ān (here, the setting of the stars etc.) are there by way of symbol, *'alā sabīl al-ramz*.[21]

There can then be no doubt about the particularity of Rāzī's theological message, nor any doubt that in presenting it he is consciously moving beyond the scholastic tradition of Ash'arī theology (albeit he repeatedly declares his allegiance to that tradition!) and some way beyond a plain (scholastic!) reading of the text. This is an avowedly symbolic reading of the Qur'ān. Nonetheless the processes are traditional: his reading is embedded in the text through the discovery of grammatical, lexical or narrative devices, transparent to the tradition, but constituting for him the cracks through which he can create a new theological space. It may be argued that neither in structure, nor form, nor procedure can his *tafsīr* be distinguished from that of Qurṭubī; and yet it is quite remarkably different. The difference can be related to a single external discipline which Rāzī has brought into the game: it is the philosophico-mystical discipline, derived from Avicenna, and marked in this work not only by its specific arguments but by the citation of authorities who scarcely belong within the tradition of *tafsīr:* Ghazālī and Avicenna, for example. But this difference has corollaries: a relative lack of sympathy with the established forms of *tafsīr* is marked also by a very considerable diminution in named authorities. He cites of course some scholars (al-Wāḥidi, Zamakhsharī, 'Abd al-Jabbār and more ancient authorities, such as Ibn 'Abbās) but more often than not, it is the anonymous forms *qālū, al-'ulamā', aktharu 'l-mufassirīn* that mark his sense of the past. There is no corresponding diminution of polyvalent readings, since these can be adequately listed under these anonymous formulae. Rāzī is quicker to express preferences and choices than Qurṭubī, but, who wasn't?[22]

Under the verse, 'When Abraham said to his father *āzar...*', Rāzī proposed eight heads of discussion. At least four of these bear the stamp of his own idiosyncratic intellectuality, the other four being more or less conventional. Of the latter, one was the narrative problem related to Āzar. Rāzī considers that the 'evident' reading (*ẓāhir*) should be accepted, namely that Āzar is the only proper name of Abraham's father and that other notions should be seen as alien imports. But the alternatives to this preference he gives in full and neatly schematized: (i) the two names are *ism* and *laqab*; (ii) *āzar* is an adjective; (iii) *āzar* is the name of an idol; and (iv) the reference here is not to Abraham's father but to his uncle. Each of these is provided with carefully subdivided possibilities and arguments. Rāzī is not less secure in the tradition than Qurṭubī; he worked like an intellectual diamond cutter, finding in every verse heads of discussion, each of which admitted of a sharply-defined multi-faceted exploration. His analyses have a hard, scintillating quality, giving his work a scholastic strength which made it a preferred source for many later authorities – even when they were suspicious of his theology (which, however, gradually became acceptable to the Sunnī world of thought – partly perhaps because of this *tafsīr*).[23]

In comparing Qurṭubī and Rāzī, it should not be imagined that because the latter has a foregrounded theology, the former has none. The foci of Qurṭubī's theology were the text of the Qur'ān and the experience of the community. If Rāzī was sustained by an intellectual vision of God as necessary being and infinite light, Qurṭubī was no less sustained by an appreciation of the quranic text as a packed container of meanings, unpacked less by individual scholars than by the diachronic community. Rāzī's finest passages reveal his own intellectual convictions, Qurṭubī's his sense of the organically growing experience of the Muslim community in confrontation with scripture. Sharing the same literary tradition and forms, these two exegetes yet symbolize a tension between the authority of the intellect and that of the community. Ibn Kathīr was to add another, a different, focus of tension.

6

> When night came upon him, he saw a star. He said, This is my Lord; but when the star set, he said, I do not like things that set. / When he saw the moon rising, he said, This is my Lord. But when it set, he said, If my Lord does not lead me right, I shall be one of those who stray. / When he saw the sun rising, he said, This is my Lord, this is greater. But when it set, he said, My people, I am free of your idolatry. / I turn my face to the one who created the heavens and the earth, a *ḥanīf*; I am not one of the idolaters.
>
> (Qur'ān 6.76–9)

Quranic style has been compared to a torso,[24] a comparison which suggests incompleteness but also continuity of detail and inflexible solidity. More illuminating perhaps is a comparison to a Chinese painting. When, in such a painting, a high pagoda or a mountain top emerges into the sky, the observer is compelled to fill the adjacent absences with rural valleys or firm foundations. Nor in this exercise is the imagination free: the heights of a pagoda do not rest on a set of Corinthian pillars, and the lower slopes of a Chinese hill are resistant to details derived from a landscape by Constable. The independent structures of Chinese poetry inform us that bamboo, lotus and cherry blossom, and a lonely scholar dreaming of his distant home are precisely what lies in the emptinesses of a Chinese landscape. Likewise when quranic narrative offers its usual provision of incomplete detail, the imagination has never been simply free to fill the gaps; the filling has to be measured against independent structures.

Abraham's sequent claims of the star, the moon and the sun that these were his Lord, can be read as a deduction. Initially ignorant, he deduced from observation of the world, that it did not contain his Lord and proceeded thence to an understanding of the world's creator. In the process, he went through a phase of believing, of the star, the moon and the sun, that these were his Lord. This reading of the material is confirmed by the story of Abraham's birth, a familiar component of the *qiṣaṣ al-anbiyā'*, rich in wonder and in miracle. Nimrod, warned by the astrologers of a miraculous birth and the end of his dominion, devised stratagems for the prevention of pregnancy and the slaughter of babies. Abraham's mother, pregnant and fearful, gave birth in a cave. Young Abraham, temporarily abandoned, was tended by angels, sucked honey and milk from his fingers, and matured with the passing of weeks as if with the passing of years. Already, still in the cave, inclined to pester his mother for information about his Lord, he was finally permitted to emerge, when he saw, amongst other things, a star. The details are richly various, arbitrary precipitate of a world of oral story-telling, Arabic versions of an ancient cycle.[25] As with all such stories, the narrative is in part its own end and carries in part a theological burden. Ibn Kathīr had great objections to it.

For him, the passage in the Qur'ān was in truth (*al-ḥaqq*) an example of a debating technique and not a deduction (*munāẓara: naẓar*). Understood properly, the narrative passage in Qur'ān 6.74–9 revealed two arguments, arranged to correspond to their chronological use. First, an argument against the worship of idols (Āzar, do you take idols as gods?), and then, a different stage, an argument against the worship of the stars. The two major types of paganism are thus covered and the quranic text neatly explained. In his *Qiṣaṣ al-anbiyā'*, Ibn Kathīr proposes that the geographical location of the later debate must be Harran, where, as is well known, they worshipped the stars. By these devices it is rendered clear that the passage relates not to Abraham's first discovery of God – as implied in the story tradition, but to a much later period in his life. How is it possible, Ibn Kathīr asks, for Abraham to be required to deduce the truth, when God has said of him 'We gave him guidance before' (Qur'ān 21.51) and 'He was a model – *umma*, loyal to God, a *ḥanīf*' (Qur'ān 16.120) and 'Behold my Lord has guided me to a straight path... the religion of Abraham. He was never an idolater' (Qur'ān 6.161). Furthermore, there are *ḥadīth*s, in Bukhārī and Muslim, which state that Muslims are born in a state of *fiṭra*, or that God has created all people as *ḥanīf*s. This being the case, how could Abraham be an exception?[26] In another context, Ibn Kathīr describes the story as one of the tales of the Banī Isrā'īl, one of those which contain lies and is opposed to the truth.[27] What causes this intemperate accretion of argument around this narrative detail? It is again a problem of narrative versus theology. There are two items of theological belief which precipitate Ibn Kathīr's radical rejection of this story – a rejection which has nothing to do with its origins, but with its content, and, to a degree, with its mode of preservation (below, section 7). According to an established Sunnī view, in opposition to a view that was associated with the philosophers, prophets are chosen by God; they do not achieve the status of prophecy through their own efforts or through deduction. Furthermore, prophets are *ma'ṣūm*; it was therefore unthinkable that Abraham could have worshipped a star. There were nuances to these beliefs.

Objections to the story of Abraham's birth, concealment and youthful speculation had emerged at least as early as Ṭabarī. He gives the narrative in full, in a version from Ibn Isḥāq. The objectors he characterizes – pointedly – as *min ghayri ahl al-riwāya*, meaning 'not preservers of tradition'. They deny a story which comes from the companion Ibn 'Abbās. They claim that it is inconceivable that God should have sent a prophet who, being mature (!), should at any time have worshipped anything other than the one true God. According to them, if this happened, it would not be permissible for God to choose such a one; for God's choice must be based on that person's being distinguished from other unbelievers by his excellence, etc. These arguments restrict what the Sunnīs preferred to see as God's free choice of a prophet to a choice conditioned by prior merit. For these objectors, Abraham's words, 'This is my Lord', must be understood either as a debating technique, conceding a false premise with a view to demonstrating its falsity; or as a rhetorical question, lacking an overt question-marker, as is not uncommon in Arabic diction. Ṭabarī cites the arguments in full but is not convinced. He thinks they are refuted by the presence in the text of the words, 'If my Lord does not lead me right, I shall be one of those that stray'. This he considers incompatible with the assumption that these words are an argument. For him, the plain meaning of the text is that this is a deduction: *al-ṣawāb min al-qawl fī dhālik al-iqrār bi-khabar Allāh alladhī akhbara bihi 'anhā wa'l-i'tirāḍ 'ammā 'adāhu*.[28]

The pertinent theological points implicit in Ṭabarī's argumentation are:

1 That the objectors restrict God's free choice of prophet.
2 That, if Abraham erred, it was in his youth, prior to full responsibility; this is hinted at in the phrase 'being mature', *wa-huwa bāligh*, incorporated in the argument of the objectors (possibly an interpolation).
3 That the objectors do not know tradition, *riwāya*, here implying narrative; this must be understood as a claim for the validity of prophetic narrative as a discipline relevant to the understanding of the Qur'ān.

It is around these points that the tradition developed.

The *tafsīr* of Tha'labī is not available in full. His attitude to story, however, is evident from his *Qiṣaṣ al-anbiyā'*, which is certainly the most positive and lively presentation of prophetic tales within the academic tradition. Generous in the citation of sources, rich in the multiplicity and variety of detail, it is little constrained by theological dogma. The impression is strong that for Tha'labī the Qur'ān must be read in the light of the established discipline of story, and could not be understood without it. He tells the story of the cave in detail and relates 6.76 to a deductive process in Abraham on leaving the cave.[29]

Baghawī is highly dependent on Tha'labī for his presentation of narrative[30] and, like him, is remarkably unembarrassed by theological complications. His retelling of the story of Abraham's birth is rich in detail, in variants and in named authorities (Ibn 'Abbās, Suddī, Ibn Isḥāq etc.). When Abraham emerged from the cave, he contemplated (! *tafakkara*) the creation of the heavens and the earth, moving from an initial assumption as to the Lordship of a star to a triumphant conclusion as to the existence of the creator-God. Presenting the story in such detail, it is evident that Baghawī's loyalties lie with those who accept it, but he gives their arguments in careful balance with those of the opposing group. In search of guidance and knowledge of divine unity, Abraham was granted guidance by God: *ātāhu rushdahu* – a phrase recalling Qur'ān 21.51. (Alluded to here in an interpretation of Abraham's words as deductive; the same verse was used later by Ibn Kathīr to deny just this.) There was, according to those who accept the story, no harm in reading this passage as a mode of deduction (*istidlāl*); and, besides, being at a time before Abraham's maturity, it did not constitute unbelief. The opposing arguments, mostly based on the discovery of rhetorical and grammatical subtleties in the text, are also given. On balance, Baghawī – though he enjoys the grammatical and rhetorical arguments – holds on to the narrative and a reading of the quranic passage as deductive.[31]

Ibn al-Jawzī rather reverses the balance, though not less judiciously. He provides an authoritative version of the story, from Ibn 'Abbās and Abū-Ṣāliḥ. On the specific reading of the words, 'This is my Lord', as applied to the stars, etc., he provides refutations: (i) because those chosen for prophecy will be preserved from such unbelief; (ii) because the argument from 'If my Lord does not guide me...' (Ṭabarī) is invalid; and (iii) because other quranic verses, notably 'We have given him guidance' (! Qur'ān 21.51 but cf. Baghawī) and 'We show him the power of the heavens...', imply that he was protected against such confusion. The impression given is that Ibn al-Jawzī would accept the story, to which he offers no objection, but reads the quranic text as argument not deduction; a tricky position.[32]

Fakhr al-Dīn al-Rāzī knows there are objections to the story as a whole, but does not accept them: the story is perfectly possible (*kullu dhālika muḥtamal fī 'l-jumla*).[33]For him, the objection to the story had been formulated in relation to the theological view that miracles may not precede the time of a prophet's summons – a view designated *irhāṣ* and associated with the (Mu'tazilī) Qāḍī 'Abd al-Jabbār. The Ash'arīs however have no objections to *irhāṣ* and consequently doubts about the truth of the story are refuted. It remains then to discuss whether the words *hādhā rabbī* could have been uttered by Abraham, as deduction, in his maturity. Neatly discriminating twelve points, Rāzī denies this possibility (it is difficult to believe that any one within the *tafsīr* tradition had ever affirmed it). This leaves two possibilities: either these words were uttered by Abraham after maturity, as an argument (*munāẓara*) – a view for which Rāzī offers seven arguments – or Abraham uttered them before maturity but near it. Rāzī is visibly torn here, for he believes passionately in the possibility of deducing from observation of the world the existence of God; but he also delights in discriminating intellectual debate. If these words were uttered as a deduction, it is to be understood that Abraham, having been chosen by God and provided with perfect intellect and pure understanding, discovered for himself and prior to revelation a formal proof for the existence of God (it is of course the proof deriving the necessary existence of a non-contingent being from the essential contingency of the world!). There is, says Rāzī, no harm in this supposition (*lā ba's bihi)*, though he prefers the view that these words were part of an argument.[34]

Qurṭubī offers nine variant interpretations of these verses with no indication of his preferences. His first variant accepts that it was a deduction in accord with the story from Ibn 'Abbās, and no sin, Abraham being under the age of *taklīf*. His second gives the opposition view, citing Zajjāj. His third variant harmonizes, accepting that these words were uttered by Abraham when he left the cave, but proposing that the words, 'This is my Lord', imply reference to the light through which God manifests himself: they constitute not idolatry (*shirk)*, but an attribution of light to his Lord – *wa-laysa hādhā shirkan innamā naṣaba al-ḍaw' ilā rabbihi*. And so on.[35]

From Ṭabarī to Qurṭubī, no exegete within the Sunnī tradition relinquishes the story. The majority, conscious of arguments against it, deliberately defend it, draw it inside the tradition and have no problems whatsoever in reconciling it with theological dogma: the dominant motif here is the concept of maturity and responsibility. Ibn al-Jawzī alone is negative, though not unduly excitable about the matter. All present a balanced reading in which some weight is given to the reading of the text as deduction and some to its being read as argument. The stresses vary. It is possible that Ibn al-Jawzī held that form of the doctrine of *'iṣma* which states that prophets are preserved from sin from birth. But even this will not quite explain the uniquely vehement rejection of story that characterizes Ibn Kathīr, whose approach is exemplified in the following.

> We gave Abraham his guidance before (Qur'ān 21.51). God provides information here concerning Abraham, namely that he gave him guidance before, that is, in his childhood; he inspired him *(alhamahu)* with the truth and with proofs against his people; as in God's word, 'That is our proof, we gave it to Abraham against his people' (Qur'ān 6.83). The stories related about Abraham concerning his father's putting him into a cave while he was a suckling, his emergence after a number of days, his looking at the stars and created things and his contemplation of them, these stories and other details related by many exegetes are, all of them, tales of the Banī Isrā'īl *(aḥādīth banī isrā'īl)*. Of this material, whatever is compatible with the truth as we have it from the sinless [prophet Muḥammad], we accept it, because it matches what is true. But whatever is opposed to any detail [of this truth] we reject it. Whatever displays neither agreement nor disagreement, we neither declare it true nor false; we suspend judgement. Many of the *salaf* have declared a dispensation with regard to transmitting material of this type. Much of it however is of no use or value in practical matters of religion (*lā fā'ida fīhi wa-lā ḥāṣil lahu mimmā yantafi'u fī'l-dīn*): if it did have a use accruing to God's servants *(mukallaf)* in their religion, then this perfect and comprehensive *sharī'a* would have explained it. The method we follow in this *tafsīr* is to abandon many of the Isrā'īliyyāt because they constitute a waste of time *(limā fīhā min taḍyī' al-zaman)*, and because many of them contain lies imposed upon [the Banī Isrā'īl] owing to their lack of distinction between true and false. This has been explained by the authorities of our community, those who preserve [its bases] and have achieved certainty *(al-a'imma al-ḥuffāẓ al-muttaqinūna min hādhihi 'l-umma)*.[36]

The concluding reference to the authorities of the community should not hide the fact that Ibn Kathīr has little respect for the intellectual tradition of Islam as expressed in the literature of *tafsīr*, or indeed in any of the scholastic disciplines. He was an expert on *ḥadīth* and a disciple of Ibn Taymiyya – together adequate symbols of his intellectual affiliation. His concept of truth is locked into the notion of what 'we have from the sinless prophet Muḥammad', that is prophetic *ḥadīth*, the *ipsissima verba*. In the passage just quoted he states in effect that 'many exegetes' have wasted their time and passed on lies, an opinion reflecting a lack of faith in every major exegete from Ṭabarī to Qurṭubī. The reference to the 'perfect and comprehensive *sharī'a*' in a sense that implies more than just the law and, apparently, a satisfaction with his understanding of this thing, could only be made by someone antagonistic to the play of intellectual speculation that marks the genius of the juristic and exegetical traditions in Islam. And it sits comfortably with Ibn Kathīr's general attitude to the past that he should consider that whatever is 'of no use or value in practical religion' should be abandoned. This grim theologian could hardly have found any pleasure in the exuberant uncertainties of Qurṭubī, or in the visionary intellectualism of Rāzī. Here, his dogmatic certainty on one item of the theological agenda – which might have been harmonized with story – is used like a blunderbuss, not only against the status of narrative as a discipline but correlatively against the literary tradition of *tafsīr* as it had developed prior to his time. No exegete prior to Ibn Kathīr used the term *isrā'īliyya* as he used it. No Sunnī exegete had denied the value of the story.[37]

The characteristic motifs of condemning the literary tradition, rejecting story, and finding contamination from external sources (Jewish lies) emerge frequently in Ibn Kathīr and may be represented here with one further example. Which son did Abraham intend to sacrifice: Isaac or Ishmael?

Already, in Ṭabarī, authority was finely balanced on this question.[38] He adduced seventeen statements which, in one way or another, favoured identification of the victim as Isaac. One of these was a prophetic *ḥadīth*, reduced, like many parallel *ḥadīth* from companions and successors, to a simple assertion, *al-dhabīḥ huwa Isḥāq*. Of more circumstantial accounts, two took the form of statements attributed to Moses and two of statements attributed to Joseph. There was also a long narrative from Ka'b rendered in such a way as to demonstrate its acceptance by Abū Hurayra. On the other side, Ṭabarī offered twenty-four statements from authorities of similar weight and standing, in favour of Ishmael. Ibn 'Abbās figures in both lists. So does the Prophet, represented in the pro-Ishmael list in the form of a comment on his nickname, Ibn al-Dhabīḥayn.

Ṭabarī himself preferred, without being unduly dogmatic *(awlā al-qawlayn bi'l-ṣawāb)*, to recognise Isaac as the victim. This he considered to be the plain meaning of the quranic text *'alā ẓāhir al-tanzīl*. For the victim of the sacrifice was clearly the one about whom Abraham was given the good news by God *(bushshira bihi)*, and in every reference in the Qur'ān to the good news (*tabshīr*), the son intended was Isaac. This argument is extended by reference to Abraham's request, *hab lī min al-ṣāliḥin*, which is deemed to confirm the fact that the good news (*tabshīr*) referred to Isaac.

Authority and tradition being more or less equally divided on the matter, Ṭabarī went on to defend his preferred position against the three major rational objections (*'illa/i'tilāl*) which, in his time, had been raised against identification of the victim as Isaac. The first of these stated that since God had promised Abraham a son, Isaac, who would produce descendants, he could not have then commanded the sacrifice of this son (i. e. before he produced descendants). To this Ṭabarī replies, by pointing to the quranic phrase, *balagha ma'ahu al-sa'y*, implying, for him, age and capacity and so making it possible[39] that Isaac had by the time of the sacrifice produced not only a child but children. The second objection focuses on the fact that immediately after the story of the sacrifice, in the Qur'ān, there is repetition of the *tabshīr* – *wa-bashsharnāhu bi-Isḥāq nabiyyan*. Now, if the first reference was taken to be to Isaac, how could the second reference be possible, granted that Isaac had already been born, grown up, produced children, and been subject to the sacrifice? The first reference must therefore be to Ishmael, who is thereby recognized as sacrifical victim. To this Ṭabarī replies by pointing to the specificity of the second *tabshīr*, which states that Isaac will be a prophet. The news, specifically, of Isaac's being a prophet came to Abraham and Isaac, after the sacrifice, as a mark of honour from God because of their respectively submitting to the trial he had imposed upon them. The third objection pointed out that the horns of the ram that was eventually sacrificed were hung up in the Ka'ba, a situation allegedly consistent only with the assumptions, (i) that the sacrifice was planned to take place in Makka, and (ii) that the intended victim must have been Ishmael, who alone of Abraham's sons was concerned with that place. Ṭabarī replies simply that the horns could have been transported from Syria to Makka.

Historically, identification of the victim as Ishmael and siting of the sacrifice in Makka were part of a process whereby an established narrative about Isaac and Jerusalem came to function within a narrative structure intended to defend and justify the sanctuary at Makka. This process took place within religious circles in a milieu characterized by oral transmission of tales and *tafsīr*. It is the oldest versions of the story and those that are relatively free from religious influence that preserve the identity of Isaac and the siting of the sacrifice in Jerusalem.[40] There may have been some consciousness of this amongst Muslim intellectuals of the calibre of Ṭabarī, and it may have influenced his preference. Certainly, the only other intellectual of standing who is known to have considered the matter, prior to Ṭabarī, Ibn Qutayba, also preferred Isaac, and put forward as the ground of his preference that so he had found it in the Torah.[41] (Muslim scholars from Ibn Qutayba to Ibn Kathīr were not averse to checking the Bible on occasions such as these, though their judgements on its value and reliability varied.) Within the tradition of *tafsīr*, the impetus provided by Ibn Qutayba and Ṭabarī ensured, on balance, and within the scholarly tradition, that the preference for Isaac consistently, if marginally, outweighed a preference for Ishmael in this context. It is likely that the opposite was true at a popular level.

Baghawī notes that there are many authorities for both views, that both are related from the Prophet, and that both are backed with arguments based on the quranic text. He states no preference of his own. Ibn al-'Arabī also notes both views, and affirms that the matter is of no great import, being one of the niceties, the relatively unimportant points of religious belief *(min maḥāsin al-sharī'a wa-tawābi'ihā wa-mutammamātihā lā ummahātihā)*. Ibn al-Jawzī affirms that there are arguments on both sides, and adds that his companions prefer the view that Isaac was the victim. Qurṭubī too prefers Isaac. He notes that Isaac is preferred by seven companions, numerous successors, the two peoples of the Book (Jews and Christians) and several exegetes, including Naḥḥās and Ṭabarī. The Prophet, it is true, appears for both views, but, according to Qurṭubī, more for Isaac than for Ishmael. Qurṭubī repeats Ṭabarī's argument from the general implications of the quranic *tabshīr* as relating to Isaac; he knows opposition arguments, broadly those known to Ṭabarī, but thinks they are not decisive, *wa-hādha 'l-istidlāl kulluhu laysa bi-qāṭi'*. Having identified two views and indicated his preference, Qurṭubī finishes with a cheerful, possibly ironic, and very succinct indication of a third view: *qāla al-Zajjāj Allāhu a'lam ayyuhumā al-dhabīḥ wa-hādha madhhab thālith*.[42]

The scholarly tradition is characterized then by an even-handed approach to the matter. It is not allowed to become divisive, or to be a focus of extreme, or damaging, or disparaging comments. Ibn al-'Arabī deliberately states its relative unimportance. Ṭabarī and Qurṭubī, at least, plainly enjoy the diversity and the opportunity to construct and refute well-expressed arguments. Where a preference is stated, it is for Isaac.

Ibn Kathīr is not with the tradition. For him, it was Ishmael who was sacrificed. Ṭabarī's argument against this view – namely that all the references to a *tabshīr* in the Qur'ān were to Isaac – he set aside on the basis of information derived from the Bible (!). There he learnt that Abraham was informed by God of both his sons. Accordingly the first *tabshīr* in *Sūrat al-Ṣāffāt* (Qur'ān 37.101) must refer to Ishmael and the second, as stated in the text, to Isaac. In the Bible, too, Ibn Kathīr learned the supplementary information that Ishmael was born when Abraham was eighty-six and Isaac when he was ninety-nine[43] Apropos of Gen. 22.1–2 (the introduction to the story of the sacrifice), Ibn Kathīr performs a very creditable piece of textual analysis, suggesting that the word Isaac has been interpolated (*aqḥama* – to cram or stuff in) and this is a lie *(kadhb wa-buhtān)*. The Jews interpolated the word Isaac because he is their forefather, whereas Ishmael is forefather to the Arabs. They were jealous. The biblical phrase 'his only son' could only have been used at a time when it would have had a true point of reference, i. e. before the birth of Isaac. And so on. A powerful argument based on a (justified but isolated) critique of the biblical text. Though transmitted by a number of the learned, even by a group of the *salaf* and companions, the preference for Isaac, he claims, is not in Qur'ān or *sunna* (!); it was received from the *ahl al-kitāb*, without consideration of proof *('an ikhbāri ahl al-kitāb wa-akhdhi dhālika musallaman min ghayri ḥujja)*. The two sequential *tabshīrs* in the text of *Sūrat al-Ṣāffāt* (when read in the light of the biblical evidence) are a sufficient proof for the point. This is the 'plain' meaning of the Qur'ān. Giving a survey of the authorities on both sides, Ibn Kathīr finds fault with the *isnāds* of the prophetic *ḥadīth* which favour Isaac. He denies the arguments of Ṭabarī. Much of this is repeated in his *Qiṣaṣ al-Anbiyā'*, where again those who favour Isaac are deemed to be finding support in *isrā'īliyyāt*.[44]Ibn Kathīr's use of the Bible, like his use of the term *isrā'īliyyāt*, is controlled entirely by his prior theological convictions. Where information in the Bible, or information provided in the broader tradition of prophetic tales is useful, he accepts it; where it conflicts with his faith, he rejects it.

Ibn Kathīr's *Tafsīr* has many merits; but he has little respect for the intellectual tradition; he barely recognises its authority and is indifferent to the fact that the positions he takes up imply at least a disrespect for his predecessors. He does not generally like polyvalent readings, but argues vehemently for a single 'correct' reading. He is not even-handed in respect of the Islamic sciences, markedly preferring the dogmatic agenda over narrative. In fact, he can barely see the point of story (of no practical benefit etc.). Further, grammatical and rhetorical virtuosity are minimally acknowledged in the quranic text, and certainly do not act, as they do in Qurṭubī, in such a way as to enhance its possibilities; they rather clamp it to a single meaning.[45]It is difficult to avoid the conclusion that, in Ibn Kathīr's view, God has considerably less literary skill than the average human being, and very little imagination. It may be remarked that an overleaping of the intellectual tradition in favour of a dimly defined *salaf*, a stringent reading of revealed texts, and a rigid dogmatic agenda is the major intellectual gift to Islam of Ibn Taymiyya; not that he originated this kind of fundamentalism, but, putting his considerable intellectual powers into the service of a naive faith, he gave and still gives this kind of view respectability. Ibn Taymiyya too is apparently responsible for bequeathing to Ibn Kathīr his casual and disparaging use of the term *isrā'īliyyāt*.

Much of Ibn Kathīr can be read as implying that wherever possible the text should be set up against mere stories, developing *ikhtilāf* and theological speculation. Sometimes this leads to insensitive readings of the text,[46] nearly always to a minimal expression of narrative. The point may have its final exemplification in a comparison between the *Qiṣaṣ al-anbiyā'* of Tha'labī and that of Ibn Kathīr.

Tha'labī is interested in stories, in narrative variants and in the varied authorities who guarantee these stories. It is the established richness of the narrative tradition that he aims to convey. Reference to the Qur'ān in this work – it should be remembered that he also wrote a *Tafsīr* -is nearly always secondary. In formal presentation of citations, the preferred introductory formula (of some antiquity) is *fa-dhālika qawluhu*, which marks the citation as illustrative and post-narrative. Sometimes the quranic text is only alluded to, without formal citation, and sometimes a citation tails off into an etc. There is no attempt to introduce all the relevant quranic narrative. In the story of Abraham's birth and early debates, for example, there are no references to the version in *sūra* 29 (*'Ankabūt*), only three verses from 26 (*Shu'arā'*), and only partial and allusive coverage of the versions in 21 (*Anbiyā'*) and 37 (*Ṣāffāt*). Read as argument, his book affirms the independent importance of narrative, a point conveyed also in his introduction.

Ibn Kathīr is in most respects the reverse of this. He cites all the relevant quranic passages in full. His comment follows these passages, much of it in the form lemma plus comment. The preferred device for introduction of citations is *qāla Allāh* (or *qawluhu* or *yukhbir Allāh*) and comment follows, either with or without formal juncture (*ayy* or *ya'nī*). This technique, too, is ancient but used flexibly by Ibn Kathīr not simply to register a formal foregrounding of the quranic text, but to ensure that the quranic text limits and controls the quantity of story that is introduced.[47]

The chronology of events in the quranic version of Abraham's biography is of course unknown, owing to its fragmentary and disparate mode of presentation. Tha'labī allows the independent structures to establish some kind of chronology; Ibn Kathīr allows dogmatic considerations to dominate. Thus, for Tha'labī, 6.80–3 (*An'ām*) precedes 19.42–8 (*Maryam*); i. e. the debate with his father's people precedes the debate with his father. Ibn Kathīr reverses this, making the debate with his father first, thereby ensuring that the allusions to the star, sun and moon must be argument, not deduction.

> It is clear that this address of Abraham regarding the stars was to the people of Harran, for they used to worship stars. This refutes the arguments of those who claim that Abraham said these words when he came from the cave as a child, as recorded by Ibn Isḥāq and others. This story is based on *isrā'īliyyāt (mustanad ilā akhbār isrā'īliyya)* which are not to be trusted especially if they are opposed to the truth.

The story of Abraham's being thrown into the fire is minimally dealt with in the Qur'ān, and so prompts a more than usually detailed presentation by Ibn Kathīr, which is still clearly an abbreviation of available material. In general then, Ibn Kathīr allows the minimal needs of the quranic text to dictate the quantity of story that is useful to the community. The rest is useless. By contrast, in the *tafsīr* tradition at large, narrative, guarded by authority, has an independent existence, and, appropriately harmonized with the other disciplines, is allowed to enrich the possibilites of the quranic text: it becomes multivalent. Ibn Kathīr aspires to a monovalent reading. Further limiting Ibn Kathīr's presentation of story is his sense of dogmatic conviction.

In terms of the structures set out in sections 1 to 3 of this paper, deemed to constitute an adequate description of the literary genre of *tafsīr*, Ibn Kathīr is clearly a *mufassir*. His work deals with the complete canonical text of the Qur'ān; he refers to authorities and, marginally, permits of multiple readings; he measures the text against the Islamic disciplines. But when compared with other great names in the tradition, he has by far the least respect for continuity and authority within the genre (hence only a grudging admission of multiple readings) and his skills within the independent disciplines are extraordinarily limited. From Ṭabarī to Qurṭubī the major *mufassirs* relied on the independent disciplines to enrich the quranic text by infusing it with the play of argument and *ikhtilāf*, of layered meanings, of grammatical and rhetorical virtuosity. Ibn Kathīr by contrast uses the quranic text to impoverish the disciplines, and consequently to impoverish the text itself.

Curiously imbalanced then, at first sight, is his focus on the story of the ghecko. This relates to the day of Abraham's being cast into the fire. All the animals participated in an effort to put out the fire, except the ghecko which blew upon it in an effort to keep it going. The Prophet used to order the killing of the ghecko for this reason. In the *Qiṣaṣ al-anbiyā'* this story is given in four versions, one from Bukhārī and three from Aḥmad Ibn Ḥanbal; other versions are referred to from Muslim, Nasā'ī and Ibn Māja. *Isnāds* are given in full, all of which go back to the Prophet of God. Here in fact is the real key to Ibn Kathīr's exegetical works, both the *Qiṣaṣ al-anbiyā'* and the *Tafsīr*. His aspiration to render a minimal version of story is countered by an aspiration to include all that is relevant and contained in the established collections of *ḥadīth* from the Prophet. The story of the ghecko could hardly be more trivial or more marginal in relation to the story of Abraham; but, guarded by *isnāds* that take it back to the Prophet, it deserves multiple repetition and extensive formal presentation.

7

> Why should I fear what you associate [with God] when you have no fear, though you associate with him [gods] for which he has given you no authority? Which of the two groups has more right to security, if you know? / Those who believe and have not mixed their faith with injustice, they have security and they will be guided right.
>
> (Qur'ān 6.81–2)

Verse 82 raises at least three questions. First, who uttered it in its presumed historical context? Second, to whom does it refer? And third, what does it mean? All of the major terms might be and were questioned: 'mixed', 'faith', 'injustice' and 'security', but, throughout the medieval period and into the modern, the focus was predominantly on the word *ẓulm* (=? injustice).

Ṭabarī knew of two proposals as to who uttered this sentence. Either it was the idolaters, for they clearly were addressed at verse 81 and might reasonably be expected to reply, in a form, which, as it happens, must be read as a confession of guilt. Or, God himself provided directly, as in justice only he could, an answer to Abraham's apostrophe. Ṭabarī preferred the latter view. A little reflection and some familiarity with rhetorical technique will suggest a third possibility, namely that Abraham posed the question rhetorically and himself provided the answer. This view was added to the list by Qurṭubī who found it recorded on the authority of Ibn 'Abbās. Amongst those who, reacting against polyvalent readings, here recorded only one possibility were, unsurprisingly, Ibn Kathīr, who asserted that these words came from God, and, more surprisingly, Fakhr al-Dīn al-Rāzī, who asserted equally dogmatically that they were uttered by Abraham as a debating device. Not only the single reading, but also the selections are revealing. Both of these, in different ways, were theologians with a highly specific message, more intent on the message than on listening to the tradition or even to the text – which is not markedly antagonistic to any of the three views.

It might have been suggested that this verse referred solely and specifically to the historical group who, in Abraham's time, followed his summons to recognize one God. However, even before Ṭabarī, the verse had been hijacked for theological purposes and was caught in a network of argument from which it could hardly be extricated. Ṭabarī, indeed, knew some – unnamed – who, supported by a report from 'Alī, proposed that reference here was to Abraham's people and had nothing to do with the Muslim community; and some – also unnamed – who thought the reference was specifically to the *muhājirūn*. These views were eclipsed. The verse was understood to have a universal significance: it stated for all time that security *(amn)* belonged to those who (i) had faith *(āmanū)* and (ii) did not mix their faith with *ẓulm*. But what did that mean?

In truth the verse had no meaning that could be imposed on theology, it was rather an excuse for restating or exploring independently existing theological dogma. It was found to contain reference to the old familiar problem of faith, works and salvation, part of the common currency of monotheist debate. The Mu'tazilite position, easily identifiable as that of Ṭabarī's opponents, and restated by Zamakhsharī, affirmed that the word *ẓulm* here meant sin *(ma'ṣiyya)*. Security (i. e. against punishment) belonged to those who had faith and avoided sin. For the Mu'tazilites, the grave sinner shared with the non-believer the expectation of eternal punishment. The Sunnī tradition states that *ẓulm* here means idolatry *(shirk)*. Security (of salvation) belongs to those who believe and avoid idolatry. All believers who do not indulge in idolatry are secure of eternal salvation, though they may undergo a period of punishment for their sins. Sins may affect punishment, but not salvation – except the sin of *shirk*. The argument was lexical, linguistic, logical, a matter of heat, a matter of indifference, and enduring. The most complex and interesting Sunnī arguments come late in the tradition and are in large part derived from a partial acknowledgement of Zamakhsharī's argument and a subtle concession to the possibilities of his view.[48]

According to Ibn Kathīr, this verse refers to those who have devoted worship to God alone, excluding all association *(shirk)*. They will be secure on the day of resurrection; they are guided right in this world and in the next. That hardly faces squarely the theological problems that crowded round the verse, and, indeed, it does not conclude Ibn Kathīr's commentary, though it is his last word *in propria persona*. He adds to this comment a series of *ḥadīth*, derived from a variety of sources. These *ḥadīths* may be analysed into four groups.

The first group confirms that *ẓulm* here means *shirk* and not *ma'ṣiyya*.

Three sources are used: Bukhārī, Aḥmad and Ibn Abī Ḥātim. The *ḥadīth* given in Bukhārī had been known also to Ṭabarī. It presents the companions as puzzled by the verse and inclined to read it with *ẓulm* = *ma'ṣiyya*, which, since none are free from sin, *ayyunā lam yaẓlam nafsahu*, bodes ill for eternal salvation. The Prophet puts them at ease by pointing to the words of Luqman, *inna al-shirka la-ẓulmun 'aẓīm*. *Shirk* is *ẓulm* and (!) *ẓulm* is *shirk*; and Muslim believers are secure of salvation. The *ḥadīth* cited from Aḥmad is a variant, and the extensive text cited from Ibn Abī Ḥatim contains two further variants of the same prophetic *ḥadīth*, plus another version, *marfū'*, from 'Abd Allāh ibn 'Abbas, and a list of other authorities who are known to have asserted that *ẓulm* here means *shirk*.

The second group consists of only one *ḥadīth*, cited from Ibn Mardawayh. It states quite simply that when this verse was revealed the Prophet said of it, 'I have been informed that I am one of them'. These words of the Prophet, unlike the previous, suggest that the verse has a narrow field of reference. It refers to the Prophet (who is known to be sinless, etc.); does it also refer to all Muslim believers?

The third group consists of three versions of a single story, two derived from Aḥmad, one from Ibn Abī Ḥātim. The main features of the story are this, that a bedouin comes to the Prophet asking to be taught about faith *(īmān);* the Prophet informs him that it means to bear witness that there is no god but God and that Muḥammad is the Prophet of God; further, to perform prayer, *zakāt*, fasting and pilgrimage. The man announces his acceptance of this programme, *aqrartu*, but, immediately afterwards, his camel stumbles and he is killed. The Prophet then announces that he has gone straight to paradise and makes explicit reference to this verse: here is one whose faith has not been mixed with *ẓulm*. Now, the story loses all point except on the (Mu'tazilite!) assumption that *ẓulm* = sin for it is sin which the bedouin, dying so conveniently, avoids, and which, had he lived longer, might have prevented his rapid ascent to paradise. (Most Muslims avoid *shirk* but do not therefore go straight to paradise.)

The fourth group consists again of only one *ḥadīth* derived from Ibn Mardawayh. According to this *ḥadīth*, the Prophet said that those who, being given, give thanks, and, being refused, are patient, who, sinning, seek pardon, and sinned against, forgive, they are the ones to whom this verse refers.

Ibn Kathīr's comment is minimal. His achievement is to set beside a segment of text all the material relevant to it that can be extracted from reliable collections of *ḥadīth*.[49] This material is almost exclusively prophetic in its ascription.

Ibn Kathīr's *Tafsīr*, in sum, cannot be adequately described in terms of the formal structures set out in sections 1 to 3 above; something else is required. Any systematic reading of his work will reveal that his primary objective is to measure the text of the Qur'ān against the established collections of prophetic *ḥadīth*; his concern to measure it against the established scholastic disciplines is minimal. The authorities to whom he looks for support are not those who work in the great intellectual traditions of exegesis or law or *kalām* but those responsible for the great collections of *ḥadīth* and those who figure in their *isnāds*: these are *al-a'imma al-ḥuffāẓ al-muttaqinūn* to whom he referred when justifying his attitude to *isrā'īliyyāt*. The Islamic concept of revelation, as is well known, is dual: it includes the text of the Qur'ān *(waḥy matlū)* and the words of the Prophet *(waḥy ghayr matlū)*. In its second aspect, it was, for centuries, without specific canonical limitations, though a gradual acknowledgement of standard sources was being worked out. Ibn Kathīr's *Tafsīr* is a comparison of canons, a juxtaposition of the two modes of revelation. It is the primacy of this effort over any effort to master the specific discipline of *tafsīr* as it had developed prior to himself that accounts for much of the idiosyncratic bias that marks this work. That it is a work of *tafsīr* need not be disputed; the forms that govern the genre are adequately present, though the mood is frequently intemperate. But in many respects Ibn Kathīr was an interloper. He borrowed the external forms of a genre – to which he was not notably sympathetic – and added to them a new formal task which, simply in terms of quantity, quite eclipsed the older forms and, wrapped in an argument of authority, seriously compromised the status of the old tradition. Here begins a possibility of *al-tafsīr bi'l-ḥadīth* which retrospectively casts the whole tradition into the shade of *al-tafsīr bi'l-ra'y*.[50]

It is not the case that Ibn Kathīr's *Tafsīr* is invariably narrower than some others. In respect of the verse, 'Those who believe and have not mixed their faith with injustice', his drawing in of the various *ḥadīth* that he cites actually demands a more complex and, in some ways, more uncertain resolution of the problem of faith and works than had previously accrued around that verse. But Ibn Kathīr does not undertake the intellectual task of exploration or reconciliation. As with Ibn Taymiyya, his capacity to master an academic discipline is apparently coupled with a distrust of complex resolutions. For both of these, the diversity of the intellectual tradition counted against it and prompted a search for a single truth deemed to be present in a narrow and exclusive definition of 'whatever is compatible with the truth as we have it from the sinless Prophet', i. e. in the *ipsissima verba* of *ḥadīth* and not in the tradition of intellectual exploration: the latter, for them, led to confusion and variety.

Ibn Kathīr's work may be distinguished within the tradition by reference to two features: (i) a measuring of the quranic text against prophetic *ḥadīth* and (ii) a reduction of complexity, of detail, of *ikhtilāf* in favour of a relatively 'simple' dogmatic agenda – not an achievement of but an aspiration towards a monovalent reading of the Qur'ān. It may be argued that the use of prophetic *ḥadīth* was a feature of all earlier *tafsīrs*. This is of course true. But earlier *mufassirs* appealed to *ḥadīth* which were already embedded in discursive or narrative structures. Ibn Kathīr, benefitting from the gradual emergence of canonical *ḥadīth* collections, drew on a body of *ḥadīth* which was separated from any context. His primary aim was to juxtapose revelation and revelation. To the basic structures of *tafsīr* set out in sections 1 to 3 above he added the novel idea of providing side by side with scriptural revelation (Qur'ān) the whole body (? in so far as he could control it) of prophetic revelation (*ḥadīth*). This was perhaps an expansion of revelation but it was accompanied, less commendably, by an intellectual and imaginative narrowness quite foreign to the *tafsīr* tradition as a whole.

It was suggested above that the works of Qurṭubī and Rāzī may be described as representing respectively allegiance to two major principles of authority. Qurṭubī represents appeal to the authority of the community, and Rāzī to the independent authority of the intellect. Ibn Kathīr, in turn, represents appeal away from these and towards the authority of the revealed texts themselves – an assertion of their sufficiency, adequacy and unified significance. He and his mentor Ibn Taymiyya are in the strictest sense of the word fundamentalist: distrustful of the intellectual tradition of Islam and of the accumulated experience of the community, they look for salvation to a new (!) reading of the fundamental texts. Their arguments were not irresistable. They were neutralized in any case by the intrinsic acquisitiveness of the *tafsīr* tradition, which struggled to contain the whole of a complex and developing past. And counter-arguments displaying a superior appreciation of what the *tafsīr* tradition was about had already been developed; as will be demonstrated in the next section.

8

1. [From the Prophet of God: He who talks on the Qur'ān on the basis of opinion, let him take up his seat in Hell.] Abū Bakr Muḥammad b. al-Qāsim al-Anbārī said... This *ḥadīth* has two explanations (*fussira... tafsīrayn*). Firstly, he who speaks on problematic passages of the

> Qur'ān (*mushkil al-Qur'ān*) uttering opinions that are not known from the early generations (*madhhab al-awā'il*), namely, the companions and the successors, he is exposed to God's anger. Secondly – and this is the firmest and most correct of the two explanations – he who speaks on the Qur'ān, uttering opinions which he knows to be untrue (*ya'lam anna al-ḥaqq ghayruhu*), let him take up his seat in Hell.
> 2. [From the Prophet of God: He who talks on the Qur'ān on the basis of opinion, even if he achieves a correct judgement, he has erred.] Ibn 'Aṭiyya said: The meaning of this is that a man asks himself concerning the significance of a passage in God's Book and conceives an answer on the basis of opinion without due consideration of the expressed statements of the *'ulamā'* and the requirements of the scientific disciplines such as grammar and the principles of interpretation (*bi-ra'yihi dūna naẓar fīmā qāla al-'ulamā' wa'qtaḍathu qawānīn al-'ilm ka'l-naḥw wa'l-uṣūl*). This *ḥadīth* does not relate to linguists who explain its language, or grammarians who explain its grammar, or *fuqahā'* who explain its significances as long as each one bases his statements on *ijtihād* founded on the rules of science and deduction (... *ijtihādihi al-mabnī 'alā qawānīn 'ilm wa'l-naẓar*). One who speaks thus is not speaking merely on the basis of opinion.[51]

This is Qurṭubī dealing with the notorious problem of *al-tafsīr bi'l-ra'y*, characteristically by citation of named authorities. The points he makes are clear. Responsible exegesis is not limited to merely preserving the opinions of the pious ancestors (1). Responsible exegesis lies in appropriate consideration for the statements of the *'ulamā'* and for the rules of the established disciplines; this is a matter of *ijtihād*, and likely therefore to produce variety (2). These points constitute a justification of the literary genre and academic discipline of *tafsīr*, and indeed a suggestive description of it. For, as I have argued in this paper, it is a discipline characterized by multiple citation of authority, systematic comparison with the scholastic disciplines, both implied if not fully worked out in Ibn 'Aṭiyya's comments. These deserve to be compared with a comment on *tafsīr* by Ibn Taymiyya:

> He who turns away from the opinions of the companions and Successors and their *tafsīr*, adopting what is opposed to that, he is in error; indeed he is an innovator (*mubtadi'an*), for they were more knowledgeable as to the *tafsīr* of the Qur'ān and its meanings.[52]

Ibn Taymiyya clearly aligns himself with the narrower interpretation of the prophetic *ḥadīth* which condemns *al-tafsīr bi'l-ra'y* , the interpretation relegated by Anbārī/Qurṭubī to second position. It is a characteristic view of Ibn Taymiyya, implicitly denying the value of the intellectual tradition in favour of the *salaf*. The procedures of Ibn Kathīr must be seen, too, as consistent with this, the narrower view of the possibilities of *tafsīr*, and product of Ibn Taymiyya's influence. The importance of the alternative view, that of Qurṭubī and of Anbarī, is that it created the possibility of an inclusive unity, a tradition that held even Ibn Kathīr inside it (whereas Ibn Taymiyya's view tends towards the exclusion of, say, Qurṭubī and Rāzī). The tradition remained, in spite of Ibn Taymiyya and Ibn Kathīr, fundamentally acquisitive. In succeeding centuries the exegetes looked back to a tradition of authority which included Qurṭubī, Rāzī and Ibn Kathīr. Fossilized components of an acquisitive tradition, they added, all of them, to its possibilities.

This acquisitiveness is an integral part of the tradition, a concomitant of that respect for the past that is marked by the formal process of citation of named authorities and acceptance of polyvalent readings. This characteristic, however, engendered strains. Tensions were part of the tradition, precisely in fact what it set out to resolve; but they were bound to grow, and might become intolerable. 'Things fall apart; the centre cannot hold; / Mere anarchy is loosed upon the world.' In the balance of centripetal and centrifugal forces that marks a discipline (or a society) committed to a hermeneutic approach to the intellectual sciences, the danger must always seem to be that the periphery flies into fragments, that meanings scatter into an unassimilable multiplicity; the canon cannot sustain the commentary.

The effort is frequently made to understand Ibn Taymiyya in terms of the political and social needs of his time and place. A purely cultural (or psychological) assessment of his intellectual adventure is also a possibility, and perhaps preferable. Acutely conscious of fission, his effort was to reconstitute the centre, to assert the centripetal forces against the centrifugal. And likewise for Ibn Kathīr. His focus on dogma, on monovalent readings, on rejection of the unnecessary and impractical, his marking of boundaries and identity (Jewish sources for lies, etc.), his focus on the Prophet at the expense of the intellectual tradition, should perhaps be seen as a reaction to the countervailing forces of geography, time, imagination and ever-accumulating experience. These contrary trends are timeless, and can be seen to be worked out in all ages, and even in one oeuvre. Wāḥidī's production of three *Tafsīrs*, *al-Basīṭ*, *al-Wasīṭ* and *al-Wajīz*, illustrates the point, but so, in a more complex manner, does Suyūṭī's several works of and on *tafsīr*. The temptations of Ibn Kathīr's approach are great, and so, evidently, is its solace. A sufficient appreciation of the tradition, however, suggests his limitations, as well as his importance. He is concerned to reconstitute even to enlarge the centre (by combining two corpora of revelation). What suffered in Ibn Kathīr was the unity of the diachronic community (so many great thinkers fall outside his definitions) and the independence of the disciplines. The basic structures of the genre, established by Ṭabarī, exemplified everywhere, affirm the opposite: the experience of the community – deemed to be represented in the intellectual and scholastic traditions – was the measure of the packed meanings of the quranic text. Citation of authority and sensitivity to the varied disciplines mark the genre and are the medium of personal and artistic achievement. Those senses of authority which I have tried to symbolize with the competing terms, community, intellect and text, characteristic respectively of Qurṭubī, Rāzī and Ibn Kathīr, suggest the ends to which the structures might be manipulated. The limitations of the *tafsīr* tradition are precisely those of the scholastic disciplines. Implicit in the restraint of all the major writers within the tradition is condemnation of mere meditation on the text (without authority), and of mystical and allegorical readings. These biases are intrinsic and were for the most part transcended only in literary disciplines which are clearly not *tafsīr*, or, indeed in a variety of sectarian traditions, invariably deemed heretical. Of those clearly within the Sunnī tradition, only Fakhr al-Dīn al-Rāzī pushed against these limitations – for which he was frequently criticized. The clarity and intellectual control which mark his theological vision, however, distinguished it from the merely personal or the vaguely mystical; and his scholastic rigour is overwhelming. Ibn Kathīr's intemperate restrictions and his wholesale adoption of Islam's second canon afforded him an easy popularity. Qurṭubī remains the better measure of what the tradition could achieve.[53]

NOTES

1 Selection of Ibn Kathīr to mark a period is justified in the course of this paper. Ṭabarī is conventionally recognized as marking both the end of the formative period and the beginning of classical *tafsīr*. The literary characteristics of *tafsīr* in its formative period are analysed in J. Wansbrough, *Studies*, pp. 118–246.

2 Reference information on all exegetes will be found in Bibliography A; all other reference information in Bibliography B. The use of the word *tafsīr* to refer to a literary genre co-exists with a less precise usage whereby *tafsīr* refers to any argument based on quranic proof-texts. In Goldziher's *Koranauslegung* reference is made to only a small selection of works that belong to the genre; his concern is with the broad development of Qur'ān based argumentation in a limited number of theological disciplines. The whole of his section on mystic exegesis, for example, is devoted to quranic arguments emerging in a genre (or genres) formally quite distinct from the genre of *tafsīr*. Ghazali's *Iḥyā'* is not a work of *tafsīr*: it belongs to a genre whose antecedents include certain

works by Muḥāsibī and the *Qūt al-qulūb* of Abū Ṭālib al-Makkī. There are mystic *tafsīrs*, e. g. that of Sahl al-Tustarī (for which, see Böwering, *The mystical vision*). This work does not exhibit the whole text of the Qur'ān, nor even a significant canonically-ordered chunk. This alone would make it a marginal work within the genre. Application of the arguments about form and structure developed in sections 2 and 3 of this paper will probably confirm the marginal status of this work and similar ones. Only exceptionally, and probably only in the later period, after Ibn Kathīr, did the discipline of *taṣawwuf* become systematically incorporated into standard works of *tafsīr*.

3 Personal meditation on the text of the Qur'ān, even over a longish segment, is probably not *tafsīr*. The status of some works has been debated. 'How elastic can the definition of *tafsīr* be?' John Burton asks (*BSOAS*, LII, 2, 1989, p. 340) apropos of Todd Lawson on 'The Qur'ān commentary of the Bāb' (in Rippin, *Approaches*). Lawson does not address himself systematically to the questions of form and structure which, in my view, alone might provide an answer.

4 See A. Rippin, 'Lexicographical texts', p.164. The work of Dīnawarī is the well-known *Tafsīr of Ibn 'Abbās*, also ascribed to Kalbī and now reassigned by Rippin: see 'Al-Zuhrī, *Naskh al-Qur'ān*', pp. 23–4 and his forthcoming '*Tafsīr* Ibn 'Abbās' in *Jerusalem Studies in Arabic and Islam*.

5 The references are to Hans-Georg Gadamer, Harold Bloom and Jacques Derrida. It would of course be possible on the basis of the theoretical approaches of these (and other) writers to devise a typology of approaches to the hermeneutic task: Derrida-an, Bloomian etc. While no academic effort is free from a proselytising aspect, their programmes are probably too didactic and ideological for the normal (Anglo-Saxon!) approaches to literary description. In the field of Jewish and, in particular, rabbinic studies, the central task of description – with all that implies of analysis and interpretation – has been consistently brought to the fore through the works of J. Neusner, A. Goldberg, P. Schäfer and P. Alexander (*inter alios*). It is worth remarking that my proposed description of *tafsīr* works also (with minor emendations) for *midrash*, reflecting, not influence, but common literary responses to the central role within a community of a divine book.

6 G. Vermes, 'Bible and Midrash'.

7 See further, J. Wansbrough, *Studies*, pp. 100–2, 168–9 and 202ff. Also, illuminatingly, J. Burton, 'Linguistic errors'. Outside of the Qur'ān those linguistic problems in which Rāzī recognized a sign of the intellectual weakness of man would always be recognized as simply errors; *ibid*. p.196.

8 Wansbrough, *Studies*, p. 119ff.

9 For a general account of the Islamic disciplines in relation to *tafsīr*, Wansbrough, *Studies*, chapter 4 is invaluable; but see the specific discussion of symbol and allegory, pp. 239–46.

10 The major works of *qiṣaṣ al-anbiyā'* allied to the *tafsīr* tradition are the works of that title by Tha'labī and Ibn Kathīr, discussed below, pp.115ff. Much less academically controlled – and in some ways more exciting – are the *Qiṣaṣ al-anbiyā'* of Kisā'ī and those versions preserved in the encyclopaedic work, *Nihāyat al-arab* by Aḥmad b. 'Abd al-Wahhāb al-Nuwayrī. For the *'iṣma* of the Prophet, see *EI2*.

11 This *ḥadīth*, as recorded by Ṭabarī, can be found *ad* 37.88 (vol. XXII, p. 71). The distinction between the two types of lie is on consideration very unclear. One effort at explaining it may be found in Ibn al-'Arabī vol. 3,

p. 1264ff. ; cit. in Qurṭubī *ad* 6.62–3 (vol. XIII, p. 301). I would suggest that the distinction emerged in consideration of the fact that two of the lies are mentioned in the Qur'ān, and one is not.

12 Below, section 6, p.117.

13 That the dogma emerged before the *ḥadīth* is obvious. For the priority of story to litany, see Wansbrough, *Studies*, pp. 122–48 (also 46–8); *Milieu*, ch. 1; Calder, 'From midrash to scripture'.

14 This observation in a less developed form and much of the following discussion derives from Ibn al-'Arabī, vol. III, pp. 1264–5.

15 See a possible example in section 6 below, p.123

16 Rāzī, vol. IV, p.105.

17 Rāzī, vol. IV, pp.105–6.

18 Cf. G. H. Box, *The Apocalypse of Abraham*.

19 Rāzī, vol. IV, pp. 106–8.

20 Rāzī, vol. IV, pp. 108–9. For Avicenna and his theory of *wujūb al-wujūd*, see any standard introduction to Islamic Philosophy, e. g. Majid Fakhry, *History* and Leaman, *Medieval Islamic Philosophy*. Rāzī's rewriting of Avicenna's *Tanbīhāt wa-ishārāt* under the title, *Lubāb al-ishārāt* is illuminating (published in one volume, Tehran 1339); and, here, the play on *ishrāq* and *shurūq* is significant.

21 Rāzī, vol. IV p. 113ff. The reference to quranic diction as symbolic is on p. 115.

22 For Ghazālī and Avicenna, p. 116; al-Wāḥidī (*et al.*), p. 113 and 109; Zamakhsharī, p. 109; 'Abd al-Jabbār al-Qāḍī, p. 106 and 113; Ibn 'Abbās, p. 106. Muḥsin 'Abd al-Hamid provides a list of Rāzī's authorities in *Al-Rāzī mufassiran*, pp. 87–102; it is not a complete list, omitting for example Wāḥidī, who was undoubtedly a major influence. Making only anonymous reference to the standard Sunnī tradition and, conversely, expanding references to the Mu'tazilite thinkers is a peculiar feature of Rāzī's *Tafsīr*. It brought him much criticism. The Shī'īs too come into the constellation of his authorities more frequently than in the tradition at large. These features are partly due to his social milieu and geographical location but should certainly also be interpreted as an effort to expand the possibilities of the tradition. Of all the *tafsīrs* I know, his has the largest sense of what can be contained within the 'Sunnī' tradition. His greatest weakness is probably in juristic materials; though it is evident too that in merely scholastic approaches to grammar and syntax he is heavily dependent on his authorities.

23 See, e. g., al-Qāsimī's play on *wujūb al-wujūd ad* 6.74 (p. 2386), derived from al-Muhāyimī; also the reference to Rāzī at bottom of same page, and again at 2371–2. Ālūsī, by contrast, refers disparagingly to Rāzī at 195.3–4; of Rāzī's interpretation of the present tense *nurī* at 6.85 he gives a summary, introduced by the anonymous *qīla* and followed by the disparaging dismissal, *wa-laysa bi-shay'*!

24 Wansbrough, *Studies*, p. 45.

25 A neat summary of rabbinic sources on Abraham's life is given in G. H. Box, *Apocalypse*, at the appendix. See also G. Vermes, *Scripture and Tradition*, ch. 8; the *Sefer ha-yasha* already exhibits conflict on the question whether Abraham knew God in his youth or discovered him after a period of idolatry.

26 Ibn Kathīr, *ad* 6.76–9. See also his *Qiṣaṣ al-anbiyā'*, p. 198.

27 Ibn Kathīr, *ad* 21.51 (vol. III, p. 181), translated below, p.120.

28 Ṭabarī, *ad* 6.76 (vol. VII, p. 248–50).
29 Tha'labī, *Qiṣaṣ al-anbiyā'*, p. 63–5; see also his introduction for his assessment of the usefulness of *qiṣaṣ al-anbiyā'*.
30 Baghawī, vol. I, p. 28. Here Baghawī explains that he has followed Tha'labī for most of the information he transmits from early exegetes.
31 Baghawī, *ad* 6.76. (vol. 2, 108ff.).
32 Ibn al-Jawzī, *ad* 6.76 (vol. 2, p. 73–4)
33 Rāzī, vol. IV, p.113.
34 Rāzī, vol. IV, pp.109–13.
35 Qurṭubī, *ad* 6.76. It is perhaps worth remarking that outside of the *tafsīr* tradition there were few inhibitions about using this passage to justify intellectual argument and deduction (*naẓar, istidlāl*); see Abu Isḥāq al-Shīrāzī, *Kitāb al-ishāra*, p. 18, line 10.
36 Ibn Kathīr, *ad* 21.51 (vol. III, p. 181). For a parallel assessment of the value of *isrā'īliyyāt*, see also his introduction, vol. I, p. 4; cf. McAuliffe, 'Quranic hermeneutics', pp. 56–8, in Rippin, *Approaches*.
37 Gordon Newby, 'Tafsīr Isra'iliyyat' fails in my opinion to make any of the distinctions that are required for a reasonable understanding of Muslim attitudes to *isrā'īliyyāt*. The word *isrā'īliyyāt* has nothing to do with the actual origins of a story, which might or might not be Jewish, might or might not be known to the Muslim exegetes; it always indicates a theological objection to some narrative detail and is mostly used carelessly and polemically. (Ibn Kathīr's methodological summaries suggest the possibility of sound or neutral *isrā'īliyyāt*, but, in practice, he only uses the term when he is faced with narrative details to which he objects.) I cannot find that the word has any systematic currency in the *tafsīr* tradition before Ibn Kathīr. (I am informed by A. Rippin that it is found in Ibn Taymiyya's *Muqaddima fī uṣūl al-tafsīr*.) There is no necessary co-ordination between use of the word *isrā'īliyyāt* and having recourse to biblical material; Ibn Kathīr, one of the most frequent users of the term, is also one of the most assiduous readers of the Bible whose contents, when he approves, he transmits; see e. g. *Qiṣaṣ*, pp. 191–2, and below, p. 123. Newby's assertion of Ibn Qutayba that he was loath to accept *isrā'īliyyāt* (p. 636) is nonsense without further indication of what Newby means by this word and whether Ibn Qutayba (also a frequent user and transmitter of biblical material) ever used it. See also A. Rippin's article in this volume at note 20. The best survey of Muslim approaches to *isrā'īliyyāt* is contained in al-Qāsimī, *Maḥāsin al-ta'wīl*, vol. I, pp. 40–50.
38 Ṭabarī, *ad* 37.107 (vol. XXIII, pp. 81–6).
39 The text is garbled here; delete *ghayr* at p. 86, line 1.
40 See Calder, 'From Midrash to Scripture'.
41 Ibn Qutayba, *Al-Ma'ārif*, p. 17.
42 Baghawī, ad 37.101ff. (vol. IV, p. 32); Ibn al-'Arabī, ad loc. (vol IV, p. 1617); Ibn al-Jawzī (vol. VII, p. 67–8); Qurṭubī (vol. XV, pp. 99–101).
43 Ibn Kathīr, ad 37.99ff (vol. IV, 14ff). The biblical references are Gen. 17.1 and 17.24–5; he perhaps missed 21.5.
44 Ibn Kathīr, *Qiṣaṣ*, pp. 232–3.
45 Any systematic comparison of Ibn Kathīr with Qurṭubī and Rāzī will suggest the poverty of his reading; even the less outstanding exegetes like Baghawī and Ibn al-Jawzī allow the disciplines to impart to the text a richness quite

absent from Ibn Kathīr. He is at his most interesting when fighting against *isrā'īliyyāt*, at his most expansive when citing *ḥadīth*; see further section 7.
46 Compare Ibn Kathīr's comments on the word *ummī* with those of Ṭabarī, Rāzī and Qurṭubī; cf. Calder, 'The *ummī*', p. 112, note 2.
47 Tha'labī, *Qiṣaṣ*, pp.65–9; Ibn Kathīr, *Qiṣaṣ*, vol. I, pp. 191ff.
48 The relevant arguments will be found in any Tafsīr *ad* 6.82. The most interesting material seems to me to be contained in the standard Sunnī commentaries on Zamakhsharī, cited in all relevant detail in Ibn al-Qāsimī's *Maḥāsin*, ad loc. The *Tafsīr al-Manār*, too, is acutely aware of the problem and plays with the Mu'tazilite view at some length, abandoning it only reluctantly. For a general account of Muslim theology of faith and works, Wensinck, *The Muslim Creed*.
49 The canonical six works had barely in the time of Ibn al-Kathīr established themselves. They do not represent the limits of his sources, as witness the references to Ibn Mardawayh and Ibn Abī Ḥatim. See Goldziher, *Muslim Studies II*, pp. 214–44 for the historical emergence of the six books.
50 For which, see section 8.
51 Qurṭubī, vol. I, pp. 32–3.
52 Cited in Ibn al-Qāsimī, Maḥasin, vol. I, p. 21. A. Rippin informs me that this quotation is derived from Ibn Taymiyya's *Muqaddima fī uṣūl al-tafsīr*.
53 I should like to express my thanks to my colleague Dr Philip Alexander whose conversation on and formal studies of Jewish *midrash* have influenced my perception of *tafsīr*; and to Professor A. Rippin who read the first draft of this paper with great care and proposed numerous improvements of argument and expression.

BIBLIOGRAPHY A: TAFSĪRS (REFERRED TO OR MENTIONED) – IN CHRONOLOGICAL ORDER

Al-Ṭabarī, Abū Ja'far, (d. 310/922), *Jāmi' al-bayān 'an ta'wīl āy al-Qur'ān*, Cairo 1373/1954.

Al-Tha'labī, Aḥmad b. Muḥammad, (d. 427/1036), *Qiṣaṣ al-anbiyā'*, known as *'Ara'is al-majālis*, Dār iḥyā' al-kutub al-'arabiyya, Cairo n. d.

Al-Wāḥidī, 'Alī b. Aḥmad Abū 'l Ḥasan al-Nīsāpūrī (d. 468/1076), *Al-Basīṭ; Al-Wasīṭ; Al-Wajīz*.

Al-Baghawī, al-Ḥusayn b. Maḥmūd al-Shāfi'ī, (d.516/ 1122), *Ma'ālim al-tanzīl*, Beirut 1407/1987 (2nd printing).

Al Zamakhsharī, Maḥmud b. 'Umar Abū 'l-Qāsim, (d. 538/1144), *Al-Kashshāf 'an ḥaqā'iq ghawāmid al-tanzīl*, Cairo 1385/1966.

Ibn al-'Arabī, Muḥammad b. 'Abd Allāh Abū Bakr, (d. 543/1149), *Aḥkām al-Qur'ān*, Cairo 1392/1972 (2nd edition).

Ibn al-Jawzī, 'Abd al-Rahman b. 'Alī, (d. 597/1201), *Kitāb Zād al-maṣīr fī 'ilm al-tafsīr*, Cairo 1384/1964.

Al-Rāzī, Muḥammad b. 'Umar Fakhr al-Dīn, (d. 606/1209), *Mafātīḥ al-ghayb*, Cairo 1289 (8 vols).

Al-Qurṭubī, Muḥammad b. Aḥmad Abū 'Abd Allāh al-Anṣārī, (d. 671/1272), *Al-Jāmi' li-aḥkām al-Qur'ān*, Cairo 1387/1967.

Ibn Kathīr, Abū 'l-Fidā' Ismā'īl, (d. 773/1371), *Qiṣaṣ al-anbiyā'*, Beirut 1402/1982 (2nd printing).

Ibn Kathīr, Abū 'l-Fidā' Ismā'il, (d. 773/1371), *Tafsīr al-Qur'ān al-'aẓīm*, Cairo n.d. (4 vols).

Al-Bayḍāwī, 'Abd Allāh b. 'Umar, (d. 791/1389), *Anwār al-tanzīl wa-asrār al-ta'wīl* (ed. H. O. Fleischer) Leipzig 1846.

Al-Suyūṭī, Jālal al-Dīn 'Abd al-Raḥmān, (d. 911/1505), *Tafsīr al-Jalalāyn*.

Al-Suyūṭī, Jālal al-Dīn 'Abd al-Raḥmān, (d. 911/1505), *Al-Durr al-manthūr fī'l-tafsīr bi'l-ma'thūr*, Beirut n. d. (? reprint of Cairo 1314).

Al-Ālūsī, Maḥmud b. 'Abd Allāh, (d. 1270/1854), *Rūḥ al-Ma'ānī fī tafsīr al-Qur'ān al-'aẓīm wa'l-sab' al-mathānī*, Beirut n. d. (2nd edition).

Al-Qāsimī, Muḥammad Jamāl al-Dīn, (d. 1332/1914), *Maḥāsin al-ta'wīl*, Cairo 1376/1957.

BIBLIOGRAPHY B: other references

Muḥsin 'Abd al-Ḥamīd, *Al-Rāzī mufassiran*, Baghdad 1394/1974.

Gerhard Böwering, *The mystical vision of existence in classical Islam: the Qur'anic hermeneutics of Sahl al-Tustari (d. 283/896)*. Studien zur Sprache, Geschichte und Kultur des Islamischen Orients: neue Folge, Band 9, Berlin and New York 1980.

G. H. Box, *The apocalypse of Abraham*, London and New York 1910.

John Burton, 'Linguistic errors in the Qur'an', *JSS*, XXXIII, 2 (1988).

Norman Calder, 'From midrash to scripture: the sacrifice of Abraham in early Islamic tradition', *Le Muséon*, CI, 3–4 (1988).

Norman Calder, 'The ummi in early Islamic juristic literature', *Der Islam*, LXVII, 1 (1990).

Majid Fakhry, *A history of Islamic philosophy* (2nd ed.), London and New York 1983.

Reuven Firestone, *Journeys in Holy Lands: the evolution of the Abraham-Ishmael legends in Islamic exegesis*, Albany, N. Y. 1990.

Ignaz Goldziher, *Die Richtungen der islamischen Koranauslegung*, Leiden 1920.

Ignaz Goldziher, *Muslim Studies* (tr. and ed. S. M. Stern and C. P. Barber). Vol. I, London 1967. Vol. II, Albany, N. Y. 1971.

'Abd Allāh b. Muslim Ibn Qutayba, *Kitāb al-Ma'ārif* (ed. M. I. A. al-Sawi), 2nd Printing. Beirut 1390/1970.

Muḥammad b. 'Abd Allāh al-Kisā'ī, *Qiṣaṣ al-anbiyā'*, 2 vols, Leiden 1922–3.

B. Todd Lawson, 'Interpretation as revelation: the Qur'an commentary of Sayyid 'Alī Muḥammād Shīrāzī, the Bāb (1819–1850)', in A. Rippin, *Approaches*.

Oliver Leaman, *An introduction to medieval Islamic philosophy*, Cambridge 1985.

J. D. McAuliffe, 'Quranic hermeneutics; the views of al-Ṭabarī and Ibn Kathīr', in A. Rippin, *Approaches*.

Gordon D. Newby, 'Tafsir Isra'iliyyat', *Journal of the American Academy of Religion*, XLVII, 4 (1979). (Thematic issue: studies in Qur'ān and *tafsīr*.)

Aḥmad b. 'Abd al-Wahhāb al-Nuwayrī, *Nihāyat al-arab fī funūn al-'arab*, Cairo 1342/1923 *et seq*.

Andrew Rippin (ed.), *Approaches to the history of the interpretation of the Qur'an*, Oxford 1988.

Andrew Rippin, 'Al-Zuhri, *naskh al-Qur'ān* and the problem of early *tafsīr* texts', *BSOAS*, XLVII (1984).

Andrew Rippin, 'Lexicographical texts and the Qur'ān', in A. Rippin (ed.), *Approaches*.
Andrew Rippin, '*Tafsīr Ibn 'Abbās* and criteria for dating early *tafsīr* texts', forthcoming in *Jerusalem Studies in Arabic and Islam*.
Ibrāhīm b. 'Alī Abū Isḥaq al-Shīrāzī, *Kitāb al-ishāra ilā madhhab ahl al-ḥaqq*, in Marie Bernand, *La profession de foi d'Abū Isḥāq al-Shīrāzī* (Supplément aux annales Islamologiques, 11), Cairo 1987.
G. Vermes, 'Bible and Midrash: early Old Testament exegesis', *Cambridge History of the Bible* (i), Cambridge 1970.
G. Vermes, *Scripture and tradition in Judaism*, Leiden 1961.
John Wansbrough, *Quranic Studies: sources and methods of scriptural interpretation*, (London Oriental Series, 31) Oxford 1977.
John Wansbrough, *The sectarian milieu: content and composition of Islamic salvation history*, (London Oriental Series, 34) Oxford 1978.
A. J. Wensinck, *The Muslim creed: its genesis and historical development* (2nd imp.), London 1965.

V

THE *SA'Y* AND THE *JABĪN*: SOME NOTES ON QUR'ĀN 37:102-3

I

The phrase *fa-lammā balagha ma'a-hu al-sa'y* (37:102) was glossed by Ṭabarī (d. 310) in accord with the exegetical tradition he inherited as follows: *fa-lammā balagha al-ghulām alladhī bushshira bi-hi Ibrāhīm ma'a Ibrāhīm al-'amal wa-huwa al-sa'y wa-dhālika ḥīna aṭāqa ma'ūnata-hu 'alā l-'amal*, 'When the youth who had been promised to Abraham reached with Abraham the working (*sic*), that is the striving (*sa'y*), that is when he was able to help him in his work'.[1] This establishes clearly the subject of the verb *balagha* and the meaning of the word *sa'y* and makes the whole phrase a description of the youth's age. It may leave in some readers a disquiet as to the position of the phrase *ma'a-hu*/*ma'a Ibrāhīm*, but what Ṭabarī meant is clear. Ṭabarī cites as agreeing with him Mujāhid (d. 104), who is quoted as glossing the phrase as follows: 'When he became a youth such that his capacity matched that of Abraham in work', *lammā shabba ḥattā adraka sa'yu-hu sa'ya Ibrāhīm fī l-'amal*. Zamakhsharī (d. 538) endorsed Ṭabarī's view and glossed the phrase as meaning: 'when he reached [the age when] he could work (*sa'y*) with his father in his activities and his business'. Zamakhsharī, however, had a sharper eye than Ṭabarī for grammatical niceties and raised the very reasonable question as to what precisely, grammatically, the phrase *ma'a-hu* was linked to. There were, he suggested, only three possibilities: either it went with *balagha*, or with *sa'y*, or with something elided (*maḥdhūf*). If the prepositional phrase is linked to *balagha*, the whole clause must be translated as 'when he together with him reached, etc.' i.e. 'when they both reached ...' Zamakhsharī rejects this precisely because it would imply that they both together reached the age

[1] *Jāmi' al-bayān*, (Cairo, 1321-8), *ad* 37:102.

of working – which is unacceptable. He also, however, rejected the possibility that it could be linked to *al-sa'y* 'because the preposition going with a *maṣdar* (*ṣilat al-maṣdar*) does not precede it', *li-anna ṣilat al-maṣdar lā tataqaddam 'alay-hi*. He proposes therefore that the phrase *ma'a-hu* be understood as an 'explanation' (*bayān*) in response to an implied question as to who precisely the boy had reached the age of working with. Though Zamakhsharī explains in some detail why he felt it may have been desirable to specify in this instance that it was the father who was in question, and not someone else, his explanation does not to my mind do away with the problem as to why the prepositional phrase precedes the verbal noun.[2] Bayḍāwī (d. *c.* 700) agrees with Zamakhsharī that the prepositional phrase *ma'a-hu* cannot be linked directly to *al-sa'y* 'because a preposition going with a *maṣdar* does not precede it' and he too proposes an elided/implied question, 'with whom?' to which the answer is provided, 'with him'.[3] The whole clause remains astonishingly clumsy, requiring to be interpreted something like: 'When he reached – I mean with his father – the age of working'. And still one would prefer the prepositional phrase after the verbal noun.

In the *K. al-Tījān* of Wahb b. Munabbih, available in the recension of Ibn Hishām (d. 218), we read about the prophet Hūd that he had a vision one night in which a figure came to him and said: 'Should there be wafted to you or to one of your progeny the scent of musk, coming from some part or other of the world, then let him who detects the scent of musk follow in that direction that breeze; when it ceases he should settle there (*nazala*); that will be his abode and it will be for the people a *sa'y*', *dhālika mustaqarru-hu wa-li-l-nās sa'y*.[4] *Sa'y* here is a parallel to *mustaqarr* and must be interpreted as a noun denoting a place. In this context, the reference is specifically to Mecca, and is representative of the strong Meccan sanctuary tradition which

[2] *al-Kashshāf* (Cairo, 1385/1966), III, 347. Perhaps Zamakhsharī's statement of the rule governing the position of prepositional phrases should be read as relating only to defined *maṣdars*. Professor A. F. L. Beeston has pointed out to me in a letter (11.4.85) that examples of the prepositional complement preceding an *undefined maṣdar* are known; e.g. *hum ashaddu minnā fī dhālika raghbatan*.

[3] *Anwār al-tanzīl*, ed. Fleischer (Leipzig, 1878), II, 175.

[4] Ibn Hishām (from Ibn Munabbih), *K. al-Tījān fī mulūk Ḥimyar* (Ḥaydarābād, 1347), 31.

permeates the *K. al-Tījān*. In the early pages of that work there is evidence of the process whereby Mecca attracted to itself sanctuary traditions which had an otherwise Palestinian and specifically Judaic context. In particular, we read that Adam and his children used to go on the *ḥajj* from Jerusalem to Mecca and that they used to offer sacrifice (*qurbān*) at Jabal al-Ṭūr – located for the purposes of this narrative at or near Mecca. In this context it is stated that he whose *sa'y* was accepted would see his sacrifice eaten by a heavenly fire, *fa-man qubila sa'yu-hu nazalat nār min al-samā' ... fa-akalat-hu*. This phenomenon is described at some length, involving the use of the word *sa'y* four times, always in close association with *qurbān*. One example: 'when the fire ate his sacrifice, he knew that his *sa'y* had been accepted', *idhā akalat al-nār qurbāna-hu 'alima anna sa'ya-hu maqbūl*. In all four instances, apparently, where the Yemeni manuscript of this text reads *sa'y*, the British Museum manuscript has *ḥajj*.[5] This substitution reflects no doubt some discomfort at the unfamiliar use of the word *sa'y*, but does not significantly help the meaning. I would propose – and will further justify in the course of this article – that *sa'y* be understood here as implying striving specifically in order to please the deity, and so be translated as 'worship', equivalent to standard Arabic *'ibāda*. In the passage about the prophet Hūd, where *sa'y* seems to be a noun denoting a place, it would be translated as 'place of worship'.

That *sa'y* does in fact function in such a way as to denote a place may be illustrated from other contexts. In the *K. Akhbār Makka* by al-Azraqī (d. 250), there are quoted a number of Traditions describing the siting and the manner of the running (*sa'y*) between Ṣafā and Marwa, in which for the most part *sa'ā* is used only as a verb. However, Jābir b. 'Abdallāh, we read, asked on a certain occasion about the *sa'y* and received the reply: 'The *sa'y* is the bed of the valley', *al-sa'y baṭn al-masīl*.[6] Here *sa'y* cannot mean the act of running; that would require a preposition, the *sa'y* is *in* or *along* the valley floor. It must mean the place of running; the place of running is the valley floor. In the *K. al-Umm* of al-Shāfi'ī (d. 204), he discusses the conditions under which one might acquire in full degree reward for one's

[5] *Ibid.*, p. 14-15; see also footnote.

[6] *K. Akhbār Makka*, in *Die Chroniken der Stadt Mekka*, ed. F. Wüstenfeld (Göttingen, 1858), I, 178.

actions at Ṣafā. 'If [the participant] fails to ascend both [hills] or fails to ascend one of them, or if he does not utter the *allāhu akbar*, or if he does not call out, or if he does not run in the *sa'y*, then he has lost merit and he is not permitted to repeat', *in lam yaẓhar 'alayhimā wa-lā 'alā wāḥid min-humā wa-lam yukabbir wa-lam yad'u wa-lam yas'a fī l-sa'y fa-qad taraka faḍlan* ...[7] I do not think *sa'y* here can be read as a verbal noun: 'if he does not run in the act of running...' I would prefer to read *sa'y* as the name of the place, between the two hills, where the running takes place: 'if he does not run in the place of running'. I recognise, however, that it might mean, as a technical term, the act of performing the *sa'y*: 'if he does not run during that act of worship known as the *sa'y*'.

The more frequent noun of place from *sa'ā* is *mas'ā*. In the *Musnad* of Ibn Ḥanbal there is a Tradition from Ibn 'Abbās which states that when Abraham was ordered to carry out the rites of pilgrimage, the devil appeared to him at the *sa'y* (*'inda al-sa'y*). This is corrected (?) in the new edition to read *mas'ā*, which is also the reading of the version in Suyūṭī's *al-Durr al-manthūr*.[8]

A very curious version of the narrative of Abraham's sacrifice may be found in the *Biḥār al-anwār* of Majlisī. He quotes from the *Tafsīr* of al-Tabarsī (d. *c*. 548) the following narrative on the authority of Muḥammad b. Isḥāq b. Yasār. 'When Abraham used to visit Ismā'īl and Hagar, he was carried on Buraq: he would leave Syria in the morning, rest in Mecca and return in the evening from Mecca to spend the night with his family in Syria. Until when he reached the *sa'y* he was shown in a dream that he should sacrifice him ...', *ḥattā idhā balagha al-sa'y uriya fī l-manām* ... It is clear in this version that Abraham is the subject of the verb *balagha*, and the *sa'y* is a place where Abraham had a dream. In fact, the *sa'y* here, as in the other instances I have cited of *sa'y* as a noun denoting a place, is Mecca. In this version of the story, the transition at *ḥattā* 'until' is very abrupt, and one might guess that something has got lost or that two narratives have been loosely yoked without much effort at tidying the juncture. The new edition of Ṭabarsi's *Tafsīr* (Qum, 1355/1937) has corrected (?) the reading here and brought it closer to the

7 *K. al-Umm* (Cairo, 1388/1968), II, 178, l. 13.

8 Ibn Ḥanbal, *Musnad* (Cairo, 1313), I, 297-8; see also new ed. A. M. Shākir (Cairo, 1949-), IV, 2702; cf. Suyūṭī, *al-Durr al-manthūr* (Beirut, n.d.), V, 280.

Quranic formulation by adding the prepositional phrase *maʿa-hu* (and this edition reads *raʾā* in place of Majlisī's *uriya*): *ḥattā idhā balagha maʿa-hu al-saʿy raʾā fī l-manām*.[9] Now, I suspect that this is a scribal (editorial?) insertion reflecting the normative influence of the Quranic text. In its present context it does not make it any easier, however, to read this sentence as having any person other than Abraham as subject of the verb *balagha*. Even if we disregard all that goes before the uneasy juncture at *ḥattā*, the most natural reading, uninfluenced by the exegetical tradition, would be to assume that the same person was subject of *balagha* and the following verb *raʾā/uriya*.

I would propose then that Ṭabarsī's text, notwithstanding the problems it exhibits of transmission and collocation, represents the original narrative context of the Quranic *wa-lammā balagha maʿa-hu al-saʿy*, which would thus be interpreted: 'When Abraham brought him – his son – to the place of worship'. This obviates all the grammatical problems detected by Zamakhsharī and Bayḍāwī, and is consistent with an established function of the noun *saʿy*.

I have proposed 'place of worship' as the appropriate translation of *saʿy*, partly on analogy with the use of *saʿy* in the *K. al-Tījān* mentioned above, but also in accord with a variant strand of the exegetical tradition. Ṭabarī had proposed *saʿy* as meaning 'work' (*ʿamal*) and had been followed in that view by Zamakhsharī and Bayḍāwī. However, one of the alternatives which he recorded was the opinion of Ibn Zayd, who stated that *saʿy* here meant *ʿibāda*.[10] The problematic *Tanwīr al-miqyās min Tafsīr Ibn ʿAbbās* of Kalbī/Dīnāwarī/Fīrūzābādī[11] glosses the phrase *fa-lammā balagha maʿa-hu al-saʿy* in the following words: *al-ʿamal li-llāhi wa-bi-l-ṭāʿa; wa-yuqāl al-mashy maʿa-hu ilā l-jabal*, 'working for God and in obedience to him; and some say, going with him to the mountain'. This gloss thus offers two items of information: first, the word *saʿy* implies working for the sake of God and in obedience, etc., a concept not far removed from *ʿibāda*; and second, the whole phrase (?) gives expression to the

[9] See Majlisī, *Biḥar al-anwār*, new ed. (Tehran, 1376-93/1957-73), XII, 136; also Ṭabarsī, *Majmaʿ al-bayān* (Qum 1355/1937), IV, 455.

[10] Ṭabarī, *ad loc.*

[11] On this work, see A. Rippin, 'Al-Zuhrī, *Naskh al-Qurʾān* and the Problem of Early *tafsīr* Texts', *BSOAS*, XLVII (1984), 23-4. I have used the edition, ascribed to Muḥammad b. Yaʿqūb al-Fīrūzābādī (Cairo, 1380/1960); see pp. 278-9 *ad* 37:102.

bringing of somebody (the victim?) to the place of sacrifice, here a mountain or hill. Now, whatever its precise date, it is generally recognised that this *tafsīr* is independent of and prior to that of Ṭabarī. It is interesting then to note that a text uninfluenced by the decisive intervention of Ṭabarī in the exegetical tradition reflects (albeit in two separate glosses) precisely the connotations that I would propose as original to this phrase, namely the bringing of the child to the place of worship.

In other versions of this story there are other phrases, of which I take this one to be a parallel, indicating that Abraham brought the child to the place of scrifice. In a version attributed to al-Suddī we read: *inṭalaqa maʿa-hu ḥattā idhā dhahaba bi-hi bayn al-jibāl*..., 'he set off with him until when he had brought him amongst the mountains ...'[12] Notice how the *ḥattā idhā* phrase parallels the version in Ṭabarsī, *ḥattā idhā balagha maʿa-hu al-saʿy*. And in a version derived from ʿAbd b. Ḥamīd (d. 249): *dhahaba bi-Isḥāq maʿa-hu fa-lammā balagha haythu arāda an yadhbaḥa-hu*... 'he brought Isḥāq with him, and when he reached the place where he intended to sacrifice him ...'[13] The Quranic phrase *fa-lammā balagha*, etc. may thus be interpreted as reflecting a narrative context in which originally Abraham (not the son) was subject of the verb *balagha* and the word *saʿy* was a noun denoting a place, probably Mecca.

II

The Quranic narrative of Abraham's sacrifice, brief and allusive though it is, is nonetheless recognizably not derived directly from the Biblical narrative. Central to the Quranic version is the fact that Abraham informs his son that he is to be the victim, and the son consents and submits. This motif is not Biblical, but it is a well-known and distinctive feature of Targumic and Midrashic versions of the story, as well as of certain Hellenistic Jewish versions. Rabbinic influence may also be detected in the Quranic *wa-lammā aslamā*. This is of course a reflex of Genesis 22:8, 'they went both of them together'; but a tendentious one insofar as it implies, which the Biblical text does not, that they both knew and both submitted to God's command. Rabbinic

[12] Cited in Ṭabarī, *op. cit.*, *ad* 37:102.

[13] Cited in Suyūṭī, *al-Durr al-manthūr*, V, 283-4.

exegesis in its concern to assert that Isaac knew and voluntarily submitted to God's command had long before interpreted the Biblical text in just this way.[14]

Given, then, the general familarity of the Quranic narrative, one phrase remains oddly puzzling: *wa-talla-hu li-l-jabīn* (37:103). This was universally recognized by Muslim exegetes as meaning 'he threw him down on his forehead/temple'. There is no precedent for any such detail in earlier Judaic or Christian exegesis. Midrashic sources lay considerable stress on the fact that Isaac was looking up, and indeed the requirements of ritual sacrifice are such that it would be very difficult to carry out the appropriate actions if the victim actually had his forehead (or even his temple) on the ground. The Muslim exegetes knew this and were notably inventive in their reactions to this phrase. One source cited by Ṭabarī glossed *talla* as *akhadha*: *akhadha jabīna-hu li-yadhbaḥa-hu.*[15] *Talla*, though like *jabīn* a *hapax legomenon* in the Qur'an, in fact means *ṣara'a* 'to throw down'. Less arbitrary than *talla* = *akhadha*, but equally characteristic, is the following version of the crucial events according to al-Suddī: 'He drew the knife across his throat but the knife did not cut – God had placed a sheet of copper over Isaac's neck; when [Abraham] saw that he threw him onto his forehead (*jabīn*) and struck at the back of his neck (*qafā*)'.[16] Here the Quranic phrase is made to describe the second stage in the act of sacrifice, posterior to an initial and more conventional attack on the throat.

In addition to having an odd meaning, it seems to me that this phrase also exhibits a grammatical peculiarity. Use of 'the forehead' rather than 'his forehead', if not actually unknown in Arabic, in this type of context (?), is nonetheless not the most usual formulation (cf. *kharartu li-wajhī*, Abū Hurayra in *Selections from the Ṣaḥīḥ of Bukhārī*, ed. C. C. Torrey (Leiden, 1969), 4). In fact, although no exegete makes explicit comment on this, nearly all exegetical glosses tacitly 'correct' this phrase and provide the possessive pronoun. From Ṭabarī: Mujahid, *waḍa'a wajha-hu li-l-arḍ*; Qatāda, *wa-kabba-hu li-fī-hi*; Ibn Zayd *jabīni-hi*, *akhadha jabīna-hu*. Zamakhsharī offers *ṣana'a-hu li-shiqqi-hi*, and is

[14] See for post-Biblical Jewish commentary on Gen. 22, G. Vermes, *Scripture and Tradition in Judaism* (Leiden, 1961), *ad* 'Redemption and Genesis 22'. For Rabbinic influence on Muslim scripture and exegesis, see J. Wansbrough, *Quranic Studies* (Oxford 1977), 134-7, and *opera cit.*

[15] Ibn Zayd, cited in Ṭabarī, *ad* 37:103.

[16] Cited in Ṭabarī, *ad* 37:102..

followed by Bayḍāwī (*ṣanaʿa-hu ʿalā shiqqi-hi fa-waqaʿa jabīnu-hu ʿalā l-arḍ*). And the *Tafsīr Ibn ʿAbbās*: *kabba-hu li-wajhi-hi, wa-yuqāl li-janbi-hi*. In every instance, the Quranic 'he threw him down on *the jabīn*' is glossed as 'he threw him down on *his* face/side/ forehead, etc.'

The common Semitic root *jbn* has amongst its range of meanings that of 'curve, mound, hump or elevation' (Hebrew, Aramaic, South Semitic). If this meaning could be extended to *jabīn*, one might then read the word as meaning 'hill' and see in it a reflex of the Biblical Mount Moriah, site of this particular sacrifice; or, perhaps, more generally, as a reflex of the Biblical 'high places', sites of sacrifice and worship. The Arabic lexicographical tradition does not appear to know any meaning for *jabīn* except forehead/temple. A. Jeffery writes: 'The sole occurence of this word is in the story of Abraham preparing to sacrifice his son... The exegetes got the meaning right but neither they nor the Lexicons have any satisfactory explanation of the origin of the word from a root *jbn*'.[17] It is not clear that the exegetes did get it right.

The dictionaries give a relevant range of meanings for the words *jabbān* and *jabbāna*. These terms would appear to mean areas of land in the desert, probably elevated land, associated with cemeteries and places of prayer. *Jabbāna* appears frequently as an element of place names in the region of Kūfa, e.g. Jabbānat Sālim, Jabbānat Maymūn, etc. These areas are directly contrasted in Yaʿqūbī with other areas known as *Ṣaḥrā'*: Ṣaḥrā' ʿUthayr, Ṣaḥrā' Banī Yashkur, etc.[18] No doubt the former were elevated areas and the latter flat desert. In the *Naqā'iḍ Jarīr wa-l-Farazdaq*[19] we read that Malik b. Mismaʿ went up (*ʿalā*) the *jabbān* in the district of Mirbad.

Altogether more striking and directly relevant is a thoroughly anomalous instance of the word *jabīn* in the *Musnad* of Ibn Ḥanbal. In a Tradition from Muʿādh b. Jabal, he relates that the Prophet, after giving him some advice about his mission to the Yemen, sent him on his way, saying *fa-nzil bayn al-jabīnayn al-Sakūn wa-l-Sakāsik*. Sakūn and Sakāsik are provinces (*mikhlāf*) of the Yemen, both well-known to the Arabic

[17] *The Foreign Vocabulary of the Qur'ān* (Baroda, 1938), 101.

[18] Yaʿqūbī, *K. al-Buldān*, ed. M. J. de Goeje in *Bibliotheca Geographorum Arabicorum*, VII (Leiden, 1892), 311-12; cf. *EI*² art. 'al-Kūfa' (Hichem Djaït).

[19] Ed. A. A. Bevan (Leiden, 1907-12), I, 731.

geographical tradition. Clearly, these words can only mean: 'Go down (to the Yemen) between the two "upland areas" or "hills" Sakūn and Sakāsik'.[20]

(It may be remarked in passing that an alternative linguistic route to the same result, *jabīn* = 'hill', is to consider that *jabīn* may be an anomalous derivative of *jab'* = 'hill'.[21])

It will be recalled that Kalbī/Dīnāwarī glossed the phrase *fa-lammā balagha*, etc., as 'taking him to the hill (*jabal*)'; and indeed, specification of a hill as the site of the sacrifice is very common. In the version of al-Suddī quoted above, we read that Abraham took his son 'between the hills (*jibāl*)'. In a version ascribed to 'Aṭā' b. Yasār (d. *c.* 100) we read: 'Abraham set off until when he was upon a hill (*jabal*) ...'[22] In the popular *Qisas al-anbiyā'* of Kisā'ī (date unknown) and in the cultural encyclopaedia of Nuwayrī (d. 732), the site of the sacrifice is Jerusalem, and in both versions Abraham invites Isaac to go with him to the hill (*jabal*), and indeed the sacrifice takes place on the hill (*ra's al-jabal*, Nuwayrī).[23]

I would therefore propose that the narrative and linguistic problems associated with the word *jabīn* in Qur'an 37:103 be resolved by recognising that in its original usage it meant hill. In its oldest forms, the narrative would be situated in Jerusalem and the hill in question would be Mount Moriah, equated in Rabbinic tradition with the hill of the Temple.

Both the items, which I have investigated here are locatory. They have acquired their Quranic context as a result of a lengthy transmission process in which different versions of the story developed and influenced each other in a variety of ways.[24]

[20] *Musnad* (Cairo, 1313), v, 235. The Sakūn and the Sakāsik are also known as tribal groups within Kinda, cf. C. E. Bosworth, 'Rajā' ibn Ḥaywa al-Kindī and the Umayyad Caliphs', *IQ*, xvi (1972), 37 n. 4.

[21] Cf. J. Blau, *The Emergence and Linguistic Background of Judaeo-Arabic* (Jerusalem, 1981), 171 *ad* n. 2. It may be worth mentioning also at this point the compelling and sometimes arbitrary nature of the Quranic need for rhyme, which has one of its classic instances only a few lines later at 37:130, *salāmun 'alā il-Yāsīn*. This would help account for the selection of a word undoubtedly used here in a rare sense.

[22] Cited in Suyūṭī, *op. cit.*, v, 284, ll. 5 ff.

[23] See Kisā'ī, *Qiṣaṣ al-anbiyā*, ed. J. Eisenberg (Leiden, 1922-3), i, 150 ff; and Nuwayrī, *K. Nihāyat al-arab fī funūn al-adab*, xiii (Cairo, 1357/1938), 120 ff.

[24] I hope to discuss the transmission history of this story in a future essay.

My proposal has been that *sa'y* meant originally place of worship and *jabīn* hill. It is interesting to note that when Saadya, a contemporary of Ṭabarī, came to translate Genesis 22 into Arabic, he chose as a translation of Mount Moriah the words *jabal al-'ibāda*.[25]

[25] *Version arabe du Pentateuque*, ed. H. Derenbourg (Paris 1893), *ad* Gen. 22:2. I should like to thank Professors A. F. L. Beeston and C. E. Bosworth for comment and criticism on an earlier draft of this work.

VI

ḤINTH, BIRR, TABARRUR, TAḤANNUTH: AN INQUIRY INTO THE ARABIC VOCABULARY OF VOWS

Professor M. J. Kister, in a justly celebrated article on the meaning of the word *taḥannuth,* takes notes only casually of the related word *ḥinth,* which, he implies, means sin.[1] Montgomery Watt had previously noted that '*ḥinth* is properly the violation of or failure to perform an oath, and so more generally sin.'[2] These are of course correct reflections of the Muslim lexicographical tradition. But, I shall argue in this essay, they do not exhaust the connotations of the word *ḥinth:* indeed they are probably secondary developments from the meaning which I shall explore here. It is not the least benefit of my proposal that it may—after a lengthy exploration of juristic vocabulary—cast new light on the meaning of the word *taḥannuth,* for so long a crux in the academic study of the biography of the Muslim Prophet.

1.

Ḥinth is part of the technical terminology of juristic discussion of oaths and vows. In the *tour de force* of juristic skills which is the *Kitāb al-Jāmi' al-Kabīr* of Muḥammad b. Ḥasan al-Shaybānī, the word functions systematically in the elaboration of juristic problems more than usually recondite.

1.1. A man says to his wife, If I speak to you [again] you are divorced; this at a time when the marriage has not been consummated. If he repeats this phrase to her three times she is once divorced, he is *ḥānith* in (?) his oath (*ḥanitha fi yamīni-hi*) and he ceases to have legitimate rights over her (*wa-laysat fi milki-hi*).[3]

This is a tricky thought. At the risk of explaining the obvious I should point out that by repeating to his wife his oath—not to speak to his wife—the man in question is in fact speaking to his wife. He is *ḥānith* in respect of his oath, and, apparently, what he has sworn becomes effective: she is divorced. The man is required to repeat the phrase three times in order to achieve a single divorce because the marriage is unconsummated. Had the marriage been consummated then the first repetition of the phrase would produce a single (revocable) divorce. I render the verb *ḥanitha* as to be/become *ḥānith* in accord with the not infrequent occurrence of phrases like *huwa ḥānith* as variants of *ḥanitha/yaḥnathu.*[4] Shaybānī continucs:

1.2. If [having divorced her once as a result of his vow] he takes her back (*tazawwaja-hā ba'da dhālik*) [as he has a right to do] and then speaks to her [as he has four times sworn not to do] he does not become *ḥānith* (*lam yaḥnath*).

Clearly the remarriage has broken the power of the vow and the man can safely

[1] Kister, '*Al-taḥannuth*', 227. For a list of the main sources used in this article see p. 239 below.
[2] W. Montgomery Watt, *Muhammad at Mecca* (London, 1953), 44; cit. in Kister, op. cit., 229–30.
[3] Shaybānī, *Jāmi'*, 26.
[4] ibid., 52, line 17; also Shāfi'ī, vol. 7, 66, line 11 (*arā-hu ḥānithan* = I consider him *ḥānith*); 68, line 20 (*naqūl . . . inna-hu ḥānith*); also Saḥnūn, vol. 3, 78, line 22 (*inna-hu laysa bi-ḥānith*), etc.

speak to his wife without thereby divorcing her, as long as he is not foolish enough once again to utter damaging vows. Shaybānī gives another instance of a similarly problematic occasion:

1.3. If he had said to her [still assuming that the marriage is unconsummated], If ever I swear an oath on the basis of divorcing you, you are divorced (*in ḥalaftu bi-ṭalāqi-ki fa-anti ṭāliq*); then if he repeats these words three times she is divorced.[5]

By repeating these words he is in fact swearing on the basis of divorcing her, and so incurs the penalty of his vow. Subsequent examples include instances of a consummated marriage where the first repetition of this type of oath creates a single divorce. I have used the clumsy 'swearing on the basis of' because if, in English, we say 'he swears to divorce her', etc. it fails to catch the conditional nature of these oaths which, as will become evident, is a characteristic (not an inevitable) feature of many oaths discussed in *fiqh* literature. In such oaths a man typically specifies the conditions under which his oath becomes effective.

It may be clear already that the form of these oaths is not such that the English concepts of 'breaking' or 'violating' an oath can be easily accommodated. The oaths are in fact acts of commitment (here to divorce) which are conditionally suspended; when the condition is fulfilled the man is committed, the vow is activated and, in this case, the man is divorced. Here and in all types of conditional vow (and, I shall argue, also elsewhere) the conceptual formulation of vows points towards *ḥanitha* as meaning 'to become committed' or 'bound' or 'liable', or, more generally, 'to incur liability'.

1.4. A man says, His wife is divorced if ever he marries womankind [*al-nisā'*—defined plural]. The oath is construed as referring to one woman . . . But if he said, [His wife is divorced] if ever he marries women [*nisā'*—undefined plural] . . . then the oath is construed as referring to three. But if he intended in the first instance . . . womankind, all of them (*al-nisā' kullahum—sic*) then he never becomes *ḥānith* (*lam yaḥnath abadan*).[6]

A man cannot fulfil the condition of marrying all women, so he cannot become bound or liable to the consequences of this vow—here, an effective divorce. To argue that there is concern here with breaking or violating an oath requires a change in the formulation of oaths that would clearly be invalid.

1.5.

(*a*) A man says to his two wives, If you two enter this house (*in dakhaltumā*) you are both divorced. He does not become *ḥānith* (*lam yaḥnath*) until they both enter together . . .

(*b*) If he says to them both, If you two enter this house and you two enter this house [indicating two different houses] . . . then you are both divorced. The two of them are not divorced (*lam tuṭallaqā*) until each one of them enters both houses.[7]

Note here how the phrase *lam yaḥnath* is a parallel to *lam tuṭallaqā*. Both phrases are intended to indicate that the man has become liable to his own vow: he is divorced.

1.6. A man says, If I possess anything other than 50 dirhams my slave is free. If he possesses only ten dirhams then he is not *ḥānith* (*lam yaḥnath*). But if

[5] Shaybānī, *Jāmi'*, 27.
[6] ibid., 28.
[7] ibid., 37.

he possesses 50 dirhams and [in addition to this] either ten dinars or something to trade with or grazing animals, then he is *ḥānith* . . .[8]

Insofar as the man is deemed to have fulfilled the condition he imposed upon himself, he is bound by his vow and his slave is free. If he is not deemed to have fulfilled the condition, then he is not liable, his slave is not free.

Divorcing wives and freeing slaves are peculiar problems because these are, in Islamic law, performative utterances: simply uttering the correct words in the correct form can produce a change of status in others. To become *ḥānith* in these cases means simply that one's slave is free, one's wife divorced—and, thereafter, one is no longer *ḥānith*. This concern with personal status is the reason for the predominance of this kind of oath in the *fiqh* works: it was necessary to know whether a wife was divorced or a slave freed for sound practical reasons, such as inheritance, ownership, etc. There were other types of commitment and I offer one example from Shāfi'ī's *Umm*.

1.7. A man is owed something by another man and he swears, If you pay me my due on such and such a day I will give you a slave from that day. He then pays him his due, all of it, except for a *dirham* or a *fils*, in the course of that day, all of it. [The swearer of the oath] is not *ḥānith* (*lam yaḥnath*); and he does not become *ḥānith*, except he be paid his due in full, before the passing of that day . . . and [not being *ḥānith*] he does not give him a slave (*wa-lā yaḥnath illā bi-an yaqdiya-hu haqqa-hu kulla-hu . . . wa-lā yahib la-hu 'abdan*).[9]

The question at issue is whether, lacking a *fils* or a *dirham* of his money, the swearer of the oath is technically bound by his oath, in which he specified payment in full. He is not bound. Consider also the phrase *kullu ma ḥanitha fi-hi* below, *ad* 3.5, meaning ' everything to which one may become bound ' or *man ḥanitha bi-'itq* meaning ' he who becomes liable to emancipation ' (*Umm*, vol. 7, p. 71, l. 31).

The following however, from Shaybānī, is more problematic.

1.8. A man says, So-and-so shall not leave this house without my permission. He then gives permission but so-and-so does not leave, until the man once again forbids him. So-and-so then leaves. The man is not *ḥānith*.[10]

Shaybānī, clearly performing here for advanced level students, gives us the difficult problem. It is worth reconstructing the simpler case. A man says, So-and-so shall not leave without my permission. So-and-so leaves without permission. The man is *ḥānith*. This case is assumed by Shaybānī who then considers a related complex question involving permission granted, then rescinded (but presumably not in the form of a vow): the man is not *ḥānith*. My preferred translation for that last phrase is ' the man has not incurred liability '. The consequences of incurring liability in cases such as this are atonement (*kaffāra*).[11] If it be understood then that amongst the possible consequences of a vow is an act of atonement, there are, I think, no instances in *fiqh* literature where ' to incur liability ', etc. will not suffice as a translation of *ḥanitha*. One final example:

[8] ibid., 43.
[9] Shāfi'ī, *Umm*, vol. 7, 68, lines 15 f.
[10] Shaybānī, *Jāmi'*, 33.
[11] Modes of atonement naturally varied slightly or even markedly throughout *fiqh* literature. Shaybānī sums the matter up concisely in his *Aṣl*, vol. 3, 196: ' If a man swears an oath and becomes *ḥānith* in respect of it, then he is subject to whichever of the modes of *kaffāra* he prefers: he may emancipate a slave, or he may feed ten poor, or clothe ten poor. If he cannot manage any of these, he should fast for three successive days.' See also, Shāfi'ī, vol. 7, 58–61 and Saḥnūn, vol. 3, 118–27.

1.9. A man swears that he will not enter this house. It reverts to desert. He enters [the place where it used to be]. He is *ḥānith* (*ḥanitha*).[12]

Here a man swears that he will not do a thing, which he is subsequently deemed to have done and so he is liable (to *kaffāra*). But here too a translation of the type ' he has broken his oath ' is perfectly possible. Outside of ' advanced ' works like the *Kifāb al-Jāmi' al-Kabīr,* simple oaths of this kind are probably the most commonly discussed in the *fiqh* tradition. In such contexts *ḥanitha* systematically functions with the meaning ' to incur liability as a result of breaking an oath ', i.e. of failing to do what one has sworn to do, or doing what one has sworn not to do. This usage predominates in later *fiqh* literature, perhaps to the point of excluding the sense of liability; (I am not sure that it disappears entirely, but that is another essay.) [13] It is however important to note that the meaning ' to violate an oath ' (or, better, ' to be or enter into a state of oath-violation ') is a secondary development deriving from the meaning ' to incur liability '. If the latter meaning tended to disappear it was in part because its use in certain situations created linguistic puzzles that could best be avoided by abandoning the word *ḥinth* in certain contexts (see below *ad* 2.4–2.7).

2.

To be *ḥānith* is to be in a state of liability, oath-liability. The examples adduced so far show that it is the swearer of the oath who becomes *ḥānith,* no one else. His oath may have repercussions for others, as in the cases of divorce and emancipation, but these precisely are performative utterances of a unique kind, as explained above. This state of oath-liability (*ḥinth*) has, naturally, as a conceptual correlative the state of being free from liability. The verb expressing this in juristic literature is *barra* (noun and adjective, *birr*).

2.1. A man says, By God I shall not enter this house or I shall not enter this house [two houses]. Whichever of the two houses he enters, he becomes *ḥānith* (*ḥanitha*). He says, By God I shall indeed enter this house or I shall enter this house. Whichever of the two houses he enters, he becomes *birr* (*barra*).[14]

What is at issue here is the different effect of positive and negative sentences in the context of vows. When a man swears *not* to do a deed, he does not become *ḥānith* till he actually does it. And if he never does it, he never becomes *ḥānith*. Conversely, when a man swears that he *will* do a deed, he is committed (*?ḥānith*) and can only free himself from this state (= become *birr*) by doing what he has sworn to do. The problem as formulated by Shaybānī is characteristically complicated: he is concerned with the effect of the conjunction ' or '. The point, however, is clear enough.

The following cases, aside from their qualities as linguistic conceits, further exemplify the usage of *ḥinth* and *birr*.

2.2. A man says, By God I shall not enter this house ever or I shall indeed enter this second house today. If he enters the first house, he is *ḥānith* (*ḥanitha*). If he does not enter the first house and fails also to enter the second house until that day has passed, he is *ḥānith*. But if he enters on

[12] Shaybānī, *Jāmi'*, 54.

[13] As an example of a later Ḥanafī writer, see Sarakhsī, Abū Bakr Muḥammad b. Abī Sahl, *Al-Mabsūṭ*, 30 vols., Cairo, 1324, (repr. Lebanon, 1406/1986), vol. 8, 126 ff.; and, as an example of a Shāfi'ī writer, Shīrāzī, Abū Isḥāq Ibrahīm b. 'Alī, *Al-Muhadhdhab*, 2 vols., Beirut, 1379/1959, vol. 1, 242 ff. and vol. 2, 129 ff.

[14] Shaybānī, *Jāmi'*, 84.

that day the second house, he becomes *birr* and his oath is null (*barra wa-saqaṭat yamīnu-hu*).[15]

That requires a bit of thought. The problem illustrates the question: what happens when you have a positive vow and a negative vow conjoined by ' or '?

2.3. A man says, By God I shall not enter this house or enter this house or enter this house [three houses] (*lā adkhulu hādhihi 'l-dār aw adkhulu hādhihi 'l-dār aw adkhulu hādhi 'l-dār*). If he enters any one of the last two, the oath becomes null and he becomes *birr* (*saqaṭat yamīnu-hu wa-barra*). If he enters the first before entering one of the last two, he becomes *ḥānith*.

Readers will enjoy working this out for themselves.

In spite of their complexity, these oaths are composed of juxtaposed simple statements of commitment either to do or not to do something. It therefore happens that *ḥinth* is used consistently with breaking and *birr* with fulfilling a vow. Of the usage expected in line with my analysis of *ḥanitha,* namely, that a man might be described as *ḥānith* when he commits himself to do something, there is no sign. It may be that the developing tradition avoided this usage because it created complications. Consider the following, taken from the *Mudawwana* of Saḥnūn:

2.4. [Saḥnūn] said: Consider; a man says, By God I shall not beat so-and-so.

(*a*) Ibn al-Qāsim replied: He does not become *ḥānith* till he beats so-and-so. The root of all this according to Mālik is this: He who swears with regard to a particular thing that he will do it, he is subject to *ḥinth* (*huwa 'alā ḥinth*) until he does it. For we do not know whether he will or will not do it. Consider; a man says to his wife, You are divorced if I do not enter so-and-so's house or if I do not beat so-and-so. [This is to be construed as a positive vow, equivalent to: By God I shall enter so-and-so's house, etc.] This man is separated from his wife [by his words] and he must be instructed thus: Do what you have sworn to do (*if'al mā ḥalafta 'alay-hi*) or you will be subject to *īlā'* [divorce attendant on a vow]. This proves that he is *ḥānith* until he becomes *birr* (*anna-hu 'alā ḥinth ḥatta yabirr*) because we do not know whether he will or will not do what he has sworn.

(*b*) But he who swears with regard to a particular thing that he will not do it, he remains *birr* (*huwa 'alā birr*) until he does it. Consider; a man swears on the basis of divorce that he will not enter so-and-so's house. This does not occasion separation from his wife. This is what Mālik said. And this proves that he is *birr* until he becomes *ḥānith* (*anna-hu 'alā birr ḥattā, yaḥnath*). All of this is what Mālik said.[16]

And all of this is usefully clear. A man swears a positive oath and thereby, as Mālik puts it, is subject to *ḥinth;* that is, I take it, is liable to carry out what he has sworn, or to atonement, or, indeed, to whatever consequences accrue, to one who does not fulfil a vow. When he swears a negative oath, he only becomes *ḥānith* when he breaks it, and then he is subject to atonement, or to whatever consequences accrue, etc. This is what Mālik said. And if any reader is willing to follow systematically the repercussions of this argument, and to compare it with the examples set out in Section 1 above, he will begin to see how linguistic problems piled up for the *fuqahā'*. These conditional vows can clearly be approached from different angles. Here, in section (*a*), Ibn al-Qāsim treats a

[15] ibid., 85.
[16] Saḥnūn, vol. 3, 114–15.

conditional vow as if it were a commitment to enter so-and-so's house: the man is *ḥānith* in respect of entering the house, if he wants to avoid divorce. Had the same vow occurred to Shaybānī while he was writing the *Kitāb al-Jāmi' al-Kabīr,* he would have considered this vow a conditional commitment to divorce, and he would have described the man as *ḥānith* (in respect of the divorce!) only when he entered so-and-so's house. There is no real inconsistency here. A man is *liable* to divorce only if he does X, but if he wishes to avoid divorce, then he is *liable* or *committed* to do X. It is important with this word *ḥinth* to specify the angle of approach.

Consider the following two examples from a little later in the *Mudawwana:*

2.5. Mālik said: A man swears, on the basis of emancipating slaves or divorcing wives, that he will indeed pay so-and-so his debt by Ramaḍān. The swearer then dies in Rajab or Sha'bān [i.e. before Ramaḍān]. Mālik said: He is not subject to *ḥinth* (*la ḥinth 'alay-hi*) in respect of slaves and wives, because he died while in a state of *birr* (*māta 'alā birr*).[17]

2.6. I asked Mālik about a man who says to his wife, My slave is free if I do not beat you by the end of the year. His wife then dies before the year is up. Is he subject to *ḥinth* in respect of the slave (*hal 'alay-hi ḥinth . . .)?* Mālik replied: No, because he was in a state of *birr* when she died before the stated period.[18]

These problems share the characteristic of specifying a term for the fulfilment of a positive vow (I shall pay, I shall beat). According to Ibn al-Qāsim, at 2.4 (*a*), the man in question should be considered subject to *ḥinth,* he has after all quite decidedly sworn that he will do something (at least at 2.5). The resolution lies in specifying clearly the angle of approach. Following Ibn al-Qāsim, we can say, of the man who has sworn that he will pay his debt, that he is *ḥānith,* in respect of paying his debt, from the moment he makes his oath; but (following Shaybānī?) he does not become *ḥānith* in respect of freeing his slaves or divorcing his wives until Ramaḍān, and then only on condition that he has not paid his debt. Mālik is clearly correct: dying in Rajab or in Sha'bān, the man is not subject to *ḥinth* in respect of slaves or wives. He is however, I submit, in a state of *ḥinth* in respect to paying his debt. A similar analysis may be applied to example 2.6.

It is clearly not possible to resolve all the word-play in these examples without holding on to the fact that *ḥinth* implies liability and *birr* absence of liability. It is also worth stressing here that in a context of conditional vows, or vows on the basis of . . ., simple statements of the type that a man is or is not *ḥānith* will not adequately clarify the situation. One has to ask in respect of what he is *ḥānith.* Consider the following two juxtaposed sentences in Shāfi'ī's *Umm:*

2.7. He [Shāfi'ī?] said: We say, concerning one who swears, on the basis of emancipating his slave (*man ḥalafa bi-'itq ghulāmi-hi*), that he will indeed beat him, we say that this prevents him from selling his slave, because he is subject to *ḥinth* till he beats him (*li-anna-hu 'alā ḥinth ḥattā yaḍraba-hu*). Shāfi'ī said: He may sell him if he wishes; it does not prevent him from selling him, for he is in a state of *birr* (*li-anna-hu 'alā birr*).[19]

Yes, indeed. The problem might well be left there, but tricky concepts merit extensive demonstration, so, without apology, here is Shāfi'ī again on *ḥinth* and *birr.*

[17] ibid., 148–9.
[18] ibid., 149.
[19] Shāfi'ī, vol. 7, 71, line 29.

2.8.

(*a*) If a man swears that he will not divorce his wife and then gives her control over her own affairs and she divorces herself, he does not become *ḥānith* . . .

(*b*) If he swears that he will beat his slave and then orders some one else to beat him, he does not become *birr* . . .

Note: a man swears a negative oath, he will not do X; if he subsequently does X he becomes *ḥanith*. And so, at 2.8 (*a*) the question is whether he does or does not become *ḥānith* if his wife divorces herself. A man swears a positive oath; the problem is how to become *birr*. And so, at 2.8 (*b*) the question is whether, getting someone else to act for him, this man does or does not become *birr*.

2.9. Likewise, if he swore not to beat him and then ordered someone else to do it, he would not become *ḥānith* . . . Rabī' [the *rāwī* of Shāfi'ī's *Umm*] said: Shāfi'ī had another view on this. A man swears that he will beat his slave. If he is the kind of man who deals with things with his own hands, then he does not become *birr* until he beats him with his own hands. But if he is an authority within the community (*wālī*), or someone who does not deal with things with his own hands, then the prevalent view is that he normally orders [things to be done]; and if he orders [the slave to be beaten] he becomes *birr*.[20]

It will be of some consequence to bear this in mind. If one binds oneself by a positive oath, the problem is how to become *birr*, that is, how to free oneself from the liability that one has created and imposed. If one binds oneself by a negative oath, the problem is how to avoid *ḥinth*.

The correlative terms *ḥinth* and *birr* are paralleled in Islamic usage by another pair of correlatives, namely *ithm* and *birr*.[21] It is not too difficult to perceive that a similar kind of contrast may be involved. To be in a state of sin is to be removed from a state of safety; there is danger (of God's displeasure); there are consequences (punishment is possible, repentance required). A man in a state of sin is ' liable ' to certain consequences. *Birr*, it appears, is a concept implying freedom from liability, and does not of itself have implications as to the nature of the liability from which one is free, oath-liability or sin-liability. Although there may be cases where to be *ḥānith* and to be a sinner may overlap, it is always possible at a conceptual level to distinguish these terms. And, of course, in very few of the cases I have cited is it possible to confuse in any degree these concepts. None the less the Arabic dictionary tradition does confuse them. I would suggest that this is due to a transfer of connotations from *ithm* to *ḥinth* due to the fact that they are both ' opposites ' of *birr*. (This transfer was much helped by the Arabic exegetical tradition relating to Qur'ān 56: 46.) It is my very tentatively held view that *birr* meaning freedom from liability is a stage in the semantic development that led to *birr*, meaning *pietas*, piety. However, I doubt that Arabic users of the ninth century were aware of this and I shall treat *birr* = piety and *birr* = freedom from liability in the next section as homomorphs, having quite distinct meanings.

3.

Troublesome and demanding to the *fuqahā'* was the undoubted fact that oaths, if their power to bind was conceded, might conflict directly with the

[20] ibid., 70–1.

[21] Several examples of this contrast may be found in Traditions. See Wensinck's *Concordance*, for e.g. *sa'altu rasul allāh 'an al-birr wa-'l-ithm;* and *al-birr ḥusn al-khalq wa-'l-ithm mā ḥāka fi nafsi-ka;* and *al-ghanīma min kull birr wa-'l-salāma min kull ithm et al.*

demands of God, whose power to bind should be absolute. This problem may be illustrated from Shaybānī who, in the instance I quote, does not seem to notice that a problem exists.

3.1. A man swears (*ḥalafa*) that he will not fast the month of Ramaḍān in Kufa. This is construed as referring to the whole month's fasting. If he is in it (i.e. in Kufa) and does not fast, he does not become *ḥānith* (*lam yaḥnath*).[22]

This problem is embedded in a series of other problems which share the linguistic feature of specifying both a place and a time for the fulfilment of a vow. None, however, raise the peculiar problem this one raises: if the man, being in Kufa, is to avoid becoming *ḥānith* he must disobey God's law by failing to fast in Ramaḍān. There is conflict between the absolute imperatives of God's law and the artificial, or arbitrary or accidental imperatives created by a vow. Few early *fuqahā'* were unaware of this problem, not even Shaybānī who, if he missed it here, did so only because his attention was focused on the implications of adverbial phrases of place and time conjoined. Of the early *fuqahā'* the one who dealt most directly, most insistently and most radically with this problem was Shāfi'ī.

I have used the English words ' oath ' and ' vow ' more or less synonymously to translate the Arabic *yamīn*. There is however another Arabic word, *nadhr*, which in various contexts is apparently synonymous with *yamīn*.[23] Some writers, however, distinguished, notably Shāfi'ī. In his *Kitāb al-Umm* vows are discussed twice, once under the heading *nudhūr* and once, more generally, under the heading *aymān*.[24] The second section repeats material from the first.

3.2. A man swears (*ḥalafa*) not to talk to X (*fulān*) or not to provide for X (*lā yaṣil fulānan*). What is called *ḥinth* in an oath (*yamīn*) is better for you [in this case] than *birr*, so perform atonement and become *ḥānith* (*kaffir wa-'ḥnath*). For, you disobey God in abandoning him [i.e. X, *fī hijrati-hi*] and you abandon virtue in the matter of providing for him (*fī mawḍi' ṣilati-hi*). This is what the Prophet meant when he said, Let him perform what is better and let him give atonement for his oath (*fal-ya'ti alladhī huwa khayr wal-yukaffir 'an yamīni-hi*).[25]

Here the notion that words have the power to make a man liable is both conceded and subverted in the cause of a higher morality. A man is urged in effect to break his oath (to make himself liable, *ḥinth*) rather than be true to his oath (*birr*) if he has sworn to do something which may be thought contrary to God's law. The man is urged to discharge his liability (incurred by breaking a negative oath) by means of atonement. And a prophetic *ḥadīth* is adduced to justify this. Immediately following this passage, Shāfi'ī continues:

3.3. Likewise with all acts of disobedience (*ma'ṣiyya*) to which a man swears (*ḥalafa*). We command him (! *amarnā-hu*) that he leave the disobedience,

[22] Shaybānī, *Jāmi'*, 57.

[23] The *Kitāb al-nudhūr* in Saḥnūn's *Mudawwana* begins with the terminology *nadhara* and *ḥalafa nudhūran* (p. 77). There is a later section (p. 104) in which the terms *qasama, ḥalafa, shahida* are all described as constituting (in appropriate circumstances) *yamīns;* on p. 105 an oath utilizing the term *nadhr* is also assimilated to the category *yamīn*, as also on p. 109. The relationship between *yamīn* and *nadhr* becomes clearer in what follows.

[24] Shāfi'ī, vol. 2, 227 for *Kitāb al-nudhūr;* vol. 7, 55 for *al-aymān wa-'l-nudhūr*.

[25] ibid., vol. 2, 55; I begin at line 6 of *Kitāb al-nudhūr*. The *Umm* is made up of discrete judgements juxtaposed, generally in a skilful and appropriate manner. I omit lines 2–4, which, in addition to a small misprint, seem to exhibit a scribal omission; and lines 4–6 because the point made there becomes clear in the lengthy passage translated as 3.2–3.6.

> become *ḥānith* and perform an act of obedience (*ṭā'a*). But if he swears to carry out an act of piety (! *idhā ḥalafa 'alā birr*) we command him to perform the *birr* and not to become/remain *ḥānith* (*amarnā-hu an ya'tī al-birr wa-lā yaḥnath*).[26]

The Arabic word *birr*, in addition to the connotations which I have been primarily concerned with in this essay, has connotations corresponding to those of Latin *pietas:* it implies dutiful and appropriate piety towards parents and relatives, by extension, good moral conduct towards the world at large, and towards God in particular; thence it takes on almost the exact significance of contemporary English ' piety ' and ' act of piety '. In the passage just quoted I have opted to translate *birr* in its first appearance as meaning ' act of piety '; I cannot see that ' freedom from liability ' will work here. In its second usage we are presented with a pun. The man here is conceived as having sworn a positive oath to carry out a pious act (*birr*). He is therefore bound with respect to that act until he carries it out. On carrying it out he becomes *birr*, free from liability. Shāfi'ī has here so organized the expression of the situation that an act of *birr* (piety) is an act of *birr* (release from liability). The last sentence then is an untranslatable pun: we command him to bring about the act of piety/the act of discharging himself from liability and so not become *ḥānith.*

He continues:

3.4. For example: By God, I shall fast today; or: By God, I shall pray so-and-so many additional *rak'as*. [These are examples of oaths committing to acts of piety, *birr*, and in these cases] we say: Clear yourself in respect of your oath (*birr yamīna-ka*), and obey your Lord. Further [in these cases] if a man does not do [what he has sworn] he is *ḥānith* and he should perform atonement. The root of our opinion lies in this that a *nadhr* is not a *yamīn* (*aṣlu ma nadhhab ilay-hi . . .*). For he who swears (*nadhara*) to obey God, should obey God. But he who swears to disobey God (*an ya'ṣī allah* = to perform an act of disobedience) should not do so, and he need not perform atonement (*lam ya'ṣi-hi wa-lam yukaffir*).[27]

It seems that the last sentence here contradicts what was argued at 3.2 and 3.3. Here we learn that oaths are binding when they are in accord with the law and failure, under these circumstances, to fulfil the oath requires atonement. We also learn that oaths which bind to acts of disobedience are not binding, and do not require atonement when they are not fulfilled. But this contradicts 3.2 where an oath to perform an act of disobedience was not to be obeyed *but required atonement*. The contradiction can be resolved by taking note of terminology: a *nadhr* is not a *yamīn*; (in fact it is evident that a *nadhr* is a *yamīn*, but not just any *yamīn*, rather a special kind of *yamīn*). I am inclined to detect a considerable quantity of redactional interpolation in this passage but whether a school redaction, post-Shāfi'ī, or a personal redaction, by Shāfi'ī, I do not know. And for the present it is immaterial. The overall intention is clear. The power of oaths to bind when they bind to acts contrary to God's law is undermined; at 3.2 by denying that one should fulfil such an oath (*yamīn*) but affirming its efficacy to the point of requiring atonement; at 3.4 by denying that such an oath (of the *nadhr* type) has any validity whatsoever: it is not to be fulfilled and atonement is not required. It may be remarked that all the concepts here (*ḥinth, birr, yamīn,* etc.) are being subtly modified in their connotations as they participate in Shāfi'ī's argumentation.

[26] ibid., 227, line 9.
[27] ibid., 227, line 10.

It is also worth pausing over the phrase *birr yamīna-ka* which clearly means 'be true to your oath', i.e. fulfil it. I am inclined to detect in this phrase an underlying meaning of 'become free' or 'clear yourself' in respect of your oath. Even more tentatively I would propose that the phrase *birr umma-ka* (be pious, dutiful towards your mother) should be understood as meaning at, as it were, an older level of language, 'become free' or 'clear yourself' in respect of the duty you owe your mother. The IVth form verb *abarra* also means, by whatever semantic route, to carry out or fulfill an oath.[28]

Shāfi'ī's efforts to distinguish a typology of oaths continue:

3.5. If a man swears (*ḥalafa*) on the basis of anything—except emancipation and divorce—as for example, This my wealth is [to be distributed] in the way of God (*fī sabīl allāh*) or, This my house is [to be given] in the way of God . . .; then, if this be my way of an oath (*yamīn—idha kāna 'alā ma'ānī al-aymān*) 'Aṭā's opinion was the following: Oath atonement requites him in this respect (*yujzī-hi min dhālika kaffārat yamīn*). Those who hold this view hold it on any matter to which one may become liable by oath—*kullu ma ḥanitha fī-hi*—except divorce and emancipation.[29]

Things to which one may become liable are divorce, emancipation, alms-giving, pilgrimage, prayer, etc.; on the basis of these one can become *ḥānith*. On other matters (*ma'ṣiyya,* etc.) one does not become *ḥānith*. The point of Shāfi'ī's argument here (following 'Aṭā) is that all valid oaths (i.e. specifying approved actions)—except those specifying divorce and emancipation—may be subverted by atonement. This is quite consistent with the general tenor of his work which is to subvert the binding power of oaths. Here, oaths to perform approved actions are brought into the same category as oaths to perform non-approved actions as defined at 3.2 above. One may avoid the commitment created by an oath by appropriate atonement; and one may take this avoiding action even when the commitment is to an action permitted by God's law. (Divorce and emancipation are exceptions because they are performative utterances, immediately effective: there is no time for atonement.)

Shāfi'ī goes on:

3.6. A man swears on the basis of giving his wealth as alms (*ṣadaqa*), and becomes *ḥānith* [i.e. liable to carry out what he has sworn]. If he intended a *yamīn*, then oath-atonement [suffices] (*in kāna arāda yamīnan fa-kaffārat yamīn*). But if he intended a *tabarrur* (!? *in arāda bi-dhālika tabarruran* . . .) as that he says, By God, I commit myself to giving all my money as alms (*li-llāhi 'alayya an ataṣaddaqa bi-mālī kulli-hi*); then he should give it as alms. For the Prophet of God said, He who swears (*nadhara*) to obey God, let him obey him.[30]

Essentially, this continues the argument above. Here is a man who has sworn on the basis of something permissible, indeed approved of, alms-giving. If he

[28] See *Lisan al-'Arab*, s.v. *brr*. The root *brr* in Hebrew is associated with clarity, brightness, cleanness and purity. This notion of unsulliedness is clearly the basic connotation of Arabic *birr*, giving rise to freedom from oath- and sin-liability. The meaning 'piety, dutifulness' may be construed as a natural development from *birr* = purity. As an 'opposite' of sin and disobedience *birr* came to connote piety and obedience. The phrases *birr umma-ka* and *birr yamina-ka*, I am inclined to see as parallels meaning 'become clear' in respect of duties owed to your mother, or created by oath. However I have the impression that eighth/ninth century writers (of *fiqh*) had little or no sense of the semantic connexion between *birr* = purity, freedom from liability and *birr* = dutifulness. I suspect that for them both the above mentioned phrases would be construed as 'be dutiful in respect of mother/vow'; while *birr* = freedom from liability would be perceived as an anomalous technical term.

[29] Shāfi'ī, vol. 2, 228, line 1.

[30] ibid., line 7.

intends a *yamīn*, he may (should?) perform atonement. But if he intends a *tabarrur*, he should carry it out. In the typology of oaths, Shāfi'ī has distinguished:

(*a*) an oath to commit a *ma'ṣiyya* which must be rejected in favour of atonement (3.2). This is a view superseded by

(*b*) an oath to commit a *ma'siyya* which must be rejected and does not require atonement (3.4). These oaths are to be distinguished from

(*c*) an oath to commit an act of piety and obedience, which can be neglected but only with atonement (3.5). And

(*d*) An oath to perform an act of piety which should not be neglected, but must be fulfilled (3.6). This last oath seems to be called a *tabarrur*. It is provided with an example which takes the form of a simple commitment by an individual, in the name of God, to perform a specific act of obedience. The appended prophetic Tradition rather suggests that a *tabarrur* is a *nadhr*. There are then two types of oath involving an act of piety: one is a *yamīn* which may be neglected on performance of atonement; the other is a *tabarrur* or a *nadhr*, which should be fulfilled. I cannot at present detect any further distinction between a *yamīn* and a *nadhr/tabarrur* other than that the former is revocable with atonement and the latter is not. The distinction is created by intention (here *arāda* rather than the expected *niyya*). The problem of distinguishing a *nadhr* from a *yamīn* is reflected in Tradition literature, which in the end offers nothing more illuminating than that a *nadhr* is a very serious *yamīn*.[31]

The immediately following section is headed *bāb nadhr al-tabarrur*, chapter on *tabarrur* oaths. Most of the material of this section is repeated in the section *man nadhara an yamshī ilā bayt allāh*, on swearing to walk to the Sanctuary, much later in the *Umm*.[32] It is not necessary to consider that chapter headings or the organization and juxtaposition of discrete rulings are due to Shāfi'ī himself. I am inclined to consider the *Umm* (and all other early works of *fiqh*) as school redactions. This section begins (in both versions):

3.7. He who swears a *tabarrur* (? *man nadhara tabarruran*) to walk to the Sanctuary should do so if he is able . . .

This is perfectly in accord with our understanding of Shāfi'ī's typology: a *tabarrur* oath must be carried out. The narrator of the *Umm* intervenes at the end of the ruling:

3.8. Rabī' says: Shāfi'ī had another view on this, namely: If a man swears (*ḥalafa*) to walk to the Sanctuary and becomes *ḥānith*, then oath-atonement suffices him. That is, if he meant by his words a *yamīn* . . .

This view, in accordance with 3.5 above is ascribed to 'Aṭā b. Abī Ribāḥ.

3.9. Shāfi'ī says: A man swears on the basis of walking to the Sanctuary. There are two views on his position. One is implied by 'Aṭā's opinion that every man who swears (*ḥalafa*) on the basis of a ritual act (*nusuk*) whether fasting or *ḥajj* or *'umra*, may perform atonement for this in the form of oath-atonement (*kaffārat yamīn*) if he becomes *ḥānith*. He is not thereafter subject to *ḥajj* or *'umra* or fasting. His ruling [i.e. 'Aṭā's] is that acts of piety (*a'māl al-birr*) towards God (*li-llāh*) should not take place except as a duty (*farḍ*) performed by the one upon whom God has imposed it; or as a *tabarrur* (! a freely given or supererogatory act of piety?) intending closeness to God [*yurīd allāha bi-hi*]. As to that which is based on the

[31] See e.g. 'Abd al-Razzāq, vol. 8, nos. 15837–45 and 15853–6.

[32] For 3.7 to 3.11, compare Shāfi'ī, vol. 2, 228, lines 11 ff. and vol. 7, 61, lines 13 ff.

improper extravagance of oaths, it does not constitute a *tabarrur* [a freely given act of piety] for a *tabarrur* is only carried out for reasons other than improper extravagance.

It must be said that that translation is more than usually an act of interpretation. It is easy enough down to the sentence beginning ' His ruling is that acts of piety ...'; thereafter I have had to make a decision about the meaning of *tabarrur* which has to be distinguished from *farḍ* on the one hand, and cannot with any claim to logic be made an oath. The writer provides the clue by glossing it at one point with the words *yurīd allāha bi-hi*, indicating that it is an act of piety, distinguished from a *farḍ*, hence, freely given. The last sentence beginning ' As to that which ...' is garbled in one or both versions. The key term is that translated as ' improper extravagance '. This appears in vol. 2 as *' ammā ma 'alā 'uluwi 'l-aymān '* (as to that which is ' high ' as oaths are high; ? high = excessive). And in vol. 7 as *' ammā 'alā ghalq al-aymān '* (as for [things] based on the locking [power] of oaths?). In either case it is evident that acts of *tabarrur* are not ideally carried out for the sake of this ' excess ' or ' locking [power] ' that is associated with oaths.

3.10. [Authorities] other than 'Aṭā' say: Such a man should walk to the Sanctuary as would be incumbent upon him if he vowed it (*nadhara-hu*) *mutabarriran* (! intending that kind of oath which is called a *tabarrur*).

A pun is a pun, but Shāfi'ī (or his redactors) certainly created an argument here that takes a deal of unravelling. It is worth recapping. 'Aṭā claims that all oaths creating a liability to an act of piety may or should be revoked by an act of atonement. This is justified on the grounds that acts of piety towards God should take the form either of duties (*farḍ*), carried out because imposed by God's law, or of freely given acts of piety (*tabarrur*), carried out for the sake of God. Shāfi'ī (at 3.6, 3.7 and, anonymously, at 3.10) modifies 'Aṭā's argument by proposing a residual category of vows which do not permit of atonement and must be fulfilled. These are associated with the terms *nadhr* and *tabarrur*, in opposition to *ḥilf* and *yamīn*.

I do not think it is possible to make sense of the passage 3.9–3.10 without acknowledging two quite distinct meanings for *tabarrur* along the lines I have proposed.

In the next sentence Shāfi'ī provides a definition of a *tabarrur*.

3.11. A *tabarrur* is that one should say, By God, I commit myself, if God cures X, or if X arrives safely from his journey ... I commit myself to performing the pilgrimage for his sake, as a *nadhr*. This is a *tabarrur*. (*al-tabarrur an yaqūl li-llāhi 'alayya in shafā 'llāhu fulānan aw qadima fulānun min safari-hi ... an aḥijja la-hu nadhran fa-huwa al-tabarrur*).

A *tabarrur* then for Shāfi'ī is a kind of vow, more or less synonymous with a *nadhr*, and to be distinguished from a *yamīn*. The distinction is amplified in the next sentence: ' As for the man who says, If I do not pay you your debt I shall walk to the Sanctuary. This belongs to the category of *aymān* not *nudhūr*.' Clearly a vow carelessly uttered in the course of a bargaining session is a *yamīn;* a vow thoughtfully uttered at a serious moment is a *tabarrur*. A *tabarrur* creates a liability to an act of piety which is not revocable. A *yamīn* may create a similar liability but is revocable by atonement.

The distinction between a *tabarrur* oath and a non-*tabarrur* oath (the latter creating a liability which can be pre-empted by *kaffāra*, except in the case of emancipation and divorce liability to which cannot be pre-empted) occurs elsewhere in the *Umm*, at least once. (See vol. 5, p. 249, lines 2 ff., *ad īlā'*.) But I have found no further evidence which explains the form or the derivation of this word. The argument of the *Umm*, which I have set out in the preceding pages is both complex and not fully resolved. I need hardly repeat: it is my opinion that the *Umm* is a school redaction. Deficiencies in the argument are due to the fact that ideas and problems that arose over a period of time have been incorporated into the text by a process of juxtaposition. One could certainly make an attempt to establish the chronological layers of such a text, but I am not convinced it would be a fruitful exercise. My present concern in any case is merely to establish the existence and the significance of certain terminological items.

Shāfi'ī (or his redactors, as ever,) did not invent the word *nadhr* but he certainly exploited it and imposed on it a meaning which it did not have outside of his work. The same, I would suggest, is true of *tabarrur*. I am inclined to see the root of this word as *birr*, meaning freedom from oath liability; *tabarrara* would then mean ' to make oneself free from oath-liability '. It will be recalled that when a man swears a positive oath his problem is how to recover *birr*. The act he has sworn to do is the act by which he frees himself from liability (= ? *tabarrara*). I would speculate then on the existence of a verbal form, to swear an oath of *tabarrur, nadhara tabarruran* or *nadhr al-tabarrur* (forms both found in Shāfi'ī, but with specialized meaning) implying simply to swear to do a particular act. Generation from this of a verb *tabarrara*, meaning to bind oneself to a particular act is not far-fetched. This speculation, however, is not strictly necessary: we know that the word *tabarrur* is used by Shāfi'ī to mean a kind of oath. For him, it is an oath particularly associated with acts of piety and it is uniquely binding.

4.

In this paper I have discussed in Section 1 the meaning of *ḥinth* and in Section 2 the meaning of *birr*. In Section 3 I have pointed to a certain subversion of the binding power of oaths for theological reasons and to an attempted development of vocabulary involving a distinction between a *yamīn* and a *nadhr/tabarrur*. The network of conceptual terms related to *ḥinth* deserves still more exploration. In the present section I shall be concerned primarily with vows related to pilgrimage and visiting Mecca. Here too it will be possible to see the development of juristic resistance to the binding power of oaths, this time arising out of concern for established ritual practice.

In the simplest and most general conceptualization of the problem it was agreed that if a man, having vowed on the basis of walking to the Sanctuary, becomes *ḥānith*, then he should walk to the Sanctuary. This raised problems if a man was old or sick or, for any other reason, incapable of carrying out his vow. Some strands of thought were rather rigorous and not at all sympathetic. Ibn Wahb records a Tradition from Sālim b. 'Abdallāh who was asked about the case of a man who had committed himself to walking to the Ka'ba a hundred times. ' Let him walk a hundred times ', said Sālim.[33] If, having sworn to walk, a man was forced, by incapacity or exhaustion, to ride part of the way, he should repeat the journey and walk where formerly he rode and ride where he walked. He should also sacrifice something in compensation for his failure to conform precisely to his vow.[34] Sacrifice as a mode of compensation for imperfect

[33] Saḥnūn, vol. 3, 77.

[34] ibid., vol. 2, 225–6; vol. 3, 77–81 provides a number of examples of sacrifice in compensation for inadequate fulfilment of oaths.

fulfilment of a vow is commonplace. This represents already a significant disregard for the precise binding power of words.

Compulsion was a problem:

4.1.

(*a*) [Ibn al-Qāsim:] I asked [Mālik] about a man who says, If I visit my father in the next so-many months, then may I be subject to walking to the Ka'ba. Then his friends compel him and bring him into his father's presence. He says: My friends compelled me.

(*b*) [Mālik] replied: Let him walk to the Ka'ba.

(*c*) Saḥnūn said: I only mention this as evidence in the face of those who claim that if a man swears, on the basis of walking [to the Ka'ba], that he will not do a particular thing, whether an act of obedience (*ṭā'a*) or disobedience (*ma'ṣiyya*), and then does it, [they claim that] he is not subject to anything (*lā shay' 'alay-hi*).

(*d*) For my own part I say that the act of a person under compulsion is not an act and he is not *ḥānith* [under these circumstances.]

(*e*) Sufyān relates . . . that Ibrahīm was asked about a man who swore on the basis of walking to the Ka'ba that he would not visit another man, and was then compelled to visit him. Ibrahim said, He is subject, i.e. to walking [to the Ka'ba] (*'alay-hi ya'ni al-mashy*).[35]

It is already clear from earlier examples that the *Mudawwana* is a school redaction, written in layers. Generally each layer is provided with a tradent. Here Saḥnūn records the words of Ibn al-Qāsim (*a*) who relates his conversation with Mālik (*a–b*). Saḥnūn gives his own opinion (*d*) and a relevant *ḥadīth* is added at the end (*e*). Saḥnūn does not actually agree here with the recorded opinion of Mālik; but he gives Mālik's rather rigorous view, he says (*c*), in order to show up an unnamed group who had so undermined the binding power of oaths that they declared a man totally free of liability when he swore not to do a thing under the conditions specified. This may be a polemical reference to Shāfi'ī's group, who had not in fact gone so far. It is notable that here it is the oldest layer of the tradition which acknowledges the greatest power to the binding form of words. Mālik and Ibn al-Qāsim seem quite content that a man should be bound by his words even when there is a clear act of immorality (compulsion) intervening to make him bound against his will or intention. Saḥnūn has found a way out: he subverts the power of oaths, in the light of morality.

If Mālik was, in these circumstances, unwilling to alleviate the binding power of words there were none the less a whole series of circumstances in which he too was perfectly willing to subvert that power.

4.2. [Ibn al-Qāsim:] What's your view? A man says, I commit myself to walking to the Sanctuary, barefoot, on foot. Must he walk? And what if he wears shoes? [Mālik:] Let him wear shoes. And if he gives sacrifice (*ahdā*) [as compensation] it is good. But if not then it is of no consequence. The matter is trivial.[36]

Here the man's words are not construed as binding, at least in so far as they

[35] ibid., vol. 3, 78–9.
[36] ibid., vol. 3, 83.

involve a departure from favoured practice. This is not just a casual concession. Systematically, personal commitment to excessive ascetic practices is undermined. A Tradition is added immediately after the above passage:

4.3. Ibn Wahb: ... A woman of those who had become Muslims vowed (*nadharat*) to walk and to perform pilgrimage barefoot, and with her hair loose. When the Prophet of God saw her, he veiled himself from her ... [and when they explained] he said, Command her to veil herself and to wear shoes; then let her walk ...[37]

And:

4.4. Mālik reports on the authority of Hamīd ... that the Prophet of God saw a man standing in the sun. The Prophet said: What's he doing? They said, He vowed (*nadhara*) not to talk, not to seek shade, not to sit down, and to fast. The Prophet said, Tell him to speak, to seek shade and to sit down; but let him complete his fast.
Mālik said: It has not reached us that the Prophet ordered him to perform atonement. But he ordered him to complete [that part of his vow] which constituted obedience to God (*ṭā'a*) and to abandon that part which constituted *ma'ṣiyya*.[38]

Here is evident the same process as we detected above in Shāfi'ī's *Umm*. The binding power of oaths is not conceded when it binds to acts that are disapproved of within the tradition. Not only does one disregard the oath, but one does not perform atonement. This distaste for ascetic practices during the pilgrimage is manifest throughout all the ancient works of *fiqh*. The man who swore not to talk, seek shade, sit down, etc. was identified in other (later!) Traditions as Abū Isrā'īl. The Tradition was exploited by Rabī', the redactor (?) of the *Umm*, who intervened at a certain point in Shāfi'ī's exposition of what was implied by a vow to walk (*al-mashy*) to the Ka'ba.

4.5. Rabī' said: This is true, if walking does not harm (*yaḍurr*) the one who walks. If it does harm him, he should ride, and he is not subject to anything [i.e. in spite of his having sworn to walk]. [This argument is based on] the parallel that the Prophet commanded Abū Isrā'īl to complete his fast and to take shelter from the sun. He commanded him to perform what was *birr* (piety) and did not hurt him; and he forbad him to subject himself to punishment (*nahā-hu 'an ta'dhīb nafsi-hi*). For God has no need of self-punishment. Likewise, if walking constitutes [self-]punishment (*ta'dhīb*) which harms, one should abandon it and one is not subject to anything.[39]

Rabī', here, pretty nearly does away with one of the commonplace oaths of early *fiqh* literature, that of walking to the Sanctuary. In so far as it constitutes a self-punishment, an act of conspicuous ascesis, it is undermined.

Equally striking is the concern of the juristic tradition to define the limits of permitted ritual by denying the power of oaths to create a liability that will conflict with established practice.

[37] ibid. See also the following *hadīths*.
[38] ibid., vol. 3, 113. This section, beginning at p. 111, might be interpreted as a Mālikī response to the question of vows based on *ma'ṣiyya*. A Tradition which names Abu Isrā'īl is also given (pp. 110–1) but its tradent (Ibn Wahb), its form (full of circumstantial detail) and its *isnād* (many-stranded) all suggest that it is later than the passage I cite. The *Mudawwana*, like the *Umm*, is composed of discrete rulings; but the *Mudawwana* preserves at least some of its tradents. Both works are school redactions. I hope to describe the formal structure of such redactions in a later essay.
[39] Shāfi'ī, vol. 7, 62, line 29.

4.6.

(*a*) Mālik: A man swears to walk to the Prophet's mosque [in Medina] or to the mosque in Jerusalem. Mālik says: Let him go to these two, riding. And he is not subject to anything (*wa-lā shay' 'alay-hi*). He who says, I commit myself to walking to the Sanctuary (*bayt allāh*), he alone should walk.

(*b*) He who says, I commit myself to walking to any place other than these three mosques, he is not required to visit such a place. E.g., if he says, I commit myself to walking to Basra mosque or Kufa mosque to pray there 4 *rak'as*. He [?Mālik] says: He is not required to visit these places; let him pray where he is 4 *rak'as*.

(*c*) Mālik: A man swears to walk to Jerusalem mosque. He must ride to Jerusalem mosque and pray there . . .

(*d*) A man of Medina or Mecca or Jerusalem says: By God, I commit myself to fasting in Ascalon or Alexandria for a month. Let him go to Ascalon and Alexandria and let him fast as he has sworn.

(*e*) Mālik: A man says, By God, I commit myself to going (*atā*) to Medina or Jerusalem, or to walking (*mashy*) to Medina or Jerusalem. He is not bound at all (*lā shay' 'alay-hi*). Unless he intended (*nawā*) by his words prayer in the mosques . . . If that was his intention (*niyya*), then he must go, riding. It is not required that he walk, even if he swore to walk, and he need not sacrifice an animal [give blood—as compensation].[40]

Juxtaposition of discrete rulings, accumulated no doubt over a period of time, outlines none the less a distinct argument. Vows to walk to Mecca are fully valid; and Mecca is the only place accorded this distinction (*a*). Vows to walk to the mosques at Medina and Jerusalem have at (*a*) a kind of secondary validity: one should go but one should ride. At (*e*), similar vows (to go to the cities, not the mosques!) are denied all binding power except in so far as they contain (by *niyya*) an element of accepted worship to which one may bind oneself. The idea of a mixed vow, containing an element to which one can bind oneself and an element to which one cannot bind oneself, emerges at (*b*). There, one is required to disregard the non-binding element (walking to Basra, etc.) but to perform the binding element (4 *rak'as*), without geographical movement. At (*d*), there is another example of a vow which contains a binding and a (less-clearly articulated) non-binding element. Here, movement to the specified site is permitted, even *from* the acknowledged centres of pilgrimage. At (*e*) it is made clear that vows that commit one to going, or walking, to even such eminent places as Medina and Jerusalem have no validity, in respect of that commitment. But if they include (by *niyya*) a commitment to perform a permitted ritual act (prayer, etc.) one should go and one should carry it out—but one should disregard the non-permitted part of the vow (walking) to the extent of deliberately riding and not performing any act of reparation.

It will be acknowledged that the technique of juxtaposed discrete rulings creates a subtle and flexible argument. It may not be fully resolved (especially as between 4.6*b* and 4.6*d–e*) but absence of a narrow final decision may be regarded as one of the great strengths of the Islamic juristic tradition. The *point* of these rulings is never in doubt. The juristic tradition plays its role in fostering and creating a hierarchy of sanctuaries.

It may be assumed that the *fuqahā'* respond thus in the face of actual practice. They elaborate controlling rules because people did go to or vow to go

[40] Saḥnūn, vol. 3, 86–7.

to mosques other than that in Mecca, and because practices existed which threatened (or simply conflicted with) the practices favoured by the *fuqahā'*. These texts are part of a process of control. Practices that develop amongst the people are interpreted, ordered and shaped by legal theory. I do not of course wish to suggest that the legal theory always, as it were, wins: it would certainly be possible to show that in some instances the tendency of the juristic tradition to, for example, ban or mould a particular practice has to be abandoned over time. Both social practice and juristic theory are products of a tension between the relative disorder of reality and the ordering principles of normative theory. Each influences the other. Developing practice is the ultimate basis of juristic speculation; and juristic speculation affects developing practice. Juristic theory is never a rigid or inflexible structure; if it were it would not be able to respond to, or capture or control the social developments that it aspires to order. What was expressed in *fiqh* literature in normative form was re-expressed (generally later) in narrative form as *hadith* with an equal (indeed greater) absence of narrow final decision. Consider for example, in relation to the sanctuary rules discussed here, the famous ' three mosques ' Tradition,[41] (which is not known to the *Mudawwana*).

The same struggle (to control and limit the sites of pilgrimage) is evident in Shāfi'ī.

4.7. A man swears (*nadhara*): I commit myself to walking to Ifriqiyya or to Iraq or to other countries. He is not bound at all. For there is no obedience to God (*laysa li-llāhi ṭā'a*) in walking to just any country. For, walking is valid only to places in which there is hope of *birr* (pious action) and that is the Sanctuary (*al-masjid al-harām*).
It is preferable to me, if a man swears to walk to the mosque of Medina, that he should walk; and if to walk to the mosque of Jerusalem, likewise. Because the Prophet said, Do not bind your saddles but for three mosques ... But it is not as clear to me that I should declare the walking to Medina or Jerusalem mandatory as it is clear that I should declare mandatory the walking to the Sanctuary. For the piety (*birr*) in visiting the Sanctuary is a duty (*farḍ*), and that in visiting the other two is a *nāfila* (supererogatory action).
If a man swears to walk to the mosque of Miṣr, he is not bound to walk to it ...[42]

In a very similar way the *fuqahā'* intervene to restrict the sites near Mecca which can be specified as object of a vow.

4.8. [Saḥnūn:] What is your opinion of one who commits himself to walking to Ṣafā or Marwa.
[Ibn al-Qasim:] I do not recall anything from Mālik on this; but walking is not incumbent on such a one.
[Saḥnūn:] What of one who specifies walking to Minā or 'Arafat or Dhū Ṭuwā?
[Ibn al-Qasim:] If he specified these or other sites in Mecca (*ghayra dhālik min mawāḍi' Makka*), he is not bound at all (*lā yakūn 'alay-hi shay'*).
[Saḥnūn:] What of one who swears, saying, I commit myself to walking to *bayt allāh* or the Ka'ba or the Ḥaram or Ṣafā or Marwa or the Haṭīm or the Stone or Qu'ayqa'ān or one of the hills of the sacred area (*ba'ḍu jibāl*

[41] For which see Kister, ' You shall only set out for three mosques ', *Le Muséon*, 82, 1969; (also in *idem*, *Studies in Jahiliyya and early Islam*, London, 1980).
[42] Shāfi'ī, vol. 2, 230.

> *al-ḥaram*) or other sites in Mecca, what of one who swears thus and becomes *ḥānith?* Must he go or not?
> [Ibn al-Qāsim:] I am of the opinion that a man who swears on the basis of walking anywhere other than Mecca or the Ka'ba or the Mosque or the Bayt, he is not bound.[43]

Here, whole lists of oaths are deemed non-binding because they do not adequately reflect the emerging juristic consensus on the terminology and topology of pilgrimage. And again, it is worth noting: the motive for juristic consideration of these formulae is not that systematic concern for words or logic which affected Shaybānī when he discussed vows in his *Jāmi'*. These are, rather, responses to practice. We may imagine that at least some people, some of the time, when they bound themselves to walking to the holy land of Mecca, did so with specific concern for this site or that (Dhū Ṭuwā or Ṣafā or one of the hills nearby) rather than for the particular complex of rituals and sites that was endorsed by the emerging juristic consensus. Shāfi'ī agreed with the Mālikī tradition in deeming that vows to go to single sites must be construed either as implying pilgrimage proper or as not binding.

4.9. If a man swears (*nadhara*) to go to a place within the *ḥaram* area, whether walking or riding, then he must approach the *ḥaram* as a pilgrim performing *ḥajj* or *'umra*. If he swears to go to ' Arafat or Marrā ' (*sic*) or a place near the *ḥaram* which is not [part of the] *ḥaram*, he is not bound to anything because this constitutes an oath (*nadhr*) to do something which is not *ṭa'a*.[44]

It is clear that the jurists did not acknowledge the binding power of oaths where the actions to which they bound were in conflict with (or simply liable to compromise) other rulings deemed superior. In particular, practices associated with pilgrimage and deemed to be *farḍ* were not to be compromised by (e.g. ascetic) practices that were not accepted. And specification of sites that were either only part of the accepted ritual complex or external to it was also not accepted. The movement of thought for and against ascetic practices, for and against pilgrimage to sites other than Mecca, for and against the emergence of local sites in or near Mecca, is of course reflected also in Tradition literature.[45]

Of the historical background implied by these rules, all that can safely be said is that some people, some of the time, around the year 800, swore oaths of the types that were forbidden. I do not feel it necessary to assume that the jurists are defending the established pre-eminence of Mecca as a centre of pilgrimage. It seems to me that they are creating that pre-eminence. The historical development that I would propose (as a tentative hypothesis) has its key in the general acceptance that all mosques were *bayt allāh*. Vows to walk to *bayt allāh* could always be construed as local.

4.10. [Saḥnūn:] If a man says, I commit myself to walking to *bayt allāh* intending (*yanwī*) thereby some mosque or other (*masjid min al-masājid*), is this intention valid according to Mālik? [Ibn al-Qāsim] said: Yes.

4.11. [Shāfi'ī:] If he vows to walk to *bayt allāh*, and has no particular intention (*niyya*) [at the time] then he may choose to walk to *bayt allāh al-ḥarām*

[43] Saḥnūn, vol. 2, 230; cf. vol. 3, 87–8.
[44] Shāfi'ī, vol. 7, 63, line 15.
[45] 'Abd al-Razzāq records Traditions where Hirā' is the site of ascetic practices (*Kitāb al-aymān w'al-nudhūr*, no. 15824; cf. no. 15858, which records a similar practice associated simply with a hill, *jabal*, vol. 8).

(i.e. Mecca); but that is not incumbent unless he expresses this intention (*illā an yanwī-hi*), for mosques are *buyūt allāh* (*al-masājid buyūt allāh*).[46]

In the immediately following sentence Shāfi'ī disallows the formula *masjid miṣr*: a vow incorporating that phrase is not binding. This is a complex resolution whereby vows specifying *bayt allāh* may be construed as referring to local mosques or to Mecca; but vows specifying any other mosque are disallowed (with the partial exception of Jerusalem and Medina). Now, I would imagine that the actual practice of binding oneself to walk to mosques was both local and regional (Jerusalem, Mecca, Medina, perhaps also Kufa, Damascus *et al.* See Kister, op. cit., at note 41 above). Only gradually, as a result of processes political, social, juristic, etc. did there emerge a single pre-eminent centre. Likewise, I would imagine that within and near Mecca there were a number of separate, independent, holy sites which only gradually became established as a pattern or sequence in the form we now know.[47] The *fuqahā'* did not challenge the status of local mosques as a legitimate object of vows because these were no threat to the preferred mosques. Presumably, as soon as a local mosque gained regional status, they would disallow it (hence Shāfi'ī's objection to vows specifying *masjid miṣr*).

In this section I have tried to provide illustrations of the tendency of the *fuqahā'* to deny the binding power of oaths when they bind to actions that conflict with or compromise rulings given a higher priority. I hope that I have also shown that juristic rulings are responses to social practice and that they provide, albeit obscurely, some indication of some forms of actual practice at the time these books were written or compiled. Now, religious practices to which one might bind oneself by oath included not only pilgrimage but also prayer, fasting, alms and *jihād*, all of which were also recognized as, in certain circumstances, *farḍ*, duties. Anomalous, therefore, in this respect is the practice of *i'tikāf* (seclusion?) which was never accepted by the jurists as a *farḍ*, but proved acceptable to them as a duty which only became *wājib* as the result of an oath.[48] Works of *fiqh* are characteristically uncertain whether *i'tikāf* must include fasting and abstinence from sexual relations or merely might include these things. There was agreement that it could only take place in a mosque, preferably in a *masjid jāmi'*. I would be inclined to see this as product of juristic structuring imposed upon a less controlled practice which was not originally restricted to mosques. In a Tradition recorded by Shāfi'ī, we read that 'Ā'isha practised *i'tikāf* on Thabīr, one of the hills near Mecca.[49] This indicates that in the early ninth century it was possible to conceive of someone practising *i'tikāf* on a hill near Mecca, in spite of a juristic tendency acting against this practice. Perhaps, in the early ninth century, at least some people did so practise *i'tikāf*.

Closely related to the practice of *i'tikāf* was that of *jiwar*. In the developed

[46] Saḥnūn, vol. 2, 230 and Shāfi'ī vol. 7, 63, line 5.

[47] See further Hava Lazarus Yaveh, *Some religious aspects of Islam: a collection of articles*, Leiden, 1981, ch. ii, 'The religious dialectics of the *hadjdj*', p. 21. *ad* n. 11. The gradual emergence of Mecca as the Muslim sanctuary, and the attraction to that sanctuary of features (proper names, stories, myths) which had emerged elsewhere is the theme of G. R. Hawting, 'The origins of the Muslim sanctuary at Mecca', in G. H. A. Juynboll (ed.), *Studies in the first century of Islamic society*, Southern Illinois University Press, 1982; and *idem*, 'The disappearance and rediscovery of Zamzam and the "well of Ka'ba" ', *BSOAS*, XLIII, 1, 1980. Also relevant, if only in a very general way, is the model of community development proposed by John Wansbrough in *Quranic studies*, Oxford, 1977 and in *The sectarian milieu*, Oxford, 1978.

[48] See e.g. Shāfi'ī, vol. 2, 92, line 6: *wa-'l-i'tikāf al-wājib an yaqūl lilāhi 'alayya an a'takif kadhā wa-kadhā* ... Cf. also below *ad* 4.10 (*c*).

[49] ibid., vol. 7, 57, line 22. Women, slaves and travellers were allowed by Shāfi'ī to practise *i'tikāf* wherever they wished as they were not bound to attend Friday Prayer (whereas a man would have to leave his place of *i'tikāf* to go the *masjid jāmi'*).

juristic tradition all mention of a practice named *jiwār* has been obliterated except (as far as I have been able to ascertain) for a short passage in the *Mudawwana* and a brief reference in the *Muwaṭṭa'*.

4.10.

(*a*) Mālik: If a man vows with regard to [a certain number of] days that he will perform *i'tikāf* in them, that vow is binding (*lazima-hu dhālika 'l-nadhr*).

(*b*) Mālik: *I'tikāf* and *jiwār* are the same (*sawā'*). Except with respect to one who vows an act such as the *jiwār* of Mecca (*nadhara mithla jiwāri makka*), whereby he performs *jiwār* during the day (*yujāwir al-nahār*) and returns at night to his own home. He said: One who performs *jiwār* of this kind, whereby he returns to his own home at night, is not bound to include fasting in his *jiwār*.

(*c*) [Saḥnūn:] Did Mālik require a man, if that man performed *jiwār* in Mecca, if he expressed intention to do so, did Mālik require him to undertake *jiwār* on the basis of intention (*niyya*)? [Mālik] said: No, [*jiwār* becomes required] only if he vows it (*nadhara*). If he vows to perform *jiwār*, and intends not *i'tikāf* but the *jiwār* that I have described, returning at night to his own home as do the *mujāwirūn* at Mecca, that is binding.

(*d*) Ibn al-Qāsim: The *jiwār* of Mecca is a practice whereby one becomes near to God, like *ribāṭ* and fasting.

(*e*) [Saḥnūn:] If a man swears to perform the *jiwār* of a mosque similar to the *jiwār* of Mecca, but not in Mecca? [Ibn al-Qāsim] replied: That oath is binding in whichever district he is, if he lives in that district. But if he is not living there, Ibn al-Qāsim stated, in the context of oaths (? *fi rasm ḥilf*): If a man vows to perform fasting in a place such as Iraq or such-like, a place wherein there is no nearness to God (*qurba*), then he should fast where he made the vow. [i.e. he should not travel to the designated place.]

(*f*) Mālik said: If a man swears to fast in one of the *sawāḥil* such as Alexandria or Ascalon or Jerusalem, even if he is from Mecca or Medina [? he should go].
He said: As to every coastal town or place where it is possible to come near to God, I consider that he should fast, as specified, in the place which he mentioned in his vow, even if he is from Mecca or Medina.[50]

This is about as much as can be learnt from the printed redaction of the *Mudawwana* about *jiwār*. In the *Muwaṭṭa'*, which is much more stringently redacted than the *Mudawwana*, the discussion is reduced to one sentence: *i'tikāf* and *jiwār* are the same, *al-i'tikāf wa-'l-jiwār sawā'*.[51]

Jiwār, then, is a technical term covering roughly the same semantic field as *i'tikāf*. But it has a specialized meaning, referring to a practice specifically associated with Mecca. This practice implies involvement during the day and return to one's house at night. It does not require fasting (*b*). It could only become binding as the result of a vow (*c*). Ibn al-Qāsim permitted the specialized kind of *jiwār*, the so-called *jiwār* of Mecca, in a mosque outside of Mecca (*e*). At this point the redactor introduces a flurry of views (*e* and *f*) from Ibn al-Qāsim and from Mālik on vows to fast when they involve a travelling component.[52] These views are designed to respond to the problem of vows to

[50] Saḥnūn, vol. 1, 232.
[51] Mālik, *Muwaṭṭa'*, 214.
[52] These are of course discrete rulings juxtaposed here and so rendered relevant, but borrowed from another context; cf. 4.6 (*d*) above.

perform *jiwār*, when they contain a travelling component. Ibn al-Qāsim and Mālik are at odds. The *jiwār* of Mecca as discussed at (*a*)–(*e*) does not include any reference to mosques. It is therefore strictly impossible to say on the basis of this evidence where this *jiwār* took place. Subsequent discussion of *i'tikāf* does specify mosques as the appropriate site for this practice. The disappearance of the word, *jiwār*, from other works of *fiqh* of roughly the same period must be due to redactional activity. The Mālikī tradition ruled that *i'tikāf* involved fasting and abstinence from sexual intercourse.[53]

The development of a juristic theory of *i'tikāf* reflects certain tensions. As an item of current practice the jurists did not condone it wholeheartedly. They did not make it mandatory and they could argue strongly that it was not part of established tradition.[54] This distrust may be due to its ascetic connotations; for, as we have seen, the jurists had a general distrust of ascetic practice. The Mālikī tradition preserved its association with fasting and abstinence; (*hadīth* literature suggests practices more extreme). But Shāfi'ī removed even these moderately ascetic aspects. There was general agreement on restricting permissible sites of *i'tikāf* to only Friday mosques. Practice was perhaps both more ascetic and less restricted. The term *jiwār* indicated either the same as or a specialized form of *i'tikāf*. These were practices to which Muslims could commit themselves by vow.

5.

In this section I shall be concerned with the term *taḥannatha*. This term, it must be admitted, does not occur in works of *fiqh*. These works demonstrate the existence of verb-forms *ḥanitha, aḥnatha* and *hannatha*. The last two are technical terms of jurisprudence meaning 'to consider or declare someone *ḥānith*'. Shāfi'ī, in the course of an argument, refers to one or some jurists with whom he disagrees as *man ḥannatha-hu,* those who consider him or declare him to be *ḥānith.*[55] Works of *fiqh* are, however, only a tiny part of a linguistic iceberg: the non-appearance of *taḥannatha* is not significant. Kister has shown that the word is not so very rare in *ḥadīth* literature.

And indeed, bearing in mind the connotations I have set out, perhaps it is not so very obscure.

> The Prophet used to perform *jiwār* in Ḥirā' for a month every year. This was a practice to which Quraysh made themselves liable by vows (*taḥannatha*) when they were still ignorant of Islam (*fī 'l-jāhiliyya*), etc.[56]

This passage contains no concepts which would not be recognizable and comprehensible to a ninth-century audience. Even if that audience has read or heard nothing but the discussions of *fiqh,* and thereby missed the verb *taḥannatha,* they would naturally perform a familiar linguistic exercise in reading a *tafa''ala* verb-form as the reflexive-passive of a *fa''ala* form. This could give no other meaning here than 'to make oneself *ḥānith*' and we know that he who binds himself by oath to carry out a particular act makes himself

[53] Saḥnūn, vol. 1, 236–7.

[54] ibid., 237. Mālik points out that no eminent figure, neither Abū Bakr nor 'Umar, 'Uthmān, Ibn Musayyib, Ibn 'Umar, etc., has ever practised *i'tikāf.*

[55] In present tense form, it is of course impossible to distinguish *aḥnatha* and *ḥannatha*, hence my selection of a past tense item to demonstrate Shāfi'ī's usage, vol. 7, 73, line 3. See also 66, line 7 (*inna-hum tuḥannithūna-hu*) and line 29 (*innama anẓur ila makhraj al-yamīn thumma uḥannithu ṣāḥiba-ha aw ubirru-hu,* I consider the outcome of the oath then declare the swearer *ḥānith* or *birr*). The *Mudawwana* prefers *aḥnatha*, vol. 3, 115, *li-mā aḥnathta-hu*, why have you declared him *ḥānith*?; see also e.g. 137, line 4 and 139, line 14.

[56] Ibn Hishām, *al-Sīra al-nabawiyya*, Beirut, 1975 (4 vols.); vol. 1, 218. See also Kister, '*Al-taḥannuth*', p. 223 and edition cited there at n. 1.

ḥānith. We further know that *jiwār* is a technical term more or less equivalent to *i'tikāf*. It implies absence from home and attendance in a holy place. *Fiqh*-works restrict permissible places to mosques, but this, I have surmised, is a normative tendency acting against popular practice (which recognized *i'tikaf* e.g. in Thabīr, a hill, like Hirā', near Mecca). *I'tikāf/jiwār* also included fasting and abstinence from sexual intercourse, mandatorily according to the Mālikī tradition. The tendency amongst some *fuqahā'* to make these ascetic elements optional is part of a consistent juristic distaste for asceticism. Actual practice of *i'tikāf* in the ninth century no doubt included fasting during the day, sexual abstinence (which *pace* Kister does not require complete avoidance of one's wife)[57] and a general turning away from the normal exigencies of daily life. We read in this passage that this was a practice to which Quraysh made themselves liable by vows; and it was conceded by the *fuqahā'* that *i'tikāf/jiwār* only became binding as the result of a vow. Mālik had specifically denied that *jiwār* could become binding on the basis of *niyya* (intention)—presumably because *niyya* was a technical term describing formal preparation to perform a *farḍ*, and *jiwār* was not a *farḍ*: it became mandatory as the result of a vow, *nadhr*.

Everything then makes sense. The life and activities of the Prophet are described by the story-tellers of the late eighth and early ninth centuries in terms of concepts and practices familiar to them and to their audience. The Prophet performs *jiwār* because this was an act of ascetic piety familiar to an Arabic-speaking audience around the year 800. He goes to Ḥirā' because visiting the hills near Mecca, as holy places, is a practice known to that audience. Quraysh are described as binding themselves by oaths (*taḥannatha*) because this is the normal, indeed the only way of imposing *jiwār/i'tikāf*, around the year 800. And, perhaps, the practice is described as part of the *jāhiliyya* because it was already evident that these contemporary practices of the early ninth century were being left behind as normative Islam developed in other directions.

Kister points to a number of parallel versions of the story in which this episode in the prophet's life is variously realized as *tanassaka* (*ad* n. 20), *i'takafa* (n. 27) and *nadhara an ya'takifa* (n. 26). These variants have of course nothing to do with historical facts, not at least historical facts of the seventh century. Variant versions of a particular narrative incident reflect the milieu of oral narrative out of which were crystallized the fixed forms in which these narratives have come down to us. The primary characteristics of oral narrative, as is well known, are the absence of a fixed form and the creative originality of every version. The story-teller elaborates his narrative in response to the demands of the occasion, the audience, the mood, etc.[58] Of the versions that once existed one must assume that only a few have survived, perhaps only a pale reflection of a version in performance. It is clear none the less that the story-tellers relied upon contemporary concepts and practices to recreate the life of the Prophet. And the concepts they preferred for this event were *jiwār* and *i'tikāf*, which, we know, are synonyms.

It will be necessary to make a few comments about the more difficult of the passages assembled by Kister in which the word *taḥannatha* occurs. First, however, in order to further establish the meaning of the word it will be useful to

[57] Kister, op. cit., 230. Curiously, Kister also denies that *taḥannuth* (as he conceives of it) could include fasting, since the Prophet used to take provisions. But he forgets the Muslim concept of fasting: the Mālikī tradition enjoins fasting as an element of *i'tikāf*, from dawn to dusk in the usual way (Saḥnūn, vol. 1, 225). Fasting did not mean starving to death.

[58] See A. B. Lord, *The Singer of Tales*, Cambridge, Mass., 1960. See also my comments on oral tradition in 'From midrash to scripture: the sacrifice of Abraham in early Islamic tradition', in *Le Muséon*, 101, (ii), 1988.

cite the only easily accessible Tradition in which the word occurs to which Kister does not refer. It appears in Bukhārī.

> 'Ā'isha related that 'Abdallah b. Zubayr said, concerning a sale or a gift that 'Ā'isha was donating, By God, 'Ā'isha shall most certainly desist or, I shall most certainly prevent her. She said, Did he say that? They said, Yes. She said, By God, I commit myself by oath (*nadhran*) that I shall not talk to Ibn al-Zubayr ever again. Ibn al-Zubayr pleaded with her [through intermediaries] when he had been neglected for a long time [*ṭāla hijratu-hu*]. But she said, No, by God, I shall not be conciliated in this matter ever, nor shall I .... my oath (*wa-lā ataḥannathu ilā nadhrī*).[59]

The story has a happy ending, for the estranged heroes are brought together and 'Ā'isha performs atonement by emancipating a slave (*a'taqat fī nadhri-hā*). All parties acknowledge that a Muslim should not swear an oath of this kind, for the Prophet forbad it. We have, since the time of Schacht's *Origins*,[60] become familiar with the fact that legal Traditions are generally a response to (not a cause of) juristic dispute. This Tradition neatly encapsulates in narrative form the juristic problem which we earlier saw Shāfi'ī deal with in normative form (*ad* 3.2 above). Muslims must not swear oaths not to talk to their companions and, if they do so, they must free themselves from such an oath by atonement. Since Shāfi'ī also developed the view that one need not perform atonement in cases of this kind, one would expect to find Traditions embodying this view too.

This Tradition is not cited in the earliest works of *fiqh*.

The phrase *wa-lā ataḥannathu ilā nadhrī* must mean: I shall not make myself *ḥānith* in respect of my oath. It is to be recalled that 'Ā'isha has sworn a negative oath: she is therefore not *ḥānith* unless or until she breaks it. When she says she will not be conciliated, she means that she will not be persuaded to break her oath, she will not make herself *ḥānith*. *Taḥannatha* means to make oneself *ḥānith*, that is, liable in respect of an oath, and this situation may be created either by swearing a positive oath or by breaking a negative oath or failing to fulfil a positive oath or becoming liable to a conditional oath.

It is perfectly easy in most instances of the verb *taḥannatha* assembled by Kister to read it as having the meaning I propose. In the light of one or two rather difficult cases, however, I would like to concede the possibility that the word may indeed be one of the *aḍdād*, meaning not only to make oneself *ḥānith* but also to rid oneself of *ḥinth*.[61] At present, it seems to me largely a matter of taste whether one considers this meaning likely or necessary. But, once conceded, it becomes almost impossible to distinguish, in any given case, which meaning is intended.

In a variety of instances Kister notes that the concept *taḥannuthu* is closely related to that of *birr* and its derivatives *tabarrur* and *abarra*.[62] In all cases he interprets these words as denoting or connoting ' piety '. Now, I certainly would not claim that it is always possible to disentangle the conceptual reference of the root *birr*, above all when it is used in close association with words connoting vows. However, I would be most unwilling to concede that ' piety ' is the most likely aspect of the root to spring to mind in a context close to *taḥannatha*. In

[59] Bukhārī, *Saḥīḥ*, Cairo, 1313 (9 vols.), vol. 8, 22.

[60] Joseph Schacht, *The origins of Muhammadan jurisprudence*, Oxford, 1950.

[61] See Kister, *'Al-taḥannuth*, 227, *ad* n. 24. One such difficult case is the version of Balādhurī (Kister, *ad* n. 21). Feeding the poor, frequently associated with *taḥannuth* is one of the more important ways of removing *ḥinth;* it is a mode of *kaffāra*, see n. 8 above.

[62] ibid., 226 *ad* n. 18 and 234–5. Kister is led to believe that *taḥannuth* is identical with *birr*. But the semantic complexity of this word precludes any conclusion so easy.

the passage cited above from Ibn Isḥāq, I proposed the translation, ' [*jiwār*] was a practice to which Quraysh made themselves liable by vows . . .' The current text of Ibn Isḥāq provides a gloss at this point, indicating that *taḥannuth* is the equivalent of *tabarrur*. I would assume that the glossator knew what he was doing and that he was more familiar than us with the semantic possibilities of the root *birr*. If he did not actually know the work of Shāfi'ī (where *tabarrur* denotes a kind of religiously approved oath) then he must have known the wider linguistic usage from which Shāfi'ī derived his usage. I would imagine then that, in stating that *taḥannatha* meant *tabarrara*, the glossator intended to convey that *taḥannatha* meant to make an oath or to bind oneself by oath, and specifically by that kind of oath designated a *tabarrur*, meaning acceptable in form and binding. Later commentators (or other commentators), finding *taḥannatha* glossed as *tabarrara*, misunderstood the connotations of the latter word (for it also undoubtedly was related to the concept *birr* = piety) and so provided the supergloss or alternative gloss *ta'abbud*. This I think was an error. None the less, out of this erroneous gloss there developed the lexical tradition that makes *taḥannatha* equivalent to *ta'abbada*.

(At the risk of multiplying hypotheses which can perhaps never be confirmed, it may be worth considering that *tabarrara* as used by Ibn Isḥāq's glossator has, not the extended meaning found in Shāfi'ī, but the natural semantic implications of a *tafa''ala* verb form; i.e. *tabarrara* means ' to make oneself *birr* ' that is ' to free oneself of *ḥinth* '. In this case, the intention of the glossator is to convey that *taḥannatha* here, being one of the *aḍdād*, means not to bind oneself by oath, but to free oneself from oath liability. In this case it becomes necessary to consider the ritual of *jiwār* at Ḥirā' as an act of atonement. That a particular ritual act might constitute a bloc-cleansing of accumulated liability (whether due to not fulfilling a positive or violating a negative vow) is not unknown to Semitic religious practice.) [63]

Kister notes that there is a group of Traditions relating to Ḥakīm b. Ḥizām b. Khuwaylid in which the verb *taḥannatha* appears a number of times.[64] The whole group of Traditions [65] constitutes a picture of a man, a trader, who is good, pious, participates in the rituals of the Ka'ba, is probably monotheist but is not initially Muslim. He is a Jāhilī Arab and the question he symbolizes is: How does a good Jāhilī stand when he becomes a Muslim? The question is characteristically transposed into a historical and diachronic form: Ḥakīm lived 60 years in the Jāhiliyya and 60 years in Islam. But the relevance is of course contemporary and synchronic (and perennial). In the late eighth and ninth centuries there were Jāhilīs (Arabic-speaking peoples, participating in traditional religious practices, perhaps monotheist) who, on cleaving to the developing religion of Islam, wanted to know whether their previous good actions counted to their credit. The good actions that were in question were such as participation in the rituals of Mecca, including the sacrifice of animals (nos. 630, 648), the emancipation of slaves (648, 637), alms-giving (637—*ṣadaqa*, 631—*ṣilat raḥm*, 644, 645 *et al.*), and other forms of generalized good action (e.g. at 631, *kāna yaf'alu 'l-ma'rūf*). It is noteworthy that Ḥakīm is frequently portrayed

[63] Consider the evening prayer of the Jewish Day of Atonement (see *Encyclopaedia Judaica*, s.v. '*kol nidrei* '). ' All vows, obligations, oaths or anathemas . . . which we shall have vowed, sworn, devoted or bound ourselves to, from this day of atonement, until the next day of atonement . . . we repent aforehand of them all; they shall all be deemed absolved, forgiven, annulled, void and made of no effect.'

[64] Kister, ' *Al-taḥannuth* ', 233.

[65] A representative group of such Traditions is conveniently gathered in Zubayr b. Bakkār, *Jamharat nasab Quraysh*, Cairo, 1381/1961, 353–77. In the following discussion I have referred to the Traditions by the numbers given them in this edition.

as binding himself by vows, e.g. at nos. 639, 641, 642 and 648. If it is acknowledged that *taḥannatha* also means to bind oneself by vows, one may add nos. 637, 645 and 654. I would translate at no. 637, *ashyā' kuntu ataḥannathu bi-hā,* as ' things to which I used to bind myself by vow . . . such as alms-giving, emancipation of slaves, helping relatives . . .'. And at no. 645, *kullu mā rabihtu taḥannathtu bi-hi,* as ' all my profits, I bound myself by vow in respect of them (sc. to donate them as charity, etc.) '.[66]

I am tempted to infer from this group of Traditions in conjunction with the evidence of the *fiqh* works (Sections 1 to 4 above) that in the late eighth and early ninth centuries popular religious practice amongst the Arabic-speaking community included, as a significant if not a major component, the practice of self-commitment by vows to established religious and pious practices. And, further, that the transition to formal/juristic Islam was characterized by a displacement of vow-orientated activities towards a more peripheral position (in the practical expression of religious commitment).

In two Traditions Ḥakīm is portrayed as deeply concerned with *birr;* at no. 631, *kāna . . . yaḥuḍḍu 'alā 'l-birr* and, at no. 644, *kuntu u'āliju 'l-birr. Birr* certainly means piety; but it also means the state of freedom from oath-liability that is achieved after one has carried out an action to which one has bound oneself. And it means the act of fulfilling (clearing) an oath (*birr yamīna-ka*). In view of the frequency of oath-related concepts in the biography of Ḥakīm, I would prefer to translate e.g. the words cited for no. 644 as ' I took great pains to fulfil [my oaths] ' or ' to achieve freedom from oath liability ' [*sc.* by carrying out actions to which I had bound myself, etc.]. Since *birr* may further have the more general connotation of ' freedom from liability (oath- or sin-liability) ' or simply ' purity ' one might read Ḥakīm's concern for *birr* as a general concern for purity. This he achieved by actions which were recognized as having a purifying effect: feeding the poor, emancipating slaves, etc. The term for such actions came to be (probably under Jewish influence?) *kaffāra*, atonement. By *kaffāra* one achieved (or re-achieved) the status of *birr* (purity, freedom from liability), a status which could be interrupted by oath-liability, sin-liability or the liability incurred when one broke the natural bonds of family life (*'uqūq*).

In this essay I have tried to analyse the meaning and the connotations of concepts that occur in literature of the late eighth and early ninth centuries. Some of these connotations have not been noted by Western scholars; some, indeed, have been very nearly eliminated from the Arabic lexical tradition. The elimination of certain semantic strands from the tradition is due to pressures arising out of the development of new connotations as the words were squeezed and moulded by the academic traditions of jurisprudence, theology and exegesis (not to mention, what is almost invisible to us, social practice). Of the processes involved I have studied here only a few, and those only partially. In many specific instances (especially in Tradition literature, which is much less structurally controlled than *fiqh* literature) I am unable to offer a decisive suggestion as to what meaning was intended. Perhaps in the telling of a story it did not much matter whether *taḥannatha* or *tabarrara* meant to bind oneself by oath or to free oneself from *ḥinth* (for both seem to mean both) since each of these actions implied, in any case, an act of conspicuous piety, whether of ritual form (*jiwār, i'tikāf, ḥajj*) or of social charity (alms-giving, emancipation). These were actions to which one might bind oneself, or by which one might free oneself

[66] Granting that *taḥannatha* is one of the *aḍdād*, one might also try, for 637, ' things whereby I used to free myself from *ḥinth* ' (i.e. from oath- or sin-liability) . . . such as alms-giving . . .'; and, for 645, ' all the profits I made I dedicated to freeing myself from *ḥinth* . . .'. Cf. nn. 8, 61 and 63 above.

from the liabilities one had incurred (whether by oath, by sin or by duties (e.g. filial) unfulfilled).

I need hardly point out that by demonstrating that the word *birr* means to be free of liability (or to be pure or clear) I have brought it into semantic parity with its Hebrew cognate. The development from there to *birr* = piety or dutifulness seems to me initially a natural development, but in time so buttressed by the needs of a theological tradition that its earlier connotations were largely lost.

Concepts of the late eighth and early ninth centuries reflect the social and academic situation of that period. Writers and scholars used available concepts to describe and control their world, and, naturally, to describe and create (or re-create) the life of their prophet and his contemporaries. Professor M. J. Kister's masterly and fascinating studies of early *ḥadīth* are all infused with the conviction that the elucidation of a concept will illuminate history. He is, of course, correct. I am not convinced that the history in question will be that of events that occurred more than 150 years prior to the establishment of the texts which are the object of our study.[67]

[67] I should like to thank G. R. Hawting and A. Rippin who criticized and commented upon an earlier draft of this paper.

Major sources

(*a*)
Kister, M. J. '*Al-taḥannuth:* an inquiry into the meaning of a term', *BSOAS*, xxxi, 2, 1968, 223–236. (Repr. in Kister, *Studies in Jāhiliyya and early Islam*, London, 1980.)

(*b*)
'Abd al-Razzāq al-Ṣan'ānī, *Al-Muṣannaf*, 11 vols., Beirut, 1390/1970.
Mālik b. Anas, Abū 'Abdallah, *Al-Muwaṭṭa'*, (ed., Aḥmad Rātib 'Armūsh), Beirut, 1404/1984 (8th edition).
Saḥnūn, *Al-Mudawwana al-Kubrā*, 16 vols., Cairo, 1323–4.
Al-Shāfi'ī, Muḥammad b. Idrīs, *Kitāb al-Umm*, 7 vols., Cairo, 1388/1968, (reprint of 1321 edition).
Al-Shaybānī, Muḥammad b. Ḥasan, *Kitāb al-Jāmi' al-Kabīr*, (ed. A.-W. al-Afghani), Cairo, 1356.
Al-Shaybānī, Muḥammad b. Ḥasan, *Kitāb al-Aṣl*, 3 vols., (ed. A.-W. al-Afghani), Hyderabad, 1386/1966.

(*Note:* Mālik died in 179, Saḥnūn in 240, Shāfi'ī in 204 and Shaybānī in 189. The form certainly and a good deal of the content of the works attributed to Mālik, Shāfi'ī and Shaybānī result, I think, from an ongoing school tradition. In spite of this I have, in this essay, referred to the contents of these works as if they were authored by Mālik, Shāfi'ī, etc.)

VII

FROM MIDRASH TO SCRIPTURE: THE SACRIFICE OF ABRAHAM IN EARLY ISLAMIC TRADITION

> Each performance is the specific song, and at the same time it is the generic song. The song we are listening to is «the song»; for each performance is more than a performance, it is a re-creation... Both synchronically and historically there would be numerous creations and re-creations of the song(*).

> Thus there may exist provisional origins, which practically and in fact form the first beginnings of the particular tradition held by a given community, folk or communion of faith; and memory, though sufficiently instructed that the depths have not actually been plumbed, yet nationally may find reassurance in some primitive point of time and, personally and historically speaking, come to rest there(**).

The origins of this story or that are indeed not accessible though they may, for convenience, be sited here or there. The Muslims of course found the origins of the story of Abraham's sacrifice in the Qur'an but that was provisional, and the best of their scholars at least were indeed sufficiently instructed to recognise other origins and, overtly or covertly, to appeal to older versions for the establishment of details[1]. For them, as for us, the oldest version of this story, available in fixed form, was *Genesis* 22. Crystallised there out of an indeterminate oral past, and invested with authority, that version imposed no doubt a steadying pattern upon the continuing oral tradition. But, being fixed, it no longer bent to the demands, social or literary, that were put upon it. In synagogues and churches, in academies and schools, the story was re-dissolved and re-moulded to diverse purposes in Hebrew and Aramaic, in Greek and Syriac, as *Midrash* or *Targum*, as commentary, homily or

(*) A. B. Lord, *The Singer of Tales*, Cambridge, Mass., 1960, p. 101.

(**) Th. Mann, *Joseph and his Brothers* (Penguin Modern Classics), U.K., 1978, p. 3.

[1] Ibn Qutayba, *Kitāb al-Ma'ārif*, Beirut, 1390/1970, p. 17, appeals to the *Torah* for identification of the victim. Abū Jaf'ar al-Ṭabarī, *Jāmi' al-bayān 'an ta'wīl āy al-Qur'ān*, Cairo, 1373/1954, vol. 23, *ad* 37:107, p. 85-86 (hereafter Ṭabarī, *Jāmi' al-Bayān*), also recognises that it was Isaac but argues on the basis of context and cross-reference in the Quranic text.

history, and no doubt, still, in market places and street corners, as popular tale and sermon[2]. In the course of the 7th century when Arabic speaking peoples found themselves ruling the ancient polyglot culture of the Near East, and came thereby to constitute a new market and a new demand for story, old cycles were new-translated, amongst them the tales of the patriarchs and prophets of the Old Testament. Something of that process of Arabisation may be illustrated, for the Biblical tales, by reference to the extensive antiquarian activity of Muslim scholars in the 9th century, scholars who collected in the form of Traditions (*aḥādīth*) snippets and fragments of what the community recalled or ascribed or invented or preserved and deemed relevant to their understanding of religion. Many versions may be found of the story of Abraham's sacrifice in collections whose purpose was avowedly scriptural (Quranic) exegesis, and whose context was therefore academic[3]. These are the versions which, for the most part, I cite in this essay. But the continuing tradition of popular narrative may best be seen in that version reported on the authority of Ka'b in Kisā'ī's *Qiṣaṣ al-anbiyā'*[4]: that version has a charm, an exuberance and a pathos not to be found in the scholarly versions. It demonstrates, in some degree of contrast to the versions I shall cite, all the processes of expansion, elaboration and ornamentation that may be recognised as part of oral creativity (which is also literary creation)[5]. It is however with the scholarly tradition that this paper is concerned and it is from that tradition that I offer a small

[2] For the development of this story in Christian and Jewish tradition, see D. LERCH, *Isaaks Opferung christlich gedeutet* (*Beiträge zur historischen Theologie*, 12), Tübingen, 1950; S. SPIEGEL, *The Last Trial*, New York, 1967; G. VERMES, *Scripture and Tradition in Judaism: Haggadic Studies*, Leiden, 1961, ch. 8, *Redemption and Genesis 22* (hereafter: VERMES, *Scripture*); and, for the Syriac Christian tradition, S. BROCK, *Sarah and the Aqedah*, in *Le Muséon*, 87 (1974), p. 67-77; *Genesis 22 in Syriac Tradition*, in P. CASETTI et *al.*, eds, *Mélanges Dominique Barthélemy: études bibliques*, Fribourg and Göttingen, 1981 (hereafter: BROCK, *Genesis 22*); and *Two Syriac verse homilies on the binding of Isaac*, in *Le Muséon*, 99 (1986), p. 61-129. For the Muslim tradition, see Y. MOUBARAC, *Abraham dans le Coran* (*Études Musulmanes*, 5), Paris, 1958.

[3] A convenient encyclopaedia of Traditional material related to *tafsīr* is JALĀL AL-DĪN AL-SUYŪṬĪ's *Al-Durr al-manthūr fī 'l-tafsīr bi-'l-ma'thūr*, Beirut, n.d., 6 vols., (?a reprint of Cairo, 1314) (hereafter: SUYŪṬĪ, *Durr*). I have used it extensively as a source for many of the versions cited in this paper.

[4] MUḤAMMAD IBN ABDALLĀH AL-KISĀ'Ī, *Kitāb Qiṣaṣ al-anbiyā'*, ed. I. EISENBERG, Leiden, 1922-3, 2 vols., vol. 1, p. 150 (hereafter: KISĀ'Ī).

[5] See A. B. LORD, *The Singer of Tales* (*Harvard Studies in Comparative Literature*, 24), Cambridge, Mass., 1960, *passim*, but see especially chap. 5, p. 99-123 (hereafter: LORD, *The Singer*). I hope to demonstrate in what follows that the versions I cite are part of, or product of, a tradition of oral narrative. They are not «sung», nor did they emerge in a milieu free from literary influence. But, pending further development of scholarship in the field of oral literature, the analysis of forms provided by LORD is adequate for the rather elementary purposes of this essay.

selection of sacrifice narratives. I refer to Kisāʾī's version (which it is impossible to date) only to illustrate how certain tendencies could, in appropriate circumstances be developed.

I

Version 1. Source: Ṭabarī, *Jāmiʿ al-Bayān, ad Qurʾān*, 37:102; Suyūṭī, *Durr*, V, 282-3, cited from Ṭabarī and Ibn Abī Ḥātim (d. 327/928). Attributed in both sources to Al-Suddī (d. 128/745). The two sources exhibit minor variations of outline or pointing, and Suyūṭī's version omits two short phrases present in Ṭabarī. The sacrifice is explained as the result of a vow by Abraham; this is differently expressed in the two sources.

[When Abraham heard that he was to be granted a son by Sarah, he swore he would sacrifice the child to God, hence ...]

1. When Isaac grew up
2. Abraham was visited in a dream and told to fulfil his vow ...
3. So he said to Isaac: Let us go and offer sacrifice to God (*inṭaliq nuqarrib qurbān ilā allāh*)
4. He took a knife and a rope and set off with him (*inṭalaq maʿa-hu*) until when he had taken him amongst the hills
5. the youth said: Father, where is your sacrifice (*qurbān*)?
6. He said: My son, I see in a dream that I sacrifice you; consider what is your view? He replied: Father, do as you are commanded; you will find me, God willing, submissive. (*Qurʾān*, 37:102).
7. Then Isaac said to him: Father, bind me tightly lest I tremble. Draw your robe back from me lest it be spattered with my blood, and Sarah see it and be grieved. Draw the knife quickly across my throat so that death be light upon me. When you return to Sarah, give her my greeting.
8. Abraham approached him, kissing him (var. turning him over), having bound him; he was crying and Isaac was crying such that the tears became [like] a swamp on Isaac's cheek (*ḥattā istanqaʿ al-dumūʿ taḥta khadd Isḥāq* — not in Suyūṭī).
9. Then he drew the knife across his throat but the knife did not cut; God had placed a sheet of copper (*nuḥās*) upon Isaac's throat. When he saw that he turned him onto his forehead (jabīnihi) and cut at the back of his neck (*qafā-hu*).
10. Hence [God's] words: When they both submitted, that is, submitted the affair to God. And he threw him down on the *jabīn* (?forehead/hill).

11. There was a call (*nūdiya*): Abraham you have fulfilled the vision, truthfully (*bi-l-ḥaqq, var. bi-Isḥāq*).
12. He turned round and there before him was a ram (*kabash*)...
13. Hence God says: We ransomed him with a great sacrifice...

This passage functions primarily as narrative. There are few formal markers indicating that this is or might be exegesis of an otherwise known text. The inform-accept motif (l. 6) is couched in precise Quranic diction, but is not marked as such. Conversely, at l. 10 and l. 13 there is an introductory formula signalling a quotation from revelation: *dhālika qawlu-hu, li-dhālika yaqūl allāh.* This type of introductory formula, which will be seen again in other versions, characteristically introduces a scriptural (Quranic) segment as commentary on or parallel to a preceding narrative. Another characteristic device, which again will be seen more extensively used below, may be detected at l. 10 where the Quranic text *fa-lammā aslamā* is immediately followed by a parallel phrase which explains (elsewhere repeats, modifies etc.) the text. This too, though not unambiguous, must be recognised as a formal device which signals the presence of a scriptural quote, the latter being always the first of a pair of parallel phrases. The phraseology at l. 11 is almost Quranic, differing in the form of the verb «to call», here *nūdiya*, in contrast to Quranic *nādaynā-hu*. This passage is not marked as scripture. It is to be noted that the passages marked as scripture at l. 10 and l. 13 are secondary; scripture acts as appendage or decorative or comment on a narrative complete in itself. Functionally at least, here, the narrative precedes the scripture.

Of the motifs in this passage some are clear reflexes of Biblical narrative. For example, the youth's question at l. 5 «Where is the sacrifice?» is a reflex of Gen. 22.7. Other motifs, notably the inform-accept motif at l. 6, are Rabbinic not Biblical (and not indeed Christian). Most of Isaac's last requests at l. 7 are also reflexes of Midrashic motifs. The request to be bound, Isaac's worries lest he tremble, his concern for Sarah, his urging haste are all explicitly available in Midrashic sources — though differently motivated and contextualised. The tears at l. 8 are also a Midrashic motif; even the exaggerated Arabic phrase that the tears became like a swamp recalls an equally exaggerated Hebrew expression that Abraham's whole body swam in tears[6]. There is however here no question of translation or of direct

[6] For a general survey of Rabbinic and Christian developments, see the works cited at note 2 above, together with their bibliographies. For specific Midrashic details I have utilised M. M. Kasher, *The Encyclopaedia of Biblical Interpretation*, tr. H. Freedman,

borrowing. These motifs in their present context function solely as elements that heighten drama, pathos and emotional involvement. In an expanded and ornamented version they can become a central item in the story-teller's charge upon the emotions of his audience. Consider Kisā'ī's version:

1. Strip me of my garment lest my loving mother see it and cry long over me.
2. Look to my bonds that they be firm lest I tremble before you and cause you pain.
3. When you place the knife upon my throat turn your face away from me lest pity overcome you and you fail in your task.
4. Seek help from God at my loss.
5. When you return take my garment to my mother that she might find consolation therein.
6. And convey to her from me a greeting ...[7].

This goes on for several more lines. I note in passing that it is characteristic of oral delivery that there should be an unreconciled element of contradiction, between items 1 and 5. Clearly the story-teller has piled up here all the last-requests motifs that he knows; we shall see them recur below. Had he remembered, perhaps, to mention blood at the «strip me of my garment» motif, he might have distinguished better between the function of the garment as an incentive to grief and as a consolation.

In Rabbinic texts these same (or similar) motifs function in the same way, i.e. as having dramatic value; but, there, are demonstrably related to textual or ritual problems that were of particular interest to the Rabbis as expounders of the Torah. In a Rabbinic context the inform-accept motif and the request to be bound were a formal presentation of the fact that Isaac was a willing and a knowing victim — an issue of dogmatic import only within the Judaic tradition. The trembling motif was related to ritual practice and the need for an unblemished victim; and Isaac's concern for Sarah provided a narrative link to Genesis 23 where her death had to be explained[8]. Kisā'ī's version exhibits further motifs which first emerged in a Midrashic context. The request that

New York, 1953. All references hereafter are to KASHER, vol. 3, page number, followed by paragraph number: request to be bound, 144 (52), 146 (65); trembling, 146 (65); concern for Sarah, 143 (50), 144 (52); urging haste, 143 (50); tears, 143 (50), 147 (68).

[7] KISĀ'Ī, vol. 1, p. 151.

[8] KASHER provides two instances where Isaac specifically refers to his mother as likely to die on hearing the news: 143 (50) and 144 (52). For the conditions affecting Rabbinical development of Biblical material, see VERMES, *Scripture*, p. 193-209.

something be taken back to his mother as a consolation is related, for example, to a Rabbinic version that specifies that the ashes be taken back. It recurs at version 6 below. Both the possibility of grief on the part of the father (as a motivation for binding and preventing trembling) and of compassion (as likely to work against the speedy fulfilment of God's command) had emerged in Midrashic materials. Reference to the father's compassion recurs in versions 6, 7 and 8 below[9].

It is further to be noted that the Rabbinic sources contain many technical details and narrative motifs, which had emerged for specific exegetical reasons, which are nowhere transferred into Arabic. What came into Arabic were those details that could serve the purpose of successful dramatic narrative. I do not know of any Midrashic source that expresses concern for Abraham's garments (as at l. 7) or Isaac's (as in Kisā'ī and elsewhere) but the motif may be a reflex of priestly ritual which in at least one Christian Syriac writer became a specific mention of priestly vestments[10]. The motif of the copper plate and that of turning the victim onto his forehead I shall discuss later.

Version 2. Source: Suyūṭī, *Durr*, V, 283-4, cited from ʿAbd ibn Ḥamīd (d. 249/823) and attributed to ʿUthmān ibn Ḥāḍir.

1. When Abraham desired to sacrifice (*yadhbaḥ*) his son Isaac, he left his mother at the Masjid al-Khayf [at Mecca] and took Isaac with him (*dhahaba bi-Isḥāq maʿa-hu*).
2. When he reached (*balagha*) the place where he desired to sacrifice him,
3. Abraham said: Stay behind, you (*ista'khirū minnī*). He took the hand of his son Isaac and took him apart (*ʿazala-hu*).
4. He said: My son, I see in a dream that I sacrifice you; consider, what is your view? Isaac said to him: Father, did my lord command you (?*rbby 'mrk*)? Abraham said: Yes, Isaac. Isaac said: Do as you are commanded; you will find me, God willing, submissive.
5. When they both submitted to God's command and he threw him down (*talla-hu*),
6. Isaac said to his father: Father, bind me tightly lest I lead you astray (?*lā ṭīsh bika*, read *aṭīsh*).
7. There was a call (*nūdiya*): Abraham, you have fulfilled the vision.
8. And the ram came down to him from Thabīr [a hill near Mecca].

[9] Midrashic sources for these motifs, see Kasher, 143 (50), 146 (65) and 147 (68).

[10] Brock, *Genesis 22*, p. 12-13; note 61 there gives further reference to Jewish sources which specify that Abraham was acting as a priest.

This passage contains a certain quantity of Quranic phraseology though none of it is marked as such. The inform-accept motif at 2.4 exhibits precise Quranic phraseology but with the addition of two extra lines which interrupt the Quranic version while adding little to the meaning. The call «You have fulfilled the vision», at 2.7, is again Quranic but introduced by the non-Quranic *nūdiya*. The phrase *lammā aslamā* at 2.5 is Quranic but the following phrase *wa-talla-hu* is shorn of its Quranic complement *li-l-jabīn*.

The contents of the story here exhibit certain peculiarities. The details at 2.3, namely Abraham's addressing a command to an unknown plurality of companions, and his taking the child apart, are reflexes of Gen. 22.5 and/or Midrashic commentary on it. In the process of transmission all other mention of these matters has got lost. At the end of this pericope in the version cited by Suyūṭī there is an additional remark from the original source, Ibn Ḥāḍir. It takes the following form: «Abraham said to his Lord: Which of my two sons am I to sacrifice? And his Lord revealed (*awḥā*): The one most loved by you (*aḥabbu-humā ilay-ka*)». This is of course a reflex of Gen. 22.2 but only as mediated through Midrashic commentary[11]. These strongly Judaic/Rabbinic elements of the story are set in a context, provided at 2.1 and 2.8, which reflects the influence of Meccan sanctuary tradition. In fact, as is well known, within the Islamic scholastic tradition (though not necessarily outside of it, cf. Kisā'ī) the geographical setting of this story was dictated by its use to justify the Meccan sanctuary and some of its rites. The (independent) attraction of Isma'īl narratives into this same setting ultimately affected the sacrifice story and caused a change in identity of the victim, from Isaac to Isma'īl. This feature is evident in the next version.

Version 3. Source: Suyūṭī, *Durr*, V, 281; cited from Al-Ḥākim (? al-Nīsāpūrī) (d. 405/1014) and attributed to 'Aṭā' ibn Yasār (c. 100/718).

['Aṭā' asked Kuwāt ibn Jubayr about the identity of the victim and he replied:]

1. Isma'īl; when he reached (*balagha*) seven years old, Abraham saw in a dream that he sacrificed him;
2. this was at his house in Syria — so he rode to him on Burāq until he came to him and found him with his mother.
3. He took him by the hand and set off with him (*maḍā bi-hi*) to do what he had been commanded.

[11] Kasher, 133 (17).

4. The devil came in the form of a man etc. [This story is not completed in this source; there is according to Suyūṭī's editor a blank in the ms.]
5. So he cut (*dhabaḥ*) the two sides of his throat; but he was cutting (*naḥar*) into copper (*nuḥās*). So he sharpened the knife two or three times on a stone and still it did not cut.
6. Abraham said: This matter is from God.
7. He raised his head and there was a mountain goat (*waʿl*) standing before him. Abraham said: Up, my son, your ransom is revealed (?*nazala*, has come down).
8. So he sacrificed (*dhabaḥ*) it there at Mina in Mecca.

This version contains no Quranic phraseology, and only a handful of vocabulary items that recall the Quranic version, e.g. *balagha, dhabaḥ*. The broken-off item at 3.4 is a commonly occuring narrative of the devil's attempt to seduce Abraham and/or Isaac/Ismaʿīl and/or Sarah/Hagar from obedience to God's command. It is available in full in a variety of Arabic versions, e.g. version 4 below, and it is derived directly from a number of Rabbinic narratives of this event[12]. In this version Abraham does not receive a call to interrupt the attempt at sacrifice, he realises for himself that this matter reflects divine intervention (3.6). The details given at 3.2 are intended to set the story within the context of the story of Hagar and Ismaʿīl and thereby site the sacrifice at Mecca, as is stressed at 3.8.

VERSION 4. Source: SUYŪṬĪ, *Durr*, V, 284, lines 5ff. Cited from Saʿīd ibn Manṣūr (227/801) and Ibn al-Mundhir (319/931); attributed to ʿAṭāʾ ibn Yasār (c. 100/718).

1. Abraham set off (*kharaja*) with his son Ismaʿīl and Isaac [sic].
2. The devil appeared to him in the shape of a man... [devil tempts first Abraham, then his son].
3. Abraham continued on his way (*inṭalaqa*) until when they were upon a hill
4. He said to his son: My son, I see in a dream that I sacrifice you; consider, what is your view? He said: Do as you are commanded; you will find me, God willing, submissive.
5. And, father, bind me tight lest my blood spatter upon you.
6. Abraham advanced upon him with the knife and pronounced a blessing over him (*barraka ʿalay-hi*).

[12] KASHER, 139 (36) and 142 (49).

7. All that lay between his throat and upper chest was changed into copper (*nuḥās*), which the knife could not penetrate.
8. Then Abraham turned round and there before him was the ram.

Here the inform-accept motif is Quranic but there are no other instances of Quranic phraseology. The story inserted at 4.2 is Rabbinic in origin. The siting of the sacrifice on a hill (4.3) is Biblical and/or Rabbinic. The blessing at 4.6 and, perhaps, the concern for blood spattering (upon vestments?) may be reflexes of priestly ritual. It is again to be noted that there is here no divine intervention: Abraham, prevented from carrying out the sacrifice by the magical transformation of the victim's body, simply discovers the ram. Except for some uncertainty about the identity of the victim (4.1) this version is uninfluenced by Meccan sanctuary tradition (but shorn also of any reference to Jerusalem).

Version 5. Source: Ya'qūbī, *Ta'rikh*, I, 25-6[13]. This work was written before 278/891. Ya'qūbī gives no source for his version.

1. And God commanded the sacrifice of his son...
2. [The tradition (*riwāya*) is at variance on whether it was Isma'īl or Isaac...]
3. When Abraham went in the morning to Mina, he said to the youth: Accompany me to the House (? *zawwir-ni bi-'l-bayt*).
4. He said to his son: God has commanded me to sacrifice you. He said: Father, do as you are commanded.
5. So he took a knife and set him down (*aḍja'a-hu*) on the Jamrat al-'Aqaba; and put below him the saddle blanket of an ass (*qurṭān ḥimār*).
6. He placed the knife on his throat and turned his face from him; but Gabriel turned the knife over (*qalaba*). Abraham looked and there was the knife turned over (*maqlūba*). He did this three times.
7. Then there was a call: Abraham, you have fulfilled the vision.
8. The ram came down from the hill of Thabīr; so he put it under him and sacrificed it.

This version is emboxed within an account of Abraham's visiting his son Isma'īl, at his home in Mecca, and building there the Ka'ba. There are other Arabic versions which put the sacrifice in the same context[14]. The inform-accept motif (5.4) is here not Quranic; indeed the words of

[13] *Ta'rīkh al-Ya'qūbī*, ed. M. Th. Houtsma, Leiden, 1883, 2 vols., vol. 1, p. 25-26.
[14] See, e.g., below, p. 397-8.

Abraham deviate considerably from the Quranic version. The expression of supernatural intervention at 5.6 is expressed in the familiar passive (*nūdiya* not *nādaynā-hu*). There are no other reflexes of Quranic vocabulary. Reference to a donkey at 5.5 is perhaps a distant reflex of a biblical detail; it is not a detail that I know from elsewhere in the Arabic tradition. Angelic intervention to prevent the slaughter of the son is familiar also from Rabbinic versions[15]. The assertion that the knife was changed/turned over (*maqlūba*) is almost certainly a reflex of a Midrashic detail, variously realised as [the knife] «became lead», «was dissolved» or «turned back to its raw state». (See further below, p. 400-2).

Version 6. Source: Ṭabarī, *Ta'rīkh*, (ed. de Goeje), I, 303-5; (ed. Ibrahim), I, 274-5. Also (in a slimmer version) in Ibn al-Athīr, *Al-Kāmil*, I, 111-2[16]. Attributed to Ibn Isḥāq (151/768).

1. Abraham, when ordered to sacrifice his son, said to him: Take the rope and the knife and let us go (*inṭaliq bi-nā*) to this valley (*shiʿb*) to collect firewood for your wife (*li-ahlika*).
2. He said this before mentioning anything of what he had been ordered.
3. As they directed themselves towards the valley the devil appeared...... [tempts first Abraham, then Ismaʿīl, then Hagar].
4. When Abraham was alone with his son in the valley, namely, they say, Thabīr
5. He said to him: My son, I see in a dream that I sacrifice you. He replied: Do as you are commanded; you will find me, God willing, submissive.
6. Then Ismaʿīl said: Father, if you desire to sacrifice me, bind tightly the ropes that nothing may spatter upon you (IA of my blood) and so my value diminish. For death is severe and I cannot be sure that I will not tremble at it, when I feel its touch. When you lay me down (*aḍjaʿta-nī*) to sacrifice me, lay me down on my face, on my *jabīn* (forehead), and not on my side — for fear, if you look on my face, you will be overtaken by compassion... If you consider that to return my garment to my mother may be more consoling to her, then do so.

[15] Kasher, 148 (73), 149 (75) and 149-50 (77).

[16] Abū Jaʿfar al-Ṭabarī, *Ta'rīkh al-rusul wa-'l-mulūk*, ed. M. J. de Goeje, Leiden, 1964; ed. M. A-F. Ibrahim, Cairo, 1960-69; Ibn al-Athīr, *al-Kāmil fī 'l-ta'rīkh*, Beirut, 1385/1965.

7. Abraham said: You are the best of helpers, O my son, in obeying God's command.
8. So he tied him as Isma'īl had suggested and bound him tight; then sharpened the knife; then laid him down on the *jabīn* (*talla-hu li-l-jabin*), fearing to look on his face, then brought the knife against his throat. But God turned it (*qalaba-hā*) onto its back (*li-qafā-ha*)...
9. There was a call: Abraham, you have fulfilled the vision...

The version given in Ṭabarī's *Ta'rīkh* which is the one I have given is rather longer than that in Ibn al-Athīr (IA). The major exception to this is at 6.5 where Ṭabarī's version has an incomplete rendering of the Quranic form of the inform-accept motif. IA gives the full Quranic text (perhaps editorial intervention?). Otherwise, at 6.6, IA adds a reference to blood to explain the spattering. The extra items in Ṭabarī all have the look of explanatory glosses and interpolations into what must have been originally a slimmer text. For example 6.2 is not in IA; the words «they say» at 6.4 are omitted; likewise the clause «and I cannot be sure... when I feel its touch» (6.6) is not in IA. The Ṭabarī text contains a whole cluster of interpolations aimed at explaining the peculiar phenomenon of laying the sacrificial victim on his *jabīn*. The IA text reads simply: «When you lay me down, lay me on my face, for I fear...». I am inclined to suggest that either IA got his version from an independent source going back to Ibn Isḥāq, or, if he derived it from Ṭabarī, he had access to a different ms. tradition from the one now available to us.

Of Quranic diction this version, other than the incomplete Quranic form of the inform-accept motif, exhibits only the phrase *talla-hu li-'l-jabīn* at 6.8 and the familiar call to Abraham, introduced as usual in the passive (*nūdiya*), at 6.9. Of Midrashic detail this version exhibits the now familiar story of the devil's temptation, the inform-accept motif and a handful of familiar last-request motifs (binding, trembling, paternal compassion, consolation for the mother). Evident for the first time in the versions I have cited is the reference to loss of value on the part of the victim. This is explicitly available in Midrashic sources where it reflects Rabbinic concern with an unblemished victim[17]. This detail is perhaps not fully integrated into the Arabic narrative. At 6.8 the verb *qalaba* (transmute/turn over) is provided with a gloss, *li-qafā-hā*, indicating that it must be translated as «turn over». This version is further affected a. by Meccan sanctuary tradition which affects both the

[17] KASHER, 146(65).

location of the site and the identity of the victim, and b. by the incidence of problematic vocabulary (*jabin*?) which prompts a certain amount of creative re-shaping by the narrator (and, in Ṭabarī, the redactor).

II

Now, material of the type adduced so far in this paper is not susceptible to precise dating, and has been subject in the process of transmission and collection to various types of oral and scribal deformation. Nonetheless certain generalisations about form, content and historical environment may be possible. A preliminary and necessarily rather broad assessment of dates must be essayed. Most of the material adduced here, and many more fragments similar in form and content, were collected in the course of the 9th century. Version 1, mediated through Ṭabarī and Ibn Abī Ḥātim, was collected, in the version we now have, in the late 9th or early 10th centuries. And version 3, cited from al-Ḥākim al-Nīsapūrī(?) seems to have been collected only late in the 10th century. However all of this material is attributed to sources in the 8th century (except Yaʿqūbī's version, no. 5, which is not attributed at all). Of the 8th century sources, some (?ʿAṭā' b. Yasār, c. 100/715, at nos. 3 and 4) may be oral sources subject to a lengthy period of oral transmission; while some (Ibn Isḥāq at no. 6, perhaps also al-Suddī at no. 1?) may have achieved written status around 800. In either case, the stories will have been subject to development, both deliberate (in response to environmental demands — time place, audience etc. — or to doctrinal demands — siting of the sacrifice, identification of the victim etc.) and accidental (faulty transmission, scribal error etc.) Even after achieving written form in a major 9th century collection a certain amount of editorial intervention and scribal error continued. These constraints need not however induce despair. For the form of the stories, the many parallel versions, and the obvious absence of a fixed inviolate text clearly indicate that they emerge from a general environment of oral narrative. This supposition is of course confirmed by the sources themselves where the tradents characteristically indicate oral transmission. Since the time of Alfred Lord's *The Singer of Tales*[18] we have become used to the fact that oral narrative is marked by instability of form and detail from version to version, and by an appropriate

[18] See note 5 above.

creative flexibility which makes of every rendering a unique work of art. Many of the versions cited here have a curious baldness. This may be due to the fact that at some point the professional narrator was constrained to dictation, perhaps in response to the demands of an academic, at least to the demands of a scribe. This remains true even if the narrator was, as it were, dictating to himself, making his own notes. The actual realisation of a story, in performance, with an audience, would no doubt be appropriately elaborate; for «the essential element... that influences the form of the poetry is the variability and instability of the audience»[19]. One might add to that the demands of the occasion, the mood of the teller etc. I have already indicated my opinion that Kisā'ī's version, in spite of written redaction, at least recalls a more elaborate and ornamented oral performance.

These materials may broadly be described, then, as the written precipitate of a widespread story-telling tradition, which existed in the 8th century and continued into the 9th century. It is futile to search for or even to assert the existence of original versions. Every realisation was a new creation. In the course of the 9th century this oral tradition became less important. No doubt it continued, but it had ceased to have great significance for the collectors, who had, after a time, transferred much or most of it from its original environment into a new academic environment where it was subject to special constraints. And, no doubt, the moulding and fixing of the story in an academic tradition imposed a controlling pattern upon popular forms. Nonetheless Kisā'ī's version in the *Qiṣaṣ al-anbiyā'* and the version in Nuwayrī's *Nihāyat al-arab*[20] (?a deveopment of Kisā'ī) indicate that the story-telling tradition did continue in a lively and creative manner and relatively free from academic (religious) constraints; for these versions preserve not only the identity of Isaac as victim but also of Jerusalem as site of the sacrifice, in spite of the total elimination of the latter and the partial elimination of the former from the exegetical tradition.

These stories may be described as Judaic and specifically Rabbinic in content and as narrative (not exegetical) in form (with the exception of those elements specified at version 1). The material borrowed from Judaic sources is for the most part characterised by its capacity to serve a recognisable dramatic or emotional purpose in its new narrative environment. Occasionally redundant elements of the Biblical narrative have been retained as at 2.3. And certain details, like the relationship

[19] LORD, *The Singer*, p. 16.

[20] AḤMAD B. 'ABD AL-WAHHĀB AL-NUWAYRĪ, *Nihāyat al-arab fī funūn al-adab*, Cairo, 1342/1923 *et seq.*, vol. 13 (1357/1938), p. 120.

between the request to be bound and loss of value of the victim (6.6) were perhaps not fully comprehensible outside a Rabbinic context of concern for the ritual of sacrifice. Interfering with the Rabbinic details are items, related to the Meccan sanctuary tradition, designed to site the sacrifice in Mecca, and, in time, to identify the victim as Ismaʿīl, (the story of Hagar and Ismaʿīl being subject to a parallel process of incorporation into the geographical context of the Meccan sanctuary).

As formal narrative (not scripture, not exegesis), it seems to me these stories may, perhaps must, be interpreted as having developed independently of the Quranic text. Certain items of that text are not seen at all in the narratives I cite. I have given no examples of the Quranic phrase *lammā balagha maʿa-hu al-saʿy*. There are versions which offer parallels to this phrase but I suspect, on the basis of arguments printed elsewhere, that the phrase was gradually eliminated or changed because not fully understood[21]. The Quranic fillers «Thus we reward the righteous», «This was the clear test» etc. do not appear in the narratives. Other phrases, *lammā aslamā, talla-hu li-'l-jabīn*, are sporadically available: in versions 1 and 2 but not in 3, 4 or 5. Version 2 has *talla-hu* not *talla-hu li-'l-jabīn*; (the truncated form is also in version 7). Version 5 exhibits the parallel formula *adjaʿa-hu* which is clearly a variant of *talla-hu*, expressing the same notion; it appears in a variety of versions. Version 6 has both *aḍjaʿa* and *talla*. I have stressed above the Rabbinic origins of the inform-accept motif. This motif occurs in versions 1, 2, 4, 5 and 6. Diction is generally Quranic but extended by two lines at 2.4, abbreviated at 6.5 and simply not Quranic at 5.4. I would suggest that this motif was realised in Arabic originally in a variety of forms (corresponding to the variety of realisations of other motifs in this story) but has in most cases been corrected in the light of normative Quranic diction. The variants from Quranic diction are the remnants of older forms. The same process of normative correction affects the phrase *talla-hu* wherever it occurs, but has not quite ousted an independent form which did not specify *li-'l-jabīn*. The actual wording of the call to Abraham, where it occurs (versions 1, 2, 5, 6), is always Quranic but invariably introduced by the non-Quranic *nūdiya*. The assumption must be that a standard narrative formula indicating the irruption of the supernatural has been edited and reformulated as *nādaynā-hu* for inclusion in a work ascribed directly to God[22]. The Quranic version, if my argument is correct, is

[21] See N. CALDER, *The saʿy and the jabīn: some notes on Qur'ān 37:102*, in *Journal of Semitic Studies*, 31 (1986), p. 17-26 (hereafter: CALDER, *The saʿy*).

[22] Cf. J. WANSBROUGH, *Qur'anic Studies: Sources and methods of scriptural interpretation*, Oxford, 1977, p. 13-16, on the attribution of the Qur'an to God as speaker; and *The*

secondary to and dependent on the narratives. The stories, it may be remarked, freely refer to God as subject of action (1.9, 1.13, 5.1, 6.7 *et al.*). Had they been dependent on a pre-existing Quranic text there would have been no reason to avoid mentioning the there explicitly identified caller.

The idea that the Qur'an achieved its present form only late in the 8th or early in the 9th centuries is of course familiar, if still controversial, as a result of the works of John Wansbrough[23]. For my own part, I find the burden of his argumentation perfectly satisfactory, and indeed consistent with what scholars working on the forms of prayer or scripture have come to expect. Such materials do not spring fully fledged into existence in their final form: they achieve a canonical form gradually over a period of time. Clearly the sacrifice narratives, if they do not actually *require* a late date for the canonical text of the Qur'an, are at least consistent with such a date, c. 800. There are however other relevant materials to be considered.

III

Version 1 exhibited at two points two distinct formal devices that marked certain passages as exegetical, that is, as related to an independently existing formula that required integration into a narrative context. There are other versions which exhibit similar features.

Version 7. Source: Suyūṭī, *Durr*, V, 280, lines 20ff. Cited from Ibn al-Mundhir (319/931) and al-Ḥākim (405/1014); attributed to Mujāhid (119/722) from Ibn ʿAbbās.

0. And of his followers Abraham / the followers of Noah in his practice (*minhāj*) and his customs (*sunan*).
1. He reached with him the *saʿy* / he became a youth such that his striving (*saʿy*) reached (*balagha*) that of Abraham in working.
2. And when they both submitted / submitted to what they both had been commanded.
3. And he threw him down (*wa-talla-hu*) / placed his face upon the ground.

Sectarian Milieu: Content and composition of salvation history, Oxford, 1978, p. 79, where Wansbrough's assessment of the development from Traditional *muyassar* to scriptural *sa-nuyassir* corresponds to my assumptions regarding *nūdiya* and *nādaynā-hu*.

[23] See works cited in note 22, especially *Qur'anic Studies* (hereafter: Wansbrough, *Studies*).

4. i. And he said: Do not sacrifice me while looking at my face lest you feel compassion for me and fail to take my life.
   ii. And if I regret [my decision] and shrink [from the deed] and struggle against you, [then fear not].
   iii. But tie my hands to my neck then place my face upon the ground.
5. When he moved his hand to sacrifice him, the knife had not yet reached [its mark] when
6. There was a call (*nūdiya*): Abraham, you have fulfilled the vision.
7. So he withdrew his hand.
8. Hence [God's] word: We redeemed him with a great sacrifice / a great ram / acceptable.

This version, like that of al-Suddī (version 1), displays a mixed style, exhibiting both independent narrative and dependent exegesis. Here the exegetical mode dominates at 7.0-7.3. Each passage consists of scriptural text directly juxtaposed to a parallel phrase which repeats and to some degree elaborates the scriptural phrase. Except at 7.0 the juncture between scripture and paraphrase (here marked by an oblique) is zero; at 7.0 it is *qāla*. The exegetical style is interrupted at 7.4 by a pure narrative style which continues to 7.7. The resumption of exegetical style at 7.8 is marked by the phrase *fa-dhālika qawlu-hu*, which introduces a scriptural item. These are the same two types of formal exegetical device as were noted in version 1. Functionally the scriptural texts in this passage serve as pegs for an ongoing narrative. The breakdown of exegetical style at 7.4 may be related to the inadequacy of the liturgical skeleton to support, as it were, the flesh of the full narrative. The exegete, lacking a peg for his narrative, reverts to the story-telling style. He re-establishes himself in the exegetical mode by a now familiar technique — *wa-dhālika qawlu-hu* — which introduces a scriptural phrase as comment on or appendage to preceding narrative. The narrative passage at 7.4-7.6 is made up of perfectly familiar motifs.

Recovery of scripture/liturgy (*qur'ān*) from this passage reveals a number of peculiarities. First, the phrase *balagha maʿa-hu al-saʿy* lacks the Quranic *lammā* as introductory. Likewise the phrase *talla-hu* lacks its scriptural complement *li-'l-jabīn*. The inform-accept motif is missing, together with what I have called the Quranic fillers. And the call of supernatural intervention is not marked as scriptural; it appears in the narrative section, introduced by *nūdiya*. Extrapolation of liturgy however reveals a remarkably satisfactory form.

— And of his followers was Abraham

— He took [his son] to the *sa'y*[24]
— And when they both submitted
— And he threw him down
— We ransomed him with a great sacrifice.

Though elliptic this would function adequately as one item in a litany of prophets. Presumably a number of prophets were named in sequence and for each one a cluster of phrases or sentences were provided designed to recall an event or some events in the life of each. An example of just such a litany may be found in the present form of Qur'an 37; also in, for example, Eccles. 44 («Let us now praise famous men ...).

One of Suyūṭī's sources for that Tradition was al-Ḥākim al-Nīsapūrī whose *Al-Mustadrak* has been published in Haydarabad[25]. The version in the *Mustadrak* is itself significant of how the tradition deals with these things. It is substantially the same pericope. There are two insignificant scribal/editorial variants (*sunna, sunan* at 7.0; *taṣil, taḥikk* at 7.5). At first sight the *Mustadrak* has the Quranic *talla-hu li-'l-jabīn* but this is certainly an instance of (probably unconscious) editorial submission to normative Quranic diction. For the same *ḥadīth*, cited in the *Talkhīṣ al-Mustadrak* which is printed in the same volume, is given the form *talla-hu* (without *li-'l-jabīn*). The Haydarabadi text omits the clumsy but not unfamiliar or incomprehensible passage at 4ii.

VERSION 8. Source: SUYŪṬĪ, *Durr*, 280, lines 10ff. Cited from 'Abd ibn Ḥamīd (249/823), Ibn Abī Ḥātim (327/938), Ibn Jarīr al-Ṭabarī (310/923), Ibn al-Mundhir (319/931); attributed to Mujāhid (119/722).

1. And when he reached with him the *sa'y* / when he became a youth so that his striving (*sa'y*) matched (*adraka*) that of Abraham in work.
2. And when they both submitted / submitted to what they both had been commanded.
3. And he threw him down upon the *jabīn* (? forehead/hill) / placed his face upon the ground.
4. i. He said: Do not sacrifice me while looking at my face lest you feel compassion and fail to take my life.
   iii. Tie my hands to my neck and place my face upon the ground. He did so.
5. When he moved his hand to sacrifice him

[24] I translate this phrase in accord with my argument in CALDER, *The sa'y*.

[25] AL-ḤĀKIM AL-NĪSĀPŪRĪ, *Al-Mustadrak 'alā 'l-Ṣaḥīḥayn*, Haydarabad, 1334-42, 4 vols., vol. 2, p. 340-1.

6. There was a call (*nūdiya*): Abraham, you have fulfilled the vision.
7. So he withdrew his hand, raised his head and saw the ram ... so he sacrificed it.

This, like version 7, is attributed to Mujāhid; it is indeed clearly a variant of the same pericope, though exhibiting significant differences. Here, the liturgical component has been improved in the direction of the canonical text. The Quranic *fa-lamma balagha* is given at 8.1 and *talla-hu* is provided with its canonical complement at 8.3. Perhaps also the commentary has been improved: at 7.1 the commentary repeated the scriptural *balagha*, but at 8.1 this becomes *adraka*. Given the peculiar qualities of this exegetical style, this may be thought superior. The same reversion to narrative is exhibited at 7.4 and 8.4 and, except for removal of 4ii, and some minor details, the narrative follows the same pattern. The inform-accept motif is still missing and the supernatural intervention is still expressed in the passive (*nūdiya*) and unmarked as scripture. The published version of Mujāhid's *Tafsir* exhibits the same scriptural framework as these two versions[26], in of course correct Quranic form. The inform-accept motif is still omitted, as are the Quranic fillers («Thus we reward the righteous» etc.). Further, the account of divine intervention has there disappeared from the abbreviated narrative component; is this perhaps because it was expressed in the non-Quranic *nūdiya* form?

This exegetical style, characterised by scriptural text and juxtaposed gloss is familiar. It is the style of those *Tafsīrs* thought to be by Muqātil (150/767) and Kalbī (146/763). These works have been studied by John Wansbrough who has described their formal literary characteristics in more detail than I need attempt here[27]. He too demonstrates the Rabbinic origins of narrative detail both in the text of the Qur'ān and in the narrative elements of these commentaries. He suggests as *Sitz im Leben* for these works the popular sermon. In both commentaries, as now available, the Quranic text is provided in full, in (more or less) correct canonical form. J. Wansbrough however is inclined to see this as the result of a lengthy and complex redaction history, which was marked in both cases by the provision of a tidied and completed text of scripture. The Muqātil text as related to Qur'ān 37.102-7 conveniently incorporates a gloss referring to al-Farrā' (207/822) which helps to confirm that this is indeed a late redaction[28]. It contains the whole of

[26] *Tafsīr Mujāhid*, ed. A-R. AL-ṬĀHIR AL-SŪRATĪ, Qatar, 1976, *ad* 37:102, p. 543-4.
[27] WANSBROUGH, *Studies*, p. 122-80.
[28] Cf. WANSBROUGH, *Studies*, p. 143.

the canonical text with only one slight deviation from the canon at v. 102 where it reads *lammā balagha ma'a abī-hi al-sa'y* (instead of *ma'a-hu*); but this is nothing more than exegesis incorporated into the text. The basic pattern is that of text plus gloss or paraphrase. Aside from the lengthy intervention by Farrā' the exegetical components are not particularly extended. The principle is however loosely applied and permits of considerable recapitulation of narrative items; nonetheless the last-requests motif, having no liturgical peg, is omitted[29]. The Kalbī text confirms Wansbrough's description in being a much neater more refined example of the style.

Version 9.

1. And when he reached with him the *sa'y* / working for God and in obedience. (Some say: taking him to the mountain.)
2. Abraham said / to his son Isma'īl. (Some say: Isaac.)
3. My son, I see in a dream / I have been ordered in a dream.
4. That I sacrifice you; consider, what is your view / what do you advise and command.
5. He said: Father, do as you are commanded / as to sacrifice.
6. You will find me, God willing, submissive / to sacrifice.
7. So when they both submitted / agreed and submitted to God's command.
8. He threw him down upon the *jabīn* / laid him down upon his face. (Some say: his side.)
9. We called out: Abraham, you have fulfilled the vision / you have carried out what was commanded in the dream.
10. Thus / in this way (*innā kadhālika* / *hākadhā*).
11. We reward the righteous / in word and deed...

It is unnecessary to quote more of this passage. The whole of canonical scripture is correctly cited. The style is remorseless to the point of being senseless (as at 9.10). Material that cannot be introduced on a canonical peg has disappeared, as e.g. the last requests of the victim. There are some signs of interpolated material (bracketed) at 9.1, 9.2 and 9.8 but the basic form is clear. Scripture, canonical scripture is here primary. It might be said that the style, thus developed, is designed to foreground the sacred text even at the expense of narrative. In this

[29] See *Tafsīr Muqātil*, ms., Ahmad III, 74 pt 2, ff. 112a-112b. I am grateful to A. Rippin for providing me with a photocopy of the relevant portions of this manuscript.

respect it is different not only from the pure narrative versions (versions 1-6) but also from versions 7 and 8 where still it is the story teller whose concerns are dominant. There can be no doubt that this, as Wansbrough argues, is not 8th century material. Something of its complex redaction history may be guessed at in the light of the fact that it is ascribed not only to Kalbī but also to Dīnāwārī (308/920) and to Fīrūzābādī (817/1415)[30]. Setting aside the varied ascriptions of this text, it is clear that it is a developed and polished version of the style exhibited in versions 7 and 8 and attributed to Mujāhid. Those versions are characterised not only by a dominant concern for narrative but also by a scriptural framework or skeleton which has not reached the familiar canonical form and by narrative items which have not yet been elevated to/edited as scripture.

The Quranic version of the story is of course familiar.

Qur'ān 37, 101-7:
101.
And we gave news of a wise youth
102.
When he reached with him the *sa'y* he said: My son I see in a dream that I sacrifice you; consider, what is your view? He said: Father, do as you are commanded; you will find me, God willing, submissive.
103.
And when they both submitted and he threw him down on the *jabīn*.
104.
We called out, saying, Abraham
105.
You have fulfilled the vision; thus we reward the righteous.
106.
This was indeed the great test.
107.
And we ransomed him with a great sacrifice.

The inform-accept motif inserted at v. 102 (and not present in the proto-scripture of versions 7 and 8) occasions a lengthy and disturbing delay in achievement of the rhyme. The established narrative expression of supernatural intervention *nūdiya* is changed at v. 104 to *nādyanā-hu*.

[30] On this work, see A. Rippin, *Al-Zuhrī, naskh al-Qur'ān and the problem of early tafsīr texts*, in *Bulletin of the School of Oriental and African Studies*, 47 (1984), p. 23 and note 15. Version 9 is taken from *Tanwīr al-miqyās min tafsīr Ibn 'Abbās*, attributed to Muḥammad Ibn Ya'qūb al-Fīrūzābādī, Egypt, 1380/1960, p. 278.

The last part of v. 105 is a formulaic filler having the right form and rhyme for the context. Similarly, v. 106 is a formulaic locution, peculiarly appropriate to the life of Abraham, and adapted here to a particular context, rhyme scheme etc. The formulaic part of v. 105 and the following verses, 108 and 109, function in this *sūra* as refrains, imposing a patterned uniformity on the litany of prophets which is its subject matter. Setting aside the formulaic items, the narrative here may be described as a skeleton, secondary to, possibly excerpted from some pre-existing forms. Some familiar topoi have disappeared (last requests, Abraham's attempt to do the deed); others have achieved a highly reduced form, invested with a peculiar allusive density, because they suggest rather than tell the story. Cut off from a detailed narrative context, this narrative skeleton is not only allusive but also elusive. I have attempted to show elsewhere how the phrases *lammā balagha ma'a-hu al-sa'y* and *talla-hu li-'l-jabīn*, being themselves the fossilised components of older narratives, were re-interpreted by the tradition for different narrative purposes[31].

All early Arabic versions of the sacrifice narrative may, then, be analysed as built primarily out of narrative materials derived ultimately from Rabbinic sources; and as exhibiting, secondarily, interference from Arabian (Meccan sanctuary) traditions. These narrative materials may be found in forms extremely close to their literary origins (2.3) or in highly expanded and freely imaginative versions (Kisā'ī). Most items lie between these extremes. In literary form, the Arabic versions may be analysed as exhibiting two extreme types: pure narrative and pure liturgy; and an intermediate type: mixed scripture and narrative exegetically linked. The mixed type would appear to have been predominantly narrative in mood until a very late date. Indeed the change in mood, exhibited in Kalbī/Dīnāwārī, is probably due to academic interference in an otherwise essentially oral medium. The versions of this story which remain available are the crystallised fixed precipitate of a larger oral tradition which was in existence in the 8th century and continued into the 9th. The transfer of motifs from Hebrew and Aramaic (possibly also Greek) into Arabic, and the development of a multiplicity of parallel versions such as can be inferred from the material presented here are processes requiring time. An extensive Arabic language tradition of story-telling based on Biblical material is unlikely to have existed before say 700; and its major development would be later. The attribution of the versions given here, and of numerous other versions,

[31] See CALDER, *The sa'y*.

do not point much beyond the 8th century as moment of origin; (except for a handful of attributions to Ibn ʿAbbās, which need not be taken seriously — as at version 7). It is theoretically possible that Rabbinic motifs had become part of a general pool of popular oral narrative even prior to the Arabic conquests. However, the consistency of Rabbinic over, say, Christian reference, and the closeness of much of the material to its Rabbinic origins (the undigested quality of some of the motifs) suggest that the process of transfer from Jewish academic to popular use was posterior to the Arabic conquests.

The liturgical forms of the material, that is versions recited (*qur'ān, qirā'a*) in a cultic context, do not differ from the pure narrative forms in terms of content. No doubt there was constant interaction between popular narrative and cultic recitation. The liturgical material is certainly best seen as secondary to (borrowed or excerpted from) popular narrative. Understanding (even imperfect understanding) of the recited forms (canonical or pre-canonical) must have depended upon the audience being already familiar with the narrative. Chronological priority for the canonical text of scripture seems to me unlikely: the versions studied here are not really consistent with the assumed prior existence of a fixed, invariable and authoritative text in constant use for prayer. The Quranic version of the sacrifice narrative may be interpreted as product of a long process of development during which narrative and liturgical versions interacted.

The two literary types in which the story comes down to us correspond to two social types about whose existence the historians inform us, viz the *qāṣṣ* (story-teller) and the *qāri'* (reciter). These terms are functional and do not necessarily indicate a distinction of personnel: the same man could no doubt be both *qāṣṣ* and *qāri'*. To me at least it seems clear that their productions have all the characteristics that we now associate with creative oral literature. Each rendering of the story was a unique creative enterprise quite free from any concern with a standard text. I see no reason to distinguish between the liturgical and the narrative realisations of the story in proposing these conclusions.

In the course of the 9th and early 10th centuries these materials achieved the fixed and frozen forms in which we now find them. This reflects the gradual emergence of an academic elite who both captured the materials of *qāṣṣ* and *qāri'* and, in time, ousted them from social (or religious) respectability.

IV

The multiplicity of parallel versions and the literary form of these stories together suggest that they emerged in an aural/oral environment, not bound by fixed written forms. It seems likely that details were aurally received, stored in the memory and orally delivered. There may have been notes as an aide-memoir but each delivery would be a unique creation. The story of Abraham presumably existed as part of a cycle of prophetic stories (*qiṣaṣ al-anbiyā'*/Legends of the prophets); and this cycle existed alongside others (Iranian heroic myth, the Alexander legends, the Bidpai fables etc.) Kisā'ī's *qiṣaṣ al-anbiyā'*, however much redacted, seems to represent the type of a prophetic cycle.

It seems quite clear that long narratives were built up by juxtaposing (or emboxing) independent or near-independent narrative units. By a narrative unit I mean for example items like the story of Abraham's sacrifice, which took its place with a number of other narrative units as the regular components of the biography of Abraham. It would not be necessary that any particular item within the biography be always included; it might be omitted, contracted or expanded depending on the situation and mood of the story-teller and his audience. Another «narrative unit» of which several examples have been adduced (3.4, 4.2, 6.2) is that of the devil's attempt to seduce Abraham and/or his son or his wife from obedience to God's command. This essentially self-contained story was optionally emboxed within the sacrifice story, and might be curtailed or expanded as occasion demanded. The sacrifice narrative could itself be emboxed within other narratives; it appears for example on several occasions as an element in the description of Abraham's first pilgrimage to Mecca. This is the context of version 5 above and a similar emboxed version may be found in a Tradition from Ibn ʿAbbās given in Ibn Ḥanbal's *Musnad* and again in Ṭabarī[32]. In that version, Abraham is commanded to perform the *manāsik* (the rituals of pilgrimage), runs a race with the devil, sees the devil at Jamrat al-ʿAqaba and Jamrat al-Wusṭā and stones him. At this point, the following reduced version of the sacrifice story is given:

— Then he threw him down upon the *jabīn*
— Ismaʿīl was wearing a white garment
— He said: Father, I have no cloth to serve as shroud other than this one, so take it off and shroud [my body] in it.

[32] IBN ḤANBAL, *Musnad*, Cairo, 1395, vol. 1, 297-8; ṬABARĪ, *Jāmiʿ al-Bayān*, vol. 23, p. 80.

— He turned round and there was a mountain goat ... so he sacrificed it.

The story here, in conformity with its context story, is justificatory of Meccan sanctuary rituals. The victim is Isma'īl and the familiar last requests motif is reduced to express significant concern for a single, white garment worn by the victim.

Just as the larger cycle was made up of self-contained narrative units which could be juxtaposed or emboxed in the manner described, so each unit in turn was made up from a cluster of smaller items, narrative motifs, from which the story-teller drew in order to create his current version. The basic motifs of the sacrifice narrative might be analysed as follows:

1. age/identity of victim
2. vision of Abraham
3. inform-accept motif
4. journey to site of sacrifice
5. disposition of victim on site
6. last requests of victim
7. execution, failure, reaction (execution, failure ...)
8. supernatural intervention
9. provision of substitute

Many of these motifs could be expressed with extreme brevity. Number 5 for example might be found simply in the form of *aḍja'a-hu* or *talla-hu*. Number 6 might be reduced to non-existence or considerably expanded and ornamented. In Kisā'ī's version of number 7 the knife is laid upon the throat three times, each failure followed by respectively an exclamation, a sharpening of the knife and an explanation from the knife (!) as to why it refused to cut. The effect is a considerable heightening of interest and suspense. No realised version need include all motifs and within limits the order was flexible. Versions 2-4 given above exhibit the following combinations of motifs:

Version 2: 1, 4, 3, 5, 6, 8, 9.
Version 3: 1, 2, 4, 7, 8, 9.
Version 4: 1, 4, 3, 6, 7, 9.

These versions are of course not simple combinations of the narrative motifs. They exhibit, for example, unexplained remnants from an older narrative tradition (version 2) or interference from the story of Hagar and Isma'īl (version 3) or interpolation of a whole optional unit, the story of the devil's seduction (version 4).

My description of these stories in terms of «units» and «motifs» corresponds, *mutatis mutandis*, to what Alfred Lord calls «themes» and «formulae» in his analysis of Yugoslavian oral epic — a very different genre of material. Lord describes his «theme» as a group or grouping «of ideas regularly used in the telling of a tale». A theme, he notes, may be realised in a short form, or omitted, or elaborated as the occasion demands. He notes also that a theme «can be broken down into smaller parts». Ultimately, it seems clear, the building blocs of a particular theme are «formulae». In defining these Lord incorporates a metrical limitation which is certainly not necessary for my purposes (and perhaps not for his). His discussion of a formula is such that it seems to vary from a fairly stable word or small cluster of words (expressing e.g. a name, an action, a time or a place) to a less stable and more complex word-cluster. This corresponds to my «motif». It must be admitted however that ultimately the difference between a narrative unit and a narrative motif is one of degree. Amongst the variables affecting form, selection and juxtaposition of motifs (formulae), according to Lord, are acoustic pattern, syntactic pattern and semantics (narrative)[33]. Particularly illuminating are his remarks on the redundant formula: «It is possible that a formula that entered the poetry because its acoustic pattern emphasised ... a potent word or idea was kept after the peculiar potency was lost ... It is then that the repeated phrases ... began to lose their precision ... Meaning in them became vestigial, connotative rather than denotative»[34]. I have suggested above that this phenomenon of acoustic inertia, accompanied by a loss of semantic precision, is exemplified in the Quranic phrases *balagha ma'a-hu al-sa'y* and *talla-hu li-'l-jabīn*. But the process did not end there: for the increased difficulty in understanding these phrases prompted new creative efforts to explain them and so occasioned new narrative motifs.

In its original narrative context, I have argued elsewhere[35], the word

[33] See Lord, *The Singer*, chap. 3, on the formula; chap. 4, on the theme. It has been objected to my description of how these stories were built that the process I envisage is too mechanical and anything but creative. This is perhaps an inevitable feature of analytic description. Lord was aware of the same problem and compares the mechanical aspects of story-telling to the mechanical aspects of formal grammar and syntax. Any description of these must be extremely mechanical, but the «rules» of grammar are not experienced as either mechanical or unduly restrictive: they do not inhibit creativity. See further Lord, *The Singer*, p. 65.

[34] Lord, *The Singer*, p. 65.

[35] Calder, *The sa'y*.

jabīn meant hill or mound and must be understood as a reflex of the Biblical Mount Moriah. However because *jabīn* also meant, and was (no doubt very early) taken to mean, «forehead» this item had a disproportionate effect on the narrative. Sacrifices were not normally carried out with the victim's head on the ground. In a version provided by Suyūṭī (V, 283, lines 27 ff.) a more normal method of sacrifice is described as part of the last requests of the victim:

> Father, take me by the forelook and take up a position
> behind me lest I harm you when I feel the fire of the knife.

In version 1 above, the difficult phrase *talla-hu* is transferred from its original location (describing the disposition of the victim on the site) and attracted to the execution-failure-reaction motif, where it proved useful as a possible reaction to initial failure: failing to cut his throat from the conventional angle, Abraham throws his son onto his forehead etc. The following example of the attraction of a word or phrase from one motif to another has a particularly complex history.

A number of versions exhibit the emergence of copper (*nuḥās*) as a detail in the narrative. In version 1 this takes the form of a sheet of copper interposed between Isaac's throat and the knife. In version 3 Abraham cutting into the throat finds himself cutting into copper. In version 4 all that was between the victim's throat and chest became copper (*ju'ila mā bayna labbati-hi ila manḥari-hi nuḥāsan*). In all versions the copper functions as an explanation of Abraham's failure to execute his son. In a Tradition from 'Abd ibn Ḥamīd (249/823) attributed to Abū Ṣāliḥ (mid 1st/7th century!) and given in Suyūṭī (*Durr*, V, 283, lines 31-32) the copper motif has a different form. There we read: When he placed the knife upon his throat, it (the knife) was transformed (*inqalabat*); it became copper (*ṣārat nuḥāsan*). Now this can certainly be interpreted as a reflex of Midrashic material. For the following interpretation of Rabbinic evidence I am much indebted to my colleague Dr. Philip Alexander. The earliest reference to the knife changing seems to be *Genesis Rabah*, 56.7. «*Do not stretch out your hand against the lad.* But where was the knife? The tears of the angels had fallen upon it and it had ...». The next word *shāḥāh* is a *crux*. The problem arises because, earlier, Abraham stretched out his hand and took the knife. Here we read only «Do not stretch out your hand», so what had happened to the knife? Clearly the answer must explain a disappearance. The word *shāḥāh* is normally translated as «melt» — the knife had melted. In *Midrash ha-Gadol*, a much later compilation, we read «and the knife was turned to lead (*'oferet*)». This is apparently an attempt to make sense of the problematic *shāḥāh*. The original exegetical problem has now been forgotten: we are no longer concerned with the disappearance of the knife but with the fact that it has become lead, that is, blunt. It seems that this process can be interpreted as internal to the Jewish tradition and as generated by a midrashic reading of scripture. The steps are as follows:

1. Exegetical problem: Where is the knife at Gen. 22.12?
2. Answer: the angels have ————ed it with their tears.
3. Problem: what exactly did the angels do?
4. Answer: they changed its nature, made it lead.

Turning to the Arabic sources, we read at 5.6 that the angel Gabriel did something to the knife — *qalaba-hā*. This could mean either «transformed or transmuted it» or «turned it over». Since in fact, here, Abraham carries out his action three times and, apparently, each time finds the knife *maqlūba*, it becomes necessary to translate *qalaba* as «turn over». The same verb *qalaba* is found at 6.8 with God as subject and with a gloss *li-qafā-hā* (onto its back) indicating that, again, the verb must be translated as «turn over». However, in the last version, cited above, the same verb, this time in the VIIth form, *inqalaba*, indicating the passive, is provided with a gloss *ṣārat nuḥāsan* necessitating a translation «was transformed».

It seems quite clear that the root of the problem lies in *Genesis Rabah* and in the verb *shāḥāh*. Both the Arabic and the later Hebrew traditions exhibit attempts to deal with this event, originally associated with the angels' tears. I would be inclined to suggest that the Arabic verb *qalaba* was introduced into the story originally to describe what the angels did to the knife (as at version 5). However since this verb offered two divergent semantic possibilities it generated two divergent glosses or gloss-traditions; one indicating that the knife was turned over, the other indicating that it had become copper, indicating bluntness. By this analysis the emergence of copper is explicable in terms of problems that arose within the Arabic language tradition, i.e. in response to a question «What does *qalaba* mean here»? If this is correct then I would interpret the lead knife of *Midrash ha-Gadol* as a reflex of popular narrative. Arabic language stories would of course be common to all religious communities and the Jewish community of the Yemen (who compiled the *Midrash ha-Gadol*) would not have lacked opportunity to hear these stories. Further, I would imagine that some external prompting was required to make them forget that the original exegetical problem lay in the knife's disappearance.

Be that as it may, the emergence of copper as an item in the Arabic-language versions of the story was to prove particularly useful. For when the narrators wished to explain why the boy was laid on his *jabīn*, or, alternatively, why Abraham didn't succeed in killing his son, granted that he tried, they found the notion of copper at hand and moved it from the knife to the victim. Thereby they created a new motif which gave to the story an added magical element.

It is then clear that all motifs and narrative items in the Arabic versions of the sacrifice story (whether narrative or liturgical) can be explained in terms of the following four processes:

1. Mediation of items from Rabbinic sources, the mediators being popular story-tellers, selection of items being related to usefulness in their narrative context (and not to their importance in the Rabbinic context).

2. Interference from Arabian sanctuary traditions associated with Mecca, affecting both the location of the sacrifice and the identity of the victim.

3. Resolution of linguistic and narrative problems arising in the process of translation and transmission.

4. Natural development of narrative technique, leading to elaboration of items that increased tension, interest, emotional involvement etc.

VIII

The *Ummī* in Early Islamic Juristic Literature

In Section 1 of this paper I discuss academic understanding of the word *ummī*; in Section 3, the form and structure of an early juristic text. Collocation of these disparate discussions in one paper is excused by their several but direct relationships to the lengthy passage from the *K. al-Aṣl* of the Ḥanafī jurist, Muḥammad ibn Ḥasan al-Shaybānī (189/805), translated in Section 2.

Section 1

That the word *ummī* came to mean illiterate – a development almost certainly product of sectarian dispute about the probative value of miracle in the Muhammadan biography – is well-known. Amongst the earliest and neatest expressions of the doctrinal point is that found in the *K. al-Dīn wa-l-Dawla* by 'Alī bin Rabban al-Ṭabarī (c. 250/864). That work includes a chapter *fī ummiyyat al-nabī wa-anna al-kitāb alladhī anzala-hu allāhu 'alay-hi fa-anṭaqa-hu bi-hi āyatun li-l-nubuwwa* – "On the Prophet's illiteracy and the fact that the Book which God revealed to him and caused him to utter is a sign of prophecy". Here, the Arabian recipient of revelation is desbribed as *ummī*, this term being glossed as, "not knowing in the least either the art of writing or that of rhetoric" – *lam ya'rif kitābatan wa-lā balāghatan qaṭṭ.*[1])

Quranic usage of the term does not confirm this meaning. Of the six instances of this word in the Qur'ān, two suggest a contrast between *ummī* and People of the Book (3:20 and 3:75). It is probable that the same contrast is involved at 62:2: *huwa alladhī ba'atha fī 'l-ummiyyīn rasūlan min-hum.* At 2:78 the reference is to a

---

[1]) 'Alī bin Rabban al-Ṭabarī, *Kitāb al-dīn wa 'l-dawla*, Beirut, 1979, p. 98–9. It may have taken some time for the assertion that the prophet was *ummī* (= illiterate) to become a standard feature of debate. Abu Bakr Muḥammad al-Bāqillānī (403/1013), while arguing for the miraculous nature of the eloquence (*balāgha*) evident in the Qur'an, makes no mention of its having come from an illiterate person; see *Kitāb al-Bayān 'an al-farq bayn al-mu'jizāt wa-'l-karāmāt*, ed. R. J. McCarthy, Beirut, 1958, paras. 29–36. Bāqillānī does however reveal that for him *ummī* means illiterate; see para. 81, p. 70, where *ummī* = *ta'adhdhur al-kitāba wa-'l-qirā'a.*

group of Jews who do not know the Book (= Torah): *wa-min-hum ummiyyūn lā ya'lamūn al-kitāb.* The remaining two instances, at 7 : 157 and 7 : 158, take the form of the phrase *al-nabī al-ummī*, grammatically placed in apposition to a preceding noun *al-rasūl/rasūlu-hu*: these are probably examples of interpolative gloss. In a recent paper Isaiah Goldfeld has shown, by analysis of the authority statements contained in the *Tafsīr* of Abū Ja'far al-Ṭabarī (the exegete, d. 310/923), that the exegetical understanding of this word in the period before Ṭabarī focussed on the contrast between *ummīs* and People of the Book. *Ummī* is understood to be a term indicating a nation or a people who do not (yet) have a divinely inspired Book, in particular the pagan Arabs. Goldfeld seems to feel that from the time of Ṭabarī onwards the dogma of Muḥammad's illiteracy dominated the interpretative process. This however is not the case: the *mufassirūn* were the most willing accepters of polyvalency and the more thoughtful make it clear that for the key passages (3 : 20 and 3 : 75) they are as capable as their European counterparts of taking context into consideration. It was the passage at 2 : 78 that carried the dogmatic burden.[2])

The usage *ummī* = nation without a Book is neatly illustrated in two passages which transmit the opinions of the jurist Muḥammad ibn Idrīs al-Shāfi'ī (d. 204/820) on a question of *jihād*. As reported by al-Muzanī in his *Mukhtaṣar*, Shāfi'ī said:

> God gave victory to the religion of his Prophet over all other religions in that he revealed to all who follow it that it is the truth, and that religions opposed to it are false. And he gave it victory in this: the totality of idolatry is two religions, the religion of the People of the Book and the religion of the Ummīs (*dīn ahl al-kitāb wa-dīn ummiyyin*). The Prophet conquered the Ummīs, so that they submitted, willy nilly, to Islam. The People of the Book he killed and captured until some submitted to Islam and some paid the *jizya*.

As reported by Rabī' bin Sulayman, Shāfi'ī cited Q 5 : 19 (Oh People of the Book, a messenger has come to you . . .) and Q 62 : 2 (He it is who has sent to the *ummīs* a messenger from their midst . . .) and explained: In [these verses] there is proof that he was sent to the [whole of] creation, for they [creation] consist of either

---

[2]) Isaiah Goldfeld, "The illiterate Prophet: an inquiry into the development of a dogma in Islamic tradition", *Der Islam*, 8 (1980), p. 58 ff. Goldfeld is not primarily concerned with the later *tafsīr* tradition but remarks on pp. 58, 62 and 67 leave the impression that the idea of illiteracy dominated the exegetical reading of the *ummī* passages. For counter examples, see Ṭabarī, Zamakhsharī and Qurṭubī *ad* 3 : 20 and 3 : 75; also, more briefly, Al-Jalālayn and Abū Su'ūd al-'Allāma *ad* 3 : 75. Ṭabarī certainly reads *ummiyyīn* at 62 : 2 as meaning people without a Book and Qurṭubī, while making this passage an excuse for discussion of the Prophet's illiteracy, makes also a graceful gesture towards polyvalency by beginning with a citation from Ibn 'Abbas: the *ummīs* are the Arabs, those who can and those who cannot write, because they were not People of the Book.

People of the Book [Jews and Christians] or *ummīs* [pagans including the Arabs].[3]) The same point is made in Shāfi'ī's *Risāla* more elaborately (*ba'atha-hu wa-l-nās ṣinfāni*) but there without reference to 62 : 2.[4])

A minority strand of the ancient *tafsīr* tradition was found by Goldfeld to hold the view that the *ummiyyūn* were, not pagans, but Jews who were ignorant of their own scripture. This view was particularly associated with Q 2 : 78, prompting from Goldfeld the following remarks: "It seems that Q 2 : 78, forming part of a group of verses referring to the people of Moses . . ., had gradually become detached from the general and coherent notion of *ummiyyūn* in the Qur'an. The reference in this verse was taken to be to the Jews."[5])

The independent evidence of Kalbī (d. 146/763) and Muqātil (d. 150/767) confirms what was found in Ṭabarī: the early Muslim exegetical tradition understood *ummī* generally to mean pagan, non-Jew, non-Christian, and in particular pagan Arab, except at Q 2 : 78 where *ummī* was understood to mean Jews ignorant of (reading and writing) the Torah.[6])

Western scholars, relying on Quranic context alone, naturally came to the same conclusions as their early Muslim counterparts; they were, after all, reading the same texts – or something very like the same texts. In only one respect did they have something to add and that was in detecting a Hebrew/Jewish antecedent for the Arabic/Muslim usage of the word *ummī*.

Nöldeke pointed out that *ummī* in Quranic usage must be understood as counterpart to *ahl al-kitāb*, and must accordingly mean a people or peoples without a divinely inspired Book. Schwally suggested that *ummī* was derived from *umma* = nation, people, and pointed to parallels with Greek *laikos* (lay) from *laos* = people and Aramaic (in fact Syriac, see Payne-Smith's Thesaurus Syriacus) *'ālmāyā* (*saecularis*) from *'ālmā* = *mundus, saeculum*. The latter is in fact probably a translation (a calque) of Latin *saecularis*. It does not seem to me that these parallels are anything other than vaguely suggestive. Schwally's further reference to Hebrew *'am ha-areṣ* confuses rather than clarifies. Is this just another word indicating the masses (the people, the world) and connoting (?) secular, lay; or does he suggest something more? It is not clear. A relationship between *ummī* and *'am ha-areṣ* had previously been pointed out by Geiger (1833). It remains true that *ummī* in Quranic usage does not indicate lay or secular, and has connotations of ignorance only at 2.78. Horovitz ventured to clarify the issue. The analogy with *'am ha-areṣ* he considered "inappro-

---

[3]) Muḥammad ibn Idrīs al-Shāfi'ī, *al-Umm*, Beirut, n. d., 8 vols., (a copy of Bulaq, 1321–25, but with different pagination) vol. 4, p. 159, lines 19ff.; (corresponding to Bulaq, vol. 4, p. 83). The passage from al-Muzanī may be found in the Beirut *Mukhtaṣar*, vol. 9 of the *Umm*, p. 276.

[4]) Muḥammad ibn Idrīs al-Shāfi'ī, *al-Risāla*, Cairo, 1388/1969, paras. 9ff.

[5]) Goldfeld, *op. cit.*, p. 65.

[6]) Goldfeld, *op. cit.*, p. 67. I would follow John Wansbrough (*Qur'anic Studies*, Oxford, 1977, pp. 122–148) in thinking that the texts of Kalbī and Muqātil are in fact redactions belonging to the 3rd/9th century; they remain independent of Ṭabarī.

priate". "We are not concerned with a contrast between *ḥaber* or the *talmid ḥakam* and the *'am ha-areṣ*, but with a contrast between Israel and the *ummot ha-'olam.*" But, – like the early exegetes – for Q 2 : 78 he made exception: here perhaps there was confusion with *'amme ha-ares.*[7])

Subsequent comment, though plentiful, represents no progress. Both C. C. Torrey (*The Jewish Foundations of Islam*, N.Y., 1935, p. 38) and A. Katsh (*Judaism in Islam*, N.Y., 1954, p. 75–6) display a common tendency to see *ummī* as meaning *goy/goyim*, i.e. non-Jew, even at 2 : 78. The comments of Rabin and Wansbrough may be taken to typify Orientalist approach. For Rabin, the phrase *al-nabī al-ummī* "has long been recognised to mean 'the gentile prophet' derived from [sic] the M[ishnaic] H[ebrew] *ummot ha-'olam.*" Two pages later, referring to 2 : 78, he suggests that "here *ummiyyūn* probably = *'am ha-areṣ*". and refers to Horovitz.[8]) Wansbrough takes an extra step: for him, reference to Jews at 2 : 78 is to be understood "in the sense of exclusion". Sectarian divisions imply both ignorance and exclusion from the community, and *ummiyyun* may therefore, even in this context, be linked to *ummot ha-'olam.* Conversely, the locution *al-nabī al-ummī* suggests "in its common interpretation" (!) "a parallel to if not a calque of *'am ha-areṣ.*" The latter postulate is, I think, intended to be rejected. The equivalence *ummī* = *'am ha-areṣ* is to be understood as an exegetical (tendentious) development from 2 : 78, associated with a dogmatic impulse to describe the Arabian prophet as unlearned.[9])

For Western scholarship, then, the tension between *ummī* = pagan outsider and *ummī* = ignorant insider has come to be understood in terms of a tension in Hebrew between *ummot ha-'olam* and *'am ha-areṣ.* There is a distinct tendency (post-Horovitz), on the basis of Quranic contextual usage, to assume that *ummī* is more likely to be related to *ummot ha-'olam* than to *'am ha-areṣ.* One may assume that the possibility of linguistic development from *ummot* to *ummī* has affected this preference. The point is made by Rabin, but also by Horovitz, who thereby leaves in his text an unresolved contradiction, for he also states that *ummī* is derived from *umma.* There is further a tendency, not fully worked out, to assume that the problematic 2 : 78 should be interpreted so as to bring this usage into line with usage elsewhere in the Qur'an. The result is that the meaning "ignorant" is denied and the relationship to Hebrew *'am ha-areṣ* is played down. I shall argue in what follows that this is not the correct path to follow. The word *ummī* has to be understood as an Arabic word which covers the same semantic spectrum as Hebrew *'am ha-areṣ*; but the details of this link have to be set out with rather more care than has been achieved so far.

In the passage translated in Section 2 of this essay, taken from the *K. al-Aṣl* attributed to the Ḥanafī jurist Muḥammad ibn Ḥasan al-Shaybānī, the word *ummī* is used to describe a Muslim who is ignorant of scripture, or, more precisely, a Muslim

---

[7]) J. Horovitz, "Jewish proper names and derivatives in the Qur'an", *HUCA*, 2 (1925), p. 190–1. See also T. Nöldeke and F. Schwally, *Geschichte des Qorans*, 2 vols., Leipzig, 1909–19, vol. 1, p. 14 and further bibliography in Horovitz and Goldfeld.

[8]) Ch. Rabin, *Qumran Studies*, Oxford, 1957, p. 123 and 125.

[9]) J. Wansbrough, *Qur'anic Studies*, Oxford, 1977, p. 53–4 and 63.

who is incapable of even that small quantity of recitation which is the minimum necessary for prayer. *Ummī* here is the functional opposite of *qāri'*. This usage is detectable also within the Shāfiʿī juristic tradition. Within the Ḥanafī tradition, as a result of the Shaybānī text, the word *ummī* continued in use as a technical term, indicating inadequate knowledge of scripture, at least until the time of Muḥammad ibn Aḥmad al-Sarakhsī (d. 483/1090 or 490/1097). This represents a new aspect of usage which must be added to scholarly understanding of the word *ummī*. At Q 2:78 the reference was to *ummīs* (= ignorant) amongst the Jews; in Muslim juristic literature, *ummī* refers likewise to ignorant, but to members of the Muslim community, who are ignorant of scripture. In this respect, it may be analysed as a Muslim naturalisation of the Rabbinic concept of *ʿam ha-areṣ* in one of its more common usages.

That locution, much cited by scholars in this context, is hardly of simple or univalent usage. In Rabbinic writings, it designates either those who are ignorant of or not practising purity laws (*ʿam ha-areṣ le-misvot*) or those who are ignorant of scripture (*ʿam ha-areṣ la-torah*).[10]) Now, the Muslim juristic usage which I have pointed to reflects the latter usage and must certainly revitalise the argument that *ummī* is a reflex of Hebrew *ʿam ha-areṣ* — that is in designating one ignorant of scripture. One can go further. Horovitz's introduction of *ummot ha-ʿolam* into the argument must be seen as something of a red herring. Biblical usage of *ʿam ha-areṣ* (especially in the plural, *ʿamme ha-areṣ/ha-araṣot*) refers predominantly to non-Jews, to foreigners in contrast to Israel. And Biblical usage was not lost in spite of the developing semantic equation *ʿam ha-areṣ* = ignorant (of purity laws, of Torah). Nor was there any systematic attempt by Rabbinic exegetical tradition to read back into Biblical contexts the later linguistic development. Midrash Rabbah adduces Deut. 28:10 (*ʿamme ha-areṣ*) as proof text in the context of a discussion of heathens, star-worshippers (*ʿovede kokhavim*) and adduces 1 Kings 7:43 (*ʿamme ha-areṣ*) in the context of a discussion of "the nations of the world" (! *ummot ha-ʿolam*).[11]) Rabbinic understanding of *ʿam ha-areṣ*, in other words, included both heathen outsiders and ignorant insiders, and, in this respect, it precisely parallels Arabic Muslim usage of *ummī*. *Ummī*, at Q 2:78 refers to ignorant Jews, elsewhere in the Qur'an to non-Jews. This is precisely how *ʿam ha-areṣ/amme ha-areṣ* functions in Rabbinic literature. The Muslim juristic usage (*ummī* = Muslim incapable of reciting scripture) represents an interiorisation of the concept: it no longer represents the ignorant of the Jewish community, but the ignorant of the Muslim community. In both cases ignorant does not mean illiterate, but, quite specifically, ignorant of scripture.

The nature and mode or context of linguistic transfer is not so easy to define; but for an understanding of sectarian borrowings (linguistic, doctrinal etc.) in the

[10]) See P. Oppenheimer, *The Am ha-aretz*, Leiden, 1977; also A., Buchler, *Der galiläische ʿam-haʿareṣ* des zweiten Jahrhunderts, Vienna, 1906, discussed in Oppenheimer, 5–10; and S. Zeitlin, "The Am haarez", *JQR*, 23 (1932), discussed in Oppenheimer, 3–4.

[11]) Midrash Rabbah, English translation, eds., H. Freedman and M. Simon, London (Soncino Press), 1939, 10 vols;

a. adduces Deut. 28:10 in vol. 3, Exodus, ad 15:6, p. 167.

b. adduces 1 Kings 8:43 in vol. 5, Numbers I, ad 1:3, p. 8–9.

early Islamic period it is the works of John Wansbrough which constitute the most useful and suggestive analyses. In particular, I am inclined to follow him in thinking that the time and the place of borrowing is the 8th and early 9th centuries and the Fertile Crescent, and not 7th century Arabia. "Borrowing" of course may not be the right word. Diffusion of Rabbinic (and other) religious terminology within the increasingly Arabic-speaking "sectarian milieu" of the 6th to 8th centuries is an instructively different model from that which suggests direct influence or (deliberate) borrowing, and, still more so, from that which suggests continuity (Islam as an aberrant Judaism). It may become possible in time to distinguish what is diffused from what is borrowed. For the present, I would suggest that it simplifies our understanding of the processes at work – whatever they were – if we recognise that Arabic *ummī* is in all its usages (except of course the later development, *ummi* = illiterate) a reflex of Hebrew *'am ha-areṣ*, meaning not only ignorant jew (2:78), and non-Jew (+ non-Christian) but also, in its fully naturalised meaning, ignorant Muslim, ignorant, that is of scripture. The only social context for the emergence of this word would seem to be a Rabbinic Jewish community who spoke Arabic. Whether that could be the Jews of the Arabian Peninsula in the 7th century is a moot point.

Schwally suggested that *ummī* (= unlearned?) was derived from *umma* in a way parallel to Greek *laikos* from *laos*. A. J. Wensinck puts forward the same view for *ummī* (= foreign) this time pointing to Greek *ethnikos*, from *ethnos*[12]). Apt though these both are I would prefer to see *ummī* as an Arabic naturalisation of Hebrew *'am/'amme ha-areṣ*, and not as a natural development from *umma* (itself a loan-word? see Horovitz *ad ummī*). Since the transfer from Hebrew *'am* to Arabic *ummī* must be assumed to have taken place at a popular (colloquial?) level the transition from a Hebrew *'ayn* to Arabic *hamza* presents no insuperable linguistic problems.

Section 2

The following passage is a subsection within the *kitāb al-ṣalāt*, contained within the collection of juristic materials known as the *Kitāb al-Aṣl* and attributed to Muḥammad ibn Ḥasan al-Shaybānī[13]).

> 1. Q. Consider, an *ummī* prays with [i.e. leads in prayer] some *ummī* people; amongst them some who can recite [as well as] some who can't (*man yaqra', man lā yaqra'*).
>
> A. Their prayer is corrupt (*fāsid*).
>
> 2. That is the view of Abū Ḥanīfa. Muḥammad (al-Shaybānī) says: the prayer of those who can recite is corrupt, but the prayer of those who cannot is perfect (*tāmm*). This is also the view of Abū Yūsuf.
>
> 3. Q. Consider, if he opens prayer with them, being *ummī*, and prays one or two *rak'as*, then is taught [? learns, *'lm*; var. *t'lm*] a *sūra* and recites it at

---

[12]) A. J. Wensinck, *The Muslim Creed*, London, 1965, p. 6.

[13]) Muḥammad ibn Ḥasan al-Shaybānī, *Kitāb al-Aṣl*, (ed. A–W al-Afghānī) Haydarabad, 1386/1966 et seq., vol. 1, 185–9.

the third and fourth *rakʿas*, does this suffice him and those who pray behind him (*a-yujzī-hi wa-yujzī man khalfa-hu*)?

A. It does not suffice them; their prayer is corrupt.

4. Q. And is it the same if he prays three *rakʿas* and then is taught [*ʿlm*; var. *tʿlm*] a *sūra*?

A. Yes.

5. In the *Imlā'* from Abū Yūsuf, it is written that Abū Ḥanīfa used to say, concerning the *ummī* who learns a *sūra* during his prayer, that he should recite it and he should build [i. e. build on what he has already done, as opposed to starting again *ab initio*]. Later he abandoned this view.

6. Q. If he opens prayer with them, being *ummī*, and prays the whole prayer, and then, when he sits back for the duration of the *tashahhud*, but has not yet uttered the closing *salām*, he is taught a *sūra* – [does his/their prayer suffice]?

A. This and the earlier problems are the same.

7. Q. If there are behind him a group incapable of recitation (*qawmun lā yaqra'ūna*) and he opens the prayer with them, he being *ummī*, and when he has prayed one or two *rakʿas* is taught a *sūra* and recites it in the remainder of the prayer [what then]?

A. It does not suffice them; they must repeat the prayer.

Q. Why?

A. Because he 'built' his prayer on non-recitation (*banā ṣalāta-hu ʿalā ghayri qirā'a*) and then he learnt a *sūra*, hence he must repeat the prayer *ab initio*.

8. This is the view of Abū Ḥanīfa. Abū Yūsuf and Muḥammad say: As to us, we consider that if an *ummī* prays with a group of *ummīs* together with a group who can recite; and if he prays with them the whole prayer, and then sits back for the duration of the *tashahhud*, then learns a *sūra*, his prayer suffices him and those behind him who cannot recite. But as for those who can recite, their prayer is corrupt.

9. Q. If the *imām* is one who cannot recite (*lā yaqra'*) and he opens prayer, then becomes ritually impure (*aḥdatha*) before he prays anything at all, and if he then puts forward [in his place] one who can recite, [what then]?

A. The prayer of the [new] *imām* and the prayer of those behind him is corrupt – according to Abū Ḥanīfa.

Q. Why?

A. Because he is subject to whatever the first *imām* was subject to [representing a continuation of the first *imām's* authority], and the first *imām* was not able to recite.

10. Q. Consider, if the first *imām* prayed one *rakʿa* then became ritually impure and put forward the other *imām*, [what then]?

A. This and the first problem are the same.

11. Q. If the first *imām*, when he opened prayer, learnt a *sūra* and pray two *rak'as*, reciting during these *rak'as* that *sūra*, and then became ritua impure and put forward a man who could not recite, [what then]?

A. This and the earlier problem are the same.

Q. And if he put forward someone who could recite?

A. This and the earlier problem are the same.

12. Q. If an *ummī* opens prayer with a group of *ummīs*, and prays w them one or two *rak'as*, then learns a *sūra*?

A. Their prayer is corrupt.

Q. Likewise if there were amongst them some who could recite?

A. Yes.

13. Q. A man enters prayer with an *imām*, having missed one *rak'a*. T man is *ummī*. When the *imām* finishes his prayer, he [the *ummī*] stands to make-up [for the missed *rak'a*]. Do you prefer that he recite in remainder of his prayer?

A. Yes.

Q. But if he cannot recite [*lam yuḥsin an yaqra'*)?

A. By *qiyās* his prayer is corrupt. But I will abandon *qiyās* and by *is san* declare that it suffices him.

Q. Why?

A. Consider, if he were dumb, and he missed one *rak'a*, and then st to make-up, would his prayer not suffice?

Q. Yes.

A. This and the other are the same.

. . . [misplaced section]

14. Q. An *ummī* opens the noon-prayer, prays, completes his prayer, utters the closing *salām*. He then recalls that he made a slip in his pra and so performs a [compensatory] *sajda*. He then learns a *sūra* before final [compensatory] *sajda*. [What then?]

A. His prayer is corrupt; he must repeat.

Q. What if he did not make a slip in his prayer, but prayed four *rak* sat back after the fourth *rak'a* for the duration of the *tashahhud*, then taught a *sūra* before he uttered the closing *salām*?

A. This and the earlier problem are the same.

15. This is the view of Abū Ḥanīfa. Abū Yūsuf and Muḥammad say: A us, we consider that if he sits back for the *tashahhud*, then learns a *sūra*, prayer is perfect.

In this translation Q(estion) translates *qultu* and A(nswer) translates *qāla*; English "consider" translates *a-ra'ayta*. This is the longest discussion of proble relating to the *ummī* in early *fiqh* literature. (A further problem may be found pp. 215–6 of the same work.)

The problem of whether it is or is not appropriate for one capable of recitin pray behind one incapable of reciting is not raised in the *Muwaṭṭa'* of Mālik, in recension of Yaḥyā. It does however occur, briefly, in the *Mudawwana* of Saḥnūn (240/854). The phrase indicating capacity to recite is *yuḥsin al-qur'ān* (cf. para. 13 above), the word *ummī* is not used. In Shāfi'ī's *Umm*[14]), the subject is discussed twice; once at vol. 1, p. 102 under the heading *bāb man la yuḥsin al-qirā'a* and again at vol. 1, p. 167, *bāb imāmat man lā yuḥsin al-qirā'a wa-yazīd fī 'l-qur'ān*. . . Shāfi'ī argues that individual Muslims should ideally acquire a minimum of seven verses for purposes of prayer and those who have that or less than that should not be recognised as prayer-leader by those who have more than the minimum. The word *ummī* does not occur in the first section. In the second section, immediately after the heading, the discussion begins thus:

> If a man leads prayer who is an *ummī* or who cannot recite the *umm al-qur'ān*, even if he can recite other parts of the Qur'ān . . ., it is not permissible for one who can recite the *umm al-qur'ān* to pray behind him. (*Idhā amma al-ummī aw man lā yuḥsin umm al-qur'ān* . . .)

An *ummī* evidentely is one who has no Qur'ān at all, and he is here classed with one who, in particular, does not know the Fātiḥa. This usage, *ummī*= ignorant of the Qur'ān, is to be contrasted with the alternative, *ummī* = non-Jew, non-Christian, pagan, also used in the *Umm*, in the context of *jihād*, and cited in Section 1 of this essay.

Within the Ḥanafī tradition, the presence of that lengthy discussion in the *K. al-Aṣl* ensured that the word remained in use for some time. In his *Mukhtaṣar*, Abū 'l-Faḍl Muḥammad al-Marwazī (334/945) summarised Shaybānī's position thus:

1. An *ummī* prays with a group including both *ummīs* and reciters (*qāri'*); the prayer of the *imām* and the group, all of them, is corrupt.

2. An *ummī* [prayer-leader] learns a *sūra*, having prayed part of his prayer, then recites it in the remainder of his prayer; his prayer is corrupt, like that of the others [praying behind him].

3. An *ummī* follows a *qāri'* [reciter] after he [the *qāri'*] has [already] prayed one *rak'a*; when the *imām* finishes, the *ummī* stands to complete his prayer [i. e. the omitted *rak'a*; his prayer is corrupt, by *qiyās*.[15])

The *K. al-Mabsūṭ* by Sarakhsī is a commentary on the Marwazī text; it expands the discussion without any sense of embarassment at the meaning of the word *ummī* which is accepted as indicating one incapable of reciting any scripture, or incapable of reciting a quantity of scripture adequate for prayer.

Section 3

In an earlier paper, also related to Islamic legal literature, I suggested that in dealing with texts attributed to Mālik, Shāfi'ī, Shaybānī *et al.* one should not imme-

---

[14]) References are to Beirut edition, see footnote 3 above; (corresponding to Bulaq, vol. 1, p. 88 and p. 147).

[15]) I have access to the *Mukhtaṣar* of Marwazī only in so far as it is the base text of Sarakhsī's *Mabsūṭ*, which takes the form of a commentary on Marwazī. For the passages cited, see Shams al-Dīn al-Sarakhsī, *Kitāb al-Mabsūṭ*, 30 vols., Cairo, 1324, vol. 1, p. 181 and 182.

diately assume that these texts are "by" the named authors.[16]) They are frequently school texts, product of organic growth over a considerable period of time, and subject to complex procedures of redaction, interpolation, excision, re-formulation etc. These processes are easily detected, less easily explained. Pending a more lengthy investigation into some of these early juristic texts, I offer here a brief analysis of the passage translated above from Shaybānī's *K. al-Aṣl*. The argument presented there may be divided into five sections represented by (1) paras. 1–6, (2) paras. 7–8, (3) paras. 9–11, (4) para. 12 and (5) paras. 13–15.

(1) Paras. 1–6. Para. 1 establishes the condemnation of all those who pray in mixed groups (i. e. of *ummīs* and *non-ummīs*) behind an *ummī* prayer-leader. Their prayer is not valid. When Marwazī read his version of the *Aṣl*, he understood precisely this: "the prayer of the *imām* and the group, all of them, is corrupt (*fāsid*)". Para. 2 however is an interpolation. The first few words ("That is the view of Abū Ḥanīfa") represent a relegation of the ruling to the more distant authority of Abū Ḥanīfa and make way for a new ruling brought in under the authority of Muḥammad al-Shaybānī and Abū Yūsuf. The practical effect of the new ruling is, as it were, favourable to *ummīs*, but one may suspect that the real motive for its introduction lies in considerations of juristic logic. The distinction introduced at para. 2 creates a satisfying sense of logical refinement.

Para. 2 also, of course, disrupts the Q and A format of the text, and, logically, disrupts the sequence of argument. Paras. 3, 4 and 6 are to be understood as following on from para. 1; the more refined view attributed to Muḥammad and Abū Yūsuf is not effective within the text. Of the five manuscripts consulted by the editor at this point, only three exhibit the interpolated para. 2; the other two, lacking para. 2, exhibit a second interpolated passage at para. 5, which, in turn, is missing from the first three. This suggests an original text consisting of 1. 3. 4. and 6. differentially developed; acquiring in one school para. 2 and in another para. 5. (The editor is not always so careful in describing the state of his manuscripts.)

Paras. 3. 4. and 6. raise the question what happens when the *ummī* prayer-leader is taught (or learns) a *sūra* in the course of prayer. The answer is nothing: the blanket ruling is reaffirmed throughout. The prayer is corrupt for all participants, the *ummī imām*, and all other participants, *ummī* or otherwise. It is worthy of remark that the sequence of questions at 3. 4. and 6. is, in an mechanical way, logical but not very sensible. First the *ummī* leader is conceived of as learning a *sūra* after two *rakʿas* and as inserting it for the remainder of his prayer. This avails nothing; he must repeat *ab initio*. Then he is conceived of as learning this *sūra* after three *rakʿas*, when there is even less remaining prayer in which to exercise this new-found skill. Finally he is conceived of as learning the *sūra* after all four *rakʿas*, when there is no time at all to practise this skill. It seems clear that once a negative answer had been established at para. 3 there was really no possibility of a different answer for paras. 4 or 6.

---

[16]) See N. Calder, "*Ḥinth, birr, tabarrur, taḥannuth*: an inquiry into the Arabic vocabulary of vows", *BSOAS*, 51.2 (1988), pp. 214–239.

How did this come about? Most tentatively I would suggest that the Q and A format (*qultu/qāla*) characteristic of some (not all, basically the early) books of the *Aṣl* has been imposed upon an originally normative and possibly disparate series of rules. Reconstructing these, they might have included something like: If a man, being an *ummī*, leads prayer, then learns a *sūra*, after two, three or four *rak'as*, it does not suffice; his prayer and that of those behind him is corrupt. The Q and A redactor has split this – or some such passage – into three questions whose sequential arrangement considered carefully must puzzle. The mechanical exploitation of a practical redactional skill would seem the most likely cause of this feature. Marwazī's summary of the argument seems impeccable: "An *ummī* [prayer leader] learns a *sura*, having prayed part of his prayer, then recites it in the remainder of his prayer; his prayer is corrupt, like that of the others [praying behind him]." It is permissible to wonder whether the text he had before him was also couched in the Q and A format. One wonders too whether it contained the interpolations: these he either ignored or did not know.

Para. 5, as explained above, is another interpolation. It introduces an alternative ruling by a form of authority slightly different from that represented at para. 2. Here Abū Ḥanīfa's authority is adduced for both rulings, represented as an earlier and a later position. It is possible that this interpolation is misplaced; for it seems to refer to the problem of the *ummī* and his own prayer, i.e. it belongs rather to group (5) composed of paras. 14–15. Paras. 1–6 deal with the quite specific problem of a mixed group praying behind an *ummī*. It is difficult to see just what difference the alternative (older) ruling could have in this situation (unless of course we begin to introduce the distinction created at para. 2 – but this para. is in no manuscript tradition combined with para. 5).

(2) Paras. 7–8. Para. 7 does not refer to the same problem as para. 3. Envisaged here is a group of *ummīs* praying behind an *ummī*. It is to be understood that could they but get to the end of their prayer without any change of status in any participant, all would be well. Change of status, however, here on the part of the prayer-leader, renders the continuation of that prayer invalid, and requires a new prayer *ab initio*. This new prayer will now take the form of a *qāri'* leading *ummīs* – which is legitimate. Para. 8 is an interpolation and at first sight confusing; for it seems to imply that we are still dealing with a mixed group of followers. As at para. 2, the first phrase relegates the previous ruling to Abū Ḥanīfa and opens the way for the double authority of Abū Yūsuf and Muḥammad. Further, this para. makes the same distinction as was introduced at para. 2 between *ummīs* and non-*ummīs*: it is only the prayer of the non-*ummīs* which is invalid if carried out behind an *ummī* prayer-leader. Change of status in the *ummī* prayer-leader however does not have the negative effect envisaged at para. 7 (the view relegated to Abū Ḥanīfa). The new ruling is that even if he learns a *sūra* during prayer, his prayer is valid and so is that of the *ummīs* behind him (not, however, the reciters).

It is clear that the interpolations at paras. 2 and 8 are from the same hand, or from the same school. They give expression to the same authority structure (Abū Ḥanīfa: Muḥammad and Abū Yūsuf) and they introduce the same distinction between *ummīs* and *qāri's* as followers of an *ummī imām*. Again, I am inclined to stress that these interpolations can be probably should be read as product of concern for refinement of logical thought. The practical benefits accruing to *ummīs* (hardly a significant group of people, and becoming less so with the passage of time) is not the issue; logic is.

(3) Paras. 9–11. These paragraphs deal with the problem of delegation. At para. 9 we are again dealing with a mixed group, led by an *ummī*. If the *ummī* prayer leader, having opened the prayer, but not entered at all into the ritual, delegates to a *qāri'*, this makes no difference. The new *imām*, in spite of his personal status, represents continuity of the *ummī imām's* authority, and so, following para. 1, the prayer of all concerned is invalid. Para. 10 deals with the same type of situation and exhibits the same characteristics as were noted above at 3. 4. 6.: the sequential arrangement of the questions is absurd. If the intervention of a delegated *qāri'* right at the beginning of a prayer does not validate it, his intervention at a later stage is hardly likely to do so. Mechanical redactional ingenuity seems again best to account for this feature. A kind of mad versatility in the elaboration of questions, an almost senseless exploration of available permutations, accounts too for para. 11. Following the logical principles set up at paras. 1. 3. 4. and 6. (and not those of the interpolations) it is perfectly plain that prayer under the conditions envisaged will not be valid: an *ummi* prayer-leader, having learnt a *sūra* and wishing to validate his prayer and that of those behind him, must repeat *ab initio*. Further, granted that he has a mixed group of followers, he probably should not appoint an *ummī* as his delegate, and, even if he appoints a *qāri'*, the appointee represents a continuation of the first *imām's* authority, and so the prayer remains invalid in any case. These are logical games, but here pretty pointless ones. Though a unified group of problems is at issue here (9–11) they represent as a bundle an ingenious but thoughtless formal procedure for the multiplication of questions, the last one having no clarificatory value whatsoever.

(4) Para. 12. This para. though exhibiting the familiar Q and A format is simply a doublet. The first part asks the same question as para. 7 and the second part the same question as paras. 3, 4 and 6. Conflation of texts that arose perhaps originally in different schools, followed by a unifying redactional procedure (producing the Q and A format) may account for the present form of the printed text.

(5) Paras. 13–15. These no longer deal with the *ummī* as prayer-leader, but with the *ummī* as follower (13) or praying by himself (14). The rather rigorous *qiyās* argument of para. 13 requires that the *ummī*, having started his prayer as a functional *qāri'* (participating in the authority of the prayer-leader), cannot finish it in a changed status, and so should repeat his prayer as an *ummī* throughout. This may be a logical consequence of para. 7. The *istiḥsān* argument is certainly more sympathetic, and not by any means lacking in logic. Para. 14 is clear enough but one may suspect another example of sequential misarrangement. The second question represents the simpler case. An *ummī*, having learnt a *sūra* while still within the sacred time of prayer (not yet having uttered the closing *salām*), is required to repeat *ab initio* in order to achieve valid prayer (cf. paras. 3, 4, 6 and 7). The first question is much more complex. Here, the *ummī*, having completed his prayer, including the closing *salām*, and started on a series of compensatory *sajdas*, is again required to repeat *ab initio*. At least three logical steps are required in order to explain this.

1. If one learns a *sura* within the sacred space of prayer, it invalidates, and one repeats.

2. If one learns a *sura* after the completion of prayer, it does not invalidate.

3. If one learns a *sūra* after the closing *salām*, but during compensatory *sajdas*, it invalidates the whole prayer, and one repeats.

The point which is being made is that compensatory *sajdas*, though taking place after the closing *salām*, are to be considered continuous with the prayer. It would certainly make the argument easier, if the questions had been asked in reverse order, i. e. moving on from the question about learning within established prayer-time, to the question about extended prayertime. The whole discussion is of course pointless if one accepts the ruling of the interpolated passages at 5 and 8.

Para. 15 repeats the interpolated argument. It follows 2 and 8 in form and it confirms the point made at 8 that an *ummī* who learns a *sūra* during prayer can build on what he has already completed and does not have to repeat. None of these interpolated passages at 2, 5, 8 and 15 are reflected in Marwazī's summary; nor indeed is the point made at para. 14.

This passage, then, as a a whole, exhibits signs of interpolation, conflation, and redactional activity involving a possible reordering of material, the imposition of a standard editorial format, and, perhaps, the ingenious elaboration of new material as a result of exploring the imposed editorial format. Further, extraneous material (not translated here) has crept in between paras. 13 and 14. There are hints of an original logical arrangement of material: this consists of problems related to 1. *ummi* prayer-leader + mixed group; 2. *ummi* prayer-leader + *ummi* group; 3. *ummi* praying by himself. But this has been partially broken down both by a mechanical reediting in Q and A format and by later interpolations which disrupt the argument. Establishing either a location or a date for this text is clearly difficult (except in the trivial sense of locating it in India in the 20th century, since no manuscript exhibits the full text as given here). The *Mukhtaṣar* of Marwazī does not help much. It suggests that the tradition he exploited was substantially the same as that in our text. But it can tell us nothing about the form of his sources, and it leaves open the possibility that his text or texts did not contain the items identified above as interpolated. It will be possible to say a little more about texts of this type, to establish a suggestion of dates and social milieu, but that must wait on further analyses, and preferably comparative analyses, of several early juristic texts.[17])

---

[17]) It is worth remarking that scholars in the parallel field of Judaic studies are much more habituated than Islamic scholars to authorless ("organic") texts. Peter Schäfer, in a recent study of scholarly approaches to Rabbinic literature, says much that is relevant also to Islamic studies, and proposes a programme of research which, while more ambitious than is easy to conceive of in the world of Islamic studies, is nonetheless suggestive of directions that might be taken. See P. Schäfer, "Research into Rabbinic literature: an attempt to define the status quaestionis", *Journal of Jewish Studies*, 37 (1986), p. 139–51.

I should like to thank my colleague Dr. Philip Alexander who discussed with me several of the issues raised in this essay.

IX

THE *QURRĀ'* AND THE ARABIC LEXICOGRAPHICAL TRADITION

Scholars have long been puzzled by the word *qurrā'* which figures repeatedly in accounts of the expedition to Bi'r Ma'ūna[1] and of socio-political movements in Southern Iraq, culminating in the Battle of Ṣiffīn[2]. Heavily glossed and subject to much interpolation, these accounts in their present form insist on the equation *qurrā'* = Qur'ān reciters but the nature of this group's intervention in political and military events has been found to be irredeemably at odds with this interpretation and has promoted efforts to find an alternative interpretation. M.A. Shaban's suggestion, given a nuanced acceptance by G.H.A. Juynboll, that *qurrā'* means villagers (*ahl al-qurā*) has much merit, at least in so far as it tackles the problem resolutely[3]. It has however inspired opposition from those who believe that the derivation of *qurrā'* from *qarya* has not been established as a genuine or even likely linguistic possibility. In this paper I would like to propose that the answer to the problem lies in the most obvious place of all, namely in a standard Arabic dictionary. I offer in what follows an account of what is contained in the *Lisān al-'Arab*[4] under the root *q-r-'*, maintai-

[1] See M. J. Kister, 'The expedition of Bi'r Ma'ūna', in G. Makdisi (ed.), *Arabic and Islamic Studies in Honor of H.A.R. Gibb* (Leiden 1965), 337-357; repr. in Kister, *Studies in Jahiliyya and Early Islam* (Variorum Reprints, London 1980).

[2] See *Ḳurrā'* in *EI*[2] and bibliography. The *qurrā'* figure also in accounts of Badr and 'Aqrabā.

[3] See M.A. Shaban, *Islamic History, a New Interpretation. A.D. 600-750* (Cambridge 1971), 50-51; G.H.A. Juynboll, 'The Qurra' in Early Islamic History', *JESHO* XVI (1973), and 'The Qur'ān Reciter on the Battlefield and Concomitant Issues', *ZDMG* CXXV/1 (1975). The remarks of John Wansbrough, in *The Sectarian Milieu* (Oxford 1978), 69, to a degree parallel those of Juynboll in 'The Qur'ān reciter'.

[4] Muḥammad b. al-Mukarram, Ibn Manẓūr, *Lisān al-'Arab* (Beirut 1300), I, 128-132.

ning that only a small leap of imagination is required to make it directly relevant to the problem.

Western scholars are inclined to accept that the verb *qara'a* = to recite and its derivatives, *qur'ān, qirā'a*, etc. are loan words[5]. While A. Jeffery prefers a Syriac origin, it seems likely that contemporary scholars will re-align themselves with Geiger and Nöldeke in preferring Hebrew or, possibly, Aramaic[6]. The appropriate range of meanings is contained not of course in Biblical, but in Talmudic, Hebrew[7]. It has however not been noted that the borrowed range of meanings, associated with cultic recitation, exists now in Arabic side-by-side with an indigenous range of meanings, which can only with difficulty be reconciled to the borrowed range. This difficulty is reflected throughout the standard lexicographic discussions.

Unsurprisingly, discussion in the *Lisān* on the root *q-r-'* begins with the word *qur'ān* as applied to God's revelation. Abū Isḥāq al-Naḥawī is cited as claiming that the meaning of this word in this context is *jam'*, gathering. It is called Qur'ān because it gathers (*jama'a*) and combines (*ḍamma*) chapters. This is reflected in Qur'ān 75:17, *innā 'alay-nā jam'u-hu wa-qur'ānu-hu*, glossed here, unhelpfully, as *jam'u-hu wa-qirā'atu-hu.* This verse and this perception of its meaning is a dominant factor affecting all discussion of the verb *qara'a*, in the end marginally preventing the lexicographers from perceiving just where their extended exemplification points; (see also n. 10, below). The equation *qara'a* = *jama'a* is thought to be confirmed by the following couplet: *hunna 'l-ḥarā'iru lā rabbātu aḥmiratin / sūdu 'l-maḥājiri lā yaqra'na bi 'l-suwari.* Accepting the very firm guidance of the *Lisān* text (*jama'a, ḍamma ba'ḍa-hu ilā ba'd*), it would appear that the noble ladies with black-ringed eyes are contrasted on the one hand with those who tend herds of donkeys (*rabbāt aḥmiratin*) and on the other with those who put together enclosures (? *yaqra'na bi 'l-suwari*). Also alleged to illustrate the equation *qara'a* = *jama'a* are sentences of the type

[5] A. Jeffery, *The Foreign Vocabulary of the Qur'ān* (Baroda 1938), 223-224, s.v. *Qur'ān.*

[6] A decisive reorientation of scholarship away from concern with a Christian background to Islam towards a sectarian but predominantly Jewish background is contained in Wansbrough, *Quranic Studies* (Oxford 1977).

[7] See M. Jastrow, *A Dictionary of the Talmud* (London and New York 1903), s.v. *q-r-'*.

mā qara'at hādhihi 'l-nāqatu salan qaṭṭ, or *mā qara'at janīnan qaṭṭ*, both implying that the female camel has not become pregnant/given birth. In an effort to establish what is required, these phrases are said to mean that the camel's womb has not 'gathered' or 'encompassed' a foetus, *lam yaḍṭamma raḥmu-hā 'alā walad*. This meaning is also thought to be reflected in the hemistich *hijān al-lawni lam taqra' janīnan*. It seems to me that it is only with some effort that these examples can be related to the verbs *jama'a* and *ḍamma*. There is special pleading going on.

In subsequent discussion, the equation *qara'a* = *jama'a* is scarcely sustained through a variety of exempla and authorities which cover both the form of the word (with or without the *hamza*) and its uses (more or less directly related to recitation and ritual practice, *nāsik, tanassuk*, even *tafaqquh*). In all of this it is the loan meaning derived from Hebrew/Aramic that dominates, and the alleged equation *qara'a* = *jama'a* is not systematically asserted — and probably could not be. Reversion to a number of secular non-ritual usages is marked by consideration of this root in relation to statements about poetry (130a, bottom). One may say *aqra'tu fī 'l-shi'r*, not glossed. Or, this poem is based on the *qar'* of that poem, meaning based on its manner or example, *hādha 'l-shi'r 'alā qar' hādha 'l-shi'r ayy 'alā ṭarīqati-hi wa-mithāli-hi*. Furthermore, *qar'* is used in relation to time (*waqt*) as in the couplet: *idhā mā 'l-samā'u lam taghim thumma akhlafat / qurū'a 'l-thurayya an yakūna la-hā qaṭru*. The *qurū'* of the Pleiades refers to the time of their storms, *waqt naw'i-hā*. The word *qar'* is used in relation to a fever, to one who is absent or distant, and refers also to periods of menstruation (*al-ḥayḍ*) and to the periods of purity between menstruations (*al-ṭuhr*). All of this is explained by the fact that *qar'* refers to time, *wa-dhālika anna 'l-qar' al-waqt*...

Abū 'Ubayd is cited as having noted that the word *qar'* is used both to refer to the period of menstruation and to the period of purity, between menstruations, *yaṣiḥḥu li 'l-ḥayḍ wa 'l-ṭuhr*. He adds the remark, 'I think it comes from *aqra'at al-nujūm*, meaning, the stars set (*ghābat*)' (130b, middle). The connection is perhaps not immediately apparent. But Abū 'Ubayd is also cited as authority for the plural form *aqrā'*, meaning periods of menstruation or periods of purity, and for the phrase *qad aqra'at al-mar'a* meaning both, her period has started and, her 'purity' has started. The basis of all this, he says, is the approach of the time of a thing (*dunuww waqt al-*

*shay*ʿ) (131a, middle). Abū ʿUbayd comes very close here to a revealing perception of the semantic relationship between these various phrases. Other authorities are unhappily torn between a narrow focus on the word *waqt* or an equally narrow focus on the word *jamaʿa* or both. A citation from Abū Isḥāq epitomises the problem. He prefers *qaraʾa* = *jamaʿa* and sees this as explaining the following phrases: *qaraytu (sic) al-māʾ fī 'l-ḥawḍ*, meaning gathered (*jamaʿtu*); *qaraʾtu 'l-qurʾān*, meaning *lafaẓtu bi-hi majmūʿan*; and *al-qird yaqrī* (!), meaning the monkey gathers food (*yajmaʿu*). Hence too, for him, *qarʾ* (= menstrual cycle) means the gathering (*ijtimāʿ*) of blood in the womb. This of course takes place in the period of purity prior to menstruation and so justifies Quranic usage of the plural form *qurūʾ* to mean periods between menstruation. The root *jamaʿa* is certainly being made to work excessively here[8].

Lengthy discussion of the word *qarʾ* and its plural and verbal forms in the context of menstruation is to be accounted for partly because of Quranic usage and partly because it offers an interesting even bewildering variety of exempla. Summarising a lengthy discussion, it is evident that *qarʾ*, pl. *qurūʾ* and *aqrāʾ*, refers to both the period of menstruation and the period between menstruation (*al-ḥayḍ wa 'l-ṭuhr*), while the verbal forms *qaraʾat* and *aqraʾat* signal the inception of a new period either of menstruation or of purity. Not surprisingly, some authorities consider the word to be one of the *aḍdād*. In attempting to explain this, the authorities betray a characteristic preference for the words *jamaʿa* and *ḍamma*. Thus al-Aḥfash offers *aqraʾat al-marʾa* meaning she began menstruating and *mā qaraʾat ḥayḍa*, apparently meaning that she had not begun menstruating (referring either to the onset of maturity or to a particular menstrual period) but cumbrously glossed *mā ḍamma raḥmu-hā ʿalā ḥayḍatin* (131b; middle). Later, al-Aḥfash is seen to distinguish between *aqraʾat* (she has reached the age of maturity, of menstruation) and *qaraʾat* (she has begun menstruating) (132a, top). Other examples reveal that this distinction was not real and that both verbs were used freely to indicate entering a period of menstruation or a period of purity.

[8] And one cannot be at all happy about his confusing the roots *q-r-ʾ* and *q-r-y*. The confusion is common enough, since *q-r-y* is also explained in terms of gathering, with more reason; hence *qarya*, place of gathering. Cf. the examples given in Zamakhsharī, *al-Fāʾiq fī gharīb al-ḥadīth* (Cairo 1356/1947), II, 332ff., s.v. *q-r-ʾ*.

Now, this exemplification together with the supplementary material to be given below suggests a range of meanings different from the notions of *jamaʿa* and *waqt* preferred by the lexicographers. The semantic force of the root *q-r-'* clearly lies in the notions of recurrence, periodisation and segmentation. It is this that is suggested on the occasions when an authority manages to combine *jamaʿa* and *waqt* in a revealing manner, notably, for example, in the citation from al-Zamakhsharī given below, at n. 10. The recurrent cycles of a woman's life are called *qar' (qurū'/aqrā')* and so are the recurrent cycles of the stars (their periods of absence, possibly also their periods of being visible), and the recurrent rhythms of poetry. A female camel who has not carried young (*hijānu 'l-lawni lam taqra' janīnan*, etc.) has not entered a period of pregnancy, or not entered the period of capacity to bear young; see further below. And the Quranic phrase *ʿalay-nā jamʿu-hu wa-qur'ānu-hu* means 'Ours is the gathering of it and its segmentation', meaning its division into periods or chapters or its segmentation through rhythm and rhyme; see again below. Finally, the noble ladies with black-ringed eyes are contrasted with tenders of donkeys, those who *yaqra'na bi 'l-suwari*. If *suwar* here means enclosures, then the *qar'* is the periodical to-and-fro of taking out to graze and returning to base. This, however, leaves a problem with the preposition *bi* (markedly problematic too for the lexicographers!). It is probable, in fact, that *suwar* here has the sense it has in the phrase *suwar al-ibil*, meaning the excellent ones of the camels. Herders of donkeys, they take the fine ones out [in the morning] and back [in the evening][9]. The two halves of the image thus combine: *hunna 'l-ḥarā'iru lā rabbātu aḥmiratin / sūdu 'l-maḥājiri lā yaqra'na bi 'l-suwari*. The notion of cyclical recurrence, periodization, thus unifies all the major strands of reference. The verbal forms *qara'a* and *aqra'a* indicate transition, irrespective of the areas of transition; *aqra'at al-*

[9] I should like to thank Professor A.F.L. Beeston for proposing that *suwar* here has the sense it has in *suwar al-ibil* (Lane); it seems to me to offer the best reading of this verse. The *rabbāt aḥmiratin* also evoked for him a memory which is worth quoting: 'While driving through some bare rocky hills in a very unfrequented area east of Dhamar in North Yemen, we suddenly came out into a most delightful little plain (in local parlance a *qāʿ*) surrounded by the hills, thickly covered in luscious grass, and here grazed a herd of some forty fine looking donkeys attended by three women' (Personal letter, October 1989).

nujūm, the stars set; *qara'at* or *aqra'at al-mar'a*, she started menstruating or started an inter-menstrual period; *yaqra'na bi 'l-suwari*, they go out to [and come back from] pasture.

Following the extensive discussion of *qar'* and its uses in relation to menstrual cycles, the *Lisān* embarks on what might appear to be a disparate assortment of further uses. Most of the material constitutes a more extensive exploration of uses already remarked; some of it is new (132a, top ff.). It will be convenient to set out this material and show that it can be explained in terms of the semantic notions I have proposed.

The first set of materials refers to poetry. On the submission of Abū Dharr to Islam, someone said, 'I have set his words to the *aqrā'* of poetry', *la-qad waḍa'tu qawla-hu 'alā aqrā' al-shi'r*. *Aqra'* here is glossed as *ṭuruq* and *buḥūr* (*'ala ṭuruq al-shi'r wa-buḥūri-hi*). Al-Zamakhsharī, more precise, suggested that the *aqrā'* of poetry were the rhymes (*aqrā' al-shi'r qawafī-hi*), so-called because they mark the divisions and the limits of verses (*maqāṭi'u 'l-abyāt wa-ḥudūdu-hā*). The notions of gathering (*jama'a, ḍamma*) are not mentioned at this point in the *Lisān*, but they had been interestingly conjoined by al-Zamakhsharī, the source of this material, in what I would consider to be by far the most precise statement of the semantic value of *qar'* made available within the Arabic tradition. Al-Zamakhsharī's initial concern is with *qar'* = menstrual cycle. The root of this, he adds, is the notion of gathering, *jam'*; further, the time of a thing, *waqt al-amr*, is called its *qar'* or its *qāri'* because times are vessels containing and gathering what is in them, *li-anna 'l-awqāt ẓurūf tashtamilu 'alā mā fī-hā wa-tajtami'u-hā*. The association of the root *q-r-'* with the notions of rhyme and rhythm clearly offer the best explanation of *qur'ān* at Qur'ān, 75:17[10].

The use of the word *qar'* or *qara'a* in relation to pregnancy and birth implies either the rhythmic alternation of periods of

[10] For Zamakhsharī's discussion, see *op. cit.*, 332. The application of the term[s] *qar'* [and *qur'ān*!] to poetry in the sense of segmentation, what Zamakhsharī calls the provision of rhyme and the marking of boundaries, may also be detected in Ibn Qutayba's remarks on a critique of another poet by Ru'ba. Ru'ba said 'His poetry has no *qirān*/*qur'ān*'. Ibn Qutayba prefers *qirān*, meaning, 'the verses do not match', *lā yuqārin al-bayt shibha-hu*. But amongst his companions are some who prefer *qur'ān*. Ibn Qutayba does not like this, but I too prefer it. See *al-Shi'r wa 'l-shu'arā* (Leiden 1902), 26. There were of course theological reasons for not admitting that the word *qur'ān* had a specifically poetic sphere of reference and this undoubtedly affects much of the lexicographical discussion.

pregnancy and periods between pregnancy or the larger cycle of child-bearing capacity as contrasted with immaturity. The same smaller and larger segmentation is implied in usages associated with menstruation. Hence the phrase *qara'at al-nāqatu* or *qara'at al-shātu* means to become pregnant, *ḥamalat*. The same meaning will serve for the hemistich *hijān al-lawni lam taqra' janīnan*, and for the phrase *mā qara'at salan qaṭṭ*, both repeated here, the latter being glossed as, she has not been impregnated, *mā ḥamalat malqūḥan*. Further discussion reveals particularities which parallel some that have already been discussed. The verbs *qara'at* and *aqra'at* both exist with no clear difference in meaning. Also, there is doubt whether these verbs imply to become pregnant (*ḥamalat*) or to give birth (*waladat, asqaṭat waladan*). They should probably be understood as indicating a moment of transition either from a period of pregnancy (= give birth) or from a period between pregnancies (= to become pregnant). In roughly the same area of usage we have, from Ibn Shumayl, the sentence, *ḍaraba al-faḥlu al-nāqata ʿalā ghayri qur'in* (*sic*; read *qar'in*), the male camel mounted the female without causing impregnation[11]. The phrase *qar' al-faras* refers to the time when mares are on heat and ready for mating, *ayyāmu wadāqi-ha* or *ayyāmu sifādi-ha*. This whole sequence of usages can be explained by noting that *qar'* refers not specifically to pregnancy or birth or being on heat but to all of these things in so far as they represent recurrent periods in the life of pastoral animals.

The phrase *aqra'at al-nujūm* begins a new section and is glossed as *ḥāna maghību-hā*, meaning the time of their setting has arrived. It also means that the rain (associated with a particular constellation) is late, *ta'akhkhara maṭaru-hā*. The phrase *aqra'at al-riyāḥ* means that the winds blow on time or arrive on time (*fī awānī-hā*). The noun-form *qāri'*, glossed as time (*waqt*), is also known and exemplified in a couplet from Mālik b. Ḥarth: *karihtu 'l-ʿaqra ʿaqra Banī Shalīli / idhā habbat li-qāri'i-hā 'l-riyāḥu.* 'How I hated the place called ʿAqr, ʿAqr of the Banī Shalīl / When the winds blew, at their habitual season'. Throughout all this, the verb *aqra'a* refers to seasonal recurrence. The addition

[11] Ibn al-Mukarram seems, in the light of the immediately following example, to imply that this means, while she was not on heat; this is unlikely. Cf. Zamakhsharī, *loc. cit.*, *al-nāqa fī qar'i-hā*, meaning the fifteen day waiting period after putting a stallion to a she-camel. If she is not discovered to be pregnant in this period, the stallion is put to her again.

of a sense of lateness or tardiness is not unusual in such locutions, like English, Spring is due now, implying, but where is the nice weather? Hence, the Pleiades have set, implying, there should be rain now, but where is it?

The phrases *aqra'a amru-ka* or *aqra'at ḥājatu-ka* are glossed with the verb *danā* (to be near) or, alternatively (*qīla*), with the verb *ta'akhkhara* (to be late). A possible English translation here would be, 'Your time has come' or 'Your turn has come' or 'Your luck has turned', implying that a new phase or a new cycle is starting. Again, the added connotation of lateness is not difficult to understand: the sense of imminence slips very easily into a sense of tardiness.

The last three sentences given in the *Lisān* and to be discussed in this study are *aqra'a min ahli-hi, aqra'a min safari-hi* and *aqra'tu min safarī*, glossed respectively with the verbs *danā, raja'a* and *inṣarafa*, which is not really very satisfactory. Indeed, there is clearly a problem: *aqra'a min ahli-hi*, glossed *danā*, is thereby alleged to mean, 'he approached his family', whereas *aqra'a min safari-hi*, glossed *raja'a*, is implied to mean 'he returned from his journey'. That one phrase *aqra'a min* should indicate both movement towards and movement from is not of course impossible, but better explanations might be found. We have seen that the verbs *qara'a* and *aqra'a* mark moments of transition in a cycle which in some way or another is recurrent. Here, then, I would suggest that *aqra'a min safari-hi* means that he ended a period of journeying and entered upon a period of staying at home, hence, reasonably, he returned from his journey. But *aqra'a min ahli-hi* must mean, not he approached, *danā*, his family, but that his period of staying with his family ended and he entered upon a period of being away from them, e.g. on a journey, or (aha!) on military service. It is useful to recall at this point that, when discussing the *qar'/qurū'* of the Pleiades, the text of the *Lisān* noted that the word *qar'* is used also in reference to fevers (i.e. they have their season, and their recurrence) and to one who is absent or distant (*yuqālu...li 'l-ghā'ib qar'un wa-li 'l-ba'īd qar'un*). Clearly, absence and distance are things which, like the Pleiades and menstruation, come in cycles and mark a periodisation in life. The verb *aqra'a* marks either a beginning or an ending to a period of absence.

That concludes the information provided in the *Lisān al-'Arab*. No significant expansion is available in other dictionaries, nor indeed in other obvious sources: the lexicographers have for the most part ransacked these for all they have to say. It must then be admitted that there is no direct reference here to the *qurrā'*; however, it will be evident from the last paragraph just how the information given may be made relevant.

The noun *qar'* and its associated verbs *qara'a* and *aqra'a* refer to a variety of cyclical and recurrent phenomena, including, most significantly for our purposes, periods of absence from home (or from the family or the tribe). In this context, the *Lisān* offers only examples using the verb *aqra'a*, but we have seen that in other contexts that verb alternates with *qara'a*, with little or no discernible difference of meaning. Thus *qara'a min ahli-hi*, like *aqra'a min ahli-hi*, would mean he ended his season at home and started his season away. A person involved in this cyclical process would be a *qāri'*, plural *qurrā'*. The period itself is presumably a *qar'*. At least one purpose for which a man, or a group of men, might leave home (or family or tribe) regularly would be to take part in military activity. I would propose therefore that the word *qurrā'* used systematically in a context associated with military expeditions, troop activities and battles must be a reference to temporary or seasonal troops (tribal levies, militia, conscripts, etc.) as opposed to full-time professionals, the standing army[12]. A person engaged in such activities is *qāri'*, meaning that he has left home to spend a period or season, a *qar'*, on military service.

That, however, must not be taken too dogmatically. A word that serves so many purposes must be interpreted in the light of information provided by context. The narratives of ʿAqrabā, Bi'r Maʿūna and Ṣiffīn, product as they, to me, evidently are of a long period of organic growth, exhibit several levels of narrative development. My proposal is that the oldest layers of narrative used the word *qurrā'* to indicate 'periodical' troops, those on a period of duty, probably away from home. Misunderstood, this word prompted glosses and narrative developments based either on *qara'a* = to recite (dominant for Bi'r Maʿūna and Ṣiffīn) or on *qarya* (*ahl al-qurā* = villagers) (dominant for ʿAqrabā?). The consistency of these narrative developments varied, but has always left a sense that another meaning

12 For a suggestive discussion of how a tribal society might deal with the universal problem of combining a regular army with an irregular militia, see Y. Yadin, *The Scroll of the War of the Sons of Light against the Sons of Darkness*, Eng. tr. (Oxford 1962), 79-86.

is required. It is my contention that the necessary meaning is provided in the dictionaries, it needs only teasing out.

The systematic application of this suggestion to specific historical narratives is not part of the aims of this essay. Nonetheless, a few remarks would seem not out of place. I limit my observations here to the accounts of Bi'r Maʿūna, most of which have been collected and analysed by M.J. Kister. These accounts are remarkable in that they agree about almost nothing in the assumed sequence of events. Though European comments on this material have been concerned exclusively with what did or did not actually happen[13], my own immediate response is that whereas these materials, appropriately analysed, might reveal much about the development of narrative, they will never reveal much about what happened. The expedition of Bi'r Maʿūna exists as a bundle of narratives. In several versions the introductory motif of the narrative is a request for military help, directed to the Prophet, by a faction within a neighbouring tribe. In two versions, from Anas b. Malik, cited in the *Musnad* of Ibn Ḥanbal, the foreign party is described as having submitted (*qad aslamū*); they wanted help against their own tribe (*istamaddū ʿalā qawmi-him*); and the Prophet provided help (*amadda-hum*) in the form of seventy of the Anṣār. According to Anas, We used to call them (the contingent of Anṣār) *qurrā'* in their time — *kunnā nusammī-him fī-zamāni-him al-qurrā'* or *kunnā nusammī-him al-qurrā' fī zamāni-him*[14]. Now, I would propose that this means that when members of the tribe (or confederation) were appointed to spend a period away from home on military activity, they were called *qurrā'*. On departing, it would be said of an individual concerned, *qara'a* or *aqra'a*; having departed, he was *qāri'*, that is, spending a season or *qar'* on military service. The phrase *fī zamāni-him*, though it may mean 'at that time' or 'in their day', I am inclined to read as 'during their period of service'. *Kunnā nusammī-him fī zamāni-him al-qurrā'*: 'we used to call such people during their period of service *qurrā'*'.

In these accounts, the reference to *qurrā'* is immediately

[13] See Kister, *op. cit.*, 346-348.

[14] Aḥmad b. Ḥanbal, *Musnad*, III, 109, 255. There are other versions of this story from Anas on pp. 111, 137, 167 and 270. Some version(s) similar to or the same as those of Anas clearly lie behind al-Wāqidī and Ibn Saʿd; Kister, 340-342. *Pace* Kister, it is not evident that it is Samarqandī's version that is referred to and refuted by Wāqidī; Kister, 350.

followed by a gloss, clearly intended to explain a usage which was puzzling: these people used to forage by day and pray by night, implying, they were called *qurrā'* because of their exceptional piety. This is only one of numerous glosses, which, introduced into a military context, impose upon the word *qurrā'* a religious connotation. In another version: *yuqālu la-hum al-qurrā' ... yaqra'ūna 'l-qur'ān wa-yatadārasūna bi 'l-layl wa-kānū bi 'l-nahār yajī'ūna bi 'l-mā'*[15]. In the course of time and through varied re-telling, the word *qurrā'*, misunderstood or misinterpreted, provoked creative efforts to reorganize the narrative. Eventually, in some versions, a military contingent was transformed into a pious and dedicated group of missionaries. In an account preserved by Abū al-Layth al-Samarqandī (393 AH), the first sentence records that ʿĀmir b. Malik wrote to the Prophet, saying, Send me men to teach us the Qur'ān and to instruct us in religion[16]. What started as a gloss has become the introductory motif for the narrative. Underlying much of the work of M.J. Kister, whose effort and erudition in the analysis of early sources is remarkable, lie a couple of methodological principles which are unsatisfactory: items that do not find their way into the main-stream tradition are assumed to be (a) ancient and (b) true. 'In the light of the version recorded by al-Samarqandī, which was omitted in the traditional accounts, ... some suggestions about this expedition may be propounded'[17]. The suggestions are of course eminently plausible; but there is in fact no reason for giving Samarqandī's version pride of place: his version is later than those from Anas, cited above and preserved in the *Musnad* of Ibn Ḥanbal. These too are versions of a story, not necessarily records of historical fact[18].

[15] Ibn Ḥanbal, 270.

[16] Kister, 348-350.

[17] *Ibid.*, 354-355. I would account for e.g. the considerable reduction of participants *apud* Samarqandī on the grounds that in significant ways it enhances the narrative: not warriors, but missionaries, the band was small and vulnerable...

[18] My thanks to Professor A.F.L. Beeston and to Professor G. Rex Smith who read and commented helpfully on an earlier draft of this paper.

X

THE BARĀHIMA: LITERARY CONSTRUCT AND HISTORICAL REALITY

John Wansbrough's rebukes to historians find their wittiest expression in his '*Res ipsa loquitur*', an essay in which the nub of the problem seems to be this, that he thinks historians are writing novels and they think they are presenting the facts. Accused of engaging with language games, narrative structures and creative mimesis, a wise historian might decide to be flattered, and stick to his last. Wansbrough, after all, is also a historian: a typological assessment of his work will not (yet) find that he has slipped into the genre of novel, or theology. Even his extensive exercises in literary criticism are part of an effort to tell the history of a community. His objections are to the arbitrarily privileged position of 'reality', the tyranny of some narrative structures, the eschewal of interpretative versatility, and a lack of methodological and literary self-consciousness. Significant criticisms, but presented in a context which implies not only serious concern with but enjoyment of the achievement of these historians, novelists *malgré eux*.

If historians have been disturbed to find themselves classified with novelists, contemporary Muslims have also been disturbed on being informed that what they thought was history was actually (often) theology (disguised as narrative, etc.). Muslims and Orientalists, regretfully not in collusion,[1] find themselves caught in the same methodological impasse, its result a hunger for facts. Whether this desire for a real referent is a general result of human psychology, or a temporary result of peer-group conditioning, it is under pressure from the methodologies of late twentieth-century thinking. For the group of academic historians sometimes called Orientalists, the message is (or should be) pressing. The irredeemable caducity of historiographical discourse and the insidious temptations of a 'detachable conclusion',[2] together with a large number of other factors intrinsic and extrinsic (like the pressures of a politically controlled career structure), encourage a focus on story (history) at the expense of process (interpretation), and it is the latter which, surely, is the real value of historical effort.

An insignificant but pleasant enough example of the scholars' search for a real referent and consequent eschewal of interpretative versatility may be found in the story, or the history, of Western scholarship's engagement with the tantalizing Barāhima. Discovered in a scatter of heresiographical fragments and theological texts, this word, by a long process of thought that began with Paul Kraus in 1934, was finally recognized as 'authentically' reflecting 'the reality of Indian–Muslim debates, and the lasting impression these debates made on Islam'.[3] That was Sarah Stroumsa in 1985, effecting a closure of academic discourse by equating text and reality; and bringing Western scholarship back into harmony with Ibn Ḥazm and Shahrastānī (collusion again). These Brahmins were odd but at least they were real. Paul Kraus had initiated the debate by suggesting that they were so odd they could not possibly be real: someone had to be lying (or writing a novel).

[1] cf. Wansbrough, '*Res ipsa loquitur:* history and mimesis' (Albert Einstein Memorial Lecture, Israel Academy of Sciences, Jerusalem, 1987), 9.

[2] ibid., 23–5.

[3] Sarah Stroumsa, 'The Barāhima in early Kalām', *JSAI*, 6, 1985, 241.

Kraus observed that the characteristics attributed to the Barāhima in a number of late Muslim theological texts do not correspond to the familiar characteristics of the Indian Brahmins. Discovering in an Ismāʿīlī source (the *Majālis Muʾayyadiyya* of al-Muʾayyad fīʾl-Dīn Hībat Allāh al-Shīrāzī, d. 470/1077) excerpts from the *Kitāb al-Zumurrud* of Ibn al-Rāwandī (fl. third/ninth century), he presented these as the earliest known references to the Barāhima, and perhaps the source for all later references (more limited in 1934 than now). The peculiar nature of these Barāhima, whose doctrines betray no link with the real Brahmins, might be explained, he suggested, on the assumption that the author, a notorious heretic, used the Barāhima as a mouthpiece for his own ideas. They were a dialectical construct, or, simply, a lie.[4]

Josef van Ess objected to this. He showed that Ibn al-Rāwandī's reputation was not uniformly bleak: the Māturīdīs approved of him. Furthermore, Kraus (following an admittedly obscure source), had taken Ibn al-Rāwandī's dialectical doxologies to represent his own ideas, which they do not. For Van Ess, following Māturīdī (d. 333/944), the real proponent of the ideas attributed to the Barāhima was Abū ʿĪsā al-Warrāq (fl. early third/ninth century). Can they be linked to the Brahmins? Van Ess proposes that Abū ʿĪsā's ideas display an Iranian anti-Arabism and a Manichaean objection to blood sacrifice. That last point can be linked to the Hindu principle of *ahimsā*. On this slender base, Abū ʿĪsā, now replacing Ibn al-Rāwandī as the subtle liar (novelist), built a picture of the Barāhima, as a cover for his own views.[5] (As presented by Māturīdī, Abū ʿĪsā's ideas are not in fact linked to the Barāhima.) In a subsequent article Van Ess expressed some doubt about Abū ʿĪsā's bad reputation: 'we are not quite sure whether he really was the Crypto-manichaean as which he is depicted in most of our sources.'[6] Still, with due measure of 'ifs' and 'perhapses', someone was lying, and it was probably Abū ʿĪsā. 'If we assume' that Māturīdī used Ibn al-Rāwandī's *Kitāb al-Zumurrud*, then 'it seems' that Abū ʿĪsā 'hid himself behind the Brahmins'. Ibn al-Rāwandī 'may' have quoted from Abū ʿĪsā's *al-Gharīb al-mashriqī*, and this 'stranger from the East' was 'perhaps depicted as a Brahmin'.[7] All of this is somehow more compelling if we recall that the problem of inflicting pain upon animals (cultic sacrifice) corresponds well to the Hindu doctrine of *ahimsā* and to Abū ʿĪsā's Manichaean leanings (if, of course, we can be sure that he really was the Crypto-Manichaean, etc.). Furthermore Abū ʿĪsā's putative knowledge of the Brahmins is made more secure by the fact that he came from a region where Manichaeanism and Buddhism (not Hinduism) were 'a living reality'.[8] Abū ʿĪsā—the conclusion is compelling, is it not?—could have derived enough knowledge about Hindus to use the notion of Brahmins as a cover for his own ideas, which can be shown to reflect (in a very imperfect reflection) one single aspect of Hindu belief. Van Ess admits to being 'euphorical' when he writes about Ibn al-Rāwandī,[9] and he is rebuked by Sarah Stroumsa: 'Van Ess's too personal reading . . . does not carry conviction.'[10]

David Thomas in a study and edition of Abū ʿĪsā's 'Against the Trinity' (quarried from a later source) was not so worried. That 'stranger from the

[4] Paul Kraus, 'Beiträge zur islamischen Ketzergeschichte: das *Kitāb al-Zumurrud* des Ibn al-Rāwandī', *RSO*, 14, 1934, 343f. ('Von den Brahmanen des Ibn al-Rāwandī gibt es keine Brücke zu denen der indischen Wirklichkeit.') See also pp. 356–7, where Kraus suggests reasons why Ibn al-Rāwandī should have chosen the Barāhima as a front for his own views.

[5] Josef Van Ess, 'Ibn ar-Rēwandī, or the making of an image', *Al-Abḥāth*, 27, 1978–79, 15–21.

[6] Van Ess, 'Al-Fārābī and Ibn al-Rēwandī', *Hamdard Islamicus*, 3/4, 1980, 4.

[7] ibid., 7.

[8] ibid., 8.

[9] Van Ess, 'Ibn ar-Rēwandī', 21.

[10] Stroumsa, 'The Barāhima', p.231, n.8.

East' was very effective: 'If this rather neat identification is correct (and any alternative strains coincidence), etc.'[11] What is known about Abū ʿĪsā's *al-Gharīb al-mashriqī* is in fact very little, and does not include the meaning of its title, still less the presence in it of a Brahmin, or a Hindu, or even the Barāhima.[12] The train of academic thought, however, that brought us to this point is at least as engrossing as that of a good detective novel.

Shlomo Pines, independently of Van Ess, took a different route to discover that Ibn al-Rāwandī was not lying (or not very much). He pointed out that the references to the Barāhima in al-Qāsim b. Ibrāhīm (d. 246/860) (not there identified as the Barāhima) and in Saadya (d. 330/942) could not derive from nor be the source of the information in the *Kitāb al-Zumurrud*. There must have been a wider range of information about the Barāhima; and it could be linked to India. For, the stress on Adam (*sic*), and on his law (a feature present in al-Qāsim and in Saadia, but not in the *Zumurrud*) recalls the doctrine of Manu, the first man, and the Manusmriti, his code of law. 'The similarity . . . is unmistakable.'[13] For Pines, with this slender link to the real Brahmins, Ibn al-Rāwandī (and Pines admits it is only a possibility) used the Barāhima in order to express his own views. Not lying, just embellishing the truth.

From even this indictment, S. Stroumsa set out to clear Ibn al-Rāwandī. Following the trail back to Abū ʿĪsā, she was able to add the evidence of Abū Muṭīʿ Makḥūl al-Nasafī, a contemporary of al-Māturīdī.[14] But not to much effect: Abū Muṭīʿ tells us about the *harābidha* of Balkh, who, in addition to having views very reminiscent of those of the Barāhima, recognize Abraham as a prophet. They are mentioned under the heading Rāwandiyya, but the link is unclear, and there is no explicit reference to the Barāhima. (The temptation to indulge in creative structure building is of course intense, and not easy to resist; see below, n. 34.) The evidence of Dāwūd b. Marwān al-Muqammis (Jewish theologian, fl. third/ninth century) may be more telling. He too knows the Barāhima and formulates their central theses in a way that (also) cannot depend on the *Zumurrud*.[15] So, from about the middle of the third/ninth century there were at least three observers (Abū ʿĪsā, al-Muqammis, and al-Qāsim ibn Ibrāhīm) who, apparently independently, describe the Barāhima. (Except that nowhere in our present sources are the views of Abū ʿĪsā linked to the Barāhima, while al-Qāsim does not call his group the Barāhima. Fortunately, 'it stands to reason' that Abū ʿĪsā 'must have ... connected the Barāhima' with his arguments against prophecy.[16] Of the other two early writers, Ibn al-Rāwandī is (presumably) dependent on Abū ʿĪsā; and Saadya (rather later) offers nothing substantially different from al-Qāsim (the whole being limited to not much more than a theory of Adam as prophet).

Perhaps Muqammis too depends on Abū ʿĪsā (who would then be unmasked as the grand perpetrator of a lie about Brahmins)? Not so, says Stroumsa. There exist two Geniza fragments which 'seem to contain hitherto lost passages' of Muqammis's work, the *ʿIshrūn maqāla*. These passages do not appear in any known manuscript of that work. They raise an interesting argument of reason against those who find value in prophets. Why should not

[11] David Thomas, *Anti-Christian polemic in early Islam: Abū ʿĪsā al-Warrāq's 'Against the Trinity'* (Cambridge, 1992), 25.

[12] ibid., 22.

[13] Shlomo Pines, 'Shīʿite terms and conceptions in Juda Halevi's Kuzari', *JSAI*, 2, 1980, 220–3. The link from Manu to Adam had been made earlier by A. Christensen; see Bruce B. Lawrence, *Shahrastānī on the Indian religions*, (Religion and Society, 4, The Hague and Paris, 1976), p.89, n.248.

[14] Stroumsa, 'The Barāhima', 232.

[15] ibid., 234–6.

[16] ibid., 237.

God take immediately to heaven a perfect being such as a prophet and so provide him immediately with his promised reward, rather than leave him to fulfil his mission on earth? A tricky question no doubt, but routine stuff, one would imagine, for a Jewish, or a Christian, or a Muslim theologian; if no one formulated it for them, they might have done it themselves, as a way into a defence of prophecy. Stroumsa however, assuming (amongst so much else) that the Barāhima are the polemical adversary here, detects a significant link to a topic of theological dispute between Hīnayāna and Mahāyāna Buddhism; yes, Buddhism. Given these anonymous Geniza fragments, the link to Buddhism, the actual references to the Barāhima in Muqammis's *'Ishrūn maqāla*, and a further reference in the same book to a refutation of the *aṣḥāb al-budud* (which can be linked to the *aṣḥāb al-bidada*, identified as a sub-group of the Barāhima by Shahrastānī—only some 250 years later, and clearly Buddhists), a conclusion emerges. All of this 'seems to reflect authentic knowledge of Indian religious groups, generically referred to as Barāhima'. So, if the agenda of beliefs attributed to the Barāhima does not coincide with known beliefs of the Brahmins, no matter; the reference is generic and covers any Indian religion. Abū 'Īsā, it is now obvious, was not lying, he collected and handed down the opinions of the Barāhima, 'as he knew them' (as Brahmins, or Buddhists, or whatever). Kraus's problem, namely, the discrepancy between the theological Barāhima and the real Brahmins, is also solved, because 'such a discrepancy does not exist in al-Qāsim b. Ibrāhīm's Barāhima'. (Al-Qāsim did not actually call them Barāhima, but whoever they were they did believe in Adam, and Adam, obviously, was Manu, etc.). And (summarizing much) there are 'basic assumptions' and a 'stable world view' that will hold everything together. Furthermore, we apparently know, in any case, of Indian–Muslim encounters in the formative years of Muslim theology, and the lack of any explicit reference to Indian mythological and theological conceptions is not surprising because the rules of debate prevented such reference. (Unless, obviously, the referents were disguised as Judaeo-Christian prophets like Adam–not to mention Seth, Noah, Abraham and Idris/Enoch.) Hence, early *kalām* references to the Barāhima 'authentically reflect . . . the reality of Indian Muslim debates, and the lasting impression those debates made on Islam.'[17] A detective story, surely; though the plot lacks variety. (And there is more than a hint of a circular argument: if we assume that the Barāhima were Brahmins, then . . . the Muslims debated with Brahmins . . .)

This focus of interest exclusively on the Brahmins distracts from discussion and observation of other issues. It would not have been less interesting to discover, right at the beginning, with Kraus, how the Barāhima functioned in the overall structure of al-Mu'ayyad's work, or in that of Muqammis (who wants to prove the necessity of God's sending prophets) or in Saadya (whose concern is with abrogation). In all cases, as also in the cases of the early Sunnī writers who deal with the same motif, the Barāhima are a foil for polemical argument and for defence of faith. (This *was* a sectarian milieu.) The literature perhaps reflects real debates, but the translation into literary form has conditions. There is no free play of argument here. In Jewish texts, the Jewish protagonist manipulates all motifs in favour of his faith, and in Muslim texts, the Muslim protagonist does likewise. The motifs that are manipulated in these highly stylized defences of faith bear some relationship to reality, but not much.

A reconstruction of Judaism from the *Tamhīd fī 'l-radd* of Muḥammad b.

[17] ibid., 237–41.

al-Ṭayyib al-Bāqillānī (d. 403/1013) would point to a very limited agenda of dogmatic points, in which Jews would recognize fragments, but only fragments, of their faith. Bāqillānī's presentation depends on a slight but logically coherent set of propositions: that Moses was a prophet, that his prophecy was proven by miracles, that knowledge of these depends on reliable transmission. The only further point relevant to Muslim–Jewish debate was Jewish denial of abrogation.[18] The Muslims willingly conceded the prophecy and the miracles of Moses, and claimed only that they were superseded by the miracles and the prophecy of Muḥammad. Christian–Jewish debate had (earlier) centred on the same points. Saadya's interest in the Barāhima responds to this polemical situation, and is limited only to establishing that the Barāhima have made no claim to a prophetic law which is non-abrogable. If they received a law (*amr*) from Adam, then they did not claim that it would never be abrogated.[19] This point was important to Saadya because his public defence of the Jewish faith required that that position be the exclusive prerogative of the Mosaic law. No other early writer deals with the Barāhima from this point of view, and we are consequently unable to judge whether they held any significant or systematic views on abrogation, or whether, if they did, it was a major, a minor, or an insignificant part of their faith. Saadya uses them only as a foil to build up an argument that will secure the defensive foundations of the Jewish faith.

Bāqillānī identified two different groups within the Barāhima. The first rejects prophets completely, arguing (apparently) that it is not permissible for God to send a prophet, and there is no respect in which it is valid for man to receive a message from the Creator. The second group admits either that God has sent no prophet except Adam, or no prophet except Abraham. Bāqillānī deals with the first group at very great length, not because they are important, or the dominant group (though they may be), but because the arguments he attributes to them, when systematically refuted, serve his purposes, namely, to demonstrate the true and firm foundations of the Muslim faith. Only at the end of his refutation does he reintroduce that group who follow Adam and/or Abraham, not to discuss them, but to dismiss them, for the logic of their position is dealt with elsewhere:

> As to those of the Barāhima who affirm the prophecy of Adam while denying the prophecy of those after him, and those who affirm the prophecy of Abraham while denying those after him, they have admitted the permissibility of sending prophets, and that they have existed and their message been transmitted, although they dispute with us on the prophecy of particular individuals. The claim of this group is not that of those who deny prophecy absolutely. We say to them, What is your proof for the prophecy of Adam or Abraham? If they say, The appearance of signs at their hands, we say, What is your proof for the validity and truth of these signs—granted that we have not witnessed them, nor met those who did so? If they say, It is the transmission of those whose numbers guarantee them against lying, then they are opposed by like arguments in respect of Moses, Jesus and Muḥammad. And the dispute with them takes the form of the dispute with the Jews.[20]

Bāqillānī focuses on one group within the Barāhima, the group who rejected prophecy, because the refutation of their argument could be exploited by him

[18] al-Bāqillānī, Muḥammad b. al-Ṭayyib Abū Bakr, *al-Tamhīd fī'l-radd ʿalā 'l-mulḥida*, ed. Khudayri and Abū Rayda (Cairo, 1366/1947), 131–40, 140–7; cf. Wansbrough, *The sectarian milieu* (Oxford, 1978), 110–14, 150–4.

[19] Saadya, apud Pines, 'Shīʿite terms', 221.

[20] al-Bāqillānī, *Tamhīd*, 113–14; and see all of 96–114.

to build up a logical defence of the Muslim faith. Saadya had focused on (? the other group) those who accepted the prophecy of Adam, because their argument, wrongly (!) understood, blocked his argument about abrogation.

It is obvious, and has been noted elsewhere, that the motifs of inter-sectarian debate differ from the motifs of intra-sectarian development.[21] Given the highly specialized social context of the documents under discussion, and the technical manipulation of argument they display, it seems unlikely they will tell us much about the real Barāhima (just as Bāqillānī would be a quite hopeless source for the history of Rabbinic Judaism, almost none of its distinguishing characteristics being acknowledged by him). The Barāhima are in effect transformed into a limited set of motifs which are important because they can be refuted and turned into a defence of another faith, either Islam or Judaism. It was a sure prompt to imaginative effort that these motifs included the apparently irreconcilable claims that the Barāhima both denied prophecy and acknowledged some prophets.

Bāqillānī's Jews, Christians and Zoroastrians were real groups, even if their historical and social complexity was compromised for polemical purposes. What about the Barāhima? In his monograph *Shahrastānī on the Indian religions*, Bruce Lawrence offers an elaborate analysis of Shahrastānī's chapter, 'On the opinions of the people of India'. Much of his commentary takes the form of literary history, detective work on Shahrastānī's sources, and on the cognitive and theological structures that dictated his understanding and organization of material. Lawrence's section on the Barāhima gives an overview of Western scholarship on this issue, and includes neat summaries of Bāqillānī, 'Abd al-Qāhir b. Ṭāhir al-Baghdādī (d. 429/1037) and later Muslim writers. He does not use Van Ess, Pines or Stroumsa. It is interesting therefore to note that, though the main focus of his interest is Indian religions, he points to no similarity between the views ascribed to the Barāhima in the theological tradition and the known views of the Brahmins/Hindus. He follows Kraus in accounting for the whole tradition by referring to Ibn al-Rāwandī 'or his anonymous predecessor(s)' using the Barāhima 'as a front' for a particular rationalist view.[22] He persuades himself that there was some logical ground for Ibn al-Rāwandī's action in that the Indian Brahmins would have seemed like strict rationalists to Muslims.[23] Just why this is so, he does not explain. The Nestorian Christian al-Kindī (dated by Kraus to the early tenth century C.E., but of uncertain date) had already (more correctly) observed that, from a rationalist standpoint, the liturgical and cultic practices of Muslims, Buddhists and Brahmins were equally repugnant.[24]

There is in fact nothing in the early texts to link the Barāhima to India. Not Muqammis, nor Ibn al-Rāwandī, nor anything attributed to Abū 'Īsā (the only sources of the third/ninth century, leaving for the moment Qāsim b. Ibrāhīm) make that link; nor does Saadya, and nor do the earliest Muslim writers, Bāqillānī and Baghdādī. In spite of the efforts of Van Ess, Pines, and Stroumsa, there is not a single dogmatic item in the agenda of Barāhima beliefs that evokes the beliefs of Hinduism. But there are numerous items that situate the group within the Judaeo-Christian-Muslim tradition. Most obviously there are the references to prophets (Adam in Saadya, Adam and Abraham in Bāqillānī). The further concern with reason as an epistemological category

[21] See e.g. Jacob Neusner, *Aphrahat and Judaism* (Leiden, 1971).

[22] Lawrence, *Shahrastānī*, 85.

[23] ibid., 84.

[24] ibid., 77; cf. Kraus, 'Beiträge', 337–9. See for this al-Kindī ('Abd al-Masīḥ b. Isḥāq), *EI* (2nd ed.), ad 'Kindī'.

(evident in Saadya, Muqammis, Bāqillānī and Baghdādī) is in no way foreign to that tradition. Evoked in Jewish texts of the third/ninth century, it recalls the milieu of the Rabbanite–Karaite dispute; and in Muslim texts of the same period and later, the Sunnī-Muʿtazilī dispute. Bāqillānī is in no doubt about the intellectual affiliations of his Barāhima: they are assumed to be monotheists, sharing the basics of Judaeo-Christian belief and the technical terminology of Judaeo-Christian-Muslim debate (*sharʿ, samʿ, maṣlaḥa, luṭf, ʿāda*), and they are closely allied to the Muʿtazila.[25] Baghdādī makes the same broad assumptions (though he has lost sight of any group within the Barāhima who acknowledge prophets), and adds an interesting elaboration of their theory of human actions. These, according to the Barāhima, are the product of rational thought (*ʿaql*) and of *khawāṭir*. Rational human beings are subject to the influence of two *khāṭirs*, one from God inciting him to reflection and to acknowledgement of God, the other from the Devil, inciting him to evil. Baghdādī assumes that this view was also held by the Qadariyya (Muʿtazila), and gives a variant account of it from al-Naẓẓām.[26] It is in fact recognizably a reflection of the Jewish tradition of the two *yezer*, the 'inclinations' to either good or evil, situated, like the *khawāṭir* of the Barāhima, in the human heart.[27] I know of no echoes to these ideas in Hinduism.

Taking into consideration only the early sources, the most obvious conclusion is that the Barāhima were a sect completely explicable in terms of the Islamic environment and its Judaeo-Christian heritage, and not Indians at all. Beyond that we know little about them: a large or a small group? a group of intellectuals? with or without a long historical pedigree? still extant in the fourth/tenth and fifth/eleventh centuries? There are some tantalizing clues scattered in the sources, but they hardly promise knowledge.

My postulate is then that we have here one word with two distinct referents—a Judaeo-Christian-Muslim group and the Brahmins. Such a postulate has some merits: it frees scholarship from the need to assume that someone was lying, and from the need to build insubstantial bridges from the Islamic to the Indian sectarian milieu. Bearing this postulate in mind, the peculiar confusion and error of later Islamic descriptions of the Brahmins in India (the Barāhima), is explained. They conflated the information of the theological tradition (the Islamic Barāhima) with the information provided by geographical and travel literature (the Indian Barāhima). The Barāhima of Ibn Ḥazm (d. 456/1064) are located in India, and have the correct Indian attributes of superior caste and sacred thread. They also, in conformity with the theological tradition, deny the occurrence of prophecy. The Barāhima of Juwaynī (d. 478/1085), by contrast and in conformity with the early theological tradition, are not situated in India and have no Indian characteristics; they have only—like the Barāhima of the older tradition—several versions of the arguments about the sufficiency of reason and the denial of prophecy.[28] The Barāhima of Muḥammad b. ʿAbd al-Karīm al-Shahrastānī (d. 568/1153) are a complex bunch, not least because he uses the term generically and so introduces a great deal of accurate information, e.g. about Buddhism, under the general heading. His initial description of the theological agenda of the Barāhima is however that of the Judaeo-Christian (Islamic) group, not an Indian group. In his

[25] Bāqillānī, *Tamhīd*, 104.3 and 107.20 (*Fa-in qālū aw qāla ikhwānu-hum min al-Muʿtazila*); 108.8 (*al-Barāhima waʾl-Muʿtazila*); 110.1 (*wa-in qāla al-fariqānī wa-man tabaʿa-hum*), etc. Cf. Lawrence, *Shahrastānī*, 88.

[26] al-Baghdādī, ʿAbd al-Qāhir b. Ṭāhir Abū Manṣūr, *Kitāb Uṣūl al-dīn* (Istanbul, 1346/1928), 154–5.

[27] See Schechter, *Some aspects of Rabbinic theology* (New York, 1909: repr. 1961), 242–63.

[28] For Ibn Ḥazm and Juwaynī, see Lawrence, *Shahrastānī*, 96–8.

introductory sentences, Shahrastānī refers to some who maintain that the Barāhima are so called because they name themselves after Abraham (Ibrāhīm). This he describes as an error, though, he claims, there are some Indian dualists who believe in the prophecy of Abraham. (The Arabic/Muslim confusion of Brahman and Ibrāhīm was of some antiquity.[29]) The Barāhima, according to Shahrastānī, are named after a man called Barhām. (Ibn Ḥazm had done better here, if it is indeed the Indian Brahmins who are at issue, with a reference to Brahma.)[30]

The mixture, not to say muddle, of Indian and Judaeo-Christian elements can be usefully illustrated from the *Kitāb Uṣūl al-dīn* of the Māturīdī scholar, Muḥammad b. Muḥammad al-Bazdawī (d. 493/1099). His concern, like that of Bāqillānī earlier, is really with the refutation of the argument against prophecy, but his introductory remarks are revealing.

> The Sumaniyya [text reads Shamaniyya]—they are the learned class of India—say that the sending of prophets is not permissible, basing their argument on reason; and they deny all prophets. Some of them claim that it is permissible, based on reason, and they affirm the prophecy, exclusively, of Adam. Some of them affirm the prophecy of Adam and Abraham, denying all subsequent prophets. The Barāhima, of the learned class of India, affirm the prophecy of Noah, Abraham and Idrīs, denying all other prophets. Because of this they are called Barāhima. They say, We are not the children of Adam; Adam was after us; he settled in our country and died there.[31]

That passage presents numerous difficulties (and prompts several strategies) of interpretation. The Barāhima are classified as a group who affirm the prophecy of Noah and Idrīs (Enoch) as well as Abraham. This information is new to the tradition and one must wonder where Bazdawī got it from. There is no obvious answer. (Did he perhaps know some Barāhima?) The major theological arguments attributed by Bāqillānī, Baghdādī, Juwaynī, etc. to the Barāhima (or a group within the Barāhima)—the arguments of reason that deny the necessity or the possibility of prophets—are now relegated to the Sumaniyya/Shamaniyya. Why did Bazdawī do this? Did his information about the Barāhima contradict what had been so frequently asserted about them—namely, that they denied the possibility of prophets? (Sumaniyya was an established term indicating Buddhists; but they had been deemed to have a prophet, Būdāsaf, etc., as early as Ibn al-Nadīm.[32]) In the conventional *kalām* arguments subsequent to this passage, all relating to the sufficiency of reason and the foolishness of prophecy, the Barāhima are (carefully?) not mentioned. They are re-introduced at the end, where they are classified, together with Jews and Christians, not as those who deny prophecy, but as those who affirm some, while denying other, prophets.[33] Bazdawī has clearly undertaken some deliberate and clever structuring in order to dissociate the Barāhima from the very set of ideas that had been, in earlier (and subsequent) Muslim theology, most characteristically theirs. His motives are at present simply unclear (though authoritative information about the Barāhima—a group acknowledging a number of Jewish prophets—might account for his carefully elaborated schema).

[29] See Lawrence, *Shahrastānī*, 90.
[30] Lawrence, *Shahrastānī*, translation, 38–9; commentary, 90–1.
[31] al-Bazdawī, Muḥammad b. Muḥammad Abū 'l-Yusr, *Kitāb Uṣūl al-dīn*, ed. Hans Peter Linss (Cairo, 1383/1963), 90–1.
[32] See Lawrence, *Shahrastānī*, 106–7.
[33] al-Bazdawī, *Kitāb Uṣūl al-dīn*, 96.

The two references to India in this passage are (significantly?) parenthetical. Further, in order to understand the reference to the group's name, the reader must disregard the immediately preceding phrase, and focus on Ibrāhīm, the middle item in a group of three. Could this be evidence of interpolation? Why are the groups who affirm the prophecy of Adam, or Adam and Abraham, classified with the Sumaniyya? Are they not precisely one of Bāqillānī's divisions of the Barāhima? It is possible to interpret this passage as product of clever logical manipulation of facts that are known, inherited, acquired and guessed at, in search of harmonization; or (and?), as product of expansion, interpolation and scribal deformation. Or is it just a muddle? It is a muddle, but product of an effort to make sense of recalcitrant materials. At least one factor that has acted to create that muddle is the conflation of ideas that refer—perhaps—to one group, the Islamic, Judaeo-Christian, Barāhima, with those that refer to another group, the Barāhima who are the learned class of India.[34]

If the Barāhima were an Islamic (Judaeo-Christian) sect, then their name offers the obvious explanation of being associated with Ibrāhīm. The point is made here by Bazdawī, and was known to Shahrastānī. It may be implicit in Bāqillānī (and if the Rāwandiyya/Harābidha of Nasafī are Barāhima, then it is there too).[35] Unfortunately, conflation of Brahma and Ibrāhīm was easy for Muslim observers, even when the object observed was, explicitly, Hindu belief. In a (bad) Persian translation of Bīrūnī's Arabic version of the Yogasūtra of Patanjali, the name Ibrāhīm is substituted for that of Brahma.[36] Perhaps the most significant evidence favouring the idea that the Islamic Barāhima were followers of Abraham is found in Al-Qāsim b. Ibrāhīm. He does not refer to the Barāhima, but to a group called the Ibrāhīmiyya. They are recognizable as Saadya's Barāhima because they share with that group significant focus on the prophet Adam. Al-Qāsim, having the same kind of sectarian purpose as is evident in all other references to the Barāhima, is concerned with the question of a *waṣiyya*, bequeathed from Adam to Seth and not subsequently abrogable. The terminological focus is of course Ismāʿīlī and creates a foil for the establishment of the truth of the Ismāʿīlī faith. Al-Qāsim also says of the Ibrāhīmiyya that they are a group from India, the lords of that country.[37] If this is not an interpolation (in this case a more than usually tempting recourse), it is the only text prior to Ibn Ḥazm that situates the (theological, Judaeo-Christian) Barāhima in India.

[34] Bazdawī's disassociation of the Barāhima from the notion of the denial of prophecy is so deliberate and so odd that it perhaps justifies the following speculation. One of his known sources was Abū Mūtīʿ Makḥūl al-Nasafī (an early proponent of the Hanafī-Māturīdī school of theology which was also Bazdawī's—see M. Bernand, 'Le *Kitāb al-Radd ʿala l-bidaʿ* d'Abū Muṭīʿ Makḥūl al-Nasafī', *Annales Islamologiques*, 16, 1980, 41–5). The unique manuscript of Nasafī's heresiographical work identifies, under the general heading of the Qadariyya, a group known as the Rāwandiyya. His discussion of that group is just sufficient to link them to the Barāhima, a point already noted by Stroumsa. While discussing this group Nasafī specifies that he has met and debated with the spokesman for the Harābidha of Balkh. But why should the Harābidha of Balkh—the word signals Zoroastrians—be cited in the context of a group who are otherwise identified as Rāwandiyya and Qadariyya? The manuscript (Oxford, Pococke 271) quite clearly reads *harābidha*, but, dated 847 (A.H.), it is a late exemplar. The possibility of a scribal malformation deriving from an original outline reading *barāhima* should perhaps be entertained; though nothing more for the moment than that. Entertaining the thought, one merely notes that the group actually existed in Balkh in the fourth century and had a spokesman (*mutakallimuhum*) who debated with Nasafī.

[35] See n.34. I see no problems in the move from Ibrāhīm to either Ibrāhīmī or Barhamī (cf. Abū Ḥanīfa, Ḥanafī), and likewise no problems with the plural form Barāhima (cf. Ḥanafī, Aḥānifa).

[36] Lawrence, *Shahrastānī*, 90. The work referred to is by Abū 'l-Maʿālī, and can be dated to 485/1092. Later than Ibn Ḥazm, and roughly contemporaneous with Bazdawī, the work reflects what was clearly a widespread confusion.

[37] Al-Qāsim b. Ibrāhīm, apud Pines, 'Shīʿite terms', 220f.

This detective story does not become easier, and, with two groups sharing one name, has taken on some characteristics of Renaissance drama, or later farce. Western scholarship, responding initially to the highly charged accusation of lying which was intrinsic to Kraus's study of the Barāhima, followed only one path, that which led from the Barāhima to the Brahmins of India. Their disregard of the other alternative, that which leads from the Barāhima to Islamic and Judaeo-Christian Abrahamites, is merely arbitrary. The problem had always been a simple one: why do the (early theological) Barāhima bear no significant relationship to the Brahmins? Available but unacknowledged was the answer proposed here: they were not Brahmins. There is evidence for an Abrahamic movement in the pre-Islamic Near East, a movement based on rejection of the prophecy of Moses, Jesus, and, later, Muḥammad. It is also certain that a distinguishable Abrahamic movement, sometimes associated with the *ḥanīfs*, played some part in the formative period of Islamic doctrine.[38] It is not easy to relate these movements to the highly intellectual Barāhima, closely allied to the Muʿtazila, of the third/ninth century and later; and, without further evidence, it is probably pointless to make the effort (though it would not be greater than that expended on linking the—theological—Barāhima to India).

If the interpretation proposed here is speculatively entertained, some at least of the consequences and reformulations that it prompts will be obvious. Two are worth mentioning. Abū ʿĪsā, whose works and opinions are so imperfectly preserved, and so arduously quarried from later sources (and who still—or therefore?—emerges as an astonishing intellectual genius), appears to have views which are identical with those of the (Islamic) Barāhima. He was perhaps, not using the Indian Brahmins as a cover, but simply an Abrahamite. This would at least explain the mystery of his obscure religious affiliation, and is consistent with a rationalist monotheism which dispassionately observes and usually condemns all other religious positions.[39] A major paradox of Barhamī belief is that they apparently both deny the validity of prophets, and affirm the prophecy of Adam, Abraham, etc. Bāqillānī, in affirming the existence of two groups, each holding one of these incompatible opinions, is perhaps dealing with this paradox. Bazdawī, in spite of the theological tradition, effectively denies that the Barāhima had rejected the whole notion of prophecy. But perhaps the two ideas are not incompatible. It is possible so to define prophecy that a prophet is one who reaches, through reason and reflection alone, the highest possible knowledge and understanding of monotheist belief. (This notion is of course associated with the philosophical tradition, but perhaps not exclusively.) Some versions of the Abraham myth, in its Arabic and Muslim versions, suggest that he could be understood as this kind of prophet.[40] And some such theory of prophecy might be discovered in positions attributed to Abū ʿĪsā.[41] But here, for the moment, speculation must stop.

In the later tradition of Islamic theology (*kalām*) the Barāhima became,

[38] See *inter alia* Michael Cook, *Muhammad* (Oxford, 1983), 80–1; Yehuda Nevo and Judith Koren, 'The origins of the Muslim descriptions of the Jāhilī Meccan sanctuary', *JNES*, 49, 1, 1990, 41f; Uri Rubin, 'Hanīfiyya and Kaʿba: an inquiry into the Arabian pre-Islamic background of *dīn Ibrāhīm*', *JSAI*, 13, 1990.

[39] See Thomas, *Anti-Christian polemic*, 9–30, for a lengthy analysis of Abū ʿĪsā's possible religious affiliation; I do not myself find that the arguments that point to 'distinctly Shīʿite sympathies' (p.22) are all that obvious.

[40] See Calder, 'Tafsīr from Ṭabarī to Ibn Kathīr: problems in the description of a genre', in G. R. Hawting and A.-K. A. Shareef (ed.), *Approaches to the Qurʾān* (London, Routledge), 115–27.

[41] This may be implied in the distinctly unclear set of arguments attributed to Abū ʿĪsā in Muḥammad b. Muḥammad Abū Manṣūr al-Māturīdī, *Kitāb al-Tawḥīd*, ed. Fathalla Kholeif (Beirut, 1970), 191–2. See Thomas's interpretation, *Anti-Christian polemic*, 28 ad. n. 95.

for the most part, simply a peg for the notion of denial of prophecy. That was their central, and in many contexts, their only characteristic. Where expansion took place, a complex of other motifs had to be dealt with, deriving from India, or from the irritating fact that the Barāhima also acknowledged some prophets. In these circumstances the most obvious recourse was multiplication of entities. ʿAbd al-Raḥmān Ibn al-Jawzī (d. 596/1200) was primarily concerned with the Barāhima as denying prophecy, but, clearly prompted by his multiplicity of sources, had to acknowledge a number of sub-sects (*madhāhib*). There were some who believed in the prophecy of Adam and Abraham (Bāqillānī is the probable source here); another group, described by Nawbakhtī, claimed that their prophet (*sic*) was an angel with four hands and twelve heads, who commanded (amongst other things) the veneration of fire and the worship of cows; still another group practised self-immolation by fire.[42] Indian and Judaeo-Christian elements here converge and separate, perceived as division within one community.

The effort of ʿAbd al-Karīm b. Ibrāhīm al-Gīlānī[43] demonstrates a different approach. In his *Al-insān al-kāmil fi maʿrifat al-awākhir wa-ʾl-awāʾil*, a work whose main purpose is to set forth the mystic philosophy of Ibn ʿArabī, he mentions, towards the end, a list of communities who have failed to achieve truth. There, the Barāhima figure as those who claim that they belong to the religion of Abraham and are his descendants.

> The Barāhima worship God in an absolute sense, not with reference to prophets or messengers (*nabī, rasūl*). They claim that there is nothing in existence which is not a part of God's creation. They affirm the unity of God as to existence (*muqirrūna bi-waḥdāniyyat Allāh fī ʾl-wujūd*). But they deny prophets and messengers absolutely. Their worship belongs to that type of worship characteristic of messengers (*rusul*) prior to receiving their message (? *ʿibādatu-hum nawʿ li-ʾl-ḥaqq min ʿibādat al-rusul qabl al-irsāl*). They claim that they are the children of Abraham, and affirm that they have a book written by Abraham, while making no claim that it is from God. The book contains truths (*al-ḥaqāʾiq*) and is in five parts. As to the first four, it is permitted for all to read them. As to the fifth, it is permitted only to some individuals within that community because of its profundity. It is well known amongst them that anyone who reads the fifth part will have to interpret its contents as referring to Islam, and will join the religion of Muḥammad. This group constitutes most of those found in the land of India. But there are some people who steal their clothes, claiming that they are the Barāhima [text: Ibrāhima], but they are not so. They are in fact well-known to worship idols, and those who worship idols are not considered by them to be of this group.[44]

In this description, some familiar motifs are joined to some new ones (familiar, the rejection of prophecy; new, the book that comes from Abraham and its five parts). The problem, already several times signalled, of a group that is perceived both to deny prophecy and to affirm the prophecy of Abraham is dealt with in a novel manner. The reference to *waḥdāniyyat Allāh fī ʾl-wujūd* is tendentious and reflects Gīlānī's own philosophy rather than that of the Barāhima. And the notion of false Barāhima who, though idolaters, steal the

[42] Ibn al-Jawzī, Abū ʾl-Faraj ʿAbd al-Raḥmān, *Talbīs Iblīs*, ed. M. M. Isṭambūlī (Damascus, 1396/1976), 65 and 69–70. Cf. Kraus, 'Beiträge', 342–59.

[43] For whom see R. A. Nicholson on 'The Perfect Man' in his *Studies in Islamic mysticism* (Cambridge, 1921), 77–142.

[44] al-Gīlānī, ʿAbd al-Karīm b. Ibrāhīm, *al-Insān al-Kāmil fī maʿrifat al-awākhir waʾl-awāʾil* (Cairo, 1368/1949), II, 80.

clothes (and the name) of the real Barāhima, is a nice variant on Ibn al-Jawzī's multiplication of entities. Just what the whole represents in terms of independent knowledge, harmonizing and creative rational guesswork, and tendentious presumption it is difficult, completely, to assess. This scholar too is engaged in language games and creative mimesis: he has his own novel to write.

Wansbrough, in reference to his experiment (the term is precise) in studying the historiography of the seventh-century Hijāz, ruefully concluded that 'to historians the factor of ambiguity is not especially welcome'.[45] He meant modern historians, though they are not, in this respect, different from their medieval Muslim colleagues. It may be possible, however, to be reconciled to ambiguity. Modern novels (like modern films), sometimes, eschew narrative closure. Modern historians, if they are fully aware of the hermeneutical nature of their discipline, and of its epistemological limitations, may have to do the same.

[45] Wansbrough, '*Res ipsa*', 15.

XI

IKHTILÂF AND IJMÂ‘ IN SHÂFI‘Î 'S RISÂLA

The characteristic aspiration of Islamic jurisprudence (1) to encompass all spheres of human activity was already evident in the structural rubrics of Mâlik's *Muwaṭṭa'* and was explicitly formulated by Shâfi‘î: "There is no event that befalls the people of God's *dîn* but that there is an indicator *(dalîl)* in the Book of God as to the path of guidance therein (48)". (2) This depiction of all human acts and activities as worthy of God's interest and object of his commands was a sacralisation of the human condition; but was also and inevitably a mode of social control and an articulation of authority. The term 'Book of God' as used by Shâfi‘î referred not simply to scripture (Quranic material) but ultimately to all forms of divine revelation. (3) The limits of that revelation, its modes and its valid principles of interpretation constitute the subject matter of the *Risâla*, as indeed of all of Shâfi'î's polemical writings. Such epistemological considerations defined, however, not

(1) For the intellectual background to the development of Islamic juristic literature, see Wansbrough, *The Sectarian Milieu*, Oxford, 1978 and *Quranic Studies*, Oxford, 1977; for a detailed analysis of early juristic literature and a survey of Shâfi‘î's achievement, see J. Schacht, *The Origins of Muslim Jurisprudence*, Oxford, 1950.

(2) Figures in brackets refer to paragraph numbers in M. ibn Idrîs al-Shâfi‘î, *Al-Risâla*, ed., A. M. Shâkir, Cairo, 1309. See also on this point para. 1326; and Schacht, *op. cit.*, 136, n. 6.

(3) In the *Risâla* paras. 53-78 constitute a preliminary assessment of what is meant by *kitâb allâh*, but see also 96-100. See, on typology of revelation, Wansbrough, *Studies*, 51-2, 174-5.

only the nature and limits of knowledge *('ilm)* but defined also its possessors and the extent of their authority.

Knowledge *('ilm)*, Shâfi'î asserts, is of two types (961). The first type is *'ilm 'âmma*—the knowledge belonging to a generality: it is a knowledge such that it is not permissible for an adult who is sane to be ignorant of it. Examples of this knowledge include the five daily prayers the fact that God exacts fasting in Ramadan, the pilgrimage, *zakât* on wealth, the fact that God has forbidden fornication, killing, stealing and wine, and other things of this kind *(wa-mâ fî ma'nâ hâdhâ)*, things that is wherewith God has charged *(taklîf)* his servants either to know, or to give, or to abstain from. This type of knowledge is found textually *(naṣṣan)* in the Book of God or generally *('âmman)* amongst the people of *Islam (ahl al-islâm)*; it is transmitted by the generality of them *('awâm-muhum)* from the generality; they relate it on the authority of the prophet of God and they do not dispute *(wa-lâ yatanâ-za'ûn)* as to its being related nor as to its being incumbent on them. This 'general' knowledge *(al-'ilm al-'âmm)* is that kind of knowledge wherein error is not possible neither with respect to its reported form *(khabar)* nor interpretation *(ta'wîl)*, nor is dispute permissible therein *(wa-la yajûz fîhi l-tanâzu')* (961-965).

The second type of knowledge consists of subsidiary duties and questions of detail *(furû' al-farâ'iḍ, khâṣṣ al-aḥkâm)* which concern God's servants; this is a type of knowledge on which there is no scriptural text *(naṣṣ kitâb)* nor with respect to most of it is there a text of Tradition *(naṣṣ sunna)*, though there is Tradition *(sunna)* on part of it. It consists only of the reports of the specialists *(akhbâr al-khâṣṣa)*, not those of the generality *(akhbâr al-'âmma)*. This type of knowledge is susceptible to interpretation *(ta'wîl)* and is to be understood by deduction/analogy *(qiyâs)* (966-7). Further, this is a degree of knowledge to which the generality do not attain nor indeed are all of the elite *(al-khâṣṣa)* charged *(taklîf)* with attaining it. With regard to the elite who can attain this degree of knowledge, it is not permissible for all of them, *in toto*, to neglect it, but if, of the elite, a sufficiency *(kifâya)* attain this degree of knowledge, then those who have neglected it incur no sin; but there is a reward *(faḍl)* for those who attain it over and against those who neglect it (971). (1)

Now, this exposition of the nature of knowledge was worked out as part of the dialogue which constitutes the basic literary format of Shâfi'î's *Risâla.* The function of the interlocutary persona in this work was to provide opportunities of repetition and explanation, intended to enhance or clarify the argument. Having heard about the two types of knowledge, the interlocutor demanded "something of the same kind *(fî ma'nâhu)* that might stand as analogy *(li-yakûn qiyâsan 'alayhi)*" (972). Shâfi'î thereupon proceeded—at a tangent—to discuss the nature of the incumbency of *jihâd* and *nafîr* (=going forth to struggle in the way of God). The incumbency of *jihâd* was proved by reference to Qur'ân, Sûra 9, vv. 111, 36, 5, 29 (in that order, the relevant command being expressed by some derivative of the root *qtl*) and by a Tradition from the prophet (again using the root *qtl, qâtala*) (973-6, 977). Shâfi'î then cited Sura 9, vv. 38, 39, 41 which command a 'going forth' *(nfr)* in the way of God. Now, these dicta, divine and prophetic, may, according to Shâfi'î, be taken to imply that *jihâd* as a whole and *nafîr* in particular are incumbent on every obedient servant of God in the same way as prayer and pilgrimage and *zakât* are incumbent on every individual. Or, Shâfi'î suggests, it may be that the meaning of incumbency *(farḍ)* in this case is different from that in the case of prayer. That is, the aim of the incumbency may be a sufficient aim *(qaṣd al-kifâya)* such that those who sufficiently undertake *jihâd* achieve the execution of the incumbency and the supererogatory benefits, and they release those who neglect *jihâd* from sin (980-1). Sûra 4, v. 95 was then adduced to demonstrate that those who avoided *jihâd (al-qâ'idûn* as opposed to *al-mujâhidûn)* were not sinners, but achieved a reward even if it was a lesser reward than those who exerted themselves. Lingering doubts on the part of the interlocutor were dispelled by citation of 9, 122:

(1) See Schacht, *op. cit.*, 136 for his comments on this passage.

(for it were better) if of every group a party did not go out to fight so that they might become learned in religious law, so as to warn the people when they return, that they might be aware.

This shows, says Shâfi'î, that *nafîr* is incumbent on some not others, and that *tafaqquh*—being learned in the law—is incumbent on some not others (988). Thus it is in every duty *(farḍ)* where the aim is to achieve a sufficiency *(qaṣd al-kifâya)* in whatever befalls: i.e. if a sufficiency of Muslims undertake the business then the rest are free from sin (990).

This exposition of the nature of a *farḍ kifâ'î* promoted the development of that term in its technical usage opposed to a *farḍ 'aynî* (a term not found in Shâfi'î's work). (1) Its immediate structural purpose, however, was to define the nature of the second type of knowledge, which was thus a kind of *'ilm al-kifâya*, such that if a sufficiency of Muslims attained it the rest were free from sin in not striving to achieve it.

It may be noted that the two types of knowledge which were thus distinguished were not provided with a clear objective demarcation: Shâfi'î did not immediately offer a distribution of juristic knowledge under the heads he had suggested. He implied, it is true, that demarcation might be based on analysis of sources: what is prescribed in the Book of God or in 'general' Traditions is part of *al-'ilm al-'âmm*. But it is not clear that 'general' Traditions are easily identified as such: it is analysis of incidence of dispute which reveals whether a Tradition is or is not 'general'. Further the words of the Book of God though identified as 'general' are not always easy to understand: the injunction to fight unbelievers for example in Sûra 9 required considerable interpretation before its meaning became clear. Equally in need of interpretation (taking one example from many in the *Risâla*) are the words of the Book of God on *waṣiyya* (393-420). But interpretation, Shâfi'î has informed us, is a characteristic of specialist knowledge. It would appear to be the case that it is the general injunction to fight unbelievers that is known *'âmmatan 'inda ahl al-islâm*; the conditions

(1) See *ibid., loc. cit.,* n. 5.

and qualification depend on interpretation by the elite. It is the possibility (or general notion) of *waṣiyya* that is clear from the Book of God; its conditions and limits are part of the knowledge of the elite. The major structural features of the law (prayer, fasting, pilgrimage, etc) are known to the generality; the details are known to the elite. Such at least would appear to be what is implied. If there is nonetheless some difficulty in demonstrating with precision what Shâfi'î meant, it may of course be because the conceptual distinction he introduced was a product more of feeling than analysis, and/or because its explanatory value was directed at a slightly different problem.

The 'general' knowledge, according to Shâfi'î, does not admit of error, interpretation or dispute; that of the elite does. The knowledge of the elite is based on Traditions which only the elite transmit and is open to interpretation *(ta'wîl)* and *qiyâs*. But the knowledge of the elite is relevant to all: the *'âmma*, it would thus appear, are dependent on the *khâṣṣa* for information as to how to act or refrain from acting. Shâfi'î's definition of knowledge in this respect implies a theory of authority. Everyone has an idea of the structure of the law based on the Book of God and 'general' Traditions, but there is an elite whose knowledge is precise and detailed and whose duty it is to advise and warn the ordinary Muslims. The knowledge which the elite possesses is subject to interpretation, *qiyâs* and dispute: variation amongst the *'ulamâ'* as to the details of the law is not to affect their authority. The effect of this definition of knowledge is to guarantee clerical authority on the one hand and to legitimise dispute on the other. It may be thought that these aims were more pertinent to Shâfi'î's manipulation of logic and concepts than objective description of juristic knowledge.

Having asserted a fundamental typology of knowledge it may be shown that Shâfi'î devoted the whole of the subsequent part of the *Risâla* to analysis of the second type, the knowledge of the elite. The interlocutor demands to know the least that constitutes a *ḥujja* in the way of *khabar al-khâṣṣa* (reports of the elite, also isolated reports, *akhbâr al-âḥâd*), thereby initiating a lengthy discussion of the definitions, conditions, and reasons for the acceptance of isolated Traditions (998ff.). [1]

The problem of conflicting *khabar wâḥid* emerges in para 1250, (where it is confused with the problem of a single *khabar* permitting two possible meanings (1251)). A rudimentary scheme of preference is brought forward (1251) but whether it would be sufficient to ensure that all *fuqahâ'* would always prefer the same *ḥadîth*, (or the same interpretation of an ambiguous *ḥadîth*) might well be doubted. The interlocutor, still puzzled by the nature of *khabar wâḥid* as a juristic proof, is made to ask about the meaning of *ḥujja* (proof). The problem, it becomes clear, lies in this that the term is applied to 'general' Traditions and to 'isolated' Traditions, though they are clearly different, not least because isolated Traditions may give rise to a multiplicity of views which have to be resolved. It transpires that there are two types of *ḥujja.* On the one hand there is a clear scriptural text *(naṣṣ kitâb bayyin)* or a *sunna* on which consensus has been achieved *(sunna mujtama' 'alayhâ)*: these constitute proofs in which all possibility of excuse *('udhr)* is cut off; doubt as to either of these two sources is not permissible and anybody who refuses to accept a proof of this kind is required to repent *(ustutîb)* (1256-9). But as to a *sunna* derived from an isolated report, a *sunna* that is, concerning which the report *(khabar)* may vary, whether because the report *(khabar)* permits of interpretation or because it is transmitted by a unique chain of transmitter ; in such matters the *ḥujja* is different. Nevertheless, it is, in Shâfi'î's opinion, incumbent on scholars to accept such reports, because they constitute a text of revelation (they are *manṣûṣ*) even if what is accepted in this manner does not constitute certainty *(iḥâṭa)* (1260). If, in matters of this kind, someone doubts then he is not required to repent *(lam naqul lahu tub)* but:

> we say to him: you may not, if you are *'âlim* doubt in this matter, just as you may not do other than judge on the basis of the witness of just witnesses, though that witness is subject to error: you judge on that basis because of the appearance

(1) On which, see *ibid.*, 50ff.

(al-ẓâhir) of truthfulness on their part; God is responsible for what you do not know about them (1261).

The two types of *ḥujja* obviously correspond to the two types of knowledge. The first type of *ḥujja* is fundamental and serves to define the basic structure of the law, such that any rejection of this *ḥujja* or of the knowledge arising from it necessitates repentance. The other type of *ḥujja*, that based on a *khabar wâḥid*, is susceptible to interpretation, variable and does not produce certainty. It is incumbent on a learned man to accept the evidence of a *khabar wâḥid* in spite of the fact that it does not produce certainty. It may seem then that variant opinions are inevitable (though they may be minimised by systematic analysis of *isnâds*, etc.) and are built into the system. By arguing for the acceptance of the *khabar wâḥid* as a *ḥujja* Shâfi'î was providing justification for the incidence of *ikhtilâf*.

Shâfi'î's concept of knowledge, I would suggest, was intended to embody a distinction between structural features and peripheral or subsidiary features, of defining features and non-defining features. The usefulness of such an analysis in an era of juristic sectarianism was that it afforded a principal of unity which transcended, while acknowledging, the incidence of dispute. Abrasive contact between local schools was neutralised by recognition that fundamentally they were all the same *(ahl al-islâm)* and that such differences as did exist did not affect the bases. The bases were precisely, as it were by definition, that which the local schools had in common. The unity which Shâfi'î aspired to assert was not an exclusive but an inclusive and tolerant one whose ultimate ground was the common interest and the legitimate authority of the clerical class.

The distinction between two types of knowledge and its relation to *ikhtilâf* was impressed upon the interlocutor/reader by repetition. It emerged again in Shâfi'î's discussion of *qiyâs* (1321-76). *Qiyâs* and *ijtihâd*, he asserts, are two words with one meaning (1324). (They represent, in effect, the intellectual process whereby a finite body of revealed texts may be rendered relevant to the infinite complexity of human events.)

> Every event that befalls a Muslim has its necessary religious value *(ḥukm lâzim)*, and there is evidence as to the true path in that matter. It is incumbent on the Muslim if there is a specific ruling on a matter to follow it. If there is no specific ruling then evidence as to the true path must be sought by *ijtihâd*. And *ijtihâd* is *qiyâs* (1326).

The interlocutor betrays his habitual puzzlement at Shâfi'î's statement and raises a whole series of highly charged questions which prepare the way for a comprehensive survey of the nature of specialist knowledge and the qualifications of the specialists.

> Do you consider that *'âlims* when they excercise *qiyâs* achieve certainty *(iḥâṭa)* thay they have understood God's truth? Is it permissible for them to vary in matters subject to *qiyâs*? Are they obliged *(taklîf)* in every matter to follow one (true) path or are there several different (true) paths? What proof is there that they can exercise *qiyâs* on the basis of surface appearance (when they are ignorant of) fundamental realities *(al-ẓâhir dûn al-bâṭin)*, or that they may vary in their opinions *(yatafarraqû)*? Is their obligation *(taklîf)* with respect to themselves different from that with respect to others? Who may exercise *ijtihâd* and *qiyâs* with respect to himself but not others, and who with respect to himself and others? (1327).

The answer to all this depends—we are no longer surprised to discover—on understanding that knowledge is essentially of two kinds: expressed here as, on the one hand, certainty, based on comprehending both surface appearance and underlying reality *(iḥâṭa fî l-ẓâhir w'al-bâṭin)* and, on the other, truth based on appearance only *(ḥaqq fî l-ẓâhir)* (1328).

The first type of knowledge, that which constitutes *iḥâṭa* certainty, is based on either a revealed text of God's command *(naṣṣ ḥukm li-lâh)* or on a *sunna* transmitted from the generality to the generality. It is not permissible to be ignorant of this knowledge or to have doubts about it (1329). The other type is of course *'ilm al-khâṣṣa*, that is a *sunna* based on *khabar al-khâṣṣa*, a *sunna* known only to the *'ulama'*, such that they alone are obliged *(taklîf)* to know it, a *sunna* found only amongst them or some of them, based on the truthfulness of the individuals who transmit something from the prophet. It is incumbent on the *ahl al-'ilm* that they have recourse to it. It constitutes a truth based on external appearance only, without understanding of inner realities. It is like killing on the basis of two witnesses: (that too is *ḥaqq fî l-ẓâhir* for it is always possible for two witnesses to err) (1330). Knowledge based on *ijmâ'* is also of this kind (1331); (1) as is knowledge based on *ijtihâd* by *qiyâs*. This *(ijtihâd* by *qiyâs)* is a search for truth *(al-ḥaqq)*, but it is truth based on what is apparent *(ẓâhir)* to the *qâ'is* irrespective of what is apparent to the generality of the *'ulamâ'*. God alone knows what cannot be seen (1332).

(If knowledge is sought on the basis of *qiyâs* and if *qiyâs* is rightly exercised the *muqâ'isûn* will be agreed on most matters but we may find them at variance (on others). There are in fact two types of *qiyâs*, one based on essential principles *(fî ma'nâ l-aṣl)* and one based on matters of similarity: only the second type permits of variation. The first type is exclusively arguments *a maiore ad minorem*, or *a minore ad maiorem*.) (2)

The interlocutor naturally requires some clarification and seems particularly perturbed by the phenomenon of variant views being equally permissible. The well-established (well-established, that is, by Shâfi'î in the *Risâla*) response to this related to the fact that, for people who are out of sight of the Ka'ba at prayer-time, all that is required from them is that they make the effort based on whatever indicators are available or known to them to pray in the right direction. But another response is found in this that permission to marry, to inherit, to act as witness is granted on the appearance of justice, though a man may inwardly *(fî l-bâṭin)* be unjust. Two men with different knowledge may be constrained to act differently with respect to the same individual: "the duty incumbent on us with respect to one man is found to differ

(1) See further on *ijmâ'*, below.
(2) For further discussion of Shâfi''îs views on *qiyâs/ijtihâd* see *ibid.*, 120ff.

(mukhtalif) depending on the degree of our knowledge and the knowledge of others" (1350-6). In like manner, with respect to a matter on which there is no binding textual rule, Shâfi'î asserts that a learned Muslim must seek the truth by *ijtihâd* and he is obliged *(taklîf)* to follow the truth (as it appears) to him (1358). The interlocutor continues to express doubt about this "judging a single matter in various ways" (1359) but is reduced temporarily to silence by a further example of court procedure, yet another citation of the *qibla* situation, and a number of Quranic quotations which assert the limitations of man's knowledge (1361-76). The main aim of the argument is to establish *qiyâs* as a valid source of (juristic) knowledge but not an infallible source: it permits, indeed precipitates *ikhtilâf.*

It is by now clear from the structure of Shâfi'î's argument that his real concern is to account for and justify the phenomenon of *ikhtilâf.* An extended discussion of *ijtihâd* permits him to make explicit this concern.

The interlocutor demands reassurance about the permissibility of *ijtihâd* and prompts Shâfi'î to adduce yet again the case of facing the *qibla* during prayer when out of sight of the actual Ka'ba. Each individual can only act on the basis of such signs *(dalâ'il)* as he is familiar with, so that two individuals familiar with different signs may face in different directions (1381). The interlocutor perceives as it were where the argument is going and is made to bring forward objections as follows:

Interlocutor: If I grant you this I grant that in certain circumstances there is *ikhtilâf.*

Shafi'i: State your opinion on this matter.

Int: I say this is not permissible (i.e. I do not grant *ikhtilâf*).

Sh: Imagine it is you and I, and we are both knowledgeable as to the means (of finding the Ka'ba). I say: this is the *qibla*; and you say something different. Which one of us must follow his companion?

Int: Neither.

Sh: What must be done?

Int: If I say it is not incumbent on them to pray until they attain certain knowledge *(iḥâṭa)*, (that is impossible) for they can never know for certain what they cannot see. Then, they must either neglect prayer, or the duty of facing the *qibla* is removed. But I cannot maintain either of these views. I see no alternative to asserting that each one may pray in whatever direction he considers right, and that they are not charged *(taklîf)* with anything else. Alternatively, I may say they are charged with finding the right answer based on both appearance and inner reality *(al-ẓâhir wa'l-bâṭin)* but any error as to the reality as opposed to appearance is discounted *(wuḍi'a 'an-humâ)*.

Sh: Whatever you say, it is proof against you; for you have distinguished between *ḥukm al-bâṭin wa'l-ẓâhir*, which was what you (tried to) deny! (1382-9).

This dialogue is nicely organised to serve its particular dramatic purpose: the interlocutor is brought to admit that there must be in certain circumstances *ikhtilâf* and there may be no way of reconciling two views which, though different, can be neither harmonised nor disproved.

The dialogue proceeds with the interlocutor inclined to assume in a case of *ikhtilâf* that one or both positions must be in error *(khaṭa')*, but the error is *mawḍû'*, set aside, discounted (1389-93). Shâfi'î clearly dislikes the use of the term *khaṭa'* and proceeds to demonstrate that *ikhtilâf* is quite inevitable in certain circumstances. His first example is based on the use of the term *mithl* in Qur'ân, 5, 95 (1394-1401). The second example is based on the choice of a 'just' man *('adl)* to act as witness, etc.: such a choice can only be based on external appearance. Sins and good actions are always both present in an individual's life so there is no escape from the necessity of *ijtihâd* as to which predominates; "this being the case, it is quite inevitable that *mujtahids* will be at variance in their opinions" (1402-1405) (واذا كان هذا هكذا فلا بدّ أن يختلف المجتهدون فيه). Or, for example, two judges may judge one affair, one by accepting, one by rejecting; this is *ikhtilâf*, but each one has acted as was incumbent upon him (1406-7). Furthermore, there is a *ḥadîth* confirming the validity of *ijtihâd* (1409) [1]:

اذا حكم الحاكم فاجتهد فاصاب فله اجران و اذا حكم فاجتهد ثم أخطأ فله اجر

The interlocutor objects to this on the grounds of its being an isolated Tradition, an objection quickly dismissed; he then points to the prophetic use of the term *khaṭa'*.

Int: In the Tradition you have given the prophet mentions error and right *(khaṭa', ṣawâb)*.

Sh: That is proof against you.

Int: How?

Sh: The prophet said that one of them was rewarded more than the other. But there can be no *reward* for what is not permissible, nor can there be a *reward* for an error (even if it is) discounted.

The point Shâfi'î desires to make is that 'error' cannot merit 'reward'. He expresses himself rather clumsily:

> If a person were told to exercise *ijtihâd*, granting the possibility of error, and then did so, as he was commanded, on the basis of external appearance, then any error he committed would be set aside—as you (the interlocutor) have said. But if that were the case then punishment, for an error, would be more appropriate (than reward); the best that could be expected (for an error) is that a man might be pardoned his error; and it is inconceivable that he could obtain a *reward*, for an error (1420).

Shâfi'î's intention is clear: all decisions based on *ijtihâd* are equally valid, and there should be, as far as possible, no talk of 'errors'; if one is rewarded for an action that action cannot be 'wrong' *(khaṭa')*. The interlocutor is not unnaturally still puzzled: what, he asks, is then the meaning of *ṣawâb* and *khaṭa'*? (1422):

(1) As a way of transcending dispute similar devices were not unknown in other areas, cf. Wansbrough, *Studies*, 111.

> One is charged *(taklîf)* with *ijtihâd* only on matters which are not evident. So, if one does that (i.e. exercises *ijtihâd*) one has done right *(aṣâba)* in so far as one has responded to an obligation *(taklîf)*. Hence that (action based on *ijtihâd*?) is 'right' *(ṣawâb)* on the basis of appearance *(al-ẓâhir)*. God alone knows the *bâṭin*. If two people differ in facing the *qibla*, though they are both 'right' *(aṣâbâ)* by *ijtihâd*, yet, while they differ in aiming for the same point, they cannot both be 'right' with respect to the point, but they are 'right' with respect to *ijtihâd* (1425-6).

One may be pardoned for thinking Shâfi'î is here over-subtle; but it is clear what he is struggling to express: he wishes to eliminate from the incidence of *ikhtilâf* all sense of error or sin. A variety of views is permissible and acceptable. Paradoxically all are 'right'.

Succeeding generations coined the apophthegmatically satisfying "*kullu mujtahid muṣîb*"; a decisive slogan which obviously had not emerged while Shâfi'î was writing, but which clearly derives from his thinking. Likewise later generations discovered what Shâfi'î lacked, a relevant Tradition: "*ikhtilâf* is a blessing", again obviously in part a result and product of clerical exploration of this theme. [1]

It has already been noted, that the function of the interlocutor in the *Risâla* is to provide Shâfi'î with the opportunity to reiterate with slight variation the same points. In particular, instances of apparent obtuseness on the part of the interlocutor lead Shâfi'î constantly back to the distinction between two types of knowledge and to the incidence of *ikhtilâf*. Indeed the quality of conviction conveyed by the argument depends perhaps more on repetition than on logical consistency.

"I find the people of knowledge both in the past and recently are at variance in certain matters. Is this permitted?" (1671). So the interlocutor introduces an argument specifically related to *ikhtilâf*. The question elicits the by now familiar answer:

(1) See further Schacht, *op. cit.*, 95-7, esp. 96, n. 2; also, Goldziher, *The Zahiris*, tr. W. Behn, Leiden, 1971, 89ff. Shâfi'î's argument about the absence of *khaṭa'* in the exercise of *ijtihâd* became a standard theme, taken up e.g. by Muḥammad 'Abduh, see G. Hourani, 'The basis of the authority of consensus', *SI*, 1964, p. 42.

ikhtilâf, Shâfi'î explains, has two aspects. From one point of view *ikhtilâf* is forbidden but "I cannot say that about the other" (1672). *Ikhtilâf* is forbidden in all spheres where God has provided a *ḥujja* in his Book, or on the tongue of his prophet, textually and explicity *(manṣûṣ, bayyin)*. But with regard to such texts as permit of interpretation *(ta'wîl)* or are to be understood by *qiyâs* in such a way that the interpreter or *qâ'is* accepts what is implied by a *khabar* or *qiyâs* even if another differs from him in his interpretation: in such a case, "I do not say that variation is forbidden, as it is in textually explicit cases." (1675) The interlocutor continues to doubt; he demands further proof as to the existence of these two types of *ikhtilâf*, the one forbidden, the other not forbidden. Shâfi'î quotes the Qur'ân:

98,4 Those who have been given the Book were not divided except after they were vouchsafed a clear proof.

3,105 Be not like those who were divided and were at variance after they were granted clear proofs.

The relevance of this is, Shâfi'î explains, that God has criticised *ikhtilâf* in matters *concerning which there are clear proofs...*! (1679). Shâfi'î goes on to give examples of established *ikhtilâf*, and to give his own suggestions for a possible (but not definitive?) resolution of various questions (1681-1804). The introduction of a distinction between *'ilm 'âmma* and *'ilm khâṣṣa* may be seen as directed entirely at this end, to explain and justify *ikhtilâf*. The argument is, perhaps inevitability, not free from circularity. In spite of Shâfi'î's attempts to distinguish the two knowledges by reference to their sources, in practice, it seems to me they can only be separated by reference to the existence of *ikhtilâf*; the distinction once established is used to explain *ikhtilâf*.

Schematically Shâfi'î's position may be summed up thus. The Book of God and 'general' Traditions give rise to a type of knowledge, also 'general', which is known to all the community. This general knowledge represents the fundamental unchanging verities of the Islamic juristic system. Around this fundamental structure there is a more nebulous structure of laws and rules, details and particulars, permitting variation, even, by new interpretation, change. This is the specialist knowledge, the monopoly of the learned classes, derived from isolated/specialist Traditions, *qiyâs/ijtihâd* and *ijmâ'*. In spite of the fact that the general knowledge is presented as somehow primary or dominant, the truth is that in every instance specialist knowledge affects and conditions general knowledge. I have pointed to two examples above—*jihâd* and *waṣiyya*—where though the legal source is 'general' the precise significance of these terms in a juristic context depends on qualification and interpretation by the learned class. Such examples could be multiplied very easily. The knowledge of the specialists qualifies, conditions and judges the general knowledge of the masses. The nature of this knowledge and its specific susceptibility to *ikhtilâf* is explained by Shâfi'î in a lengthy, coherent and well-organised argument, within which repetition is meaningful and varied, never merely otiose, stretching from para. 961 *(Bab al-'ilm)* to the end of the *Risâla*. Final demonstration of the coherence of his argument depends upon the provision of a context for his work, and analysis of his notion of *ijmâ'*.

* * *

Shâfi'î's analysis and exposition of Islamic epistemology was in one sense monolithic and totalitarian. All human events could and must find their resolution in God's law. (1) Both psychologically and sociologically this was an ennoblement of the human condition: nothing in human life or society was so mean or so insignificant that it was unworthy of God's interest and command. This interest and command were mediated to man through a prophet, who left to his (in time universal) community the tangible evidence of his mission, the exegetical source for the knowledge of God's will, scripture and Tradition, both aspects of divine revelation. (2) The first part of the *Risâla* is concerned with the identification

(1) See note 2, p. 55.

(2) The development of these ideas in Islam is nowhere better analysed than in Wansbrough, *Studies*, chaps. 1 & 2.

of Qur'ân and *ḥadîth* as aspects of revelation and valid sources for the discovery of God's law. (1) But perhaps the major intellectual effort in the first part of the *Risâla* was directed towards the identification of two 'objective' sciences which could be applied to the texts of revelation in order to discover 'scientifically' what they meant: linguistics and history. The former provided the exegetical principle of *'âmm* and *khâṣṣ* (179 ff.), the latter that of *al-nâsikh wa'l-mansûkh* (106 ff.). The second part of the *Risâla*, which I have analysed in some detail in this essay, is devoted entirely to the problems of *'ilm*, *ikhtilâf* and associated problems deemed to arise out of the nature of the revealed texts, or out of meditation on their meaning. Two further 'objective' sciences are in this context introduced which may be brought to bear on revealed texts; biography, as a check on *isnâds (ad* the *khabar wâḥid)* and logic *(qiyâs)* as a means of extending the scope of a given text. The whole work is dedicated to the service of a series of ideas which represent the monolithic, totalitarian all-embracing nature of the Islamic juristic impulse. All events have their resolution in God's law; all knowledge is therefore knowledge of God's law, (hence *'ilm* is defined as relating only to knowledge of the law; (2)) all sources of knowledge are revealed sources; (3) all authority is clerical authority, arising from clerical custody and learned interpretation of the revealed sources.

Quite remarkable in this context is the complete absence of any reference to the intellect as itself, independently of God's revelation, a source of knowledge in the moral/juristic sphere. The characteristic Mu'tazilî distinction between contingent (revealed) and non-contingent (rational) law may well have found expression by the time of Shâfi'î's writing. If that is the case, the very absence of reference in the *Risâla* may itself be a polemical comment, a refutation of those who asserted a role for reason in this sphere. (4)

(1) See further J. Burton, *The Collection of the Qur'an*, Cambridge, 1977, 21-29; also Wansbrough, *Studies*, 43-52, 77-8, 148-202; and *Milieu*, 71-87.

(2) Or, 'of the Book', cf. *Risâla*, paras. 43-5.

(3) For *ijmâ'*, see below.

(4) See on the Mu'tazilî position, Schacht, *op. cit.*, 40 and 258-9; Wansbrough,

Shâfi'î's discussion of *ikhtilâf*, based on his distinction between two types of knowledge, in no wise mitigated the totalitarian aspect of Islamic jurisprudence: quite the reverse, for in the course of that discussion he repeated and reaffirmed the dogma that all human eventualities were subject to God's law, and his distinction between two types of knowledge served only to confirm that all knowledge was based on revelation. Nevertheless, his defence and justification of *ikhtilâf* established a kind of flexibility and tolerance (already perhaps implicit in some earlier juristic literature) in so far as the notion of variation was now built into the system and its negative implications neutralised. ([1]) The subtlety of intellectual endeavour, the constant repetition, the consistency of effort, which are all demonstrable behind the scholastic dryness of the text, reflect a considerable concern to give force to his contention: *ikhtilâf* is permissible and to be expected. The motives for the concern though no doubt multivalent, are not obscure. He was clearly responding to a contemporary need to forge for the geographically and ideologically various ancient schools a principle of transcendent unity whereby they could recognise in themselves a unified and catholic body. At the same time he enabled the contemporary scholars to associate themselves with traditions, or traditional figures of the Islamic past, going back to and including all of the *aṣḥâb*, irrespective of recorded deviation or divergence in juristic conclusions. This desire for an inclusive catholicity manifests itself throughout the second part of the *Risâla*. The issue on which there was no compromise and which represents as it were the common denominator subscribed to by all the ancient schools, the focus of their loyalty, was that of clerical authority. The articulation of a typology of *'ilm* was also a defence and justification of a gulf between those who know (the specialists) and those who depended on those who know (the 'generality'). Thus, abdication of certainty *(ikhtilâf)* went hand in hand with assertion of prerogative.

Milieu, 110-13; for a later period, G. Hourani, *Islamic Rationalism*, Oxford, 1971, chap. 6.

(1) A point already noted by Wansbrough, *Milieu*, 91.

The juristic closing of ranks, evident in the *Risâla*, was, I have surmised, a response to the Muʿtazilî challenge. The epistemological focus of that challenge lay in the denial of the jurists' monopoly of knowledge/authority: (epistemology in Islam was always a discussion of authority). Revelation, for the Muʿtazilîs, was not the sole source or type of knowledge; reason was a parallel and independent source. Divine law as such had a strictly limited sphere of validity. It was partly at least because they thus defined a sphere of knowledge/authority free from the influence of the *fuqahâ'* that the Muʿtazilîs found frequent favour at the court of the caliphs. Though not explicitly enunciated, the *Risâla* functions as a refutation of Muʿtazilî epistemology: revelation, it asserts, is a necessary, an exclusive and a sufficient source of knowledge for all human purposes—and its interpretation is the prerogative of the *fuqahâ'*.

* * *

Acknowledgement and justification of *ikhtilâf* had a still wider significance: in Shâfiʿî's writing it emerged as a functional juristic concept which guaranteed the practical infallibility *(ʿiṣma)* of the community. This characteristic *(ʿiṣma)* on an ideological or metaphysical level was usually associated with *ijmâʿ*, (1) but that concept *(ijmaʿ)* in a juristic context was of limited, that is strictly qualified, value. There was a grand metaphysical value in the assertion that the Islamic community could not unite on an error and a more prosaic usefulness, in view of the evidence of recorded dispute, in the assertion that the community remained infallible even when it did not achieve *ijmâʿ*, even when it held and promulgated divergent juristic views. Divergent views emerging within the community could all be considered, with appropriate qualifications, to be right. It was this continued rightness of variant views that guaranteed the infallibility of the community.

Ijmâʿ in fact as a juristic concept represents principles

(1) See Wansbrough, *Milieu*, 86 and *opera cit.* there; the term 'metaphysical' is of course W's.

of rigidity and immutability dangerously opposed to the flexibility and tolerance which, I have suggested, Shâfi'î tried to build into the system by his analysis of *'ilm* and *ikhtilâf*. Schacht has demonstrated Shâfi'î's considerable distate for the concept of *ijmâ'* as used by the ancient schools—that is, pre-eminently and perhaps exclusively as a term indicating the *consensus doctorum (ijmâ' al-'ulamâ')*—(though he continued to resort to that idea on a casual and *ad hoc* basis). (1) This distaste may be related to a number of factors, not least that, since the *'ulamâ'* cited were invariably local *'ulamâ'* and *ijmâ' al-'ulamâ'* emerged in polemical contexts as a local *ijmâ'*, it was a concept which tended to foster entrenched positions and irreconcilable opposition between local schools. Regional variation if justified by appeal to *ijmâ'* would tend to be divisive, each region presenting itself as a self-contained community, denying the validity of alternative views or the soteriological status of other communities. Shâfi'î by accounting for regional and other variation as a result (a permissible and inevitable result) of interpretation of revealed texts defused tension and diminished conflict. *Ijmâ' al-'ulamâ'* was a concept which he considered so absurd (or dangerous) that he was tempted to deny its existence (cf. 1556-9) as well as its validity.

In the *Risâla* Shâfi'î's major discussion of *ijmâ'* is situated in the middle of his extended discussion of the elements which make up *'ilm al-khâṣṣa* after the discussion of *khabar wâḥid* and before the discussion of *qiyâs/ijtihâd.* I have already tried to demonstrate that that argument is generally both coherent and purposeful: the distinction between the two types of knowledge is elaborated and applied with varied reference to *khabar wâḥid*, *qiyâs*, *ijtihâd* and *ikhtilâf* (all these being notions related to *'ilm al-khâṣṣa*) and with cumulative impact. The structure of the argument is meticulous and the situation of *ijmâ'* within that argument makes it clear that we are to take *ijmâ'* as an element in *'ilm al-khâṣṣa.*

The *ijmâ'* discussed in the *Risâla* (1309-20) is consensus on

(1) See Schacht, *op. cit.*, 88-95.

a matter not referred to in any revealed text (to be distinguished therefore from a *sunna mujtamaʿ ʿalayhâ*—already established as part of the knowledge of the generality. (1) The interlocutor asks:

> What is your proof that you may follow the consensus of the people *(mâ jtamaʿ al-nâs ʿalayhi)* in a matter on which *there is no text of God's command and which they do not relate from the prophet*? Do you claim what others claim, namely that the *ijmâʿ* does not exist except on the basis of a valid *sunna* even if they do not actually relate it?

Shâfiʿî explains that if the people have achieved consensus on a particular matter and they specify that it is based on a *ḥikâya* from the prophet, then what they say must be accepted (1310).

> As to what they do not specify in this manner (i.e. do not specify as a transmission, *ḥikâya*, from the prophet) then the case may be either that what they say is a transmission *(ḥikâya)* from the prophet (2) or the case may be otherwise. In fact, however, it is not permissible to consider (a matter based on *ijmâʿ*) to imply a transmission *(ḥikâya)* (if the people do not actually specify that) because it is not permissible to relate something except on the basis of what one has heard, nor is it permissible to relate something merely imagined (1311).

Now, this approach to the concept of *ijmâʿ* relates clearly to two questions. First, when a problem arises, concerning which there are no revealed texts of any kind, is it permissible to turn to the people? And, second, does the existence of an *ijmâʿ* amongst the people—an *ijmâʿ* devoid of revealed support—imply the existence of a prophetic Tradition which has somehow got lost? Both these questions had previously emerged in the Jewish juristic tradition with respect to the concept *minhag*. The question of what to do in cases where

(1) See above, esp. *ad Risâla*, 1259 and (below) 1815.

(2) The text is garbled: read either أن يكون ما قالوه or أن يكونوا قالوه: see editor's footnote.

texts of revelation provided no guidance was answered in the Talmud, as it was answered by Shâfi'î, in terms of turning to the people. ("Go out and see what the action of the people is and act likewise", TJ, Pe'ah, 7:5, 20c.) It would appear to be the case that one way of explaining the validity of custom *(minhag)* as a source of law was on the grounds that a previously extant transmitted tradition had in the course of time become forgotten. Both aspects of the debate may be detected in a well-known narrative concerning Hillel the Elder. When asked what the law was in a particular case, he said: Leave it to Israel; if they are not prophets, they are the sons of prophets. This represents the assertion and justification of *minhag* as a valid source of law. When he had seen how the people acted, Hillel thereupon 'recalled' the *halakhah* and said: Thus have I received the tradition from Shemai'ah and Avtalyon (TB, Pesahim, 66a). This may be taken to represent the assertion that a custom of this kind is due to a 'lost' tradition. Shâfi'î's discussion of the concept *ijmâ'* echoes this Rabbinic debate. For him it was a question of whether *ijmâ'* (of the type specifically defined by him in this context) implied the existence of a transmission *(ḥikâya)* which had subsequently vanished from the community. He informs us that he had previously held that view but had now changed his mind because of his intellectual conviction that Traditions from the prophet could not altogether vanish from the community (1312). *Ijmâ'* was a valid source implying nothing about the existence of a 'lost' transmission. (To have said otherwise would have been to impair the hierarchical ranking of revelation: community *ijmâ'* if it implied a revealed text would be on a par with revelation.) The validity of *ijmâ'* derived from the fact that the *'âmma* could not unite on something opposed to the prophet of God (1312). (1)

(1) For the Jewish concept *minhag* see, *Encyclopedia Judaica*, 1971, *ad minhag*. The process whereby Rabbinic and other Judaeo-Christian ideas became available to Muslim scholars has been extensively discussed throughout Wansbrough's two books, *cit.*, note 1. Shâfi'î's conviction that no Tradition could disappear from the community is related to his notion of language, *Risâla*, 133ff., esp. 138-40. His notion of *ijmâ'* was later subsumed under the juristic concept of *'âda*.

Evidence for that conclusion, revealed proof that is for the validity of *ijmâ'* as an independent source of law, was found in two Traditions referring to *luzûm al-jamâ'a*, cleaving to the community. (The 'My community shall not unite on an error' Tradition obviously emerged later than and partly as a result of Shâfi'î's work.) The concept of cleaving to the community, like the concept of *ijmâ'* independent of revelation, immediately provoked clarificatory remarks which might be interpreted again as reflecting a dispute. Shâfi'î was quick to point out that by *luzûm al-jamâ'a* he understood a juristic concept ("for *taḥlîl* and *taḥrîm*") not a physical movement from place to place in order to join a particular physically defined body of people *(jamâ'a)* (1319). It may thus be legitimate to infer that the concept of *luzûm al-jamâ'a* had earlier been associated with a context not quite so centrally juristic. One might refer at this point to that (literary) group or tendency—isolated by Wansbrough—whose dominant notion of soteriology was membership of the community. (1) In practice however Islamic ideology, formulated as a result of sectarian/ confessional debate, probably associated the notion of cleaving to the community with sectarian movements, specifically Khârijî. (2) Shâfi'î's insistence that he did not mean cleaving physically to a group may represent an attempt to dissociate himself from the conventional vision of Khârijî sectarianism. One might in sum see Shâfi'î's notion of *ijmâ'* as the integration of a specific juristic concept (?Judaic) with a metaphysical concept (the soteriological community) which had already emerged in an Islamic context.

It may be instructive here to repeat that there are two distinctions to be borne in mind while reading Shâfi'î on *ijmâ'*. First there is the distinction, noted by Schacht, between *ijmâ' al-'ulamâ'* and *ijmâ' al-âmma*; then there is the distinction

(1) Wansbrough is inclined to see membership of the community as the earliest expression of Islamic soteriology, intercepted later by the idea of submission to the law as the dominant mode of salvation. Shâfi'î's ranking of *luzûm al-jamâ'a* below revelation as source of law, may be thought to symbolise this change; see *Milieu*, 87-91, and chap. IV.

(2) Cf. Wansbrough's comments, *ibid.*, p. 119-20.

between *ijmâ'* on a matter dealt with in a Tradition or in the Book of God and *ijmâ'* on something not dealt with in revelation, both of these being *ijmâ' al-'âmma*. Now, *ijmâ' al-'âmma*, if it is based on an element of revelation, is not only part of *'ilm al-'âmma* but is the defining feature of that type of knowledge: it is the absence of dispute or presence of *ijmâ'* which permits the definition of an item as *'âmm* not *khâṣṣ*. *Ijmâ' al-'âmma* however, when it is on a matter not provided with a textual base, is clearly to be understood as part of *'ilm al-khâṣṣa*. This may be inferred from the context of Shâfi'î's discussion of *ijmâ'*, but, lest there be doubts, it may be worth referring again to paras. 1328-32. Shâfi'î there defined what constituted certainty *(iḥâṭa)* (1329) and what did not, viz., *akhbar al-khâṣṣa* (1330), *ijmâ'* (1331) and *ijtihâd bi-qiyâs* (1332). Though the reference to *ijmâ'* is laconic, it may not be simply dismissed: *ijmâ'* (as a separate source, distinct from revelation) is part of *'ilm al-khâṣṣa*. A final confirmation and perhaps explanation of this may be derived from the last few paragraphs of the *Risâla*. The discussion of *'ilm* and *ikhtilâf* analysed in this essay gave place to a lengthy series of examples of *ikhtilâf* (1681-1804). To this was added a brief appendage on whether *aqâwîl al-aṣḥâb* might function as sources of knowledge (1805-11). Then, another appendage was added, constituting a final resume of the argument about two types of knowledge. The interlocutor was yet again puzzled:

> So, you make juristic decisions *(ḥakamta)* on the basis of *kitâb* and *sunna*; but on what basis do you make decisions by *ijmâ'*, and then make decisions by *qiyâs*? Do you set these two up on a par with *kitâb* and *sunna*?

With these words Shâfi'î provided himself with another opening for his unwearying reiteration of the same argument. The basis of the decision is different in each case.

> Decisions may be based on scripture *(kitâb)* or Tradition-on-which-there-is-consensus *(al-sunna al-mujtama' 'alayhâ)*; on such matters there is no *ikhtilâf* and we may say: we have judged the truth with respect to both external appearance and inner reality *(ḥakamnâ bi'l-ḥaqq fî l-ẓâhir wa'l-bâṭin)*.

Alternatively, decisions may be based on a *sunna* related by isolated paths, a *sunna* upon which the people *(al-nâs)* have not reached consensus. Concerning this we say: we have judged the truth on the basis of external appearance only *(ḥakamnâ bi'l-ḥaqq fî l-ẓâhir)*, error being possible on the part of the transmitters. Furthermore, decisions may be based on *ijmâ'*, and *qiyâs*, which are (as sources) weaker than the others, though necessary; for *qiyâs* is not permissible when a report *(khabar)* is available... (Just as purification using sand is only permissible when water is not available). So, what comes after a *sunna* (in the hierarchy of sources) constitutes a *ḥujja* only if a *sunna* is lacking (1815-18).

The complete hierarchy of sources would thus appear to be:
— *kitâb* and *sunna*-on-which-there-is-*ijmâ'*,
— *sunna* on which there is no *ijmâ'* (isolated or specialist Traditions),
— *ijmâ'* and *qiyâs*.

Only the first group there corresponds to the knowledge of the generality; the other sources constitute the knowledge of the specialists. The *sunna*-on-which-there-is-*ijmâ'* relates to a consensus achieved as the result of and specifically related to a prophetic Tradition. Consensus, *eo ipso*, is a lower proof and constitutes a *ḥujja* only if there is no revealed text available. This consensus, on a matter not dealt with in a revealed text, is, we know (1309-20) a consensus of the *'âmma.* (1) Why then is it defined, as it clearly here is defined, as part of the knowledge of the *khâṣṣa*? An explanation is not difficult to find. Consensus, when it is not based on a revealed text, is a weaker source than a revealed text; but custody of revealed texts, in particular of specialist or isolated Traditions, lies with the *'ulamâ'*. Hence it is the *'ulamâ'*, and only the *'ulamâ'* who are in a position to accept or deny or otherwise qualify a consensus of the people, a consenus, that is, not related to a revealed text. A consensus of the generality must give way before a text. The point is of course that Shâfi'î was concerned to assert revelation as the primary source of law. Generally speaking in the event of conflict between custom

(1) *Pace,* the editor of the *Risâla*, p. 599, note 10.

(ijmâ') and revelation he desired that revelation should prevail; revelation should prevail in fact even where it could not decisively remove doubts or *ikhtilâf.* He permitted however, as a residual source, appeal to the practice of the community, if it could be shown to be a universal practice, in areas where revelation provided no guidance. Custom/consensus was not to prevail over revelation; where an element of revelation could be rendered relevant by a scholar then revelation took precedence over *ijmâ'*. Knowledge of the area where custom might prevail could only belong to the scholar who knew the limits and the finer details of revelation. The area of valid *ijmâ'*, that is the area not covered by revelation, was known only to scholars and was therefore part of *'ilm al-khâṣṣa.* Shâfi'î's dealing with *ijmâ'* is fully consistent with his general principles which are *(a)* to assert a primary role for revealed texts in the assessment of the law, and *(b)* to preserve and bolster the authority of the *'ulamâ'*.

That Shâfi'î derived his notion of *ijmâ'* more from a theoretical tradition of juristic/epistemological debate than from the practical exigencies of juristic decision-making may be inferred from the fact that he gives no examples of knowledge based on it (in spite of his reference to *taḥlîl* and *taḥrîm* (1319)). Its practical usefulness juristically (? a Judaic notion) was limited but its metaphysical import (? Khârijî) was immense —as a tag or slogan reflecting the unity and infallibility of the community. (1) A powerful and attractive idea of marked relevance to the sense of community identity was not rejected (as it might have been in view of its possibly sectarian origins) but was integrated into a juristic structure and as it were taken on board.

Shâfi'î's analysis of *ikhtilâf* and *ijmâ'* was a personal one, inspired by social experience, conditioned by an academic tradition and reflecting his own intellectual insights and development. His manipulation and definition of these concepts were not final but subject inevitably to change and interpretation. Later writers for the most part abandoned

(1) Wansborough, *ibid.*, 70-71, 86, 121ff.

the notion of *ijmâʿ* on a matter not dealt with in revelation. They had a larger body of Traditions available and a more developed and more subtle exegetical apparatus. They were less willing to acknowledge a situation that could not be made relevant to a textual base. *Ijmâʿ* in later works of *uṣûl al-fiqh* was nearly always considered a proof together with and subordinate to revelation—and indeed was frequently understood as *ijmâʿ al-ʿulamâʾ*. As a juristic concept it functioned then as a stabilising factor defining a permanent body of basic rules ("general knowledge") and acting against change and development. *Fuqahâʾ* were constrained to assert its existence where they wished to establish or preserve a rule, and to deny its existence when they wished to change or adapt an established rule. (1) 'Progressives' and 'conservatives' varied in their estimation of how large an area of *furûʿ* was covered by *ijmâ*. (2) The purely juristic use of *ijmâʿ* (a fairly well-defined and limited technical term) subsisted with the emotional/metaphysical usage and created inevitably problems of interpretation and resolution. (3)

The process of creating or re-creating a sense of unity and identity within the Islamic community was a continuous one, necessarily opposed to intellectual rigidity. Social political and economic factors inevitably impinged on modes of literary expression, demanding resolution. New intellectual resolutions contained logical or systematic problems which, on a purely intellectual level, inspired reassessments. Given the intellectual conservatism and the group solidarity of the scholarly elite it was perhaps inevitable that change and development should rely very largely on the manipulation or refining of concepts already available but whose relevance could be changed or renewed. That is the process evident in Shâfiʿî's work. *Ikhtilâf* and *ijmâʿ* were but two notions whose significance and

(1) See the example provided in Calder, 'Zakât in Imâmî Shîʿî Jurisprudence', *BSOAS* XLIV, 1981, p. 472.

(2) Cf. Ibn Taymiyya: كثير من المسائل يظنّ فيه الاجماع ولا يكون الامر كذلك بل يكون القول الآخر ارجح في الكتاب والسنّة *Majmûʿ fatâwt Ibn Taymiyya*, 30 vols., Riyadh, 1381-3, vol. 20, p. 10.

(3) See Hourani, 'The basis of the authority of consensus', *SI*, 1964.

connotations were developed by Shâfi'î and charged with a new relevance. His literary productions, thereafter, though profoundly influential, themselves became part of a structure constantly elaborated, refined and re-interpreted. (1)

(1) I should like to record my thanks to Dr John Wansborough for reading and commenting on an earlier draught of this study; and to Philip Alexander for discussing some of the problems raised.

XII

THE SIGNIFICANCE OF THE TERM *IMĀM* IN EARLY ISLAMIC JURISPRUDENCE

Islamic juristic literature emerged towards the end of the eighth century. In its earliest phase it reveals the existence of and reflects the concerns of a clerical elite associated with one or another of the half dozen or so localities where juristic speculation took place: Medina, Mecca, Kufa, Basra, Syria and, later, Egypt. This literature is characterised by a polemical tone reflecting dispute, for the most part between the local schools, though there was also dispute within schools. Dispute no doubt emerged initially with respect to details of substantive law (*furūʿ*) but inevitably modulated to the higher order question of authority for the law – a question invariably related to the nature and value of precedent. The centrality of precedent in the complex theory of authority that gradually emerged in juristic writing is reflected in and may be demonstrated by the jurists' use of the term *imām*[1].

A relatively early and neutral (non-juristic) witness to the meaning of that term may be found in Labīd's *muʿallaqa* where he refers to a tribal hero as:

من معشر سنّت لهم آباءهم　　ولكلّ قوم سنّة وامامها

one of a band whose fathers laid down for them a *sunna*;
every tribe has a *sunna* and its *imām*[2].

[1] For the emergence of juristic literature, see J. Schacht, *Origins of Muhammadan jurisprudence*, Oxford, 1950; for the domination of precedent, see further J. Wansbrough, *The Sectarian milieu*, Oxford, 1978, ch. 2, esp. pp. 70–87.

[2] See Zawzanī, *Sharḥ al-muʿallaqāt al-sabʿ*, Beirut, 1966, p. 191. For the term *sunna*, see Schacht, *Origins*, 58–81; I. Goldziher, *Muslim Studies II*, ed. S. M. Stern, U. K., 1971, pp. 123–198; M. Bravmann, *The spiritual background of early Islam*, Leiden, 1972, pp. 123–198. Bravmann, citing the same verse, translates *imām* as rule/model; cf. A. F. L. Beeston, *JAL*, vii, 1976, p. 6. For a sampling of the Arabic lexicographical tradition see e. g. *Lisān al-ʿArab*, *ad amma*.

Sunna here refers to tribal law, the well-established customary practice of the tribe, validated by tradition and by the practice of the forefathers. Taking the pronominal element of *imāmuhā* as referring to *sunna* (not *qawm*) I would understand *imām* as referring to a tribal hero whose actions enshrine and articulate the law – that is precedent.

In juristic literature *sunna* (more specifically *sunnat al-nabī*) refers to divine law, based on the practice of the prophet which constitutes the model for the community. It is not surprising therefore that prophets in their function as law incarnate are also designated *imām*. A characteristic discussion of the term may be found in the *Tafsīr* of AL-ṬABARĪ (d. 310) *ad* Qur'ān 2:124. There, God addresses Abraham, saying: انّي جاعلك للنّاس اماما I shall make you an IMĀM for the people. ṬABARĪ interpreted that as meaning: I shall make you for the people an *imām* who provides leadership and guidance (*yu'tamm bihi wa-yuqtadā bihi*). He continued:

> God meant by the phrase *innī jāʿiluka* etc: I shall make you such that you lead those who come after you who believe in me and my prophets; you will go before them and they will follow your guidance and they will find their *sunna* in your *sunna* (*yastannūna bi-sunnatika*) which you perform in accord with my command and my revelation . . .

An *imām* was thus a person whose actions constituted *sunna*, became models, that is, of right conduct for later generations. The same explicit linking of *imām* and *sunna* had been made a generation or so earlier by IBN QUTAYBA (d. 276) who interpreted the same Quranic verse as implying *yu'tammu bika wa-yuqtadā bi-sunnatika* lead by you and guided by your *sunna*[3].

The term *imām* was not restricted to prophets. Varied recognition of diverse *imāms* was one of the means whereby sectarian groups (including the local schools of law, as will become clear) defined their identity. The particular direction of Shīʿī beliefs in this context is well known: their *imām par excellence*, after the death of the prophet, was ʿALĪ IBN ABĪ ṬĀLIB. Later dogmatic development among the Shīʿa tended to obscure the original connotation of the term *imām*, as designating legal precedent, but that connotation may still be found, clearly expressed, in a poem cited

[3] Ibn Qutayba, *Ta'wīl mushkil al-Qur'ān*, Cairo, 1954, p. 345.

by Mas'ūdī (d. 346). The poem is ascribed to a seventh century follower of 'Alī.

We accept (*raḍīnā*) God's authority and none other
  We accept God as Lord, and the Prophet, and the Warning
We accept the hero, the guide, 'Alī, our *imām*
  We accept this leader in ease and in hardship
We accept him, living or dead, for he
  Is the *imām* of guidance, who has the status to command and forbid[4].

This poem established a constellation of authorities: God, Prophet, the Qur'ān (Warning) and 'Alī. For the Shī'a it was the last authority, 'Alī, the Imām, who explained the others and so gave the definitive articulation of the law in his commands and prohibitions. The reference to "living or dead" confirms that the commands and prohibitions of an *imām* are permanent models of right conduct whose value and significance continue after his death.

Recognition of 'Alī as the *imām* was a peculiarly Shī'ī formulation. Other sectarian groups offered alternative constellations of named *imāms*. The group known as the Murji'a, in a text entitled the *Kitāb al-Irjā'* and ascribed to Ḥasan ibn Muḥammad ibn al-Ḥanafiyya (d. c. 100) summed up their position with regard to their authorities as follows:

فانّا قوم الله ربّنا والإسلام ديننا والقرآن إمامنا ومحمّد نبينا . . . ونرضى من أئمتنا بأبي بكر وعمر . . . ونرجيء منهم أهل الفرقة الأول

We are a people such that God is our Lord, Islam our law, the Qur'ān is our *imām* and Muḥammad our prophet . . . We accept of our *imāms* Abū Bakr and 'Umar . . . and of them we reserve judgement on the first people of the *firqa*.

This definition of authorities parallels in some respects that of the Shī'ī poem e. g. in its inclusion of God, prophet and Qur'ān, and in its use of the root *raḍiya* to indicate "acceptance". The nearer authorities however are Abū Bakr and 'Umar; 'Uthmān and 'Alī are rejected as *imāms* because they were involved in the civil confrontation (*firqa*) which ended the charismatic unity of the Muslim community[5].

[4] Al-Mas'ūdī, *Murūj al-dhahab*, (4 vols in 2), Cairo, 1384/1964, II, 410.

[5] For the text, see J. van Ess, „Das *Kitāb al-irǧā'* des Ḥasan ibn Muḥammad ibn al-Ḥanafiyya", *Arabica*, XXI, 1974. The date of the document is a matter of dispute, see M. Cook, *Early Muslim dogma*, Cambridge, 1981 and

That Murji'ite text names two *imāms* who were also caliphs, leaders of the Islamic community, and illustrates a tendency whereby the term *imām* took on a specific technical meaning (*imām* = caliph) which in time and in certain contexts blurred or ousted the equally technical but more general meaning *imām* = juristic precedent. The former meaning has dominated Orientalist writings on the imamate which is usually seen as a synonym of caliphate[6]. That notion derives of course from a strong Muslim tradition which made the same equation and which led to a peculiar textual problem in the *Kitāb Ikhtilāf Mālik wa-l-Shāfi'ī*[7]. In that work SHĀFI'Ī is writing about the Medinese whom he portrays as defining their law and justifying it by reference to the precedents established by a number of Companions and Successors. These included ABŪ BAKR, 'UMAR and 'UTHMĀN as well as, for example, ABŪ HURAYRA, IBN 'UMAR and 'UMAR IBN 'ABD AL-'AZĪZ. The caliphs in this work, though they function as precedents, are given no particular preeminence. And yet the work contains numerous generalisations – almost a refrain – to the effect that Medinese law is based on the practice of "the *imāms*", ABŪ BAKR, 'UMAR and 'UTHMĀN. Some lists add 'ALĪ. This generalisation which is usually at odds with the specific details of the text creates an incongruity which was noticed by Joseph Schacht who concluded that SHĀFI'Ī had "forced the concept of the practice of ABŪ BAKR, 'UMAR and 'UTHMĀN upon the Medinese". It is difficult to believe that SHĀFI'Ī's argumentation could be so slipshod. I am inclined to see the list of names as a later gloss on the term *a'imma* which by itself would create no problems. In fact, on several occasions, the gloss was omitted leaving the term *a'imma* or *a'immat al-nās* as a general term referring to all the authorities of the Medinese – a perfectly appropriate usage[8].

N. Calder, *JSS*, XXVII (i), 1983. See further Cook's translation of this passage, *ibid.*, pp. 27–8.

[6] See e. g. *imām* and *khalīfa* in EI (ii).

[7] Contained in Al-Shāfi'ī, *Al-Umm*, (7 vols.), Bulaq, 1321–5, vol. VII, 177–249; designated by Schacht in *Origins*, *Treatise III*.

[8] Schacht, *Origins*, 24; unglossed examples of the term *a'immat* (*al-nās*) may be found in *Umm* VII, 188, lines 14 and 17, also pp. 240–1. Schacht is probably wrong in thinking that Shāfi'ī considered the decisions of the first caliphs as "more authoritative": the text he relies on for this view (p. 18) is discussed below, 260–261.

A quite specific instance of Medinese usage of the term *imām* to mean juristic exemplar – on this occasion referring to ṬALḤA IBN ʿUBAYD ALLĀH – may be found in MĀLIK's *Muwaṭṭaʾ*, in the chapter on Pilgrimage (*ḥadīth* no. 10). ʿUMAR IBN AL-KHAṬṬĀB saw ṬALḤA IBN ʿUBAYD ALLĀH wearing a dyed robe while in a state of ritual purity for the pilgrimage and rebuked him, saying, "You people are *imāms* by whom the masses are guided, . . . so don't wear coloured robes".

إنّكم أيها الرهط أئمّة يقتدى بكم الناس . . . فلا تلبسوا أيها الرهط شيئاً من هذه الثياب المصبّغة .

An *imām* was a person whose example the people followed in matters of religious law.

The pre-eminence of the first four caliphs, as leaders of the community and Rāshidūn, naturally ensured for them a prominent position amongst those who might function as precedents. But the term *imām* retained its more general usage (*imām* = juristic precedent) in spite of the parallel process whereby it came to designate, specifically, caliphs. In IBN QUTAYBA's *Taʾwīl mukhtalif al-ḥadīth* he discusses the erroneous views of AL-NAẒẒĀM on juristic authority. In particular he defends the idea of recourse to ABŪ BAKR as authoritative precedent:

> [Abū Bakr] gave a *fatwā* on [this] because it was an affair which befell the Muslims and so they needed a decision . . . He was permitted to exercise *ijtihād al-raʾy* on something not transmitted from the Prophet, and on which the Book revealed nothing; for he is the *imām* of the Muslims and their *mafzaʿ* (recourse) in whatever befalls them . . . Likewise ʿUMAR, ʿUTHMĀN, ʿALĪ, IBN MASʿŪD and ZAYD IBN THĀBIT gave their opinions when they were asked; they are the *imāms* and recourse may be had to them when new problems arise[9].

Thus even late in the 3rd/9th century the term *imām* continued to be used to designate an authority, or a number of authorities, whose actions, commands or opinions might be used as source or justification of the law. Though the caliphs appeared, variously, in a number of constellations of authoritative figures there was as yet no simple equation of caliph and *imām*.

[9] Ibn Qutayba, *Taʾwīl mukhtalif al-ḥadīth*, Beirut, 1393/1972, pp. 24–5.

In his *Kitāb Jimāʿ al-ʿilm*[10], Shafiʿī discussed the question of whether consensus (*ijmāʿ*) might be found amongst the leaders of the provincial law schools. Referring to the leading jurists of an earlier generation – IBN MUSAYYIB in Madīna, ʿAṬĀʾ in Mecca, ḤASAN in Basra, SHAʿBĪ in Kufa – he asserts to his interlocutor who (wrongly according to SHĀFIʿĪ) would make their agreement a basis for juristic decisions: These are the ones you have made *aʾimma fī l-dīn*[11]. He was implying that his opponents found valid precedents in the opinions of jurists. In the *K. Ikhtilāf Mālik wa-l-Shāfiʿī*, SHĀFIʿĪ described the factionalism of the local schools: Mecca found its *ḥujja* in ʿAṬĀʾ, Basra in ḤASAN, Kufa in SHAʿBĪ etc. Of these SHĀFIʿĪ concedes: All of them are *ahl ʿilm wa-imāma fī dahrihi* and they are greater than those who come after them[12]. He meant of course that their opinions were being used in the local schools to justify the law. The term *imām* was used in the local schools for all those – Prophet, Companions, Successors and jurists – who were cited as justificatory sources for the law.

The law that was thus preserved and defined in Kufa, Basra, Mecca, Medina or Syria was presented as *sunnat al-nabī*. That concept though common to all the schools was nonetheless a vessel of varying content. Schacht's designation of the local codes as "living tradition" implies not that the law "lived" in the lives of the people, but that it "lived" (and developed) in the ongoing academic discussions of the clerical elite[13]. When, in merely local circumstances, called upon to defend a particular item of positive law the jurists called first upon the juristic tradition (*sunna*) and only secondarily or casually upon specific citations from the Prophet, Companions, Successors etc. The citation and elaboration of justificatory precedents however acquired considerable impetus from the facts of abrasive contact and polemical dispute between the local

[10] Contained in Shāfiʿī, *Umm*, VII, pp. 250–62; designated by Schacht, *Treatise IV*.

[11] *Ibid.*, p. 258, line 13, also 259, 9.

[12] *Ibid.*, 246.

[13] Schacht, *Origins*, 58 ff., cf. also Wansbrough, *Milieu*, 81; note Abū Yūsuf's comment *contra* Awzāʿī in *Umm*, VII, 320: Judgement as to what is *ḥalāl* and what is *ḥarām* is not based on statements such as "the people have always done this". Most of what the people have always done is not *ḥalāl*. Judgement is based on the *sunna* from the prophet from the *salaf* of his *aṣḥāb* and from the *fuqahāʾ*.

schools. This would appear to have become severe in the early Abbasid period and may perhaps be related to the Abbasid desire to legitimize their power in part at least by patronage of the religious scholars. No doubt the local schools found themselves in competition in promoting their cause at court and in securing the benefits of caliphal indulgence. The social and cultural imperatives of the time compelled disputants to justify their juristic opinions by appeal to precedent; the intensity of dispute ensured that appropriate precedents would be found. The result was a proliferation of precedents enshrined in *ḥadīth* variously related to jurists, Successors, Companions and the Prophet. In the consequent confusion the participants lost track of whether law or precedent (*sunna* or *imām*) came first. Theoretically the *imām* by his actions gave rise to or confirmed the law; in practice the existence of known *sunna* led to the emergence of appropriate justificatory precedents. Though the tendency to make prophetic precedent decisive cannot fail to have risen early, the local schools continued to define the law in accord with local tradition (*sunna*) and to select justificatory precedents (*ḥadīth*) on the basis of what was or was not accepted in local scholarly circles.

With the gradual emergence of a technical terminology qualifying the types of prophetic *ḥadīth* in circulation, the local schools focussed their objections on those known as *akhbār al-khāṣṣa* (or *akhbār āḥād*, that is, sparsely attested Traditions). These were seen to be those most responsible for disrupting the locally established *sunna*. Abū Yūsuf (d. 182) in a lengthy reasoned argument against the acceptance of such Traditions cited a Tradition from the Prophet which included the following:

فاجعل القرآن والسنّة المعروفة لك إماماً قائداً

Make the Qur'ān and the known *sunna* a guiding *imām*[14]. By "make the *sunna* an *imām*" he meant that the locally established code, which had emerged in the course of scholarly discussion should be the criterion for accepting or rejecting Traditions.

The use of the term *imām* to refer not to an authoritative figure but to a body of material or of ideas was not a difficult transition. If a prophet such as Abraham was, as law incarnate, an *imām*, so, in the Qur'ān, the Book of Moses, as law inlibrate, was also an *imām* (Qur'ān, 11:17). The Qur'ān itself was frequently, as in the

[14] *Umm*, VII, 307–8; cf. Schacht, *Origins*, 28–9.

Tradition just cited and in the passage from the *Kitāb al-Irjā'* cited above, referred to as an *imām* – presumably because it contained and expressed and could be used to justify the law. In the atmosphere of polemical dispute within which sectarian groups of one kind or another found it imperative to define and defend their authorities (*imāms*) the term took on an added semantic significance as that which resolves dispute or *fitna*. This is reflected in the report cited by John Burton[15]. It is more clearly seen in a report concerning Aḥmad ibn Ḥanbal which states that, having collected his Traditions (the *Musnad*), he asserted:

عملت هذا الكتاب إماماً إذا اختلف الناس في سنّة عن رسول الله

I have made this book an *imām* should there be any dispute concerning a *sunna* of the Prophet[16]. He (or whoever first produced this report), as a successor and pupil of Shāfi'ī meant that prophetic *ḥadīth*, as collected in the *Musnad*, should be the ultimate source of authority for establishing the law and resolving questions in doubt. It has already been demonstrated that even late in the ninth century, in the time of Ibn Qutayba, the question of relevant and valid authorities was not that simple.

Dispute about authorities in the juristic field did have some definitive results. In particular it secured for the Qur'ān and for prophetic *ḥadīth* a primary role in the justification of the law and prompted, perhaps, the production of a fixed version of scripture[17] as well as a fixed canon of *ḥadīth* (the six books). About the role of the Companions and about the meaning of *ijmā'*, *qiyās* and *ijtihād*, I think no final results were ever secured – thus ensuring a necessary element of flexibility in the juristic tradition. A number of attempts to define a hierarchy of sources may be distinguished in the following passage from Shāfi'ī's *K. Ikhtilāf Mālik wa-l-Shāfi'ī*.

> [1.] As long as the Book and Sunna are present there is no alternative for those who hear them but to follow them. Otherwise we turn to the opinions of the Companions or one of them.
>
> [2a.] The opinions of the *imāms*, Abū Bakr, 'Umar and 'Uthmān, if we turn to them for authority (*taqlīd*) are in my view preferable.

[15] J. Burton, *The collection of the Qur'ān*, Cambridge, 1977. p. 143; cf. Wansbrough, *Quranic Studies*, Oxford, 1972, p. 45, and *Milieu*, 70–1.

[16] *Cit.* in W. M. Patton, *Aḥmad ibn Ḥanbal and the Miḥna*, London 1897, p. 19.

[17] Wansbrough, *Studies*, 148–202.

[3.] But this [is only the case] if we do not find an indication in juristic dispute (*ikhtilāf*) which suggests the closest [of the elements of dispute] to Book and Sunna; in which case we follow the opinion which agrees with that indication.
[2b.] Because, concerning the opinions of an *imām* it is well known that people cling to them; and he whose opinion people cling to is more acceptable than those who [merely] give *fatwās* ... If nothing is to be found from the *imāms* then we turn to the Companions who are of such status in *dīn* that we can accept their opinions. To follow them is better than to follow those who come after them.
[4.] Knowledge is in various degrees:

i. Book and Sunna
ii. consensus where there is nothing in Book or Sunna
iii. the opinion of one/some of the Companions where we know of no-one who opposes that opinion
iv. dispute amongst the Companions
v. analogy (*qiyās*)

There should not be recourse to anything other than Book or Sunna as long as these are present; and knowledge should be sought from the higher degree (SHĀFIʿĪ, *Umm*, VII, 246).

This passage displays not one but four hierarchic systems. Section [1.] suggests that after *kitāb* and *sunna* one should turn to the Companions. Section [2a.] and [2b.] propose an intervening layer of three primary *imāms* (caliphs); this passage may be the insertion of the anonymous glossator who at so many other points in this work glossed the term *aʾimma* with the names of the caliphs. Section [3.] is another intrusive gloss prescribing *ikhtilāf* after *kitāb* and *sunna* but before the *imāms*. Section [4.] offers a coherent system different from [1.], [2.] and [3.]. IBN QUTAYBA's hierarchy of sources, referred to above, is different in detail from any of these, though it is close to system 1. The theory of authority implied in the Murjiʾite text is different again. Dating the various levels of gloss apparent in the passage cited from *Ikhtilāf Mālik wa-l-Shāfiʿī* must be quite impossible. I do not feel that SHĀFIʿĪ could, even granted the possibility of constant revision, be responsible for them all; and none of them correspond precisely to the system set out in the *Risāla*. It may be worth noting that throughout the passage the term *sunna* clearly means prophetic *ḥadīth* which makes Shāfiʿī's lifetime the *terminus a quo*.

The various applications of the term *imām* as illustrated in this essay find a kind of resolution in a passage in SHĀFIʿĪ's *Risāla*. That work sets out a particular constellation of authorities, sometimes thought of as the 'classical' or standard system, though this is only partly true. In particular he proposed prophetic *ḥadīth* as the final arbiter in juristic dispute and so prompted the *ḥadīth* collecting activity of the ninth century. It was his contention that the Book of God (a term which he understood to comprehend also *ḥadīth, ijmāʿ* and *qiyās*[18]) contained a resolution for all events that befell the people of God's religion[19]. A full understanding of God's commands implied a particular status:

> He who grasps knowledge of God's commands in his Book, whether explicitly expressed or by inference, and to whom God grants success in enunciating and acting on that knowledge, has attained excellence in religious and worldly affairs; he is free of doubts, wisdom illuminates his heart and he merits in *dīn* the status of *imāma*[20].

He who knows God's law merits the status of *imām*. Here a traditional mode of thought which tended to recognise authority in past exemplars is given a new vitality; the authority of past *imāms* is continued in, and manifested in contemporary *imāms* (jurists), – those that is who have perfected their knowledge. It is perhaps on the basis of this idea that SHĀFIʿĪ himself, and all the major jurists of his generation were recognised after their deaths as *imāms*.

SHĀFIʿĪ's own personal attempts to express and explore the law were gathered together (by his pupils?) in a compendious work entitled *Kitāb al-Umm*. The peculiar resonance of that title, its appositeness, can only be fully appreciated in the light of the semantic implications of the term *imām* as outlined in the present essay. The title is obviously a play on the Quranic "*umm al-kitāb*" a phrase which refers on the one hand to the heavenly model or archetype of the manifest Qur'ān; and on the other to the *Fātiḥa*, the first *sūra* of the Qur'ān. Concerning the latter designation ṬABARĪ remarks:

[18] *Cf.* Wansbrough, *Studies*, 51–2, 56–7, 74–8; see also Ibn Qutayba, *Mukhtalif al-ḥadīth*, 94, where he glosses *kitāb Allāh* as "not the Qur'ān . . . but *ḥukm Allāh*".

[19] Shāfiʿī, *Risāla*, ed. A. M. Shakir, Cairo, 1399/1979, para. 48.

[20] *Ibid.*, para. 46.

It is called the *umm al-qur'ān* because the Arabs so designate anything that unites a matter, or leads a matter, such that if it has things that follow it (*taba'*) it becomes for them an *imām jāmi'* (i. e. an *imām* that unites).

A particular technical application of the term *umm* is to the standard around which and behind which an army gathers, and by which it is guided. Ṭabarī illustrates this usage with a line from Dhū al-Rumma:

على رأسه أمّ لنا نقتدي بها   جماع أمور لا نعاصي لها أمرا

At the head of (the lance) a standard whereby we are guided
It gathers together; we do not rebel against it.

An *umm* is an *imām jāmi'*, something that gathers together, unites and provides guidance[21]. When the juristic writings of Shāfi'ī were collected in the *Kitāb al-Umm* what was being claimed was that this book, (like the *Musnad* of Ibn Ḥanbal later) would provide guidance in case of dispute, because it contained full details of God's law.

The terminological usage that I have discussed here is of course only one technical application of a term which had other usages, indeed other more or less technical applications. In particular it referred also to a military leader. In the *K. Ikhtilāf Mālik wa-l-Shāfi'ī* where *imām* is most frequently used to mean precedent there exist also contexts where it clearly does not mean precedent but rather field-commander[22]. Likewise in *Siyar al-Awzā'ī*[23], the term *imām/a'imma* is constantly in use to mean military leader. Awzā'ī's usage is unambiguously clarified in Ṭabarī's *Ikhtilāf al-fuqahā'*, where, apropos of a problem related to the usufruct of captured goods, Awzā'ī's interlocutor, for clarity, demanded: "Are you not then counting the *amīr al-sariyya* (unit commander, general) as *imām*?" To which Awzā'ī replied, "Yes".

ألست تعد أمير السرية إماماً؟ قال بلى[24].

Imām then meant military leader. It's limitation to head of state or

[21] Al-Ṭabarī, *Jāmi' al-bayān*, eds. Shakir and Shakir, Cairo, 1374ff., I. 108.

[22] e. g. *Umm*, VII, 211.

[23] Contained in *Umm* VII, 303–36, (*Treatise IX*).

[24] Al-Ṭabarī, *Ikhtilāf al-fuqahā'*, (ed. Schacht), Leiden, 1933, p. 99–100. (This passage was pointed out to me by my colleague, Dr. A. A. Sharif.)

caliph was I think a later development[25], no doubt a gradual one, though a key moment in that development may be recognised in the reign of Ma'mūn. I would be inclined to see caliphal use of the term *imām* as an attempt to steal the jurists' clothes: were the caliphs too perhaps custodians of divine law?

Divine law, for the jurists, was revealed to man through the mediation of the Prophet and through scripture, both designated *imām*. Thereafter the law was preserved and expounded by the Companions, Successors and the *fuqahā'* who by their personal knowledge and implementation of the law became themselves *imāms*, to be imitated and obeyed by the rest of the community. The Prophet's role as mediator between God and the community was thus re-created from generation to generation by the *fuqahā'*. Their status was formalised in the *warathat al-anbiyā'* Tradition which recognised that the Prophet left behind him not wealth but only knowledge (*'ilm*): the *'ulamā'* were heirs of the Prophet. This notion in its extreme form recognised in the *fuqahā'* the only authorities within the community – for God's law provided, after all, for all eventualities – but in the developing tradition was variously qualified and interpreted by jurists and by other authorities. Not least, "secular" authorities like the Abbasid caliphs, though they encouraged and patronised legal studies, and at times and in order to bolster their authority "submitted to the divine law even in respect of their own persons"[26], had alternative views on the prophetic inheritance. If it was a logical conclusion of the clerical theory that they, the scholars, were *warathat al-anbiyā'*, it was a perhaps inevitable riposte that the caliph was "heir to the prophet's mantle, the prophet's staff and the authority of God" – وارث البرد والقضيب وحكم الله[27].

[25] Hence I disagree with Schacht's translation of *a'imma* in *Treatise III* as Caliphs (*Origins*, 24; cf. also 70); as well as with his translation of *imām* as governor (*Origins*, 208) where it means, I think, field commander.

[26] Goldziher, *Muslim Studies II*, 63.

[27] *Cit.* in S. Sperl, 'Islamic kingship and Arabic panegyric poetry', *JAL*, VIII, 1977.

XIII

FRIDAY PRAYER AND THE JURISTIC THEORY OF GOVERNMENT: SARAKHSĪ, SHĪRĀZĪ, MĀWARDĪ

Outstanding amongst the scholastic compendia of jurisprudence produced in the fifth/eleventh century are the *Muhadhdhab* of the Shāfiʿī scholar Abū Isḥāq al-Shīrāzī (d. 476) and the *Mabsūt* of the Ḥanafī scholar Shams al-Dīn al-Sarakhsī (d. 483).[1] These works encoded three centuries of juristic speculation while confirming and promoting the distinctive patterns of their respective law schools. Both scholars, Sarakhsī in Qarakhanid Transoxania, and Shīrāzī in Saljūq Baghdad, were involved in the politics of their day, but produced no political theory separate from their large-scale works of *furūʿ* which followed the traditional pattern of *furūʿ* literature, established as early as Mālik. The holistic approach to divine law was the dominant one in the Islamic juristic tradition and it may be thought that the conformity to type of Sarakhsī's and Shīrāzī's works helped to ensure them the classical status they acquired in the developing law-schools, and in the curricula of *madrasas*. The *Kitāb al-Aḥkām al-sulṭāniyya* of Māwardī[2] (d. 450) was in contrast, to a great extent, innovatory in subject matter and in structure, if not in juristic methodology. The difference between writers like Sarakhsī and Shīrāzī, on the one hand, and Māwardī, on the other, is not however simply formal: it includes a nicely distinguished approach to political power. The nature of this distinction might be demonstrated under a number of discrete headings selected from *furūʿ* literature. This essay is concerned with Friday Prayer (FP), a ritual generally recognized as having in some degree a political aspect.[3]

Sarakhsī distinguished two types of conditions relevant to FP: those affecting the individual participant (i.e. being male, of sound mind, free and residing in—as opposed to travelling through—a given area) (pp. 22–3) and those affecting the institution. For discussion of the latter he proposes 6 heterogeneous headings, namely *miṣr, waqt, khuṭba, jamāʿa, sulṭān* and *al-idhn al-ʿāmm* (p. 23). This essay will not be concerned with the second heading, namely, the timing of FP.

By *miṣr* Sarakhsī means that FP should take place only in a town that has acquired some size and significance. He explicitly contrasts this with the Shāfiʿī view which was that any community comprising at least 40 free males—even a village (*qarya*)—could organize and participate in FP. Sarakhsī's use of the term *miṣr* (possibly slightly archaic by the eleventh century) was conditioned by the fossilized terminology provided in the Traditions that he cited to establish his view. These (e.g. from the Prophet: *la jumʿa wa-la tashrīq illa fī miṣr jāmiʿ*) used the term *miṣr jāmiʿ*, a notion which would originally have designated a garrison town which 'gathered together' or 'united' (*jamaʿ*) the members of different tribes. In that context FP would have been a manifestation of political (military) unity transcending the different traditions and values

[1] Abū Isḥāq al-Shīrāzī, *Kitāb al-Muhadhdhab*, 2 vols., Beirut 1379/1959; Friday prayer is discussed in vol. I; page references are given in brackets in the text. Shams al-Dīn al-Sarakhsī, *Kitāb al-Mabsūṭ*, 30 vols., Egypt 1324; Friday prayer is discussed in vol. II; page references are given in text. For both scholars q.v. in *EI* (I).

[2] This work is too well-known to require comment; for a recent survey of its contents including references to all major secondary materials, see A. K. S. Lambton, *State and government in medieval Islam*, Oxford, 1981, ch. vi. Reference to Gibb, below, is to H. A. R. Gibb, 'Al-Mawardi's theory of the caliphate', in *Studies on the civilisation of Islam*, London, 1962.

[3] See *EI* (I) ad *ṣalāt* and *d̲j̲umʿa*; *EI* (II), *d̲j̲umʿa* and refs. given there.

of individual raiding parties and tribal groups. This notion of FP as a focus of unity within a political entity was preserved in the Ḥanafī tradition, where, according to Sarakhsī, the dominant view (*ẓāhir al-madhhab*) was that a *miṣr* could be defined as a town/city in which there was a *sulṭān* or *qāḍī* who could impose penalties (*iqāmat al-ḥudūd*) or implement laws (*tanfīdh al-aḥkām*). For Sarakhsī, FP is a religious ritual uniquely associated with a civic community, possessed of a (single) governor, capable of preserving law and order. The terms *sulṭān* and *qāḍī*, used to designate the governor, I am inclined to interpret at this stage (see further below) as neutral terms indicating only someone in charge. It is notable that political units larger than a city (caliphates, dynasties, *dār al-islām* etc.) are not mentioned ; smaller units (villages etc.) are excluded by definition.

The Islamic juristic tradition laid considerable stress on the fact that a single city (or community) should have only one FP. For Sarakhsī in Transoxania this was not a matter that required qualification. His discussion assumes rather than argues that there shall be only one FP in a single city ; he also makes it clear that communal prayer at noon is abhorred on a Friday, one reason for this being that it might reduce the number of participants in the FP (pp. 35–6).[4] Shīrāzī cites Shāfiʿī's view that FP should take place in only one mosque in a city no matter how big the city, or how many its mosques ; but adds qualifications relating specifically to Baghdad (p. 124). Cairo at this time was of course ruled by the heretical Fāṭimids but it too did not conform to the pattern of one city, one Friday Prayer. Notwithstanding the deviations from the norm that were imposed in practice, and the careful qualifications that were required to account for this, the Sunnī tradition continued even much later to restate the ideal. FP was a symbol of a unified political (or social) entity (whether a city, as for the Ḥanafīs, or a smaller but still distinct community, as for the Shāfiʿīs).[5]

The evidence of annalistic works suggests that in practice the *khuṭba* may have functioned as a means to symbolize the relationship between the city as a political entity (*miṣr*) and the larger political unit to which it belonged (a local prince whose control extended over more than one city, a local dynasty or the caliphate itself). Works of *fiqh* however do not provide any theoretical confirmation of this practice. Sarakhsī's discussion of the *khuṭba* (p. 24) confines itself to a formal listing of its modes and components, but without any mention of the prayer for the ruling sovereign. There can be no reason to doubt that such a prayer normally in practice took place and the failure to acknowledge it in works of *fiqh* must be seen as deliberate abstention. Shīrāzī, for the Shāfiʿīs, mentions it only to reject it (p. 119) :

> As for the prayer for the *sulṭān* it is not *mustaḥabb* because it is related that ʿAṭā' was asked about this and he said it was an innovation : the *khuṭba* was merely a reminder (*tadhkīr*).

The components of the *khuṭba*, as normally listed, are the *ḥamdullāh*, the prayer for the prophet, the *waṣiyya bi'l-taqwā* and a Qur'ānic recitation. Wensinck in *EI* (I) mentions in place of the *waṣiyya* a prayer for the faithful but this is not a usual formulation.

Under the heading *jamāʿa* Sarakhsī discusses the number of participants required in order to ensure the validity of FP. For the Ḥanafīs this was either two or three in addition to the *imām*. Shāfiʿī had specified 40 (p. 24).

[4] See further below, p. 42–3.

[5] cf. G. Makdisi, *The rise of colleges*, Edinburgh, 1981, 13 f.

The fifth condition related to FP specified by Sarakhsī (p. 24) was the presence of the *sulṭān*—a concept, as already indicated, which served also in the definition of a *miṣr*. Justification for this condition was found in the famous tradition from the Prophet via Jābir, typically, available in a variety of forms, and cited in the *Mabsūṭ* as a fundamental *ḥadīth* establishing the obligatory nature of FP. This *ḥadīth* takes the form of a statement that God has made it incumbent on Muslims to attend FP ' if/as long as they have an *imām*, tyrannous or just ' (*wa-la-hu imām jā'ir aw 'ādil*). Sarakhsī glosses this with the remark that the Prophet has made the *imām* (=*sulṭān*) a condition because of his implementing the threat (implied in the Tradition from Jābir) against one who abandons the *jum'a*. In fact it is difficult to read Sarakhsī's version as implying any threat other than that of divine sanction, so the gloss is already tendentious. Secondly, it is part of the general tradition of jurisprudence (*al-athr*) that four things (spheres of authority) belong to the *wulāt* (governors) one of which is the *jum'a*. Thirdly, Sarakhsī adduces an argument which (like the gloss of Jābir's Tradition ?) might be classified as an example of *istiṣlāḥ* :

> [The *sulṭān* is a condition of FP] because the people (*nās*) must relinquish [other forms of] communal prayer in order to perform the *jum'a*. If the *sulṭān* were not made a condition here this would lead to *fitna*, because some people would reach the Friday mosque before others and would perform the prayer [immediately] for some purpose of their own, and so others would miss it. In this there is manifest [possibility of] *fitna*. Hence this matter has been delegated (*mufawwaḍ*) to the *imām* to whom has been delegated [the administration of] the affairs of the people and [the implementation of] justice, because he is the most suitable (*aqrab*) for the settling of *fitna*.

It must be understood here that the normal communal prayers (*jamā'a* as opposed to *jum'a*) at noon in the mosques of the city are on Friday forbidden. Sarakhsī points out that in the early (?) *amṣār* the gates of the local mosques (as opposed to the *jāmi'* mosque) were closed (pp. 35–6) and the people of various factions, groups and quarters gathered in the Friday mosque. Since FP can only be performed once in the city it would be theoretically possible for one or several groups to pre-empt other groups by starting FP before they arrive. This threat of factionalism (*fitna*) (perhaps itself a theoretical construct designed to emphasize the role of FP as symbol of unity) is apparently met by making the *sulṭān* a condition—for he is the one to whom has been delegated the right to oversee the affairs of the people and to deal with *fitna*. It is assumed throughout that the term *imām* in the Tradition means governor (*sulṭān*, *wālī*) and that every city has a (separate ?) governor. The unidentified delegator is God. The terminology is formal, archaic, juristic and universal : no attempt is made to specify whatever mode of power delegation actually existed under the Qarakhanids. No political entity larger than a city is mentioned or alluded to.[6]

The final condition affecting the validity of FP and adduced by Sarakhsī is *al-idhn al-'āmm* :

> If the *sulṭān* prays with his retinue in his palace, then if he opens the gate of his palace and grants general permission (*idhn 'āmm*) to the people [to

[6] The idea of the ruler as chosen or delegated by God was common in the bureaucratic as well as in the juristic tradition : see Lambton *State and government*, 56 ff. ; also e.g. ' The dilemma of government in Islamic Persia ', *Iran*, XXII, 1984, 57.

participate in the prayer] his prayer is permissible, whether or not in fact the generality attend. But if he does not open the gates of his palace and does not grant permission to enter then his prayer does not suffice. For, making the *sulṭān* a condition is intended to guard against the possibility of [some of] the people missing it ; and this is not achieved except by general permission. Just as the generality [of the people] require the *sulṭān* to carry out prayer, so also the *sulṭān* requires them in order to accord the general permission. Thus the matter is balanced with respect to both sides (p. 24).

Now, as a set of general rules specifying the conditions under which FP may validly be performed these, by Sarakhsī, are as remarkable for the information that they fail to convey and for the issues they fail to raise as they are for their, in some respects, direct and positive concern with obviously political themes. Thus, Sarakhsī defines the city as one where there is a functioning authority (*sulṭān, qāḍī, wālī, imām ; li-iqāmat al-ḥudūd wa-tanfīdh al-aḥkām*) ; but about the proper constitution of that authority he says nothing. Indeed the wording of Jābir's Tradition—*wa-la-hu imām jā'ir aw 'ādil*—may be taken to imply that proper constitution and perhaps even appropriate implementation of the law are not relevant. It would appear to be the fact of authority not the form that counts. In discussing the *khuṭba* Sarakhsī's concern is with basic religious values (God, the Prophet, exhortation, recitation) and there is what can only be construed as deliberate restraint from exploiting an institution which might have been a key for integrating the theoretical discussions of *fiqh* and the actual forms of political practice. Further, the characterization of authority is both formal (abstract) and vague : none of the terms used has a specific Qarakhanid connotation and no consideration is given to any political entity outside the city. Civic authority is conceived of as necessary partly in order to impose God's laws—but that consideration was dispensable, as civic authority might be *jā'ir*. More circumstantially, civic authority is necessary to prevent *fitna*, that is, factionalism, within the Islamic community. What emerges from this is a minimal concept of authority, whose primary function is to protect Islamic values and Islamic unity ; it is a concept that offers few concessions to the government of the day. In effect this preserves a maximal distinction between the demands of the law and what actually happens : the law does not attempt to justify the *status quo*, it preserves its independence from it.

If within a recognizable civic community there emerges any effective government capable of imposing order, FP is valid. To this degree a kind of legitimacy is conferred on all forms of power even where that power is *jā'ir* (i.e. ? fails in some or in considerable degree to act with appropriate justice). But this ' legitimacy ' is not offered directly to bolster the influence or power of the ruler. FP is a ritual in which the whole Muslim (local) community, abandoning factional allegiances, expresses its adherence to universal Islamic values. The primary aim of the *shar'ī* formulation was to secure Islamic values : support for power was a means to that end. Power is recognized and accepted because, it is implied, only with efficient government and stability can Islam prosper and *fitna* be avoided. A corollary of this is naturally that, from the point of view of any given governor, it is at least politic to favour and support, in general, Islamic values and, in particular, Islamic jurists, because they offered—to a degree—an ideology of submission.

The fact that Islamic law seems to contain or express an ideology of submission has been frequently noted by Western scholars.[7] But any simple statement of the position will not do justice to the manifest subtleties of the juristic tradition. No item of revelation, whether the Tradition of Jābir, or any other, has intrinsic or absolute meaning : it derives its meaning from its place in a structure of thought, a structure formalized as comment on revelation and constrained certainly by the limits of revelation, but a structure demanding to be read and understood as a whole. Thus, even if it is true that Sarakhsī's views on Friday Prayer imply that the dangers of discord or civil strife are in any given city so great that any form of government is better than none at all, they do not imply that all forms of government are equal. Some forms of government are undoubtedly better than others. The work of the jurists over centuries was precisely to establish the theoretical outlines of a perfect community and, by holding it up before the people, to demonstrate the failings of what actually happened. Mainstream *fiqh*, by its very nature, was in varying degrees an expression of opposition to governments (as, of course, also to all life-styles that did not constantly and consciously aspire to the prophetic paradigm).

I have suggested above that Sarakhsī's expression of the rules related to FP included as it were an incentive for the governor to support Islamic values. In practice of course the support was frequently limited, distant, merely verbal or even non-existent. FP was carried out by a local *imām masjid*, a relatively minor appointee of the governor, and few *sulṭāns* can have been greatly exercised by their apparent duty to exist in order to ensure the validity of FP for the masses. This was not however the limit of Sarakhsī's thought, for, by making *al-idhn al-ʿāmm* a condition of the validity of FP, Sarakhsī was pointing out that the *sulṭān* too is subject to duties and constraints imposed by divine law. If his FP is to be effective for reward then he must ensure that it is available to the masses—not simply because it is useful or pragmatic to do so, but because this is an item in the law. FP therefore is a symbol too of the *sulṭān*'s submission to the law. FP became both a symbol of the fact that the civic authorities were divinely constituted (*mufawwaḍ*) and of the fact that they were subject to God's law. Recognition of their authority as God-given was coupled with an attempt to ensure that it was appropriately exercised. If the jurists seemed to advocate submission—as in the Tradition of Jābir—it was not out of pusilanimity, but because they found in that a means to constrain rulers towards (*a*) a practical justice, tending at least towards the forms of Islamic law and (*b*) practical support for the tenets of Islam in general and the members of the juristic class in particular. Sarakhsī dictated the *Mabsūṭ* to his students while imprisoned by a Qarakhanid prince, the Khaqan Ḥasan ; he remained in prison for ten years (466–77/1073–84). The biographies fail to explain this, restricting themselves for the most part to the repetition of a phrase, namely, that he was imprisoned ' for something he said to the Khaqan '—*li-kalima naṣaḥ bi-hā al-khāqān*. This remains an obscure event but it serves as a reminder that a class and an intellectual tradition which laid considerable stress on the need for functioning authority did not thereby relinquish their right to criticize and influence that authority even at the expense of personal liberty.

Statements of the law implied to a variable degree condemnation of what actually happened and, in specific contexts, this could be made explicit. In the *Mabsūṭ* ad *maks* (II, 199) Sarakhsī states : ' That which has been transmitted concerning the blaming (*dhamm*) of tax-collectors (*ʿushshār*) is related

[7] Appropriately careful expression of this may be found in Lambton, *State and government*, *passim*.

only to that part of the people's property which they take unjustly (*ẓulman*) —as in our time—and not to that which they take by right'. The small parenthesis makes it clear that the tax-collecting activities of the Qarakhanids were not *shar'ī*. Had they followed the system set out in the *Mabsūṭ* they would not be 'blamed'. It is precisely because he does not describe, does not attempt to justify, the *status quo* that Sarakhsī was able to criticize and might hope to influence. By preserving the *sharī'a* as an ideal, Sarakhsī was preserving and enhancing the authority of his social group. This accounts also for the preservation of archaic, abstract and universally applicable terminology in expressing the divine law: Sarakhsī did not want to suggest that the Qarakhanid practice was also *shar'ī* practice. Nor however did he want to incite opposition to the Qarakhanids: authority was necessary. The tradition of *fiqh* writing steered an uneasy course between the Scylla of anarchy and the Charybdis of legitimizing the inadequate. If one were to extract from Sarakhsī a notion of legitimacy one would find that it had a minimal aspect (power was legitimate in so far as it could impose order and stability and so permit Islam to flourish) and a maximal aspect (that power was fully legitimate that conformed to the *sharī'a*). It was a sliding scale. Presumably no *faqīh* would lightly suggest that any particular power had in large measure achieved *shar'ī* practice.[8]

Particular details of contemporary practice naturally found their way sometimes into works of *fiqh*, whether for praise or blame, or for some more abstruse end, not easily discerned. The remarks of Sarakhsī on *al-idhn al-'āmm* have, as far as I am aware, no precedent in the juristic tradition, and they are adduced without any backing from revealed sources or citations from earlier jurists. It is possible that they reflect some local practice whereby at least one city governor organized the Friday Prayer in his own palace, with his retinue. The point of that condition as expressed by Sarakhsī was that the *sulṭān* had a duty to the people, namely, to permit their participation, that he needed them for the validity of his prayer just as they needed him for theirs. For Sarakhsī 'the matter is balanced with respect to both sides'; both the sultan and the people are subject to the constraints of the law. If however in contemporary practice, a city governor had for some reason of his own decided to perform the FP in his own palace, whether permitting or not permitting the people to attend, then one may well imagine that his motives were not to demonstrate his need for the people, possibly indeed to demonstrate something totally other than this. The apparently bland text of Sarakhsī's discussion may conceal a deliberate undermining of secular pretensions.

Shīrāzī's discussion of FP is at first reading significantly less 'political' than Sarakhsī's. The reason for this is in large measure a purely formal one. The Ḥanafī tradition permitted reference to social conditions (*ṣalāḥ/istiṣlāḥ*) in discussion of juristic details. In the Shāfi'ī tradition by contrast it was required that justification of God's law be by formal reference to Book and Traditions. Thus presented, the law has the appearance of being completely free from social and political influence, being related only to God's word and prophetic precedent. This had its usefulness in appearing to remove the law from the political arena, while enhancing its implicit criticism of actual practice. For Shīrāzī as for Sarakhsī, FP was related to the Tradition from Jābir, including the phrase *wa-la-hu imām jā'ir aw 'ādil* (p. 116). The conditions affecting the

[8] In these paragraphs I am particularly concerned to qualify the view of Gibb that 'the efforts of jurists were necessarily directed to justifying the actual situation'; in 'Some considerations on the Sunni theory of the caliphate', in *Studies on the civilisation of Islam*, 141–2.

participants were more or less those cited by Sarakhsī. Of conditions affecting the institution, all those mentioned by Sarakhsī are discussed by Shīrāzī—with the exception of *al-idhn al-ʿāmm*. Where Sarakhsī used the term *miṣr* or *miṣr jāmiʿ* Shīrāzī refers to *balad*, *qarya* and *waṭan*, implying a community smaller than the limit envisaged by Sarakhsī. Further, these terms required no overtly political element in their definition : they are explained in terms of buildings, conglomerate and inhabited by a sufficient number to render valid FP. The concept is clarified by contrast with that area in which FP is not valid, namely, *al-baduw*, the desert where a migrant life is led (p. 117). FP is thus characteristic of a settled as opposed to a nomadic community. The number required for valid FP is 40 free males. Whereas for Sarakhsī FP is related to the existence of governing bodies, for Shīrāzī it is the existence of a settled community—rather than a functioning authority—that is the condition of FP. This turning away from government as a factor of importance in establishing the validity of FP is a constant, possibly a stressed, feature of Shīrāzī's exposition. In discussing the *khuṭba*, he specifically states that the *duʿā' li'l-sulṭān* is not *mustaḥabb* (p. 119). In discussing whether the presence of the sultan is a condition, he states the following :

> It is the *sunna* [=normal practice] that the *jumʿa* not be performed without the permission of the *sulṭān* because that may be to slight him (*iftiyāt*) ; but if it is performed without his permission, it is permissible because [*a*] it is related that ʿAlī performed the *ʿīd* prayer while ʿUthmān was besieged and [*b*] [FP] is a duty (*farḍ*) due to God and it is not specifically related to the actions of the *imām* (*wa-lā yakhtaṣṣu bi-fiʿl al-imām*) ; hence it does not require his permission [being in this respect] like other *ʿibādat* (p. 124).

This has to be construed as a very significant qualification of what may be thought to be implied in the Tradition of Jābir. The formal justification (*a*) has its value, but it is the carefully expressed juristic argument (*b*), that is striking. FP is deliberately freed from its association with government. In so far as the notion of the sultan's permission is acknowledged it is portrayed as a politeness, a matter of manners. In law, FP is no more dependent on the sultan than other acts of worship (meaning daily prayer, fasting, pilgrimage etc.). FP in this reading is not a symbol either of the existence of nor of the necessity for a functioning government : it is the communal activity of a settled community of Muslims, who thereby express their shared participation in the tenets of Islam. This shared faith of a united community is, ideally, independent of governors and their ways.

Both Sarakhsī and Shīrāzī may be interpreted as searching for a minimal political or social requirement for the preservation and expression of Islamic values. The Ḥanafī tradition looked to a city and a governor to create the basic conditions for the flourishing of Islam. The Shāfiʿī tradition looked much more to a sense of communal unity, both fostering and fostered by shared faith—and no doubt inspired and guided by the *fuqahā'*. Both traditions were of course faced with the fact that FP was in some degree a political institution which in normal practice contained explicit references to the government, and was perhaps a means whereby political messages could be conveyed to the people and political influence brought to bear. This situation was no doubt perceived as unsatisfactory not least because opposition to the government might be expressed as opposition to FP and so constitute a threat to those values and to those institutions through which the clerical class expressed their authority. Both traditions in different ways and to different degrees tried to dissociate themselves from the government. No matter how much real support the mosque gave to the *sulṭān*, or how much real influence the *sulṭān* exerted on the mosque, juristic theory preserved its independence. What actually happened was not at all, or not necessarily, or not completely, part of the law. It is arguable that precisely by this abnegation the jurists ensured the continuation of their own authority. It was precisely because they did not try to bring practice into the sphere of divine law that the jurists preserved its and their capacity to criticize and influence.

Amongst the political aspects of FP which are habitually not mentioned in juristic works is the whole question of who appointed the *imāms* of mosques and what rules there are for the running of these institutions. It is true that some aspects of this question might be clarified by adding up a number of discrete and remorselessly uncross-referenced items in standard works of *fiqh*, but these will not add up to a description of actual practice. That this was a considered abnegation is highlighted for the fifth century by the example of Māwardī who, a generation before Sarakhsī and Shīrāzī, had attempted in fact to bring the law and the bureaucratic system into some kind of harmony. Prior to analysing how he did this, it is necessary to consider further how Sarakhsī and Shīrāzī limited themselves. Both writers discuss the nature and conditions affecting prayer leaders in relation to communal prayer (*jamā'a*) not *jum'a*.[9] Sarakhsī expressed specific doubts about the capacity in such a post of the blind, the beduin, the slave, the bastard and the sinner (*fāsiq*) ; their functioning as prayer leader, *imām*, was permissible but others were preferable. The reason for this preference was that *imāma* was part of the prophetic inheritance and those chosen for this post should be as like the prophet as possible. Furthermore, it is the position from which the caliphate was derived (*huwa makān ustunbiṭ minhu al-khilāfa*).[10] The *imām*, prayer leader, should therefore be the most ' superior ' person, *man huwa a'zam fī 'l-nās*. A further reason why it is better to avoid the blind, the beduin, the slave etc. is that it is the function of the *imām* to maximize the numbers of those who participate in *jamā'a* (*takthīr al-jamā'a*) : ' and in promoting the " superior " there is maximization of those who participate in *jamā'a* '. Similarly, an attempt to promote a *fāsiq*, though permissible, is abhorred because its tendency will be to decrease those who participate in prayer (*taqlīl al-jamā'a*), for the people do not like to be led by such. This notion that the people do or do not like to be led by specific types is repeated on several occasions. Abū Yūsuf is quoted as objecting to the *imāma* of *ṣāḥib hawa* or *ṣāḥib bid'a* because ' the people do not like to be led by such '. And of slaves Sarakhsī says : ' the people rarely like to be led by slaves '. The person who should lead prayer, based on a famous Tradition from Ibn Mas'ūd, is the most capable in reciting the Book, the most learned in the *sunna*, the greatest in piety and the oldest. Sarakhsī in fact dislikes the apparent preference in the Tradition for one capable of reciting the Qur'ān over one who knows the law. He gives reasons, historical and legal, to justify his conclusion that being learned in the law is the most significant factor in assessing the worthiness of a prayer leader. He makes an exception of one who is the object of criticism in some aspect of his religion ' because the people do not like to be led by such a one '. Thus Sarakhsī produces a general legal principle for choosing a prayer leader, namely, that he should be likely to

[9] Sarakhsī, *op. cit.*, I, 40–2 ; Shīrāzī, *op. cit.*, I, 104–6.

[10] I take this to be a historical reference to the caliphate of the Rāshidūn and in particular to that of Abū Bakr ; ' caliph ' is not a term used by Sarakhsī to refer to contemporary governors.

maximize the number of participants in prayer. To this he adds the specific consideration that the most learned in *sunna* is overall the most worthy of the post.

There was another set of conditions affecting the choice of prayer leader which was distinct from and not easily harmonized with the set already discussed. It was related to ownership, a concept capable of metaphorical extension to include rulers and governors.

> It is abhorred for anyone to lead a man in prayer in his [the man's] house, except with his permission because of [*a*] the Prophet's words : A man does not lead a man in his own *sulṭān* [=sphere of authority] and [*b*] the promotion of another over him constitutes a slighting (*iftiyāt*) of the owner in the eyes of his family or relatives and that is not consistent with good manners (*ḥusn al-khalq*).[11] Unless the guest in question be a *sulṭān* [governor] in which case the right to the imamate is his wherever he may be [within the sphere of his authority].

This rule might have been extended to account for and explain the practice of governing authorities in appointing the *imāms* of Friday mosques. Sarakhsī, however, makes no further comment on the matter. It is implicit in the discussion that the second set of conditions—ownership/*sulṭān*—takes precedence over the first.

Shīrāzī's discussion of the rules and conditions affecting the leadership of FP is related like Sarakhsī's to communal prayer (*jamā'a*). He discusses various debilities which to a greater or lesser extent impair but do not necessarily invalidate prayer leadership : as, for example, being immature, or a woman or a *kāfir* or a *fāsiq*, or being incapable (through sickness or debility) of standing etc. The list of possible deficiencies is open-ended, no criteria being adduced to ensure that it is either complete or logical. No doubt these were the discrete items thrown up by the juristic tradition or produced casuistically in debate, and they were dealt with as such with no attempt to establish general principles. There is more than one instance when prayer under a particular circumstance (as e.g. when the literate prays behind the illiterate) had elicited within the tradition two views, namely, that it is and that it is not permissible. This kind of irresolution serves once again to remind the reader that a work of *fiqh*, though intended to guide conduct, did not simply lay down rules for action ; it rather explored the possibilities of divine law with a varying and unpredictable concern for what actually happened.

Shīrāzī's discussion of who in particular is the most worthy of the imamate (of prayer) parallels Sarakhsī's. He too prefers the more knowledgeable in *fiqh* (*afqahuhum*) to the more capable of reciting (*aqra'uhum*) and for similar reasons. Likewise, cutting across these considerations is the notion that within his own home the householder is most worthy of being prayer leader—and Shīrāzī cites a variation on the Tradition cited by Sarakhsī. This concept is extended to cover the *imām* of a mosque who, within his own mosque, is most worthy, and the *imām al-muslimīn* who is more worthy than either the householder or the *imām masjid* ' because his *wilāya* is general and because he is a shepherd and they are his flock and the promotion of the shepherd is better '.[12] Shīrāzī lived in Baghdad and was an associate of Niẓām al-Mulk ; he was familiar with the

[11] It is a consideration of this kind that led Shīrāzī to express his view that FP was valid without the permission of the *sulṭān*.

[12] For the ruler as ' shepherd ' see e.g. Abū Yūsuf in Lambton, *State and government*, 57.

political structures of his day but he does not clarify who is the *imām al-muslimīn*. I would assume that he meant the holder of real power, that is, the Saljūq ruler and not the caliph.[13]

Māwardī's *Al-Aḥkām al-sulṭāniyya*—usually thought of as a work of Shāfi'ī jurisprudence—is not in the same literary tradition as Sarakhsī's *Mabsūṭ* or Shīrāzī's *Muhadhdhab*, which, conversely, are clearly in the same tradition as one another, though they belong to different schools. Māwardī's was an attempt to bring the actual political institutions of his day as organized and administered by the court bureaucracy (or bureaucracies) into the sphere of *fiqh*. His organizing principle was not the concepts which, since the time of Mālik, Shāfi'ī etc. had provided the structure for large-scale works of *fiqh*, including those of Sarakhsī and Shīrāzī, but rather the major institutions of government as they existed in his day, some of which, like the wazirate, the *imāra 'alā 'l-bilād* and others had not previously featured as elements in *fiqh* discussion. Others, like the organization of *jihād*, the office of *qāḍī* and, our present concern, the imamate of prayer, had already been to a considerable extent worked out, and the parameters of relevant details and possible options had been fixed.

In his chapter entitled *fī 'l-wilāyāt 'alā imāmat al-ṣalawāt*, Māwardī provides immediately precisely the information which we noted as lacking in Sarakhsī and Shīrāzī. He distinguishes between the post of prayer leader in relation to communal prayer, Friday prayer and supererogatory prayer ; then :

> The appointment of an *imām* to lead the communal prayer is dependent on the type of mosque in which prayer is held. There are two types : *masājid sulṭāniyya* and *masājid 'āmmiyya* [government mosques and public mosques]. The *sulṭāniyya* mosques are those . . . for the supervision of which the *sulṭān* is responsible. No-one may be appointed (*intidāb*) to the imamate [in such a mosque] except one appointed (*nadab*) and invested (*qallad*) by the *sulṭān* . . . Once someone has been invested [in a post] he has more right than any other to lead the prayer *even if others are better or more knowledgeable than he.*

Māwardī explicitly states that Friday mosques are government mosques. His statement makes central two features which were either absent or obscure in the discussions of Sarakhsī and Shīrāzī. First, he provides that the *sulṭān* (the meaning of this term in Māwardī will be discussed below) shall be solely responsible for the appointment of *imāms* in Friday mosques ; and secondly, he provides that the appointee, by virtue merely of his appointment, shall have absolute precedence over all others. It is not at all impossible that these rules would be recognized as valid or reasonable by Sarakhsī or Shīrāzī ; but, though they presumably knew, or knew of, Māwardī's work, they chose not to express themselves in this way. Māwardī himself acknowledged that juristically the prayer of the people would be sufficient if they agreed amongst themselves as to who should be *imām*. In spite of all acknowledged qualifications however he repeats that once the *sulṭān* has appointed an *imām* to mosques of the government type no other person can lead prayer as long as the appointee is present : *lam yakun li-ghayrihi an yataqaddam fīhā ma'a ḥuḍūrihi*. In discussing the residual rights of the people to appoint their own *imām* if the regular *imām* is absent, not having appointed a deputy, he stresses that the exercise of choice does not infringe or pre-empt the *sulṭān*'s rights. Even in the non-governmental mosques where the imamate is normally dependent on the consent of the people, the ultimate residual right of choice, in case of dispute, lay with the *sulṭān*.

[13] There is no doubt that both in Būyid and in Saljūq times it was generally the military *amīr/sulṭān* who appointed judges and *imāms* of mosques ; see further n. 14.

Within the government mosques the *sulṭān* might further appoint more than one *imām* and specify their spheres of duty. It is clear his aim was to demonstrate that the *sulṭān*'s control of Friday mosques was *shar'ī* or, conversely, that the *sharī'a* provided for the *sulṭān*'s control of Friday mosques. It may be that he had not subverted the letter of the law, but it is certainly arguable that he had abandoned the spirit.

In discussing the qualities desirable in a prayer leader Māwardī followed the normal paths of *fiqh* discussion with the normal qualifications as to women, slaves, *fāsiqs* etc. He expresses the usual preference for a *faqīh* over a *qāri'* (other things being equal) using the same kind of argument as was used by Sarakhsī and Shīrāzī. His exploration of this kind of detail was possible because he had already established a single principle of prayer-leadership which pre-empted all others, namely, appointment by the *sulṭān*. Once the institutional arrangements for the imamate as an official post had been dealt with he was free to demonstrate his concern for and his prowess in traditional juristic methodology. It was of little concern to him whether the view of Abū Ḥanīfa or of Shāfi'ī was accepted with regard to the definition of a *miṣr/qarya* (he gave both with no indication of his own preference) since in either case any existing Friday mosque and its personnel could be controlled and organized through the government bureaucracy. However in cases where juristic variation was likely to cause administrative problems he did provide answers, invariably answers stressing the competence of the *sulṭān* to cut through juristic *ikhtilāf*. For example, he cites variant opinions on the question of how many participants are required for valid FP. This could lead to problems when the opinion of an *imām* (obviously in this case government appointed) differed from that of his congregation. The resolution lay in this that the *sulṭān* could specify in advance which juristic rule the *imām* had to follow and the *imām* was required to take steps to ensure that the specified rule was implemented, even if this meant (in the most difficult scenario) that the *imām* had to appoint under certain circumstances a deputy to undertake his duties (when the number conformed to the rule specified by the *sulṭān* but not to the rule adopted by the *imām*) or his post (*wilāya*) became null (*bāṭil*).

Māwardī's aim in writing his famous work included a desire both to make administrative practice *shar'ī* and so demonstrate that what actually happened was in fact legitimate ; and to make the *sharī'a* broader, in the sense of forcing it to take into account elements of practice which until his time had been, pointedly I would suggest, ignored, and were ignored afterwards by such as Sarakhsī and Shīrāzī. He achieved his aim first by incorporating into a *fiqh* discussion administrative posts which were not usually dealt with in works of *fiqh*. Secondly, he abandoned the normal order of *fiqh* works and produced a coherent structural description of administrative positions, where earlier works (and later) relied upon juxtaposition of discrete uncross-referenced items (a means perhaps precisely to avoid the legitimation of actual practice). Thirdly, he makes explicit the capacity of the *sulṭān* to control, appoint, invest etc. in specifically religious contexts like Prayer as well as in other areas ; this is at best implicit in mainstream *fiqh* and may there be subtly qualified (by remarks like Sarakhsī's *ad maks*), or undermined (as Shīrāzī's dissociation of FP and government). Finally he cuts through the problem of acknowledged *ikhtilāf* by asserting that the *sulṭān* could specify which of the various available options was to be the administrative one. Whether Māwardī was justified in thinking that *ikhtilāf* could, as it were, legitimately, be reduced in this way, I do not know. However, I would read Sarakhsī and Shīrāzī as rejecting these views. In their works not only was *shar'ī* recognition of the *sulṭān*'s authority kept to a minimum but the full range of *ikhtilāf* was upheld.

A final example of Māwardī's manipulation of the juristic tradition may be found in his carefully oblique reference to the *da'wat al-sulṭān* (=*al-du'ā' li'l-sulṭān*). It will be recalled that Sarakhsī ignored this and that Shīrāzī pointedly referred to its being *ghayr mustaḥabb*. Māwardī refers to this prayer only in the last paragraph of his chapter, and brackets it with another item of practice universally ignored by the *fuqahā'* :

> The wearing of black is a privilege of the *imāms* [prayer leaders] in those prayers wherein the *da'wat al-sulṭān* is performed ; this [wearing of black] being in conformity with its [the *sulṭān*'s] current insignia (*shi'ār*). Deviation in this matter is abhorred, though it is not required by the law, for it constitutes a safeguard against opposition to it [the *sulṭān*=government].

This, the sole reference to the *da'wat al-sulṭān* is made without any mention of its juristic status ; it may serve as evidence that Māwardī is capable of blurring a juristic ruling where he finds it convenient to do so. The passage may also serve to clarify the meaning of *sulṭān*. This was not in Māwardī a title belonging to any particular office or officer of state. The three chief offices of state were for him the caliph, the *wazīr* and the *amīr*. Here he refers to the wearing of black, an 'Abbāsid (caliphal) insignia, as characteristic of the *sulṭān*. My assumption is that he uses the term *sulṭān* here because of its neutral meaning, having no specific reference to either the caliph or the *amīr*. He could, had he chosen, have made clear any reference to either. He wished to refer in a general sense to the actual government, or to the *de facto* authorities, and would like no doubt that the notion of government (*sulṭān*) should be understood as combining the caliphate and the amirate in precisely the way he had outlined in the earlier chapters of his book.

Gibb's suggestion that the *Al-Aḥkām al-sulṭāniyya* was written for a caliph in the later Būyid period seems to me correct. Its argument is such as to make explicit a legitimizing role for the caliph within the Būyid state. I do not find it far-fetched to compare Māwardī's notion of the caliphate with that of a constitutional monarch : a theoretical primacy in all matters of state was combined with a real lack of power in anything. It was in practice the *amīr* who appointed even to religious offices such as judgeships or the imamate of Friday mosques, as Māwardī makes clear in his chapter on the amirate. It is possible that occasionally the caliph might have enough local power in the immediate vicinity of Baghdad to restrict the power of some *amīrs* or wrest from them certain rights, but in general throughout the domains of Eastern Sunnī Islam, the *amīr* was the *de facto* and frequently, by virtue of Māwardī's theory, the *de jure* ruler.

Māwardī's remarks on the *da'wat al-sulṭān* and the wearing of the *sulṭān*'s insignia (that is, specifically, the caliph's) are both aspects of a political initiative. The aim was to offer the Būyid *amīrs* legitimacy and so perhaps to enhance political stability, while at the same time and by the same arguments to provide a function for the caliph (the constitutional caliphate). I cannot agree with Makdisi[14] that there was any separation of powers, as between caliph and *amīr* :

[14] Makdisi, *op. cit.*, 13–14. It may be that under al-Qādir the caliph was indeed capable of controlling and appointing to the mosques of Baghdad ; Mamlūk sources and caliphal court historians would have their own reasons for stressing this. Māwardī specifically states in his chapter on the *imāra* that appointing to the imamate of communal and Friday prayers was part of the functions of the *amīr* (Cairo ed., 1973, 30). Niẓām al-Mulk confirms this for the Saljūq period in *Siyāsat-nāma*, ed. H. Darke, Tehran, 1962, 56.

the *amīr* had all the power, even in theory, and any curtailment of the *amīr*'s power locally in Baghdad and for a short time was accidental. Māwardī did not make his theory in any sense dependent on the caliph's retaining any real power whatsoever. The caliph functioned as theoretical source of authority.

Immediately after the sentence on *daʿwat al-sulṭān* etc., Māwardī writes :

> If someone gains power by force (*taghallab*) who prohibits communal prayer this constitutes an excuse for not performing it openly. But if the usurper establishes it in spite of his deviation in faith (*maʿa sūʾ muʿtaqadihi*), he should be followed therein but not followed in any *bidʿa*.

This is the last sentence in the chapter. It appears that Māwardī was acutely conscious of the fragility of power, and it may be for that reason that he proposed that the power and the administrative system should be given considerable support from the law. It is implicit in his sentence about the wearing of black that what constitutes a safeguard against opposition to the *sulṭān* (government) should be carried out. None the less, the possibility of power being seized by another (*amīr* ?), by one whose faith was inadequate, had to be recognized. It may be that he had the Fāṭimids in mind, but the situation in Eastern Islam in Būyid times was very much one of robber bands at large and the Būyids were not themselves always Sunnī. Māwardī was concerned to secure stability for whatever government existed, even at the cost of acknowledging full (or considerable) legitimacy. But if, in spite of that, the government fell, and fell to one whose faith deviated from the true faith, then Friday Prayer should as far as possible continue and the process of, as it were, seducing the *amīrs* towards the norms of Islam by the offer of legitimacy would begin again.

It is almost a commonplace of Western comment on Islamic juristic theory of government that it attempted to justify the *status quo*. I doubt this. The juristic theory of government on the whole aimed at *not* justifying the *status quo* in the manner illustrated for Sarakhsī and Shīrāzī. None the less, once Māwardī was accepted into the canon of respectable jurists (as, if doubtfully, he was) it became possible for every jurist to adopt whatever point he liked in the sliding scale of legitimacy that was produced in the juristic tradition. Between Shīrāzī's almost complete disregard of the political institution and Māwardī's almost complete adoption of it there are a considerable number of intermediate positions. My own overall impression is that the dominant tradition (at least prior to the Ottoman period) was that which attempted to dissociate the law as a theoretical structure from the practical politics of the day. Māwardī's stance, if adopted wholeheartedly, seems likely to have weakened the influence of the clerical class by bringing them into a dangerously close alliance with political power. Shīrāzī sees the religious community as something quite separate (ideally) from the political structure ; upon his remarks it would not be impossible to build an ideology of (careful) opposition whether passive or otherwise. Indeed even Sarakhsī's nice balance of government and religion was not incompatible with criticism and resistance. The law was a sufficiently flexible instrument to be used for diverse political ends.[15]

[15] My intention in this essay has been to demonstrate that Māwardī is markedly different in his aims from Shīrāzī and Sarakhsī. I have stated throughout that the latter are representative of the juristic tradition and that Māwardī is the innovator. Space has not permitted me to demonstrate this in detail ; the matter may broadly be verified by study of earlier juristic writers, such as Mālik, Shāfiʿī, Shaybānī *et al.*

XIV

Exploring God's law: Muḥammad ibn Aḥmad ibn Abī Sahl al-Sarakhsī on *zakāt*

I

Literary works within the genre of *furūᶜ al-fiqh* are characterised by two major hermeneutical constraints. The primary constraint is that of loyalty to tradition *(madhhab)*. Of jurists who produced lasting works, the vast bulk were consciously allied to a school tradition and wrote in submission to it. They were not alone before revelation (in a position of interpretative freedom or licence), but heirs to, guardians of and interpreters of a tradition of interpretation. The second constraint is that of justification by reference to revelation. The school tradition as it was understood or presented by individual jurists had to be defensible by reference (primarily) to Qur'ān and hadith. Most of the literature of the law and many of its formal elements can be characterised by reference to this dual hermeneutical activity. The formal structures of commentary, gloss, supercommentary, multiple citation of authority, and jigsaw puzzle composition (where new works were created by the juxtaposition of phrases, sentences and paragraphs derived from earlier authorities, as in the *Al-Baḥr al-Rā'iq* of Ibn Nujaym[1] or in the *Fatāwā Hindiyya*[2]) are all symbolic of the school-based hermeneutical engagement that gripped and inspired the Muslim jurists.

The individuality of particular works – their thinness or density of texture, their vitality, complexity, capacity to engage the intellect or the imagination etc. depended on a number of other tendencies which were differentially exploited by different writers at different times and places, and are much less easy to define or quantify. Language for example (at

[1] Ibn Nujaym, Zayn al-Dīn b. Ibrāhīm al-Miṣrī (d. 970/1563), author of *Al-Baḥr al-Rā'iq*, a commentary on the *Kanz al-Daqā'iq* of ᶜAbdallāh b. Aḥmad Ḥāfiẓ al-Din al-Nasafī (d. 710/1310).

[2] The *Fatāwā Hindiyya* or the *Fatāwā ᶜĀlamgīrī*, a work of Ḥanafī *fiqh* compiled under the patronage of Aurangzēb in the years 1664 - 72, its chief author being Shaykh Niẓām Burhānpūrī.

the level of word or sentence) or presentational elegance and coherence (at the level of paragraph) might be foregrounded to the point of virtuosity. There were infinite gradations of interest between a practical sense of the real consequences of the law and an imaginative exploration of its logical (or analogical) possibilities. Some jurists were at ease with a dialectical and exploratory presentation of the law; others tended towards a static monovalency. Unsurprisingly, since the world of literature is not identical with the world of everyday problems (the teaching *faqīh* is not at the same time a *muftī*) the works that have been promoted by the tradition as valuable tend to display qualities of virtuosity (of language, structure, content) that elicit reader responses that are literary (intellectual, imaginative, playful) and not merely practical. It is an evidently inadequate reader-response to treat the linguistic virtuosity of the Mālikī jurist Khalīl b. Iṣḥāq[3], or the densely textured argument of the Ḥanafī jurist Sarakhsī, as if these writers intended to produce simply a list of instructions.

The Ḥanafī jurist Muḥammad b. Aḥmad b. Abī Sahl Abū Bakr al-Sarakhsī (d. ca. 490/1097[4]) has long been perceived by Western scholars as, in some way, a distinctive writer, though little has been done in the way of characterising his distinction.[5] His method, approach and achievement will hardly be illustrated by one brief sondage, such as is attempted here, but without some beginning he will not be appreciated at all. Merely to cite Sarakhsī's preferred opinions about the law – which has been done often enough – will not uncover his peculiar genius. Something appropriately complex (and correspondingly revealing) is required. The passages translated below illustrate the play of thought and argument in that part of Sarakhsī's discussion of *zakāt* where he perceives certain tensions arising between the demands of God and the rights and

3 Khalīl b. Isḥāq (d.776/1374), author of the famous *Mukhtaṣar,* frequently published.

4 The *Kitāb al-Jawāhir al-Muḍiyya* (Ḥaydarābād, 1332/1912) by ʿAbd al-Qādir b. Abī al-Wafā' Muḥammad al-Qurashī (d. 775/1373) gives his date of death at ca. 490/1097; vol. 2, 29 (no. 85). The *Fawa'id al-Bahiyya* (Beirut? 1323) of Muhammad ʿAbd al-Hayy al-Laknawī repeats this and adds the alternative *(wa-qīla)* of ca. 500/1107; p. 158. This is probably derived from Ibn Quṭlubughā, *Tāj al-tarājim,* (ed. Flügel, Leipzig, 1862), no. 157. F Sezgin gives 483/1090 *(Geschichte des Arabischen Schrifttums,* Leiden, 1967, vol. 1, p. 443), possibly following Heffening in EI[1], ad Sarakhsī. Se now "Sarakhsī" in EI[2].

5 See Heffening in EI[1] ad Sarakhsī. Baber Johansen is probably the best of those who frequently cite Sarakhsī, but he too tends to use this work as a source of rules, rather than to discover his (Sarakhsī's) literary aims. See e.g. *The Islamic law on land tax and rent* (Croom Helm, London, 1988) passim.

duties of the *zakāt* donors, *zakāt* recipients, tax-collectors and governor. In relation to the wide span of interests represented in a work of *fiqh*, or even in those parts of it which deal with *zakāt*, that is a small topic. It has however the merit of being fairly easily defined and separated from other issues, and its problems are less intractable to 20th century analysis than some.

Sarakhsī's *Mabsūṭ* is a commentary on the work known as *Al-Kāfī* by Muḥammad ibn Muḥammad al-Ḥākim al-Marwazī[6]. That work dictates the organisational structure of Sarakhsi's work and provides a framework of basic rules. These are expanded by Sarakhsī, often by pointing to acknowledged dispute *(ikhtilāf)* within the Ḥanafī tradition or across the major schools, and by the provision of justificatory or explanatory argument. The chapter headings for discussion of *zakāt* relate to property which can be the subject of ownership: camels, sheep and goats, cattle, gold and silver, trade goods, minerals, agricultural produce. The quality of Sarakhsī's discussion might be described as ritualistic: it involves an intense and unsparing focus on detail, on typologies of goods, on nomenclature, on modes of ownership, timing of payments, expressions of intention etc., much of which is impractical, and inimical to the social end of *zakāt* (if indeed it is conceded to have one, other than accidentally). The mode of discussion is juristic but its quality is ritualistic and religious and can perhaps be accounted for by the unarticulated but pervasive sense that this is God's law, deserving of unsparing effort and constantly sharpened focus.

The nexus of responsibilities as between donor, recipient, tax-collector and governor first becomes an issue in the section on camels. The arguments there are understood to cover all pastoral animals, and not to cover gold, silver and trade goods as long as these are kept at home. If gold, silver and trade goods are carried from city to city or in any other way through the customs barriers set up by governors, they are legitimately subject to a tax conventionally termed *ʿushr*, though not necessarily realised as a tithe.[7] In this case the rules that have been stated for camels come into effect again, for it is understood that, in some way or another – and it is a matter of considerable complexity – the private religious duty of *zakāt* takes on some aspects of a public duty in so far as the governor

6 Died 334/945, or, possibly, 344/955. Both dates are given in Laknawī, *Fawā'id*, 185.

7 Sarakhsī, *Mabsūṭ*, vol. 2, 199. The *ʿushr* for Muslim traders is here specified as one fortieth.

plays his role in providing the property owner with protection (or in so far as the governor is a deputy of God etc.)[8]. (The distinction is formally between *ẓāhir* or apparent goods, and *bāṭin* or hidden goods. Curiously, this terminology, though certainly current in some juristic discussions at this time, is not alluded to by Sarakhsī.) The following discussion is based on two citations from Sarakhsī. The first, taken from the section on camels, represents an exploratory and idealistic statement of the potential rights and duties of donors, recipients, tax-collectors and governor. The second, from a later part of the same section, shows Sarakhsī coming to a narrower focus on the actual governors of his day and on the way their activities affect the actual and current fulfillment of this ritual duty. A full analysis of Sarakhsī's views, even on this limited topic, would require this analysis to be extended in order to cover also customs duties and agricultural produce, but this will not be attempted here.

II

In the following passage Sarakhsī conceives of (in fact inherits from Marwazī[9]) three situations in which the owner of camels (or other pastoral animals), faced with a demand from a tax-collector, may refuse to pay.

> 1.1. The collector arrives. The owner says, I have not had these animals for a whole year, or, I owe a debt which is greater than their value, or, These animals are not mine. He then swears that this is so. He is believed in all cases.
>
> 1.2. This is because he is responsible *(amīn)* for *zakāt* duties that are obligatory on him. *Zakāt* is an act of worship purely for the sake of God *(ʿibāda khāliṣa li-llāh)*, and the word of a responsible person is always acceptable in regard to acts of worship that are obligatory [solely] as

[8] Ibid., 199-200.

[9] The printed text of Sarakhsī's *Mabsūṭ* does not indicate the limits of the text inherited from Marwazī. It can be guessed at, and sometimes fairly securely recovered. I have not however tried to impose my guesses here on the reader. Punctuation, paragraph structure, and the provision of numbers for ease of reference have been added to the translated passages and are part of an effort at interpretative understanding.

being due to God. Hence if the owner denies that *zakāt* is obligatory, for any of the reasons just given, the collector must believe him. He is however required to swear.

1.3. The requirement to swear is not specified in one tradition from Abū Yūsuf. He said, No oath is required because oaths are irrelevant in regard to acts of worship *(ᶜibādāt)*. It is like one who says, I have fasted, or, I have prayed; he is believed without an oath. But according to the main tradition *(ẓāhir al-riwāya)*, Abū Yūsuf said, Required is the affirmation of a responsible person, together with an oath *(al-qawl qawl al-amīn maᶜa 'l-yamīn)*. In other acts of worship oaths are not relevant because there is no-one who might be deemed to be calling the worshipper a liar. But here the collector is [implicitly] denying the claim put forward by the donor. Hence he is required to swear.

2.1. The owner says, Another collector has already taken my *zakāt;* and he swears that this is so. If there has not been another collector in that year his word is not accepted.

2.2. This is because a responsible man is believed if he affirms what is probable; but if he affirms what is improbable, he is not believed. In this case, the owner affirms what is improbable. If there has been another collector that year, his word stands.

2.3. This is true whether or not the owner brings forward a certificate of payment. So, in the *Mukhtaṣar* [i.e. of Marwazī]. This is the tradition as derived from the *Kitāb al-Jāmiᶜ al-ṣaghīr* [of Shaybānī].

2.4. In the *Kitāb al-zakāt* however Shaybānī says, If he brings forward a certificate of payment. This implies that showing a certificate of payment is a condition for believing the owner in this case. This is the tradition from Ḥasan b. Ziyād from Abu Ḥanīfa. The reason for this is that the owner has affirmed something and brought evidence of its being true. The custom is that when a collector takes *ṣadaqa,* he gives a certificate of payment. Hence the owner's affirmation is accepted if accompanied by this evidence. Otherwise it is rejected. It is like the case of a woman who affirms that she has given birth: if the midwife also bears witness to it, her word is accepted, otherwise not.

2.5. The other view [that a certificate is not required] – which is the more valid view – rests on the fact that a certificate is in writing, and all writing is similar. Also the owner may inadvertently neglect to take the certificate, or may lose it subsequently. So it should not be made decisive in this matter. The rule is that the owner's word is accepted if accompanied by an oath.

3.1. The owner says, I have paid my *zakāt* directly to the poor. He is not believed and, according to our tradition, *zakāt* is taken from him [i.e. a second payment].

3.2. According to Shāfiᶜī, he is believed. This is because *zakāt* is obligatory only for the sake of the poor, as proved by (Q9.60), *Ṣadaqāt* are only for the poor, the miserable etc. Furthermore God says (Q51.19), On their wealth is a claim for the beggar and the deprived. Hence, if the due sum is transferred to the rightful recipient, and the rightful recipient has the capacity to receive that due sum, the duty of the donor is fulfilled *(bari'at dhimmatu-hu)*. It is like the case of one who buys something from an agent, and then transfers the price directly to the one who appointed the agent. In this case, the collector receives the *zakāt* in order to pass it to the poor, and the donor has relieved him of this burden by placing it directly where it belongs. So there can be no claim against him [by the collector].

3.3. The argument for our view is as follows. *Zakāt* is a financial duty implemented in full by the imam by virtue of legitimate *(sharᶜī)* authority. The person subject to the duty does not have the capacity to deprive the imam of his right to implement it. It is like the case of one subject to *jizya* [the poll tax, deemed to be specified for purposes of defence] who decides to pay it directly to the soldiers; [this is not permitted].

This argument may be explained in two ways

3.3.1. *Zakāt* is due solely for God's sake *(maḥḍ ḥaqq Allāh)*. So it can be implemented only by one who is appointed as deputy for the implementation of what is due to God *(man yuᶜayyan nā'iban fī istīfā' ḥuqūq Allāh)*. This is the imam. Accordingly, the duty of the donor is not fulfilled *(lā tabra'u dhimmatu-hu)* except by transfer of his *zakāt* to the imam. On the basis of this argument we affirm that even if the donor is known to be telling the truth when he states that he paid the *zakāt* directly to the poor, it is taken from him a second time. His duty, as between him and God, is not fulfilled by direct payment to the poor. This is the preferred view of one/some of our shaykhs, namely, that the imam has the right of choice in deciding where to distribute the *zakāt,* and the donor may not deprive the imam of this right of choice.

3.3.2. The collector is deemed agent *(ʿāmil)* to the poor. What is collected is due to the poor. But the right of collection has been transferred to the collector so that the poor do not retain the right of demand on their own behalf. Nor is it obligatory to pay them, if they request it. It is like the case of a debt due to a minor: if the debtor pays it to the minor and not to the minor's guardian [it is not valid]. According to this analysis, we affirm that a man is deemed to have fulfilled his duty as between himself and God if he pays directly to the poor.

3.3.3. The plain meaning of the phrase "he is not believed" [as used by Marwazī, author of the text which Sarakhsī is commenting on] is an indication of this position. It means that if the donor is known to be telling the truth the collector should not interfere with him. This is because the poor have the capacity to receive what is their due; though it is not obligatory to pay them on their demand. Deeming the collector to be a representative of the poor is to give him a capacity of supervision under the law. Accordingly, if the donor pays directly to the poor, when the latter make no demand on the former, the aim of the duty of *zakāt* has been achieved. It is different from the case of the minor, for he does not have the capacity to receive what is due to him, so the duty is not fulfilled by paying him directly.[10]

Each of these three paragraphs contains a rule, some kind of defence of the rule, and an item of *ikhtilāf* which, also provided with a justificatory defence, permits further exploration of the rule. The first result of this format, in relation to the base text of Marwazī, is that a relatively simple statement of the Ḥanafī code (Marwazī) is brought back into the sphere of argument and discovery - where it is assumed to have come from. The *ikhtilāf* items which are the primary generator of this phenomenon may

[10] Id. *Mabsūṭ,* vol. 2, 161-2.

be derived from inside the Ḥanafī tradition (paras. 1 and 2) or from outside it (para. 3) – a fact which has implications both for the Ḥanafī code and for the global concept of Islamic law (or *sharīʿa)*. The concise statement of the law is presumed to be distilled from a matrix of argument (Ḥanafī and Islamic) which, rediscovered and reasserted, engages the reader in the process of creative discovery – but does not offer him the licence of choice, since loyalty to the tradition is presupposed.

A second result of the commentary, in this passage, is that rules are measured against a causal nexus which, at least potentially, explains them. All three rules here are to a degree measured against the idea that *zakāt* is a pure act of worship, for the sake of God, and consequently a private responsibility (1.2). That idea is however discovered to be not sufficient to explain the rules. The duty of *zakāt,* which is ideally pure and for the sake of God, necessarily, by the internal logic of its nature, creates rights which accrue to the poor, or the tax-collector, or the imam, and so derogate from the expected rights of the donor. Since neither the rules nor the concomitant possible structures of rights are definitive, the message that can be recovered from all this is, to say the least, complex.

Para. 1 is based on a set of logical possibilities that derives directly from the rules governing the individual's liability to *zakāt.* Here, at first, responsibility is left entirely with the individual, and is justified by reference to *zakāt* as an act of worship solely for the sake of God. The need for an oath however is deemed to be a matter of *ikhtilāf,* permitting *zakāt* to be seen as precisely like other private acts of worship (prayer, fasting), or as significantly different – based on a functional right accruing to the tax-collector and so derogating from the potential full rights of the donor. Sarakhsī prefers the latter rule.

Para. 2 is also based on a logical possibility, arising out of the nature of tax-collecting on camels. Here, initially, the factual improbability of a claim is made to derogate from the private rights of the donor (2.2). In the end however Sarakhsī restates this rule so as to bring it into line with para. 1: the owner's word is accepted if accompanied by an oath (2.5). The *ikhtilāf* item focuses on a certificate of payment. The rejected view acknowledges that this can be a relevant support to a claim of this kind. The preferred view (based on grounds that would be as unsatisfactory to a medieval as to a modern administrator, 2.5) tends to bolster the idea of *zakāt* as a private responsibility and a religious one rather than merely (!) an administrative and social obligation.

Para. 3 is the most complex. In the end Sarakhsī here almost reverses the law that he inherited. As he inherited it, the donor who claimed to have paid the poor directly, was not to be believed, and would be forced to pay a second time (3.1). In his final résumé however, the donor's act will be effective "if he is known to be telling the truth"(3.3.3) . That leaves a considerable and unexplored stress on "knowing". In order to reach that conclusion, Sarakhsī first introduced an *ikhtilāf* item from Shāfiᶜī (3.2). He then stated the Ḥanafī position as he understood it (3.3). He then offered two explanations of the Ḥanafī position, implying that even if not compatible with one another (as they are not) they were both compatible with the overall Ḥanafī position. This is not obvious in the case of the second explanation which makes no overt link to the crucial concept of the imam and his legitimate authority. Sarakhsī may be assumed to be forcing the tradition more than a little when he uses the second of these explanations as a means to understand his base text. The result of course is to minimise the role of the governor/imam, in relation to what it might have been (had Sarakhsī for example chosen to use 3.3.1 instead of 3.3.2 in order to understand the base text). In the final preferred position, the donor, paying by himself, is secure as between himself and God, absolutely (3.3.2) and secure, as between himself and the tax-collector, if known to be telling the truth (3.3.3). It is not an accident that, in this paragraph, Sarakhsī introduces the Shāfiᶜī view prior to providing a defensive analysis of the Ḥanafī tradition. For the concepts which he eventually prefers as an explanation of the Ḥanafī view (at 3 3.2 and 3.3.3) are, in part, derived from the Shāfiᶜī analysis.[11]

Throughout this passage Sarakhsī is quite clearly partisan; in favour of a concept of *zakāt* which makes it a highly personal duty, between

[11] When, in the context of customs duties *(ᶜushur)*, Sarakhsī recapitulates this problem, he follows the mood of this passage at least to the extent of giving full rights of personal distribution to the donor, thereby, in this context, depriving the Imam of any.

> If a Muslim says, I have paid the *ṣadaqa* (on trade goods) direct to the poor, he is believed, as long as he swears an oath to that effect. This is different from the situation with regard to pastoral animals because on trade goods the right of payment is delegated to the owner prior to his passing through any customs barrier. [I.e. since the owner of trade goods has the general right of personal distribution it is perfectly reasonable for him to have executed that right prior to his passing through the customs barrier, and so, making that claim, he is believed – if he accompanies the claim with an oath.] But in pastoral animals the right of collection belongs to the Imam *(kāna ḥaqq al-akhdh li-l-imām. Mabsūṭ,* vol 2, p. 200.)

Just how little and how much that right of collection could mean depends on the different analyses of 3.3.1 and 3.3.2-3.

individual worshippers and God. Its social functions are, in the preferred readings, accidental (though acknowledged to be primary in a view attributed to Shāfiʿī and therefore within the possibilities of Muslim juristic argument). The emergence of rights in others (the poor, the tax-collector) and the consequent derogation of rights in the donor is also accidental, and deemed to have no implications that *zakāt* is for the sake of the poor (a view attributed to Shāfiʿī) or for the sake of the imam (as deputy to God, a Ḥanafī view acknowledged, but displaced in favour of an alternative, which is less obviously in line with the Ḥanafī tradition as presented at 3.3). By embedding his preferred views in a reticulation which contains also rejected positions, Sarakhsī gives expression to a concept of law which is dialectical, exploratory, suggestive and intellectually stimulating. The exploratory approach to *zakāt* requires the reader, more or less simultaneously, to see and consider varied possibilities. Perspective however is achieved by insisting on a dominant approach, that which is asserted to be the Ḥanafī tradition (which is nonetheless quite obviously developed/changed both at para. 2 and at para. 3). The complexity of Sarakhsī's discourse is ensured by the number of structures he brings into correlation. First, the rules of the base-text (Marwazī); then the items of *ikhtilāf;* then the explanatory framework. In addition to all this there is a trailing set of analogies (at 2.4; 3.2; 3.3; 3.3.2; 3.3.3) which compares the relationships set up in a context of *zakāt* to the relationships set up in a number of other legal situations.

This type of discussion is obviously not (directly) practical. These rules and the discussion around them do not conform to the tax-collecting situation as it existed in Sarakhsī's time, and probably could not be brought into line with any realistic social approach to tax-collecting. The passage as a whole points to ways of thinking about *zakāt,* and urges a suitable complexity of approach(es). It does not tell anyone what to do. Even the rules which initiated the commentary were not practical (a point acknowledged by Sarakhsī; see Section III, below). They were derived through logical (though not exhaustive or inevitable) processes of thought about the implications of certain hypothetical eventualities, and they gave rise to abstract thinking about the nature of *zakāt* and its capacity (whether essentially or accidentally) to engender a network of rights and duties.

III

Reflection on rules and on their implications for the nature (or natures) of *zakāt* (and for the nature or natures of political authority in respect of *zakāt*) etc. might of course serve immediate practical ends and generate a simple rule of conduct. In the following passage, Sarakhsī eventually focuses on the situation of *zakāt* donors in his own time and place. The rule he discovers however is significantly not provided by the tradition, but drawn by him out of the conceptual possibilities of the law, with evident and considerable ingenuity.

1.1 Outlaws *(khawārij)* conquer one of the lands of the People of Justice and collect the alms *(ṣadaqa)* due on their property. Subsequently the imam re-conquers the land. He may not collect these dues a second time. This is because he has failed to provide protection and "collection depends on protection" – *al-jibāya takūn bi-sabab al-ḥimāya.*

1.2 This ruling is different from that of the merchant who passes the customs officer *(ʿāshir)* of a rebel people *(ahl al-baghy)* and is taxed. If he subsequently passes the customs officer of the People of Justice he may be taxed a second time. This is because the owner exposed his own property to the rebels when he took it through their land. So he is not excused. In the former situation however the owner of property did nothing. Rather, the imam failed in his duty of protection, so he may not collect a second time.

1.3 However the ruling is issued that the owner of property in case of conquest by outlaws should pay, as between himself and God, a second time. This is because they do not collect our wealth as *ṣadaqa,* but through mere lawlessness. They do not distribute it as *zakāt* should be distributed. Hence the owner should pay what is incumbent on him for the sake of God. Whatever they took from him was mere injustice.

1.4 Likewise with respect to the Dhimmi community: if the outlaws take their poll tax, the imam may not extract from them further taxation, because he has failed to provide protection.

2. As to the collections made by the sultans of our time, these tyrants *(hāʾulāʾi al-ẓalama),* whether alms, tithes, *kharāj* or *jizya,* Marwazī

[author of the work Sarakhsī is commenting on] did not deal with them. Many of the religious leaders of Balkh promulgate the ruling that payment is required a second time, as between the owner of goods and God, as in the case of land conquered by rebels. This is because we know that they do not distribute the collected wealth as it should be distributed.

2.2 Abū Bakr al-Aᶜmash used to say that on *ṣadaqāt* they rule that repetition is required but on *kharāj* this is not so. This is because the rightful recipients of *kharāj* are the military, and these are the military: if an enemy appeared they would defend *Dār al-islām*. *Ṣadaqāt* however are for the poor and the needy, and they do not give it to the poor and the needy.

2.3 The more valid view is that these illegitimate collections fulfill for the owners of wealth the duty of *zakāt* – as long as they formulate at the time of payment the intention of giving alms to them [i.e. to the unjust sultans]. This is because the wealth that they possess is the property of the Muslims, and the debts they owe to Muslims are greater than their own wealth. If they returned to the Muslims what they owe them, they would possess nothing. Accordingly they have the status of the poor [and are therefore legitimate recipients of *zakāt*]! Muḥammad b. Salama said of ᶜAlī b. ᶜĪsā b. Yūnus b. Māhān, the Governor of Khurasan, that it was permissible for him to receive alms. He was a prince in Balkh who needed to perform atonement for an oath he had sworn (and failed to keep). He asked the *fuqahā'* how he should perform atonement. They issued the ruling that he should fast for three days [which is the mode of atonement due from a poor man; a rich person would normally be expected to feed a certain number of the poor or to free a certain number of slaves.] He wept and complained to his retinue, They say that my debts are greater than my wealth and my oath-atonement is that due from one who owns nothing. The same considerations are valid in the case of exactions collected today, as long as the donor formulates the intention at the time of payment that this is his tithe or his *zakāt*. This is permissible along the lines we have just enunciated.[12]

[12] Id., vol. 2, 180

Here too a set of rules is inherited and embedded in a causal nexus wherein the primary element is that collection depends on protection - a rule provided in a satisfyingly apophthegmatic and rhyming form (1.1). (A similar apophthegmatic form was given to the assertion, attributed to Abū Yūsuf, that, Required is the affirmation of a responsible person together with an oath – *al-qawl qawl al-amīn maʿa al-yamīn.)* Throughout para. 1 (1.1 – 1.4) the conceptual structure offers distinctions between legitimate rulers (imams) and outlaws or rebels *(khawārij, ahl al-baghy),* between pastoral peoples (who are overtaken by outlaws) and itinerant traders (who voluntarily submit themselves to the power of rebels), and between the imam's right to collect (lost if he fails to provide protection) and the donor's duty to pay (not in fact fulfilled through payment to rebels). The rules related to *zakāt* are extended also to *jizya,* the poll tax paid by non-Muslims. The whole is an abstract structure which does not describe the reality of any particular system, and provides no clues as to how to distinguish legitimate and illegitimate rulers in the real world. It does however provide an initial set of concepts for thinking about the real world, specifically in relation to *zakāt* payments (and with subsidiary reference to Dhimmis).

The principle that provision of protection is a means whereby the imam gains rights of collection is obviously of some importance. Curious then that it was not specified in the context of the previous section. There the most explicit legitimating theory in relation to the imam was that he functioned as deputy of God in the context of a duty that was owed to God (3.3.1). The activities of the tax-collectors were justified also by the contrasting assumption that they were agents to the poor (3.3.2). It is just possible that the most general statement of the imam's rights as understood within the Ḥanafī tradition (that *zakāt* is a financial duty implemented by the imam through *sharʿī* authority – *ḥaqq mālī yastawfī-hi al-imām bi-wilāya sharʿiyya,* 3.3 above) is compatible with any one of those (as indeed Sarakhsī claims) and with the further notion that collection depends on protection. It is precisely the search for compatibility between rules (potentially varied) and explanation (delicately balanced) that provides a significant part of the intellectual dynamic of Sarakhsī's text. It is not absolutely clear that generalising statements which work for one set of rules are intended to be recalled when a different set of rules is at issue. Though, no doubt, obvious contradiction would be felt to be unsatisfactory.

Para. 2 exemplifies the way in which inherited concepts may serve the need to describe and assess the real world. At 2.1, Sarakhsī states his personal conviction that the governors of his time were tyrants, belonging therefore neither to the category of legitimate imams nor to the category of rebels and outlaws. He has effectively opened up a third category which was not given him by the tradition. Tradition, represented by "many of the religious leaders of Balkh", had in fact assimilated the local rulers to outlaws and rebels (2.1). Abū Bakr al Aᶜmash had distinguished between *ṣadaqa* and *kharāj* (2.2), implying a fragmented concept of legitimacy: thc rulers were legitimate recipients of *kharāj*, illegitimate recipients of *zakāt*. Sarakhsī's own view depends on a juristic device, a *ḥīla*, whereby the tyrants could be perceived, juristically, as poor – because their wealth was stolen and could not be counted as legitimate property – and therefore potentially legitimate recipients of *zakāt*. This was not a new device, Sarakhsī had found it prefigured in a ruling by Muḥammad b. Salamah, but, applied in this context, it proved both amusing and effective. The tyrants were recognised as thieves and robbers, neither their legitimacy nor their capacity to protect (hardly evidenced in a context where they were robbers) being conceded. But the exactions forced upon a subject people could be recognised as a legitimate fulfillment of a personal duty to God.

Here we see a remarkable example of the way in which the transformation of rules into a pattern of sophisticated and subtly discriminating concepts makes possible a number of different readings of the world. Sarakhsī has a preferred reading and a preferred set of consequences but the major alternative possibilities offered by the tradition remain explicitly present and Sarakhsī's own effort may be thought an incentive to further conceptual distinctions which might lead to different consequences. As so often with this writer, the reader is left not with a sense of the law as a determinative structure, but with a sense of the law as a structure for thinking with, a structure that encourages sharply focused and conceptually sophisticated thinking.

IV

A survey of conclusions that might be gleaned from this study prompts the initial observation that Sarakhsī is not merely making a list of practical rules. It may be possible to elicit such from his work, and he demonstrates, on occasion, how this might be done. That is, by measuring the world against the conceptual possibilities implicit within the

Ḥanafī juristic tradition. This is not the same as taking a rule and obeying it; what seems to be required is to take a set of logically related rules and to understand them in relation to the tradition, each other, variant rules, and one or several conceptual explanations of their form. This may give rise to a practical rule of conduct. But it may not. Once this process of intellectual exploration is started, the discovery of a rule ceases to be an adequate end: the process offers such obvious rewards, of intellectual stimulation and literary pleasure, that it cannot be adequately explained in terms of a practical interest – which is frequently, in any case, not in evidence. Many passages of this work and of other works of *fiqh* do not result in any obvious rule of conduct. Does the process point perhaps to some other end or set of ends?

What is most obviously demonstrated in a work of *fiqh* I have already stated in the first paragraph of this study: it is loyalty to a particular tradition. It is reasonable to assume that this is not simply a fact but a message, or part of a message. Thinking Muslims, those who study *fiqh*, are being urged, or even compelled, to see themselves as committed to the past of a particular tradition, that is to the efforts of that tradition to understand God's law. By virtue of this commitment they are deprived of two freedoms: the freedom to interpret revelation for themselves as an *ab initio* activity, and the freedom simply to choose amongst variant possibilities. At least in medieval times, a Ḥanafī (whether so by virtue of birth, geography or education) did not simply set aside the teachings of the past in favour of his own study and interpretation of revelation, nor did he abandon a Ḥanafī ruling in favour of a Mālikī ruling simply because it might be convenient or desirable to do so. The positive message here is of course about authority: authority lies with tradition (represented by the scholars of a particular school) and not with the texts of revelation (important though these undoubtedly were)

Somewhat qualifying this message of particularity is the message of plurality. Sarakhsī's responses to Marwazī's more or less monovalent text include, as a primary act, the provision of a pluralist matrix for these rules. The pluralism covers both the Ḥanafī tradition, where dispute is articulated by reference to the founding fathers (Abū Ḥanīfa, Abū Yūsuf, Shaybānī and other authorities), and the non-Ḥanafī traditions of juristic thinking (Shāfiʿī, Mālikī etc.). The message thus becomes more complex. For we are required to note that the interpretative possibilities of revelation are (and have historically been) many; and of that many, some (those governed by a tradition of authority similar to that of the

Hanafī school, i.e. Shāfiᶜīs, Mālikīs etc.) offer valid, effective, and justified systems of rules which are recognised as challenging the Ḥanafī system. Within the context of Sarakhsī's work (and of all other Ḥanafī works of *fiqh)* the superiority of the Ḥanafī tradition is assumed. (And within the Ḥanafī system, it is assumed also that the major tradition is superior to minor traditions.) These things are known in advance and only require demonstration. This is the function of revelation: to be organised and interpreted in such a way that it defends and justifies a pattern of rules whose superiority was never in doubt, and was guaranteed within an ongoing school tradition.

The demand for loyalty to a particular school is then not dogmatic, in the sense of excluding others; though it is real, in the sense of being, precisely, a demand for loyalty. The relationship between the schools (and between variant traditions within a school) is dialectical. It rests on their common acknowledgement of revelation and on a common system of argument. Or so it is implied by Sarakhsī, whose systematic presentation of the views of his own school and of others is embedded in a context of explicit argument.

In many contexts of course the argument takes the form of reference to Qur'an and hadith. In the passages I have cited however the arguments are predominantly conceptual and reflect on the possibilities of relating inherited rules to the discovery of coherence within a conceptual structure. This is the loosest and most inventive part of Sarakhsī's thinking. The processes involved are at times almost uncontrolled and arbitrary. The provision of analogies of relationship between different topics of the law for example (3.2; 3.3; 3.3.2; 3.3.3) is controlled by nothing but the convenience of the writer and his ability to perceive and articulate similarities. At other times the process is controlled by a clearly desired and more or less explicit practical end (so in Section III above). At still other times, the play between inherited rules, generalising abstractions, and conceptual patterning is loose and exploratory, leading to a plurality of structures for understanding the law and/or the world (so, perhaps in Section II above). Loyalty to the tradition clearly does not mean blind loyalty, but rather thinking loyalty, or interpretative loyalty; and it does not exclude deliberate and conscious manipulation of the tradition for particular ends. (This is of course conceded in the literature of *ḥīlas,* devices for, legally, getting round the law.)

That complex of messages suggests an overarching framework (maybe a theology?) within which, topic by topic, bundle by bundle, the inherited rules of law are, on the one hand, drawn back to revelation and, on the other, drawn out into conceptual structures whose function is (apparently) to be used for thinking with. Those structures are explicitly pluralist. In so far as the problems of the law are moral (the word might be legitimately used for the problems discussed in this paper, though much of the subject matter of juristic discourse cannot possibly be brought under this heading) this has the interesting consequence that though a final moral position may be available to a juristic thinker, it will be final primarily because it is sanctioned by authority and not because it is (incontrovertibly) the right answer. It is as if only the essentially arbitrary fact of loyalty to a tradition can decide between the various interpretative possibilities that are the products of human ingenuity. The forms and structures of Sarakhsī's literary style enable his readers to play – at least in appearance – with all the inherited possibilities of the Muslim tradition, while finding some comfort in the stasis (but only relative stasis, for the interpretative process is ongoing) of the Ḥanafī tradition.

XV

[137] Al-Nawawī's Typology of *Muftīs* and its Significance for a General Theory of Islamic Law

YAḤYĀ b. Sharaf Muḥyī al-Dīn al-Nawawī (631–76/1233–77) produced in the Introduction to his *Majmūʿ*, in the section devoted to *iftāʾ*, an account of the grades and ranks of *muftīs*. This proved to be one of the most important and influential statements, within the tradition of Shāfiʿī jurisprudence, of a theory that explained and justified the activities of *muftīs*—Muslim jurists who undertook the function of giving specific answers to specific questions of law. In the course of his exposition al-Nawawī exploited the terminological inheritance of the juristic tradition (centrally evoked in the terms *taqlīd* and *ijtihād)* to suggest a general theory of Islamic law, embracing its major functionaries (teaching-jurists and *muftīs),* its literary genres *(furūʿ* and *uṣūl),* and its patterns of school affiliation *(madhāhib).* The connotations which he gives to the terms *taqlīd* and *ijtihād* permit some reassessment of the familiar problem of the closing of the door of *ijtihād.*

1.

The *Majmūʿ* is a commentary on the *Muhadhdhab* of Abū Isḥāq Ibrāhīm b. ʿAlī al-Shīrāzī (d. 476/1083). In his Introduction, al-Nawawī, [138] freed from the textual constraints that governed the commentary proper, offered a set of discussions which stand as a prologue to the study of *fiqh.* The Topics of this prologue may be characterized as follows (the section devoted to *iftāʾ* is Topic 7):

1. A statement of the general high value of *fiqh,* followed by a presentation of the particular aims and intentions of this work (512);
2. A brief assessment of the lives and achievements of al-Shāfiʿī and al-Shīrāzī (13–28);
3. A paraenetic passage advocating purity and sincerity in the undertaking of all tasks (28–29);
4. The identification of knowledge (primarily *fiqh)* as a worthy object of human endeavour (31–34), superior to acts of worship and piety (35–37),

* For copyright reasons, this article has been reset. References to the pagination of the original are indicated in square brackets.

to be sought not for worldly ends but for the sake of God (39–40), and, once (appropriately) acquired, demanding for those who have acquired it respect and freedom from criticism (40–41);

5. A typology of juristic knowledge (41–46);
6. The profession of teaching and its conventions (46–67);
7. The profession of *iftā'* and its conventions (67–95);
8. Important issues related to the *Muhadhdhab (96–116).*

Permeating and uniting these Topics are two major themes (which recur also as major themes in the account of the grades and ranks of *muftī*s, inside Topic 7). The first is loyalty to juristic school *(madhhab),* explained in terms of a dual hermeneutical loyalty, first to the texts of revelation, the common inheritance of the Muslim community, and second to the texts of the juristic tradition, the specific inheritance of the Shāfiʿī community. The second theme relates to the difference between juristic knowledge as an end in itself, leading to the profession of teacher, and juristic knowledge as a means to govern action (requiring therefore to be accommodated to a specific reality), leading to the profession of *iftā'*.

Loyalty to *madhhab.* In his first Topic, al-Nawawī acknowledged the achievement of the *'ulamā'* of the past, in particular their literary achievement, which, he claims, had left succeeding generations in a position of clarity in respect of the law.[1] The special contribution of the Shāfiʿī school was represented by the *Muhadhdhab* of al-Shīrāzī and the *Wasīṭ* of al-Ghazālī, both of which had long been the prime focus of
[139] scholarly attention.[2] Al-Nawawī had decided to produce, in his present work, a commentary on the former, in which he would express a variety of matters. This variety, in fact, is easily reducible to two spheres of activity. He would evaluate, comment on, justify, expand and add to the hadith which were cited by al-Shīrāzī. And he would present, analyse, explain and evaluate the opinions of Shāfiʿī jurists from the time of al-Shāfiʿī through the succeeding generations up to the present day.[3] He would in other words carry out the dual hermeneutical task which had become the duty and the delight of succeeding generations of scholars. It is evident, that, of these two activities, the first, that of relating law to revelation, was governed by the second. This was partly a result of quantity—the juristic texts were so much larger than the body of revelation, but in the end simply a matter of loyalty. "In the books of the Shāfiʿī tradition there is dispute and variety such that the student will not be sure that the views of a particular writer are the *madhhab* until he has read and mastered the majority of well-known books

1 Yaḥyā b. Sharaf Muḥyī al-Dīn al-Nawawī, *Al-Majmū' sharḥ al-Muhadhdhab,* 18 vols. (Cairo, n.d.), vol. 1, 6.

2 Ibid., 6.

3 Ibid., 7 –11.

within the tradition."[4] One read and mastered the books of the tradition in order to discover the *madhhab;* and one manipulated the diverse hermeneutical techniques that had been developed in the literary genre of *uṣūl* (and in related genres, e.g. of hadith criticism) in order to explain and justify the *madhhab.* This process of hermeneutical play was an intellectual pleasure:

> God has multiplied the books of our Companions and of others, in the form of *mabsūṭs* and *mukhtaṣars,* in works rare and works well-known. In this book of mine you will find such mention of earlier works as will give you delight and increase your desire to work and study.[5]

Anticipating for his readers that work and study will be a product of (and cause of) delight, al-Nawawī, in his second Topic, invited the contemplation of two models of work and study: al-Shāfiʿī founder of the *madhhab,* linked to the Prophet by lineage, knowledge and interpretative skill, and al-Shīrāzī, author of the *Muhadhdhab,* linked to al-Shāfiʿī by study and commitment.

The emblematic significance of this allusive re-creation of the *ṭabaqāt* genre is worked out in the last Topic, which al-Nawawī entitled "Important issues related to the *Muhadhdhab".* The issues are in fact [140] hermeneutical. They relate to problems of harmonization and reconciliation within a continuous and ongoing tradition of interpretative loyalty. Problems related to the understanding and manipulation of prophetic hadith and Companion statements are presented first, followed by problems related to the use and exploitation of opinions attributed to al-Shāfiʿī, to the early masters of the school, and to later masters. These three layers of school tradition had a corresponding technical terminology: *qawl,* meaning an opinion of al-Shāfiʿī, *wajh,* meaning a view associated with an early companion or successor (of al-Shāfiʿī), *ṭarīq* referring to dispute and variety within the later tradition. References to the *aṣḥāb al-wujūh* here and in the text translated below indicate the first generations of the pupils of al-Shāfiʿī. The contemporary jurist had to respond to both revelation and school tradition. While these are temporally continuous, in the sense that prophetic words give way to those of Companions and Successors, and these in turn to the words (works) of the professional jurists, they are objectively realized as two bodies of texts—the totality of which creates a duty of loyalty, demanding to be preserved and integrated within (and constituting a source for) the ongoing tradition. The processes of intertextual reference to which the jurist was committed gave rise to a shorthand vocabulary of allusion, familiar in so far as it relates to Book and hadith, less familiar in its reference to tradition. Al-Nawawī's discrimination of *qawl, wajh* and *ṭarīq* was in fact a stricter application

4 Ibid., 9.

5 Ibid., 10.

of a more flexible earlier usage.[6] The totality of textual material deriving from the time of the Prophet and his successors through the time of al-Shāfiʿī and his successors was subject to problems of variation, dispute, and qualitative assessment. These were the subject of this Topic. They represented for skilled and thinking jurists an area of intellectual play and the enactment of a religious duty, a means for the integration of the diachronic and the synchronic community.

Teaching jurists and *muftīs*. Knowledge as a religious duty was the theme of Topic 4. Introduced by an injunction to purity and sincerity in the general undertaking of tasks (Topic 3), it closed with an injunction to respect and not to blame or criticize the *fuqahāʾ*—those, that is, who undertook, as a high and fitting object of human endeavour, the pursuit of knowledge, in purity and sincerity, and for the sake of God. In order to demonstrate the high value of knowledge, al-Nawawī cited [141] authorities from the religious and from the poetic world.[7] In the former context he referred to a number of mostly familiar, conventional, arguments which established the superiority of knowledge over acts of worship and piety. Two of these deserve mention. Those who achieved knowledge were heirs to the prophets, in contrast to those who dedicated themselves to ritual and ascetic acts. The latter remained subordinate to and dependent on *(tābiʿ, muqtadin, muqallid)* the *ʿālim*. It was incumbent on them to obey him but not vice versa. Further, knowledge was a *farḍ kifāya,* a religious duty capable of being and requiring to be fulfilled by one or some of the community on behalf of the rest. Al-Nawawī quoted al-Juwaynī:[8] A communal duty *(farḍ kifāya)* is superior to an individual duty *(farḍ ʿayn)* because the former is enacted on behalf of the community and relieves it of a burden *(yasaddu masadd al-umma wa-yusqiṭ al-ḥaraj ʿan al-umma)*.[9]

In his typology of juristic knowledge (Topic 5) al-Nawawī distinguished knowledge of individual duties, of communal duties and of supererogatory duties, this totality of knowledge being the prerogative of the jurist. Turning then to the topic of teaching, his discussion was enriched with explicit or implicit echoes of what had already been established—the complexity and delight of *fiqh,* the high value of knowledge, the superior status of those who devoted themselves to it, the fulfillment of a communal duty, and an aspiration to embrace all spheres of life. The scholar-jurist was the guardian of the community's knowledge and his highest aim was to compose learned works.

---

6 Ibid., 107. See also 11, 107–08, 111–12, 115; and paras. 3.3, 4.1, 4.2 in Section 2 below.

7 Compare ibid., 31–37 with 37–38.

8 ʿAbd al-Malik b. ʿAbdallāh Abū al-Maʿālī al-Juwaynī Imām al-Ḥaramayn, d. 478/1085. See Ibn Qāḍī Shuhba Abū Bakr b. Aḥmad, *Ṭabaqāt al-Shāfiʿiyya,* 4 vols. (Haydarabad, 1398/1978), vol. 1, 275–77.

9 Compare with the Ḥanafī view, as in Muḥammad Amīn Ibn ʿĀbidīn, *Ḥāshiyat radd al-muḥtār,* 8 vols. (Beirut, 1386/1966), vol. 1, 42–43. Ibn ʿĀbidīn prefers the view that a *farḍ ʿayn* is superior to a *farḍ kifāya,* but he presents both views, together with an anonymous allusion to al-Juwaynī's formulation.

> He should engage in writing if he is suited to the task. For, in so doing, he will attain a finer understanding of the truth and the subtleties of knowledge, in that he will be compelled to investigate, study, analyze and master areas of dispute and argument, matters clear and obscure, opinions valid and invalid. By this means the successful participant will attain the quality of a *mujtahid (wa-bi-hi yattaṣif al-muḥaqqiq bi-ṣifat al-mujtahid)* ... And let his writing be in that area where its usefulness will be most general and the need for it greatest; let him devote himself to the *madhhab.* For it is, in terms of benefit, the greatest of disciplines and through it the able writer masters the majority of other disciplines. [10]

[142] For al-Nawawī, the scholar achieved his highest purpose, and possibly, in some sense, the attribute of *ijtihād,* through writing; and the best form of writing was derived from and related to the *madhhab.*[11]

Turning from this high purpose, al-Nawawī offered his analysis of *iftā*ʾ (Topic 7). In his first sentence he signalled his commitment to tradition by identifying his sources. These were three masters of the Shāfiʿī school, namely al-Khaṭīb al-Baghdādī,[12] al-Ṣaymarī,[13] and Abū ʿAmr Ibn al-Ṣalāḥ.[14] He had studied and would now summarize their books, adding extra material from the scattered writings of other scholars.[15] *Iftā*ʾ, he begins, was a duty of high value: the *muftī* too was heir to the prophet and carried out a communal duty—but his task was subject to a specific danger, that of error. The first sequence of citations to which al-Nawawī exposes his reader relates to great scholars and jurists of the past who approached with trepidation, or refused, the task of responding to specific questions on the law. The difference between the author-jurist and the *muftī* (though they might in practice be the same person) is that the former "investigated, studied, analyzed and mastered areas of dispute and argument", while the latter had a duty to give a specific answer, thereby mediating between God and his creation.[16]

---

10 Al-Nawawī, *Majmū*ʿ, vol. 1, 49–50.

11 See also the ideal syllabus of students, ibid., 64–65.

12 Aḥmad b. ʿAlī Abū Bakr al-Khaṭīb al-Baghdādī, d. 46311071; Ibn Qāḍī Shuhba, *Ṭabaqāt,* vol. 1, 254–56.

13 ʿAbd al- Wāḥid b. al-Ḥusayn Abū al-Qāsim al-Ṣaymarī, d. after 386/996 (var. after 405/1014); Ibn Qāḍī Shuhba, *Ṭabaqāt,* vol. 1, 177–78.

14 ʿUthman b. ʿAbd al-Raḥmān Abū ʿAmr Ibn al-Ṣalāḥ, d. 643/1245; Ibn Qāḍī Shuhba, *Ṭabaqāt,* vol. 2, 142–46. For more on Ibn al-Ṣalāḥ, see now Wael B. Hallaq, "*Ifta*ʾ and *ijtihad* in Sunni legal theory: a developmental account" in *Islamic legal interpretation: muftīs and their fatwas,* ed. M. K. Masud, B. Messick, D. Powers (Cambridge: Harvard University Press, forthcoming, 1996).

15 That he did not use any of the great works of *uṣūl* from inside the Shāfiʿī tradition is significant. These did not serve his legitimizing purpose. They offered a technique for legitimizing the *madhhab.* His problem was how to legitimize, within the *madhhab,* the actual activities of *muftīs.* See n. 29 and Section 5 below.

16 Al-Nawawī, *Majmū*ʿ, vol. 1, 67. See further below, Sections 4 and 6, on the distinction between the scholar and the *muftī.* For a discriminating discussion of the role and functions of the *muftī,* contrasted

The two themes that I have identified as constituting the dominant message of al-Nawawī's Introduction were not only stated but enacted in the process of text creation. Al-Nawawī's discourse is highly segmented, consisting for the most part of juxtaposed citations (direct, or indirect in the form of paraphrase and summary) appropriated here to the creation of a new text and argument. Some of the texts are [143] derived from revelation (Qurʾan and hadith) or from Companions and Successors, but the bulk are from the juristic heroes of the Shāfiʿī tradition. Out of his dual loyalty, enacting it, al-Nawawī creates an argument which he presents as a continuation (not a disruption) of the tradition. At the same time, and precisely by virtue of the distancing effect of citation (by juxtaposing statements that are not fully harmonized, by acknowledging dispute and variety, by selective abnegation in declaring preference etc.), he enacts the role of the author-jurist and not that of the *muftī.*

2.

The passage which relates to the grades and ranks of *muftīs* divides *muftīs* into two categories, offers a four part subdivision of category 2, and, in a series of supplementary questions, identifies three further types of (so-called) *muftīs*. This gives a total of eight Types distributed across, effectively, three Categories. Al-Nawawī's typology can be presented as follows:

Category 1 (Type 1): The independent *muftī.*
Category 2 (Types 2, 3,4 and 5): The affiliated *muftī.*
Category 3 (Types 6, 7 and 8): The deficient *muftī.*

The terminology which characterizes Category 2 includes *muntasib* (affiliated), *muqayyad* (limited or qualified), *muqallid* (submitting to the authority of the founding—independent—*muftī),* and *mujtahid* (creative, but within the bounds of the *madhhab).* The passage is translated below. Punctuation, paragraph division and numeration are interpretative devices, and, like the numbering of Types (in square brackets), intended to facilitate reference.

1.0 Abū ʿAmr [Ibn al-Ṣalāḥ] said, *Muftīs* are of two categories, independent and otherwise.

1.1 Category 1 [Type 1]: The independent *muftī.* The conditions of the independent *muftī* are [as follows]:

---

with those of the *qāḍī,* see also A. Kevin Reinhart, "Transcendence and social practice: *muftīs* and *qāḍīs* as religious interpreters", in *Annales Islamologiques,* 29 (1993), 5–28.

1. He should have acquired knowledge of the proofs of *sharʿī* rules ... ; these have been elaborated in works of *fiqh,* and so become easy of acquisition, praise be to God;

2. he should know the conditions and aspects of proofs and how to derive rules from them ... ; this can be acquired from works of *uṣūl al-fiqh;*

3. he should be familiar with Qurʾan, hadith, the rules of abrogation, language and linguistics, dispute and variation amongst scholars ... ; [144]

4. he should be possessed of knowledge and experience in these matters;

5. he should know *fiqh* and be master of its major problems and divisions.

One who acquires these qualities is an independent and absolute *muftī (al-muftī al-muṭlaq al-mustaqill),* through whom the communal duty *(farḍ kifāya)* is discharged.

1.2 He is independent and absolute because he freely manipulates arguments without submission to or limitation by any *madhhab (bi-ghayr taqlīd wa-taqyīd bi-madhhab aḥad).*

1.3 Abū ʿAmr said, The condition of his learning the problems of *fiqh* is not laid down in many famous books. This is because it is not a condition of the rank of *ijtihād,* for *fiqh* is the result of and posterior to *ijtihād,* and what is posterior to a thing cannot be a condition of it. But Abū Isḥāq al Isfarāʾīnī,[17] Abu Manṣūr al-Baghdādī [Ibn al-Sabbāgh],[18] and others have made it a condition. That knowledge of *fiqh* is a condition in the *muftī* through whom the communal duty of *iftāʾ* is discharged is the valid view, though it is not a condition in the independent *mujtahid.*

1.4 It is not a condition in the *muftī* that all the rules of the law should be in his head. It is sufficient that he should memorize the majority and be capable of getting at the rest quickly ...

1.5 Further, the condition of acquiring all the knowledge we have itemized is relevant only to the absolute *muftī,* one who covers all topics of the law. As to the *muftī* who works only in a specific area, like pilgrimage, or inheritance, it is sufficient that he know that area. This is according to al-Ghazālī, his companion [Ibn] Barhān,[19] and others. There are some who have denied it absolutely, but Ibn al-Sabbāgh permitted it in inheritance, and the more valid view is that is is permitted absolutely.

---

17 Ibrāhīm b. Muḥammad Abū Isḥāq al-Isfarāʾīnī, d. 418/1027; Ibn Qāḍī Shuhba, *Ṭabaqāt,* vol. 1, 158–60.

18 Aḥmad b. Muḥammad al-Qāḍī Abū Manṣūr Ibn al-Sabbāgh al-Baghdādī, 494/1101; Ibn Qāḍī Shuhba, *Ṭabaqāt,* vol. 1, 284–85.

19 Aḥmad b. ʿAlī Abū al-Fatḥ Ibn Barhān, d. 520/1126; Ibn Qāḍī Shuhba, *Ṭabaqāt,* vol. 1, 307–09.

2.0 Category 2. There have been no independent *muftīs* for ages past. *Fatwās* belong now to those affiliated to the imams of the accepted *madhhabs*. The affiliated *muftī* is of four grades *(li-'l-muftī al-muntasib arba'at aḥwāl).*

2.1 Grade 1 [Type 2]. This *muftī* does not submit *(taqlīd)* to his imam [145] either in *madhhab* or in proofs, because he has the quality of independence. He is linked to him only because he follows the imam's method of *ijtihād.*

2.2 Abū Isḥaq [al-Shīrāzī] claimed this quality for our companions. But he said of the companions of Mālik, Aḥmad, and Dāwūd, and most of the Ḥanafīs, that they belonged to the tradition *(madhhab)* of their imams by virtue of submission *(taqlīd).* Then he said, The correct stance is that adopted by our companions, namely that they follow the *madhhab* of al-Shāfi'ī but not in submission to him *(lā taqlīdan la-hu).* Rather, finding his method of *ijtihād* and analogy the most sound, and granted there is no escape from *ijtihād* , they followed his path and sought knowledge of rules by the method of al-Shāfi'ī. Abū 'Alī al-Sinjī[20] said much the same, namely, We follow al-Shāfi'ī to the exclusion of others, because we find his opinions the weightiest and most just, not out of submission to him *(lā anna qalladnā-hu).*

2.3 I [al-Nawawī] say, These opinions of Abū Isḥāq and Sinjī are in agreement with the command of al-Shāfi'ī which is reported by al-Muzanī[21] in the introduction to the *Mukhtaṣar,* and by others, namely that he announced the prohibition of submission *(taqlīd)* whether to him or to others.

2.4 Abū 'Amr said, The claim that they absolutely did not practice *taqlīd* is not sound, nor consonant with their practice or the practice of most of them.

2.5 A certain master of *uṣūl* in our tradition states that there has been no independent *mujtahid* since the time of al-Shāfi'ī. This being the case, the *fatwā* of a *muftī* of this type is like the *fatwā* of the independent *muftī* in respect of acting on it, and in respect of its being assessed for *ijmā'* or in juristic dispute.

3.1 Grade 2 [Type 3]. He is a *mujtahid* limited to the *madhhab* of his imam, but independent in the establishment of his principles by proof *(mujtahid muqayyad fī madhhab imāmi-hi mustaqill bi-taqrīr uṣūli-hi bi-'l-dalīl).* However, he does not in his proofs go beyond the principles and methods of his imam.

3.2 It is a condition in this *muftī* that he know *fiqh, uṣūl,* and the arguments that lead to judgements; that he understand the methodology of proofs and analogies; that he be experienced in deducing and deriving rules *(al-takhrīj wa-'l-istinbāṭ),* and capable of relating what is [146] not textually recorded from the imam to the imam's principles. He is not free from the taint of *taqlīd* since he lacks some of the tools of the independent *muftī,* lacking expertise for example in hadith and Arabic; these are frequently lacking in the limited *muftī (al-muqayyad).* Further, he takes the texts of his imam as a basis for deriving rules, just as the independent *muftī*

20 Al-Ḥusayn b. Shu'ayb Abū 'Alī al-Sinjī, d. 427/1036 or 430/1039; Ibn Qāḍī Shuhba, *Ṭabaqāt,* vol. 1, 208–09.

21 Ismā'īl b. Yaḥyā Abū Ibrāhīm al-Muzanī, d. 264/878; Ibn Qāḍī Shuhba, *Ṭabaqāt,* vol. 1, 7–8.

does with the texts of the law; and he may well be content with the proofs of his imam in disregard of opposing opinions, like the independent *muftī* in respect of his texts.

3.3 This is the quality of our companions, those whose opinions are preserved *(aṣḥāb al-wujūh);* the imams of our tradition are, most of them, thus. One who acts on the *fatwā* of such a one submits *(taqlīd)* to his imam and not to him.

3.4 The apparent meaning of the words of our companions is that the communal duty of *iftā'* is not discharged by a *muftī* of this type. But Abū ʿAmr said, With such a *muftī,* the discharge of the communal duty is evident in respect of *fatwā,* but not in respect of the renewal of the sciences which support the giving of *fatwās*. This is the case because he takes the place of his independent imam, as deduced from a valid principle, namely the permission of submission *(taqlīd)* to a dead person.

3.5 The limited *(muqayyad) muftī* may be independent in a specific question or topic of the law as explained above. He may issue *fatwās* on matters on which the imam has left no text, based on deduction *(takhrīj)* from his principles. This is the correct view which corresponds to practice; it has been the recourse of *muftīs* for ages past.

3.6 In these circumstances if he delivers a *fatwā* based on his deduction *(takhrīj),* the questioner is *muqallid* to his imam and not to him. This is what the Imām al-Ḥaramayn said ... Abū ʿAmr said, This should be construed in the light of a dispute reported by Abū Isḥāq al-Shīrāzī and others, as to whether it is permissible to attribute to al-Shāfiʿī the deductions *(takhrīj)* of our companions. The more valid of the two views is, no.

3.7 At times he will deduce *(takhrīj)* from a specific text of his imam and at times he will not find such a text and he will deduce based on his principles ...

4.1 Grade 3 [Type 4]. He does not reach the rank of the early scholars whose views are preserved *(aṣḥāb al-wujūh)* but he has a trained intelligence *(faqīh al-nafs),* knows the *madhhab* of his imam, is familiar with his proofs and can deploy them, and is generally capable of organizing and presenting arguments towards a juristic preference. He [147] falls short of the former types because of his deficiencies in knowing the *madhhab,* or in experience of inference, or in knowledge of interpretative argument etc. This is the quality of many of the moderns up to the end of the fifth century *(ilā awākhir al-miʾa al-rābiʿa),*[22] author jurists, who organized and presented the *madhhab,* and wrote the books which are the prime focus of scholarly study today. They do not match the previous types *(alladhīna qabla-hum)* in *takhrīj.*

---

22 The reference is to jurists like al-Shīrāzī and al-Ghazālī; so *al-mi'a al-rābiʿa* must be a reference to the 400s and not to the fourth century.

4.2 As to their *fatwās,* they produced these in a manner the same as or close to the manner of the others, using analogy for untransmitted problems, and not limiting themselves to overt analogy. Amongst them are some whose *fatwās* have been collected but, in their integration within the *madhhab,* they do not reach the quantity of those of the scholars of the early generations *(aṣḥāb al-wujūh).*

5.1 Grade 4 [Type 5]. He masters the learning, transmitting and understanding of the *madhhab,* in its clear and its difficult aspects, but he has some weaknesses in control of argument and organization of analogy. His transmission and his *fatwās* based on it depend on the writings of the *madhhab* as he reports them, whether the texts of the imam or the elaborations of the *mujtahids* within the *madhhab.* What he does not find in transmitted form ... he may link to transmitted material and give *fatwās* on this basis; likewise in respect of whatever can be brought under an established principle in the *madhhab.* In cases different from this, he must abstain from giving *fatwās.* Such cases are rare, however, for it is very unlikely, as the Imām al-Ḥaramayn said, that a problem will arise which has no textual reference in the tradition, or which cannot be linked to the meaning of a text, or brought under a principle.

5.2 The conditions of this *muftī* are that he have a trained intelligence (*faqīh al-nafs*), and that he have mastered a large quantity of *fiqh.* Abū ʿAmr said, with regard to this and the previous type of *muftī,* that it is sufficient for him to have the bulk of the rules in his head, and that he be able in time of need to get at the rest quickly ...

6.1 [Type 6] Question *(in qīla):* What of one who has learned one book or several within the tradition, but is deficient, lacking the qualities of those described above; if the layman (*ʿāmmi*) can find no other in his town, may he have recourse to such a one? Answer: If there is a *muftī* in another town such that he can get to him, he must, in so far as it is possible, approach him. Otherwise he should mention his problem [148] to the deficient person, and if the latter finds it, quite specifically, in a reliable work, and if he is one whose reporting is acceptable, then he should transmit it to the questioner in its textual form. The layman is then *muqallid* to the founder of the *madhhab.*

6.2 Abū ʿAmr said, I have found this in the writings of a certain scholar and evidence supports it. If he does not find the specific problem written out he may not use analogy on other written sources to which he has access; this is true even if he believes it to be an example of analogy with no element of distinction, for he may imagine this to be the case where it is not. 7.1 [Type 7] Question: May a *muqallid* give *fatwās* in areas where he is *muqallid?* Answer: Abū ʿAbdallāh al-Ḥalīmī,[23] Abū

23 Al-Ḥusayn b. al-Ḥasan Abū ʿAbdallāh al-Ḥalīmī, d. 403/1012; Ibn Qāḍī Shuhba, *Ṭabaqāt,* vol. 1, 170–71.

Muḥammad al-Juwaynī,[24] Abū al-Maḥāsin al-Rūyānī,[25] and others have declared it definitively forbidden *(ḥarām)*. But al-Qaffāl al-Marwazī[26] has said it is permitted.

7.2 Abū ʿAmr said, Those who prohibited it intended only that the *muqallid* should not transmit his ruling in his own name; he should rather attribute it to the imam to whom he is *muqallid*. On this basis, we acknowledge *muftīs* who are *muqallids*. They are not real *muftīs (laysū muftīna ḥaqīqatan)*, but since they take the place of real *muftīs* and perform their functions, they are counted amongst them. They should only say, for example, The *madhhab* of al-Shāfiʿī is such and such. Even if they fail to make this attribution, it is to be understood as a situation too familiar to require overt expression; there is no harm in that.

8.1 [Type 8] The author of the *Ḥāwī*[27] said, If a layman knows the ruling on a particular problem, with its attendent evidence, there are three opinions [on his giving *fatwās* in this area]. Firstly, it is permissible for him to give *fatwās*, and it is permissible to submit to his rulings *(taqlīd)*, because he has acquired knowledge in this field just as the scholar has. Secondly, it is permissible only if the evidence is either the Book or sunna, otherwise not permissible. Thirdly, it is not [149] permissible, absolutely; and this is the most valid view. God knows best.[28]

At the end of para. 5, which concludes his assessment of Category 2—the affiliated *muftī*, in a passage not translated, al-Nawawī recapitulated briefly, stating that for all of Types 1 to 5, a trained intelligence *(fiqh al-nafs)* and a knowledge of the school tradition *(ḥifẓ al-madhhab)* were required. Types 6, 7 and 8 are understood to be at a lower level, implying absence of these qualities. The whole set of categories and types is clearly intended, synchronically, to justify the activities of real contemporary *muftīs*, even those of a low level of knowledge, and, diachronically, to justify the tradition which gave rise to, dominated, and was the focus of loyalty for contemporary *muftīs*. The practical orientation of the passage (its acknowledgement of school affiliation, interpretative thinking within the school tradition, the relative ignorance of some practitioners of *iftāʾ*; and its indifference

24 ʿAbdallāh b. Yūsuf Abū Muḥammad al-Juwaynī, d. 438/1046; Ibn Qāḍī Shuhba, *Ṭabaqāt*, vol. 1, 213–15.

25 ʿAbd al- Wāḥid b. Ismāʿīl Abū al-Maḥāsin al-Rūyānī, d. 501/1108 or 502/1109; Ibn Qāḍī Shuhba, *Ṭabaqāt*, vol. 1,318–19.

26 ʿAbdallāh b. Aḥmad Abū Bakr al-Qaffāl al-Ṣaghīr al-Marwazī, d. 417/1026; Ibn Qāḍī Shuhba, *Ṭabaqāt*, vol. 1, 175–76.

27 Muḥammad b. Saʿīd Abū Aḥmad, known as Ibn al-Qāḍī, Ṣāḥib al-Ḥāwī, d. after 340/951; Ibn Qāḍī Shuhba, *Ṭabaqāt*, vol. 1, 106–07.

28 Al-Nawawī, *Majmūʿ*, vol. 1,70–75.

to theological problems) marks its difference from the major tradition of discussion of *iftā'* up to that time, namely that of *uṣūl* literature.[29]

3.

Al-Nawawī's elaboration of *iftā'* is also a demonstration of affiliation *(intisāb)*, which is a part of the situation that made the elaboration necessary. Everything he says is, at least overtly, drawn out of the Shāfiʿī tradition of thought. Abū ʿAmr Ibn al-Ṣalāḥ dominates, but through him and independent of him, there are further layers of citation and reference, encompassing a totality of fourteen named scholars together with a number of anonymous and group references. The style marks engagement in the interpretative process, not only in the sense that this text interprets the tradition, but also in the sense that it creates a new pattern and texture of discourse, itself demanding to be interpreted. The text both carries and creates ambiguities. It frequently avoids disambiguating techniques (such as naming or circumscribing referents, highlighting distinctions, or decisively taking sides in a dispute). This ambiguity is not an evasion of message but a richness of message and an invitation to interpretation. The richness emerges here, perhaps, because the material was controversial, not yet fully integrated into the tradition. It displays, even in this mediated version, the markedly [150] creative interpretative activities of Abū ʿAmr. This ambiguity and richness can be related to certain features of style which would be developed and manipulated naturally by skilled participants in this mode of discourse. Central to these features of style are those that depend on manipulation of citations.

Al-Nawawī both legitimizes Abū ʿAmr by citing him, and distances himself by selective re-introduction of the formula, "Abū ʿAmr said". A whole series of obviously creative arguments, displaying some degree of opposition to the tradition, are introduced into the text carefully governed by this formula (at 1.3, 2.4, 3.4, 6.2, and 7.2). Much of the rest of the material is also from Abū ʿAmr, but, where it is less contentious, al-Nawawī allows it to merge with his own discourse. In spite of the frequent use of the formula, "so-and-so said", it is not possible, with certainty, to disambiguate the overall contribution to the text of al-Nawawī, Abū ʿAmr, and other jurists.

Careful use of formulae and citations enables al-Nawawī to preserve two or more views while prompting, but not compelling, a particular preferred reading. At para. 2.2, Abū Isḥāq al-Shīrāzī claimed *(iddaʿā*, the term implies doubt) that most of the Shāfiʿī scholars were *muftīs* of Type 2, a claim justified by Shāfiʿī rejection of the word *taqlīd*. Al-Nawawī intervenes to explain why the Shāfiʿīs have rejected this word (2.3) and then introduces Abū ʿAmr to propose that Shāfiʿī scholars do in fact

29 See note 15 above, and, for more on this, Section 5, below.

practice *taqlīd* (2.4). At 3.3, in contrast, without any overt formula of attribution or distancing *iddaʿā*, al-Nawawī identifies Shāfiʿī scholars of the rank of *aṣḥāb al-wujūh* (i.e. Shāfiʿī scholars of the first generations after al-Shāfiʿī) as in fact of Type 3. At 4.1, the great scholars of the fifth century *(al-mutaʾakhkhirūn)* are identified as of Type 4. Al-Nawawī, it seems, offers Type 2 because it is part of the tradition-he inherited it from his authority; but his presentation suggests that it is not a necessary and perhaps not a possible category (since al-Shāfiʿī, the *aṣḥāb al-wujūh* and *al-mutaʾakhkhirūn,* i.e. Types 1, 3 and 4, exhaust the tradition). That pattern of offering and taking away is a mark of commitment and development. Al-Nawawī demands from his readers an interpretative assessment, which he prompts but does not compel. Al-Suyūṭī, some two and a half centuries later, with specific reference to this passage, claimed for himself Type 2 status, but he both re-named and re-assessed the Type (and indeed, in respect of his scholarly achievement, historical context, and hermeneutical development probably justified his claim).[30]

[151] A third possibility which arises from the processes of multiple citation relates to the way that particular terms are allowed to carry layers of meaning and connotation which may be strictly incompatible, but have to be held simultaneously by the attentive reader. In this passage, the words *taqlīd* and *ijtihād* are not decisively established as having just one area of meaning, nor definitively valued as good, or neutral, or bad. In paras. 2.1 to 2.3, a claim is made that Shāfiʿī *muftīs* are totally free from *taqlīd* (here clearly a bad thing) and that they are in this respect different from other juristic traditions. But Abū ʿAmr thinks they do display *taqlīd,* a term which for him carries no opprobrium, but simply marks the dependence (in some sense or another) of the affiliated *muftī* on the independent *muftī.* Para. 3 discusses a *muftī* who is *mujtahid* and limited or qualified *(muqayyad)* by his adherence to the *madhhab.* Here, *taqyīd* is clearly an attempt to avoid the word *taqlīd,* though this *muftī* too is "not free from the taint of *taqlīd*" (3.2). Abū ʿAmr argues, however, that through this *muftī* the communal duty of *iftāʾ* is fulfilled because the *muftī* takes the place of the independent imam in the sense that he is *muqallid* to him, *taqlīd* of a dead imam being permissible. *Taqlīd* in this case is a necessary mediation of authority; not just a neutral fact but a legitimizing agency, making it possible to claim for the community that the communal duty of *iftāʾ* has been and is being discharged. The reader has to hold it in mind that *muftīs* of Types 2 and 3 are, in some sense or another, *muqallid,* while at the same time being, in some sense or another, *mujtahid.* Neither of the terms *taqlīd* and *ijtihād* are used in

---

30 Al-Suyūṭī, *Kitāb al-radd ʿalā man akhlada ilā ʾl-arḍ wa-jahila anna ʾl- ijtihād fī kull ʿaṣr farḍ.* (Cairo: Maktabat al-Thaqāfa al-Dīniyya, n.d.), 38–42. Al-Suyūṭī designates this Type, *al-mujtahid al-muṭlaq,* with no authority from al-Nawawī. See further, E. M. Sartain, *Jalāl al-Dīn al-Suyūṭī: Biography and background* (Cambridge, 1975), 61–72.

the descriptions of Types 4, 5, and 6; but nor is there any disambiguating denial of these qualities. Type 7, however, is *muqallid,* clearly in some absolute sense, implying retrospectively that Types 2 to 6, if they are *muqallid,* are not *muqallid* to this degree. In fact Type 7 *muftīs* are not "real" *muftīs* (7.2), a claim which again, retrospectively, implies that higher Types are "real" and, in that respect, perhaps, participate, in some degree, in *ijtihād.*

This type of discourse demands that the reader be continually alert to the way terms are used. There is clearly no simple distinction or contrast of *muqallid* and *mujtahid.* There is rather one type of *mujtahid* who is completely free of *taqlīd* (Type 1) and one (or two) types of *muftī* who are completely free of *ijtihād* (Types 7 and 8), while all the intermediate grades are (perhaps, because al-Nawawī does not [152] intervene to compel our interpretation) mixtures. *Taqlīd* from a certain angle may be perceived as a weakness and taint, to be avoided and disapproved of; from a different angle, it is a necessary principle of mediation whereby the community derives the benefits of the activities of past jurists, and achieves the fulfillment of a communal duty. Al-Nawawī in offering this text demands that it be read dynamically by a reader whose mind is open to systematic ambiguity and hermeneutically engaged. Though it is a text which depends crucially on the earlier (and in many respects innovative) work of Abū ʿAmr Ibn al-Ṣalāḥ, it is neither summary nor plagiarism. Al-Nawawī plays his part in accommodating the achievement of Ibn al-Ṣalāḥ to the ongoing tradition.

4.

The principle of authority that is promoted throughout this passage has its focus in the notion of the absolute and independent *mujtahid* or *muftī,* that is the founder of a school tradition. It is conceded that such *muftīs/mujtahids* no longer exist, indeed (with a probably anti-Ḥanbalī polemical intent) that none has existed since the time of al-Shāfiʿī (2.0, 2.5). All subsequent ranks of *muftīs* are intermediaries. No matter how great their creative input their views are constrained by tradition, by the fact of affiliation, and the petitioner *(mustaftī)* who adopts their views is *muqallid,* not to the intermediating *muftī,* but to the founding imam. This is explicitly stated with respect to Type 3 *muftīs* (3.3 and 3.6), and is *a fortiori* true of Types 4 to 8, though explicitly articulated only at Type 6. It is probably also true of Type 2, who is certainly affiliated, if only ambiguously *muqallid* (compare 2.1 and 2.4).

The absolute and independent *muftī* then, by virtue of his knowledge, skills, experience, and his direct creative confrontation with the texts of revelation, is the mediator of authority to the affiliated *muftīs.* These in turn are the mediators of authority—specifically his authority—to the ordinary people, who, in accepting the authority of the affiliated *muftīs,* are *muqallid,* not to these *muftīs,* but to the imam, the founder of the school. Absolute *ijtihād* belongs to the imam, and absolute *taqlīd* to the masses (and to the lowest ranks of *muftīs).* The intervening *muftīs* are channels of authority participating in various degrees of *ijtihād* and *taqlīd.*

The terms *mujtahid* and *muftī* may designate the same person, and even, sometimes, the same activity, but there is a conceptual distinction that can be and sometimes must be maintained. Al-Nawawī stressed in his interjection after para. 5 that it is a condition in all *muftīs* of Types 1 [153] to 5 that they have knowledge of the *madhhab.* That condition (paradoxically) includes Type 1, who is the creator of the *madhhab.* Abū ʿAmr explained: knowledge of *fiqh* is a condition in the *muftī,* even the absolute and independent *muftī,* but not in the absolute and independent *mujtahid* (1.3). There is a difference between the *mujtahid* and the *muftī.* The distinction is that between the independent scholar, who, as it were, privately, for the sake of God, and in fulfillment of a communal duty, interprets the revealed texts in order to establish the structures of the law; and the same, or another, scholar, who, already in possession of those structures, i.e. having a knowledge of *fiqh,* makes himself available to the public and responds to their questions. Al-Shāfiʿī, qua scholar and author, was an independent *mujtahid;* in so far as he made himself available to respond to specific questions, he was an independent *muftī.* His mastery of the first of these functions, that is, his knowledge of *fiqh,* was a precondition for his participating in the second function.

The communal duty of *iftāʾ* is fully discharged by the activities of the independent *muftī* (1.1 and 1.3). Was it also fully discharged by the activities of the affiliated *muftīs*? The tradition apparently provided a negative answer to this question (3.4—the reference is probably to works of *uṣūl).* Abū ʿAmr, however, introduced a distinction. He distinguished the communal duty of *iftāʾ* from the communal duty of mastering and reviving the sciences. Just what that distinction entailed, al-Nawawī does not explore—though it clearly relates again to the distinction between the scholar-jurist and the *muftī.* The duty of *iftāʾ* was deemed to be fulfilled by the higher ranks of affiliated *muftīs* by virtue of their "taking the place of" and "submitting to" *(taqlīd)* the independent *muftī* (3.4). The discharge of the communal duty by the independent *muftī,* the founding imam, was mediated, through the generations and through the ranks of the affiliated *muftīs*, to the community at large. The affiliated *muftīs* did not directly, but only by virtue of their affiliation, discharge this duty. The lower ranks of *muftīs* probably could not, by themselves, discharge the communal duty of *iftāʾ*. At Type 5, for example, we learn that, although this type will be able to deal with the vast majority of cases that come their way, whether by direct appeal to juristic texts, or by "linking", or by the discovery of a common principle, there will be a residue of cases in which, because of the inadequacy of their mastery of the sources (sc. works of *fiqh),* they must abstain from giving *fatwās. A fortiori* this deficiency will be evident in Types 6 to 8. If the communal duty of *iftāʾ* [154] is to be fulfilled, these *muftīs*, when they come to the limits of their knowledge, will have to appeal to the higher ranks. Al-Nawawī is clearly here pointing to the distinction between, on the one hand, local and village *muftīs* (and salaried *muftīs* appointed and paid by the government) and, on the other hand, high-ranking scholars and teachers (like himself) who did not waste their time on the routine duties of *iftā'*, but held themselves in reserve (and in training) for the rare and tricky issue which the jobbing *muftī* would pass up for their consideration. It was through the high-ranking scholars (those who did not participate routinely in the duties of *iftā'*) that the communal duty of *iftā'* was fully discharged.

The overall effect of this passage is to legitimize and explain the actual experience of the Muslim community. This worked historically in the sense that affiliation to the *madhhab* is explained and justified by reference to the interpretative activity of the founder and the mediating function of affiliated *muftīs*. And it worked also for the real contemporary activities of low-ranking *muftīs*, even of Type 7. These legitimately issued *fatwās* precisely by virtue of being *muqallid* to the founding imam, and by virtue of appeal to the high-ranking *muftīs*. The latter, participating to a greater degree in *ijtihād,* and enjoying a different mode or degree of *taqlīd,* represent layers and degrees of intermediation, preserving—and interpreting—the saving activity of the independent imam.

Al-Nawawī's terms and concepts work at several different levels to explain both the history of the *madhhab* and its contemporary experience. His typology of *muftīs* has a synchronic aspect in that Types 3 to 8 certainly, and Type 2 possibly, may be assumed to exist at any given time; and a diachronic aspect in so far as the early generations of the *madhhab* (the *aṣḥāb al-wujūh)* were predominantly Type 3 (or possibly Type 2), while the later generations *(al-muta'akhkhirūn)* were predominantly of Type 4. The vast bulk of contemporary (and earlier) *muftīs* were presumably of Types 5 to 7. Type 8 was of uncertain legitimacy. It is my guess that al-Nawawī (following Abū ʿAmr) would put himself in Type 3, while not denying the (nevertheless unlikely) possibility that, given the right conditions, he or some other might be of Type 2. The typology can certainly also be adapted to describe the different levels of activity of a single jurist. A jurist of the standing of al-Nawawī might function (with ease) at levels (Types) 4 and 5, had the certain capacity of working as a Type 3 jurist, and might, in appropriate conditions, and in relation to some new or unexpected problems, [155] function at Type 2. A jurist would of course claim to be of the type that represented his highest capacity. Al-Suyūṭī: claimed to be a Type 2 *muftī,* but, by virtue of his terminology, his hermeneutical engagement, and his historical situation may have intended something significantly different from al-Nawawī.[31]

31 The problem of the relationship of the *muftī* to the *madhhab,* and the significance of typologies and hierarchies of *muftīs*, is discussed, from a different perspective, by Reinhart in "Transcendence and social practice", 20–23.

5.

Joseph Schacht famously asserted that the door of *ijtihād* closed about 900 A.D. Wael B. Hallaq has asserted that it did not close, or at least there was no consensus on its closure, throughout the history of Islamic law. Al-Nawawī distinguished.

Al-Nawawī distinguished *ijtihād* meaning direct confrontation with revelation (his Category 1, corresponding to my Type 1—and extinct from the time of al-Shāfiʿī)[32] from *ijtihād* meaning interpretative thinking about the law, including creative responses to new cases, within the tradition. The qualifications which circumscribed the latter were reflected in a bundle of terms *(intisāb, taqyīd, taqlīd* etc.) whose positive connotation was loyalty (to the history and experience of the community) and whose negative connotation was distance (from the texts of revelation) and mediation. In presenting *muftīs* of Types 3, 4 and 5, al-Nawawī stresses that they derive their law, including their assessment of new cases, from the *madhhab* and not (directly) from the texts of revelation. The terminology associated with Type 3 is *takhrīj* and *istinbāṭ*. This *muftī* relates what is not textually available from the imam to the imam's principles; he takes the texts of the imam as a basis for deriving rules (3.2, 3.5). Type 4 knows the *madhhab* of the imam, is familiar with his proofs, and works through the tradition towards a juristic preference. Type 5 knows the *madhhab,* derives his rulings from the writings of the *madhhab,* and, when faced with new problems, deals with them by linking *(ilḥāq)* the new case to transmitted material, and bringing the new case under a principle established within the *madhhab (indirāju-hu taḥta ḍābiṭ mumahhad fī 'l-madhhab).* The nature of the relationship between the affiliated *muftī* and his *madhhab* is summarized later, in a passage again derived from Abū ʿAmr Ibn al-Ṣalāḥ. "The texts of the *madhhab* of the imam of the *muftī* are in relation to the *muftī* like the texts of the law-giver to the independent [156] *mujtahid.*"[33] This is an acknowledgement of a historical fact: jurists within a *madhhab* draw the law out of the texts and structures of the *madhhab* and not out of the texts of revelation. Between the jurist and the texts of revelation there stood the immense creative act of the imam, who had first translated the texts of revelation into the orderly structures of the law.

In so far as al-Nawawī condoned the use of the word *ijtihād* for the affiliated *muftīs,* he meant an *ijtihād* which is associated with and not opposed to *taqlīd.* For him, the creativity of Muslim jurists in the post-formative period depends primarily on their interpretation of the tradition, and only marginally (if at all) on their interpretation of revelation. The latter function was the one designated

32 Obviously the Ḥanbalīs would not agree with this.

33 Al-Nawawī, *Majmūʿ*, vol. 1, 76.

ijtihād in the absolute sense, and it had nearly disappeared, though some space is left for it under Type 2.

The combination of creativity and independence in a Type 2 *muftī* is difficult to pin down. Of him it is asserted, initially, that he has the quality of independence, that he is free from *taqlīd,* and that he follows only the method of *ijtihād* of his imam—but he belongs to the category of affiliated *muftīs*. Now, conceding that a jurist could identify and isolate a completely new problem, I find it difficult to understand, if he is affiliated at all, even in a very weak sense, that he could act independently in the sense of looking for a solution solely to the texts of revelation. There can be few (albeit some) juristic problems which are so dissociated from the prior structures of the law, that they could be independently thought about, in a state of, as it were, complete freedom from *taqlīd.* This is perhaps what al-Nawawī and Abū ʿAmr were pointing to when they explained the motives for and cast doubts upon the traditional modes of expression: "the claim that [affiliated jurists even of the highest rank] absolutely did not practice *taqlīd* is not sound, nor consonant with their practice or the practice of most of them" (2.4 above). Al-Suyūṭī, continuing the process of hermeneutical engagement and responding to particular problems which he identified and responded to, gave new life to this category, but, significantly, in the face of vehement opposition.[34]

[157] For historians of Islamic law, the achievement of al-Nawawī (that is of al-Nawawī in and through the Shāfiʿī tradition) points towards and condones a middle position between Schacht and Hallaq. Schacht will be correct in asserting that the gate of *ijtihād* closed about 900 if he means that about then the Muslim community embraced the principle of *intisāb* or school affiliation. Hallaq will be correct in asserting that the gate of *ijtihād* did not close, if he distinguishes clearly the two types of *ijtihād*—independent and affiliated.

Schacht in fact explicitly associates his claim that the transition from *ijtihād* to *taqlīd* took place in about 900 with the idea that, about then, the notion of school affiliation took over from and pre-empted a certain type of independent reasoning in the law. This is a broadly correct observation, though he adds to it a negativity of connotation which derives from his pessimistic assessment of the later tradition.[35] He did not equate the end of *ijtihād*—in this sense—with the end of creativity in

34 I would be inclined to recognize the justice of al-Suyūṭī's claim to Type 2 status in so far as he issued a series of important *fatwās* which dealt with certain practices characteristic of the piety of the mystic orders, having the effect of integrating them into normative Islam. Because many of these were not previously embedded in the structures of *fiqh,* and because the structures of *fiqh* did not contain a pre-formed framework for their solutions, it is possible to acknowledge that he was acting, not independently, since he did not claim Type 1 status, but with a remarkable decree of creative independence. But is this what he meant?

35 Joseph Schacht, *An introduction to Islamic law* (Oxford, 1964),70–71; for his pessimism about later thought, see 75.

the law.[36] In spite of this, a generation of modern scholars, following Schacht and relying on his authority, have taken the closing of the door of *ijtihād* to mean an end to creativity, and the beginning (variously dated) of decline, decay, anchylosis etc. This is a little unfair to Schacht, but explicable because of Schacht's real failure to appreciate the later tradition, and also because he failed to provide any terminology or intellectual structure that would express the creativity that he was willing to accord to (some) later thinkers.

In a series of important essays on *ijtihād* and on juristic thinking in general, Wael B. Hallaq has, very reasonably, asserted that creative thinking about and development of the law did not cease, and did not unambiguously decline, at any period of Islamic history. Without qualifying the general tenor of his arguments, it is possible to suggest that he too, at least in his earliest papers (1984 and 1986), did not provide a terminology and an intellectual structure that fits the actual activities of Muslim jurists. And he did not systematically make the distinctions that would enable his readers to understand why this debate about the door of *ijtihād* existed.

[158] In his 1984 essay, Hallaq assumes that the discipline of *uṣūl* and the hermeneutical structures presented there have their primary function in relation to novel cases.[37] Consequently he also implies that the process of *ijtihād,* as it is described in works of *uṣūl,* where it (almost) invariably relates to direct confrontation with revelation, is, in that sense, a major part of the ongoing and creative aspect of juristic thinking. But this is not sure. The hermeneutical structures described in *uṣūl* have their most obvious (primary?) use in works of *furūʿ* where they function to explain, defend and justify the inherited structure of law (the *madhhab)* or, polemically, to impugn the claims of other schools, or, discursively, to explain and to assess *ikhtilāf* within the tradition.[38] New rules

---

36 "Whatever the theory might say on *ijtihād* and *taḳlīd,* the activity of the later scholars, after the 'closing of the door of *ijtihād*', was no less creative, within the limits set to it by the nature of the *sharīʿa,* than that of their predecessors. New sets of facts constantly arose in life, and they had to be mastered and moulded with the traditional tools provided by legal science. This activity was carried out by the *muftīs.*" Ibid., 73.

37 "The primary objective of legal theory, therefore, was to lay down a coherent system of principles through which a qualified jurist could extract rulings for novel cases. From the third/ninth century onwards this was universally recognised by jurists to be the sacred purpose of *uṣūl al-fiqh.*" Wael B. Hallaq, "Was the gate of *ijtihād* closed?" *International Journal of Middle East Studies,* 16.1 (1984), 5 (reprinted in idem, *Law and legal theory in classical and medieval Islam* (UK: Variorum Collected Studies Series, 1995)).

38 A full account of the "function" and value of *uṣūl* would also have to take into account the tendency to make of it a closed and independent science, deserving elaboration for its own sake, and irrespective (or almost irrespective) of its results. I am not sure that one could derive from Sayf al-Dīn al-Āmidī's *Kitāb al-Iḥkām fī uṣūl al-aḥkām* a system that would permit (or disallow) the derivation of a

(which were only rarely conceded to be new) responding to new situations, or derived imaginatively from the inherited structures of the law, were worked out by interpretation of, or were otherwise drawn out of, the statements and opinions of previous jurists within the school exactly as happens in the passage currently analyzed. The process of *ijtihād* as described in *uṣūl* has, accordingly, a primarily historical aspect in that it explains how the early masters and founders of schools arrived at the structures of law which are attributed to them. Subsequent scholars had to repeat (to re-create) that process from generation to generation in order to justify the structures to which they offered loyalty. It is true that the process of repetition and re-creation made space for development and the accommodation of new rules, but the inherited structures of the law governed all new thought. *Ijtihād* in the sense that it was described in works of *uṣūl* was quite evidently not the process that jurists, if they observed themselves accurately (not an easy task-for them or us), actually engaged in. This was one of the difficulties that faced al-Nawawī (and, before him, Abū ʿAmr Ibn al-Ṣalāḥ) [159] when he attempted an account of *iftāʾ*. A second difficulty was that ordinary (working) *muftī*s clearly did not reach the standard of skills laid down for the *mujtahid-muftī* who was described in works of *uṣūl*. In order to explain and justify the reality of historical development, the jurists had to move away from the theories of *uṣūl*, to create a new intellectual space that would explain and justify their activities. Hence al-Nawawī did not turn to the major tradition of *uṣūl* when he embarked on an account of *iftāʾ* and, hence too, perhaps, Hallaq, relying too heavily on the tradition of *uṣūl*, gives a subtly one-sided account of juristic thought. He emphasizes one aspect of the dual hermeneutical task, at the expense of the other (the major).

Hallaq, of course, knew the distinction between independent and affiliated jurists,[39] and acknowledged that one type of *ijtihād* had disappeared,[40] but he did not tease out the implications of these facts.[41] He was impatient of the vocabulary developed by the tradition(s) to express their sense of history (and theology)[42]

particular rule from a text; the exploratory aspect is so stressed that one feels that precisely there is the point. For al-Āmidī's work, see Bernard G. Weiss, *The search for God's law: Islamic jurisprudence in the writings of Sayf al-Dīn al-Āmidī* (Salt Lake City: University of Utah Press, 1992).

39 Hallaq, "Was the gate", 10–11, 15, 17, 24.

40 Ibid., 25.

41 Casual reference to this or that writer as embracing or abandoning *taqlīd* (ibid. 12) requires the further consideration of how the writer used that term and the connotations he gave it. Using al-Subkī as a source for asserting of some early Shāfiʿīs that they were or were not *mujtahids* has this problem, that al-Subkī was exploiting the terminological developments of al-Nawawī. Hallaq, "Was the gate", 10–11, ad notes 50, 51, 54–57; 15, ad Juwaynī.

42 "One of the most important elements that largely contributed to the deepening of this controversy is the misuse or the misunderstanding of technical terms. This was due to the absence of a common technical dictionary to which jurists would conform. Although some lawyers tried to define the terms used in describing the ranks of *mujtahids*, the majority of scholars remained confused." Ibid.,

and this impatience led to a confusing account of the terminology they exploited, confusing largely because, in aspiring to cover all the juristic traditions over a lengthy period of time, Hallaq sacrificed much of their precision and finesse.[43] Hallaq also allowed the term *ijtihād* to carry nearly the whole burden of allusion to creativity in Islamic law. Accordingly, when even he had to admit that the tradition did not perceive a real or a vital [160] continuation of *ijtihād* (after al-Suyūṭī, a period which saw a "significant decrease" or a "drastic decline" in the numbers of *mujtahids*),[44] he was forced to conclude that the Muslims were wrong in their perceptions, or at least in their words: "the methodology of *ijtihād* continued to be employed but mostly without being recognized under its proper name."[45] But the meaning of *ijtihād* depends on its use, and that varied.[46]

When Hallaq wrote his 1986 essay, "On the origins of the controversy about the existence of mujtahids", he disregarded some of the qualifications which he had previously acknowledged as necessary for understanding the history of *ijtihād*. Hence, "since *ijtihād* persisted in theory and in practice and since *mujtahids* continued to exist in the fifth/eleventh century and long afterwards, the reasons for the emergence of the question concerning the existence of *mujtahids* must be sought outside the boundaries of the legal system."[47] Hallaq finds these reasons in "the theological doctrine of the end of religion and the coming of the day of

---

25. But change and development in terminology was precisely one of the most characteristic means whereby the tradition did what Hallaq has so effectively claimed for it, namely, change, develop and adapt to new situations. The majority of scholars were not confused; they knew how to manipulate and serve the tradition of discourse which had constituted their training and their intellectual and literary tools.

43 Ibid., 25-27. The term *mujtahid muṭlaq* was used by al-Suyūṭī to designate al-Nawawī's Type 2 *muftī*, a trick of terminology, perfectly legitimate (after 250 years), though not sanctioned anywhere in al-Nawawī's text, and tending to generate connotations which al-Suyūṭī certainly wanted to exploit. Within the Ḥanafī tradition, Muḥammad b. ʿAlī al-Ḥaskafī (d. 1088/1677) and Ibn ʿĀbidīn (d. 1252/1836) use the term *mujtahid muṭlaq* to designate al-Nawawī's *mujtahid mustaqill*. Ibn ʿĀbidīn, *Hāshiya*, vol. 1, 77.

44 Hallaq, "Was the gate", 29, 31.

45 Ibid., 32.

46 Problems related to variation in the use of terminology, developments in the use of terminology, and the varying significance of terminology when it is differentially embedded in argument and exposition seem to me obscured in that methodological approach which picks terms, phrases, sentences and arguments from a large diversity of sources, representing different traditions and different periods, in order to depict "Islam" or "Islamic law", as if these were not subject to the usual processes of historical and hermeneutical development. Hallaq's earlier work (1984 and 1986) and Reinhart's "Transcendence and social practice" (n. 16 above) seem to me in some respects open to this criticism.

47 Wael B. Hallaq, "On the origins of the controversy about the existence of *mujtahids* and the gate of *ijtihād*", *Studia Islamica* (1986), 63, 134 (reprinted in idem, *Law and legal theory)*.

judgement."[48] He is correct in asserting that this was a factor affecting discussion of *ijtihād,* especially in a form which focused on the existence or non-existence of *mujtahids*. But that which prompted the discussion we see in al-Nawawī (and other discussions of the same type, including discussions about the existence of *mujtahids*) was something absolutely central to the legal system. In one sense of the word, indeed in its most characteristic use, in the signification which Hallaq most frequently assigned to it, *ijtihād* had come to an end (or nearly!). The direct and independent confrontation with the texts of revelation and the manipulation of the hermeneutical principles set out in works of *uṣūl* were not characteristic of the real practical activities of *muftīs* or author-jurists from about the middle of the fourth century onwards. This was the problem that led the Muslim jurists to a [161] crisis of self-understanding which was eventually worked out by manipulating the concepts of *ijtihād* and *taqlīd* (and *intisāb, taqyīd* etc.) in a variety of ways, differing from school to school and from generation to generation.

In his most recent paper (forthcoming, 1996),[49] Hallaq shows remarkably how he has not stopped thinking about these matters. Here, all the major questions that had demonstrably contributed to the theoretical explorations of Ibn al-Ṣalāḥ and al-Nawawī emerge too for him. The distinction between independent *ijtihād* and *ijtihād fī 'l-madhhab* is now clearly articulated and controlled, and the complete or near complete disappearance of the former is acknowledged. The real existence of *muftīs* who were actually *muqallid* and, sometimes, scarcely capable of even low-grade *ijtihād* is recognized as a factor requiring to be caught in a theoretical framework. Something emerges of the importance of Ibn al-Ṣalāḥ as an innovative and daring theoretician of affiliation *(intisāb*—though Hallaq does not mention this term which carries much of the weight of Ibn al-Ṣalāḥ's argument). The question, what then was the function of those works of *uṣūl* which offered only the high (and unreal) definitions of *ijtihād* and *iftā'?* is neatly raised, though, I think, not quite answered. Hallaq relates this question to "objective reality" and "self-perception" (Did jurists of the calibre of al-Shīrāzī and al-Ghazālī perceive clearly the real nature of the practice of jurists and *muftīs*? Did they have a clear perception of their own activities?). I have proposed above one possible answer: one function of the hermeneutical structures set out in works of *uṣūl* was to justify the structure of the *madhhab* as it was inherited. This is what al-Shīrāzī and al-Ghazālī actually did with *uṣūlī* arguments when they wrote their works of *furū'*. This is what al-Nawawī points towards when he insists that the independent *mujtahid* is the source of authority for all subsequent (affiliated) *muftīs*, that the masses are affiliated to him and not to the intermediate *muftīs*, and that independent *ijtihād* no longer exists (except marginally). It was the interpretative activities of the independent *mujtahid* which were being explored in a work of *uṣūl,* and not (except again marginally) the

48 Ibid.

49 Hallaq, "*Iftā'* and *ijtihād* in Sunni legal theory" (n. 14 above).

actual activities of living *muftīs* and jurists. But there is a second answer. Different jurists defined terms differently and incorporated them differently into structures of argument and exposition. For al-Ghazālī *taqlīd* was a radically negative concept, defined as uninformed acceptance of the opinions of others *(qubūl bi-lā* [162] *ḥujja).*[50] It seems likely that he accounted for continuity within the *madhhab* as a result of re-enactment of *ijtihād* from generation to generation, not *taqlīd.* The term *intisāb* is not, I think, used by him.

6.

In Section 1 of this paper, I identified two themes which run through the whole of al-Nawawī's introduction to his *Majmūʿ*: the theme of loyalty to *madhhab* and that of distinguishing the tasks of the teaching jurist and the *muftī.* These themes are also essential elements in his assessment of *iftāʾ*. The terminology of *intisāb, taqlīd, taqyid,* and *ijtihād fī 'l-madhhab* explains and justifies the school loyalty that was in fact, historically, constitutive of the juristic experience of Islam. The central notion that the founding imam was the only independent *mujtahid* and, for all practical purposes, the only one who derived rules directly from the revealed sources can be seen as a liberating and not as a constraining notion. It meant that the experience of the community, symbolized in the achievement of the founding imam, was built into the tradition, which achieved thereby an ongoing aspect. *Taqlīd,* so often dismissed as "blind imitation", was in fact a way of incorporating the experience of the past and giving it a dynamic aspect, for each new generation of scholars built on the achievement of the past, and became constitutive of the next generations' task. Though *taqlīd* carried connotations of absolute submission (e.g. in so far as a layman was required simply to accept the decision of a *muftī),* it was, in relation to the higher ranks of *muftīs* (who were also scholar-jurists), liberating, precisely because they did not have to return to the original texts. The independent reading of the founding imam was already accomplished and it offered a basis for further readings. This was acceptance of authority, but not blind, for it was accompanied by the cultivation of a hermeneutical system *(uṣūl)* which explained and justified the achievement of the founding imam, and continued to have an explanatory and justificatory function in respect of the ongoing tradition. Abū ʿAmr Ibn al-Ṣalāḥ had affirmed that Shāfiʿī jurists had a relationship to the texts of the *madhhab* which paralleled that of the founder to the texts of revelation. While that was in some respects a statement of the inferior position of the later jurists, it is perhaps better understood as an elevation of the status of the founding imam who had carried

50 Al-Ghazālī, *Al-Mustaṣfā min ʿilm al-uṣūl,* 2 vols. (Bulaq, 1324/1906), vol. 2, 387.

out the immense task of translating [163] revelation into juristic structure. By that act of authority he created the tradition which, thereafter—affirmed, embraced, cultivated, and interpreted—was constitutive of informed choice and freedom for his followers.[51]

The difference between the *muftī* and the teaching jurist is essentially one of function and need not be one of person. The teaching jurist had a duty to explore and master the tradition (the *madhhab)* and, if possible, to become an author-jurist, writing within and about the *madhhab.* The *muftī* had a duty to give a single answer to a specific question from a layman. This duty, unlike the task of the author-jurist, was dangerous, because it represented an arrogation of authority, making the *muftī* a direct mediator between God and man. There were sound reasons for avoiding it. The elaboration of argument for one's peers, or for the training of young minds, or simply for the sake of God, was not the same as offering a decisive and single opinion as to which of the innumerable possibilities of God's law was the correct one. This was the fearful, the inferior, but the necessary task of the *muftī.*

> The *muftī* in his *fatwa* should not restrict himself to saying, There is dispute on this question or, There are two opinions or two views or two transmissions ... For this is no answer. The intention of the petitioner is clarification of how to act, and the *muftī* should give a decisive statement of the preponderating decision *(yajzimu bi-mā huwa al-rājiḥ).*[52]

The author-jurist would consider, explore and demonstrate what was preponderating; the *muftī* would only state it. The *muftī*'s task was always in fact derivative and dependent on the author-jurist's explorations, even when the functioning *muftī* was himself an author-jurist. The derivative nature of the *muftī*'s task made it possible for *muftīs* to function adequately even when they were relatively ignorant, and made it desirable for the high-ranking author-jurist to avoid *iftā'*, at least as a mundane and quotidien duty. Through their training and mastery of hermeneutical skills, the author-jurists, precisely in their capacity as author-jurists, were guides and leaders to the low-ranking *muftīs*. This observation suggests some qualifications to the conclusions of Hallaq's "From *fatwas* to *furū'*".[53] Even if there is evidence of *fatwās* influencing [164] *furū'*, it is the controlling decision of the author-jurist to incorporate or not to incorporate the *fatwā* that counts. Conversely there is specific evidence (and I think a legitimate general presumption) that the reality of influence was mostly in the opposite direction, that is from *furū'* to *fatwās*. The authoritative explorations of the high-ranking jurists

---

51 The idea of authority and tradition as constitutive of freedom and rational choice has a contemporary authoritative exposition in the works of Hans-Georg Gadamer. See especially, *Truth and method* (London: Sheed and Ward Ltd., 1975), 235–341.

52 Al-Nawawī, *Majmū'*, vol. 1, 79.

53 Wael B. Hallaq, "From *fatwās* to *furū'*: growth and change in Islamic substantive law", in *Islamic law and society*, 1.1 (1994).

influenced, and in some circumstances transformed, the content of contemporary *fatwās*.[54]

A. Kevin Reinhart, in his characterization of the different functions of *qāḍīs* and *muftīs*, is not concerned with the further difference between the *muftī* and the teaching-jurist. This distinction may be blurred in practice, but, conceptually, it is available and clear. When Reinhart summarily refers to "the detached and speculative *muftī*" in contrast to "the engaged and practical *qāḍī*",[55] he is insufficiently discriminating. To be detached and speculative is the function of the author-jurist. The *muftī* has to give up a measure of detachment and to abandon speculation in order to carry out his particular function. It is precisely the need for this kind of discrimination that led so many of the great author-jurists of the pre-modem period to express their perceptions in terms of the graded ranks and hierarchies of *muftīs* and author-jurists.

This said, it must finally be reaffirmed that al-Nawawī belonged to his time and to his tradition. Throughout the juristic tradition as a whole, the verb *aftā* and its various derivatives had a broader range of connotation than the ones that I have insisted on in these pages. *Muftīs* did sometimes explain and justify their decisions, even inside the format of a *fatwā*—thereby obscuring the boundary between the *muftī* and the author-jurist. Some *muftīs* acquired a status, qua *muftī*, which was much higher than their contemporary author-jurists. And different schools of law at different times used different terminology to express their sense of participation within a tradition. The history of the development of ideas in the Islamic juristic traditions is not yet very advanced.[56]

---

54 I give a specific example in my forthcoming essay, "Exploring God's law: Muḥammad ibn Aḥmad ibn Abī Sahl al-Sarakhsī on *zakāt*", in *Law and the Islamic world—past and present*, ed. C. Toll and J. Skovgaard-Peterson (Copenhagen, 1995). Here, the Ḥanafī jurist, al-Sarakhsī, first summarizes the established tradition of *fatwā* in a particular area of law in the district of Balkh, and then proceeds to offer a different analysis of the law which permits a different ruling. Over time it was of course the juristic arguments of al-Sarakhsī that survived and had their influence, not the transient and forgotten rulings of the *muftīs* of Balkh.

55 Reinhart, "Transcendence and social practice", 25 (n. 16 above).

56 Cf. n. 46 above.

XVI

The ʻUqūd rasm al-muftī of Ibn ʻĀbidīn

I

John Dryden's 'Religio laici',[1] a defence in rhyming couplets of English Protestantism, is not an obvious point of departure for this study of a Muslim poem about juristic authority. There is value however in the comparison for the contrasts that emerge. Dryden's poem first defends Christianity against an Enlightenment Deism, and then situates English Protestantism between the two extremes of Papism and 'the private spirit' ('Occasioned by great zeal and little thought'). Ibn ʻĀbidīn's 'Chaplets on the mufti's task', written in the nineteenth century, is a highly condensed version of a conventional academic work of the type sometimes called 'manuals for muftis' or *adab al-muftī*. It aims to inform the professional mufti and the educated jurist of a methodology for the discovery of a rule of law. It speaks of secure authority; very different from the challenged, if triumphant, authority of English Protestantism in the seventeenth century.

Dryden's title—'A layman's faith'—reflects a familiar sensibility. For the moderate Protestant, neither an overweening reason, nor the heavy accretions of Church tradition stand against common sense applied directly to Scripture (rendered into a native tongue). The (qualified) rejection of tradition, the (equally qualified) assertion of the sufficiency of Scripture, and the personal nature of religious experience are points that recur and are interrelated:

More safe and much more modest 'tis to say
God would not leave mankind without a way;
And that the Scriptures, though not everywhere
Free from corruption or entire or clear,
Are uncorrupt, sufficient, clear, entire
In all things which our needful faith require.
If others in the same glass better see,
Tis for themselves they look, but not for me;
For my salvation must its doom receive
Not from what others but what I believe.

Not authority and tradition rule, but the free individual searches for his truth in Scriptures, within the acknowledged, but not overly constraining, boundaries of a liberal mother-church. ('Shall I speak plain, and in a nation free/Assume an honest layman's liberty?' Of course.) The Book, not tradition, is the yardstick.

The Book's a common largess to mankind;
Not more for them [the partial Papists] than every man designed.
The welcome news is in the letter found;
The carrier's not commissioned to expound.
It speaks itself, and what it does contain,
In all things needful to be known, is plain.

[1] John Dryden, *Selected poetry*, 64–78.

The new church contrasts markedly with the ill-judged hypocrisy of former times.

> When want of learning kept the laymen low,
> And none but priests were authorized to know;
> When what small knowledge was in them did dwell,
> And he a god who could but read or spell;
> Then Mother Church did mightily prevail:
> She parcelled out the Bible by retail,
> But still expounded what she sold or gave
> To keep it in her power to damn and save.
> Scripture was scarce, and as the market went,
> Poor laymen took salvation on content,
> As needy men take money, good or bad;
> God's Word they had not, but the priests' they had.

Freed at least from this, the consequences of reform were yet not all good. The private spirit was open to the unfortunate concomitance of 'great zeal and little thought'. Scripture could be, alas, too accessible.

> While crowds unlearned, with rude devotion warm,
> About the sacred viands buzz and swarm,
> The fly-blown text creates a crawling brood
> And turns to maggots what was meant for food.
> A thousand daily sects rise up and die;
> A thousand more the perished race supply ...
>
> What then remains but, waiving each extreme,
> The tides of ignorance and pride to stem?
> Neither so rich a treasure to forgo,
> Nor proudly seek beyond our power to know.
> Faith is not built on disquisitions vain;
> The things we must believe are few and plain.

The peculiar Englishness of this (small) faith and its expression should not obscure the universality of the protestant sensibility delineated here. Christianity is not alone in engendering a critique of tradition that rests on appeal to a common reading of holy texts, and a discovery of truths that are few and plain. ('Tis some relief that points not clearly known/Without much hazard may be let alone.')[2]

The point of this too brief summary of a complex poem is not simply to note that in Islam it was otherwise—though it was. But also to note that the prejudices of Dryden, in post-Reformation Europe (even amongst 'partial Papists'), remain the prejudices of modern scholars who offer academic comment on faith; and have become the prejudices of many modern Muslims (for Islam had, with Afghani and 'Abduh, its own assertion of a reasonable faith and everyman's direct approach to scripture). It is difficult to state the sensibility of the dominant traditions of pre-modern Islam without seeming to violate normality. There, the dominant traditions were contained and expressed within the successful juristic schools: the Ḥanafī, the Shāfiʿī, the Māliki and the Ḥanbalī. Neither Scripture nor common sense had (direct) authority. The interpretations of established figures stood firmly between the present and the sources. Tradition counted; and knowledge and learning (of tradition). The

[2] Dryden later converted to Catholicism, a movement back to tradition that is not without pointers in the argument and expression of his poem.

honest layman had nothing of value to say in the discovery of a juristic rule. Only the learned jurist could speak authoritatively, and not by virtue of his access to the sources, but by virtue of his control of tradition. The Book was not, in any relevant sense, a common largesse, nor was its meaning plain. None but learned jurists were authorized to know, and what they offered was not God's Word directly, but its interpretation. The Book did not 'speak itself'. The jurists' words, based on learning within a school tradition, were, for all practical purposes, the meaning of God's Word. Neither few nor plain were the things a Muslim needed to know. Sophisticated disquisitions about juristic matters not accessible to final judgement were a part of faith, and were not dismissed as 'vain'.

Ibn ʿĀbidīn spoke no less than Dryden from within the conventions of a constructed religious sensibility. It is one the West has found difficult to understand. The term which best expresses it is *taqlīd*, which is more a justified acknowledgement of authority than Western scholarship's 'blind submission'. Ibn ʿĀbidīn's poem, which offers the educated Muslim and the mufti a methodology for discovering the law, does not mention Quran and sunna; nor point to the interpretative disciplines that were explored in *uṣūl al-fiqh*. It directs the mufti and the educated jurist towards the body of juristic works (within a school tradition—Ibn ʿĀbidīn was a Ḥanafī) that had to be mastered if action was to be based on knowledge.

This brief reference to Dryden has another use. The writing of didactic poetry is not characteristic of the twentieth century, and the taste is difficult to recover. Ibn ʿĀbidīn, unlike Dryden, has no standing in the history of poetry, but his effort to cast a scientific work into poetic form was also not merely the provision of a convenient and teachable mnemonic. It was an exercise in the constructed expression of an established body of knowledge. Its value lies more in the construction and in the expression than in the message—for that was familiar enough. To enjoy it, the reader has to maintain some sensitivity to style and expression. These are qualities only distantly echoed in the following translation, to which I have nonetheless attempted to give (a kind of) poetic form.

II

Muḥammad Amīn b. ʿUmar Ibn ʿĀbidīn was a Ḥanafī-Māturīdī jurist of the eighteenth and nineteenth centuries. He died in 1252/1836, after a career spent mostly in Damascus. His greatest work was the *Radd al-muḥtār*, a commentary on the *Durr al-Mukhtār* by Muḥammad b. ʿAlī al-Haskafī (d. 1088/1677), which was in turn a commentary on the *Tanwīr al-abṣār wa-jāmiʿ al-biḥār* by Muḥammad b. ʿAlī al Ghazzī al-Timirtashī (d. 1004/1595). These are all works of *furūʿ al-fiqh*. The layered writing (commentaries on commentaries) is not a sign of failure of intellect or endeavour, but of commitment to tradition. Ibn ʿĀbidīn also wrote a number of separate treatises. Amongst these were the poem translated below (*ʿUqūd rasm al-muftī*), a commentary on the poem, and an additional special commentary on that part of the poem which refers to custom as a source of law.[3] These three works (the poem, the commentary, and the treatise on custom), together with a large section of the introduction to the *Radd al-muḥtār*[4] represent Ibn ʿĀbidīn's contribution to the literary genre of *adab al-muftī* (if indeed it is a separate genre).

[3] All contained in Ibn ʿĀbidīn, *Rasāʾil*; the poem and its commentary, 1/10–52; the treatise on custom (*Nashr al-ʿarf fī bināʾ baʿd al-aḥkām ʿala 'l-ʿurf*) 2/114ff.

[4] Ibn ʿĀbidīn, *Radd al-muḥtār*, 1/69–78.

The two major genres of juristic writing are the familiar *furū' al-fiqh* and *uṣūl al-fiqh*. Collections of fatwas are not quite *furū'*, though they have something in common; and assessment of the task and duties of a mufti are certainly not *uṣūl*, though some of the conclusions of the *adab al-muftī* tradition were incorporated into works of *uṣūl*. Specialist academic discussion of the mufti and his task was a relatively late development in Islamic juristic writing. The task and duties of the *qāḍī*, by contrast, was a topic of *furū'* distinguished and defined in the earliest known juristic works. Recognition of the mufti as a functionary of the law, different from the academic jurist on the one hand and from the judge on the other, took time. Only in later works is there a clear recognition that precisely these three functionaries constitute together, typologically, a coherent and complete account of human service of the law. The point is implicit in the monograph on *fatāwā* by the Shāfi'ī, 'Uthmān b. 'Abd al-Raḥmān Ibn al-Ṣalāḥ (d. 643/1245), is repeated by Yaḥyā b. Sharaf al-Nawawī (676/1277) in the introduction to his *Majmū'*, and is succinctly recapitulated, in precise typological terms, by 'Alī b. 'Abd al-Kāfī al-Subkī (d. 756/1357) in his *Fatāwā*. Subkī is able to state, simply and categorically, that jurists are in three ranks (*marātib*): the academic jurist, the mufti, and the qadi, in that order.[5] Within the Shāfi'ī tradition, Ibn al-Ṣalāḥ's work, though it gathers material and ideas from other sources, is the first specialist and complete monograph devoted to the subject of muftis. His achievement was recognized by Nawawī who attempted to incorporate his findings into the standard genres of juristic writing. In his *Majmū'* (a commentary on the *Muhadhdhab* of Abū Isḥāq Ibrāhīm b. 'Alī al-Shīrāzī, d. 476/1083), Nawawī made discussion of *iftā'* a part of his general introduction. In his later *Rawḍat al-Ṭālibīn* (also a work of *furū'*), he made the same material a subsection of the topic of *qaḍā'*. Major developments within the Mālikī tradition in the understanding and expression of the mufti's task belong to the same century (the 7th/13th), and can be associated especially with the work of Shihāb al-Dīn al-Qarafī (d. 684/1285).[6]

The Ḥanafī tradition shows the same late development of a fully discriminated assessment of the mufti's role; and the same ambivalence about where to discuss it. The alternatives were specialist monographs or treatises, introductions to works of *furū'*, or subsections or digressions within the juristic topic of *qaḍā'*. Ibn 'Ābidīn, writing long after the establishment of a fully discriminated juristic topic of *iftā'*, exploits all of these literary spaces. It is not strictly possible to give his work a chronology, since he worked simultaneously on all his major works (within this field) and included cross-references to all of them, within all of them. Each work was work-in-progress, adorned with references to the other works. Nonetheless, it seems likely that he wrote the poem, *'Uqūd rasm al-muftī*, first. Subsequently, he wrote the commentary to the poem, then the additional commentary on custom. The major study that is incorporated into the Introduction to the *Radd al-muḥtār* must have been started later, though references to it have been placed within the commentary to the poem. Finally, there are scattered comments on *iftā'* incorporated under the topic of *qaḍā'*, later in the *Radd*.

The topics to be covered in a discussion of *iftā'* were fully established within the tradition. They have probably their most succinct possible expression in the 74 lines of the *'Uqūd*. Nearly all of that work relates to the assessment

[5] For Ibn al-Ṣalāḥ and Nawawī, see, Calder, 'Al-Nawawī's typology of muftis'. For Subkī, *Fatāwā*, 2/122–3.

[6] For whom, see now, Sherman A. Jackson, *Islamic law and the state: the constitutional jurisprudence of Shihāb al-Dīn al-Qarafī*.

and ranking of authorities and books within the Ḥanafī juristic tradition, and to assessment and ranking of formulaic expression within the books. Where the basic processes of assessment and ranking do not provide a ruling (the *madhhab*), a number of subsidiary principles are offered, the most productive of which are probably those that refer to the needs of the time or to custom. It is just possible to recognize a residual suggestion that, when all else fails, a trained jurist might make independent assessment of the arguments in so far as they relate to the sources, but that is hedged with qualification. A jurist finds how to act by discovery of the rule that is favoured by the *madhhab*, and he does that by processes which are more or less automatic, not based on independent assessment of the sources, or the arguments, or even on independent preference for particular jurists. The preferences are those laid down by the tradition. This search for and assertion of an authority of law which is (apparently) free from personal and judgemental assessment by the jurist will not mislead those who are familiar with the sociological study of juristic and judicial processes. Such assessments are a common feature of juristic systems and do not mean that there was no creativity or flexibility within a system. Within all legal systems judges and jurists can make extremely creative decisions while maintaining that they are merely enforcing a pre-existing set of well-established rules.

The importance of Ibn ʿĀbidīn's work lies in the system of authority that it articulates. It is the authority of the *madhhab* and, though the word does not occur, *taqlīd*. The problem faced by a mufti is how to manipulate and argue about juristic books produced within the *madhhab*. Jurists did not derive their rulings from an independent study of Quran and sunna, nor did they claim to do so. The great translation from revelation to rules had been undertaken by the independent *mujtahids*, the founders of the schools of law. While their work could be understood and justified by reference to the principles of *uṣūl al-fiqh*, practising jurists and muftis were not required to apply those principles. The hermeneutical task that faced a jurist who wanted to know how to act lay not in the application of rules to revelation, but in the application of rules to the juristic tradition. The point had been made explicitly by Ibn al-Ṣalāḥ: the mufti is, in relation to the texts of the *madhhab*, like the founder in relation to the texts of revelation.[7] The point could hardly be more clearly or explicitly repeated than in the content of this poem.

III

Ibn ʿĀbidīn's poem is an *urjūza*. Each *bayt* is made up of two rhyming hemistyches, each hemistych of three *juz'*. I have used for my translation the iambic pentameter, without rhyme (and with many licenses). The original is not great poetry but it is a poem; the knowledge it offers is neatly formed, charmingly contained, and skilfully controlled. It is mostly clear and self-explanatory, but I have amplified some of the points and explained the overall structure in Section IV below. The numbered divisions within the poem correspond to those introduced by Ibn ʿĀbidīn for his commentary.

(i)
In God's name I begin this work; and with
        High praise of him who gave us rules and law.
Blessings and peace eternally I pray
        Upon a prophet who gave us the Way

[7] Calder, 'Al-Nawawī's typology of muftis', 155–6.

And on his House and his Companions true
Throughout long ages and the passing years.
And now: The indigent sinner, slave of God
Muḥammad Ibnu ʿĀbidīn entreats
The blessings of his Lord—the One, the Generous
And in the achievement of his aims success:
The composition of an ordered jewel
A necklace rare of far-refulgent pearls
Entitled 'Chaplets on the Mufti's task';
Required by muftis or by those who'ld act alone.
I now begin the appointed task, entreating
Grace from the abundant sea of Providence.

(ii)
Know there's a duty to accept what's known
To be preferred by right authority
Or written in the Manifest Transmission
If no opposing preference can be shown.

(iii)
The Manifest Transmission's books are six
In number, also known as the *Uṣūl.*
Muḥammad al-Shaybānī wrote them all,
Explained in them the Nuʿmānī school:
The two *Jāmiʿ*, known as the large and small
The two *Siyar*, known as the small and large,
The *Ziyādāt* and the *Mabsūṭ*; by sound
And clear authority transmitted—all.
His too: the questions known as 'Rarities',
Transmitted in the books by unclear paths.
And then the questions called 'Occurrences'
Deductions by the Elders of our school.

(iv)
Because in composition the *Mabsūṭ*
Is first of six, it's also called the *Aṣl.*
Then came the *Jāmiʿ* number one, the small
Which (being later) has priority.
The last that he composed was the *Siyar*,
The large; therefore relied on, being last.

(v)
The six by Ḥakīm Martyr were conjoined
In his *Sufficio*. The name's deserved.
Its finest commentary is the *Mabsūṭ*
Sarakhsī's work, a sun and by a Sun:
So sound is its transmission conduct is
Based there, and deviation not allowed.

(vi)
Know this: Abū Ḥanīfa is the source
Of high reports and rulings manifold.
Of these he chose a part and left the rest
And then his fellow jurists chose their share;
Hence all replies go back to him alone
As his companions all have testified.

(vii)
No choice being known from him, the chosen view
Is that of Abū Yūsuf Yaʿqūb.
Then Muḥammad; his views are sound. And then
Zufar and al-Ḥasan Ibnu Ziyād.
Some say that if the Two Companions are
Agreed against the Imam, the mufti chooses.
Some say the stronger proof's preferred, where there's
A mufti with the skill to uncover it.

(viii)
But in our time there is no preference based
On proof; and so opinion's based on order
If they have not preferred the opposing view—
For what seemed clear to them, we must accept.
We see that they have sometimes given preference
To a companion's view—made it prevail.
Zufar is an instance; they have preferred
His view on seventeen juristic rules.

(ix)
Thereafter, if there is no view transmitted
From these, our highly learn'd authorities
And if they disagree who later came
Then preference goes to the majority
Of such as Ṭaḥāwī and Abū Ḥafs
And Abū Jaʿfar and the famous Layth.
Where even these have no established view
And yet the need remains for a response
The mufti then must seriously strive
And fear the power of God on judgement day.
For none deficient in the skills required
Should dare to give a ruling—save a wretch.

(x)
Some principles there are accepted and
Defined by those who're qualified to rule.
In ritual acts priority is given
To our Imam; that's absolute unless
His sound transmission's not adopted—as
On purity, date wine remaining by.
For rules related to the judge's office
The view of Abū Yūsuf is selected.
In matters of inheritance they have
Based fatwas always on Muḥammad's view.

Analogy gives way to *istiḥsān*,
Save in few cases, and obscurity.
The Manifest Transmission's rules are not
To be opposed; the record there is sure.
And deviation's not allowed from rules
Where knowledge is supported by transmission.
A rule that tends to ward off unbelief
From Muslims must, though weak, be brought to bear.
A rule by right authority rejected
Is abrogated; something else required.
A rule that's been established in the Texts
Is counted sound wherever it occurs.
Superior are the Texts to Commentaries
And Commentaries above Fatāwā ranked
Unless a different rule, expressly, they
Describe as sound; that's best that's thus described.

(xi)
The first is best of variants listed in
The *Khāniyya* and in the *Multaqā*.
In other works rely on proofs that they
Put last—for that is the established way.
The custom's thus in the *Hidāya* and
Such works as that; (the learned know this fact).
Likewise, if they give reasons for one view
While disregarding all the rest, choose it.

(xii)
Where'er you find two views and one deemed sound
Then that's the one to lean on; it's secure:
Marked by such phrases as 'The fatwa's there'
or 'Closer', 'Clearer', 'Chosen', or 'More fit'.
Or yet, 'This view is sound'. 'More sound' is more
Secure, though some say the opposite is true.
Likewise, 'Fatwas are given thus', or 'Based
On this'; these two are stronger than the rest.

(xiii)
If you should find two views reported sound
Then choose the one you wish; each is allowed.
Unless one's 'sound' and one 'more sound'; or one
Declared the fatwa: preference here is known.
Also a view that's in the Texts, or is the Imam's,
Or Manifest Transmission, or adopted by
Most of the great; or it is *istiḥsān*,
Or offers to the *waqfs* clear benefit;
Or it's a view more suited to the time
Or has in argument a clearer proof.
This, only if there's conflict in assessment
Or no assessment given of the sound view.
So take the view that's marked preponderant
By factors you've now come to know. That's best.

(xiv)
Act on the meaning given for transmissions
        If not opposed to a clear established view.

(xv)
Custom has much authority in Law
        And so a rule may well be based on it.

(xvi)
To act, or to respond to a petitioner
        Using a view that's weak is not allowed. (70)
Save one who acts under necessity
        And one whose skill and knowledge is renowned.
But not a qadi, he can't judge this way;
        And if he does, his judgement does not stand.
Especially qadis now; they are restricted
        To school-established rules when they're appointed.

(xvii)
Completed are the verses I've composed.
        Praise be to God; he is the best of seals. (74)

IV

The following comments clarify reference and structure. Unless otherwise signalled, extra material is derived from Ibn ʿĀbidīn's commentary on his poem. That commentary consists mostly of citations from earlier jurists which function as justification of the positions he adopts in the poem.

Section (i). This is mostly conventional introduction and self-explanatory. Line 7 identifies the intended audience (*yaḥtāju-hu al-ʿāmilu aw man yuftī*): the mufti and those sufficiently educated to act without appeal to a mufti.

Section (ii). These two lines effectively summarize the whole of the Ḥanafī theory of juristic authority. It is a duty (*wājib*) to follow a rule that is known (*ʿulima*—the epistemological stance is important) to be preferred by those who have the right to establish preference (*ahl al-tarjīḥ*). Lying behind these is the 'manifest transmission' (*ẓāhir al-riwāya*), which is the basis of the Ḥanafī *madhhab* and must be followed—unless qualified by authoritative preference. In the rest of the poem we learn about the manifest transmission and its transformation into a literary tradition which expresses the ongoing authority of the great jurists. These are the *ahl al-tarjīḥ*.

Section (iii). Ibn ʿĀbidīn identifies the books of the manifest transmission and two further (lower) categories of books. The six books written by (or attributed to) Muḥammad al-Shaybānī[8] are the *Jāmiʿ al-kabīr*, the *Jāmiʿ al-ṣaghīr*, the *Siyar al-kabīr*, the *Siyar al-ṣaghīr*, the *Ziyādāt*, and the *Mabsūṭ* (or *Aṣl*). These books are deemed to be transmitted from Shaybānī by sound authority (*mutawātiran* or *mashhūran*). Less secure, because of inadequate transmission, are certain other books attributed to him (the *Kaysāniyyāt*, the *Hārūniyyāt*, the *Jurjāniyyāt* and the *Raqqiyyāt*) and a number of books attributed to others (e.g. the *Mujarrad* by al-Ḥasan b. Ziyād[9] and the *Kutub al-amalī* by Abū Yūsuf[10]). These are known as *masāʾil al-nawādir* (rarities). The third

[8] Muḥammad b. al-Ḥasan al-Shaybānī, d. 189/804.
[9] Al-Ḥasan b. Ziyād al-Luʾluʾī, d. 204/819.
[10] Yaʿqūb b. Ibrāhīm al-Anṣārī, d. 182/798.

category, known as *nawāzil* or *waqīʿāt* (occurrences), consists of rulings deduced by later scholars when asked about events which had not been covered by Abū Ḥanīfa and his companions. The first book to gather material of this kind is the *Kitāb al-nawāzil* by Abū 'l-Layth al-Samarqandī.[11] Later scholars continued to accumulate such material, and some jurists reproduced it mixed up with other (earlier) material, e.g. Qāḍīkhān[12] in his *Fatāwā*. Some, however, distinguished, notably Raḍī al-Dīn al-Sarakhsī[13] who recorded, in order, the *masā'il al-uṣūl*, the *nawādir*, and the *fatāwā* (i.e. *nawāzil/waqīʿāt*). (What a fine achievement this was, says Ibn ʿĀbidīn.)

Section (iv). This section establishes the principle that, of books in the manifest transmission, those produced later have higher authority; and gives some pointers towards establishing chronology. The last sentence in Ibn ʿĀbidīn's commentary on this section is derived from the commentary on Ibn Nujaym's *Ashbāh*,[14] by al-Bīrī.[15]

> If there is difference of opinion on a particular event, it is the best and the chosen view, for a *mujtahid*, that he should consider the arguments and look into the question of what is preponderant in his view. For a *muqallid*, he should follow the last book to be composed, which is the *Siyar [al-kabīr]*. Unless the scholars of later date (*al-mashāyikh al-muta'akhkhirūn*) choose something different, in which case it is a duty to act according to their choice, even if it is an opinion of Zufar.[16]

Ibn ʿĀbidīn quotes this as confirmatory of his poem. He did not believe that there were *mujtahids* (in the real sense) in his own time. Like al-Bīrī, he believed that *muqallids* should simply follow authority, meaning that of the manifest transmission, unless qualified by a clear preference from later authorities.

Section (v). This section establishes the fundamental importance of the *Kāfī* of al-Ḥakīm al-Shahīd, qadi of Bukhara[17] and the commentary on it (the *Mabsūṭ*) by Shams al-A'imma al-Sarakhsī.[18] The pivotal role of these works is due to the fact that they (correctly) summarize and expound the rules of the manifest transmission.

Section (vi). Sections (iii)–(v) dealt with books. Sections (vi)–(viii) deal with authority figures. Section (vi) is concerned to justify Abū Ḥanīfa as eponym of the school, though not all its rulings are attributed to him. Ibn ʿĀbidīn's commentary explains at length how a *mujtahid* may have two or more views on one matter, and suggests why Abū Ḥanīfa's views, as preserved, are distributed across three (or more) authorities (i.e. himself, his two major, and some minor companions). He quotes statements by the early companions which show that they did not express any opinion which was not a transmission from Abū Ḥanīfa; indeed they swore oaths to that effect (hence line 25 in the poem).

> Q. If a *mujtahid* abandons an opinion, it does not remain an opinion of his; it is as if it were abrogated (as will be explained later[19]). Therefore the

[11] Naṣr b. Muḥammad al-Samarqandī (d. 376/986).

[12] Al-Ḥasan b. Manṣūr al-Uzjandī Qāḍīkhān (d. 592/1196), author of the *Fatāwā Qāḍīkhān* or the *Fatāwā Khāniyya*.

[13] Muḥammad b. Muḥammad al-Sarakhsī (d. 544/1149), author of the *Muḥīṭ*.

[14] The *Kitāb al-ashbāh wa-'l-naẓā'ir* by Zayn al-Dīn b. Ibrāhīm Ibn Nujaym (d. 970/1563).

[15] The reference is presumably to the *ʿUmdat dhawī al-baṣā'ir li-ḥall muhimmat al-ashbāh wa-'l-naẓā'ir* by Ibrāhīm b. Ḥusayn b. Bīrī (d. 1099/1688).

[16] Ibn ʿĀbidīn, *Rasā'il*, 1/20. For Zufar see n. 21 below.

[17] Muḥammad b. Muḥammad al-Ḥakīm (d. 334/945).

[18] Muḥammad b. Aḥmad b. Abī Sahl al-Sarakhsī (d. 490/1097).

[19] The reference is to line 49.

opinions attributed to his companions, in which they are at odds with him, are not his *madhhab*. Their opinions are their *madhhab*, so how can they be attributed (*tunsab*) to him? A Ḥanafī follows (*qallada*) Abū Ḥanīfa, and is therefore affiliated (*nusiba*) to him and not to anyone else.

A. I used to find this a problem, but answered it in my commentary, the *Radd al-muḥtār*. The Imam [Abū Ḥanīfa] ordered his companions to adopt those of his opinions which seemed to them to best accord with the evidence. It follows that the opinion they adopted was an opinion of his, because founded on his principles, the ones he laid down for them; it was not an opinion abandoned in every respect.[20]

Section (vii). This section establishes a basic hierarchy of authorities. First Abū Ḥanīfa; then, when no view is known from him, Abū Yūsuf; then Muḥammad al-Shaybānī; then Zufar[21] and Ibn Ziyād (not in order). The two lines beginning 'Some say' (*qīla*) indicate views that have status within the tradition but are rejected by Ibn ʿĀbidīn.

Section (viii). The first line of this section re-affirms that the principle of hierarchy gives the ruling. The second and subsequent lines, however, point to later authority for 'they' can express a preference and, if they do, it must be followed. The first sentence of Ibn ʿĀbidīn's commentary gives the mood of the argument:

> You know that the more valid view is that the mufti who is *mujtahid* should choose, and give his fatwa based on the stronger argument; he is not required to proceed on a basis of hierarchy [*tafṣīl*, translated 'order' in the poem, l. 30]. Since the mufti who is *mujtahid* does not exist in our time, and only the pure *muqallid* remains, it is incumbent on us to follow *tafṣīl*. We give fatwas first with the view of the Imam, and then and then. [That is,] as long as we do not see that those who are *mujtahid fi 'l-madhhab* have declared something else valid, because the proof is stronger, or the times have changed, or whatever they prefer. We follow what they say, as if they were alive and had issued to us a fatwa to this effect.[22]

The poem shows that, while the principle of order is basic, it can be abandoned under 'their' authority. The preference within the *madhhab* for 17 opinions of Zufar (though contrary to all the general principles) illustrates the point.

Section (ix). This section reverts to the principle of hierarchy. Where there is no opinion transmitted from Abū Ḥanīfa and his companions, then preference is given to the majority opinion of the next generations. The examples given are Aḥmad b. Muḥammad al-Ṭaḥāwī (d. 321/933), Abū Ḥafs Aḥmad b. Ḥafs al-Bukhārī (d. 264/878), Abū Jaʿfar Muḥammad b. ʿAlī al-Hinduwānī (d. 362/973), and Abū 'l-Layth al-Samarqandī. Where even these do not provide an answer (or where a majority cannot be established), then the mufti has to give the case special consideration: *fa-'l-yanẓur al-muftī bi-jaddin wa-'jtihādi* (l. 38). This special consideration (*ijtihād*, understood to be within the *madhhab*, not the *ijtihād* of the founding Imam[23]) is based on principles, and these are set out in Section (x).

Section (x). The principles set out here are brought into play, apparently, only when the principles of hierarchy, both as applied to books (the manifest transmission), and authorities (Abū Ḥanīfa first, then Abū Yūsuf, etc.) have

[20] Ibn ʿĀbidīn, *Rasāʾil*, 1/24.
[21] Zufar b. al-Hudhayl al-ʿAnbarī, d. 158/775.
[22] Ibn ʿĀbidīn, *Rasāʾil*, 28. For the distinction between the independent *mujtahid* and the affiliated *mujtahid* (*mujtahid fi 'l-madhhab*), see Calder, 'Al-Nawawī's typology of muftis'.
[23] See previous note.

failed to produce an answer. In fact these principles sometimes simply contradict the principle of hierarchy (e.g. preference is given to Abū Yūsuf or to Muḥammad in certain areas of the law) and should be understood as having precisely that effect: of creating exceptions to the general rules. The most revealing principle is that expressed in line 50 which states that a rule that has been established in the 'texts' (*wa-kullu qawlin fi 'l-mutūni uthbita...*) is deemed to be preferred. It will be useful to pause here and consider what this implies.

Ibn 'Ābidīn's argument seems to state that when a mufti is faced with a problem he should first look into the books of the manifest transmission, taking into account their order of composition, then consider the views of individual authorities, in appropriate order, and if that does not produce an answer, look for the majority view of Ṭaḥāwī, Abū Ḥafs *et al.*, and so on. In practice, what a mufti would do first is look into the standard works of the Ḥanafī tradition, where, much of the time, he would find an answer. The details of how to find, and how to assess, an answer from those books is given through Sections (xi) to (xiii). The rules that have been given throughout Sections (iii) to (x) are not really rules of discovery; they are rules of justification.

Ḥanafī jurists had to account for the relationship between the foundation texts of the *madhhab* and the later classical and standard textbooks. How had the great classical jurists (those who produced the *mutūn*) come to state that the *madhhab* was such and such when there was a large diversity of books, rulings, and authorities which constituted the foundation texts of the Ḥanafī tradition and/but which did not fully clarify these things? The answer offered is that they had used certain principles, namely those set out here by Ibn 'Ābidīn. In relation to the classical jurists, these were principles of discovery. In relation to later jurists (Ibn 'Ābidīn himself) they were principles of justification.

The same problem (of discovery versus justification) can be discovered in the history and development of works of *uṣūl al-fiqh*. The hermeneutical principles set out in these works were, perhaps, in some earlier phases, thought to be principles for the discovery of rules of law. Later jurists (and some earlier ones) perceived more clearly that they were principles of justification for rules that were known in advance, through authority, specifically the authority of the founding Imams. Ibn Khaldūn (reflecting the accepted perceptions of his time) expressed the situation clearly. Rules that had functioned for the founding Imams as rules of deduction (*istinbāṭ*) functioned for later scholars for the preserving and guarding of established rules.[24] Likewise here. Up to Section (xi), line 49, the rules for muftis, as set out by Ibn 'Ābidīn, are conceptually prior to the emergence of the classical texts (*mutūn*), and function primarily, or even exclusively, to justify what is found in those texts.[25]

Lines 50 and 51 transfer the question of authority to, precisely, the *mutūn*. These are the texts which count and principles must now be laid down for

[24] Ibn Khaldūn, *Muqaddima*, 456–7. Ibn Khaldūn is here talking about the science of *khilāfiyyāt*, the science of identifying and defending juristic rules that are in dispute. 'The master [of this science] has to know the principles whereby one manages to deduce rules, just as the *mujtahid* needs these principles. However, the *mujtahid* needs them for deduction; the master of *khilāfiyyāt* needs them to preserve the already deduced rules from destruction by the adversary'— *li-ḥifẓ tilka 'l-masā'il al-mustanbaṭa min an yahdima-hā al-mukhālif* ....

[25] An authoritative series of studies on *uṣūl al-fiqh* by Wael B. Hallaq is now conveniently gathered in his *Law and legal theory in Classical and medieval Islam*. Generally I find that Hallaq, in all these studies, overstates the case for *uṣūl al-fiqh* as a science of deduction. Only in his most recent essay ('Iftā' and ijtihād in Sunni legal theory') does he begin to acknowledge that the science of *uṣūl al-fiqh* must be understood as primarily, maybe exclusively, a science of justification. See note 24 above.

managing them (since they too do not in a simple manner solve all problems). The details of how to manage the classical texts are set out in Sections (xi) to (xiii), though one major principle is set out here: texts are ranked above commentaries and commentaries above *fatāwā* (line 51).

In his commentary, Ibn ʿĀbidīn identifies the 'texts' as the following works. The *Mukhtaṣar* of Aḥmad b. Muḥammad al-Qudūrī, d. 428/1037; the *Bidāyat [al-mubtadi']* by ʿAlī b. Abī Bakr al-Marghinānī, d. 593/1197;[26] the *Mukhtār* by ʿAbdallāh b. Maḥmūd al-Mawṣilī, d. 682/1283; the *Wiqāyat [al-Riwāya fi masā'il al-Hidāya]* by Maḥmūd b. Aḥmad al-Maḥbūbī, d. ?7th/13th c.; the *Kanz [al-daqā'iq]* by ʿAbdallāh b. Aḥmad al-Nasafī, d. 710/1310; the *Nuqāya* (or *Mukhtaṣar al-Wiqāya*) by ʿUbaydallāh b. Masʿūd al-Maḥbūbī, d. 747/1346; the *Multaqā [al-abḥur]* by Ibrāhīm b. Muḥammad al-Ḥalabī, d. 956/1549. The commentaries, which are ranked lower than the texts, are the commentaries on these works. (The *mutūn* have a higher rank because, being shorter, they are deemed to contain the essential and undisputed parts of the law.) The *fatāwā* are those books within the Ḥanafī tradition which have the word *fatāwā* in the title, e.g. the *Fatāwā* of Qāḍīkhān.

Section (xi) identifies the general patterns of presentation adopted in the major textbooks of the tradition, and gives some first principles of how to read these texts. Section (xii) looks at the precise formulae used to identify the preferred view; phrases like *al-fatwā ʿalay-hi*, *al-ashbah*, *al-azhar*, *al-mukhtār*, *al-awjah*, *al-ṣaḥīḥ*, *al-aṣaḥḥ*, *bi-hi yuftā*, etc. The dispute recorded (and rejected) at line 59 relates to a minority view that if an opinion is recorded as the 'more sound' (*al-aṣaḥḥ*) then its opposite is sound. Section (xiii) raises the question of what to do when either there are two views recorded as sound (by whatever terminology) (line 61) or there is no assessment at all of the sound view (line 66). The principles set out here repeat to some extent the principles set out earlier. There is a residual possibility of simple choice (line 61) or (for those more competent) of assessment of argument. It is important to note that assessment of argument is the last principle to be adduced and is followed immediately by a reminder of the situation at issue: when the standard books of the tradition have unresoluble conflict or no assessment at all of the preferred view.

Section (xiv) instructs the mufti to act on the *mafhūm* of transmitted material, as it has come (through the tradition)—*wa- ʿmal bi-mafhūmi riwāyatin atā*. *Mafhūm*, literally 'meaning' or 'implication', is interpreted in the commentary as referring to basic deductions from language. The language in question is the language of the sources, and Ibn ʿĀbidīn refers his reader at this point to the discipline of *uṣūl*. Section (xv) is a very brief statement of the importance of custom (*ʿurf*), much amplified in his commentary and in his independent treatise, *Nashr al-ʿarf*.

Section (xvi) reaffirms the basic principle of *taqlīd*. Both the mufti, and one who would act on his own behalf, are bound to choose the view that is preferred in the *madhhab* (as discovered through the principles set out in this poem). Using a view that is weak (i.e. weak within the *madhhab*) is not allowed. There is exception for 'necessity' (*ḍarūra*), and the mufti can take this into account when he gives a ruling to a petitioner; and for one who has appropriate skill (i.e. to analyse the arguments for himself). This last exception applies only to one who is making a decision for himself. A mufti, giving a ruling to another, is bound by the *madhhab*, even if his own assessment of the argument

[26] Al-Marghinānī's commentary on his own work is the famous *Hidāya*. A good brief account of the influence of the *Hidāya* may be found under 'Marghinānī' in EI(2) (by Heffening).

suggests a preference for a view classified in the tradition as weak. Qadis are absolutely bound by the rules of the *madhhab*; and, for the qadis of Ottoman times, this principle was also articulated in their terms of appointment.

When Ibn ʿĀbidīn wrote the Ḥanafī *madhhab* had existed for more than a thousand years. His poem is an assessment and a justification of juristic literature within the *madhhab* throughout that period. In an unapologetic assertion of continuity, loyalty, and commitment, it links the thirteenth century to the second (the nineteenth to the eighth A.D.). The other step that was required to justify and explain the juristic tradition was to ground it in revelation. That task, however, was carried out elsewhere, within expanded commentaries on *furūʿ* and by reference to the hermeneutical rules of *uṣūl al-fiqh*. The genre of *adab al-muftī*, in this and in nearly all its examples, relates the mufti to the school tradition where he will find a rule of law. It is not expected that the mufti will exploit for himself, with a view to discovery of the law, the hermeneutical rules of *uṣūl al-fiqh*.

REFERENCES

Calder, Norman. 1996. ʻAl-Nawawī's typology of muftis and its significance for a general theory of Islamic law', *Islamic Law and Society* 3/2.

Dryden, John. 1985. *Selected poetry* (Selected by Douglas Grant with an introduction by Gamini Salgado). Harmondsworth: Penguin Books.

Hallaq, Wael B. 1994. *Law and legal theory in classical and medieval Islam*. Aldershot and Brookfield, VT: Variorum.

Hallaq, Wael B. 1996. ʻIftāʼ and ijtihād in Sunni legal theory: a development account' in Muhammad Khalid Masud, Brinkley Messick and David S. Powers (ed.), *Islamic legal interpretation: muftis and their fatwas*. Cambridge, MA and London: Harvard University Press.

Ibn ʿĀbidīn, Muḥammad Amīn b. ʻUmar. n.d. *Majmūʼat al-rasāʼil*, n.p.

Ibn Khaldūn, ʿAbd al-Raḥmān b. Muḥammad. n.d. *Muqaddimat Ibn Khaldūn*, Beirut.

Jackson, Sherman A. 1996. *Islamic law and the state: the constitutional jurisprudence of Shihāb al-Dīn al-Qarafī*. Leiden, New York and Cologne: E. J. Brill.

Al-Subkī, ʿAlī b. ʿAbd al-Kāfī Taqī al-Dīn. n.d. *Fatāwā* (2 vols), Beirut: Dār al-maʿrifa.

XVII

ZAKĀT IN IMĀMĪ SHĪʿĪ JURISPRUDENCE, FROM THE TENTH TO THE SIXTEENTH CENTURY A.D.

Māwardī said of *zakāt* that it was paid *ṭahratan li-ahlihā maʿūnatan li-ahl al-sahman*, as a purification for the donor and a support for the recipient.[1] It has thus a dual aspect. As a social tax it provides for the transfer of wealth from certain productive classes of society to certain poor or non-productive classes. As a religious duty it is of essentially the same type as *ṣalāt, ḥajj*, etc., a *farīḍa ʿala l-ʿayn*. Like these it is a ritual whose correct performance involves an attention to precise details of quantity (*naṣāb*), timing (*al-ḥawl*), and intention (*niyya*) which may be irrelevant or even inimical to the optimum fulfilment of the social aim.

The *zakāt* donors were defined as those possessed of productive wealth derived from pastoralism, agriculture or trade.[2] The recipients were divided into eight categories, five of which may be subsumed under the headings of the poor, the needy or those under particular difficulties; the other three were the tax-collecting and military classes (*al-ʿāmilūn, fī sabīl allāh, al-muʾallafa*). Sunnī jurists in general acknowledged that *de facto* rulers had a certain right to collect and distribute the *zakāt*, 'because they (the *wulāt*) are the trustees (*umanāʾ*) over the collection of *zakāt* from the donors on behalf of the recipients'.[3] Shāfiʿī (d. 204/820), however, perceived that the political rights of the *wulāt* might conflict with the individual need for religious reward. For the latter it was necessary that the *zakāt* be paid at a particular time (*al-ḥawl*): Shāfiʿī indicated that if the tax-collector did not arrive at the appropriate moment the donor should distribute the *zakāt* himself.[4] Likewise with regard to *niyya* Shāfiʿī considered it preferable (*wa-aḥabbu ilayya*) that the individual should undertake his own distribution in order to be sure about the discharge of his religious duty (*fa-yakūn ʿalā yaqīn min adāʾihā*).[5] There was thus some tension between the political rights of the ruler and the religious needs of the individual donor.

The ruler was entitled to use one part of the *zakāt* collected—that of the *ʿāmilūn*—to finance his tax-collecting bureaucracy: *wa-yuʿṭā aʿwān idārat wālī l-ṣadaqa*, it may be given to the aides in the administration of the *wālī l-ṣadaqa*.[6] There was, however, for Shāfiʿī a possibility, when the donor distributed the *zakāt* directly, that the share of the *ʿāmil* might be *sāqiṭ* (lapsed).[7] Nevertheless, on the whole, for Shāfiʿī as for later Sunnī jurists the system of religious taxation implied the existence of a government who collected and distributed. Of what was collected the government might legitimately use three out of eight parts for bureaucratic and military purposes. Shāfiʿī acknowledged, even stressed, that the individual need for salvation could pre-empt the right of the ruler to collect and distribute; and he was familiar with the possibility and the terminology of *suqūṭ*. In his works juristic rules are set out as ideals with

[1] Māwardī, *Al-Aḥkām al-Sulṭāniyya*, ed. Enger, Bonn, 1853, 195; cf. also N. P. Aghnides, *Mohammedan theories of finance*, New York, 1916, p. 323, n. 1.

[2] See, for further details, mostly common to Sunnīs and Shīʿīs, Aghnides, op. cit., 203–95.

[3] Muḥammad ibn Idrīs al-Shāfiʿī, *Kitāb al-Umm*, Cairo, 1388, I, 70.

[4] ibid., 15.

[5] ibid., 19.

[6] ibid., 61.

[7] ibid., 68; cf. Abū Yūsuf, *Kitāb al-Kharāj*, Cairo, 1352, 81.

little reference to the actual practice of the administration; later Sunnī writers, it will be shown, manifested a rather different concern to provide the greatest degree of legitimacy for the actual practice of *de facto* powers.

Works of Imāmī *fiqh* emerged only in the second half of the tenth century A.D. and first achieved a high degree of technical excellence in the writings of Muḥammad ibn Ḥasan al-Ṭūsī:[8] first, concisely, in his *Kitāb al-Nihāya* and later, expansively, in his *Kitāb al-Mabsūṭ*. Defining the Imāmī attitude to *zakāt* he declared that in the absence of the *imām* or his appointee (*man naṣabahu l-imām*) the shares of the *suʿāt/ʿāmilūn*, the *muʾallafa* and *jihād* were *sāqiṭ*.[9] The term *man naṣabahu l-imām* refers presumably to a contemporary of the *imām*, certainly in this context to an entity deemed absent. During the Ghayba, then, the Imāmīs emphasized the dissociation of the sacred from the profane by denying precisely those shares which would have served the administrative and military needs of the government. They were enabled thereby to affirm their independence of the political institution and to stress the religious rather than the political aspects of *zakāt*. Later, in his *Mabsūṭ*, Ṭūsī confirmed that the shares of the *muʾallafa* and the *ʿamil* were *sāqiṭ*, but, by providing an extended definition of *sabīl allāh*, he was enabled to affirm its contemporary operancy.[10] *Sabīl allāh* was there defined as including the building of mosques, the upkeep of bridges and other *maṣāliḥ*.[11] The scholarly class thus had a claim on *zakāt* only insofar as religious buildings were concerned.

Jaʿfar ibn Saʿīd al-Muḥaqqiq al-Ḥilli confirmed that the shares of the *ʿāmil* and the *muʾallafa* were *sāqiṭ*, accepted the extended definition of *sabīl allāh* and added to it the consideration that *jihād* might be possible even in the absence of the *imām*.[12] Ḥasan ibn Yūsuf ibn al-Muṭahhar al-ʿAllāma, a generation later, not only accepted the possibility but inferred from it that the share of the *muʾallafa*, too, could not continue *sāqiṭ*: لو احتيج الى جهاد حال غيبة الامام فالوجه جواز صرف السهم الى اربابه من المؤلفة.[13] The share of the *ʿāmil*, however, would appear to have been left as Ṭūsī had defined it: 'the share of the *muʾallafa*, the *sāʿī* and the *ghāzī* are *sāqiṭ* during the Ghayba—except when there is need of *jihād*'.[14] It is difficult to see how the exceptive phrase can have

[8] The major Imāmī *fuqahāʾ* in the period under discussion, and those of their works which constitute the main sources for the present study are: M. ibn Ḥasan al-Ṭūsī (d. 460/1067): *Kitāb al-Nihāya*, Beirut, 1970, *Kitāb al-Mabsūṭ*, Persia, 1271, n.p. (references to Ṭūsī, *Mabsūṭ*, *zakāt*, 7 indicate the seventh page of the section on *zakāt*); M. ibn Aḥmad ibn Idrīs al-Ḥillī (d. 598/1202): *Kitāb Sarāʾir al-Islām*, Persia, 1270/1854, n.p. (references given to British Museum edition where the *incipit* is p. 2); Jaʿfar ibn Ḥasan al-Muḥaqqiq al-Ḥillī (d. 676/1277): *Sharāʾiʿ al-Islām*, 4 vols., Najaf, 1389/1969, *Al-Mukhtaṣar al-Nāfiʿ*, Cairo, 1376 (Qum reprint); Ḥasan ibn Yūsuf ibn al-Muṭahhar al-Ḥillī (d. 726/1325): *Kitāb Mukhtalif al-Shīʿa*, 4 vols. in 1, Persia, 1324/1906, *Kitāb Qawāʿid al-Aḥkām*, in Karakī, *Jamiʿ al-Maqāṣid* (see below), *Kitāb Taḥrīr al-Aḥkām*, 2 vols., Persia, 1314/1896; Shams al-Dīn ibn Makkī al-Shahīd al-Awwal (d. 786/1384–5): *Al-Lumʿat al-Dimashqiyya*, in Shahīd II, *Rawḍa* (see below); ʿAlī ibn Ḥusayn ibn ʿAbd al-ʿĀlī al-Karaki (d. 937/1530–1 or 940/1533–4): *Kitāb Jāmiʿ al-Maqāṣid fī sharḥ al-Qawāʿid*, 2 vols., Tehran, 1395; Zayn al-Dīn ibn ʿAlī al-Shahīd al-Thānī (d. 960/1559): *Masālik al-ifhām fī sharḥ Sharāʾiʿ al-Islām*, 2 vols., Persia, 1310 and 1314, *Al-Rawḍat al-Bahiyya fī sharḥ al-Lumʿat al-Dimashqiyya*, Tabriz, 1271.

[9] Ṭūsī, *Nihāya*, 185. For further discussion of the term *sāqiṭ* in this kind of context, see al-Sharīf al-Murtaḍā, *Al-Shāfī*, Tehran, 1301/1884, 40–41, and Ṭūsī, *Kitāb al-Ghayba*, Najaf, 1385, 64; acceptance of the term *sāqiṭ* in this kind of context would seem to have been first justified by Ṭūsī.

[10] Ṭūsī, *Mabsūṭ*, *zakāt*, 17–18.

[11] An indication that Sunnī juristic works were part of the juristic pool drawn upon by Shīʿī jurists: cf. Abū Yūsuf, op. cit., 81.

[12] Muḥaqqiq, *Sharāʾiʿ*, I, 162. (Ṭūsī also acknowledged the validity of defensive *jihād*, but this did not affect his discussion of *zakāt*.)

[13] ʿAllāma, *Taḥrīr*, 68.

[14] *idem*, *Qawāʿid*, 22.

any relevance to the *sā'ī*; that share remains *sāqiṭ*. There is none the less an element of ambiguity about the phraseology which may have been deliberate. The ambiguity was emphasized, perhaps exploited, by Shams al-Dīn ibn Makkī, al-Shahīd al-Awwal: ومع الغيبة لا ساعي ولا مؤلفة الا لمن يحتاج اليه, during the Ghayba, no *sā'ī* and no *mu'allafa* except for one/those needed.[15] That removed the specificity of the need (*jihād*) and left it an open question whether there might not be a need for the *sā'ī* during the Ghayba. Zayn al-Dīn ibn 'Alī al-Shahīd al-Thānī was quite explicit. Commenting on the exceptive clause, *illā li-man yuḥtāj ilayhi*, he states:

> That is the *faqīh* if he is able to appoint a *sā'ī* to collect *zakāt*; and if *jihād* is necessary during the Ghayba and *ta'līf* is required that is permissible by means of the *faqīh* or someone else (*bi l-faqīh wa-ghayrihi*).[16]

By the sixteenth century the three *zakāt*-recipient categories which by Ṭūsī had initially been declared *sāqiṭ* had been re-established as operative.

That change took place exegetically and without polemic. There was no overt appeal, as justification for development, to revelation or to *ijmā'*; there was rather a gradual reassessment of the meaning of revelation, or of the dicta of earlier jurists. Adduction of the concept of *ḥāja* as justificatory reflects a diffuse and general habit of juristic appeal to related concepts, e.g. *ḍarūra*.[17] The final Imāmī assessment of the eight categories paralleled the Sunnī assessment except in this that whereas for the Sunnīs the major executive agent (for organization of collection and for *jihād*) was the *wālī* or governor, for the Shī'īs it was the *faqīh*.

Legal developments in this field benefited the *fuqahā'* in at least one other way. Although there had been amongst Imāmī jurists various views as to who was included in the categories of the *fuqarā'* and the *masākīn* the opinion prevailed that these terms meant a person whose income was insufficient to cover annual expenses for himself and his family. Shahīd II added to this the consideration that if someone was incapable of earning a living because of his endeavours in religious knowledge (*'ilm dīnī*) he might receive *zakāt*, even if he could, by leaving his studies, earn a sufficiency. In the discussion of *zakāt al-fiṭra* he added that special attention was to be given to people of pre-eminence in *'ilm* and *zuhd*: preference was to be given them over other degrees. The *fuqahā'* thus not only finally controlled the collection and distribution of *zakāt* but were also major recipients.[18]

Developments in legal theory reflect change in the aspirations of the religious class. Those in turn were affected by historical events and by ideological (juristic) conditioning. The early Imāmī image of the sacred *umma*, as presented in the *Nihāya*, is relatively free from concepts of military or bureaucratic organization. Shahīd II, on the other hand, perceived the community as ideally possessed of a tax-collecting bureaucracy and a military force, both under the control of the *fuqahā'*.

It is certain that in Buyid times the *fuqahā'* already considered themselves as judicial authorities, and no doubt were able within the Imāmī community to control some part of *zakāt* payments.[19] In the following centuries, especially

[15] Shahīd I, in *Rawḍa*, 51.
[16] Shahīd II, *Rawḍa*, 51.
[17] See Calder, 'Judicial authority in Imāmī Shī'ī jurisprudence', *British Society for Middle Eastern Studies Bulletin*, VI, 1979, 107.
[18] Shahīd II, *Rawḍa*, 49, 51.
[19] cf. Calder, art. cit.; 'Abd al-Jalīl al-Qazwīnī, *Kitāb al-Naqḍ*, ed. Muḥaddith, Tehran, 1331/1952, 164.

under tolerant and favourably inclined governments (the caliph al-Nāsir, Ilkhanids, Ṣafavids) it is probable that they consolidated their hold on their followers and increased their control of material wealth. That was reflected in the increasing stress in legal works on their general authority. By the early sixteenth century when Tahmāsp promoted the creation of a formally Shī'ī state, their aspirations and perceptions had been sharpened to a point where they presented themselves as the rightful authorities within such a state. The juristic theory of the Ṣafavid period differed significantly from the early Buyid expression in so far as it offered a determinate body which ought ideally to control or replace the actual government, in order to implement the *sharī'a*. The early doctrine of *suqūṭ* had probably developed as a means to avoid overt expression of political opposition.

According to Shāfi'ī, God had imposed on all Muslims a charge on their wealth on behalf of other Muslims.[20] *Zakāt* in general was not to be paid to non-Muslims.[21] Just as performance of *ṣalāt* was an outward symbol of adherence to the Islamic community, so was payment of or acceptance of *zakāt*. Participation in that ritual displayed membership of the community. The Imāmīs were concerned not with *islām* as the relevant category but with *īmān*; that was specified by all writers as a necessary condition in the recipient of *zakāt al-māl*. Ṭūsī suggested that in the absence of Imāmī recipients *zakāt al-fiṭra* might be distributed to *mustaḍ'ifīn* in general. Muḥammad ibn Aḥmad ibn Idrīs objected to this view and Muḥaqqiq after initial hesitation confirmed Ibn Idrīs's opinion. Thereafter no Imāmī *faqīh* appears to have denied that *zakāt al-māl* and *zakāt al-fiṭra* were to be paid within *dār al-īmān*.[22] Any Imāmī who knowingly paid *zakāt* wrongly—that is to a non-Imāmī—failed to gain reward. *Zakāt* was a community-defining ritual.[23]

'Adāla was a quality which might be required in the recipient of *zakāt*. It was a quality involving manifestation of positive virtues and was the opposite of *fisq*, a quality acquired by the commission of one or more *kabā'ir*, or persistent commission of *ṣaghā'ir*. To stipulate in the recipient of *zakāt* the quality *'adāla* suggests that the community within which that ritual was carried out was perceived as a positively virtuous community in which every individual assiduously obeyed the law. To stipulate absence of *fisq* permitted a broader definition of community, including those who were, if not conspicuously *'ādil*, yet not *fāsiq*. The matter became controversial at about the time of 'Allāma. He stated in the *Taḥrīr al-Aḥkām*:

> Ṭūsī and al-Sharīf al-Murtaḍā have specified *'adāla* but others have rejected this opinion; the latter view is stronger. The others have specified avoidance of *kabā'ir*. In our opinion it is permissible to give to a *fāsiq* as long as he is *mu'min*.[24]

The identification of the ' others ' was provided in the *Mukhtalif al-Shī'a*. In that work 'Allāma cited Ṭūsī and several of his contemporaries as specifying

[20] Shāfi'ī, *Umm*, I, 70.

[21] For both Sunnīs and Shī'īs there was much discussion about whether the *mu'allafa* might or might not be non-Muslim. See e.g. Shāfi'ī, *Umm*, 61 and 72–3: the different opinions there expressed indicate the composite nature of the *Umm*; see also Ṭūsī, *Mabsūṭ*, *zakāt*, 17; note that Shāfi'ī is cited as source of this discussion; his opinion thereafter became part of Imāmī *ikhtilāf*; cf. note 11 above.

[22] For this term see A. K. S. Lambton, ' A nineteenth century view of *jihad* ', *SI*, XXXII, 1970, 182.

[23] See Ṭūsī, *Nihāya*, 185, 192; *Mabsūṭ*, *zakāt*, 16; Ibn Idrīs, *Sarā'ir*, 106, 109; Muḥaqqiq, *Mukhtaṣar*, 59.

[24] 'Allāma, *Taḥrīr*, 69.

some variant of the root ʿ *d l*. Al-Shaykh al-Mufīd (d. 413/1022) and al-Sharīf al-Murtaḍā (d. 436/1044) both demanded positive virtues: *ṣiyāna, nazāha, taqī, ʿafīf*. According to ʿAllāma, Ibn Idrīs did not specify *ʿadāla*. But that was misreading or misrepresentation for Ibn Idrīs had in fact demanded *ʿadāla aw ḥukmuhu*. The only writers that ʿAllāma finally adduced in favour of his opinion were ʿAlī ibn Bābūya and his son al-Ṣadūq, of the generation prior to Ṭūsī. Even there the evidence was negative: they did not specify *ʿadāla*, but nor did they specify the absence of this quality: it was not for them an issue. In the face of an immense weight of tradition ʿAllāma chose to deny that *ʿadāla* was a condition required in the recipient of *zakāt*. Avoidance of *kabāʾir* was necessary but not absence of *fisq*.[25]

The point was obviously thought important, and the law was obviously uncertain and susceptible to modification. That modification was achieved again not by appeal to revelation or *ijmāʿ*, rather by asserting (unconvincingly ?) the absence of *ijmāʿ* and by appeal to the dicta of earlier jurists. ʿAllāma for reasons which are not immediately apparent wished to deny that *ʿadāla* was a condition for receiving *zakāt*. To that end he searched the sources for justification. It is manifest that his opinion was not forced upon him by the overwhelming evidence of acceptable *uṣūl*.

Shahīd II also treated the question of *ʿadāla* as a contentious issue. In the *Masālik al-Ifhām* he put forward a novel argument. All the Imāmī *fuqahāʾ* accepted that children of *muʾminīn* may be given *zakāt* to the exclusion of children of *kuffār*. Shahīd II noted that children may not possess the qualities of either *ʿadl* or *fisq*. If they do not possess *ʿadl* they should not receive *zakāt*. But everyone agrees they should receive *zakāt*. Therefore *ʿadl* cannot be a condition.[26] The logic is fair enough but the reader is not convinced that he was led to his opinion by the logic, rather his opinion required justification.

Shahīd II's commentary on the *Lumʿa* (of Shahīd I) apropos of *ʿadāla* may be given in abbreviated form as illustrative of a manner of juridical argument.

> [Shahīd I said] *ʿadāla* is to be considered in other than the *muʾallafa* . . . and it is said (*qīla*) that that which is to be considered is only avoidance of *kabāʾir*.
>
> [Shahīd II added]: as to the *muʾallafa* it is because their *kufr* prevents *ʿadāla* . . .
>
> Consideration of *ʿadāla* in the *ʿāmil* is generally agreed (*mawḍiʿ al-wifāq*).
>
> As to the consideration of *ʿadāla* in the others, that is only one of various views, though Murtaḍā claimed *ijmaʿ* . . .
>
> Some stipulate [only] avoidance of *kabāʾir* even if the *ṣaghāʾir* lead to the designation *fisq*. That is because of the text (*naṣṣ*) which denies [*zakāt*] to a wine-drinker . . . ; it does not indicate a general denial to *fāsiqs*. Other *kabāʾir* have been added [to wine-drinking] by a process of *musāwāt* (ʿ equalization ʾ). That, however, is a matter for consideration since *musāwāt* is denied and *qiyās* rejected by the Imāmīs . . . If *ʿadāla* were to be considered children would be denied *zakāt* . . .[27]

Shahīd II like ʿAllāma wanted only *kabāʾir* to be taken into consideration as denying the right to *zakāt*. He argued that *ijmāʿ*, though it had been claimed, had never existed on this issue; he questioned the interpretation of a revealed text by earlier *fuqahāʾ*; and he worried about children who might have to be

[25] *idem*, *Mukhtalif*, II, 11; cf. Ibn Idrīs, *Sarāʾir*, 106.
[26] Shahīd II, *Masālik*, I, 61.
[27] *idem*, *Rawḍa*, 50. Denial of *qiyās* was a well-established slogan of Imāmī jurisprudence.

denied *zakāt*. Commendable care for the welfare of children and for the precise meaning and exegesis of the sources may have been the only factors which led him to his conclusion; the argument, however, may also and perhaps better be understood as *post facto* justification of an opinion which emerged for other reasons.

While the precise motivation behind ʿAllāma's and Shahīd II's argumentation cannot be discerned it may none the less be remarked that removal of *ʿadāla* as a condition broadened the scope of patronage of those who distributed *zakāt*—the *fuqahā'*. Further, again, from Ṭūsī to Shahīd II there was a change in the underlying vision of the community. Ṭūsī's writings implied a community of believers (*mu'minīn*), whose actions were in accord with their faith (*ʿadāla*), a community without a formal bureaucratic or military class. Shahīd II's believers were acknowledged as participants in the community even if their actions did not reach the high standards of *ʿadāla*. He stressed the general authority of the *fuqahā'* over the bureaucratic and military classes. This view confirms the illegitimate non-*sharʿī* nature of Ṣafavid rule, while proposing that most of the people within the Ṣafavid state—insofar as they were Shīʿīs—might be brought within the ambit of practical *sharʿī* politics; or at least, in this context, they would be subject to those elements of clerical control and patronage implied in the theory of *zakāt*. The *fuqahā'* might hope within the community to exercise at least a part of the authority they conceived themselves to possess, and to make this a basis for consolidation and expansion of their practical control of affairs.

For both Sunnīs and Shīʿīs *niyya* (intention) [28] is an essential element in the attainment of religious reward (*jazā'*/*ijzā'*). ʿAllāma stated that if a man gave away all his wealth and forgot *niyya* he gained no *ijzā'*.[29] Shāfiʿī explained that since *ṣadaqa* might be either incumbent (*farḍ*) or voluntary (*taṭawwuʿ*) it is not permissible that a man gain *ijzā'* for distributing *zakāt* (the *farḍ*) except he express *niyya* to the effect that it is such.[30] *Niyya* thus for him distinguished the formal ritual of *zakāt* from superorogatory alms-giving. There was at least one modification to the requirement of *niyya*, namely that if the *wālī* (governor) took *zakāt* from a person without his consent that person still gained *ijzā'*. Shāfiʿī was led from there to conclude:

> If the *wālī* takes from a man his *zakāt*, whether the man at that point does or does not express *niyya*, whether the man is willing or otherwise, whether the *wālī* expresses *niyya* or not, it provides *ijzā'* for the donor; just as *ijzā'* is procured in the matter of distribution of *zakāt* whether the one who distributes it is his (the donor's) *walī* (= agent) or the sultan.

Shāfiʿī, however, does not in his *furūʿ* provide for an unjust sultan; the implication is that the *zakāt* will reach its legitimate recipients. He added that it was preferable that the individual should undertake his own distribution so as to be sure about the correct discharge of the duty of *zakāt*.[31]

Māwardī stated that payment of *zakāt* (on *ẓāhir* goods) [32] to the *wālī* might be either *wājib* or *mustaḥabb*; it was a matter of *ikhtilāf*.[33] That was rather

[28] See for *niyya* Schacht, *Introduction to Islamic law*, Oxford, 1964, 116–18.
[29] ʿAllāma, *Taḥrīr*, 67.
[30] Shāfiʿī, *Umm*, I, 18–19.
[31] ibid., 19.
[32] For the distinction between *ẓāhir* and *bāṭin* goods, see Aghnides, op. cit., 296–7.
[33] Māwardī, op. cit., 195.

different from Shāfi'ī who had not expressed the problem in these terms and who had considered it preferable in any case for an individual to distribute *zakāt* himself. Māwardī acknowledged that if the ultimate distribution was unjust (not in accord with the law) the individual should not in fact pay his *zakāt* to the *'āmil* but should hide it, or, if it was taken willy nilly, should repeat the *zakāt* in order to gain reward.[34] Nawawī (d. 676/1277–8) in the *Minhāj al-Ṭālibīn* admitted that, while an individual might distribute *zakāt* himself or through his *wakīl*, it was better for him to give the *zakāt* to the *imām* (i.e. *de facto* ruler) unless he was *jā'ir*.[35] The commentary on this by Shirbīnī (d. 977/1569–70) though complex, is illuminating on the tendency of Sunnī legal theory to acknowledge the authority even of tyrants (*jā'irīn*).

> *Ẓāhir* goods [may be distributed by individuals] according to the new view, [which is derived] by *qiyās* from [the situation of] *bāṭin* goods [which may at all times be distributed by individuals]; the old view is that it is incumbent to deliver [*zakāt* on *ẓāhir* goods] to the *imām* or his *nā'ib* because of . . . (Q 9.103) . . . The apparent view [arising from the qur'ānic verse] is that it is incumbent. This [is the case even] if he (the *imām*) does not demand it. If he does demand it, it is incumbent to surrender it to him even if he is *jā'ir*, as a display of obedience . . . The *jā'ir imām* is joined to the others in this rule because of the prevailing of his authority and because of his not being dismissed for *jawr*. For, if they refused to surrender it to him he would fight them, even if they claimed that they would deliver it to the recipients themselves, because of their refusal to display obedience.[36]

Here it is unambiguously stated that it is incumbent to pay *zakāt* to the ruler even if the ruler is *jā'ir*. His *jawr* would imply that the *zakāt* thus paid might not reach its *shar'ī* recipients, it remained valid *zakāt*. On *niyya* Shirbīnī acknowledged that it was required, for *ijzā'*, at the moment of payment to the sultan. However, there was a variant view:

> The donor [who pays the sultan without expressing *niyya*] gains *ijzā'* because custom indicates that what the sultan takes and distributes to the recipients is nothing other than incumbent *zakāt*. This custom removes from this religious duty the requirement of *niyya*.[37]

Here Shāfi'ī's original argument for the necessity of *niyya*—to distinguish between the *farḍ* and the *nāfila*—is turned back to front. Since Shirbīnī deems it incumbent to pay the *zakāt* (*farḍ*) to the sultan (even if he is *jā'ir*) that payment becomes itself the sign of its being the *zakāt* (*farḍ*) and it no longer has to be distinguished by *niyya*.

The various views here distinguished within Shāfi'ī *fiqh* may not represent a strictly chronological development: they may have existed side by side for some time in the works of other writers and other schools. They represent, however, a spectrum of possibilities wherein at one extreme the right and duty of the individual to gain reward for himself by paying *zakāt* is stressed while at the other extreme this right is removed and transferred to the ruler. In the view of Shirbīnī the mere collection of taxes by a tyrant ruler (who might not assess them correctly or distribute them justly), constituted *zakāt*. Neither the

[34] ibid., 209.
[35] In M. ibn al-Khaṭīb al-Shirbīnī, *Mughnī al-Muḥtāj fī sharḥ al-Minhāj*, 4 vols., Cairo, 1308, I, 402.
[36] ibid.
[37] ibid., 403.

donor nor the sultan was required to undertake *niyya*. Yet the donor gained *ijzā'*. This was nothing more than a bald assertion that religious reward was gained by mere submission to the *de facto* power of the actual ruler. His deviation from the ideal (*jawr*) did not preclude the fact that what was put into effect was a sufficient approximation to the *sharī'a* for the members of the political community to gain religious reward. The effect was certainly to render sacred (*shar'ī*) the ordinary acts of the people (who paid) but it also rendered sacred the political acts of the ruler (who exacted). The whole was an expression of the support of the religious classes for the *de facto* power and may be thought to symbolize a general Sunnī tendency to acknowledge or promote the legitimate (*shar'ī*) rule of the actual governors.[38]

For the Imāmīs, while the *imām* is present *zakāt* should be paid to him or his *su'āt* or might possibly be distributed by the donor himself. According to Ṭūsī when the *su'āt* do not come or at a time when there is no *imām* (the Ghayba) it is incumbent on the donor to undertake the distribution of *zakāt* by himself. He should not pay *zakāt* to the *sulṭān al-jawr*: ومتى لم يات السعاة او يكون فى وقت لا يكون فيه امام فعلى رب المال ان يتولى تفرقتها بنفسه ولا يدفعها الى سلطان الجور. This was qualified, however, by the acknowledgement that the donor might distribute through his own *wakīl*. If the individual undertook distribution without the intermediation of the *imām* or the *sā'ī*—as must be the case during the Ghayba—it was thought better not to appoint a *wakīl* because the individual could be sure of his own actions but only doubtful about the actions of others. On the other hand, it was permissible to deliver *zakāt* to a trustworthy member of the Shī'ī fraternity and in fact it was better (*afḍal*) to hand it over to the '*ulamā'* because they were more knowledgeable about the ' places ' of *zakāt* (i.e. the appropriate recipients).[39] There is some confusion here as it is thought ' better ' not to appoint a *wakīl*; and yet ' better ' to pay through the ' *ulamā*. Since the *imām* was absent and the *sā'ī* not relevant to the Ghayba, the role of the '*ulamā'* can best be explained (?) as trustworthy *wakīl* to the donor.

In spite of this there is for the Buyid period some evidence that the *faqīh* was already seen as to some extent replacing the *imām*. According to Murtaḍā:

> It is better to disburse *zakāt* . . . to the *imām* or his *khulafā'* representing him; and if that is impossible it is related that it should be disbursed to trustworthy *fuqahā'*.[40]

And for Mufīd:

> God has made it a duty for the *umma* to carry *zakāt* to the prophet or the *imām*, his *khalīfa*, . . . ; if the *khalīfa* is absent the duty is to carry it to one of the *khalīfa*'s associates appointed by him; and if the *sufarā'* between him and his people are not available it is incumbent to carry it to the trustworthy *fuqahā'*.[41]

The incumbency there suggested by Mufīd was not afterwards accepted. None the less it was obviously considered preferable in Buyid times that *zakāt* should be transferred to its recipients via the *fuqahā'*. It is apparent from the remarks of Murtaḍā and Mufīd that in some undefined way they took over in this field

[38] cf. Calder, art. cit., and sources cited *ad* notes 8 and 9.
[39] See for all this, Ṭūsī, *Nihāya*, 185; *Mabsūṭ*, *zakāt*, 13 (*ad niyya*), 16, 20.
[40] Al-Sharīf al-Murtaḍā, *Jumal al-'ilm wa'l-'amal*, with commentary by Ibn al-Barrāj, Mashad, 1974, 269.
[41] Cit. in 'Allāma, *Mukhtalif*, II, 16. (This text is only available to me in this rather late compendium.)

the role of the *imām* or his representatives. They were not themselves, however, referred to as representatives of the *imām* but rather as a kind of residual authority which became effective precisely in the absence of representatives. Ṭūsī's detailed *furū'* provided for distribution either through the *imām* or his *sā'ī* (both absent or *sāqiṭ*) or the *wakīl* of the donor. Presumably the *faqīh* acted as *wakīl* to the donor.

Muḥaqqiq, too, specified only three possible distributors: the *imām*, the *'āmil* and the donor. In the absence of the *imām*, *zakāt* was to be paid to a reliable Imāmī *faqīh* for he was more cognisant of its 'places'.[42] Since the *faqīh* was neither *imām* nor *sā'ī* (that category was *sāqiṭ* according to Muḥaqqiq) he must again have acted as *wakīl* to the donor.[43] The *faqīh*, however, even if his role was formally identifiable only as *wakīl* to the donor, performed the same functions as the *sā'ī* who was direct appointee of the *imām*. The impingement of some confusion on Muḥaqqiq's thought may be illustrated by a comparison of a particular remark in the *Sharā'i' al-Islām* and its parallel in the (later) *Mukhtaṣar*.

(*Sharā'i'*): اذا قبض الامام او الساعي الزكاة برئت ذمة المالك ولو تلفت

(*Mukhtasar*): اذا قبض الامام او الفقيه برئت ذمة المالك ولو تلفت

'If the *imām* or the *sā'ī/faqīh* takes the *zakāt* the donor's duty is fulfilled even if the goods subsequently perish.'[44]

Muḥaqqiq was beginning to see the *faqīh* as taking on the function of the *sā'ī*, direct representative of the *imām*.

'Allāma reaffirmed in his *Qawā'id al-Aḥkām* the traditional view. The *zakāt* might be paid to the *imām* (absent), the *'āmil* (still *sāqiṭ* ?), the poor (the recipient), or a *wakīl*. During the Ghayba it should (*yustaḥabb*) be paid to a *faqīh*.[45] Presumably again the *faqīh* acted as *wakīl* (to the donor). In the *Taḥrir*, however, 'Allāma complicated the issue by specifying not four but five modes of distribution. It might be passed either directly to the recipient, or to the *sā'ī*, or the *wālī* (= *imām*), or the *wakīl*, or, and this is new, the *ḥākim*.[46] It is known that during the Ghayba the *ḥākim* was a *faqīh* acting as direct appointee of the absent *imām*.[47] Earlier assessment had not distinguished the role of the *faqīh* in distributing *zakāt* from the role of a *wakīl* to the donor. 'Allāma's list at least suggests that the *faqīh* acted by right of his representation of the absent *imām*. The period was obviously one of transition. Both Muḥaqqiq and 'Allāma considered that *zakāt* should be paid to the *fuqahā'*. There was some doubt as to in what capacity the latter undertook to receive and distribute the *zakāt*.

According to Shahīd I:

يجب دفعها الى الامام مع الطلب بنفسه او بساعيه وقيل وكذا الى الفقيه ودفعها اليهم ابتداء افضل وقيل يجب

(*a*) It is incumbent to pay *zakāt* to the *imām* on demand whether by himself or through his *sā'ī*.
(*b*) It is said, likewise to the *faqīh*.
(*c*) Payment to those (all of them ?) voluntarily is preferable.
(*d*) It is said, incumbent.[48]

That represents considerable change. Rule (*a*) was traditional. Rule (*b*) was a

[42] Muḥaqqiq, *Sharā'i'*, I, 164–5.
[43] cf. *idem*, *Mukhtaṣar*, 60.
[44] ibid., and *Sharā'i'*, I, 165.
[45] 'Allāma, *Qawā'id*, 23.
[46] *idem*, *Taḥrīr*, 67.
[47] cf. Calder, art. cit.
[48] Shahīd I, in *Rawḍa*, 50.

direct transferral to the *faqīh* of authority which traditionally belonged to the *imām* or his *sāʿī*. The *faqīh* had a right to demand *zakāt* and it was incumbent to pay him. The justification of that view was obscured in the anonymous *qīla*. Rule (*c*) was again not novel: it had always been thought preferable to distribute *zakāt* through a *faqīh*. Rule (*d*) suggested it might be incumbent; again, the anonymous *qīla*. Shahīd I thus produced a ruling whereby *zakāt* could be a compulsory tax, administered not by the government but by the *fuqahāʾ*. Mufīd, it is true, some three and a half centuries previously, had already stated something rather like this but that statement had proved premature: it had not found general acceptance. Centuries of legal effort and a gradual refinement of the concept of clerical authority had provided a context, a structure and a justification which made Shahīd I's assessment seem both appropriate and convincing.

Shahīd II witnessed from his base in Ottoman Syria the establishment of Shīʿism as the official religion of Ṣafavid Persia. That did not represent the official implementation of the *sharīʿa* but it offered opportunities and inspired a comprehensive analysis of the nature and extent of the *faqīh*'s authority. Shahīd II's commentary on Muḥaqqiq's *Sharāʾiʿ*, with regard to *zakāt*, may be described as an incorporation of the *faqīh* into all those rules which for Muḥaqqiq had been relevant only to the *imām* or the *sāʿī*. The clarity and integrity of his view, however, is best appreciated in *Al-Rawḍat al-Bahiyya*.

> It is necessary to pay *zakāt* to the *imām* if he demands it in person or through his *sāʿī*, because of the necessity of obedience. It is said it is necessary to pay it to the *faqīh sharʿī* during the Ghayba if he demands it whether in person or through his *wakīl*, because he is *nāʾib* to the *imām* like the *sāʿī*, indeed stronger (*li-annahu nāʾib al-imām ka l-sāʿī bal aqwā*).
>
> If the donor refuses (*khalafa*) and distributes the *zakāt* himself he gains no *ijzāʾ* because of the refusal (to pay the *faqīh*) which corrupts his act of worship (*liʾl-nahy al-mufsida* (*sic*) *liʾl-ʿibāda*). To pay it to them voluntarily without demand is better because they are more knowledgeable of its 'places' . . . It is said . . . it is incumbent to pay, without demand, the *imām* or his *nāʾib* or, during the Ghayba, the *faqīh* . . . ; as proved by . . . (Q 9.103) . . ., for, rendering it compulsory for him (the *imām*) to collect requires that it be compulsory for them (the donors) to pay, and the *nāʾib* is like the *munawwib*. The more prevalent view (*al-ashhar*) is *istiḥbāb*.[49]

The more prevalent view is not necessarily Shahīd II's. This passage asserts categorically that the *faqīh* may demand *zakāt* and if he demands it, it is incumbent to pay him. He may demand it in person or through his *wakīl*. So it is envisaged that the *faqīh* may send out tax-collecting deputies to collect *zakāt*. It might be incumbent to pay *zakāt* to a *faqīh* even if he does not actually demand it. Shahīd II justifies this view with a qurʾānic quotation and with the assertion that the *nāʾib* is like the *munawwib*. That is, the *faqīh* (*nāʾib*) is like the *imām* (*munawwib*) and possesses accordingly all of his rights. The two propositions rendered available in that passage, that the *faqīh* is *nāʾib* to the *imām* and that the *nāʾib* is like the *munawwib* constitute the foundation of Shahīd II's vision of the execution of the *sharīʿa*. The seeds of that vision were not absent in Buyid times but it took almost six centuries for the full implications of the *imām's* absence to become clear. The Buyid *fuqahāʾ* perceiving that their interests were bound up with the preservation of the *sharīʿa* as ideal, free from

[49] Shahīd II, *Rawḍa*, 50.

involvement with the *de facto* power, had declared several aspects of the *sharī'a sāqiṭ*.[50] By the time of Shahīd II it had been perceived that most of the *sāqiṭ* functions should in fact be under the control of the *faqīh*. That development probably reflects a real consolidation of authority under tolerant governments and was fostered by the elusive possibility of actually forming a ' state ' subject to *shar'ī* rules and governed by the clerical class.

It will be noted that as the *faqīh* asserted his right to administer *zakāt* the individual lost his right to distribute it himself. It was gradually perceived that the authority delegated by Ja'far al-Ṣādiq to the *fuqahā'* covered not only strictly judicial activities but also control of *zakāt*. This was only part of a gradual process whereby most of the *sāqiṭ* functions of the *imām* were brought into the sphere of *qaḍa'*. That process, while enhancing the authority of the clerical classes, restricted the degree of participation of the non-clerical individual in his own salvation. Some indications in early texts (Ṭūsī, Ibn Idrīs) that the individual might be personally responsible for the fulfilment of the religious duty of *zakāt* were overlaid and finally removed by the imperatives of clerical control.

A similar process was evident in Sunnī sources.[51] There, the right to collect and distribute granted to the accepted *shar'ī* executive, the *de facto* ruler, pre-empted the right of the individual to assess and distribute for himself. For the Shī'īs the accepted *shar'ī* executive was manifestly not the *de facto* ruler but the *faqīh*. The developments in Sunnī theory, it has been shown, were accompanied by a removal of the need for *niyya* on the part of the donor. A parallel process may be discerned in Imāmī Shī'ī jurisprudence.

According to Ṭūsī, *zakāt* might be paid either through the *wakīl* of the donor or through the *imām/sā'ī*. In the former case both the donor and the *wakīl* were required to express *niyya* : if either of the two neglected it there was no *ijzā'*. In the latter case, a merely theoretical possibility, the donor had to express *niyya*, but not, necessarily, the *imām*. If, however, the *imām* took *zakāt* by force, then the unwilling donor gained *ijzā'*.[52] *Niyya* then during the Ghayba—when the *imām* cannot take *zakāt* forcibly—is absolutely essential on the part of the donor and is required twice if the *zakāt* is paid through a *wakīl*. The *faqīh* in Buyid times was probably thought of as *wakīl*, in precisely this sense. 'Allāma in his *Taḥrīr* agreed with Ṭūsī. In the *Mukhtalif*, he disagreed. Where payment was effected through a *wakīl*, *niyya* was required only once, either by the *wakīl* or the donor, not both. When payment was effected through the *imām/sā'ī* 'Allāma denied any distinction between compulsory and voluntary donation : in either case *niyya* was not required on the part of the donor.[53] It thus fell, for 'Allāma, that whether the *faqīh* as distributor of *zakāt* was *wakīl* to the donor or *nā'ib* to the *imām*, the burden of *niyya* could be removed from the donor and transferred to the *faqīh*. The religious reward (*ijzā'*) of the individual might be vicariously acquired simply by his submission to the authority of the clerical class.

According to Shahīd II :

تجب النية فى (زكاة) الفطرة وفى الماليـة من المالك او من وكيلـه عند الدفع الى المستحق او وكيله عموما كالامـام ونائبه عامـا او خاصا او خصوصا كوكيلـه ولو لم ينو المـالك عند دفعها الى غير المستحق ووكيله الخـاص فنوى القابض عند دفعها اليه أجزى.

[50] See note 9 above.
[51] Above, p. 473.
[52] Ṭūsī, *Mabsūṭ*, *zakāt*, 13 ; cf. Shāfi'ī, *Umm*, I, 19 ; another example of Shāfi'ī's influence on Imāmī *furū'* ; cf. notes 11 and 21 above.
[53] 'Allāma, *Taḥrīr*, 67 ; *Mukhtalif*, II, 21.

Though complex, both the terminology and the content of that passage are illuminating. It may be analysed as follows:

(*a*) *Niyya* is incumbent with regard to *zakāt al-fiṭra* and *zakāt al-māl.*
(*b*) (It is incumbent) from either the donor or his *wakīl* (not both).
(*c*) (It is incumbent) at the time of payment to the recipient or to his (the recipient's) *wakīl.*
(*d*) (The recipient's *wakīl* may be) *'umūm*, in a general way, i.e. the *imām* or his *nā'ib 'āmm* or his *nā'ib khāṣṣ.*
(*e*) (Or the recipient's *wakīl* may be) *khuṣūṣ*, that is, his (own personal) *wakīl.*
(*f*) If the donor does not express *niyya* on payment to anyone other than the recipient himself or the recipient's personal *wakīl*
(*g*) (i.e. if the donor fails to express *niyya* when he pays to the *imām* or the *nā'ib 'āmm* or the *nā'ib khāṣṣ*) and if the receiver subsequently expresses *niyya* on disbursement he (the donor) gains reward.[54]

It is here confirmed that if the donor pays through the *faqīh* (the *nā'ib 'āmm* of the *imām*)—and according to Shahīd II it is incumbent that he in fact do just that—he need not undertake *niyya* because he will gain reward on the basis of the *faqīh*'s *niyya* when he distributes the *zakāt.* Just as the Sunnī's religious reward depended finally simply on submission to the authority of the *de facto* governor, the Imāmī's religious reward depended simply on submission to the authority of the clerical class. They depicted themselves as responsible for the collection and distribution of *zakāt*; they further analysed the tax-situation in such a way that their control of *zakāt* was uncircumscribed by the rights or duties of donors. The donor became most certain of reward by unqualified surrender of his *zakāt* to the *fuqahā'*. The *faqīh* in this assessment of *zakāt*-distribution was seen to be not *wakīl* to the donor but *wakīl* to the recipient, a position acquired by virtue of his status as *nā'ib* to the *imām.*

The *fuqahā'* were permitted to distribute the *zakāt* in a rather arbitrary fashion. It was preferable (*mustaḥabb*) to pay something to each of the eight recipient categories. But it was not incumbent to deal equally with each group, in fact it was better to give preference to the 'superior', *bal al-afḍal tafḍīl al-murajjaḥ.* That, from Shahīd II, should be compared with his incorporation of the clerical class into the recipient categories of *fuqarā'* and *masākīn.*[55] It is permissible to pay the *zakāt* to only one of the eight categories or even to only one individual within a category. Further it was permissible to provide *ighnā'*, that is to provide more than a sufficiency: there were no limits to how much could be given as long as it was paid at one time.[56] The *fuqahā'* gave themselves a great deal of discretionary power in utilizing and distributing the taxes, payment of which to them they thought incumbent.

The locution *nā'ib 'āmm* which emerged in Shahīd II's discussion of *zakāt* had first appeared in the works of 'Alī ibn Ḥusayn al-Karakī[57] where, too, it was explicitly contrasted with the term *nā'ib khāṣṣ.*[58] The first of these terms designates a fully-qualified *faqīh*, sharing in the judicial authority delegated to

[54] Shahīd II, *Rawḍa*, 51.
[55] Above, p. 470.
[56] Shahīd II, *Rawḍa*, 50–1.
[57] For whom, see Khwānṣārī, *Rawḍāt al-Jannāt*, Tehran, 1306, 402–7; E. Glassen, 'Schah Isma'il und die Theologen seiner Zeit', *Der Islam*, 48, 1971–2.
[58] Karakī, *Jāmi'*, 130–1, *ad* Friday Prayer; see also *ad jihād*, 187. The definition of *nā'ib khāṣṣ* given by A. K. S. Lambton, op. cit., 181, footnote, reflects a later development. The use of the term *nā'ib khāṣṣ* in the *Risāla Jihādiyya* is certainly to be understood as a reference to the pre-Ghayba period, or to the *sufarā'*, Kohlberg, 'The development of the Imāmī Shī'ī doctrine of *jihād*', *ZDMG*, 1976, 82–6.

the *fuqahā'* by Ja'far al-Ṣādiq. The second term, *nā'ib khāṣṣ*, would appear to indicate the same entity as was in early Imāmī juristic works designated *man naṣabahu al-imām*, that is, a contemporary of the *imām*, or possibly the four *sufarā'*. This distinction in the typology of *niyāba*, once it emerged, was exploited, particularly by Shahīd II in his *al-Rawḍat al-Bahiyya*, for its remarkable explanatory and justificatory value within the structure of juristic argument.

The idea of the *faqīh* as *nā'ib 'āmm* to the absent *imām* became a key element in a juristic structure which denied *shar'ī* legitimacy to secular powers, while affirming the ultimate right of the clerical class to implement the *sharī'a* and promoting in practice their financial independence from the government. This was a doctrine of potential resistance, significantly different from that which existed in Buyid times,[59] but it may not be naïvely interpreted as a revolutionary theory. For, incorporated within the juristic framework of the theory were elements permitting or promoting accommodation between the ruler and the religious classes.[60] (The elaboration of the *sharī'a* in Islam was always based on the juxtaposition of formally discrete units in such a way that the full meaning of one unit only becomes clear when the various qualifications implicit or explicit in the framing of other units are taken into consideration.) Different jurists at different times laid varying stress on the notions of illegitimate government or legitimate clerical aspirations or modes of accommodation. But in general the practical result of the Imāmī theory was neither clerical rule nor necessarily clerical rebelliousness (though the latter was not unknown, and the former always possible): the Imāmī *fuqahā'* were, however, stronger, richer, and significantly more influential in the state than their Sunnī counterparts. The events of the early Ṣafavid period, and especially the biography of al-Karakī, may be thought to confirm that it was the accommodatory aspects of the *sharī'a* which were generally most relied on to promote the interest of the Imāmī faith and to enhance the power and influence of the clerical class.[61]

[59] Above, p. 469.

[60] See my forthcoming study, ' Accommodation and revolution in Imāmī Shī'ī jurisprudence : Khumaynī and the classical tradition '.

[61] I should like to thank Professor A. K. S. Lambton and Dr. John Wansbrough for their helpful suggestions in the preparation of this study.

XVIII

KHUMS IN IMĀMĪ SHĪ'Ī JURISPRUDENCE, FROM THE TENTH TO THE SIXTEENTH CENTURY A.D.

Khums was, like *zakāt*, a ritual duty incumbent on individuals, a *farīḍa 'alā l-'ayn*. Distinguished from the other *'ibādāt* by being as to immediate aim human rights and not divine ones (*ḥaqq li'l-ādamiyyīn* not *ḥaqq li'llāh*) the final aim of both *khums* and *zakāt* was none the less divine reward and more certain salvation. The qur'ānic basis for *khums* was found in the verse (8 : 41):

> Know that whatever you acquire as material gain a fifth belongs to God and to the Prophet and to those related and the orphans and the poor and the wayfarers.

The Imāmī *fuqahā'*, notwithstanding an early- or pre-Būyid assertion of a five-part division, generally inferred from this a six-part division of *khums*. After the death of the Prophet three parts belonged to the *imām* and the other three parts to the poor, orphans and *abnā' al-sabīl* of the Banī Hāshim. With respect to the last three categories, except for an isolated *taraddud* expressed by Muḥaqqiq,[1] *īmān* (Imāmī faith) was a condition required in the recipients. *'Adāla* was not generally required. Need (*fuqr*) was specified in all three categories. Ṭūsī alone was doubtful if *fuqr* was required in orphans; subsequent *fuqahā'* considered that it was. The ' wayfarers ' were deserving if they were in need during their journey even if they had a sufficiency in their homeland.

Whereas for Sunnīs *khums* was a concept applicable only to booty gained in war, the qur'ānic phrase *mā ghanimtum min shay'* was taken by the Imāmīs to refer to seven categories of goods. These categories did not change through the centuries. Those cited by Shaykh-i Bahā'ī (d. 1013/1604–5) are exactly the same as those provided by Muḥaqqiq and were all available in a slightly less systematic form in Ṭūsī's *Nihāya*. They are, from 'Allāma's *Qawā'id*: (1) booty taken in war; (2) minerals; (3) treasure-trove; (4) what is taken from the sea (pearls or treasure); (5) the profits of trade, agriculture and craft (*tijārāt, ṣinā'āt, zirā'āt*); (6) Dhimmī land if bought from a Muslim; (7) *ḥalāl* goods mixed with *ḥarām*. Category 5 was subject to *al-ḥawl*, i.e. it was an annual tax. There was considerable *ikhtilāf* on the question of *naṣāb* as applicable to categories 2, 3, or 4. *Khums* was due on booty taken in war only when the war was legitimate and that, according to Ṭūsī, had not occurred since the time of 'Alī.[2] With the gradual reassessment of *jihād* as legally viable during the Ghayba [3] it is possible that *khums* on booty became also potentially not actually viable.

As long as the *imām* was present he was personally responsible for distributing *khums*. There were no restrictions on what he might do with his own shares; he might spend them on whatever he wished, family expenses, whatever burdens he had to bear (*mā yalzimuhu min taḥammul al-athqāl*), or providing for others (*ma'ūnat ghayrihi*), etc. The remaining three shares he should distribute to the appropriate Banī Hāshim recipient categories according to

[1] For the Imāmī jurists mentioned in this study see N. Calder, ' *Zakāt* in Imāmī Shī'ī jurisprudence ', *BSOAS*, XLIV, 3, 1981, 468–80, *ad* n. 8.

[2] Ṭūsī, *Mabsūṭ, jihād*, 9; all works of Imāmī *fiqh* mentioned in this study are cited with details in Calder, op. cit., loc. cit.

[3] cf. A. K. S. Lambton, ' A nineteenth century view of *jihād* ', *SI*, XXXII, 1970; and E. Kohlberg, ' The development of the Imāmī Shī'ī doctrine of Jihād ', *ZDMG*, 1976.

their needs and annual expenses calculated on a basis of moderation (*iqtiṣād*). It was thought that if there was a surplus after disbursement to the recipients then it belonged exclusively to the *imām*: *kāna lahu khāṣṣatan.* Conversely if there was a deficiency he must make it up from his own wealth (? share of *khums*): وان نقص كان عليه ان يتم من حصة خاصته. If that meant that he was bound to use his share of the *khums* to provide for deficiencies in the recipients' shares there was some logical inconsistency in Ṭūsī's statements, since he had also stated that the *imām* might do with his share whatever he wished. The question was to become controversial.[4]

Anfāl was a term used by Imāmī *fuqahā'* to indicate goods which belonged exclusively to the *imām*. Amongst those were various types of land and material wealth as well as the *imām*'s share of *khums*. Usufruct of the *imām*'s property without his permission was thought rebellious. The *imāms*, however, had provided their followers during the Ghayba with a dispensation (*tarkhīṣ*) as to *manākiḥ*, *masākin* and *matājir*. There was considerable speculation as to the meaning of that dispensation. The idea emerged that Imāmīs alone were permitted to trade in certain goods which ideally belonged exclusively to the *imām*.[5] The dispensation did not include Sunnīs; so their trading in such goods confirmed them in rebellion. Both Ibn Idrīs and 'Allāma added to their assessment of that dispensation: 'let none imagine that if he make a profit in such trade he should not extract the *khums*'. The dispensation in other words did not effect the operation of *khums*. It provided a legitimate basis for the daily life of the Shī'a, while emphasizing the essential rebelliousness of Sunnī activities. *Khums* as a tax remained valid even in the absence of the *imām*.

Ṭūsī was uncertain about what should be done with *khums* during the Ghayba and pointed to the absence of a specific revealed text on this matter. He suggested four possibilities.

1. All goods are to be considered in the same way as *masākin*, *matājir*, etc. That is, a waiving of *khums* completely in view of the recorded dispensation. This view was dismissed as being opposed to *iḥtiyāṭ* ('caution') and constituting the usufruct of property without the owner's specific permission.

2. *Khums* is to be preserved as long as the donor is alive; when death approaches he should appoint as *waṣī* over the goods a reliable member of the Imāmī fraternity . . . and so on until the goods may be delivered to the *imām*.

3. *Khums* should be buried because the earth will disgorge what is in it on the advent of the *imām*.

4. *Khums* should be divided into six parts; the three parts belonging to the *imām* should be buried (= option 3) or consigned as *wadī'a* to someone trustworthy (= option 2). The other three parts should be distributed to the appropriate recipients.[6]

Ṭūsī then indicated very firmly his preference for option 4. He did not indicate who should undertake the distribution of the Banī Hāshim's share.[7] It is none the less highly probable that by virtue of their influence and their knowledge the *fuqahā'* were able for *khums* as for *zakāt* to exert considerable control over the matter of distribution. No role, however, at this stage was specifically asserted for the *fuqahā'* as such. Trustworthy Imāmīs (who might

[4] Ṭūsī, *Mabsūṭ*, *zakāt*, 20–1.
[5] Ibn Idrīs, *Sarā'ir*, 114–15; 'Allāma, *Qawā'id*, 24; *Taḥrīr*, 75.
[6] For *waṣiyya* and *wadī'a*, see Schacht, *Introduction to Islamic law*, Oxford, 1964, 119–20, 157.
[7] Ṭūsī, *Nihāya*, 200–1.

frequently be members of the clerical class) were under certain circumstances to look after but not to use the *imām*'s goods.

Ibn Idrīs is renowned in Imāmī biographical literature for his unmitigated attacks on Ṭūsī's *furū'*. Indeed scarcely a page of his *Sarā'ir al-Islām* does not contain some carping comment about Ṭūsī's inconsistency, his reliance on *akhbār aḥād,* his going beyond *ẓāhir al-tanzīl* or *'umūm al-āya,* his deviation from *barā'at al-dhimma.* In spite of this, large sections of Ṭūsī's *Nihāya* or *Mabsūṭ* were quoted verbatim by Ibn Idrīs. It is clear that Ṭūsī whether attacked or followed was the dominating influence. The discussion of *khums* in *Sarā'ir al-Islām* displays a polemic intensity rare in any Muslim juristic work and manifestly reflects a real contemporary concern for an issue not unapt to rouse controversy, namely, control of an extensive body of wealth. The centre of the controversy for Ibn Idrīs lay in the rule summed up by Ṭūsī as that, while the *imām* is present, if there is a surplus of the Banī Hāshim's share of *khums* it belongs exclusively to the *imām* and if there is a deficiency he must provide for it. According to Ibn Idrīs:

> If there is a surplus he [the *imām*) becomes the *ḥāfiẓ* and *mutawallī* for the preservation of that on their [the Banī Hāshim's] behalf. He may not appropriate any of it for himself for the right is theirs and he may not take any of their property.

Ibn Idrīs here was actually contradicting Ṭūsī and other earlier writers. This he acknowledged:

> [As for] that which is found in the writings of some of our companions to the effect that: the surplus belongs to the *imām* exclusively (*kāna lahu khāṣṣatan*) [— a quote from Ṭūsī]; the meaning of that is that the *imām* may look after it, protect it and manage it but he may not own it.

Ibn Idrīs defended his interpretation of his predecessors by adding a grammatical argument which suggested that it was or might be permissible to use terms indicating ownership to denote a relationship which was less than ownership. Having thus reinterpreted his predecessors he was enabled to state:

> There is no *khilāf* amongst Muslims in general nor among the Shī'a in particular that with regard to the shares of [the Banī Hāshim] . . . the *imām* has no right to any part of them, rather he has his shares and they have theirs.

That flagrant disregard of the 'plain' meaning of his predecessors' words Ibn Idrīs further defended by careful exegesis of the qur'ānic *naṣṣ* (Q 8: 41), which enabled him to claim the Qur'ān together with *ijmā'* as *dalīls* supporting his view. He acknowledged then that there were two Traditions in Ṭūsī's *Tahdhīb* which might support the opposite view but they were according to him *akhbār āḥād, mursal* not *musnad* and in the *isnād* of at least one of them there was a cursed *kāfir.* Since the generality of Traditions may be said to be in favour of separate ownership by the *imām* on the one hand and the Banī Hāshim on the other, Ibn Idrīs claimed in support of his view *sunna* as well as Qur'ān and *ijmā'.* To this he added *adillat al-'uqūl* in so far as it is not permissible to utilize without permission the property of another. That was a purely rational perception of right action.

To that four-part proof supporting his view Ibn Idrīs added *iḥtiyāṭ,* caution, with respect to *barā'at al-dhimma. Barā'at al-dhimma* refers to the most economic fulfilment of religious duty, without the addition of extra details which might be irrelevant or inimical to God's command. Caution, *iḥtiyāṭ*, requires the fulfilment of the command and the eschewing of extras.

> If there were in this matter only the way of *iḥtiyāṭ* with respect to *barā'at al-dhimma* it would suffice. For, the *dhimma* is dependent on the wealth [the *khums*] and its reaching its rightful owner; if the donor ensures that, then the fulfilment of his duty [*barā'at al-dhimma*] is certain but if he gives it to other than the owner then it is a matter of dispute and the fulfilment of his duty is not certain.

There, in fact, Ibn Idrīs betrayed his real concern: the problem was not whether the surplus from the Banī Hāshim's share belonged exclusively to the *imām* but what the donor was to do with his *khums* during the *Ghayba*. Ibn Idrīs wanted a strict separation of the *imām*'s share from the Banī Hāshim's share.

> We have not found any work by our companions in which after mentioning this problem he does not say . . . that half the *khums* should be bequeathed (*yūṣā*) to its owner [the *imām*] or preserved for its owner (*yuḥfaẓ*) or stored as *wadī'a* for its owner, with a variety of expressions. If these writers had desired that someone other than the *imām* should have a right to it during the Ghayba, or that it should be consigned to someone other than he, they would be contradicting themselves.

Ibn Idrīs desired that the *imām*'s share should not during the Ghayba be distributed to someone else, above all not to the Banī Hāshim; it was precisely the confusion of their share with the *imām*'s that he most inveighed against.[8] Presumably the opponents who called forth this extensive piece of polemic *fiqh* had advocated the distribution of *all* the *khums* to the Banī Hāshim, a view which in fact became explicit in the works of Muḥaqqiq.

When he came to discuss what precisely to do with the *khums* during the Ghayba, Ibn Idrīs followed, indeed paraphrased, Ṭūsī, indicating four possible options and his very decided preference for the fourth. Three parts should be distributed, the other three parts preserved, passed on, etc. Before leaving the subject Ibn Idrīs produced a flurry of lengthy quotations from Mufīd, Murtaḍā and Ṭūsī designed to illustrate that none of them suggested that the *imām*'s share during the Ghayba should be distributed to the Banī Hāshim.[9]

The evidence would seem to suggest that Ibn Idrīs was right: the earlier *fuqahā'* had suggested that the *imām*'s share of *khums* should be preserved as *waṣiyya* or *wadī'a* until the advent of the *imām*. Ibn Idrīs's polemic indicates the emergence of a novel contrary view that the *imām*'s share should also be distributed to the Banī Hāshim. That view was justified by exploitation of the unresolved ambiguity of expression of earlier *fuqaha'*: did the *imām* possess his share of the *khums* exclusively or was he required to provide from it for the deficiencies of the Banī Hāshim? The polemic suggests a struggle but the nature of the struggle remains unknown. It is probable that a certain income accrued to the clerical classes from both *zakāt* and *khums* throughout the Saljūq period. Part of that income was no doubt distributed in accord with the *sharī'a*, part of it certainly went into the upkeep of mosques and *madrasas* and personnel.[10] The technically unusable part of that income, the

[8] Ibn Idris, *Sarā'ir*, 114–15.
[9] ibid., 116–18.
[10] cf. e.g. 'Abd al-Jalīl Qazwīnī, *Kitāb al-Naqḍ*, ed. Muhaddith, Tehran, 1331/1952, 164.

imām's share of the *khums*, may have been stored as treasure in a mosque or shrine. That part, Ibn Idrīs suggested, should continue to be stored in perpetuity. The opposing group suggested it should be distributed to the Banī Hāshim recipients. That would be beneficial to the *fuqahā'* in general (if they were the distributors) as increasing their practical control of a usable body of wealth. It might have been particularly useful to those of the clerical class who were also Sayyids (Banī Hāshim).[11] Ideologically, any claim by the *fuqahā'* to control the *imām*'s share of *khums* differed from their control of *zakāt* in that *khums*, unlike *zakāt*, was legally the property of the *imām*. By claiming the right to distribute *khums* the *fuqahā'* asserted a certain relationship between themselves and the *imām*.

Muḥaqqiq followed Ṭūsī, and disregarded Ibn Idrīs, in acknowledging that while the *imām* was present any surplus in the Banī Hāshim's share became his, and any deficiency had to be supplied from his share.[12] This, not unnaturally, in view of Ibn Idrīs's polemic, was a preliminary to the production of a new option regarding what was to be done with the *khums* during the Ghayba. Muḥaqqiq cited the four options presented by Ṭūsī and Ibn Idrīs and added that the *imām*'s share too might be distributed to the Banī Hāshim. Justification for that view was of course that it was incumbent on the *imām* to supply any deficiency.[13] Both the premise and the conclusion had been denied by Ibn Idrīs. Muḥaqqiq confirmed his preference for the distribution of the *imām*'s share in the *Mukhtaṣar*.[14] He, like Ṭūsī and Ibn Idrīs before him, failed to specify who was to distribute the Banī Hāshim's share, but of the *imām*'s share he had this to say : يجب ان يتولى صرف حصة الامام فى الاصناف الموجودة من اليه الحكم بحق النيابة كما يتولى اداء ما يجب على الغائب. That passage is hardly perspicuous but the following translation is proposed :

> He must distribute the *imām*'s share . . . who possesses [judicial ?] authority by right of *niyāba* just as he undertakes fulfilment of what is incumbent on the absent [*imām*] ; [or : just as someone undertakes the duties incumbent on one who is absent (— a reference to *wakāla* ?)].[15]

That is admittedly tendentious but the ambiguity is Muḥaqqiq's. There is little doubt that the person in question was the *faqīh* but the tortuous reference to him reflects perhaps a real problem, namely, how to justify the clerical class's claim to administer wealth which unambiguously belonged to the *imām*. The implications of Muḥaqqiq's locution are that the acknowledged judicial *niyāba* had a general not a specific import. The *imāms* had delegated also to the *fuqahā'* control of their property or at least of the distribution of *khums*. A specific text (*khāṣṣ*) was perceived to have a more general (*ʿāmm*) denotation.

ʿAllāma in his *Taḥrīr* repeated verbatim regarding the distribution of *khums* Muḥaqqiq's *man ilayhi al-ḥukm bi-ḥaqq al-niyāba*.[16] In the *Qawāʿid*, however, he more bluntly asserted :

> ومع الغيبة . . . انما يتولى قسمة حقه عم الحاكم.
>
> During the Ghayba . . . the only one who may undertake the distribution of the *imām*'s share is the *ḥākim*.[17]

[11] For the relationship between *sayyids* and *ʿulamā'*, admittedly in a later period, see A. K. S. Lambton, ' The Persian *ʿulama'* and constitutional reform ', in *Le Shīʿisme imamite*, Colloque de Strasbourg, Paris, 1970, 164.

[12] Muḥaqqiq, *Shara'iʿ*, I, 182.

[13] ibid., 184.

[14] *idem*, *Mukhtaṣar*, 64.

[15] *idem*, *Sharā'iʿ*, I, 184.

[16] ʿAllāma, *Taḥrīr*, 74–5.

[17] *idem*, *Qawāʿid*, 44.

It was, in other words, the *faqīh* who qualified for the *ex ante* delegation of Ja'far al-Ṣādiq who had also a right to deal with and distribute the *imām*'s *khums*.[18] It was in his capacity as judge (*ḥākim, nā'ib al-imām*) that the *faqīh* distributed the *khums*. The superficial tendency of the jurisprudential argument was to assert the right of the *fuqahā'* because of the acknowledged delegation. It is not impossible that a *de facto* or generally accepted control of *khums* by the *fuqahā'* made this ritual a suitable context for asserting that the *niyāba* of the *fuqahā'* was a general one. 'Allāma did not specify for his view *ijmā'*, it was rather the strongest available option (*aqwā*).[19]

It may here be noted that the accepted mode of passing on intact the *imām*'s share of the *khums* had been *waṣiyya* and *wadī'a*. Juridically the ultimate residual authority over both of these was a legitimate judge. In the various events of a *waṣī* or *mūda'* dying, disappearing or proving incompetent or corrupt, the relevant goods fell under the control of the judge. In the course of generations it would inevitably happen that acknowledged judicial authorities would find themselves in control of a body of wealth derived from *khums* payments: as such they would seem to be acting as *nā'ib* to the owner of that wealth: not the donor, but the absent *imām*. It was perhaps thus in response to a *de facto* situation that the law developed in the way that it did. The assertion that the *fuqahā'* could actually distribute the wealth they controlled was a legal innovation, perhaps again justificatory of what actually happened, but certainly a distinct increase in the discretionary authority of the clerical class.

Shahīd I stated about *khums*:

> It is divided into six parts, three of which are for the *imām* to be paid direct to him, or to his *nuwwāb* as long as he is absent, or to be preserved (*yuḥfaẓ*) . . .[20]

That illustrates the general tendency to recognize in the *'ulamā'* deputies (*nuwwāb*) to the *imām*. The terminological distinction between *nā'ib khāṣṣ* and *nā'ib āmm* does not, however, appear to have been available to Shahīd I. He did not specify in the *Lum'a* how the *nuwwāb* were to use the *imām*'s share.

Shahīd II in the *Masālik al-Ifhām* took up the problem of the distribution of the *khums*. That problem was related to the question whether, if there was a surplus in the share of the Banī Hāshim, it belonged to the *imām*. If it did, then it became permissible to argue that, likewise, the share of the *imām* during the Ghayba belonged to the Banī Hāshim and so could be distributed.

Shahīd II introduced a complex and subtle argument to demonstrate that it was incumbent on the *imām* to make up any deficiency in the share of the Banī Hāshim.[21] That, for him as for earlier *fuqahā'*, constituted the essential premise which justified the distribution of the *imām*'s share during the Ghayba by appropriately qualified clerics. His later analysis in *al-Rawḍat al-Bahiyya* of the rules relevant to distribution of *khums* sufficiently indicate his assessment of the scope of the *fuqahā'*'s authority.

> [The *imām*'s share] is to be conveyed to him if he is present or to his *nuwwāb*; they are *al-fuqahā' al-'udūl al-imāmiyyīn*, those who possess the *sharā'iṭ al-fatwā*, because they are his *wakīls*. Thereupon, it is incumbent

[18] For the *ex ante* delegation see N. Calder, ' Judicial authority in Imāmī Shī'ī jurisprudence ' *BRISMES Bulletin*, VI, 1979.
[19] 'Allāma, *Taḥrīr*, 74–5.
[20] Shahīd I, in *Rawḍa*, 53.
[21] Shahīd II, *Masālik*, II, 68, lines 20 ff.

on them to act in accord with their *madhhab*: those who consider it permissible to distribute it to the recipients by way of fulfilling [deficiencies], which is the prevalent view amongst the *muta'akhkhirīn*, may distribute it as they see fit, generously or otherwise; those who do not accept that view should store it for the *imām* as *wadīʿa* until his appearance ... Thus, as long as the *imām* is absent; or it should be preserved (*yuḥfaẓ*) by the donor of *khums* as *wadīʿa* just as we have described for the *nā'ib* [= *faqīh*]. The donor may not distribute the *imām*'s share of the *khums* to the recipient categories under any circumstances, may not in fact give it to anyone other than the *ḥākim sharʿī*. If someone does undertake that he is held accountable (*ḍāmin*).

It is apparent from the absolute nature of Shahīd I's statement that it should be handed to the *nuwwāb* that no aspect of that share during the Ghayba is *ḥalāl* to anyone other than its group [*farīqihi* = ? the group in charge of *khums*, the *fuqahā'*].[22]

That passage as usual in Shahīd II clarifies the unresolved ambiguities of earlier writers by stressing the authority of the clerical group and minimizing if not in effect denying the rights of the individual donor. It may be noted that even if the latter stored his goods as *wadīʿa* for the *imām* they would in the long run fall into the hands of a judge. The terminology here applied to the *fuqahā'* is clear and reflects, on the one hand, the absence of any limitation to their deputed authority and, on the other, the judicial origins of that authority. They are *nā'ib* and *wakīl* to the *imām*, must possess the *sharā'iṭ al-fatwā* (i.e. those specified in the delegation traditions) and are the *ḥākim sharʿī*. A *ḥākim sharʿī* is a real judge whose authority derives from Jaʿfar al-Ṣādiq's delegation and is to be distinguished from the appointee of a *de facto* power, who might or might not be a *ḥākim sharʿī*.[23] The use of this term in this context confirms that the ultimate source of the *faqīh*'s authority is judicial. The development discussed in this study is one whereby a *sharʿī* function, which had in Būyid times floated as it were free from any firm structure of authority, was brought into the sphere of *qaḍā'* and so subject to the authority of the *fuqahā'*. A precisely similar development was demonstrated for *zakāt*[24] and might be demonstrated for most of the *sharʿī* functions which were considered *sāqiṭ* in Būyid times.[25] In the works of Shahīd II, the rightful (legitimate) executive of the *sharīʿa* in all relevant fields (*jihād*, *kharāj*, Friday prayer *et al.*) was the *faqīh*, whose function was both explained and justified by the terminology which he exploited: *ḥākim sharʿī* and *nā'ib ʿāmm*.

The details presented in this study and in the earlier study of *zakāt* illustrate both the fact and the manner of juridical development. As to the former, even if change was from generation to generation subtle and gradual, the difference between Ṭūsī and Shahīd II is sharp and clear enough. The manner of development may be summed up as exegetical and terminological innovation. The motives of development are not readily extrapolated from jurisprudential texts but may to some extent be inferred. The doctrine of *isqāṭ* elaborated by Murtaḍā and Ṭūsī suggests a cautious approach to the *de facto* political power and implies the absence of any aspiration to oppose or replace the extant power. That caution reflects the extreme degree of tension which subsisted through the

[22] *idem*, *Rawḍa*, 53.
[23] See further, Calder, 'Judicial authority'.
[24] See Calder, 'Zakāt'.
[25] See further, Calder, 'Zakāt', *ad* note 9.

Būyid and early Saljūq periods between the Sunnī majority and the minority Shī'ī community. By late Saljūq times that tension had to some extent been dissipated. The *Kitāb al-Naqḍ* (*c.* 560/1165) presents a picture of the Shī'ī community as on the whole flourishing, rich and prosperous, with a considerable number of mosques and *madrasas*, abundant wealth to be distributed in the form of *zakāt* and *khums* and increasing influence in court circles.[26] Subsequently under, for example, the caliph al-Nāṣir and then under the Ilkhānids, tolerance and patronage from the *de facto* governments provided the Shī'ī community with opportunities to consolidate its internal social structure and to establish its control of material wealth. Throughout this period friction between Sunnīs and Shī'īs though endemic does not appear to have been so violent or so intense as during the Būyid period. That may partly be related to the fact that the Shī'īs had established themselves in certain areas as the dominant community, notably in South Iraq, Baḥrayn and the East coast of the Arabian peninsula, parts of central and northern Syria (Aleppo, Ba'albek, Tripolis) and some scattered areas of Iran. The Syrian community was already well established in Būyid times [27] and might be related to the pro-Shī'ī tendencies of the Ḥamdānid princes. By the early sixteenth century the Baḥraynī community and the Syrian provided the intellectual leadership of the Shī'ī community, and by attraction and emigration they became the chief clerical dignitaries in the new Ṣafavid state.

It is probable that the internal affairs of the Shī'ī communities were managed by legitimate magistrates who emerged locally in close association with noble families (Sayyids), themselves constituting minor and local dynasties.[28] The relationship subsisting between the Shī'ī community and the *de facto* power might be compared to that described by Goitein as subsisting between the Jewish community of Egypt and their government.[29] Both the Jews and the Shī'īs constituted a community within a community, variously linked to the political structure but preserving a great degree of independence from it. The Shī'īs had their own law and their own magistrates whose authority was no doubt rendered more effective by careful cultivation of good relations with the actual ruler [30] and acquisition of his practically useful albeit technically illegal decrees of appointment. Kulaynī's delegation Traditions it may be thought reflected already a need for formal judicial sanction for the community's daily activities such as marriages, wills, resolution of dispute, etc. The real authority of the clerical class, in the course of time, with successive tolerant governments and declining friction with Sunnīs, became actually greater and was bolstered by the acquisition and control of material wealth in the form of *awqāf* as well as *zakāt*, *khums*, etc. Legal theory both justified and promoted that authority. The reality of power in turn influenced and dictated developments in legal theory. The juridical developments described above display an increasing trend to express, to defend and to promote the authority of the *fuqahā'*. That was a reflection both of their aspirations and of the reality of their achievements.

It would, however, be invidious to imagine that the only influence on the developing structure of ideas was that exerted by historical facts or social

[26] Qazwīnī, op. cit., 47–8, 164, 53–4, 71.

[27] As witness the letters of Ṭūsī and Murtaḍā to Aleppo, Tripoli, Tyre, Sidon, Damascus, etc.; Khwānsārī, *Rawḍāt al-Jannāt*, Tehran 1306, 385, 582.

[28] See e.g. Qazwīnī, op. cit., 229 ff.

[29] S. Goitein, *A Mediterranean community*, Vol. II, Berkeley, 1971.

[30] cf. Qazwīnī, op. cit., 53–4, 71.

pressures. Cultural artefacts, such as a legal system, once created, take on a life of their own, and generate, on a purely intellectual level, problems which demand resolution no less insistently than do political or social problems related to public events. Shahīd II was an academic jurist concerned as much with style and elegance as with political events. He is accredited with a significant stylistic innovation in so far as in his commentaries he mixed the *matn* and the *sharḥ* in such a way as to produce continuous prose: a practice adopted from the Sunnī tradition.[31] The *Masālik al-Ifhām*, a commentary on Muḥaqqiq's *Sharāʾiʿ*, is an early version of the style, but rough and uncertain. *al-Rawḍat al-Bahiyya*, on the other hand, with its fusion of *sharḥ* and *matn*, and its combination of *uṣūl*, *furūʿ* and polemic is an impressively written and well-ordered work which, while sensitive to the developments of previous centuries, transcends a great deal of the muddle and obscurity of earlier writers. One of the most significant signs of his concern for juridical economy and elegance was the way in which he utilized the concepts of *nāʾib ʿāmm* and *ḥākim sharʿī* to account for all the *sharʿī* functions of the *faqīh*. That was a major artistic resolution to an essentially intellectual, conceptual problem. It may be taken to represent the fact that amongst the various factors affecting juridical development was the resolution of logical and systematic problems that emerged, unrelated to external events, in the elaboration of the *sharīʿa*.

[31] See Khwānsārī, op. cit., 288–99, for the biography of Shahīd II; Shirbīnī's *Mughnī al Muḥtāj fī sharḥ al-Minhāj* is a Sunnī example of a commentary which incorporates and integrates the original text.

XIX

Accommodation and Revolution in Imami Shi'i Jurisprudence: Khumayni and the Classical Tradition

The elaboration of divine law has been for centuries a dominant mode of Islamic self-expression. The rendering of revelation into prescription, the perennial task of Muslim jurists, has produced a notion of the *shari'a* which, though never fixed in its details, has served as model and touchstone, as object of pious reflection, as justification of the *status quo* and, more rarely, as incentive to revolution. The idealistic nature of divine law was freely acknowledged particularly in spheres of political relevance. There, the practical need for government and authority promoted a complex assessment of the relationship between ideal and actuality such that, generally without compromising the existence of the ideal — which was always restated, actual practice was acknowledged in some degree satisfactory. Nevertheless the idea of a law, transcending human government and capable of implying judgement upon it, was always, in the hands of the clerical class, a means of influencing government and a potential source of resistance. A doctrine of potential resistance is not a doctrine of revolution. The modes and theories of accommodation, as developed by Sunni jurists in particular, have been to some extent documented in Orientalist literature.[1] Revolutionary interpretations of the notion of divine law have not usually been expressed by jurists nor in juristic format.

Acknowledgement of the legitimacy of *de facto* powers has been a prominent feature of Sunni political thinking. Conversely it has for some time been noted that denial of legitimacy has been an almost equally prominent feature of Imami Shi'i juristic literature.[2] Denial of legitimacy however has only rarely been associated with revolution or rebellion and it may be demonstrated that the Imami jurists were, no less than their Sunni counterparts, concerned to provide, within the structure of the *shari'a*, a means of accommodation with *de facto* powers. The recent emergence in Iran of members of the clerical class, notably Ayatallah Ruhallah Khumayni, as leaders of a revolution prompts the present consideration of Khumayni's theory of government (*wilayat al-faqih*) together with an assessment of how it is related to or differs from the classical tradition. The text studied here is taken from a juristic work, the *Kitab al-Bay'*, published in 1391/1971(?),[3] and constituting in form at least a traditional work of Imami jurisprudence, following the pattern set by Murtada Ansari[4] (1281/1864–5) in his *Kitab al-Makasib*. An all too slight and provisional account of earlier juristic theory must serve for context and background.

Early pre-Ghayba Shi'ism manifested itself primarily as a revolutionary and apocalyptic doctrine: recognition of the injustice and illegitimacy of a given ruler was accompanied by an active effort to remove him and replace him by a determinate successor, identified as one or another descendent of Ali. The establishment of the right ruler would, it was thought, inaugurate a period of just government, peace, prosperity, etc. The exigencies of practical politics ensured that successful revolution led to either the abandonment (Abbasid) or modification (Fatimid) of the revolutionary and apocalyptic ideology that had promoted its success.

The notion that the imam, the apocalyptic 'right ruler', was (temporarily or otherwise) absent may be associated with the abandonment of active revolutionary ideals; this idea emerged amongst various Shi'i groups[5] prior to its definitive adoption and elaboration in Twelver Shi'i, Imami circles. During the tenth century (AD) various theologians and jurists forged a specifically Imami religious sectarian identity by defining the number and identity of the imams, by adopting a theology and elaborating a juristic literature as flexible as that of the Sunnis.[6] The pivotal assertion that the charismatic 'right ruler', the ultimate repositary of the law, was absent (and definitively so)[7] had two major consequences. First, the clerical class became the medial expositors of the law. Secondly, the denial of any immediate threat to *de facto* powers (the rightful ruler being absent) rendered possible a variety of approaches to the government of the day.

Technically the actual government (in the tenth century, the Buyids) was and remained illegitimate (non-*shar'i*) since only the (absent) imam could validly put the *shari'a* into effect. This notion that the *shari'a* could not be fully implemented during the Ghayba is strikingly affirmed in at least two polemical works of the Buyid period, in which the idea is put forward that certain parts of the *shari'a* are during the Ghayba *saqit* — lapsed[8]. Specifically, certain functions of the imam (*hudud, jihad et al.*,) are inoperable during his absence and await, for their full and rightful implementation, the day of his return. Politically, the doctrine of the Ghayba and that of *suqut* (lapsing) indicate a denial of legitimacy but an abstention from active opposition: the *shari'a*, in its political aspects, is not being put into effect but there is no one available to implement it. Practically, the Imamis were enabled to establish a perennial *de facto* rapprochement with actual governments whether ostensibly Shi'i like the Buyids or Sunni like the Saljuqs[9].

It is a commonplace of historical analysis that ideologies develop in response and reaction to actual events, but academic theories once formulated have a life of their own and develop also in response to purely formal exigencies of logic, structure and, in the present context, juristic elegance. The very notion of the *shari'a* as a complete formal structure militated against the survival of the doctrine of *suqut*. Practical and theoretical factors combined over a period of centuries to displace that doctrine. The executive functions of the imam were gradually and piecemeal re-expressed and re-established as belonging during the Ghayba, by right (by extension of the acknowledged delegation of judicial authority) to the *fuqaha'*. By the time of the Ottoman jurist Shahid II[10] (d. 960/1559) this realisation was embodied in a terminological innovation whereby the *faqih* was recognised as *na'ib 'amm* (general delegate) of the absent imam. The only significant *shar'i* function which was not transferred to the *fuqaha'* was that of *jihad* for the sake of expansion.[11]

It is not possible to discuss here the full implications of the doctrine of *niyaba 'amma* (general delegation) but two particular factors may be mentioned. The *fuqaha'* had the right to collect and administer the *shar'i* taxes of *zakat* and *khums*. Whereas Sunni *fuqaha'* did not acknowledge the continuing validity of *khums* as a tax and recognised *de facto* governmental collections as *zakat*, the Imami *fuqaha'*, denying the *shar'i* nature of governmental collections, made themselves the focus of *shar'i* finances. In particular they were able to control and justify their control of *khums* which became, in practice, a primary source of clerical income. This financial independence from the government is one of several features distinguishing Imami *fuqaha'* from their Sunni counterparts and permitting a degree of opposition and resistance, not usually found in Sunni circles. Secondly, the theory of general delegation (*niyaba 'amma*) incorporated an element of populism in so far as recognition of a fully qualified *faqih* (possessed of *shara'it al-ifta'*[12]) depended to a large extent on public witness. While it is true that clerical opinion influenced the public in such matters the dependence of the *fuqaha'* for financial support and for recognition of their status on the people led to and still leads to a degree of demagoguery: the *faqih* frequently follows rather than leads public opinion[13].

The theory that the *faqih* is the ideal executor of the *shari'a* and the only rightful governor in the absence of the imam, though it may reflect a consolidation of clerical authority within certain spheres of life, is not a good illustration of practical political thought amongst Imami jurists. Neither before nor after the time of Shahid II did the *fuqaha'* rule; and though they were frequently influential both before and during the Safavid period they neither created nor claimed to have created an (ideal) *shar'i* state. The actual government was *de jure* illegitimate. The most practically relevant area of juristic speculation lay not in the presentation of an ideal government by the *faqih* but in the various efforts at accommodation which are visible in works of Imami *fiqh*. The principle of *de jure* illegitimacy did not prevent the emergence of a spectrum of *de facto* approaches to political power. The potential opposition implicit in the juristic theory of *niyaba 'amma* was rarely stressed but some kind of *modus vivendi* was advocated, varying from positive support for the relatively just and tolerant (but still 'illegitimate', *ja'ir/zalim*) ruler to dissociation and dissimulation (*taqiyya*) under the obviously unjust or intolerant ruler. Such matters were a constant feature of juristic speculation under the heading, 'Working for the illegitimate (*ja'ir/zalim*) governor.' Generally it was thought *mustahabb* or even *wajib* to work for (and thereby support) a relatively just governor; and undesirable but permissible to work for a relatively unjust governor under 'conditions of compulsion'[14]. Real practical support was thus offered to *de facto* powers in spite of their acknowledged illegitimacy.

One other example of accommodation may be cited here. With regard to that class of land 'conquered by force' (*maftuha 'unwatan*)[15] Shahid II notes that the ideal during the Ghayba is that the *na'ib al-imam*, the *hakim shar'i* (= *na'ib 'amm*), in so far as he can gain independent control of such land, should disburse the proceeds on the welfare of Muslims (*masalih al-muslimin*). But in so far as such land was under the control of a *ja'ir* (as in practice it always was) it is permissible (*yajuz*) to go along with him in his administration of it, and it is valid (*yasuhh*) to accept (and use the proceeds he has derived from it in the form of) *kharaj* and *muqasama*[16]. These terms in this context refer to the actual tax-collecting activities of the ruler (*ja'ir*). These activities were given a partial legitimacy in so far as they were recognised as being based on a potentially valid *shar'i* tax, but it was being administered illegitimately by a *ja'ir* governor. This idea had been developed in particular by the Safavid jurist al-Karaki (d. 937/1530–1 or 941/1533–4) in his theoretical and practical support for the *ja'ir* sultan Tahmasp: the tax-collecting activities of Tahmasp's government were acknowledged as partly legitimate[17].

These practical approaches to *de facto* power, the permission to work with illegitimate governors, the 'legitimation' of profane tax-collecting, represent a tendency in juristic speculation which might usefully be termed *de facto* recognition. The notion of a *de facto* recognition subsisting with a *de jure* illegitimacy adequately defines the range of options available to the Shi'i *fuqaha'*. *De facto* recognition and rapprochement secured considerable advantages to the Shi'a in general and to the clerical class in particular: the latter were enabled to protect and preserve their interests and those of their followers by courting the help and protection of the actual governors. At the same time the ideal vision of the perfect *shari'a* was preserved intact. Not the least benefit of the jurists' exploration of the area of accommodation was that it permitted a variable approach to the government of the day: the degree of *de facto* support offered might be greater or smaller depending on the perceived justice or tolerance of the actual ruler. This variable approach is made explicit in the discussion of the conditions under which it is *wajib, mustahabb, makruh* or *ja'iz* to work with the illegitimate ruler. Further, it was precisely by this ability to register a greater or lesser degree of support to actual rulers that the *fuqaha'* were able to exercise real influence on governmental policies.

Juristic exploration of the area of accommodation continued throughout the Qajar period. One of the most significant advances was made by Kashif al-Ghita' in the early nineteenth century. Acting in response to the threatened Russian invasion of Persia, and relying on the by now well-established theory of clerical authority (*niyaba 'amma*) he indicated his support and sanction for the defensive activities of the Shah. He thus provided the Shah with a temporary, partial and derived legitimacy[18]. The notion thus emerged in Imami jurisprudence of a legitimate secular ruler, a notion that was conceptually dependent on the prior notion of clerical authority (*niyaba 'amma*). This new development in juristic theory precipitated a terminological innovation whereby the term *na'ib khass*, previously applicable only to contemporary appointees of the imams, or to the four *sufara'*, became applicable also to a ruler who acted with the permission and sanction of the *fuqaha'*. This notion of a derived *de jure* legitimacy has this in common with the earlier elaboration of *de facto* recognition that it was variable and retractable: the *fuqaha'* could provide or withhold recognition and with this sanction might hope to influence.

It is to be noted that the present discussion is concerned only with the development of a theoretical framework for political ideas: the actual influence of the *fuqaha'* depended on other factors such as their ability to achieve a united front, the power and personality of the ruler, the economic and social factors which affected the mood of the people, etc.[19] It may further be noted that the theory of *niyaba 'amma* is a theory of *potential* resistance and, while it allowed for some real opposition to the government at times, the active opposition to tyranny was not 'a fundamental and pervasive character of Twelver Shi'ism'[20] — not, that is, if by tyranny is meant the 'illegitimate' governor, *ja'ir*. The search for a *modus vivendi* is at least as important a characteristic of the juristic tradition.

It is clear that the notion of the ideal *shari'a* implemented by an ideal ruler, a *faqih* possessed of *shara'it al-ifta'*, acting as *na'ib 'amm* to the absent imam, is a vital structural component in the tradition of Imami jurisprudence. But *in itself* that notion was visionary and apocalyptic: it threatened on the one hand violent revolution and on the other defeatist quietism. Practical constructive thinking by Imami jurists took the form of theoretical exploration of what I have called the area of accommodation. There the problem was how to establish a *modus vivendi* with actual governments, how to influence governments so as to bring them close to a practical justice or even to the acquisition of a theoretical legitimacy.

Developments in the late nineteenth and early twentieth centuries seem to betray a more active sense of opposition amongst the Imami jurists[21]. This may partly be a result (subjective) of sharpened Western interest in moments of unrest or revolution[22]; but reflects also clerical revulsion against the venality and incompetence of the Qajars, as well as, and even more important, clerical suspicion and distrust of Western influence and secularisation[23]. Nevertheless juristic speculation continued to develop primarily in the area of accommodation. The question that presented itself was how to mould or influence an illegitimate government, not how to achieve an ideal *shar'i* state ruled by a *faqih*. Increasingly the question presented itself as to what form of government — (the Western world offered some potential alternatives to monarchy) — might achieve the greatest degree of practical efficiency and practical justice.

From the point of view of theoretical speculation the events of the Tobacco Regie were relatively unimportant: a particular act or series of acts by the Shah were condemned as illegitimate and as demanding or justifying some degree of clerical and popular opposition, for the limited purpose of persuading the Shah to rescind the tobacco concession. The various events of that period were however a potent incentive to political reflection and helped precipitate the spate of political theorising which emerged during the period of the Constitutional revolution.

It is quite impossible here to do anything like justice to the variety of political opinions which were expressed at that time by members of the clerical class[24]. What I would like to stress however is that neither the proponents nor the opponents of the constitution were concerned directly with the establishment of government by the *faqih*, a government which would be fully legitimate. What they discussed was the practical merits of absolute monarchy over and against those of constitutional government; they were concerned with the potential of such forms of government to preserve and protect Shi'ite Islam, which seemed under imminent threat from the influences of foreigners on the one hand and the weakness of the government on the other. The question of how to strengthen the government against foreign influences precipitated a debate which took the form of assessing alternative forms of government as more or less likely to permit some kind of *de facto* efficiency and justice, or, possibly, *de jure* legitimacy. The practical ability of the clerical class to influence one or another form of government was also a factor affecting debate. Na'ini's very subtle analysis of the merits of constitutional government is summed up by Algar as a political theory that 'seeks to reconcile continued awareness of the occultation of the *imam*, together with the resultant impossibility of legitimacy, with the practical need for a form of government that does not grossly offend the dictates of religion'.[25] Conversely Fadlallah Nuri's support for the monarchy was based, not on any consideration of that institution's actual legitimacy, but on its greater familiarity and its established potential legitimacy. He saw in some of the democratic principles associated with constitutionalism a threat to the fundamental principles of authority associated with the *shari'a*: the sovereignty of the people in parliament was not in his view a principle compatible with the authority of the divinely revealed *shari'a*[26].

The intellectual vitality of that debate reflects the underlying flexibility of the Imami juristic tradition. The idealistic aspect of the law, the implementation of the ideal *shari'a* by a qualified *faqih*, served as the structural ground for debate, and represented the ultimate residual right of the *fuqaha'* actively to oppose, to resist or to influence. The idealistic vision *per se* did not lend itself to flexible and practical development. The real debate, the constructive political theory, took place where, in Imami juristic literature, it had always taken place, in the area of accommodation, on the assumption that the governing institution would not be synonymous with the religious institution.

Discussion in the course of the twentieth century has continued to explore the possibilities of a relationship between an illegitimate political power and a religious institution. Most of the writers on the *marja'al-taqlid* discussed by Professor Lambton[27] at least recognise that the actual government will be something distinct from the religious institution. The problem that manifested itself for them in that context was how to reform and strengthen the latter so that it might be better able to influence the actual government. In spite of some tendency to look for an identifiable ideal ruler, the general terms of the discussions were constructive. They represented a continuation of the classical tradition of search for a *modus vivendi* with the actual and essentially illegitimate governing power.

Since that time the religious institution in Iran has removed one government and set up another. The causes and consequences of the Iranian revolution are not here to be considered. The question I would like to take up is whether and how Khumayni's juristic writing reflects a revolutionary impulse and how it may be related to the classical tradition.

Khumayni's discussion of *wilayat al-faqih* begins with the following extensive argument[28]:

1. The precepts of Islam (*ahkam al-islam*) even such basic cultic practices as prayer and *hajj* have social and political aspects, directly related to this-wordly life and livelihood. The existence in Islam of economic, legal (*huquqi*, relating to rights) social and political laws (*qawanin*) reveals that Islam is not composed simply of cultic and moral precepts (*laysa 'ibaratan 'an al-ahkam al-'ibadiyya w'al-akhlaqiyya faqat*) — as some youths and even elders amongst Muslims have claimed.

2. This misconception amongst Muslims is the result of the presence of foreigners and foreign workers in Islamic lands; these have put about pernicious propaganda aimed at drawing the youth and the students of modern science away from Islam, and at creating dissension and hatred amongst Muslims. They have achieved such a degree of success that it is difficult for us to refute their claims and their accusations.

3. The pernicious influence of the foreigners demands counter-propaganda especially from the spiritual leaders (*ruhaniyyun*) and from the students of the religious sciences.

4. The main aim of the counter propaganda is to make it manifest that Islam arose to found a just government (*hukuma 'adila*) in which there are laws (*qawanin*) related to finances, the treasury and the collection (of taxes) from all classes of society . . .; and laws related to (legal) compensation whether in the form of retaliation (*qisas*) or punishment (*hadd*) or indemnity (*diyya*), laws of such a kind that were they put into effect crimes would be fewer if they did not cease entirely, and likewise the evils consequent upon (such crime) would cease, such as those consequent upon the use of alcohol . . .; and laws relating to judicial authority and legal rights, in an easy and just manner occasioning no waste of time and money such as can be witnessed in the courts of today; and laws relating to *jihad* and defence and treaties between the state of Islam (*dawlat al-islam*) and other states.

5. Islam has laid down the foundations of a government not based on tyranny (*istibdad*), whereby the opinions and desires of an individual rule society, nor based on constitutionalism (*al-mashruta*) or republicanism, systems founded on human laws (*al-qawanin al-bashariyya*) whereby the opinions of a group dominate society; but rather a government which in all spheres seeks help and inspiration from divine law (*al-qanun al-ilahi*).

6. No Islamic governor (*wulat*) may indulge in arbitrary action (*al-istibdad bi-ra'yihi*) but all that pertains to government, its affairs and its necessities, must be based on divine law.

7. However the governor (*wali*) may in certain matters act in furtherance of the welfare of Muslims (*salah al-muslimin*). This is not arbitrary exercise of opinion (*istibdad bi'l-ra'i*) because it is in

furtherance of welfare; his opinion like his action is subordinate to welfare (*tabi'un li'l-salah*).

8. Divine precepts (*al-ahkam al-ilahiyya*), financial, political or legal (*huquqi*) are not abrogated; they remain valid till the day of resurrection. The enduring (validity) of these precepts demands necesarily (*bi-darura*) a government (*hukuma*) and a governorship (*wilaya*) which will guarantee the dominance of divine law and dedicate itself to its implementation.
9. The implementation of divine law is impossible without a government to prevent chaos and confusion; further, to preserve order (*hifz al-nizam*) is a duty (*wajib*) and to neglect Muslim affairs is reprehensible, and this cannot be achieved except by a *wali* and a *hukuma*. Defence of Muslim frontiers, also a duty, based on reason and revelation, equally demands the formation of a government.
10. The Muslim need for a government is the clearest of their needs and God's neglect of that need is inconceivable . . . And reason indicates the necessity of a government to spread justice, to teach and educate, to preserve order, to remove unrighteousness and to defend the frontiers, and to prevent the excesses of foreigners.
11. Revelation confirms this:
    — Traditions show that the Qur'an and the Sunna provide a ruling for all of man's needs (pre-eminent amongst them the need for a governor/government).
    — Traditions also articulate the nature of man's need for a government; for example, from the Imam al-Rida, a Tradition embodying the following ideas:
    — people need a ruler to prevent them transgressing the law, otherwise they would not leave off what they found pleasing or useful simply on the grounds of the harm it might cause to others;
    — the evidence of other groups and sects reveals the need for one leader to fight, distribute booty, restrain the iniquitous, etc.;
    — without a leader the community would dissolve and religion (*din*) would disappear, the Sunna and religious precepts would change; Islam would be added to or subtracted from by innovators and unbelievers . . . because people are imperfect . . .; the laws and the established practices (*shara'i'* and *sunan*) and the precepts and the faith would change and that would be the destruction of mankind.

The fundamental idea which informs the movement of thought in this passage is that there exists a legal system (Islamic law) which can be put into effect, which covers all aspects of social and political life and which promises an end to disorder and chaos and even to crime and bureaucratic inefficiency, and guarantees the formation of a just government. One of the characteristics of this law is that it precludes arbitrary acts by a governor because it lays down precisely what to do; and where it does not provide clearly for particular actions another notion, that of *salah al-muslimin*, will direct the opinions and actions of the governor.

Now, all of this is visionary, part of the perennial human desire for eternal and immutable justice (nowhere better documented than in the Muslim search to define the *shari'a*), but neglectful of realities. The idea that the law precludes arbitrary or partial actions is not to be accepted. Even the most densely textured of legal systems does not permit a mechanical assessment of the relations subsisting between a particular series of facts, a particular series of laws and the actions they demand. Neither the 'facts', nor rules, nor language, nor personalities, nor modes of implementation are so easily quantifiable as to allow more than a modest hope that the consequences of the law will be predictable[29]. The much more elusive concept of *salah al-muslimin* promises no real end to dispute or to arbitrary opinion.

Further incidental details of the argument continue to betray a naïvely optimistic view of the perfectibility of law and human society. Crime might vanish under certain conditions, or a judicial system be established eliminating waste of time or money. Casual reference to *dawlat al-islam* neglects all the international political realities which make this concept for the moment a distant ideal not a present reality. Outsiders, foreigners, are easily categorised as of evil purpose, the prime source of corruption in insiders, a world-view reflecting emotional and ideological reaction rather than rational assessment. The underlying appeal of the passage, notwithstanding the juristic or logical appearance of the argument, is emotional and apocalyptic. What is asserted is only the perfectibility of human society by the implementation of Islamic law.

The one crucial and ostensibly 'logical' step that is asserted is that Islamic law because it contains rules pertaining to or which can only be carried out by a government demands necessarily the formation of a government. There are rules of social political and economic organisation which are eternally valid and which demand for their implementation a governor and a government. It is faith not logic that renders this argument permissible: it is not the existence of the law but the nature of the law that makes its implementation imperative. God's will, once recognised as such and once manifest in practical form, exacts from believers submission. Granted however the nature of the law there is still the problem of its actual existence in the required form. By implication, for Khumayni, the divine law is already realised as a tangible and practical code; and the actual (and manifestly imperfect) world is presumed to be immediately perfectible. Divine law (an ideal) is related to Islamic government (also an ideal 'to guarantee the dominance of divine law') without consideration of the relation between those ideals and their corresponding realities — a tangible code, and a functional governing institution.

Islamic political thought in general has been more careful to acknowledge a gap between ideal and reality. The argument from the existence of the law to the necessary existence of a government took the form in classical literature of the so-called *sam'i* or *shar'i* argument for the necessary existence of the caliphate. This argument first appeared in the Sunni tradition in the *Usul al-Din* of al-Baghdadi (d. 429/1037–8) and was used later by Mawardi (d. 450/1058) and other Sunni writers on political theory[30]. In the hands of these writers it became an argument for the legitimacy of the actual government, and for the admission of a variety of deviations from the ideal as being still *shar'i*. The same *shar'i* argument for the necessary existence of the caliph/imam took on revolutionary implications in the works of the Mu'tazili writer Abd al-Jabbar (d. 415/1025) and more especially in the works of his Zaydi followers[31]. The Imamis initially distrusted the *shar'i* argument for the necessary existence of the caliph/imam because it was not immediately adaptable to their notion of the imamate. But in so far as they conceded that the law required an executor they identified the latter with the imam[32]. The implications of that theory and later developments have already been discussed. Identification of the ideal executor of the *shari'a* became for them the foundation of a doctrine of potential resistance but was carefully qualified by the characteristic desire of the Imami *fuqaha'* to establish a *modus vivendi* with the illegitimate powers. For them too the *shari'a* was elaborated as an ideal, designed certainly to influence practice, but incorporating a practical acknowledgement of political realities.

Space for the moment permits of no more than the assertion that the argument from the existence of law to the necessary existence of a government has been frequently adduced in Islam, in a variety of contexts, and for a variety of purposes. Khumayni's rendering is given apocalyptic and revolutionary significance by the implication that the divine law must be and can be put into practice without compromise. The use of the term *qanun* (in addition to the more traditional terms *shari'a* or *shar'*) emphasises his vision of the law as something practical and effective: this term was earlier reserved to distinguish governmental decrees from *shar'i* prescriptions[33].

Khumayni depicts divine law as a system ready for immediate implementation, as a blueprint for action. This is not a unique interpretation of divine law in Islam but it does little justice either to the general elaboration of that notion in juristic literature or to the practical function of the *shari'a* in relation to judicial or administrative practice. With respect to the writing out of the *shari'a* not only do jurists habitually recognise and acknowledge the persistent failure to achieve in practice what is ideally required but they habitually acknowledge the existence of *ikhtilaf* and even, sometimes, the incidence of chronological developments. The unique immutable and perfect law which is God's law *par excellence*, and which is contained *in potentio* in Qur'an and Sunna, has not yet been written out. When the jurists write they strive towards a definition of the law, they approximate to it, they render it anew from generation to generation. The writing of the law is a pious exercise, an assertion of the existence of a moral order, and an attempt to define it. An academic exposition of the divine law by a Muslim jurist may better be assessed as an exploration of the theological and moral significance of the prophet's biography than as a code for implementation, a shifting model not a determinate code. The writing of the law, especially as characterised by the easy acknowledgement of *ikhtilaf*, betrays the exploratory and idealistic nature of the law as presented in juristic literature. The relationship between juristic literature and actual practice has been frequently described as partitive: only parts of the *shari'a* have generally been implemented (Schacht). But a better depiction of their relationship might be obtained by analogy with the relationship that subsisted between Natural Law and positive law in the writings of Aquinas and the Schoolmen: Natural Law served as source, touchstone and judge of positive law, but was not itself an instance of positive law[34]. Works of *fiqh* have always functioned and still function effectively as *sources* (not necessarily the major source) for the positive law of Islamic states/governments.

Khumayni's radical attitude to Islamic law is perhaps best seen in his assumption that divine law represents an effective alternative to constitutionalism or republicanism; and that indeed it excludes these other forms of governmental organisation: divine law precludes human laws. This notion that divine law and human law are mutually exclusive may be thought contradicted by the practical development of constitutional and republican, and still Muslim, states. The sense of Islamic identity, and due reverence for the *shari'a*, has not in practice precluded the elaboration of a positive law which is distinct from, while frequently based on, juristic speculation. The written constitution of Kuwait, Article 2, exemplifies the attitude of most modern Arab states: 'The religion of the state is Islam and the Islamic *shari'a* shall be a main source of legislation.' Even within the specifically Imami tradition Na'ini and those who have followed him represent the current of constitutional accommodation which has existed in Iran[35].

Reference to Muslims who have compromised, though strictly it indicates those who deny the social and political elements in Islamic law (a rare category indeed), might be taken to indicate by polemical licence those whose compromise takes the more usual form of not expecting the immediate application of the law; those who acknowledge its shifting function as ideal or source or incentive to reflection.

Khumayni however did not set out to analyse or write a historical treatise: his purpose was hortatory, to inspire loyalty and to assert an identity; not to investigate differences but to assert unity and solidarity. The emotional charge of his argument lies in a series of contrasts which are implied or explicitly rendered:

divine law	:	human law
Muslim	:	foreigner
reason and revelation	:	opinion and arbitrary action
stability and immutability	:	change and instability
justice	:	injustice
order	:	disorder

Everything in the first column is symbolised in the notion of divine law (*qanun ilahi*); the mere establishment of an Islamic government will render possible the realisation of all those notions. The message is not explicitly revolutionary (there is no mention of revolution)[36]; but the message is that perfection is attainable. One of the more interesting features of the work, exemplifying a general tendency to avoid what might be divisive, to gloss over distinctions, is his consistent use of the terms Islam/Muslim and his eschewal of the terms Iman/Mu'min, which traditionally distinguish Imamis from Sunnis.

The second major section of Khumayni's argument takes the following form[37]:

1. It remains to discuss the identity of the governor (*wali*) ... According to the true sect (*al-madhhab al-haqq*) the imams are *wulat al-amr* and they possess what the prophet possessed of 'general government' and 'total divine caliphate' (*wilaya 'amma, khilafa kulliyya ilahiyya*).

2. As to the period of the Ghayba, *wilaya* and *hukuma* have not been delegated to a specific person. But it is necessary ... that those functions continue ... because Islamic society requires them ... for the removal of dissension, the organisation of the community and preservation of the *shari'a*, etc.

3. Hence we declare that Islamic government, since it is legal government (*hukuma qanuniyya*), indeed the government of divine law (*hukumat al-qanun al-ilahi*) and since it is appointed to put the law into effect and to spread divine justice (*'adala ilahiyya*), requires a *wali* who must possess two qualities:
   — knowledge of the law (*'ilm bi'l-qanun*)
   — justice (*'adala*)

   The quality of competence (*kifaya*) is included in that of *'ilm* ... but may be considered a third quality.

4. Traditions indicate that knowledge and justice are qualities requisite in the imam; and it is generally accepted amongst Muslims ... that the imam and the caliph must know divine precepts and they must be better than others ...

5. As to justice ... reason and revelation are agreed that the *wali* must be knowledgeable of the law and just to the people and in putting the divine precepts into effect.

6. On this basis the task of *wilaya* falls to *al-faqih al-'adil*. Undertaking a government and laying the foundation of the Islamic state (*al-dawlat al-islamiyya*) is a *kifa'i* duty[38] incumbent on just *fuqaha'*.

7. If one such succeeds in forming a government it is incumbent on the others to follow him. If the task is not possible except by their uniting, they must unite to undertake it. If that were not possible at all, their status would not lapse, though they would be excused from the founding of a government.

8. So it is incumbent upon them to impose penalties where possible, to collect taxes (*sadaqat, kharaj, khums*) and to organise financial expenditure on Muslim welfare and on poor Sayyids and others and on all the needs of the Muslim people and of Islam. They possess with respect to government all that the prophet and the imams possessed.

9. Their status is not the same as that of the imams because the latter possessed spiritual qualities (*fada'il ma'nawiyya*) not shared by

others. The term 'caliphate' has two technical meanings:
— the divine creative caliphate (*al-khilafat al-ilahiyyat al-takwiniyya*), restricted to the prophet and the imams;
— the relative and functional caliphate (*al-ma'na al-i'tibari al-ja'li*), transferrable and belonging now to the *fuqaha'*.

10. Hence the *faqih 'adil* possesses all that the prophet and the imams possessed in the field of government and politics (*hukuma, siyasa*); no distinction is conceivable because the *wali*, whoever he is, puts into effect the precepts of the *shari'a,* imposes divine penalties, collects *kharaj* and other revenues and administers such revenues for the welfare of Muslims. For the prophet used to lash the adulterer 100 times, and likewise the imam, and likewise the *faqih*; they [all] collected *sadaqat* in the same way; and in accord with the exigencies of Muslim welfare they ordered the people as a governor orders and it is incumbent to obey them.

The purpose of this passage is to establish in a manner which presents itself as more or less rational (to be distinguished from direct appeal to revelation[39]) that the Islamic government can only be put into effect by a just *faqih*; and that the *faqih*, as potential executor of the *shari'a,* has in the field of government all the rights of the imams and the prophet. The compelling nature of the argument is less logical than terminological: a portentous emotional claim is built up by multiplication of abstract terms associated with divine law and Islamic government. These include: *wilaya 'amma, khilafa kulliyya ilahiyya, al-wilaya w'al-hukuma, al-hukumiyyat al-qanuniyya, ahkam al-qanun al-ilahi, ahkam al-shari'a, masalih al-muslimin, al-khilafat al-ilahiyyat al-takwiniyya et al.* The cumulative impact of this is vague and emotional, not rational or functional: all that is insistently asserted is a vision: the actualisation of the *shari'a.* It is a rallying cry, a call to solidarity, apocalyptic rather than mundane or practical. Distilled out of all this is the notion that the *wali* must be *'alim* and *'adil.* But these terms represent no logical advance, they are a restatement of the vision: to be *'alim* is to know the *shari'a* and justice (*'adala*) has no meaning outside the law, it is the law in practice. The abstract concept, the *shari'a* actualised, is transferred first to an institution, Islamic government — *wilaya, hukuma, khilafa,* then to a person, *al-faqih al-'adil.* No real distinction is envisaged between governor and government[40].

The argument from law to government and from government to governor disregards certain distinctions, commonplace in the west and not entirely unknown even in the Imami tradition. There are distinctions between academic knowledge of the law, judicial decisions about particular cases, legislative activity (corresponding in an Islamic context to the area of *masalih al-nas*) and executive action. The point here is not however Khumayni's carelessness or ignorance, neither of which are proved, but his purpose: to rally Muslims, to instil hope, to bring to the fore a possible alternative to the actual government. A well-established traditional theory has been stripped of its accommodatory aspects and put to work for new ends.

Khumayni's reading of the tradition has revolutionary implications. This is rendered possible by the isolation of the discussion of government from the disparate and fragmentary assessments of authority which constituted the structure of classical readings. Prior to the mid-nineteenth century jurists acknowledged and discussed the rightful authority of the *fuqaha'* under particular headings: *jihad, zakat, qada'*, etc. The ideal rights of the *fuqaha'* were in such contexts immediately qualified by discussion of what happens during the dominance of a *ja'ir*: what relation has actuality to the ideal? There was no established context for a full discussion of *wilayat al-faqih* as such. The first jurist to define a context for this discussion, indeed the first to develop this terminology, would appear to be Murtada Ansari in his *K. al-Makasib*, which as I have already pointed out constitutes the model for Khumayni's *K. al-Bay'*. His discussion of *wilayat al-faqih* did not have the same implications as Khumayni's. He makes generous acknowledgement of *ikhtilaf* and takes note of the tradition of accommodation. He analyses the meanings of *wilaya* with a degree of subtlety and a multiplicity of precise terminological sub-divisions which are nowhere evident in Khumayni. His assessment of what degree of general authority belongs to the *fuqaha'* is carefully qualified by acknowledgement of the difficulties of the revealed sources and by recognition of conflicting views. His work takes the form of juristic speculation. Khumayni' s is a call to action. Further, Ansari does not make any crude equation of *wilaya* and *hukuma*. For him the 'root' of *wilaya* would appear to be *waliy* (legal agent) not *wali* (governor). He is concerned with the extent of the *faqih's* right of *wilayat al-tasarruf* — that his right to act as agent for and on behalf of the people. Khumayni has indeed taken up various pointers contained within Ansari's discussion, and has produced an extreme version, and a relatively unsubtle one.

Having established that governmental authority belongs to the *fuqaha'* Khumayni defines the nature and extent of their authority by an immediate contrast with that which belongs to the imam. The unique status of the latter is a result of spiritual qualities, not of legal rights or functions. Their caliphate is divine and creative, that of the *fuqaha'* relative and functional; but the authority of the *faqih* includes everything practical. All the rights that belonged to the prophet and the imams in the field of government now belong to the *fuqaha'*: no distinction is conceivable. (The fact that the imams themselves never actually practised government is glossed over.)

Amongst the most interesting notions expressed in the above passage (para. 7) is the idea that if one *faqih* succeeds in forming a government it is incumbent on others to follow him. The idea of the subordination of all qualified *fuqaha'* to a single *faqih* who happens to gain political power is probably without precedent in the Imami tradition. (It might be compared with the position of the *marja' al-taqlid*, also not by any means an established or fully accepted Imami institution: Taliqani's remarks on the inability of one man to fulfill this post are particularly interesting[42].) More characteristic of the general tendency to permit divergent views (as less likely to be divisive) and better supported in the classical sources is the doctrine of *ijtihad*, which acknowledges the rights of all fully qualified *mujtahids* to diverge in the expression of their legal decisions (*ijtihad*).

The idea that all *fuqaha'* should unite to undertake the formation of a government is also important for its practical significance. If it is impossible for the *fuqaha'* to establish any kind of government, they retain their right though they lack the reality of power. This confirms the *de jure* illegitimacy of actual governors (other than *fuqaha'*) and restates the traditional point of view. It is possible here to detect a reversion to the principle of accommodation: the ideal government has been discussed at some length but finally acknowledgement of the possibility of accommodation re-emerges. This tendency is confirmed later in the discussion[43].

> Since there is no doubt about the rights of the just *fuqaha'* it is necessary to submit to their supervision (*dakhalat nazarihim*) ... ; and it is necessary that government be by their permission; and if they are not available or incapable it becomes incumbent on just Muslims; but they must seek permission from a just *faqih* if there is one.
>
> The idea that government belongs to the *fuqaha'* may be criticised on the grounds that they are incapable of organising political or military affairs; but there is no basis for such a criticism for we can see that organisation and administration in every state is based on the common efforts of a large number of specialists and men of insight. Sultans and presidents, from ancient times to the present day, ... were not well-versed in the arts of politics and leadership of the army; rather affairs remained in the hands of specialists ... If the man in charge of government is a just person then no doubt he will choose ministers and agents who are just and efficient — hence tyranny and corruption and transgression will grow less in the finances of the Muslims and in their goods and persons.

Here the possibilities of accommodation are to a limited extent restated: a variety of concessions to the ideal is envisaged. The 'government' of the *faqih* is re-phrased quite suddenly as 'supervision' and 'permission' — which need not at all be the same thing. A government by just Muslims, with the permission of the *fuqaha'*, is a possible alternative to government by the *fuqaha'*, and a potentially 'legitimate' alternative. Knowledge of the law is distinguished fairly clearly from ability actually to implement the various arts of government (a distinction which, pushed any distance at all, would reflect adversely on the earlier argument that the governor must know the law: it is possible that the executive agent will not also be the judicial/legislative agent). The nature of the argument has changed: Khumayni no longer presents simply an emotional appeal to the divine law and its need for actualisation, the inseparable concepts of law, government and just *faqih*. The question of whether the *faqih* is competent to organise a government or run a state is a question implying a rather different order of reality, a slightly more practical one. Divine law, Islamic government and just *faqih* are images which fuse together in an ideal Utopian apocalyptic world. The emergence of the question of competence reflects the impingement of the real difficulties of the task on the idealistic vocabulary: the effect is minimal but important. There is still a good deal of naïve optimism in the idea that tyranny and corruption will simply vanish if the leader or governor is just (though this would undoubtedly help); but the revolutionary symbolism has been qualified by a degree of accommodation. Some kind of government separate from the religious institution might be possible.

Khumayni's success as a revolutionary leader was due largely to his ability to exploit the revolutionary implications of the Imami Shi'i juristic tradition in a manner not obviously inconsistent with earlier developments. He was able thereby to secure a considerable degree of solidarity amongst the clerical class and to rally the traditional loyalty of the Iranian people. While the fundamental economic, political and social causes of the revolution must be explored elsewhere the reason for the emergence of a cleric as the obvious alternative to the actual ruler (and not for example, a colonel) may be explained by reference to purely theoretical matters. The Imami juristic tradition had for centuries preserved and propagated an idea of legitimate authority as belonging ultimately to the *fuqaha'*. When widespread dissatisfaction with the monarchy, and distrust of Western influence, reached the point of incipient revolution, the people turned to the only generally available alternative theory of authority. And at a critical moment they found a stridently revolutionary interpretation of the Imami tradition easily available in the writings and preachings of Khumayni and his followers. Clerical and popular dissatisfaction united round a particular focus of loyalty: divine law. Whether the aims of all the revolutionaries who gathered round that symbol are the same may well be doubted.

The revolutionary interpretation of the Imami tradition was based on the isolation of the notion of divine law and *shar'i* government from a well-established context of accommodation. Divine law, Islamic government and the clerical ruler became disembodied ideals functioning as apocalyptic symbols of a new just and well-ordered system. These same features given a still more frankly revolutionary reading may be detected in Khumayni's Persian language version of the *wilayat al-faqih*[44]. That work was promoted and published entirely separate from any juristic context. It was freed thereby from all the accommodatory aspects of the juristic tradition and functioned simply and exclusively as an incitement to revolution. A revolutionary reading of Islamic law, once adopted (especially when it was isolated from most other aspects of that law) rendered the religious ideology very susceptible to influences from secular revolutionary ideologies such as Marxism. Recent events in Iran have illustrated both the impingement of Marxist ideas on the modes of religious expression and attempts to purify the religious institution from secular revolutionary elements.

The tone of this essay has been such as to suggest that while the ideal notion of *shar'i* government by the *faqih* has played (and will continue to play) an extremely important functional role in the elaboration of clerical ideas and in the exercise of clerical influence, still the practical questions of government lie elsewhere. The future of Iran, and of the religious institution there, will depend on a renewed exploration of the area of accommodation. Constructive thought in this area may well still be undertaken by Khumayni but seems more likely to emerge from other thinkers without as well as within the clerical class.

NOTES

1. See for example, the relevant articles by H. A. R. Gibb in *Studies in the Civilisation of Islam*, eds. S. J. Shaw and W. R. Polk, London, 1962; Binder, 'Al-Ghazali's theory of Islamic government', *MW*, XLV, 1955; M. W. Watt, 'Reflections on Al-Ghazali's Political Theory', *Transactions of the Glasgow Oriental Society*, XXI, 1965/6, *et al.* Cf. also N. Calder, 'Judicial Authority in Imāmī Shī'ī Jurisprudence', *BRISMES Bulletin*, VI, 1979, p. 107.
2. Cf. N. R. Keddie, 'The roots of the *ulama*'s power in modern Iran', in *Scholars, saints and sufis*, ed. N. R. Keddie, Los Angeles/London, 1972; J. Eliash, 'The Ithna 'asharī juristic theory of political and legal authority', *SI*, XXIX, 1969. Cf. also Arjomand, 'Religion, Political action, and legitimate domination in Shi'ite Iran; *Archives europ. social*, 20, 1979; the value of this article is mitigated by inadequate definition of the concept of 'legitimacy' and insufficient reference to the juristic tradition, where the problem of legitimacy becomes central. See further, J. Eliash, 'Some misconceptions regarding the juridical status of the Iranian *ulama*', *IJMES*, X, 1979: the interpretation of the *maqbul* Tradition of Ibn Hanzala (for which, see also Calder, op. cit.) offered in this article appears to be Eliash's own, which is of limited relevance for discovering its value within Imami juristic literature; note, for example, Khumayni's interpretation of this tradition in Khumayni, op. cit. (note 3 below), II, 476ff.
3. Ayatallah Ruhallah Khumayni, *Kitab al-Bay'*, 5 vols., Iraq 1390–91/1970–71 (?); I had access to this work in Iran in March/April 1978, at which time it was in circulation under borrowed covers, hence the uncertainty about the dates.
4. For whom, see H. Algar, *Religion and State in Iran*, Berkeley/Los Angeles, 1969, pp. 162–5. The *K. al-Makasib* is available in lith., Persia, n.d.
5. See Muhammad ibn Hasan al-Tusi, *Kitab al-Ghayba*, Najaf, 1385, p. 18ff.
6. See further E. Kohlberg, 'From Imamiyya to Ithna 'ashariyya, *BSOAS*, XXXIX, 1976; also McDermott, *The Theology of al-Shaikh al-Mufīd*, Beirut, 1978; and Calder, *BSOAS*, XLIII (2), 1980, pp. 365–6.
7. See for example, Eliash, 'Some misconceptions', 23–4.
8. See al-Sharif al-Murtada, *al-Shafi fi l-Imama*, Tehran 1301/1884, pp. 40–41; and M. ibn Hasan al-Tusi, *K. al-Ghayba*, p. 64. Cf. for further discussion of these works, N. Calder, *The Structure of Authority in Imami Shi'i Jurisprudence*, Ph.D. thesis, London, 1979, chap. 3.
9. Cf. Kohlberg, op. cit., 533–4.
10. Zayn al-Din ibn 'Ali al-'Amili; see especially relevant sections of his *al-Rawdat al-Bahiyya fi Sharh al-Lum'at al-Dimashqiyya*, Tabriz, 1271.
11. The development of the theory of *niyaba 'amma* is discussed in detail in Calder, *The Structure of Authority*, chaps. 4–6.
12. The conditions required for giving a valid fatwa, namely *iman, 'adala,* and knowledge of *usul al-fiqh.*
13. Cf. Lambton, 'A Reconsideration of the Position of the *marja'al-taqlid*', *SI,* XX, 1964, p. 118.
14. See further Calder, 'Judicial authority'; Madelung, 'A treatise of the Sharif al-Murtada on the legality of Working for the government', *BSOAS,* XLIII, 1980; I cannot agree with Madelung's identification of the just ruler (*sultan 'adil*), in this context, at this period, as anyone other than the imam, op. cit., p. 30. Imami juristic literature of the pre-Qajar period acknowledges government during the Ghayba either by a *ja'ir* (illegitimate and actual) or by a *faqih* (legitimate and potential); see for example, Shahid II, ad. n. 16 below. The terms *ja'ir/zalim*, though linguistically inseparable from notions of tyranny and misrule, are utilised in a *shar'i* context to designate the illegitimate ruler, quite irrespective of his actual achievement of or failure to achieve some kind of practical justice or tolerance.
15. For classification of land, see further Lambton, *Landlord and Peasant,* London, 1969, pp. 19–20.
16. Shahid II, op. cit., p. 264.
17. See further on Karaki, E. Glassen, 'Schah Isma'il und die Theologen seiner zeit', Der Islam, 48, 1971/2; A. H. Hairi, *Shi'ism and Constitutionalism in Iran*, Leiden, 1977, pp. 61–2.
18. See Lambton, 'A Nineteenth Century View of *jihad*', SI, 32, 1970; also E. Kohlberg, 'The Development of the Imami Shi'i Doctrine of *jihad*', *ZDMG*, 1976.
19. Cf. Keddie, 'The Roots', 212–13: (doctrines however are never really 'disembodied').

20. H. Algar, 'The Oppositional Role of the Ulama in 20th century Iran', in *Scholars, saints and sufis*, ed. Keddie.
21. See Algar, op. cit.; Keddie, op. cit.; Lambton, 'The Tobacco Regie', *SI*, XXII/XXIII and 'The Persian 'ulama and Constitutional Reform', in *Le Shi'isme Imamite*, Colloque de Strasbourg, Paris, 1970.
22. Moments of actual opposition (the Tobacco Regie, the constitutional revolution, the recent revolution in Iran) must be assessed in the light of: a) the existence of *fuqaha'* who supported the Iranian government in each of these periods; b) long periods of comparative tranquility or accommodation; c) an extensive Arab Shi'i population (Iraq, Gulf, Lebanon) whose favoured *mujtahids* have only rarely indulged in active political opposition.
23. See op. cit., n. 21 above.
24. The best available extensive discussion of clerical speculation during the period of the constitutional revolution is contained in Hairi, op. cit.
25. Algar, 'The Oppositional Role', p. 238.
26. See further on Fadlallah Nuri, Hairi, 'Shaykh Fazl Allah Nuri's Refutation of the Idea of Constitutionalism', *MES*, 13, 1977.
27. In Lambton, 'A Reconsideration'.
28. Khumayni, op. cit., Vol II, 459–63.
29. Western literature on this topic is immense: see *inter alia* H. L. A. Hart, *The Concept of Law*, Oxford 1961, chap 7; J. Frank, *Law and the Modern Mind*, London, 1949, chap (i).
30. For details on Baghdadi and Mawardi, see H. A. R. Gibb in *Studies in the Civilisation of Islam*, pp. 151–65.
31. See especially, Abd al-Jabbar, *Sharh al-Usul al-khamsa*, Cairo, 1965, 753ff.
32. See al-Sharif al-Murtada, loc. cit., note 8 above.
33. See *Kanun* in *EI* (ii).
34. See for example, A. P. d'Entreves, *Natural Law*, London, 1970.
35. Khumayni's attitude to the constitution is at first sight inconsistent, see for example, Algar, 'The oppositional role', pp. 246–55. In fact, the habitual juxtaposition of ideal and accommodation within the Imami tradition would make it possible that in other contexts Khumayni might adopt a pragmatic attitude to the constitution. In the present context he is setting out the ideal.
36. The revolutionary message became explicit in Khumayni's Persian language edition of this argument, *Wilayat-i Faqih*, Tehran, 1357.
37. Khumayni, op. cit., 463–7.
38. A *kifa'i* duty is one incumbent on the community as a whole in such a way that, if a sufficient number implement it, it ceases to be incumbent on the rest.
39. The rightful authority of the just *faqih* can also, Khumayni declares, be proved directly from Traditions. This is extensively demonstrated in op. cit., 467–88. The key *hadith* he deals with are all susceptible to a variety of metaphorical readings and I would characterise his discussion as the elaborate deduction of preconceived opinions. The Traditions he cites are well-established in this context and are for the most part adduced in a more circumspect manner in Ansari, *K. al-Makasib*, pp. 144–6; few however have been immune to challenge either on the grounds of their *isnad* or the significance of their content as is evident from the polemical nature of Khumayni's analysis.
40. See also the transition from *nawa'ib al-wali* to *nawa'ib al-hukuma*, Khumayni, op. cit., p. 490.
41. Ansari, *K. al-Makasib*, 144–6.
42. Lambton, 'A Reconsideration', 125–6.
43. Khumayni, op. cit., 497–8.
44. See n. 36 above.

XX

LEGITIMACY AND ACCOMMODATION IN SAFAVID IRAN: THE JURISTIC THEORY OF MUḤAMMAD BĀQIR AL-SABZAVĀRĪ (d. 1090/1679)

INTRODUCTION

Few governors or rulers have failed to recognise the convenience and the stabilising influence of legitimacy as an adjunct to power. In mediaeval Islam (as elsewhere) new dynasties created and propagated normative systems designed to demonstrate their right to rule; and adopted, and where possible adapted, pre-existing normative systems to the same end. Paramount amongst the complex and competing normative systems produced within Islam was that presented by the *sharīʿ*. Nearly all literary manifestations of the Islamic juristic tradition included reference to the rights and duties of the ruler. Insofar as the elaboration of these rights and duties embraced the actual system of a contemporary governor, to that degree his administration was, from the standpoint of the *sharīʿa*, legitimate. At least some writers within the Sunnī juristic tradition developed in practice a number of characterstic devices to distance themselves from governments and so withhold legitimacy. But there was a strong and lasting tradition amongst Sunnī jurists, paradigmatically exemplified in Māwardī, so to define the law that the administrative practice of the day was acknowledged to be a possible realization of the *sharīʿa*. The Imāmi Shīʿī juristic tradition, on the other hand, when it emerged in the Buyid period, had defined the *sharīʿa* as ideally to be implemented, in those contexts where a governor was required, only by the Imam, who was absent. In this respect, it withheld from all secular powers the possibility of legitimacy. Systematic development of the Imāmī rules led, in time, to the conception that certain *sharʿī* functions, ideally administered by the Imam, had, during his absence, been delegated to appropriately qualified *fuqahā'*. This in turn led to the possibility that secular rulers, insofar as their activities were in accord with the instructions of appropriately qualified *fuqahā'*, might attain a partial and secondary or derived legitimacy.

This at least is what I have argued with respect to the Shīʿī tradition; in line, I think, with the views of Professor A. K. S. Lambton in her *State and Government in Medieval Islam.*[1] Professor W. Madelung, in a very carefully worded analysis of a legal treatise by al-Sharīf al-Murtaḍā (d. 436/1044), may be thought to deviate and has been understood to deviate from the views that I have expressed. He suggests, in analysing Murtaḍā's treatise on working for the unjust governor, that the term *al-sulṭān al-muḥiqq al-ʿādil* may be understood as a reference to the ruler who acts in accordance with the commands of the Imam. He therefore expresses doubt about the view that "according to Imāmī belief all government in the absence of the Imam is necessarily and inescapably illegitimate". He goes on to state, however, that "primary and inherent legitimacy belongs only to the rule of the Imam".[2] As it happens, I believe that terms of the type *al-sulṭān al-muḥiqq al-ʿādil,* when used in a work of *fiqh,* including the treatise of Murtaḍā, refer only to the Imam.[3] In other respects, however, the interpretation given to Murtaḍā's work by Madelung is a possible one; and in view of his conception of "primary and inherent legitimacy" as belonging to the Imam, it may be that he and I do not differ very much. I do nevertheless wish to argue that the systematic elaboration of the Imāmī juristic tradition was such as to preclude the possibility of any secular governor being the legitimate agent of the *sharīʿa*, except in a number of secondary and derived senses, expression of which will be discussed in what follows.

Hamid Enayat, in his *Modern Islamic Political Thought,* also conceives of the possibility of a just ruler in the absence of the Imam and he cites the use of the term *sulṭān al-ḥaqq al- ʿādil* by Ibn Idrīs (d. 598/1202) to demonstrate this concept in a work of *fiqh*. He also quotes a passage from Muḥammad Baqir al-Sabzavārī (d. 1090/1679) to illustrate the arguments of a "promonarchical jurisconsult".[4] Enayat too is a careful writer and, while I cannot agree with his intimation that the term *sultān ʿādil* in a work of *fiqh* can mean anything other than the Imām, I am not inclined to disagree with the gist of his argument. Yet there remains a clear need for a more discriminating and precise use of terminology, for the combination of Madelung's, Enayat's and my own writings on this subject has led in a recent work devoted very largely to the question of legitimacy in the Safavid period to confusion and muddle.[5]

It is necessary to note that the work cited by Enayat to demonstrate the promonarchical views of Sabzavārī was not a work of *fiqh*; Sabzavārī, however, did write several works of *fiqh*, amongst them a work entitled *al-Kifāya fi 'l-aḥkām*. It is my intention to analyse, in what follows, those parts of the *Kifāya* which relate specifically to those *sharʿī* functions which ideally belong to the Imam. I hope to show that, in a work of *fiqh*, this "promonarchical" jurist was not able to provide any arguments that might sustain the belief that the secular system was a manifestation (except, as we shall see, in a highly qualified way) of the *sharīʿa*. Indeed, insofar as he conceived that there had been delegation of *sharʿī* functions during the *ghayba* (occultation of the Imam) to anyone other than the Imam, he conceived of delegation only to the *fuqahā'*.

I

Judicial authority (*qaḍā'*) is described, in Sabzavārī's work, as a general authority (*wilāya ʿāmma*), acquired by delegation (*niyāba*) from the Imam.[6] The holder of such authority must fulfil certain conditions, namely that he be adult, sane, male, etc., and that he have adequate knowledge, sufficient to permit of his being a *muftī*; indeed, he should be a *mujtahid muṭlaq*, that is, an unrestricted *mujtahid*, capable of exercising judgement in all legal fields. (In the absence of anyone possessing this capacity, then a partial *mujtahid*, a *mujtahid bi 'l-tajazzu'*, might acquire judicial authority.) Justification for these rules is found in the famous *maqbūl* ("accepted") tradition of ʿUmar b. Hanẓala, together with the almost equally famous tradition of Abū Khadīja (described here as weak, *ḍaʿīf*), both of which represent the sixth Imam as stating specifically his conferral of judicial authority upon members of the Shīʿī community possessed of adequate knowledge.[7] (A view, described as recent, that *ijtihād* was not required, that only knowledge of Imāmī *ḥadīth* was necessary—probably a view deriving from the literalist Akhbārī tradition, following Astarābādī (1036/1627–8)—is described as subject to dispute and an argument adduced to refute it.)

Sabzavārī goes on to state that it may be inferred from the Traditions of ʿUmar b. Ḥanẓala and Abū Khadīja that it is not permissible to take judicial problems to *quḍāt al-jawr*, that is, the *qāḍī*s of tyranny. This phrase clearly refers to *qāḍī*s appointed to office by secular government, and deriving or pretending to derive their authority from that source. Sabzavārī adds the significant rider that this lack of permission remains "whether [the *qāḍī*s in question] are believers or not" (*sawā'an kānū mu'minīn aw lā*)[8]—where the term "believer" implies Imāmī Shīʿī. This of course would be the situation in Safavid Persia, where the governors naturally appointed believers to judicial posts: they retained nonetheless the designation *quḍāt al-jawr*, *qāḍī*s of tyranny—insofar as appointed by secular governments. It will be seen later that insofar as they fulfilled the conditions that implied participation in the Imam's delegation they might also have legitimate authority and this would overlap with their illegitimate authority.

The absence of *sharʿī* recognition of the secular system had still further implications. Thus, Sabzavārī goes on to state that it is to be inferred also from the two Traditions that it is not permissible to receive anything through *their* judgement, *bi-ḥukmi-him* (i.e. that of the *quḍāt al-jawr*), even if one has the right to that thing, *wa-in kāna la-hu ḥaqqan*. He acknowledges some dispute about this view, which is said to be clear (*ẓāhir*) with respect to debt (*dayn*) but less clear with respect to property (*ʿayn*). He concludes, however, that the requirement of the two Traditions is general and covers therefore both cases. It is not permissible to appeal to *quḍāt al-jawr* even when they are believers and even when the law is correctly implemented.

Sabzavārī's discussion is an exploration of the implications of *sharʿī* non-recognition of the secular system of judicial authority. It may be worth recalling at this point that works of Islamic law generally give expression to a certain tension between the normative and the exploratory aspects of their subject-matter. It is usually the case that a particular writer will give his own view, but not at the expense of variant views within the tradition. When there are significant and widely accepted or weighty deviations, they are cited. Accordingly, at this point Sabzavārī cites a view of al-Shahīd al-Thānī (Shahīd II, d. 966/1559) which represents a particular concession to the secular system.[9] Shahīd II and others, he explains, have made an exception in favour of the claimant who carried his problems to the *ahl al-jawr*—the people of tyranny—if it is the case that acquisition of a legal right is dependent on this step. The prohibition, according to Shahīd II, against approaching the secular system (*ahl al-jawr*) relates only to appeal to them by choice, when it is possible to achieve one's aim through the *ahl al-ḥaqq* (i.e. appropriate Shīʿī judges). When it is not so possible, then permission to act through the *ahl al-jawr* is available. Shahīd II's discussion of course related specifically to the conditions of his own time and place, and has its significance in its relevance to the position of Shīʿīs in Ottoman territory in the early sixteenth century. Sabzavārī, in the Persia of Shah ʿAbbās II (1052–77/1642–66), was not inclined to favour Shahīd II's view, which he describes as constituting help towards a sin (*iʿāna ʿalā 'l-ithm*) since, he explains, the judgement of a *jā'ir* (tyrannous [judge]) in a case affecting Shīʿīs is undoubtedly prohibited.

Sabzavārī adds three notes (*masā'il*) to his general discussion of the principles of judicial delegation. In the first note he repeats that during the Imam's presence his permission is required for judicial authority; but during his absence, the judicial authority is effective of a *faqīh* who posseses the qualities of *iftā'*. Such a one has the Imam's permission, as already explained (i.e. by reference to the Traditions of ʿUmar b. Ḥanẓala and Abū Khadīja). (Sabzavārī goes on here to discuss the rules of informal arbitration which need not concern us.) In his second note Sabzavari states that *qaḍā'* is *mustaḥabb*, that is, desirable or preferable, for one who has faith in himself to undertake the task in accord with its conditions. It is in general a *kifā'ī* duty, that is, one which, as long as it is adequately fulfilled in the community at large, does not become incumbent on individuals; but when only one qualified person is available to carry out this duty it becomes *wājib ʿaynī*, i.e. incumbent on that individual. In his third note, Sabzavārī discusses whether it is permissible for a *qāḍī* to gain, in return for his efforts, a subsistence (*rizq*) from the Treasury, *bayt māl al-muslimīn*. This is permissible, but the list of qualifications is such as to imply a considerable distaste for such payments. It will be seen later that Sabzavārī did conceive of the possibility of a kind of "legitimate" *bayt al-māl* coming into existence in the absence of the Imam through the actions of an illegitimate (*jā'ir*) governor. By "legitimate" I mean of course, having the sanction of the *sharīʿa*. The paradoxical nature of legal rulings related to the tax-collecting activities of *jā'ir* governors is generally conceded—and will be discussed below *ad kharāj*.

The broad parameters of Sabzavārī's discussion of *qaḍā* are entirely in accord with the traditional approach to that discussion in a *sharʿī* context, as it had taken place for centuries.[10] The emergence of a Shīʿī dynasty, propagating Imāmī Shiʿism within its territory, had made no significant difference. In effect, Shīʿī discussion of judicial authority refers to the existence of two judicial systems, one of which is the legitimate *sharʿī* system; the other, clearly that instituted by the secular governor of the day, is described consistently as a system of *jawr*, tyranny (*quḍāt al-jawr, ahl al-jawr* etc.). Sabzavārī expressly takes note of the fact that the presence of believers, as participants in the system, does not affect its standing; it remains impermissible to apply to that system, even when the system administers correct laws. As it happens, the wording of the two Traditions that are deemed to lie at the root of the judicial delegation does seem to point in precisely this direction. Generally speaking, it would be quite wrong to imagine that the plain reading of a root text presents insurmountable problems to a developing legal-exegetical tradition. But, to a very considerable extent, human artefacts of the type of a legal system, once established and subject to known rules, may thereafter become intransigent to at least some developments. The direct recognition of the actions of a secular governor as being the implementation of the *sharīʿa* was logically precluded by certain fundamental principles to which early Shīʿism had committed itself. The most important of these was the principle that the *sharīʿa* could only be put into effect, in those areas where a governor was required, by the Imam, who was absent. Further development of this principle led either to the conclusion that a particular function had lapsed (*sāqiṭ/suqūṭ*) pending the return of the Imam, or it had been delegated to the *fuqahā'*.[11] The exploration of tension between "lapsing" and "clerical delegation" produced a great deal of subtle and some vitriolic dispute in a *sharʿī* context. But, from Buyid to Safavid times, these two positions remained the outer parameters of dispute. Though variously combined with a more or less accommodatory attitude to government, and a greater or lesser acknowledgement of the rights of individuals, they were so firmly entrenched that, perhaps, not simply they were not, but they could not be subverted without creating a break with the tradition (indeed a sense of logical failure) that would be difficult or impossible to sustain.

Whatever value be conceded to that argument (and I am inclined to believe that legal logic was of great importance in academic juristic dispute) it is at least well known that certain accommodatory steps expressed in early Safavid times inspired violent and effective reaction. Shahīd II's gentle push towards working through an illegitimate (*jā'ir*) judicial system in Ottoman territory was paralleled by a number of accommodatory features expressed by the early Safavid jurist Karakī (d. 940/1534).[12] The immediate reaction, however, spearheaded by the jurist Qaṭīfī (d. 945/1539), who engaged in violent dispute with Karakī precisely on matters relating to accommodation with secular power, was strong enough, if not to force retreat, at least to prevent further development. The characteristic attitude of Qaṭīfī and those who followed him was quietist and non-accommodatory. The accommodatory arguments of Karakī, notably in the field of *kharāj* (a form of potentially *sharʿī* taxation) were followed by Sabzavārī, but there is no evidence at all that the accommodatory moves were such as to bring the secular government within the sphere of *sharʿī* legitimacy.

The key to *sharʿī* legitimacy lay in the acknowledged delegation of judicial authority. Sabzavārī, as demonstrated above, gave nothing to the secular system. Judicial authority lay within the class of learned jurists; there, it was diffuse and informal. There was no hierarchical system, and no institutional controls; in fact, the only control emerging from Sabzavārī's discussion, again entirely in line with the tradition, is that implied by the need for a personal or public recognition of one's abilities. A theoretical concern that the public should apply to the most learned (*aʿlam, afqah*) represents a suggestion of a hierarchical system which is not in fact explored.

The *sharʿī* discussion demonstrates the existence of a conflict of legitimating systems. The *sharīʿa* conferred authority upon a broad class of *mujtahids* and denied the authority of those appointed by the government. No doubt the government promulgated a definition of legitimacy that sanctioned the creation of judicial authority by delegation from the appropriate governor. A conflict of authority was thus built into the Safavid administrative system and may be thought to represent a constant and inalienable destabilizing factor. The description of the Safavid system provided by Sir John Chardin seems to confirm the existence of two judicial systems in some degree of conflict with one another. He notes that most Persians preferred the government courts to the *qāḍīs*' courts.[13] It will be suggested later that while the Imāmī system pointed towards conflict and destabilization the judicial theory of Ottoman jurists was such as to provide for legitimacy, cohesion and stability.

II

The acknowledged judicial delegation became the formal criterion normally adduced by Shīʿī *fuqahā'* to account for the transfer of other areas of *sharʿī* authority to the *mujtahids*. In this respect one might describe the process whereby *sharʿī* authority, in a general sense, was conceded to the *fuqahā'* as an expansion of the sphere of *qaḍā'*. The theoretical developments and the refinements of terminology attendant upon the expansion of the sphere of *qaḍā'* I have discussed elsewhere, for the *sharʿī* taxes of *zakāt* and *khums*.[14] Sabzavārī, discussing the distribution of *zakāt*, acknowledges a number of possibilities including (a) that the individual might undertake the task for himself, (b) that it is *wājib* (mandatory) and (c) *mustaḥabb* (preferable) to carry it to the *faqīh*. He states that if the Imam, being present, demands it, it is *wājib* to take it to him and he adds that the transfer of this rule to the *faqīh* is not unlikely (*lā yabʿud*).[15] His discussion, while not free from the expression of preference, tends to lay down the parameters within which one must act, rather than to specify exactly what one should do. These parameters do not include the possibility of the secular government playing any role whatever in the field of *zakāt*: where delegation is acknowledged it is to the *faqīh*. A similar situation is evident in the discussion of *khums*. Here, Sabzavārī considers at one extreme, the possibility that all goods theoretically subject to *khums* are to be declared *mubāḥ*, that is free of any charge upon them; and, at the other extreme (and preferable in his view—*al-aḥwaṭ ʿindī*), that the appropriate sums should be transferred to the rightful recipients "through the administration of the *faqīh*"—*bi-tawliyat al-faqīh*.[16] His discussion of *jihād* does not involve any explicit delegation to the *faqīh*, nor to anybody else, except when *dār al-islām* is threatened by *kāfirs*, when it becomes incumbent to fight for everyone capable of fighting.[17] In the discussion of Friday Prayer, he mentions two possibilities, namely that it was, during the *ghayba*, either *wājib* on condition of the presence/permission of the *faqīh*, or *wājib* even without the presence/permission of the *faqīh*. His discussion implies but does not clearly state a third possibility namely that it was not permissible at all during the *ghayba*.[18] This last position had been strongly argued for by Qaṭīfī and his followers, in opposition to Karakī and his followers. By omitting to mention it Sabzavārī intends no doubt to condemn it. It is to be noted, then, that in all areas where one might look for delegation, in the field of *sharʿī* juristic discussion, Sabzavārī, in so far as he conceives of delegation, conceives of it as to the *faqīh*. Where delegation of authority does not take place it may be because a function has lapsed (the omitted view on Friday prayer), or been done away with (the minority view on *khums*) or left to individuals (a possibility under *zakāt*). There is no delegation elsewhere.

Shīʿī jurisprudence of the Buyid period, when it first achieved substantive articulation, declared, in effect, that the rightful ruler—the only one capable of adminstering the *sharīʿa*—was absent, and that accordingly several *sharʿī* functions had lapsed. This was a declaration of illegitimacy for the secular ruler, but, at the same time, a rescission of challenge and revolution. From Buyid to Safavid times, the dominant tendency was to rehabilitate the *sharīʿa* by expressing a clear delegation of *sharʿī* functions to the *faqīh qua* judge (*ḥākim*/*qāḍī*). This too is not to be interpreted as a challenge to Sunnī governments; in fact significant theoretical advances seem to have taken place at times of rapprochement between governments and the Shīʿī community. I would be inclined to see this theoretical development in favour of the *fuqahā'* as reflecting the political status of the Shīʿī communities within the larger Sunnī community: they were, I would suggest, independent self-regulating communities of much the same kind as Christian or Jewish communities and they required to be administered by officers within the community. It was clearly conducive to that end that the *fuqahā'* be recognized as having the right very largely to put into effect the *sharīʿa*—excluding of course *jihād*, a function that did not have to be attended to by the smaller Shīʿī community. The development by Shahīd II of an elegant and extreme theory of clerical delegation, such that all *sharʿī* functions came within the ambit of the *mujtahid, qua ḥākim*—except *jihād*—must be seen as an expression of a desire to achieve an independent self-regulating community within the Ottoman system, having the same kind of status as was there conceded to Christian and Jewish communities.

The early Safavid jurist, Karakī, also gave expression to a very full concept of clerical authority within the sphere of the *sharīʿa* (excluding again *jihād*). Though his views definitely implied the illegitimacy of the secular government—insofar as they restricted the possible rightful agents of the *sharīʿa* to only the *faqīh* (notwithstanding the Shīʿī affiliation of the Safavid ruler)—they too are not to be understood as a challenge to the government. Karakī's personal and practical position was accommodatory; attacks on him were directed at criticizing his close relationship with secular power. The expressed alternative to his view was dissociation from government (quietist not revolutionary). It would seem then to be the case that, from the time of Karakī to that of Sabzavārī, the expression of a full concept of clerical authority within the *sharīʿa* was associated with an accommodatory approach to secular power. Those who opposed Karakī, who generally advocated a more restricted concept of clerical authority, tend to advocate dissociation from the government. I find it difficult to perceive in the whole of the Shīʿī juristic tradition up to this period any serious or sustained expression of challenge to or opposition to secular power. It seems quite clear that those who, in Safavid Iran, developed the fuller expression of clerical authority did so under the impression that it was consistent with an accommodatory alliance with government. There can be little doubt that the basis of this alliance was (a) the borrowed legitimacy available to the secular ruler insofar as he could make his sytem work through the *sharʿī* system. (To this end the *sharīʿa* had to be fully available and this may account for the fuller concept of *sharʿī* authority expressed by the accommodatory party). And (b) the obvious benefits accruing to the religious classes from alliance with power. The non-accommodatory view, represented paradigmatically by Qaṭīfī, in his dispute with Karakī, tended to restrict the possible implementation of the *sharīʿa* by e.g. denying Friday Prayer, or by denying the validity of *kharāj*. The affirmation of Friday Prayer as valid during the *ghayba* meant amongst other things the provision of institutional posts (*imām jumʿa*) that could be filled by jurists. The legitimacy of *kharāj* (even when, as will be demonstrated, administered by a *jā'ir*) meant the legitimate participation by the *ʿulamā'* in the responsibilities and in the profits of government. One of the most illuminating disputes between Karakī and Qaṭīfī is made available in anecdotal form in the *Lu'lu' at al-baḥrayn*;[19] here, Karakī is presented as arguing that it is *mustaḥabb* or *wājib* to accept gifts from sultans, while Qaṭīfī argues that it is at least *makrūh* ("disliked"). The basic polarity of this dispute is of course familiar. One group advocates the responsibilities of participation in government, at some cost to moral purity, and accepting the incidence of corruption and venality that is perhaps inseparable from practical politics. Another group withdraws from government, rejecting participation, at the cost perhaps of influence. The polarity is of course universal, and, in Persia as elsewhere, the extreme positions, adopted in the course of debate by Karakī and Qaṭīfī, gave way to nuanced middle positions. That the fuller definition of clerical authority could become a medium of challenge and opposition to government no doubt became clear in time. Whenever it emerged I would be inclined to see it as a novel possibility in the history of the Shīʿī juristic tradition, which was characteristically accommodatory and not oppositional in its earlier development.

III

I have stated so far that the Shīʿī tradition of juristic writing conferred judicial authority upon the *faqīh* or *mujtahid*, directly, and that insofar as it acknowledged the possible implementation of other *sharʿī* functions that characteristically belonged to the Imam, it did so only to an appropriately qualified *faqīh*. In developing this theory the Shīʿī jurists were well aware of the necessary illegitimacy that was thereby implied for all forms of secular government; and they developed a terminology to express that illegitimacy, the central terms being *jawr/jā'ir* and, synonymously as far as I can perceive, *ẓulm/ẓālim*. These terms were not intended to indicate practical wickedness or necessary real injustice on the part of the governor (though that was always a possibility). From earliest times discussion of working with the *sulṭān jā'ir* was combined with recognition that such a *sulṭān* might permit correct implementation of the *sharīʿa*.[20] The accommodatory aspect of the juristic tradition may best be exemplified by consideration of two *sharʿī* topics: (a) working for the unjust governor and (b) *kharāj*. Discussion of these topics can be extremely complex.

(a) Within the conservative framework of juristic writing, the first topic, working for the unjust governor, is usually discussed twice in a comprehensive work of *fiqh*: once with respect to *iqāmat al-ḥudūd* and *qaḍā'* (imposing penalties and judicial authority) and once, more generally, with respect to taking up any kind of official position.[21] *Iqāmat al-ḥudūd*, it is to be noted, is yet another *sharʿī* function characteristically belonging to the Imam, and delegated during the *ghayba* (if delegation is recognized) either to individuals (permitting, for example, householders to impose penalties on slaves and other members of their family) or to the *fuqahā'*.

Hence Sabzavari states, with respect to *iqāmat al-ḥudūd*, that this function belongs to the Imam or to one given his permission. Sabzavārī then presents an argument, in the face of some doubt implied by some early Buyid *fuqahā'*, to demonstrate that it is permissible for the *faqīh* to carry out this activity during the *ghayba*. He then quotes the enterprising sixth/twelfth century *faqīh* Ibn Idrīs:

> It is related that one appointed by a *sulṭān ẓālim* over the people and given charge of *ḥudūd* may impose them . . . and believe that he is doing this with the permission of *sulṭān al-ḥaqq*, not *sulṭān al-jawr*.

This is a neat expression of the way in which the legitimate system may work through the illegitimate system. It is in fact a quote from the *Nihāya* of Ṭūsī (d. 460/1067). Ṭūsī's argument took the usual form of expressing first that *iqāmat al-ḥudūd* was a function belong to the Imam (designated *sulṭān al-zamān al-manṣūb min qibal allāh*) or his deputy (designated *man naṣaba-hu al-imām*). Thereafter, if a man was appointed to *ḥudūd* by a *sulṭān ẓālim,* he was to believe that he was acting with the permission of *sulṭān al-ḥaqq* and not *sulṭān al-jawr.*[22] *Sulṭān al-ḥaqq* is of course another designation of the Imam—whose permission alone was of any significance. Ibn Idrīs, however, does not like the general nature of Ṭūsī's expression and continues thus:

However it is better (*awlā*) . . . to reject action in accord with this tradition; in fact it is mandatory to do so. For *ijmāʿ* is available . . . that imposition of *ḥudūd* is not permissible, and none is charged with this task except the *imāms* and their judges (*ḥukkām*) who act in accord with their permission.

Ibn Idrīs here re-states the basic *sharʿī* position (I know of no deviation from this throughout the Imāmī Shīʿī juristic tradition) that *iqāmat al-ḥudūd* belongs to the Imam(s) and those to whom they give permission. Granted this, he does not like the general formulation (derived from Ṭūsī's *Nihāya*) of permission to impose *ḥudūd* in the service of a *ẓālim sulṭān.* Having acknowledged the existence of this view, he argues against it. It is by no means clear that he understood by *ḥukkām* quite the wide sweep of authority that later jurists comprehended within this term. His expression suggests a very wary approach to the secular government. But Sabzavārī comments: "This view [of Ibn Idrīs] is valid [only] if the one appointed [by a *ẓālim*] is not a *faqīh*".[23] It thus emerges, for Sabzavārī, following Ibn Idrīs's expression (but not thereby necessarily following his intention), that if a *faqīh* is appointed by a *ẓālim,* he may impose *ḥudūd,* and believe that he is acting by permission of the Imam (*sulṭān al-ḥaqq*) not the secular power (*sulṭām ẓālim*). It becomes clearer from this example in what way the broader view of clerical (judicial) authority was of mutual benefit to rulers and jurists. If the secular government appointed to judicial tasks and to *ḥudūd*-implementing activities a fully qualified jurist then the practical workings of the system would be in accord with the *sharīʿa* and fully legitimate. For a Safavid Shah, let us say, who understood the theory, it must have been galling nonetheless to realise that insofar as his administrative system was an implementaion of the *sharīʿa* it had nothing to do with him; it derived its functional legitimacy from the belief of the participants that they were acting not on the basis of his permission (or appointment) but by virtue of the acknowledged delegation from the absent Imam. Some, perhaps, did know the theory and acknowledged it when convenient.

In the *kitāb al-tijāra* (chapter on trade), Sabzavārī, in accord with the established tradition, discusses the general question of taking up official posts, having already dealt with the specific question of *ḥudūd* and *qaḍā'.* A brief outline will suffice. When it is a question of taking up a post with a *jā'ir* (he does not even mention the possibility of taking up a post with an *ʿādil*) in conditions where one is secure against doing what is *ḥarām,* it is permissible, possibly *mustaḥabb,* perhaps *wājib* to do so. If one is compelled by a *jā'ir* to take up a post (under threat of harm to oneself, one's property, one's honour or one/some of the believers) then, if the harm is insignificant, it is *makrūh* (disliked); but if the harm is significant, it is permissible, *mustaḥabb,* indeed *wājib.*[24] These were the main parameters of Sabzavārī's discussion, and, while he had preferences within those parameters, there is nothing here that is fundamentally new to the tradition. On balance Sabzavārī was rather favourable to the principle of working with a *jā'ir* just as he was favourable to the principle of letting a *jā'ir*/*ẓālim* acquire a borrowed legitimacy by working through the fully qualified *fuqahā'* in areas where their authority was recognized.

(b) Juristic discussion of *kharaj,* the second area that I have isolated to illustrate the accommodatory aspect of Imāmī jurisprudence, is extremely complicated. I wish initially to single out for discussion only one rule. I quote it first from the classic juristic work of al-Muḥaqqiq, the *Sharā'iʿ al-Islām* (Muḥaqqiq died in 676/1277 under the Īlkhānids).

What the *sulṭān jā'ir* collects under the title *muqāsama* . . . or under the title *kharāj* . . . or under the title *zakāt,* it is permissible to buy or accept as a gift . . .[25]

The significance of this rule lies in the locution *under the title*; for the intention was to express the notion that secular tax-collecting, though it sheltered, as it were, under the terminology of *sharʿī* taxes, was not an implementation of the *sharīʿa.* This is made perfectly clear both in earlier writers who characteristically add the gloss that the sultans have no right to these taxes, and in later commentaries, which explain the phrase "under the title" on the grounds that only the Imam can implement *sharʿī* taxes. Only the Imam can implement the *sharīʿa*; the actions of a secular governor (*sulṭān/sulṭān jā'ir/ẓālim*) are not the *sharīʿa*. The rule is intended to create a dispensation whereby the products of the illegitimate tax-collecting activities of an illegitimate ruler are not subject to the usual prohibitions that would affect avowedly ill-gotten goods. These products could be bought and used within the community. I would suggest that the subtle phraseology is designed precisely to signal the illegitimacy of rulers (*sulṭān jā'ir*) and their tax-collecting activities (having only the *name* of *sharʿī* taxes). In European terms the distinction created is one corresponding to *de jure* illegitimacy, but *de facto* accommodation.[26]

The dispute about *kharāj* in Safavid times begins with Karakī. The main aspects of the dispute are provided in Madelung's "Shiite Discussion on the Legality of the *kharāj*" (1981) and of course in Tabataba'i's *Kharaj in Islamic Law*. The central argument of Karakī is that *kharāj* is a valid *sharʿī* tax, and that the broad parameters of its legitimate collection can be ascertained. Insofar as the secular rulers (usually designated *sulṭān jā'ir,* sometimes simply *sulṭān*) conducted themselves within the broad parameters of the known rules then what they collected became *ḥalāl* to the people at large; and, furthermore, the sultan acquired certain rights related to collection and distribution. I would be inclined to interpret Karakī as moving some way from the traditional view; for that clearly distrusted the tax-collecting activities of the ruler. These activities had only the *name* of *sharʿī* taxes. Karakī seems to argue that the tax-collecting activities as such were legitimate and only the agent of the activities was not the rightful agent. This was a tricky position to sustain but it seems to have prevailed with many Safavid jurists. I have described above the kind of legitimacy available to a ruler, insofar as he employed appropriately qualified *fuqahā'* for *sharʿī* tasks, as "borrowed". I would characterize the kind of legitimacy made available to him by virtue of Karakī's description of *kharāj* as, at best, "reflected" legitimacy. In neither case was the ruler provided with a secure normative base for his governing activities. What security there was, was in any case instantly undermined because Karakī's position came under intense attack first from Qaṭīfī and subsequently from such influential jurists as Ardabīlī (993/1585) and others. The dispute remained a live issue for a century or more, being still worthy of complete recapitulation and lengthy digression at the time of Sabzavārī. This dispute served in the end only to foreground the unwillingness or the incapacity of Shīʿī *fuqahā'* to recognize in the secular ruler an appropriate or rightful administrator of the *sharīʿa,* or to recognize in his administration the *sharīʿa* in practice.

Sabzavārī's discussion of land law involves extensive quotation from earlier jurists: Ṭūsī, Muḥaqqiq, ʿAllāma, Shahīd II, Karakī and Qaṭīfī. The latter two, however, are always quoted anonymously, perhaps because their articulation of the dispute was still seen to be disruptive more than one hundred years after the event. After a lengthy introduction which illustrates the existence of *ikhtilāf,* indeed violent dispute (and therefore of course an area of *ijtihād*), Sabzavārī begins his own analysis (*wa-naḥnu nadhkur al-taḥqīq* . . .) which like the preceding section very rapidly develops the form of extensive and diverse quotation accompanied by comment.[27]

The following survey is intended to indicate the conceptual bases for the discussion rather than to provide details. I restrict my comments to five headings.

1. It is instructive to raise the question why *kharāj* becomes the focus of a discussion whose real subject was the question of accommodation with secular power. I would suggest that the *sharʿī* taxes *zakāt* and *khums* had been thoroughly dealt with within the Shīʿī tradition in such a way that there was no conceptual space for accommodation in this area. By contrast, *kharāj* had been rather neglected by the Shīʿī *fuqahā'* (Tabataba'i, 1983, p. 47): for them, insofar as *kharāj* was a legitimate possibility it belonged to the Imam and insofar as the secular government collected something under this title it was not "real" *kharāj*. This function had not been definitively tidied up and transferred to the *fuqahā'*: it remained open for exploration.

It was (or seemed, at least initially,) possible that this juristic topic could be made into a device whereby the activities of a governor could be made, to a degree, legitimate. The incentive towards the discovery of such a device came about because of the new tension between Sunnīs and Shīʿīs created by the establishment of Safavid Persia in opposition to Ottoman Turkey. On the one hand the Safavid governors offered a pro-Shīʿī policy and demanded, no doubt, support. And at least some *fuqahā'* were inclined to respond positively to that demand (seeing here, perhaps, an appropriate mode of supporting their faith). On the other hand, the Ottoman government instituted anti-Shīʿī policies (Imber, 1979) and so prompted the Ottoman *fuqahā'* (Shahīd II) to clarify their accommodatory policies, and so dissociate themselves from extremists. Both parties, the accommodatory Safavid *fuqahā'* (Karakī *et al.*) and the accommodatory Ottoman *fuqahā'* made *kharāj* a focus of their theoretical explorations. But, they inspired opposition, which focussed on the same subject, representing a political stance of dissociation (to be distinguished, I think, from active opposition).

2. The discussion of *kharāj* is carried out by all participants in relation to the collecting-activities of *jā'irs* (except as qualified in section IV below). It is unnecessary for me to demonstrate this as the discussion of Madelung (1981) and Tabataba'i (1983) make it abundantly clear. It is worth, however, stressing the notions attendant upon the use of this term, which are brought out by Shahīd II with his accustomed clarity and conceptual rigour (in his commentary on Muḥaqqiq, the *Masālik al-ifhām*). Of the taxes called *muqāsama* and *kharāj*, administered by the sultan *jā'ir*, Shahīd II states that these taxes cannot become real (*lā yataḥaqqaqānī*) (= legitimate) except by specific designation from the *imām ʿādil*. In the meantime, during the time of the domination of the *jā'ir* (*fī zaman taghallubi-hi*), the Imams have given permission to deal in these collections. Shahīd II says he knows of no opposition to this view in spite of the *jā'ir*'s being *ẓālim* in collecting these taxes (*wa-in kāna ẓāliman fī akhdhi-hi*). Furthermore the *jā'ir* is not to be reproached for his manifestation of *ẓulm* in this respect (*la yuqdaḥ fī-hi taẓallumu-hu*) as long as the *ẓulm* is not realised in the form of an increase beyond the customary exaction from the people etc.[28]

Interesting though it would be to give more of Shahīd II's finely discriminating commentary, this must suffice to make the point that it is *jā'irs* who collect the taxes and that the term *jawr* is not an assertion of practical wickedness, but of conceptual status, corresponding to our "illegitimate".

In his extensive recapitulation of all the major arguments that had been adduced in the tradition on this subject, Sabzavārī gives no evidence that the term *sulṭān ʿādil* was ever used in this context. He does, however, use the term once. He is commenting on Shahīd II's remarks:

> It is manifest that the Imams, since they knew the impossibility of the just sultan's acquiring authority until the time of the *qā'im (lammā ʿalimū intifā' tasalluṭ al-sulṭān al-ʿādil ilā zaman al-qā'im)* and since they knew that the Muslims have certain rights in lands conquered by force (= *kharāj* lands) and since they knew that they would not be able to achieve these rights during that extended time (*tilka 'l-mudda al-mutaṭāwila*) except by recourse to *sulṭāns* and *amīrs*; [for all these reasons) they have declared it permissible to accept from them [the products of these taxes]. For, in declaring these things *ḥarām* there would be hardship and difficulty for them (i.e. believers/Muslims) and denial of their rights totally.[29]

Of this passage, I will merely remark that the reason for the impossibility (*intifā'*) of the just sultan's acquiring authority until the time of the *qā'im* is that only the *qā'im* (= Imam, *qua* eschatological figure) can be the just sultan (= Imam, *qua* executor of the *sharīʿa*).

3. There was thus universal agreement that it was the *jā'ir*—or illegitimate governor—who would administer the *kharāj* during the *ghayba*. Paradoxically, however, though the agent was illegitimate, the process could be legitimate. The central term in this context is *ḥalāl*. Karakī and those who followed him argued for the *ḥill* (legitimateness) of *kharāj* during the Ghayba.

Shahīd II in his *Masālik al-ifhām* does not use this argument. For him, *kharāj* was a tax administered by a Sunnī governor, the Ottoman sultan. We have already seen that for him the illegitimacy of the Ottoman ruler (*jawr*/*ẓulm*) was not a matter for blame. Indeed he proposed that there was a standard of practical equity whereby to measure and judge these illegitimate actions, namely custom. He went on to discuss the tax which was collected under the title *zakāt* (as opposed to *kharāj*). Here again his argument demonstrates that the tax actually administered is not real *zakāt*, is not legitimate (*sharʿī*). But again he proposes accommodation and a measure of practical equity: he suggests this time that the *jā'ir*'s practice should be measured by the standards of his own *madhhab*, i.e. a Sunnī *madhhab*.[30] Thus, while acknowledging the illegitimate status of the *jā'ir*, he nonetheless makes provision for an accommodatory recognition of his activities as practically just or equitable, albeit not *sharʿī*. He was thus in a position to argue that his community might deal with the government, pay their taxes and refrain from "blame" (*qadaḥ*) as long as the government demonstrated some kind of practical justice in its administration. No doubt this argument would have its uses in persuading the Ottomans that the established Shīʿī community of Syria was not deserving of the persecution that was meted out elsewhere to extremists.

Shahīd II went further and noted that his assessment of the situation was restricted to a *jā'ir* who was opposed to the Truth, i.e. a non Shīʿī ruler (*al-ḥukm mukhtaṣṣ bi-l-jā'ir al-mukhālif li-l-ḥaqq*). For if the *jā'ir*/ruler were a believer, it would not be *ḥalāl* to deal in what he collects, because of his acknowledgement that he was a *ẓālim* in this area.[31] This is a fully logical position, consistent with the juristic tradition. For the dispensation to deal in what was collected by *jā'irs* had always referred to Sunnī rulers. It was hardly a practical but certainly a logical assumption that a true believer would abandon power in favour of the Imam, the legitimate agent of the *sharīʿa*. More interesting, however, is the value of this view for propaganda purposes. Shahīd II was demonstrating a distinct lack of sympathy for events and developments in Safavid Iran, he was in fact excluding the Safavid government from the area of accommodation into which he drew the Ottoman government. It is well-known that events in Iran only stirred up trouble for him and his community in Ottoman territory, and this was his response, at least at one stage of his career: a denial of the possibility of accommodation with a government that claimed to be believers!

The *fuqahā'* resident in Safavid Iran had of course different views. Karakī and those who followed him argued that it was possible, within the context of Shīʿī law, to know the modes and conditions of imposition of *kharāj*. In this respect the activities could be, or correspond to, *ḥalāl* activities. Echoing this tradition and its arguments Sabzavārī too provides arguments *fī ḥill al-kharāj*. Commenting on Shahīd II's assertion that accommodation in the area of taxation would be restricted to non-Shīʿī governors, Sabzavārī states the following:

> The tendency manifest in Shahīd II's words to restrict the ruling on the legitimacy (*ḥill*) of *kharāj* to what is collected by non-Shīʿīs has no significance. For it is clear that the Imams' dispensation was intended to enable the Shīʿa to achieve their rights in the Treasury in accord with their knowledge that that would not be possible for them because of their incapacity and because of the sultans' gaining control over wealth (read: *li-'stīlā' al-salāṭīn ʿalā l-amwāl*, not *li-'stīlā'i-him al-salāṭīn* . . .).[32]

The pronouns there are rather carelessly distributed but the intention is clear. *Kharāj* is legitimate (*ḥalal*/*ḥill*) and the Shīʿī community has "rights" in the Treasury. It followed from this that a sultan insofar as he implemented a legitimate tax—albeit he was not the appropriate agent—himself acquired rights. Sabzavari quotes an anonymous writer (?Karakī):

> *Kharāj* and *muqāsama* are incumbent [on the owner of *kharāj* land] and these [taxes] are undertaken by the *jā'ir* (*yatawallā-humā al-jā'ir*). It is not permissible to deny [their validity], nor to refuse them, nor to have the usufruct of them without his [the *jā'ir*'s] permission. This is by agreement of our companions (*bi 'ttifāq al-aṣḥāb*).[33]

Again it is to be noted that the administrator of the taxes is to be a *jā'ir*. But the owner of land is conceived of as legitimately subject to taxes through the administration of the *jā'ir*; and the *jā'ir* acquires certain rights to the usufruct of them, at least to the extent that one is not permitted to refuse to pay or to acquire the usufruct of them without his permission.

The precise legal status of the *jā'ir* may be thought a little hazy here, but the intentions behind this elaboration are clear enough. The difficult conceptual distinctions that we are required to embrace are reflected in the remarks of a contemporary Shīʿī scholar. "What the unjust ruler takes as *kharāj* may *stand for* the actual fiscal duty of the taxpayer . . . This is the most complicated dilemma presented by the subject of *kharāj* in Shīʿī law. How can such an exception be allowed in the face of the Shīʿī doctrine concerning rulers and the invalidity of their actions?"[34] Quite. The italics in that quotation are mine and I would certainly be inclined to interpret at least some writers of what I will call the Karakī tradition as asserting that the *jā'ir's* activities not only *stood for* but *were* the actual, that is the *sharʿī*, duty of the tax-payer.

4. The concepts that regulated the discussion, as I have analysed it so far, were (a) that the *jā'ir* was not and could not be the legitimate—though he was the actual—agent of *kharāj*; and (b) that the tax itself was, or might be, *ḥalāl* during the *ghayba*.

I think none will deny that these concepts are being manipulated in search of practical results, namely what I have called practical accommodation with a ruler, Sunnī or Shīʿī. But concepts locked into a logical structure of discourse may dictate unexpected but inexorable logical consequences. Exploration of the *sharīʿa* within the Shīʿī juristic tradition was such that there was general agreement that if any of the Imam's functions continued during the *ghayba* they continued as duties and functions of the *fuqahā'*, who acted as the Imam's *nā'ib* (deputy). Once it was conceded that *kharāj* was, during the *ghayba*, *ḥalāl* or potentially *ḥalāl* the question was quite unavoidable: should not this activity, like all other *sharʿī* activities which belonged ideally to the Imam, devolve upon the *fuqahā'*? (I should stress here that this question became inevitable for logical reasons, relating to the conceptual structure of the *sharīʿa* as elaborated within the Imāmī juristic tradition. I conceive that *kharāj* became a focus of controversy in the Safavid period initially because of the (external) political concerns of the *fuqahā'* and their relations with rulers. But discussion of the concept was eventually controlled by the logical structure of juristic thought which did not in the end prove very helpful as a means of supporting or strengthening a pro-Shīʿī ruler.)

Shahīd II asks the question whether the *fuqahā'* have (ideally) control over *kharāj* in the *Musālik al-ifhām* and comes to a negative conclusion.[35] It seems that Karakī too asked the question and came, cautiously, to a positive answer.[36] The question, I have suggested, was inevitable; an initial negative answer not surprising in view of the fact that the tradition offered no specific justification for any other answer. But logic pointed in the opposite direction and we find that Shahīd II in his *al-Rawḍa al-bahiyya* states the following:

During the *ghayba* [taxes] in the hands of the *jā'ir* are permissible [etc.] . . . but that over which the *nā'ib* of the Imam, namely the *ḥākim sharʿī*, can gain independent control, that is for him to control (*mā yumkin istiqlāl nā'ib al-imām bi-hi wa-huwa al-ḥākim al-sharʿī . . . fa-amru-hu ilay-hi*).[37]

Sabzavārī cites another writer from the Karakī tradition who came to the same conclusion (*ākhar min al-aṣḥāb*):

Does the usufruct [of the products of these taxes] depend on the permission of the *ḥākim sharʿī*, if he is capable of distributing them appropriately, granted his being the *nā'ib* of the Imam, and his being vested with authority in greater matters? (*binā'an ʿalā kawni-hi nā'iban min al-mustaḥaqq ʿalay-hi al-salām wa-mufawwadan ilay-hi mā huwa aʿẓam min dhālika*) The manifest view is that this is so . . . But, when there is no such capacity [on the part of the *ḥākim sharʿī*] the matter belongs to the *jā'ir*.[38]

And Sabzavārī, giving his own view, writes:

If the *ḥākim sharʿī* can get control over (these taxes) the manifest view is that this is permissible. It is better to seek the permission of the *ḥākim sharʿī* concerning what the *jā'ir* gives one . . .[39]

The long-running high-profile dispute about *kharāj* was almost certainly initiated in an effort to provide a maximum degree of accommodation with the government. Its conceptual resolution, however, confirmed that the only legitimate agent of the *sharīʿa* during the *ghayba* was the *faqīh* (*qua* judge, *ḥākim sharʿī*); and that the activities of the ruler, even if they conformed closely to *sharʿī* rules, constituted *jawr*. The "promonarchical" jurist Sabzavārī was as unable as anyone else to escape from the terminology of *jawr* and *ẓulm*.

5. It made matters only worse that, again, the constraints of a well-established juristic tradition almost compelled an adequate expression of the anti-accommodatory party. Sabzavārī quotes, again anonymously, something from the Qaṭīfī tradition (Qaṭīfī himself?):

A recent companion has disputed this matter: he claims . . . that [to conceive of *kharāj* as *ḥalāl* etc.] is to provide support for sin (*muʿāwana ʿalā 'l-ithm*), to strengthen a *ẓālim (taqwiyat al-ẓālim)* and to acknowledge that he has authority and permission from God (*wa-qawl bi-anna la-hu wilāya wa-ʿahd min allāh*). For, in respect of one who does not derive his authority (*salṭana*) from God or from his prophet, it is permissible to oppose him in this sphere . . .[40]

Sabzavārī does not like this view. He reminds us that the terms *jawr/ẓulm* are compatible with a practical justice and need not inspire opposition, but the equivocal note remains. Up to and including Safavid times (and as far as I am aware throughout the Qajar period as well) the Shīʿī juristic tradition did not or could not create the conceptual space that might permit a secular ruler to be seen as true agent of the *sharīʿa*. Qaṭīfī was right in affirming that the secular ruler did not derive his authority from God or from his prophet: the only people for whom that privilege was claimed were the imams and the *fuqahā'*.[41] For most *fuqahā'* it did not necessarily follow that one had to refrain from providing support for a practically just (equitable) ruler; indeed they were inclined to concede that in spite of his *jawr*/illegitimacy he acquired certain rights, recognized by the law. The extent and significance of these "rights", the limits, that is, of accommodation, these were the subject of debate. If some justice is to be done in English to the kind of distinction that the Shīʿī tradition worked with, I think we need terms of the type I have used here and in earlier studies. The Shīʿī juristic tradition did not concede *de jure* legitimacy to any secular governor; it rather explored the possibilities of *de facto* accommodation. Within that sphere it eventually encompassed both a very positive accommodatory attitude, pushing hard, as it were, against the limits of illegitimacy, and at the opposite extreme, a quietistic attitude of dissociation, maintaining the purity and integrity that came from non-involvement with government. In the end too, and probably already in the Safavid period, the juristic tradition became a medium for expressing political challenge to secular power. (I have already pointed out that the main theoretical justification of challenge in modern times was, in Safavid times, associated with accommodation.) This flexibility should not surprise: throughout the centuries the academic tradition of Islamic jurisprudence has, given its varied expression, manifested itself more as a medium for the exploration of possibilities than as a dogmatic assertion of limitation.

IV

Nonetheless the Shīʿī system was distinctive and had certain practical consequences, of which I will mention here only two.

First, a literary consequence. Precluded from developing a theory of legitimacy within the literary tradition of *fiqh* (whether because of the logical structure, the weight of tradition, or the incidence of opposition) those *fuqahā'* who accepted the challenge and the difficulties of working with the government began to explore the possibilities of a different mode of writing. This, I take it, is the significance of Sabzavārī's *Rawḍat al-anwār-i ʿAbbāsī*. This is the work, written at the request of Shah ʿAbbās II, which Hamid Enayat cites to illustrate the promonarchical stance of Sabzavārī. Here, freed from the burden of a long tradition and the tendentious limitations of an established technical terminology, Sabzavārī began to explore and create a new normative system which might, as it were, embrace and justify the secular power. Here it was that Sabzavārī, who had in a work of *fiqh* specifically noted the impossibility of a just sultan's acquiring authority during the *ghayba*, was able to suggest the need for "a just and judicious king to administer and rule the world" during the Imam's absence. This was the creation and exploration of a new normative system, distinctly religious in tone, but not a work of *fiqh*.[42] This literary genre was taken up later by Muḥammad Bāqir al-Majlisī whose works—Persian in language, paraenetic, exemplary, popular—may indeed be recognized as having, in one of their aspects, a legitimizing function. Their religious tone, however varied its sources and its expression, did not involve the formulation of legalistic norms of the type characteristic of the *fiqh* tradition.

It is worthy of remark that the clerical biographies of the Shīʿī tradition do not have much faith in Sabzavārī as a *faqīh*: he is portrayed at best as dull and derivative, at worst as totally incompetent and unworthy of the title of *mujtahid*.[43] The tradition of *fiqh* writing was in decline. Interest was deflected into other fields, notably that of Tradition collecting and that of Persian language, pious, hortatory works, intended no doubt finally to confirm and mould the faith of the indigenous population. Majlisī, the most famous of the late Safavid promonarchical clerics, made no significant contribution to *fiqh* writing.

Secondly, a political consequence. The Ottoman government embraced and supported a religious tradition, which, in its most highly articulated and rational literary manifestation (*fiqh*), confirmed and promoted the legitimacy of the government. The Safavid government found itself in time allied to a religious tradition which dogmatically withheld just that. I would suggest that this difference had significant practical results. The Ottomans benefited from a theory of legitimacy which, highly articulated, conceptually sophisticated and flexible, served to justify and shape administrative practice. A major benefit gained was stability and I would propose this difference between Ottomans and Safavids as one factor (amongst many) accounting for the long duration of the Ottoman dynasty relative to the Persian dynasties of the same period.

It will be clear that the concept of legitimacy that I have been using throughout this paper is one that describes not (objectively) a government or a system, but the relationship (perceived) between a government and a normative code. According to the dominant expression of the *sharīʿa* within the Ottoman empire, the government was legitimate in the sense that its activities and institutions embodied a possible realization of the *sharīʿa*. But, for the minority Shīʿī community in Ottoman territory, this same government was not legitimate, that is, its activities did not and could not constitute a realization of the *sharīʿa*. It is of course commonplace that the *sharīʿa* was not the only normative system available within Ottoman or Safavid territory which could have legitimizing force. For example, it would appear to be the case that there existed in Safavid Iran a popular theory which recognized the legitimacy of Safavid rule insofar as the rulers were descended from the Imam, functioned as deputies of the Imam, and were perhaps *maʿṣūm* (immune from error).[44] This was a theory which contradicted, but existed side by side with that of the *sharīʿa*. Disentangling the conceptual structures and the practical uses of varied legitimizing theories in an Islamic context is an academic task as yet scarcely begun.[45] But any typology of legitimating theories will recognize a spectrum of possibilities: from a literary, conceptually sophisticated, legalistic, all-embracing theory (like that of the *sharīʿa*) to a naive, simple, popular and perhaps largely unwritten theory (e.g. that kings are divine agents and rule as such).

It is highly probably that, *mutatis mutandis*, Safavids and Ottomans had roughly equal access to popular and traditional modes of legitimacy. The Safavids, however, were precluded from precisely the most sophisticated theory that had been developed in Islam (outside, perhaps, the chanceries). At least some expounders of the *sharīʿa* in a Sunnī context had for centuries been extending the conceptual boundaries of their description so as to embrace (and make possible thereby participation in, and, in part control of) the practices of government. It is clear that judges (*qāḍīs*) within the Ottoman empire derived their authority (*sharʿī*) solely from the fact of appointment by the secular ruler. They were thus servants of the state and agents of the *sharīʿa*, not by virtue of an accidental overlap (as for the Safavids) but because these concepts fused at a practical level. The career of the sixteenth-century *shaykh al-islām* Abu 'l-Suʿūd sufficiently illustrates the tendency to make the *sharīʿa* and the administration the same thing. In his well-known *fatwā* regarding taxation in Salonika Abu 'l-Suʿūd demonstrates (or at least asserts) that the actual tax collecting activities of the government are the *sharīʿa* in practice.[46] His *fatwā*s here and elsewhere demonstrate the complementary tendencies (a) to extend the conceptual boundaries of the *sharīʿa* so as to include administrative practice, and (b) to control and restrict the activities of government by requiring that they be judged in the light of the *sharīʿa*.

It is impossible here to explore more fully the modes and consequences of Ottoman *sharʿī* legitimacy. The systematic exploitation of the *sharīʿa* to justify and to shape a highly articulated, bureaucratic and legitimate structure was, however, an option not available to the Safavids, nor to any subsequent Persian dynasty.[47]

BIBLIOGRAPHY

A. *Works of* fiqh *(in chronological order of author)*

Ṭūsī, Muḥammad b. Ḥasan, *al-Nihāya,* Beirut, 1390/1970.

Ibn Idrīs, Muḥammad b. Manṣūr al-Ḥillī, *al-Sarā'ir,* Tehran 1270/1853–4.

Muḥaqqiq, Jaᶜfar b. Ḥasan al-Ḥillī, *Sharā'iᶜ al-Islām,* 4 vols., Najaf, 1389/1964.

idem, al-Mukhtaṣar al-nāfiᶜ, Cairo 1376/1956–7 (?).

ᶜAllāma, Ḥasan b. Yūsuf b. Muṭahhar al-Ḥillī, *Qawāᶜid al-aḥkām.* in Karakī, *Jāmiᶜ,* II.

Shahīd II, Zayn al-Dīn b. ᶜAlī, *al-Rawḍa al-bahiyya,* Tabriz, 1271/1854–5.

Karakī, ᶜAlī b. Ḥusayn b. ᶜAbd al-ᶜĀlī, *Jāmiᶜ al-maqāṣid, sharḥ al-Qawāᶜid,* 2 vols., Tehran, n.d.

Sabzavārī, Muḥammad Bāqir, *al-Kifāya fī 'l-aḥkām,* Tehran 1269/1852–3.

B. *Secondary works*

Arjomand, S. A., *The Shadow of God and the Hidden Imam.* Chicago, 1984.

Calder, N., "*Zakāt* in Imāmī-Shīᶜī Jurisprudence". *BSOAS,* XLIV (1981), pp. 468–80.

idem, "*Khums* in Imāmī-Shīᶜī Jurisprudence". *BSOAS,* XLV (1982), pp. 39–47.

idem, "Acccommodation and Revolution in Imami Shiᶜi Jurisprudence". *Middle East Studies,* XVIII (1982), pp. 3–20.

Eliash, J., "Misconceptions regarding the Juridical Status of the Iranian *ᶜulamā'*". *IJMES,* X (1979), pp. 9–25.

Enayat, H., *Modern Islamic Political Thought.* London, 1982.

Hourani, A., "From Jabal ᶜĀmil to Persia". *BSOAS,* XLIX (1986), pp. 133–40.

Imber, C. H., "The Persecution of the Ottoman Shīᶜites According to the Mühimme Defterleri 1565–1585". *Isl.,* LVI (1979), pp. 245–73.

Lambton, A. K. S., *State and Government in Medieval Islam.* Oxford, 1981.

Madelung, W., "A Treatise of the Sharīf al-Murtaḍā on the Legality of Working for the Government (*Mas'ala fī 'l-ᶜamal maᶜa 'l-sulṭān*)". *BSOAS,* XLIII (1980), pp. 18–31.

idem, "Shiᶜite Discussions on the Legality of the Kharāj". *Proceedings of the Ninth Congress of the Union Européenne des Arabisants et Islamisants (Amsterdam, 1978),* ed. R. Peters. Leiden, 1981.

Tabataba'i, H. Modarressi, *Kharaj in Islamic Law.* London, 1983.

idem, An Introduction to Shiᶜi Law. London, 1984.

[1] Lambton (1981), pp. 242–53. See also Calder, *opera cit.*

[2] Madelung (1980), p. 30; cf. Lambton (1981), p. 243, n. 2.

[3] See further nn. 21 and 22 below.

[4] Enayat, p. 173, in reference to Ibn Idrīs, p. 203; see further nn. 21 and 22 below.

[5] I refer to Arjomand (1984); see also my review in *MES,* XXIII (1987) (forthcoming).

[6] Sabzavārī, p. 131a.

[7] For the ᶜUmar b. Ḥanẓala Tradition, see Calder (1979) and Eliash's article (1979), on which see also Calder (1982) (ii), n. 2. The traditions may be found in e.g. Ṭūsī, *Tahdhīb al-aḥkām,* VI (Tehran, 1390), in the *K. al-qaḍāyā wa 'l-aḥkām,* nos. 514, 516.

[8] Sabzavārī, p. 131b (l. 3).

[9] *Ibid.,* l. 4.

[10] I have discussed the Imāmī theory of judicial authority in some detail in *The Structure of Authority in Imāmī Shīᶜī Jurisprudence,* unpublished Ph.D. thesis, London University, 1979, ch. 4.

[11] This will become evident throughout the present paper, but, for further details, see *ibid., ch. 3.*

[12] For further discussion of these jurists, see also Madelung (1981) Tabataba'i (1984), Arjomand (1986) and Hourani (1986).

[13] J. Chardin, *Voyages en Perse et autres lieux de l'Orient,* 10 vols., Paris, 1811, VI, 91–6. See further, *op. cit. ad* n. 10 above, *loc. cit.* The Persians preferred the government courts, apparently, because they were more likely to bring about a definitive resolution to a problem. Decisions by *qāḍīs*' courts (which perhaps were those that emerged locally, rather than as a result of central appointment) were always subject to appeal to other similar courts (since these courts were not formally ranked).

[14] Calder (1981 and 1982).

[15] Sabzavārī, p. 20b (*maqṣad fī kayfiyyat al-ikhrāj*).

[16] *Ibid.,* p. 23a (l. 24).

[17] *Ibid.,* p. 37b (ll. 7–11).

[18] *Ibid.,* p. 10b.

[19] Yūsuf al-Baḥrānī, *Lu'lu'at al-baḥrayn,* Najaf, 1386/1966, *ad* Qaṭīfī, 160ff.

[20] Cf. Tabataba'i (1983), p. 158: "The term 'unjust' is not used in its general sense, but refers to the injustice this sort of ruler perpetrated against the Imams and their legitimate successors by usurping their legal rights."

[21] These two areas of discussion and, in particular, the latter, constitute always the *loci* from which Madelung and Enayat (see nn. 3 and 5 above) are inclined to derive the supposition that the terms *al-sulṭān al-muḥiqq al-ᶜādil* and *sulṭān al-ḥaqq al-ᶜādil* may refer to someone other than the Imam. A contemporary Shīᶜī commentator, in remarkably circumspect language, might seem to agree with them: "In earlier . . . sources . . . the term *al-sulṭān al-ᶜādil* . . . is sometimes used in such a way as to give the impression that there was some support for the concept of a just ruler who was not the imam . . ." (Tabataba'i, 1983, p. 158). This is hardly decisive. My answer to these (erroneous) suppositions lies in the kind of overall consideration of the Imāmī presentation of the *sharīᶜa* that I offer in this paper. There is no logical space in the Imāmī conception of *sharīᶜa* for a just sultan (synchronic) and there is no exploration of such a concept throughout the whole of the tradition up to and including the work of Sabzavārī (diachronic). See further n. 22 below.

[22] Ṭūsī, *Nihāya,* pp. 300–1. Ṭūsī's elegant variation in the titles/designations of the Imam may be annoying but is not confusing. That *iqāmat al-ḥudūd* belonged to the Imam was axiomatic. It is this knowledge that permits us to recognize in a variety of titles the same entity. The phrase *sulṭān al-zamān al-manṣūb min qibal allāh aw man naṣaba-hu al-imām* is the same as the more frequent *al-imām aw man naṣaba-hu al-imām.* The variation of title corresponds to English, "the Queen or one of Her Majesty's ministers". "Queen" and "Her Majesty" are the same entity. Use of *sulṭān al-ḥaqq* in this context helps us to understand Murtaḍā's *al-sulṭān al-muḥiqq al-ᶜādil* (*pace* Madelung) and Ibn Idrīs's *sulṭān al-ḥaqq al-ᶜādil* (*pace* Enayat) as designation of the Imam. This in turn reflects on how we are to read Ṭūsī, and others, in the same context (working for the *ᶜādil* and the *jā'ir*) who used the term *sulṭān ᶜādil* alone, to designate the Imam, i.e. the rightful ruler as apposed to the *jā'ir.*

I give one further (I hope decisive) example of this usage. ᶜAllāma in his *Qawāᶜid, ad* Friday Prayer, states that one of its conditions is *al-sulṭān al-ᶜādil aw man ya'muru-hu.* This is another variation on *al-imām aw man naṣaba-hu al-imām.* The entity designated *al-sulṭān al-ᶜādil* is the Imam and there could be no doubt about this, for the only entity that was ever in question in this context was the Imam. ᶜAllama's discussion naturally proceeds, having established that *al-sulṭān al-ᶜādil* is a condition, to the question of what happens in the *ghayba.* This is a logical progression only if we understand that *al-sulṭān al-ᶜādil* is the Imam (see *Qawāᶜid,* p. 14). Fortunately Karakī, who took a particular interest in Friday Prayer, decided in this instance to gloss what was obvious. He states: *al-sulṭān al-ᶜādil wa-huwa al-imām al-maᶜṣūm* (*Jāmiᶜ,* p. 130, ll. 20–1). See further Mīr Dāmād's definition of *al-sul-ṭān al-ᶜādil* as cited in Arjomand (1986), p. 305, n. 102.

[23] Sabzavārī, on *iqāmat al-ḥudūd,* p. 43a, ll. 5ff.

[24] Sabzavārī, p. 44b; this topic is discussed also in Lambton, ch. 14.

[25] Muḥaqqiq, *Sharā'i'*, I, pp. 159–60.

[26] This rule is a permanent feature of Shīʿī works of *fiqh*. Muḥaqqiq in the *Sharā'i'* refers it to the *sulṭān jā'ir*, in the *Mukhtaṣar* to the *sulṭān*. The general, unqualified, use of *sulṭān* means naturally *sulṭān jā'ir/ẓālim*; for they were the only ones that existed. Muḥaqqiq makes his meaning clear in the *Mukhtaṣar* by adding "although he (the *sulṭān*) has no right to (what he collects under the title *kharāj, zakāt,* etc.)—*wa-in lam yakun mustaḥiqqan la-hu*. This is a reflection of Ṭūsī's phraseology: he refers to *kharāj* and *ṣadaqāt* as collected by *salāṭīn al-jawr—wa-in kānū ghayr mustaḥiqqīn la-hu* (*Nihāya*, p. 358). Ibn Idrīs conveys the same idea: he refers to *zakāt* and kharāj, collected by *sulṭān al-jawr—wa-in kāna ghayr mustaḥiqq li-akhdhi shay'in min dhālik*.

[27] The analysis of *kharāj* begins in *Kifāya*, p. 38a, l. 7. The passage beginning *wa-naḥnu nadhkur al-taḥqīq* begins on p. 38b, 4 ll. from bottom.

[28] Cit. Sabzavārī, p. 39a, ll. 1–5. Most of Shahīd II's comments are echoed by Karakī in *Jāmi' al-Maqāṣid*, I, p. 207, ll. 29ff.

[29] Sabzavārī, p. 39a, ll. 18ff.

[30] *Ibid.*, ll. 8ff.

[31] *Ibid.*, ll. 15ff. See further Tabataba'i (1983), p. 163.

[32] *Ibid.*, p. 40a, ll. 33ff. (*al-baḥth al-khāmis*).

[33] *Ibid.*, 2 ll. from bottom. The substance of this passage is repeated from *ākhar min al-aṣḥāb* at p. 40b, ll. 1ff.

[34] Tabataba'i (1983), pp. 160–1.

[35] Cited in Sabzavārī, p. 39a, l. 16.

[36] Madelung (1981), pp. 195–6.

[37] Shahīd II, *al-Rawḍa*, p. 264, l. 21.

[38] Sabzavārī, p. 40b, ll. 5ff.

[39] *Ibid.*, ll. 10–11.

[40] *Ibid.*, ll. 11–13.

[41] In fact the resolution of the concept "deputy of the Imam" required a distinction between *nā'ib 'āmm* (the *faqīh*) and *nā'ib khāṣṣ* (a term with, as far as I can determine, a historical function, namely to explain and justify the recorded instances of delegation during the Imam's presence, and/or the delegation of the four *sufarā'* of the lesser occultation; see further, Calder (1981)).

[42] Praise and commendation of practically just (equitable) rulers was of course never incompatible with a *sharʿī* concept of illegitimacy; but such commendation could not be incorporated into a work of *fiqh*. See, for an example of ṣuch, ʿAllāma's introduction to his polemical work, *Minhāj al-karāma*, Tehran(?), 1296.

[43] See, e.g. Muḥammad Bāqir al-Khwānsārī, *Rawḍāt al-jannāt*, Tehran, 1390f., 8 vols., II, pp. 68ff. Khwānsārī's own criticism is implied in his observation that Sabzavārī's commentary on the *Irshād* of ʿAllāma is mostly derived from another work; he cites at great length a less restrained view of Sabzavārī.

[44] Lambton, ch. 15.

[45] But see, for a beginning on the Ottomans, C. Imber, "The Ottoman Dynastic Myth" (forthcoming in *Turcica*).

[46] See Ö. L. Barkan, *Osmanli imperatorluğunda zirai ekonominin hukuki ve mali esaslari*, Istanbul, 1943, pp. 297–300.

[47] I should like to express my thanks to the History Department of the School of Oriental and African Studies who, by inviting me to talk to them in March 1986, compelled me to think about these matters; also to Professor A. K. S. Lambton whose encouragement and comments were, as always, helpful and inspiring.

XXI

DOUBT AND PREROGATIVE : THE EMERGENCE OF AN IMĀMĪ SHĪʿĪ THEORY OF *IJTIHĀD*

Imāmī Shīʿism emerged as a distinct sectarian group in the late ninth and early tenth centuries (AD), with as its prime distinguishing tenet the notion that the Imām of the Age was absent. It seems that other Shīʿī groups had at earlier dates formulated similar theories.(1) The enduring success of the Twelver Shīʿī formulation may be related to the activities of an academic elite who asserted, manipulated and added to that theory in such a way as *a)* to exploit traditional loyalty to ʿAlī's descendants while *b)* controlling the merely revolutionary aspect of older Shīʿism and *c)* making the clerical class the focus of community authority. The first of these achievements is easily demonstrated and finds literary reflection in works of heresiography (e.g. the *Firaq al-Shīʿa* of Ḥasan ibn Mūsa al-Nawbakhtī) and biography/hagiography of the Imāms (e.g. the *Kitāb al-Irshād* of al-Shaykh al-Mufīd)—works designed to demonstrate the diachronic continuity of true faith in loyalty to the charismatic line of true Imams. The revolutionary aspect of traditional Shīʿism, implicit in the recognition of a particular living individual as the rightful alternative to the government of the day, was clearly neutralised by the doctrine of the Ghayba: the alternative governor was not available. Muḥammad ibn Ḥasan al-Ṭūsī remarked in his *K. al-Ghayba*: "The manifest acts and conditions of [all who claim to be

(1) See Ṭūsī, *Ghayba*, 29ff., 42ff., *et al.*

imām] contradict their *'iṣma* (sinlessness/infallibility) hence we know that he whose *'iṣma* is sure [i.e. the true *imām*] is absent."(2) A dispassionate observer might conclude that theoretical considerations of this kind ensured the indefinite prolongation of the Imām's absence. As to the authority of the *fuqahā'*, it was articulated both in works of *furū' al-fiqh* and in works of *uṣūl al-fiqh*. In the former it emerged in discussion of those areas of activity which in the Sunnī juristic tradition had been relegated to the secular governor.(3) In the latter it was implicit in the Shī'ī development of a methodology of jurisprudence firmly·based on the pattern provided by the Sunnī juristic tradition.

The scholarly bases of Sunnī jurisprudence had been laid down by al-Shāfi'ī in his *Risāla fī uṣūl al-fiqh*. Their essential premise was that knowledge of God's law (which affected all spheres of human activity) was dependent on custody and interpretation of a finite body of revealed texts (Qur'ān and Tradition).(4) In a remarkably short of time the Imāmī Shī'a, once they had defined the Imām as absent, came to accept the canonical text of the Qur'ān(5) and produced a canonical body of Traditions—thereby signalling their submission to the otherwise Sunnī principle that the moment of God's intervention in human affairs had passed and that continuing knowledge must be based on texts, the residue and witness of that intervention. The 'revealed' status of Imāmī *ḥadīth* is nicely exemplified in a Tradition from Ja'far al-Ṣādiq: "My *ḥadīth* is my father's *ḥadīth*, my father's *ḥadīth* is my grandfather's *ḥadīth*... and 'Alī's *ḥadīth is the ḥadīth* of the Prophet of God and the Prophet's *ḥadīth* is God's word."(6) Some of the more complex problems of relating revealed texts to the detailed structure of substantive law were first adumbrated by al-Sharīf al-Murtaḍā in polemical response to the theories of the Mu'tazilī 'Abd al-Jabbār. Murtaḍā set out his ideas in his *K. al-Shāfī*,

(2) *Ibid.*, 3.

Cf. Calder, "Zakāt in Imāmī Shī'ī jurisprudence" and "Khums in Imāmī Shī'ī jurisprudence", *BSOAS*, 1981 and 2.

(4) For the emergence of Sunnī jurisprudence see Schacht, *The Origins of Muhammadan jurisprudence*, Oxford, 1950; also J. Wansbrough, *Qur'anic Studies* and *The Sectarian milieu*, OUP 1977 and 1978.

(5) Cf. E. Kohlberg, "Some notes on the Imamite attitude to the Qur'an", in Stern, Hourani and Brown, eds., *Islamic philosophy and the classical tradition*, Oxford, 1972; and J. Eliash, "The Shi'ite Qur'an", *Arabica*, XVI, 1969.

(6) *Cit.* in G. Lecomte, "La littérature du Ḥadīth" in Colloque de Strasbourg (1968), *Le Shi'isme Imamite*, Paris, 1970, p. 96.

which was later abbreviated and adapted by Ṭūsī in his *Talkhīṣ al-Shāfī*. The somewhat confused argumentation of both these works reflects the fact that Imāmī dogma (including *uṣūl*) developed initially in the course of a polemical encounter with Muʿtazilīs and Sunnīs and were subject to all the constraints of virtuoso debate and *ad hominem* argument. They do, however, bear witness in the sphere of *uṣūl* to the existence of certain idealistic slogans which were the starting point of Imāmī debate: notably, rejection of *qiyās, ijtihād* and *khabar wāḥid*. Of *ijtihād* Murtaḍā said:

> As to *ijtihād* clear proofs reveal the falseness of what you (sc. ʿAbd al-Jabbār) call *ijtihād*. One of these proofs is that *ijtihād* in the *sharīʿa* is, according to you, a seeking for a dominant opinion *(ghalabat ẓann)* in matters which have no clear indicator *(dalīl)*. But opinion *(ẓann)* has no place in the *ṣharīʿ* and it is not valid that the juristic status of a thing (its *taḥrīm* and *taḥlīl*) should be established by opinion.(7)

And of the *khabar wāḥid*:

> The situation of these with regard to the *sharīʿa* is clearer than all that has gone before; for they do not produce knowledge *(ʿilm)* and they are contradictory, coming down to us with different and opposing rules.(8)

It was part of the polemical game, which flourished at this time in Buyid Baghdad, that one should assert that one's own group had access to knowledge *(ʿilm*, not *ẓann)* whereas one's opponent's group did not. *ʿIlm*, for the Imāmiyya, it transpires from these polemical works, depended on the Qur'an, and the Traditions of the Imāmiyya as mediated through Imāmī *tawātur* and Imāmī *ijmāʿ* and guaranteed by the continued existence, invisibly, of the absent Imām. Independent rational knowledge *(ʿaql)* constituted for the Imamiyya a further source of knowledge, as it did for the Muʿtazila.(9)

The rejection of *qiyās, ijtihād* and *khabar wāḥid* remained a part of the popular polemical definition of Shīʿism, as against Sunnism,

(7) Murtaḍā, *Al-Shāfī*, 31-2; cf. also 36, where *ijtihād* = *qiyās*; and Ṭūsī, *Talkhīṣ*, 306-7, where *ijtihād* = *ra'y*.

(8) Murtaḍā, *Shāfī*, 36.

(9) For an assessment of the Muʿtazilī attitude to "rational" law see G. Hourani, *Islamic Rationalism: the ethics of ʿAbd al-Jabbār*, Oxford, 1971; also *id.*, "Two theories of value in medieval Islam", MW 50 1960.

for some time. These items became traditional slogans in the agenda of sectarian definition, and may be found categorically expressed, in a variety of polemical contexts.(10) The development of a sophisticated methodology of *uṣūl* first introduced qualifications and finally reversed (at least for *ijtihād* and for *khabar wāḥid*) the content of those slogans.

All Islamic legal systems exhibit a common framework of juristic topics (purity, prayer, pilgrimage, *zakāt*, etc.) together with an elaborate and tortuous set of details, subject to variation and doubt within and between schools. The various juristic groups defined their position by recourse to and interpretation of a finite number of revealed texts common to them all. Imāmī Traditions and Imāmī *furū'*, as they emerged in the course of the tenth century, proved to be new variations on well-established themes. Linant de Bellefonds has noted that of the five major schools of law it is the Hanafī, not the Shī'ī, which displays the greatest deviation from the common norms of the other four.(11) Of Imāmī Traditions it is the theological rather than the juristic which deviate markedly from Sunnī norms (though even there it was frequently to assert Mu'tazilī views on an established point of debate). Hence the methodology of reconciling law and revelation which had developed in Sunnī circles since the time of Shāfi'ī was fully applicable to the similar problems which faced the Imāmīs in the tenth century: their problem was to adopt, adapt and refine from a well-established pool of exegetical technique and vocabulary.

Ṭūsī's *'Uddat al-Uṣūl* is the most significant work of juristic methodology written by an Imāmī scholar of the Buyid period. The earlier works of Murtaḍā and Mufīd were by contrast short, uncertain and lacking in detail;(12) though their views on a number of points remained as part of the tradition to be adduced and exploited by later scholars in the general process of methodologial development. The major exegetical principles adduced by Ṭūsī in the *'Uddat al-Uṣūl* were precisely those that

(10) See, for example, the introductory passage in Ṭūsī's *Mabsūṭ*; also the Persian polemical works, Qazwīnī, *K. al-Naqḍ*, Tehran, 1331/1952, 49-50 and Murtaḍā b. Dā'ī Rāzī, *Tabṣirat al-'Awāmm*, Tehran, 1313/1934, p. 191-2.

(11) Linant de Bellefonds, "Le droit Imamite", in *Le Shī'isme Imamite*, p. 184.

(12) An outline of the ideas of Murtaḍā and Mufīd in *uṣūl al-fiqh* may be found in R. Brunschwig, "Les *usul al-fiqh* imamites à leur stade ancien," in *Le Shi'isme Imamite*.

had developed in the Sunnī (and by this time in the Muʿtazilī) traditions. These principles were expressed in simple antithetical headings: *ḥaqīqa* and *majāz, awāmir* and *nawāhī, ʿumūm* and *khuṣūṣ, muṭlaq* and *muqayyad, mujmal* and *mubayyan, nāsikh* and *mansūkh.* A limited number of additional interpretative and exegetical devices demanded discussion *(barāʾat al-dhimma, qiyās, istiṣḥāb al-ḥāl, ijmāʿ)* and the problem of *isnāds* had to be analysed *(tawātur* and *khabar wāḥid).* These were the common principles of the Islamic juristic tradition, variously accepted, rejected, and qualified by schools and scholars in the process of defining an identity. The whole series reflects the exegetical premise that the sciences of linguistics, rhetoric, history, biography and logic represent independent and authoritative disciplines: appeal to them was thought not only permissible but necessary. That some or all of these sciences were in fact subordinate to the exigencies of juristic interpretation has been suggested and demonstrated.(13)

The principle of *ijtihād* which Imāmī scholars of the Buyid period categorically rejected as an invalid principle leading to *ẓann,* not *ʿilm,* had been given its first scholarly formulation in the *Risāla* of Shāfiʿī. I have suggested elsewhere that in developing his theory of *ijtihād* Shāfiʿī was concerned partly to account for and justify the phenomenon of *ikhtilāf* and partly to assert the authority of the clerical class.(14) I will suggest in what follows that the development of an Imāmī Shīʿī theory of *ijtihād* reflects a concern with the same problems: how to explain and account for variant opinions, how to assert and justify the authority of the clerical class over the masses.

The characteristic early Imāmī rejection of *ijtihād,* amply confirmed in Ṭūsī's *ʿUddat al-Uṣūl,*(15) was related to an idealistic desire for a firm clear definition of divine law free from doubt and *ikhtilāf.* The rejection of the *khabar wāḥid,* given its most extreme formulation by Murtaḍā, reflects the same impulse, and was inherited by Murtaḍā from the Muʿtazila. The Muʿtazilī rejection of *khabar wāḥid* was made possible by their conception of a considerable residual area of moral law accessible to the unaided

(13) The Islamic tradition of *uṣūl* is discussed in I. Goldziher, *The Zahiris* (Eng. tr. W. Behn) Leiden, 1971; and in the works cited in note 4 above. The most sophisticated discussion is undoubtedly that of John Wansbrough.

(14) Calder, "*Ikhtilāf* and *ijmāʿ* in Shāfiʿī's *Risāla*" SI, 58.

(15) Ṭūsī, *ʿUddat*, 59 and 290ff.

intellect. One result of the Muʿtazilī theory was to reduce the sphere of authority of the *fuqahā'*—for their authority was limited to the area of revealed law.[16] In the tension between two schemes of values, one which saw all human contingencies as necessarily subject to moral principles deducible only from revealed texts, and one which saw revealed texts as relevant only to a small number of primarily cultic matters, the *khabar wāḥid* took on a pivotal role as what might be designated marginal revelation. Rejection of the *khabar wāḥid* could be seen as a restriction of clerical authority. It is possible therefore to analyse as symptomatic of a desire to expand and preserve the area of clerical authority Ṭūsī's complex resolution of the established Shīʿī slogan, no *khabar wāḥid*. In effect, while acknowledging that *khabar wāḥid* did not give rise to *ʿilm*, he asserted nonetheless that not only was it rationally possible for acts of worship to be based on it but specific permission was available in the law *(fī l-sharʿ)*. That permission related only to those Traditions which were transmitted by a member or members of the True Sect and who possessed certain qualities including that of *ʿadāla*. He rejected the well-established arguments against the *khabar wāḥid* based on *Qur'an*, 2:169 and 17:36 and adduced to support his argument *ijmāʿ al-firqa al-muḥiqqa*, consensus of the True Sect. This at first sight astonishing assertion was based on his contention that the traditional Shīʿī rejection of the *khabar wāḥid* referred only to those transmitted by their sectarian opponents.[17] This new assessment characteristically denied the validity/authority of alien sources while defending and upholding Imāmī sources.

But Ṭūsī's concern to establish the *khabar wāḥid* as a source of law had graver implications. The (imaginary) interlocutor of the *ʿUddat al-Uṣūl* posed the question whether acceptance of the *khabar wāḥid* did not lead to the conclusion that truth layin two different directions *(jihatayn mukhtalifatayn)*. Denial of this conclusion the interlocutor claimed was well known on the part of Shīʿī scholars and elders. Ṭūsī naturally had his (novel) reply at the ready: "What is well known is that the truth may not lie both with [the Shīʿa] and with those who oppose their faith. As to its being well known that the truth cannot lie in two directions if it emerges from two variant *khabar*, we have demonstrated that this

(16) Cf. Calder, "Ikhtilāf and ijmāʿ", p. 70-2.

(17) For Ṭūsī on the *khabar wāḥid*, see *ʿUddat*, 41-57.

is known."[18] Such a situation indicated the necessity and the permission to choose. Ṭūsī's concern to establish an area of choice may be interpreted as a desire to incorporate as harmoniously as possible the divergent characters and views which had been gathered into the nascent Shīʿī tradition. Acknowledgement of choice as an option in the assessment of legal values was in effect a confession of doubt and brought the Shīʿa very close to the Sunnī theory of *ijtihād* which nonetheless tradition required that Ṭūsī reject. He was himself aware that the distinction between choice and *ijtihād* was at best a subtle one:

> Some say [in a case requiring choice] that each *mukallaf* (person subject to God's command) should act in accord with his own *ijtihād*, but that would lead to the supposition that *kull mujtahid muṣīb*, which we do not accept. Only choice is possible.[19]

"All *mujtahids* are in the right" was a slogan ascribed by the Shīʿa to other sects, and taken to be symbolic of their juristic weakness. It is patent however that every *chooser* was in some sense *muṣīb*.

Ṭūsī's consciousness that *ikhtilāf* was a serious problem may further be inferred from the fact that he made that phenomenon itself a justification for the acceptance of *khabar wāḥid*. The evidence of Shīʿī *ikhtilāf*, explained as arising out of the use of *khabar wāḥid*, proved that the latter was a valid source. He pointed out that *ikhtilāf* amongst the Shīʿa was greater than that between Abū Hanīfa, Shāfiʿī and Mālik. "In spite of their great divergence of opinion, I have found the Shīʿa such that not one has cut the bond of association, nor accused his opponent of going astray or being corrupt; nor has anyone severed himself from the dissenting opinion."[20] This claim to have detected in the past history of the Shīʿa a broad tolerance in legal affairs reflects a contemporary concern both to justify the past and to establish for the present and the future a similar broad tolerance. Just as Shāfiʿī had elaborated a theory of *ijtihād* in order to assert a unity that transcended and included difference of opinion (intercepting and cancelling its capacity to divide) so Ṭūsī recognised the same problem and dealt with it by asserting an area of choice—

(18) *Ibid.*, 53.
(19) *Ibid.*, 21.
(20) *Ibid.*, 56-7.

introducing doubt and flexibility into a system ostensibly concerned with certainty *('ilm*, not *ẓann)*. Ṭūsī's technical use of the term choice was closely related to his use of the term *tawaqquf* (suspending decision) and may be found illustrated elsewhere in the *'Uddat al-uṣūl* (e.g. *ad mushtarak* expressions, p. 21, or *ad* absence of *ijmā'*, p. 192).

In the very work wherein he argued in favour of recourse to the *khabar wāḥid* (suitably defined), Ṭūsī was still able to assert: "action based on the *khabar wāḥid* is not valid as we have explained."(21) This was not contradiction but a product of his own interpretation of the meaning of *khabar wāḥid* and the safeguards he introduced against its misuse. What he desired was the preservation of a slogan (continuity) with a change in its practical application (development and flexibility). The same problem faced him and his successors with regard to other established slogans of Shī'ī *uṣūl* (no *ijtihād*) as also with the polemical assertion of certainty *('ilm)* over and against the allegedly erroneous and heretical recourse to *ẓann*. Small points of terminology were made to bear considerable epistemological weight as Ṭūsī and later thinkers strove to reconcile the rigour of polemical slogans with their perception of the importance of doubt, *ikhtilāf*, etc.

With the advent of the Saljuqs, the removal of Ṭūsī to Najaf and the gradual cessation of meaningful polemical debate between sects, it became impossible to sustain the hard edge of sophisticated argument. Shī'ī *uṣūl* like all other branches of Shī'ī intellectual activity entered a period of stagnation designated by Imāmī writers a period of *taqlīd* (imitation), by which they meant *taqlīd* of Ṭūsī. Problems of continuity, flexibility and *ikhtilāf* were obscured by a general uncritical submission in legal affairs to the views propounded by him. Intellectual revival began with the work of Ibn Idrīs al-Ḥillī and may possibly be related to the increasing political liveliness of the Shī'a in the late Saljuq period, especially during the time of the caliph al-Nāṣir (d. 622/1225) during whose reign Ibn Idrīs died. In the introduction to his *Sarā'ir al-Islām* Ibn Idrīs presented the apathy and ignorance of the Shī'a as the motive for his producing that work, which contained in the event a broad and frequently petty re-

(21) *Ibid.*, 230.

interpretation of details of the *sharīʿa* and an intense attack on Ṭūsī. The attack was characterised by an unremitting critique of Ṭūsī's use of the *khabar wāḥid* and an appeal from Ṭūsī's interpretation of *uṣūl* to Murtaḍā's. His detailed justifications of *sharʿī* precepts involved frequent dismissal of Traditions as *khabar wāḥid* and a repeated and idiosyncratic application of the principles of *barā'at al-dhimma*.(22) His work, introduced with an attack on *taqlīd*, was concluded with a peroration on the same theme, culminating in a striking plea for flexibility and development:

> It is not fitting for one who has understood those who have preceded him in certain affairs that he considers that superiority belongs to them ... for they err where they err because they have exhausted their minds and used up their time on other things; then they have turned to those things wherein they erred with minds worn out and spirits ravaged and little time. Those who come after them benefit without effort from the achievements of earlier thinkers ... and so, being in full possession of their faculties and with plentiful time and unburdened by weariness, they notice what their predecessors did not notice and consider what they did not consider. Hence it is that the *muta'akhkhirūn* are superior to the *mutaqaddimūn* and knowledge increases with the increase of men and the progress of time ...

That plea for progress and development found general acceptance amongst later writers(23) but was initially perceived, in conjunction with the attack on Ṭūsī, as disruptive of continuity.

Disruption prompted mediation and harmonisation, tasks undertaken and successfully carried through by Jaʿfar Ibn Ḥasan al-Ḥillī, known as al-Muḥaqqiq and his pupil Ḥasan ibn Yūsuf ibn al-Muṭahhar, known as al-ʿAllāma. Muḥaqqiq's efforts in that direction are exemplified in his *Nukat al-nihāya*, (24) a commentary on Ṭūsī's work in which he justified against the critique of Ibn Idrīs the anomalies, contradictions and isolated opinions which the latter had found there. His general concern to heal Ṭūsī's reputation and to establish a compromise position is further evident in his attitude to the *khabar wāḥid*. In his *K. al-Muʿtabar*, he asserted with regard to this problem that there were extreme

(22) For *barā'at al-dhimma*, see e.g. Calder, "Khums", *BSOAS* XLV, 1982, pp. 41-2.

(23) E.g. it is quoted in al-Ḥurr al-ʿĀmilī, *Amal al-Āmil* (2 vols), Baghdad, 1385 I 7-8.

(24) Contained in Khwansārī, ed., *Al-Jawāmiʿ al-fiqhiyya*, Tehran, 1276/1860.

Traditionists *(hashawiyya)* who accepted all *khabar wāḥid* irrespective of their contradictions, and there were the opposite extremists who rejected all *khabar wāḥid.* But *tawassuṭ* was best. *Tawassuṭ* meant acknowledgement of those *khabar wāḥid* which had been accepted by the companions (Imāmī *fuqahā'*) or confirmed by other indicators.(25) That was a modified restatement of Ṭūsī's view. But perhaps the most striking feature of Muḥaqqiq's discussion of *uṣūl* in this work is the evidence it provides of the impingement of doubt as to the content of the divine law. His *Mu'tabar* is addressed to a certain Muḥammad ibn Muḥammad al-Juwaynī, apparently both scholar *(muqarrir qawa'id al-īmān)* and official (*ṣāḥib dīwān al-mamālik*, etc.), and begins with a section on advice *(waṣāyā)*:

> I warn you against the *hashawiya* and the *muqallida* of the scholars, for they may cheat you in order to attract you into their ignorance... Let it not worry you that such a one should say: The truth is visible, there is no doubt, the way is clear... For it is not difficult to answer him: All that may be known may validly be described as clear even if the path is hard and the [ascertainment of] truth difficult... If you considered the variation [of opinions] amongst the excellent in legal matters, that would indicate to you the difficulty of achieving [an answer] without study and reflection...(26)
> Hence if a matter seems to you distinct and certain then express it, otherwise cling to suspension of decision *(tawaqquf)* for that is the shore of perdition.(27)

(فاذا تعيّن لك الوجه فهناك فقل والاّ فاعتصم بالتوقّف فانّه ساحل الهلكة)

Clearly, for Muḥaqqiq, the *sharī'a* was not a structure, easily known, of order and stability; it was uncertain, shifting and doubtful. The awesome nature of the *muftī*'s responsibility as articulator of divine law, coupled with the warnings discovered in Q2.169 and 10.59 were brought forward as incentives to caution on the part of the *muftī*. To declare as certain that which has not been established to be so is "to invent a lie concerning God."(28) That the law was doubtful and that scholars should be cautious in expressing their views or should suspend decision

(25) Muḥaqqiq, *Mu'tabar*, 6, lines 3-8.
(26) *Ibid.*, 3, lines 25ff.
(27) *Ibid.*, 4, lines 1-2.
(28) Qur'an, 10:59.

(tawaqquf) were opinions that reflected Muḥaqqiq's careful mediation of past and present, his justification of *ikhtilāf*, his balancing of continuity and flexibility. The disadvantage of his position was perhaps that suspension of decision, the shore of perdition, represented an abdication of authority and a withholding of guidance.

If Muḥaqqiq's work betrays the impingement of doubt, 'Allāma's represents its establishment and exploitation. His achievements in juristic theory may be summed up by reference to two spheres of innovation. First he proposed a new (within Shī'ism) terminology for the organisation and evaluation of Traditions. Second, he adapted the technical terminology of Shī'ī *uṣūl* in such a way as to render its central principle that of *ijtihād*. The essence of his conclusions there was that the actions of ordinary people *(mukallaf/muqallid)* could and should be based on the mere opinion *(ẓann)* of *mujtahids*. Both innovations were essentially terminological and both owed much if not everything to Sunnī tradition.

According to M. Ṣādiq Baḥr al-'Ulūm, 'Allāma was a distinguished writer in the science of *ḥadīth* but his writings on that subject have been lost. It is nonetheless known that he was the first Shī'ī scholar to adopt a technical terminology for the division of Shī'ī Traditions into the categories of *ṣaḥīḥ, ḥasan, muwaththaq* and *ḍa'īf*, all of them well-known from Sunnī sources.(29) It is clear that 'Allāma was trying to deal with the vexed question of the *khabar wāḥid* and that he felt the introduction of more subtle distinctions would help. From the point of view of certainty the results of his analysis were apparently depressing: it is possible that his low estimate of Shī'ī Traditions accounts for the disappearance of his works in this field. Mīrzā Muḥammad al-Astarābādī (d. 1036/1626-7) whose work entitled *al-Fawā'id al-Madaniyya* became an early expression of the Akhbārī position accused 'Allāma of claiming that most of the Shī'ī Traditions were *ghayr saḥīḥ*.(30) 'Allāma himself in a passage made available in Ḥasan ibn Shahīd II's *Ma'ālim* stated:

> As to the Imāmiyya, the *akhbārīs* of them have relied in *uṣūl al-dīn* and *furū' al-dīn* only on isolated traditions *(akhbār āḥād)*; and

(29) See Muḥammad al-Mahdī Baḥr al-'Ulūm, *Al-Fawā'id al-rijāliyya* (ed. Baḥr al-'Ulūm), 4 vols, Najaf, 1385-6/1965-7, vol. II, p. 260 (commentary).

(30) Astarābādī, *Fawā'id*, f. 3a.

> the *uṣūlīs* such as Ṭūsī and others have agreed in accepting the isolated tradition *(khabar wāḥid)*. None have rejected it except Murtaḍā and those who followed him.(31)

It appears that 'Allāma understood most of the Shī'ī Traditions to be *āḥād*. Some clarification of what he meant by this may be had from his definitions of *tawātur* and *āḥād*. In defining the former he rejected the idea that it depended on a specific number of transmitters, and claimed that the only significant factor was whether it did or did not produce certainty. Likewise, a *khabar wāḥid* was one which gave rise merely to opinion *(ẓann)*, irrespective of the number of transmitters.(32)

Now, discovery of whether certainty or merely opinion had in fact been achieved depended, not at all on *isnāds*, but on assessment of the juristic tradition, and the degree of unanimity it manifested. In this way, 'Allama made the experience of the community (or more specifically, the clerical class) the major criterion for the assessment of the value of revelation. It was largely then the evidence of the community's experience, the cumulative evidence of *ikhtilāf* and non-certainty, that led 'Allāma to his pessimistic assessment of Shī'ī Traditions.

Most of the law, for 'Allāma, was in a state of doubt. He found no difficulty in providing an elaborate argument for the use of the *khabar wāḥid* as a proof *(ḥujja)*, based this time on Quranic sources, as well as *ijmā'*, and much more sophisticated than either Ṭūsī's or Muḥaqqiq's arguments.(33) His system as a whole freely acknowledged a complete lack of certainty in the law. This feature of his thought may best be illustrated by quotation. At

(31) Ḥasan ibn Shahīd II, *Ma'ālim al-dīn*, 191. On the question of the origins of the Akhbārī and Uṣūlī controversy there remains much study to be done. It is my belief that the terms used in this passage do not have a "party" or "sectarian" significance but a much vaguer sense of "Traditionist" and *jurisprudens*. I think the Akkbārī movement is best understood as beginning where the Shī'ī historians see its beginnings, with the attack of Astarābādī on 'Allāma's innovation. They defined themselves against primarily 'Allāma and did not begin to do so until the time of Astarābādī. Buyid, Saljuq and Mongol texts occasionally refer to *uṣulīs* and *akhbārīs* but to what extent these can be aligned with Uṣūlīs and Akhbārīs is not clear. But cf. Madelung, "Imamism and Mu'tazilite theology", in *Le Shi'isme Imamite*, 20-1.

(32) 'Allāma, *Mabādi'*, 201-3. There had been Sunni definitions of the same kind, cf. Aghnides, *Mohammedan theories of finance*, New York 1916, 39-44.

(33) E.g. 'Allāma, *Mabādi'*, 203-5.

the beginning of his *Tahdhib al-wuṣūl ilā ʿilm al-uṣūl* he defined the word *fiqh*:

الفقه لغة الفهم وعرفا العلم بالاحكام الشرعية الفرعية المستدلّ على اعيانها بحيثلا يعلم كونها من الدين ضرورة فخرج العلم بالذوات وبالاحكام العقلية وكون الاجماع وخبر الواحد حجّة وعلم المقلّد والاصول الضرورية كالصلوة والزكوة.

> *Fiqh*, in its basic linguistic meaning, is understanding. Conventionally, it is knowledge of detailed *sharʿī* values the status of which is inferred in so far as their being part of religion is not known by immediate certain knowledge *(ḍarūratan)*. Hence [the following] are excluded: knowledge of essences, of rational [as opposed to revealed] values, that *ijmāʿ* or *khabar wāḥid* are valid proofs in legal matters, the knowledge of the *muqallid* and the fundamental premises [of the law] *(al-uṣūl al-ḍarūriyya)* such as *ṣalāt* and *zakāt*.(34)

This passage distinguishes two types of juristic value: inferred *(mustadall)* and immediate/certain *(ḍarūrī)*. The latter type belongs to a totally different category of known things from the former and is exemplified in such things as prayer and *zakāt*. *Fiqh* is a term referring to the inferred not to the immediate/certain type of knowledge.

A similar definition was given at the beginning of the *Taḥrīr al-Aḥkām*. There, too, one of the exceptions, not to be included in *fiqh*, because it was part of *ḍarūrī* knowledge, was knowledge of *uṣūl al-sharīʿa*,(35) a concept exemplified by "such things as *ṣalāt* and *zakāt*." In the *Tahdhīb*, under the heading, *fī l-mujtahad fīhi*, that is, "on the sphere of *ijtihād*," he said:

> [This includes] every legal value *(ḥukm sharʿī)* on which there is no definitive indicator *(dalīl qaṭʿī)*; hence it excludes rational values; and [the existence of] a definitive indicator excludes [also] those elements of the law which are known *ḍarūratan*, such as the incumbency of *ṣalāt* and *zakāt*.(36)

(34) *Id.*, *Tahdhīb* (1501), f. 2b-3a.
(35) *Id.*, *Taḥrīr*, 2.
(36) *Id.*, *Tahdhīb* (1501), f. 205a-b.

For 'Allāma knowledge of the law was thus of two types. There was an immediate necessary knowledge *(ḍarūrī)* which related to what I would call structural elements such as the incumbency of *ṣalāt* and *zakāt*. This knowledge was provided with definitive indicators, *dalīl qaṭ'ī* or *dalīl qāṭi'*. The other type of knowledge, devoid of definitive indicators, concerned detailed *shar'ī* values, *(al-aḥkām al-shar'iyya al-far'iyya)* and was the prerogative of the *fuqahā'*. It is to be noted that since he defined *fiqh* as a word relevant only to the inferred type of knowledge, which was also the sphere of *ijtihād*, the terms *faqīh* and *mujtahid* would be synonymous.

It is clear that this division is precisely the same as was enunciated by Shāfi'ī, who used, to express that division, the terms *'ilm 'āmma* and *'ilm khāṣṣa*. The latter type of knowledge was for Shāfi'ī the preserve of the *fuqahā'* and was the sphere wherein there could be no certainty.[37] 'Allāma's debt to Sunnī models was acknowledged by later and frequently hostile (Akhbārī influenced) Shī'ī sources, but he himself made little secret of it: his discussion of *ijtihād* contained at least one reference to Shāfi'ī's argumentation.[38] The overall conclusion of 'Allāma's observations was that whereas there was a basic structure to the law, known *bi-l-ḍarūra*, the details were at the very least less certain; in fact, they belonged not to the category of *'ilm*, but, as we shall see, to the category of opinion *(ẓann)*.

The term *ḍarūrī* deserves first however some comment. It is used generally to describe a type of knowledge which inspires such a degree of certainty that it cannot be shaken; paradigmatically it is exemplified in simple sensual observation or basic intellectual principles: (this is a table, 1+1=2). According to 'Allāma, a *khabar mutawātir* gives rise to *ḍarūrī* knowledge. This is based on the fact that:

> Our certainty as to the happening of great events, such as the existence of Muḥammad, is no less than our knowledge that the whole is greater than a part and other basic principles [of *ḍarūrī* knowledge]. Further, this knowledge is present amongst the masses *(al-'awāmm)* and those who do not practice deduction *(istidlāl)* so it is not subject to doubt.[39]

(37) *Cf.* Calder, "Ikhtilāf and ijmā'", 55-69.

(38) 'Allāma, *Tahdhīb* (1501), f. 203b.

(39) *Id.*, *Mabādi'*, 199-200; cf. Bāqillānī, *Tamhīd fī l-radd*, Cairo, 1366/1947, 162ff. and for Baghdādī, Wensinck, *Muslim creed*, London, 1968, 256-7.

This extension of the meaning of the term *ḍarūrī* is probably to be traced to the work of Bāqillānī. When ʿAllāma classed "things such as *ṣalāt* and *zakāt*" as part of *ḍarūrī* knowledge, he meant that knowledge of these legal duties (the general principles, not the details) was a knowledge based on *tawātur* and found amongst the masses. It is to be noted that though there would be *ijmāʿ* also on such knowledge, the *ijmāʿ* would be construed as posterior to and a result of the *tawātur*. This *tawātur/ḍarūrī* knowledge was found on such things as the incumbency of prayer and *zakāt*. The other type of knowledge was an inferred *(mustadall)* and uncertain *(ẓannī)* type, the exclusive preserve of the *ʿulamāʾ*.

Ijtihād was defined as a word indicating expenditure of effort by a *faqīh* in order to acquire an opinion *(ẓann)* on a *sharʿī* value *(ḥukm)*. Neither the prophet nor the *imāms* were permitted to act on the basis of *ijtihād* for they were capable of gaining *ʿilm*, in which case action on the basis of *ẓann* was not permissible. The *ʿulamaʾ* however were permitted to deduce *ẓannī* values by *ijtihād*.(40)

The statement, *kull mujtahid muṣīb*, which had been a particular object of Ṭūsī's denunciation was still rejected as a characteristic Ashʿarī belief: in fact, God had only one answer for each problem. But the erring *mujtahid* was understood to be forgiven. *Ijtihād* in effect was a reasoned effort to state the law, and wrong conclusions were not subject to penalties.(41) The process however was undertaken seriously and piously. In arriving at his conclusion it was necessary that the *mujtahid* be able to demonstrate a justificatory methodology, based on revelation and exegetical technique. If he reached only one view free of opposing views *(muʿāriḍ)* then action upon it was incumbent; if there was an opposing view and if one of the two was clearly predominant *(rājiḥ)* then action was incumbent on the basis of the predominant; if there was no visible criterion of preference *(tarjīḥ)* then it was a matter of choice (as for Ṭūsī) or *tasāqut* (as for Murtaḍā; that is, both lapse and recourse is had to reason). In either case—and this was perhaps the main aim of the argument—a practical juristic value/decision *(ḥukm)* was established and any-one who neglected it was a sinner.(42)

(وعلى كل تقدير فالحكم معين فالمخالف له مخطئ)

(40) ʿAllāma, *Tahdhīb* (1501), f. 201b-203a; *Mabādiʾ*, 240-1.
(41) *Id.*, *Tahdhīb*, f. 205b-206a; *Mabādiʾ*, 244-5.
(42) *Id.*, *Tahdhīb*, f. 206a; *Mabādiʾ*, 245-6.

Insistence on the establishment of a juridical rule which could and should be acted upon was 'Allāma's answer to problems of abdication of authority inherent in Muḥaqqiq's advocation of suspended decision *(tawaqquf)*. 'Allāma's perception that the law was based on opinion was combined with a perception that guidance was necessary: although the decision of the *mujtahid* was based on opinion, action in accord with it was necessary and he who abandoned action was a sinner. The essence of the system was expressed in a pithy axiomatic form probably coined by 'Allāma and adduced by him at the beginning of his *Tahdhīb*, and again at the beginning of his *Taḥrīr al-Aḥkām*:

ظنّية الطريق لا تنافي علمية الحكم

The elegance of that slogan defies adequate translation but means something like, "a method based on opinion is not inconsistent with a juristic value based on knowledge."(43) That paradox conceded that the *mujtahid*'s sources were matters of opinion and his conclusions therefore susceptible to variation but the conclusion once given was"known" and action in accord with it was necessary.

The way in which Shī'ī acceptance of *ijtihad* was accompanied by a general acknowledgement of doubt, if not a complete abandonment of certainty, may be illustrated from Ḥasan ibn Shahīd II's *Ma'ālim al-dīn* He presented a series of arguments of by then well-established import explaining why *tawātur* Traditions were a source of knowledge.(44) He then raised the question whether the *khabar wāḥid* could be used as a basis for defining the law.(45) A positive answer was provided by exegesis of the two Quranic passages formerly adduced by 'Allāma (9:122 and 49:6), by appeal to agreement of the elders *(iṭbāq qudamā' al-aṣḥāb)*, and by the following argument:

> The sphere of definitive knowledge of those legal values which are not *ḍarūrī* in religion and in the Shī'ī sect is in our time cut off. For, that which is found in the indicators of juristic values *(adillat al-aḥkām)* produces only *ẓann* because of the lack of *mutawātir* proof, and the absence of any method of ascertaining *ijmā'* other than transmission of *khabar wāḥid*; and because it is evident that *iṣālat al-barā'a* produces

(43) *Id.*, *Tahdhīb*, f. 3b; *Taḥrīr*, 2.
(44) Ḥasan ibn Shahīd II, *Ma'ālim*, 183-5.
(45) *Ibid.*, 188-92.

> [also] only *ẓann* and the Book is *ẓannī al-dalāla*. If the cutting off of knowledge *('ilm)* be granted with regard to legal values *(ḥukm shar'ī)* then God's commission *(taklīf)* must be based on opinion *(ẓann)*.(46)

That passage concedes that there can be no certain knowledge about matters not already established and accepted, and that all available sources of knowledge give rise only to opinion. Even intellectual principles *(iṣālat al-barā'a)* produce only *ẓann* and the Book (although *mutawātir* of transmission) was only an indicator of opinion *(ẓannī al-dalāla)*.

This establishment and confession of doubt as part of the essential character of divine law should be contrasted with the idealistic aspiration to *'ilm* and rejection of *ẓann* that characterised Imāmī *uṣūl* of the early Buyid period. This development (from *'ilm* to *ẓann*) may be seen as response to a number of social and academic factors. There was first of all a need to provide for the harmonious integration or at least peaceful juxtaposition of past and contemporary *ikhtilāf*; closely related to this there was a need to provide at least some scope for development and flexibility. Furthermore the authority of the clerical class was enhanced by the recognition of a large area of doubt, since it was only within that area that they could prescribe (clearly, what was for all time "known" offered no scope for choice/authority). On a more general level it may be noted that for many Muslim scholars (not only the Shī'a) the *sharī'a* was not so much a law to be followed—though it was certainly to be aimed at—as a meditation upon an unattainable ideal. That ideal could hardly be defined let alone put into practice.(47) The minute and detailed elaboration of doubts was an expression of piety and worship—and of course of tolerance. The intangible and indefinable law became a reflection of the transcendent and ineffable deity.

***

Ijtihād was a terminological innovation which, by naming, justified doubt and uncertainty but it justified also a distinction between the clerical class and the rest of the community. That

(46) *Ibid.*, 192; for *iṣālat al-barā'a*, see note 22 above; the development of the Imāmī theory of *ijmā'* may be followed in Calder, PhD, see note 62.

(47) Cf. Becker's remarks, *cit.* Wansbrough, "On recomposing the Islamic history of North Africa", *JRAS*, 1969, pp. 163-4.

distinction with all that it implied of authority and submission had been first elaborated in Shāfiʿī's *Risāla*. Shāfiʿī's *ʿilm al-khāṣṣa* was re-expressed by ʿAllāma as uncertain (not *qaṭʿī* inferred *(mustadall)*, doubtful *(ẓannī)* and *ijtihādī*. It was this knowledge which was the subject of *fiqh* and the preserve of the *fuqahāʾ*. The acknowledgement of *ikhtilāf* within the sphere of that knowledge rendered this theory one of the cornerstones of the charismatic community; it was inerrant because individuals, appropriately qualified, might differ. Opinions, once offered and justified, could not be rejected but were preserved and recorded assiduously against the day they might be useful.(48) The right to express an opinion depended on knowledge which was the essential quality separating the *ʿālim* from the *ʿāmmī*, and accounting for the authority of the former over the latter.

Though the Shīʿa initially avoided the terme *ijtihād*, the distinction between the *ʿāmmī* and the *ʿālim* was already implicit in one of Kulayni's Traditions.

> Abū ʿAbdullah was sitting in the circle [of students] of Rabīʿa, when a bedouin came and asked Rabīʿa a question. Rabīʿa answered. When he finished speaking the bedouin asked him: Is it your responsibility *(a-huwa fīʿ unqika?)*. Rabīʿa did not reply. The bedouin repeated the question but received the same response... [Finally] Abū ʿAbdullah said: it is his responsibility.(49)

The chapter heading for that was: That the *muftī* is responsible. The point was that the inquirer had only to obey; responsibility for right or wrong lay with the *muftī*. The implications of that Tradition were confirmed in Ṭūsī's *ʿUddat al-Uṣūl*. In that work he asserted that there were two views on a person incapable of juristic deduction (that is, an *ʿāmmī*, someone incapable of deriving the law from revelation):

> (i) It is related from the Baghdādīs that such a one may not follow by *taqlīd* a *muftī* but must merely refer to him so that he may direct him to the path of *ʿilm* concerning the problem in question. (ii) The Baṣrīs and most *fuqahaʾ* say that the *ʿāmmī* may accept the statement of the *muftī*... That which we follow is that it is permissible for the *ʿāmmī*... to follow by *taqlīd* the *ʿālim*.(50)

(48) Cf. Wansbrough, *Sectarian Milieu*, 87, 91.
(49) Kulayni, *Furūʿ al-Kāfī*, II 358.
(50) Ṭūsī, *ʿUddat*, 293.

The division of society into *muftīs* and *muqallids* was there acknowledged. Ṭūsī justified his opinion by reference to precedent: the generality of the sect *('āmmat al-ṭā'ifa)* had always sought and received *fatwās* from the *'ulamā'*. Though permissible in matters of *furū' al-fiqh*, *taqlīd* was not generally thought permissible in matters of *uṣūl al-dīn*, albeit there were various qualifications to that view.(51)

As the *fuqahā'* consolidated their position within the community and bolstered it by giving expression to it in *furū'* and *uṣūl*, or by establishing real control of judicial and other community affairs, their perception became sharper of their unique status. Muḥaqqiq in his *Mu'tabar* noted that the constant appearance of new problems *(ḥawādith* and *mawāni')* required a class which would specialise in the law *(tafaqquh)*: this he related to Q9.122 (after Shāfi'ī)(52) and to various Traditions urging the quest for knowledge. A paeon of praise for the learned was summed up by reference to a Tradition from 'Alī: Study *fiqh* for the *fuqahā'* are the heirs of the prophet.(53) This preceded and led to an assessment of the uncertainty of the law and an assertion that the *muftī* in giving a *fatwā* is speaking on behalf of his Lord and with the tongue of his law *mukhbir 'an rabbihi wa-nāṭiq bi-lisān shar'ihi*. The markedly charismatic view of the clerical class that emerged in Muḥaqqiq's work is apparent also in 'Allāma's writing,(54) and was institutionalised by adoption of the theory of *ijtihād*. The essence of that theory was that it was both permissible and incumbent for the *muqallid* to act on the basis of the opinions *(ẓunun)* of the *mujtahid*.

> It is permissible for the *'āmmī* to act by *taqlid* on the decision of the *mujtahid* in *furū' al-shar'*, based on *law la nafara* (Q9.122) wherein God has rendered learning incumbent on part of the community and permitted to the rest *taqlīd*.(55)
> It is incumbent on the *'āmmī* to act by *taqlīd* if he is incapable of *ijtihād*.(56)

(51) *Ibid.*, 294; for a later synoptic survey see Ḥasan b. Shahīd II, *Ma'ālim*, 237-9.

(52) Shāfi'ī, *Risāla*, Cairo, 1338/1969, paras. 988ff.

(53) Muḥaqqiq, *Mu'tabar*, 3, lines 1-2; cf. the *warathat al-anbiya'*, Tradition amongst the Sunnis.

(54) See e.g. 'Allāma, *Taḥrīr*, 3-4.

(55) *Id.*, *Tahdhīb* (1501), f. 207b-208a.

(56) *Ibid.*, 208a-b.

In the matter of choosing a *muftī/mujtahid* the *mustaftī/muqallid* was required, it is true, himself to exercise *ijtihād*. The criteria of choice were to be assessed according to public opinion *(bi-mashhad min al-khalq)* and correspond precisely to the criteria affecting the choice of a judge. A *mujtahid* was *ipso facto* a *shar'ī* judge and capable of giving judicial decisions.(57) His fame and influence depended largely upon his ability to find favour in the eyes of the people, a factor which lent a certain 'populist' quality to his leadership. The *muqallid* was required as far as possible to choose the more pious and the more learned as his *mujtahid*; where there was conflict between these two, preference was to be given to the more learned. Oral or written communication of a *mujtahid*'s opinion to a *muqallid* was permissible. The *ijtihād* of a dead *'ālim* was not binding.(58) These considerations, all of them adduced by 'Allāma, became the essential elements of all subsequent articulations of *ijtihād*. Though elements of *ikhtilāf* grew up there were from 'Allāma's time to the early Safavid period, few significant developments.(59) In other words, the parameters of things relevant to a discussion of *ijtihād* were so finely perceived by 'Allāma that later writers had little or nothing to add. There can be little doubt that the perfection of his formulation was due to extensive study in, borrowing from and re-interpretation of Sunnī sources. His debt to Sunnī sources was, in fact, acknowledged in biographical works of the Safavid period.

The qualities formally required in a *mujtahid* did not differ markedly from those adduced by Ṭūsī for a *muftī*, and were the same as those required for a *qāḍī*. 'Allāma thought they could be reduced to one consideration, namely that he should be able to deduce *aḥkām* from *dalā'il shar'iyya*.(60) Shahīd I gives a detailed assessment of those qualities purportedly deduced from the famous *maqbūl ḥadīth* of 'Umar ibn Hanẓala.(61) They may be summed up as knowledge of the various exegetical devices mentioned above backed by appeal to the 'independent' evidence provided by the

(57) Cf. Calder, "Judicial authority in Imāmī Shī'ī jurisprudence", *Bulletin of the British Society for Middle Eastern Studies*, VI 1979.

(58) 'Allāma, *Mabādi'*, 247-9.

(59) For a later assessment of *ijtihād*, see Ḥasan b. Shahīd II, *Ma'ālim*, 235-42.

(60) *Mabādi'*, 241-2.

(61) Shahid I, *Dhikrā*, 3; for the Tradition of Ibn Hanẓala, see Calder, "Judicial authority" and Eliash, "Some misconceptions regarding the juridical status of the Imāmī *'ulama'*", *IJMES* X 1979.

sciences of grammar, rhetoric, history, biography and logic. These factors rarely constitute a real methodological constraint on the possible options of the *faqīh*.

What did represent a real constraint was the inalienable structure, common to all Islamic legal systems, corresponding to those parts of the law designated by 'Allāma as known *bi-l-ḍarūra* by Shāfi'ī as *'ilm 'āmma*. That society consisted of a group of people who performed purification and prayer, paid *zakāt*, waged religious war, fasted in Ramaḍān, bought and sold, married, divorced, judged and carried out all such and other daily activities consciously in the eyes of God and in accord with his command was an assumption never questioned. The development of Imāmī *uṣūl* from the 10th to the 16th centuries may be characterised as movement from the idealistic desire for *'ilm* throughout the law, to a recognition that its basic structure subsisted with a mass of details (whose boundaries were never, perhaps could never be, defined) subject to variation and doubt. Within this area of doubt the social, political, economic and personal factors that affected a *mujtahid*'s choice are not easily, perhaps not at all, quantifiable. It is to be noted that the tension between elements that can be known and elements that may be chosen was constant, though the terminological description of that phenomenon was more sophisticated and the acknowledgement of its existence and scope more generous after adoption of the theory of *ijtihād*. This development found its culmination in the *Ma'ālim al-dīn* of Ḥasan ibn Shahīd II (d. 1011/1602-3), a work giving the clearest possible expression to a methodology of doubt. That, however, was not without its dangers, for, misused, or misunderstood, the authority of the *mujtahid* could seem to be merely arbitrary, implying too casual or too cavalier an attitude to revelation. It is accordingly hardly surprising that Ḥasan ibn Shahīd II's summation of the tradition was scarcely complete but it was attacked by the idealism of Mīrzā Muḥammad al-Astarābādī whose *Fawā'id* laid the foundations of a literalist reaction. The subsequent struggle between Akhbārīs and Uṣūlīs dominated Imāmī jurisprudence throughout the Safavid period and beyond.([62])

(62) This essay is adapted from chaps 6-9 of Calder, unpublished PhD thesis, *The structure of authority in Imāmī Shī'ī jurisprudence*, London University, SOAS, 1979.

SOURCES

KULAYNĪ, Muḥ. b. Ya'qub (d. c. 328/940), *Furū' al-Kāfī* (2 vols in 1), Iran 1315/1898.

AL-MURTAḌĀ, 'Alī b. Ḥusayn al-Mūsawī (d. 436/1044), *Al-Shāfī fī l-imāma*, Tehran 1301/1886.

AL-ṬŪSĪ, Muḥ. b. Ḥasan (d. 460/1067), *Talkhīṣ al-Shāfī*, in Murtaḍā, *Shāfī*; *K. al-Ghayba*, Najaf 1385; *'Uddat al-Uṣūl*, Tehran 1314.

IBN IDRĪS, Muḥ. b. Aḥmad (d. 598/1202), *Sarā'ir al-Islām*, Iran 1270/1854.

AL-MUḤQQIQ, Ja'far b. Ḥasan (676/1277), *K. al-Mu'tabar*, Iran 1318/1901.

AL-'ALLĀMA, Hasan b. Yusuf (d. 726/1325), *Mabādi' al-wuṣūl ilā 'ilm al-uṣūl*, Najaf 1970; *K. Taḥrīr al-aḥkām* (2 vols), Iran 1314/1896; *K. Tahdhīb al-wuṣūl ilā 'ilm al-uṣūl*, MS. India Office, Ar II 1501 and 1502.

AL-SHAHĪD AL-AWWAL, Shams al-dīn b. Makkī (d. 786/1384-5), *Dhikrā al-Shī'a fī aḥkām al-sharī'a*, Persia, n.d.

ḤASAN IBN AL-SHAHĪD AL-THĀNĪ (d. 1011/1602-3), *Ma'ālim al-dīn fī l-uṣūl*, Qum n.d.

ASTARĀBĀDĪ, Mīrzā Muḥammad Amīn (1026/1626-7), *Al-Fawā'id al-madaniyya*, MS. India Office Ar II 1507.

INDEX OF TECHNICAL TERMINOLOGY

INDEX OF ARABIC AUTHORS CITED

INDEX OF QUR'ĀN CITATIONS